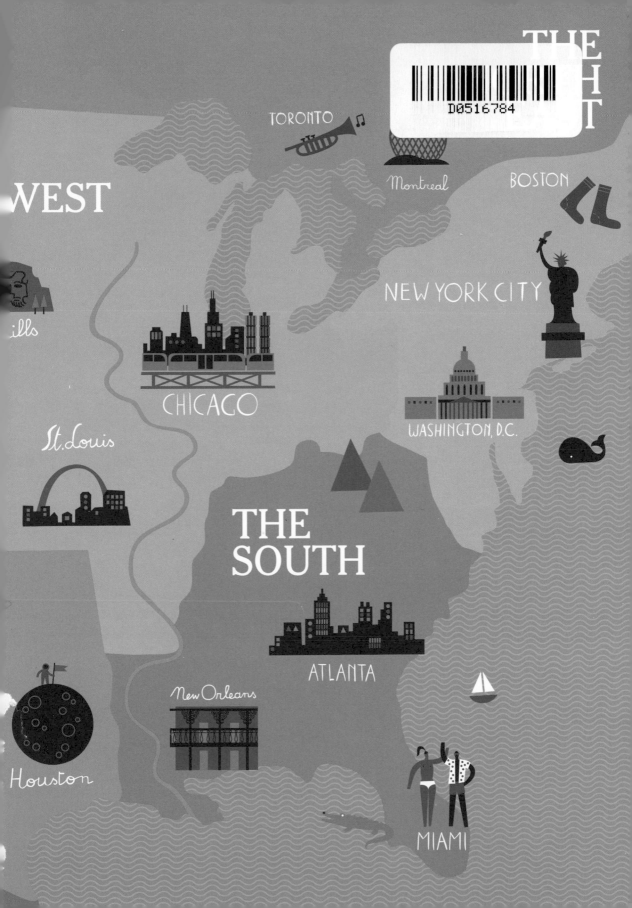

The New York Times

36

HOURS

EDITED BY BARBARA IRELAND

The New York Times

36

HOURS

150 WEEKENDS IN THE USA & CANADA

TASCHEN

Contents

THE NORTHEAST

THE SOUTH

THE MIDWEST

THE SOUTHWEST

THE WEST

Foreword

The 36 Hours *column made its first appearance on the pages of* The New York Times *in 2002, became an immediate hit with readers, and has been inspiring trips, wish lists, and clip-and-saves ever since. Created as a guide to that staple of crammed 21st-century schedules, the weekend getaway, it takes readers each week on a carefully researched, uniquely designed two-night excursion to an embraceable place. With a well-plotted itinerary, it offers up an experience that both identifies the high points of the destination and teases out its particular character.*

As one of the dozens of editors who have worked on 36 Hours *over the years — along with hundreds of writers, photographers, graphic artists, and designers — I've come to feel that the column's popularity is based on its special feeling of accessibility. Whether it is serving as a guide for actual exploring or as a vision to dream on,* 36 Hours *differs from much traditional travel writing in this vital respect: rather than recounting a trip the writer took, it offers up a trip the reader can take.*

36 Hours *lives in the realm of the possible. The framework is the weekend. The audience is broad — with a little adapting, these itineraries are meant to work for both the backpacker and the jet-setter. And the destination might be anyplace where there is fun to be had and a quirk or two to discover.*

This book brings together 150 new and updated 36 Hours columns for locations in the United States and Canada. Amid all the richness of this vast territory, from glittering cities and eccentric small towns to heart-stopping mountains and seacoasts, even 150 places is not very many, and the task of selecting them was not always easy. Some, of course, were obvious musts: the marquee metropolises like New York, Montreal, and Los Angeles; the world-famous natural wonders at Niagara Falls, the Grand Canyon, and the Bay of Fundy; the national icons of Washington, D.C., and Quebec City.

But the process of choosing among all the rest brought home to me how much more there is to find and see over a territory stretching from Juneau to Miami and Newfoundland to Kauai. There had to be a spot for Clarksdale, Mississippi, where the blues are deep and authentic, and one for the Laurel Highlands of Pennsylvania, where Frank Lloyd Wright's masterpiece, Fallingwater, is hidden away in the woods. So-called "secondary" Rust Belt cities like Duluth and Detroit turn out to be rich repositories of spirit and culture. And the work of some of the best and most renowned Times *staff writers was ready to be plucked for the book, too — David Carr on his former home city of Minneapolis, Ariel Kaminer on Lower Manhattan, Sam Sifton on Brooklyn, Mark Bittman on Death Valley.*

This book is not a conventional guidebook, and 36 Hours *was never intended to replicate the guidebook formula. It was meant from the beginning to give a well-informed inside view of each place it covers, a selective summary that lets the traveler get to the heart of things in minimal time. Travelers who have more days to spend may want to use a* 36 Hours *as a kind of nugget, supplementing it with the more comprehensive information available on bookstore shelves or on the locally sponsored Internet sites where towns and regions offer exhaustive lists of their attractions. Or, since the book is organized regionally, two or three of these itineraries could easily be strung together to make up a longer trip. (I did this myself in Kentucky and eastern Tennessee, using the* 36 Hours *columns for Louisville, Lexington, and Gatlinburg.)*

Whatever the journey or the wanderer's choice, the star of the book is North America itself, shining out page after page in all of its amazing variety, energy, and grandeur.

— BARBARA IRELAND, EDITOR

PAGE 2 The Statue of Liberty, icon and inspiration since 1886, lifts her famous torch in New York Harbor.

OPPOSITE Delicate Arch at sunset in Arches National Park outside Moab, Utah.

Tips for Using This Book

Plotting the Course: Travelers don't make their way through a continent alphabetically, and this book doesn't, either. Each of its sections is based on a region — Northeast, South, Midwest, Southwest, and West — and introduced with a regional map. Each begins in a prominent city or destination and winds from place to place the way a touring adventurer on a car trip might. An alphabetical index appears at the end of the book.

On the Ground: Every *36 Hours* follows a workable numbered itinerary, which is both outlined in the text and shown with corresponding numbers on a detailed destination map. The itinerary is practical: it really is possible to get from one place to the next easily and in the allotted time, although of course many travelers will prefer to take things at their own pace and perhaps take some of their own detours. Astute readers will notice that the "36" in *36 Hours* is elastic, and the traveler's agenda probably will be, too.

The Not So Obvious: The itineraries do not all follow exactly the same pattern. A restaurant for Saturday breakfast may or may not be recommended; after-dinner night life may be missing. The destination dictates, and so, to some extent, does the personality of the author who researched and wrote the article. In large cities, where it is impossible to see everything in a weekend, the emphasis is on the less expected discovery over the big, highly promoted attraction that is already well known. In New York, for example, the Metropolitan Museum of Art is left for art lovers to find on their own.

Travel Documents: The United States and Canada are friendly neighbors, but they are still separate countries. A passport is required for travel between them; and where a visa is required, travelers should be prepared to show that, as well, at the international border. Goods and luggage may be inspected by customs agents.

Seasons: The time of year to visit is left up to the traveler, but in general, the big cities are good anytime; the smaller northern towns are usually best visited in warm months, unless they are ski destinations; and the Deep South and Southwest may be unpleasantly hot in July and August. The most tourist-oriented towns are often seasonal — some of the sites featured in Provincetown or Bar Harbor, for example, may be closed from November to April.

Updates: While all the stories in this volume were updated and fact-checked for publication in fall 2011, it is inevitable that some of the featured businesses and destinations will change in time. If you spot any errors in your travels, please feel free to send corrections or updates via email to 36hoursamerica@taschen.com. Please include "36 Hours Correction" and the page number in the subject line of your email to assure that it gets to the right person for future updates.

OPPOSITE The fantasyland skyline of Las Vegas, the uniquely American oasis of hope, abandon, and glittering commercialism in the Western desert.

THE BASICS

A brief informational box for the destination, called "The Basics," appears with each *36 Hours* article in this book. The box provides some orientation on transportation for that location, including whether a traveler arriving by plane should rent a car to follow the itinerary. "The Basics" also recommends three reliable hotels or other lodgings.

PRICES

Since hotel and restaurant prices change quickly, this book uses a system of symbols, based on 2011 United States dollars.

Hotel room, standard double:
Budget, under $100 per night: $
Moderate, $100 to $199: $$
Expensive, $200 to $299: $$$
Luxury, $300 and above: $$$$

Restaurants, dinner without wine:
Budget, under $15: $
Moderate, $16 to $24: $$
Expensive, $25 to $49: $$$
Very Expensive, $50 and up: $$$$

Restaurants, full breakfast, or lunch entree:
Budget, under $8: $
Moderate, $8 to $14: $$
Expensive, $15 to $24: $$$
Very Expensive, $25 and up: $$$$

TORONTO

Montreal

Mont TREMBLANT

Burlington

Stowe

Niagara Falls

Lake Placid

Cooperstown

Buffalo

PITTSBURGH

the Laurel Highlands

NEW YORK CITY

I ♥ NY

the Brandywine Valley

Princeton

BALTIMORE

PHILADELPHIA

WASHINGTON, D.C.

Annapolis

CAPE MAY

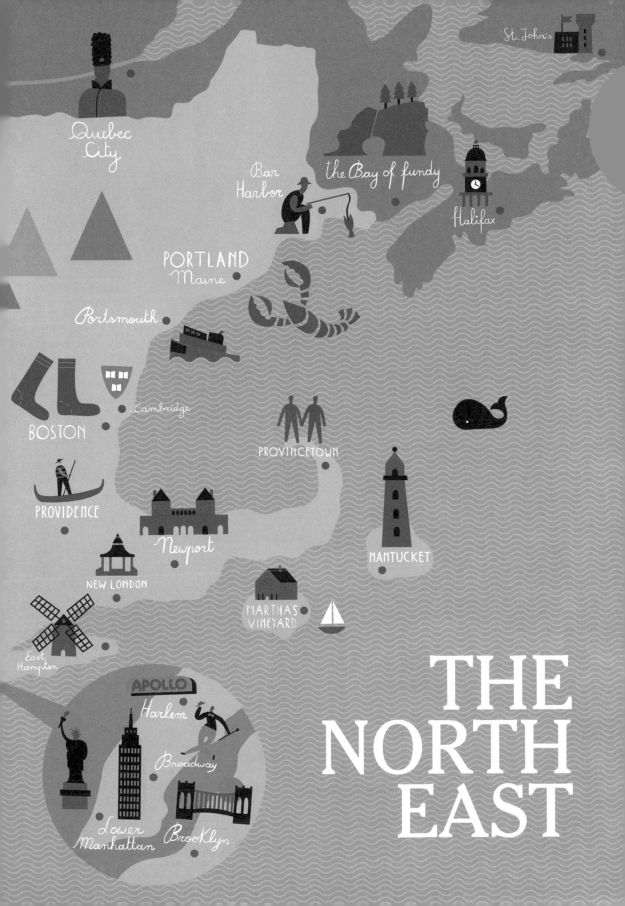

St. John's

Quebec City

Bar Harbor

the Bay of Fundy

Halifax

PORTLAND
Maine

Portsmouth

Cambridge

BOSTON

PROVINCETOWN

PROVIDENCE

Newport

NANTUCKET

NEW LONDON

MARTHA'S VINEYARD

East Hampton

APOLLO

Harlem

Broadway

Lower Manhattan

Brooklyn

THE NORTH EAST

New York City

In New York City, a continent opens its doors and urban renewal never stops. Someone new is always getting off the bus, train, or plane, some new idea is always catching fire, and the skyscrapers just keep on rising. If it's your first time in town, you'll feel the buzz — this is energy central for American culture. If you are returning after a couple of years away, change is what you'll find: crowds explore a hot new park, familiar landmarks have gotten face lifts, and the center of cool has shifted innumerable times (but it's probably still somewhere in Brooklyn). — BY AMY VIRSHUP

FRIDAY

1 *Get Your Tickets* 5 p.m.

The refurbished **Lincoln Center** (Broadway between 62nd and 63rd Streets; lincolncenter.org), includes not only a new fountain with 353 custom-made, computer-controlled nozzles, but a new visitors' center and ticketing space, the **David Rubenstein Atrium** (that's what you get when you give $10 million). The box office sells same-day discount tickets at 25 to 50 percent off regular prices, with a two-ticket-per-person limit, for the Metropolitan Opera, the New York Philharmonic, the New York City Ballet, and the City Opera. Check to see what's on and pick up a pair for tonight.

2 *Pre-theater Prix Fixe* 6 p.m.

Daniel Boulud's New York culinary empire now runs from the Bowery to the Upper East Side. Just across from Lincoln Center, his **Bar Boulud** (1900 Broadway near 64th Street; 212-595-0303; danielnyc.com; $$$) is the perfect perch for a pre-performance meal. Terrines, sliced meats, and cheeses (the last divided into categories like Bloomy, Stinky, and Old & Hard) are the heart of the menu, but there's also a three-course prix-fixe option that includes such classic choices as a salade niçoise, roasted chicken breast, and house-made ice cream or sorbet. For the full experience, sit at the

charcuterie bar, where the view includes fromage de tête Gilles Verot (that's headcheese for those who don't speak French). Afterward, grab a drink at the **Alice Tully Hall** lobby bar before curtain time at Lincoln Center.

SATURDAY

3 *Breakfast, Retro-Style* 10 a.m.

Find the **Standard Grill** at the base of the Standard Hotel (848 Washington Street at West 13th Street; 212-645-4100; thestandardgrill.com; $$). Despite the hotel's Brutalism-Meets-Miami-Beach exterior, the dining room is pure retro: a tile-vaulted ceiling, penny (as in real pennies) floor, red leather banquettes. The menu is pleasingly retro, too: warm cinnamon-and-sugar-crusted doughnuts made on the spot, for example, or ultra-sweet French toast with bananas and rum sauce.

4 *Upside of the Tracks* 11 a.m.

Just down the block at the corner of Gansevoort and Washington Streets are the southernmost stairs to the **High Line** (thehighline.org), the immensely popular linear park recently created on what was once an abandoned freight rail line. On a summer weekend thousands of people might be walking on it, but it's fun even in winter, when it has a quieter, almost derelict

OPPOSITE Manhattan at dusk.

RIGHT The Lake in Central Park. Weather permitting, rowboats can be rented during the summer from the Loeb Boathouse near Fifth Avenue and 72nd Street.

beauty, with bare tree limbs and the seed heads of grasses swaying in the wind off the Hudson.

5 *Brooklyn Browsing* 1 p.m.

Once known as the city of churches, Brooklyn these days might be called the borough of boutiques. For a taste, take the 2/3 or 4/5 subway train to Borough Hall and walk to Court Street in the Cobble

ABOVE The High Line rises above Chelsea along a former elevated train track.

BELOW Foot traffic at Herald Square, where Broadway meets Sixth Avenue in Midtown Manhattan.

Hill neighborhood. At tiny **Fork & Pencil** (221a Court; 718-488-8855; forkandpencil.com) look for imaginative housewares, toys, and antiques. The proceeds go to support local charities. **Papél New York** (225 Court; 718-422-0255; papelnewyork.com) sells sleek paper goods, including sheets of wrapping paper that will class up even the smallest of gifts. Need to refuel? The Stumptown Coffee at **Cafe Pedlar** (210 Court; 718-855-7129; cafepedlar.com) is roasted nearby in Red Hook, and you can pick up a bag of Hair Bender blend beans along with your espresso. Or stop at the **Chocolate Room** (269 Court; 718-246-2600; thechocolateroombrooklyn.com) for homemade chocolate caramel popcorn.

6 *New Yorkers at Play* 6 p.m.

You've hiked the new park; now stroll the old standby. To see the real New Yorkers at play in **Central Park** late on a Saturday afternoon, enter

well north of the touristy horse-drawn hansom cabs and schlock art vendors on Central Park South. Here's one good route: Use the 77th Street entrance from Central Park West (across from the American Museum of Natural History) and wind your way south along the Lake, detouring to Strawberry Fields if you're a John Lennon fan, and then east to Bethesda Fountain. Climb the stairs, walk south on the Mall (look out for tango dancers), and wind your way to Columbus Circle. The paths are easy to get lost on, so take a map or keep one handy on your cellphone (Google's isn't bad).

7 *Seafood on the Park* 8 p.m.

Sleek and highly polished, **Marea** (240 Central Park South; 212-582-5100; marea-nyc.com; $$$), just east of Columbus Circle, is like some movie version of New York except, yes, that really is a fallen mogul pitching new investors at the table next to yours. The menu is devoted to an Italian spin on fish. Share an order of the unctuous ricci (sea urchin, lardo, and sea salt draped bruschetta-like over toast), then choose among the crudo (raw fish), oysters, and antipasti.

ABOVE Columbus Circle, just off Central Park.

RIGHT The Metropolitan Opera House at Lincoln Center. Discounted same-day tickets can be purchased at the David Rubenstein Atrium.

For a main course you can get a whole fish roasted or sautéed, then choose your sauce and side dish.

8 *Cocktails and Codes* 10 p.m.

If you're talking cocktails in New York these days, you need to know two words: speakeasy and artisanal. In dark, hidden spots, behind hard-to-find entrances, bartenders are mixing up concoctions with names like Corpse Reviver No. 2 (gin, Cointreau, Lillet Blanc, lemon, and absinthe) that only seem

old-fashioned. That particular drink was assembled by the garter-sleeved bartenders at **Little Branch** (20 Seventh Avenue South at Leroy Street; 212-929-4360). Cash only.

SUNDAY

9 *Comfort Breakfast* 10 a.m.

The name is an oxymoron and the kitchen is probably smaller than yours, but **Little Giant** (85

OPPOSITE An exhibition at the New Museum of Contemporary Art.

ABOVE Economy Candy on the Lower East Side.

BELOW Speakeasy-style cocktails are served up at Little Branch in the West Village.

Orchard Street at the corner of Broome; 212-226-5047; littlegiantnyc.com; $$-$$$) turns out slightly refined comfort food that has crowds piling up on the sidewalks of the gentrifying Lower East Side. Little Giant serves a Trucker's Breakfast, but the bacon with it will be hand-sliced and the mushrooms cremini. Weekend brunch is cash only.

10 *Art Under Construction* 11 a.m.

The anchor of the Lower East Side art scene is the **New Museum of Contemporary Art** (235 Bowery at Prince Street; 212-219-1222; newmuseum.org), designed by the Japanese firm Sanaa to look like a

series of off-kilter boxes, which opened to raves in 2007. Examine the art inside and then stroll outside to look for more. A growing number of storefronts in the Lower East Side are studios where artists and gallerists with big ambitions work small for now.

11 *Sugar Rush* 1 p.m.

A giant Gummi rat. How New York is that? You can pick one up to take home, along with giant pixie sticks, wax fangs, Mallo Cups, and classics like Hot

Tamales and Mike and Ikes at **Economy Candy** (108 Rivington Street; 212-254-1531; economycandy.com). Crammed with what seems like every candy bar ever known, plus hard candies by the pound, nuts, and dried fruits, it's a playground for the sugar-obsessed.

ABOVE A view of New York Harbor.

OPPOSITE New York's iconic Flatiron Building, at the confluence of Fifth Avenue and Broadway.

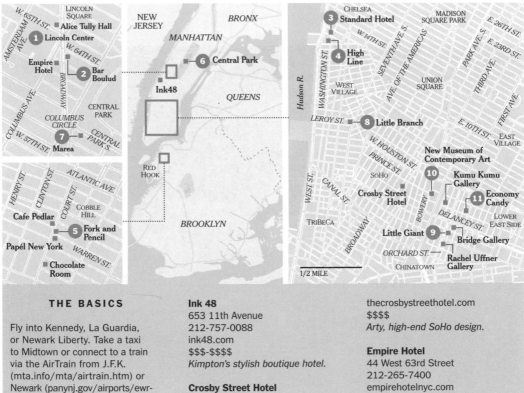

THE BASICS

Fly into Kennedy, La Guardia, or Newark Liberty. Take a taxi to Midtown or connect to a train via the AirTrain from J.F.K. (mta.info/mta/airtrain.htm) or Newark (panynj.gov/airports/ewr-airtrain.html). Taxis are plentiful. The subway is convenient and safe.

Ink 48
653 11th Avenue
212-757-0088
ink48.com
$$$-$$$$
Kimpton's stylish boutique hotel.

Crosby Street Hotel
79 Crosby Street
212-226-6400

thecrosbystreethotel.com
$$$$
Arty, high-end SoHo design.

Empire Hotel
44 West 63rd Street
212-265-7400
empirehotelnyc.com
$$$
Steps from Lincoln Center.

Lower Manhattan

Welcome to Lower Manhattan. You're already behind schedule. Here in the pre-grid city, where Broadway started as a path and Wall Street once really had a wall, the streets may be old but the pace is quick and the outlook is young. Bond traders and bohemians, tai chi practitioners and adventurous just-minted college grads are all sprinkled into the mix. Was it really just a decade or so ago that people wondered if the area would ever recover from the shock of the attacks that took down the World Trade Center? Since then the pace of development has only intensified. Thirty-six hours seems far too little time to cover it all. But it's a great start. — BY ARIEL KAMINER

FRIDAY

1 *Hang Out* 3:30 p.m.

On a tiny platform 23 feet off the ground, every natural impulse tells you to stay away from the edge. But Jonah, a rather dreamy trapeze instructor, tells you to lean over it — way over it — and so you lean. Then he tells you to bend your knees and jump off. And so, against all reason, you jump. What follows is something close to flying, accompanied by the incomparable sensation of zoom and the sound, perhaps, of your own giddy scream. That first step is a doozy all right, but the odd collection of charming teachers at the **Trapeze School New York** (Pier 40, Hudson River Park opposite Houston Street; 917-797-1872; trapezeschool.com; $57 for a two-hour beginner class, plus $22 registration fee) make it fun. The school has several locations; this one, open in the warm months, sits right on the river, with peerless views of the Statue of Liberty and the skyline. What better way to situate yourself in Lower Manhattan than while hanging from your knees and swinging a 70-degree arc?

2 *Footing the Bill* 6 p.m.

Feel wobbly? Time for acupressure massage at the **Fishion Herb Center** (107 Mott Street; 212-966-8771; fishionherbcenter.com), a cramped warren of fluorescent-lighted cubicles that's far, indeed, from the Swiss apple stem cell facials of uptown spas, not just in ambience but (delightfully) in price. Settle into a cracked old wing chair while a Chinese masseur bears down on the tip of your fourth toe, or the area right inside your heel, tiny spots said to correspond to precise parts of the body. Check the laminated chart and note that he's put his hands on not only your "liver" and "spleen" but also places — hello! — not fit to name in a family newspaper. What's the standard tip for that?

3 *Bridge to the 19th Century* 8 p.m.

Depending on whose story you believe, the **Bridge Café** (279 Water Street; 212-227-3344; bridgecafenyc.com; $$-$$$) may be the city's oldest drinking establishment, tracing its ancestry to 1794. It wears its history lightly, with a low-key New American menu and friendly setting (seared diver scallops; grilled petite lamb chops). After dinner you can wander the almost ridiculously picturesque streets just south of the Brooklyn Bridge (but north of the dreaded South Street Seaport mall), cobblestone alleys right out of a Walt Whitman poem. Or, if you haven't seen it, walk a few blocks west to the World Trade Center site and take some time to ponder.

OPPOSITE Brunch at Blaue Gans, a Viennese-style coffee house on Duane Street.

RIGHT Open since 1794, the Bridge Cafe on Water Street at the foot of the Brooklyn Bridge.

4 *Admission to the Bar* 10 p.m.

Lower Manhattan is also the seat of the city government, so fight the lure of yet another *Law & Order* rerun and go see the real thing in action. The gritty night session of New York Criminal Court, at 100 Centre Street, is open to the public, but applause and/or booing is strongly discouraged. Afterward, go to **Forlini's** (93 Baxter Street; 212-349-6779) to have a Scotch with the only team that always comes out on top: the lawyers. Or, take a short perp walk toward the Tombs, Lower Manhattan's very own jail, and find **Winnie's** (104 Bayard Street; 212-732-2384), a gloriously, garishly seedy dive bar where tough customers and painted ladies drink cocktails and sing karaoke into the morning.

SATURDAY

5 *Tai Chi Theater* 9 a.m.

Full-body exercise can be a great start to the day, especially when you're not the one doing it. Every morning in Chinatown's Columbus Park, old men, young students, and graceful women of a certain age gather in their own little groups to perform tai chi. Whatever its spiritual or physical benefits, it makes for beautiful spectacle, with everyone moving in perfectly choreographed slow motion, as though performing water ballet on land.

6 *Vienna Goods* 11 a.m.

By Saturday night, **Blaue Gans** (139 Duane Street; 212-571-8880; kg-ny.com; $$), an update on the classic Viennese coffee house, is a crowded scene restaurant. But at this hour it's peaceful, sunny, and oh so European, from the newspapers dangling from a bentwood rack to the soccer match on TV to the counter filled with pastries expressing principled dissent from American diet trends. Order some Wiener schnitzel the size of Poland or Kaiserschmarren (what might have been called French toast before the Franco-Prussian War) and enjoy the most elaborate coffee presentation since the days of the Habsburgs.

7 *Art and About* 1 p.m.

Big scary galleries and august museums may hardly take notice, but new cultural activity still thrives amid Lower Manhattan's condo sales offices. TriBeCa is sprinkled with galleries, among them **apexart** (291 Church Street; 212-431-5270; apexart.org), a small nonprofit space that emphasizes group shows with a political theme; **Art in General** (79 Walker Street; 212-219-0473; artingeneral.org), an old-timer by comparison, which commissions work that might not find a home in other venues; and **Ethan Cohen Gallery** (14 Jay Street; 212-625-1250; ecfa.com), which specializes in contemporary Chinese art.

OPPOSITE The view of Lower Manhattan from across the East River, at Brooklyn Bridge Park in Dumbo.

RIGHT The Staten Island Ferry cruises by the Statue of Liberty at dusk.

BELOW Tourists gather around the Wall Street Bull along Broadway in the Financial District.

8 *And Staten Island, Too* 5 p.m.

Is there any greater cliché than a sunset ride on the **Staten Island Ferry**? No, and so what? Grab a beer at the snack bar and a spot on the bow and toast Lady Liberty standing among all the tribes she spawned: dudes in fake Gucci, biddies back from the Met, and, on one visit, a lumbering Goth goddess hiding behind elaborate facial tattoos. (Ferries run 24 hours; siferry.com; fare, free.)

9 *Dine and Wine* 9 p.m.

TriBeCa has more than its share of multistarred restaurants, but they're booked, expensive, and awfully serious. Take the bistro route without denying yourself the white tablecloths by dining at the **Harrison** (355 Greenwich Street, at Harrison Street; 212-274-9310; theharrison.com/harrison.php; $$-$$$). Expect modern American fare like seared skate wing or updated twists on roasted chicken, and plan to linger a while.

10 *Sofia on the Hudson* Midnight

If you can choose only one Bulgarian hipster bar this weekend, **Mehanata** is the way to go. This freakish little hybrid is at Broadway and Canal (113 Ludlow Street; 212-625-0981; mehanata.com), but at times it feels like a different country, or planet. The crowd is a mix of cute college girls, sullen artists, and burly Eastern Europeans—with the odd whirling dervish thrown in for good measure. As a D.J. spins

something trendy, everyone drinks and dances, and soon enough the night slides over the edge into genuinely weird terrain. Food is available but in no way advisable.

SUNDAY

11 *Why Is It So Bright?* 11 a.m.

There's something about dancing tabletop with a band of crazed Bulgarian hedonists that changes a person—but how, and for how long, it's best not to ask. Much better plan: brunch at **Smorgas Chef** on Stone Street, a pretty cobblestone lane in the Financial District (53 Stone Street; 212-422-3500; smorgas.com/index_wallstreet.htm; $$). Bring a stack of newspapers but do not read them. Instead, treat yourself to smoked salmon eggs Benedict, administer frequent doses of coffee, and ignore the ringing in your head. It will subside eventually. It has to.

ABOVE Stone Street, said by some to be the oldest paved street in New York City. Today it's a spot for bars, lofts, and Sunday coffee.

OPPOSITE Flying high at Trapeze School New York.

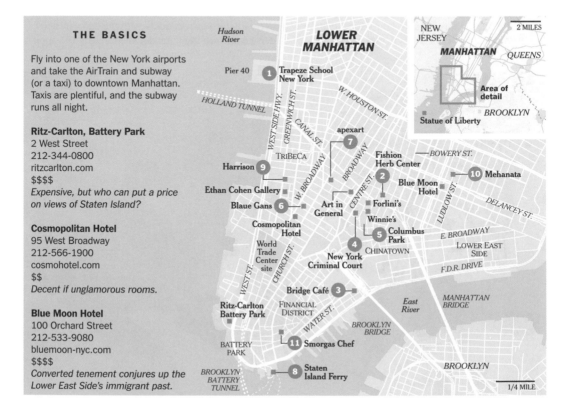

THE BASICS

Fly into one of the New York airports and take the AirTrain and subway (or a taxi) to downtown Manhattan. Taxis are plentiful, and the subway runs all night.

Ritz-Carlton, Battery Park
2 West Street
212-344-0800
ritzcarlton.com
$$$$
Expensive, but who can put a price on views of Staten Island?

Cosmopolitan Hotel
95 West Broadway
212-566-1900
cosmohotel.com
$$
Decent if unglamorous rooms.

Blue Moon Hotel
100 Orchard Street
212-533-9080
bluemoon-nyc.com
$$$$
Converted tenement conjures up the Lower East Side's immigrant past.

Broadway

Four plays in one weekend? Why not? On Broadway, the best of American theatrical talent comes together in 41 theaters within a tight cluster of walkable New York City blocks. The schedules are right, the marquees are bright, and the variety of the productions gives you plenty to choose from. Between shows, follow celebrity footsteps into some hangouts of the theater people and learn some Broadway history. This district has been home of the best (and worst) of what the New York stage has to offer for more than a century.

— BY MERVYN ROTHSTEIN

FRIDAY

1 *Ticket Strategy* 2 p.m.

Lengthy treatises have been written about how to get Broadway tickets. One option is to join the line at the discount **TKTS** booth at the north end of Times Square (tdf.org/tkts), sponsored by the nonprofit Theater Development Fund. The latest hits aren't likely to show up here, but good productions well into their runs may be available, and savings can be 25 percent to 50 percent. Lines form well before the booth opens at 3 p.m. Whether you buy at TKTS, pay full price at a theater box office, or book weeks ahead through **Telecharge** (telecharge.com) or **Ticketmaster** (ticketmaster.com), study the reviews and listings first. To span the Broadway experience, plan to see a mix of shows — light and serious, traditional and daring.

2 *Evening Joe* 6:15 p.m.

Join pre-theater crowds at **Joe Allen's** (326 West 46th Street; 212-581-6464; joeallenrestaurant.com; $$). It's a very busy, very New York place. While you're eating your meatloaf or pan-roasted Atlantic cod, check out the wall displays of posters for the biggest flops in Broadway history. You no doubt know the book, and the movie, of *Breakfast at Tiffany's*. But did you know there was also a 1966 musical version? It starred Mary Tyler Moore and

OPPOSITE Times Square is at the heart of Broadway and home to the TKTS booth for discounted theater tickets.

RIGHT A production of *The Book of Mormon*, one of Broadway's success stories, at the Eugene O'Neill Theater.

Richard Chamberlain. The world may have forgotten, but the stars no doubt haven't.

3 *Song and Dance* 7:45 p.m.

Get your theater weekend off to a high-energy start with a musical. Broadway is most famous for its musicals, and the top 14 longest running shows in Broadway history (No. 1 is *The Phantom of the Opera*) are creatures of song and dance. A tip: musicals that have been playing for years can sometimes be tired, with sets shopworn and stars long gone. Choose one that's still fresh, and arrive early. Latecomers are despised almost as much as people who forget to turn off their cellphones.

4 *Fisticuffs Optional* 10:30 p.m.

Head off for a drink at **Angus McIndoe** (258 West 44th Street; 212-221-9222; angusmcindoe.com), where producers, critics, stagehands, directors, and sometimes even actors show up to discuss what's playing, what's in rehearsal, and what's in trouble. A notorious incident here: the director David Leveaux, angry with Michael Riedel of *The New York Post* for making snide comments about his show at the time, a 2004 revival of *Fiddler on the Roof*, pushed, or maybe it was punched, Riedel. It's unlikely there will be another boxing match, but you never know.

SATURDAY

5 *45 Seconds Away* Noon

The legendary **Cafe Edison** (Hotel Edison, 228 West 47th Street; 212-840-5000; edisonhotelnyc.com; $)

looks like a plain deli, but to Broadway it is something like what the Polo Lounge is to Hollywood. Producers, writers, even old-time comedians have been known to hang out here — yes, that could have been Jackie Mason you saw here once, telling a bad joke. Neil Simon wrote a play called *45 Seconds From Broadway* about the Cafe Edison, but the restaurant is better than the play. August Wilson used to sit for hours over coffee working on his dramas. And another kind of star — Joe DiMaggio — lived at the Edison when he was hitting the kind of home runs that aren't just a metaphor for success. The cafe is also known as the Polish Tea Room, but you can order much more than tea — from bagels and lox to potato pancakes and applesauce to pastrami on rye.

6 *Get Serious* 1:45 p.m.

You want to see at least one meaty serious play, the kind with a chance of showing up someday on college reading lists. Schedule it for today's matinee, and you'll leave yourself time afterward to think about what you've seen and maybe even discuss it over dinner. While you're waiting for the show to begin, check out the "At This Theater" feature in your *Playbill* to see what giants of yesteryear appeared on the stage you'll be viewing. Humphrey Bogart became a star at the Broadhurst in 1935 in *The Petrified Forest*. Marlon Brando made his Broadway debut in 1944 in *I Remember Mama* at the Music Box (which was built by Irving Berlin) and astonished audiences as Stanley Kowalski in *A Streetcar Named Desire* in 1947 at the Ethel Barrymore.

7 *Dinner Break* 6:15 p.m.

Rebuild your strength with a French-inspired dinner at **Chez Josephine** (414 West 42nd Street, 212-594-1925; chezjosephine.com; $$$). It's run by Jean-Claude Baker, the adopted son of the chanteuse Josephine Baker. There's a pianist accompanying the meal — and whoever's playing that evening counts among his predecessors Harry Connick Jr. If you'd rather go Japanese, try **Kodama Sushi** (301

West 45th Street; 212-582-8065; $$), a home away from home for chorus lines, supporting casts, stage managers, and other theatrical types. Stephen Sondheim and William Finn have been spotted at the sushi bar, and the autographed posters on the wall from recent hits (and misses) add to the ambience. It's a neighborhood place, but the neighborhood is Broadway.

8 *Seeing Stars* 7:45 p.m.

For the biggest night of the week, find a show with top-tier leads. Then file in with the rest of what's likely to be a full audience, and share the night with the other star watchers. Seeking autographs? Head for the stage door right after the curtain drops, and don't be dismayed if you're part of a crowd. Celebrity actors are usually willing to pause before entering their limos and sign all of the *Playbill* copies thrust at them. Before the show, check out the theater itself: many Broadway houses are stars in their own right. Notice the ornate decoration, and remember the history. **The Lyceum** on West 45th Street, for example, dates to 1903 and was put up by a producer named David Frohman. The story has it that he built

ABOVE A cluster of theater marquees along West 45th Street between Eighth Avenue and Broadway.

BELOW Breakfast at Cafe Edison on West 47th Street, a regular gathering spot for Broadway royalty.

OPPOSITE Queuing for theater tickets at the TKTS booth in Time Square.

an apartment high up inside with a small door for observing the stage — and that he would wave a white handkerchief to warn his actress wife, Margaret Illington, that she was overacting.

9 *And More Stars* 11 p.m.

The post-performance star gazing is usually good at **Bar Centrale** (324 West 46th Street, 212-581-3130), where actors often retire for a cocktail after two or three hours of performing. It's run by Joe Allen, above his eponymous restaurant. Don't seek autographs here, though — the performers expect post-play privacy.

SUNDAY

10 *Brunch, Anyone?* 12:30 p.m.

If the weather's good, the idyllic garden of **Barbetta** (321 West 46th Street; 212-246-9171;

barbettarestaurant.com; $$$), is an enchanting space for a light pasta and a lighter wine, giving you a feel of northern Italy.

11 *Grand Finale* 2:45 p.m.

Make your last play memorable. Broadway and its audiences have fallen under the spell of Hollywood-style special effects, and if you want something splashy, you can probably find it. In theater, you're seeing the pyrotechnics live (despite all the publicity, accidents are rare), and producers can't rely as much on computer-generated sleight of hand. Sit back and enjoy the spectacle.

THE BASICS

Taxis, trains, buses, and subways all converge on Times Square. Everyplace in the theater district is walkable from anyplace else in the theater district.

Marriott Marquis
1535 Broadway
212-398-1900
marriott.com
$$$-$$$$
In the heart of Broadway, with a theater inside.

W Times Square
1567 Broadway
212-930-7400
starwoodhotels.com
$$$-$$$$
Stylish and luxurious.

Hilton Times Square
234 West 42nd Street
212-840-8222
hilton.com
$$$-$$$$
Spacious rooms, many amenities.

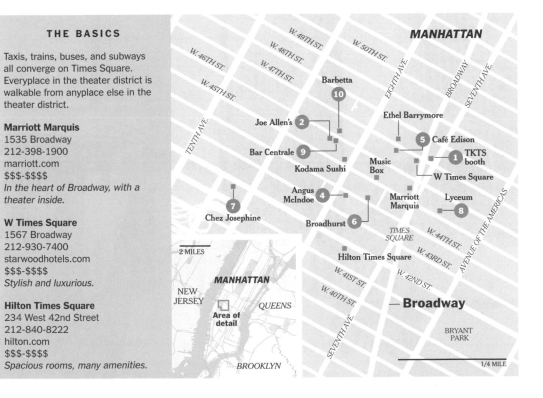

Harlem

In Harlem, the first decade of the 21st century may best be remembered for a seismic demographic shift: an influx of whites and a drop in the black population that put it below 50 percent for the first time in decades. This shifting landscape has brought with it a new cultural scene with a distinct cosmopolitan vibe. But even with the arrival of new doorman buildings, luxurious brownstone renovations, and chichi boutiques and restaurants, this swath of Upper Manhattan still brims with the cultural landmarks that made it the capital of black America. — BY JOHN ELIGON

FRIDAY

1 *The Collector* 4 p.m.

Stop in at the **Schomburg Center for Research in Black Culture** (515 Malcolm X Boulevard; 212-491-2200; nypl.org/locations/schomburg), a trove of manuscripts, rare books, photos, videos, and recordings. Its exhibitions have included photos of early-20th-century Harlem life, private papers of Maya Angelou, and an exploration of the influence of jazz on the visual arts. It is named for Arturo A. Schomburg, a visionary Puerto Rican-born black private collector who amassed a significant portion of this material before his death in 1938. Check the schedule for films, lectures, discussions, and musical performances.

2 *Strivers' Row* 6 p.m.

The timing may not have been great when a group of elegant townhouses went up in Central Harlem in the late 19th century — it was shortly before an economic panic. But the development, on 138th and 139th Streets between Adam Clayton Powell Jr. and Frederick Douglass Boulevards, survived. Today it is one of New York's most graceful and integrated examples of period architecture. Stroll past Italian-palazzo and neo-Georgian former homes of the high achievers like Scott Joplin and Bill Robinson (Bojangles) who gave this section its nickname, **Strivers' Row**. Don't miss a nod to the

past, painted on some of the entrances to the rear courtyard: "Private Road; Walk Your Horses."

3 *Culinary Eclectic* 8 p.m.

Marcus Samuelsson, true to his heritage as Ethiopian born and Swedish raised, has done with his restaurant, **Red Rooster Harlem** (310 Lenox Avenue; 212-792-9001; redroosterharlem.com; $$), what few can: attracted a clientele diverse in both color and age. The menu pulls from all cultural corners (blackened catfish, lemon chicken with couscous, steak frites with truffle Béarnaise). Stick around after dinner for a drink at the horseshoe-shaped bar or in the basement lounge.

4 *Old-world charm* 11 p.m.

After eating at Red Rooster, head downstairs to Samuelsson's other creation, **Ginny's Supper Club**. Although both are housed in the same building, Ginny's has its own unique speakeasy vibe and a different menu of creative small plates and cocktails. With a DJ spinning tunes, you can dance off your dinner.

SATURDAY

5 *The Main Drag* 10 a.m.

The 125th Street corridor stands at the convergence of old and new. On the sidewalks, vendors sell fragrant oils and bootleg DVDs. Indoors, you can find shops like **La Scala NYC** (254 West 125th Street; 212-678-7889), an outlet for Ferragamo, Prada, and Dolce & Gabbana, and **S&D Underground** (136 West 125th Street; 212-222-1577), which stocks favorite urban brands. In the midst of it all is the **Apollo**

OPPOSITE Italianate and neo-Georgian townhouses line Harlem's Strivers' Row, once home of Scott Joplin.

RIGHT Named for one of New York's first black-owned bars, 67 Orange Street is on Frederick Douglass Boulevard.

Theater (253 West 125th Street; 212-531-5300; apollotheater.org), where black entertainers have gotten their start for generations. Group tours are available by appointment; if you're not traveling with a pack, you may be able to tag along with one. (Call to check availability.) To catch the famed Amateur Night, return on a Wednesday.

6 *El Barrio* Noon

Harlem's east side is El Barrio, a repository for Spanish culture. Have an authentic Puerto Rican meal at **La Fonda Boricua** (169 East 106th Street; 212-410-7292; fondaboricua.com; $$), which started as a lunch counter and expanded with a simple dining room. There is no printed menu, but you can't go wrong with the pernil (roast pork). Walk off lunch with a tour of the murals on nearby buildings. A mosaic at 106th Street and Lexington Avenue honors Julia de Burgos, a 20th-century poet. The four-story-tall *Spirit of East Harlem*, on Lexington at 104th Street, includes men playing dominoes, a woman holding a baby, and the Puerto Rican flag. Stop at **Justo Botanica** (134 East 104th Street; 212-534-9140), a musty store founded in 1930 that offers spiritual readings and sells African and Native American carvings as well as prayer cards, candles, and beads. For a history of Spanish Harlem, visit **El Museo del Barrio** (1230 Fifth Avenue; 212-831-7272; elmuseo.org).

7 *The New Renaissance* 3 p.m.

The true Harlem Renaissance was centered on art, and now new galleries and art spaces are popping up again. **Casa Frela Gallery** (47 West 119th Street; 212-722-8577; casafrela.com), in a Stanford White brownstone, exhibits small collections and screens films. The **Renaissance Fine Art Gallery** (2075 Adam Clayton Powell Jr. Boulevard; 212-866-1660; therfagallery.com) and the **Dwyer Cultural Center** (258 St. Nicholas Avenue; 212-222-3060; dwyercc.org) celebrate black culture through art. **The Studio Museum** (144 West 125th Street; 212-864-4500; studiomuseum.org) shows fine art, photography, and film.

8 *The Scene* 6 p.m.

Hard to believe, but the stretch of Frederick Douglass Boulevard where the 1970s drug lord Frank Lucas boasted he made $1 million a day selling heroin is now Harlem's Restaurant Row, a stretch of inviting restaurants and lounges. If the weather's nice, enjoy a drink in the neighborhood's best outdoor space at **Harlem Tavern** (No. 2135; 212-866-4500; harlemtavern.com). Find an ode to multiculturalism at **bier international** (No. 2099; 212-280-0944; bierinternational.com), a twist on the German beer garden. Check out **Moca Restaurant & Lounge** (No. 2210; 212-665-8081; mocalounge.com) for the latest in hip-hop tracks. At No. 2082 and

named for the address of one of New York's first black-owned bars, **67 Orange Street** serves up exotic cocktails and a speakeasy vibe.

9 *Soul Food* 8 p.m.

Those who know soul food know that it is best prepared at home. So it should come as no surprise that good soul food restaurants are difficult to find even in Harlem. **Sylvia's** (328 Lenox Avenue; 212-996-2669; sylviassoulfood.com) gets the most buzz, but it's more about the restaurant's history than the food. Better options are **Amy Ruth's** (113 West 116th Street; 212-280-8779; amyruthsharlem.com; $), where dishes are named for famous blacks, or **Miss**

Mamie's Spoonbread Too (366 West 110th Street; 212-865-6744; spoonbreadinc.com; $-$$) and its sister restaurant **Miss Maude's** (547 Lenox Avenue; 212-690-3100). Perhaps the best hidden secret in Harlem soul food — and music — is **American Legion Post 398** (248 West 132nd Street; 212-283-9701; $). Every other Saturday, and on some other nights, the post hosts a jazz jam session in the basement of the brownstone it calls home. There is no cover for this can't-miss live show, and the drinks are cheap, as are the favorites like fried chicken and meatloaf, served on Styrofoam plates.

10 *A World of Music* 11 p.m.

For a great combination of live music and dance space, take a seat at **Shrine** (2271 Adam Clayton Powell Jr. Boulevard; 212-690-7807; shrinenyc.com), a no-frills restaurant and bar where everyone feels like a local. This is a true melting pot of music. Jazz, reggae, hip-hop, pop, and more might be played by the live

OPPOSITE Manuel Vega's mosaic tribute to the poet Julia de Burgos at East 106th Street and Lexington Avenue.

ABOVE The Abyssinian Baptist Church, where the Sunday-morning service is as theatrical as a Broadway production.

LEFT Dr. Harold Cromer puts on a tap dance show at the Dwyer Cultural Center.

bands on a single night. And with lots of floor space to maneuver in, you'll be dancing until your feet are sore.

SUNDAY

11 *Gospel and Brunch* 11 a.m.

Gospel churches are a staple of Harlem visits. A tourist favorite is **Abyssinian Baptist Church** (132 Odell Clark Place; 212-862-7474), a megachurch with a Broadway-like music production. For something

more serene, yet still inspiring, attend a service at **Mount Olivet Baptist Church** (201 Lenox Avenue; 212-864-1155). Afterward, have your Sunday brunch at **Kitchenette Uptown** (1272 Amsterdam Avenue; 212-531-7600; kitchenetterestaurant.com; $$). The restaurant is designed like a rural porch, providing a home-style feel with hearty dishes to match. Try the baked crème brulee French toast, turkey sausage, or one of the thick omelets.

ABOVE A Rafael Ferrer exhibit at El Museo del Barrio in Spanish Harlem.

OPPOSITE Interior of Mount Olivet Baptist Church, 201 Lenox Avenue, at 120th Street, formerly Temple Israel.

THE BASICS

Harlem spans a section of northern Manhattan roughly from 110th Street to 155th Street.

Get around on the subway, or hail taxicabs.

Aloft Harlem
2296 Frederick Douglass Boulevard
212-749-4000
alofthotels.com/harlem
$$
A bona fide luxury hotel to represent Harlem's changing face. High design in contemporary style.

The Harlem Flophouse
242 West 123rd Street
347-632-1960
harlemflophouse.com
$$
Charming four-room bed and breakfast in an 1890s brownstone.

Mount Morris House
12 Mount Morris Park
917-478-6214
mountmorrishouse.com
$$$
Four-room B&B in a restored mansion with elegantly carved woodwork.

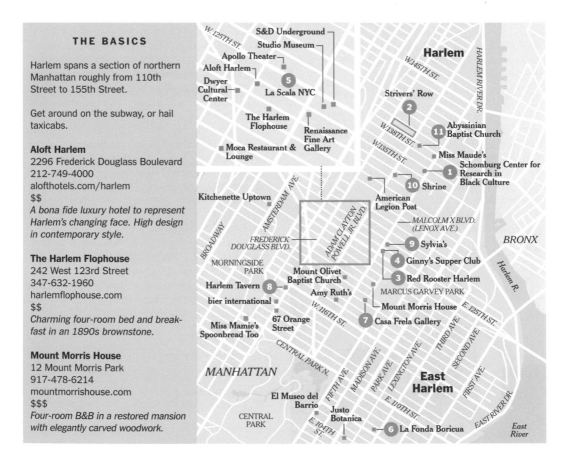

Brooklyn

The Brooklyn Cruise Terminal on the Buttermilk Channel has picturesque views even when the Queen Mary 2, *which docks there regularly, is at sea. There is verdant Governor's Island across the water and, behind it, the heaving, jagged rise of Manhattan. To the north are the great bridges of the East River. To the west, the Statue of Liberty. And to the east, beyond chain link and forbidding streets, there is Brooklyn itself, New York City's most populous borough, a destination in its own right.* — BY SAM SIFTON

FRIDAY

1 *Waterfront Stroll* 4 p.m.

The cobblestone streets under the Manhattan Bridge are home to small shops and shiny new condominium buildings, and to **Saint Ann's Warehouse** (38 Water Street, at Dock Street; 718-254-8779; stannswarehouse.org), a theater that has been a mainstay of the Brooklyn arts scene for more than three decades. Located across from Fulton Ferry State Park, it is an excellent destination after a walk along the **Promenade** in Brooklyn Heights (parallel to Columbia Heights, a grand old street of towering brownstones, running from Remsen to Orange Streets). Check ahead to see what's playing and then wander down to the box office to pick up your tickets.

2 *Walk in the Park* 5 p.m.

Alternatively, head inland, toward the leafy precincts of Fort Greene, for a show at the **Brooklyn Academy of Music** (bam.org) or the **Mark Morris Dance Group** (markmorrisdancegroup.org). Atlantic Avenue, which runs deep into the borough, will lead you most of the way, through a stretch of antiques shops and restaurants.

3 *Pretheater Dinner* 6:30 p.m.

Once you get strolling, it is difficult not to drift into other pretty residential neighborhoods: Cobble Hill and Carroll Gardens nearby and, slightly farther

OPPOSITE Brownstone-lined streets invite long strolls in Park Slope and Prospect Heights.

RIGHT Boutiques like the Brook Farm general store flourish in Brooklyn's Williamsburg and Greenpoint neighborhoods.

afield, Park Slope and Prospect Heights. There is excellent eating along the way. At the bottom of Court Street in Carroll Gardens: **Prime Meats** (465 Court Street at Luquer Street; 718-254-0327; frankspm.com), a chic Germanish steak and salad restaurant. A block or so farther south, on the corner of Huntington Street: **Buttermilk Channel** (524 Court Street; 718-852-8490; buttermilkchannelnyc.com), where you can get local cheeses and pastas and a superlative duck meatloaf. Ten minutes before the end of your meal, have the host call for a car, and go to the performance you've chosen.

4 *Drink after the Curtain* 10 p.m.

Fort Greene abounds in bars suitable for a late-evening drink. A cocktail at the minimalist and homey **No. 7** is no-risk (7 Greene Avenue at Fulton Street; 718-522-6370; no7restaurant.com). Those seeking rougher charms can venture to the **Alibi** (242 DeKalb Avenue between Clermont Avenue and Vanderbilt Avenue), where there are cheap drinks, a pool table, and a crowd that runs equal parts artist and laborer.

SATURDAY

5 *Breakfast Paradise* 9 a.m.

Tom's Restaurant in Prospect Heights (782 Washington Avenue at Sterling Place; 718-636-9738) has been a crowded, friendly mainstay of this neighborhood for decades, and is a winning place to begin a day in Kings County (that's Brooklyn, to you outsiders; each of New York City's five boroughs

is a separate county). Eat pancakes and waffles in a room filled with tchotchkes and good cheer, and watch the marvelous parade.

6 *Parks and Arts* 10 a.m.

A Tom's breakfast provides a strong foundation for a visit to the exhibitions of the nearby **Brooklyn Museum** (200 Eastern Parkway at Washington Avenue; 718-638-5000; brooklynmuseum.org). It is also useful in advance of a walk through the **Brooklyn Botanic Garden** (900 Washington Avenue; 718-623-7200; bbg.org), a 19th-century ash dump that is now home to some of the best horticultural displays in the world. And of course there is **Prospect**

Park (prospectpark.org), Frederick Law Olmsted and Calvert Vaux's triumphant 1867 follow-up to Central Park in Manhattan. Those with children may wish to visit the zoo (450 Flatbush Avenue near Empire Boulevard; 718-399-7339; prospectparkzoo. com), where the daily feedings of the sea lions are a popular attraction.

7 *A Visit to Hipchester* 2 p.m.

Boutiques, coffee bars, and restaurants continue to flourish in Williamsburg and Greenpoint, north Brooklyn's youth-culture Marrakesh. Amid these, **Brook Farm**, a general store in south Williamsburg, offers an aesthetic of farmhouse cosmopolitanism (75 South Sixth Street, between Berry Street and Wythe Avenue; 718-388-8642; brookfarmgeneralstore.com). **Artists and Fleas** is a weekend market where artists, designers, collectors, and craftspeople showcase their work (70 North Seventh Street between Wythe Avenue and Kent Avenue; artistsandfleas.com).

ABOVE A storefront on Eighth Avenue in Brooklyn's Chinatown, in Sunset Park.

LEFT The much loved and well used Prospect Park, designed by Frederick Law Olmsted and Calvert Vaux after they completed Central Park in Manhattan.

OPPOSITE Diners in the back room of Williamsburg's Fatty 'Cue, the Southeast Asian inspired barbecue restaurant.

And **Spoonbill and Sugartown, Booksellers** offers an eclectic mix of art and design books and academic tracts (218 Bedford Avenue at North Fifth Street; 718-387-7322; spoonbillbooks.com). For a pick-me-up or a new coffee machine for home, try **Blue Bottle Coffee** (160 Berry Street between North Fourth and North Fifth Streets; 718-387-4160; bluebottlecoffee. net), an impossibly nerdy outpost of the original Oakland coffee bar. Siphon? French press? Cold drip? All available, along with all the crazy coffee talk you like. Get your geek on.

8 *Dinner for Kings* 7:30 p.m.

Those enamored of the Williamsburg scene may stay in the neighborhood for a smoky dinner at **Fatty 'Cue**, Zak Pelaccio's antic and awesome Southeast Asian barbecue joint (91 South Sixth Street between Berry Street and Bedford Avenue; 718-599-3090; fattycue.com). In Greenpoint, there is the excellent and slightly more adult-themed **Anella**, where the chef Joseph Ogrodnek works marvels with vegetables and duck (222 Franklin Street at Green Street; 718-389-8100; anellabrooklyn.com). Parents with children might try the pizzas at **Motorino** (319 Graham Avenue at Devoe Street; 718-599-8899; motorinopizza.com) or scoot back to Park Slope, where the brothers Bromberg offer a welcoming family atmosphere with food to match at their **Blue Ribbon Brooklyn** (280 Fifth Avenue, between

First Street and Garfield Street; 718-840-0404; blueribbonrestaurants.com).

9 *Pazz and Jop* 10 p.m.

Brooklyn's music scene continues to expand. Three places to hear bands are **Union Pool** in Williamsburg (484 Union Avenue at Meeker Avenue; 718-609-0484; unionpool.blogspot.com); **Brooklyn Bowl**, also there (61 Wythe Avenue between North 11th and North 12th Streets; 718-963-3369; brooklynbowl.com); and **Southpaw**, in Park Slope, (125 Fifth Avenue, between Sterling Place and St. Johns Place; 718-230-0236; spsounds.com). Jazz heads should make their way to **Barbès** in Park Slope (376 Ninth Street at Sixth Avenue; 347-422-0248; barbesbrooklyn.com), where a rich calendar of readings and concerts can take a visitor from early Saturday evening well into Sunday morning.

SUNDAY

10 *Dim Sum à Go-Go* 10 a.m.

Brooklyn's Chinatown, along Eighth Avenue in the Sunset Park neighborhood, is not as large as Manhattan's. But it offers great pleasures. Arrive early for a dim sum meal at **Pacificana** (813 55th Street at Eighth Avenue; 718-871-2880), and watch as the dining room fills into an approximation of a rush-hour subway car. Then stop in at **Ba Xuyen** (4222

Eighth Avenue, between 42nd and 43rd Streets) for a banh mi brunch sandwich and a Vietnamese coffee, or at the tiny **Yun Nan Flavour Snack** (775A 49th Street at Eighth Avenue) for a fiery sweet and sour soup with dumplings.

11 *History in the Ground* 1 p.m.
    Walk off all the food with a tour of **Green-Wood Cemetery** (500 25th Street at Fifth Avenue; 718-768-7300; green-wood.com), the hilly and beautiful

parkland where generations of New Yorkers have moved after death. Admission is free, as are the maps available at the entrance. Look for Boss Tweed, for Jean-Michel Basquiat, for Leonard Bernstein and other once-boldfaced names, as parrots (really!) fly about and the wind ruffles the trees and that view of Manhattan opens up in the distance once more. It appears smaller from this vantage, as if placed in perspective.

ABOVE The view of Manhattan from the Battle Hill Monument at Green-Wood Cemetery, which was a popular tourist attraction in the 19th century.

OPPOSITE The pedestrian path on the Brooklyn Bridge.

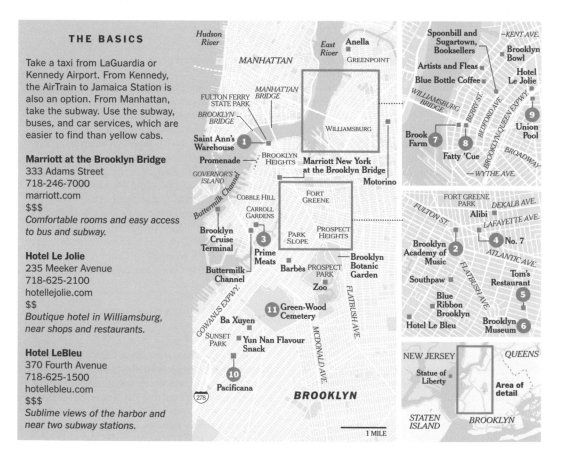

THE BASICS

Take a taxi from LaGuardia or Kennedy Airport. From Kennedy, the AirTrain to Jamaica Station is also an option. From Manhattan, take the subway. Use the subway, buses, and car services, which are easier to find than yellow cabs.

Marriott at the Brooklyn Bridge
333 Adams Street
718-246-7000
marriott.com
$$$
Comfortable rooms and easy access to bus and subway.

Hotel Le Jolie
235 Meeker Avenue
718-625-2100
hotellejolie.com
$$
Boutique hotel in Williamsburg, near shops and restaurants.

Hotel LeBleu
370 Fourth Avenue
718-625-1500
hotellebleu.com
$$$
Sublime views of the harbor and near two subway stations.

Hudson River

MANHATTAN

East River Anella GREENPOINT

FULTON FERRY STATE PARK
MANHATTAN BRIDGE
BROOKLYN BRIDGE

Saint Ann's Warehouse **1**
Promenade BROOKLYN HEIGHTS
GOVERNOR'S ISLAND WILLIAMSBURG

Marriott New York at the Brooklyn Bridge
Motorino

Buttermilk Channel
COBBLE HILL
CARROLL GARDENS
FORT GREENE

Brooklyn Cruise Terminal
Prime Meats **3**
PARK SLOPE PROSPECT HEIGHTS

Buttermilk Channel
Barbès PROSPECT PARK
Brooklyn Botanic Garden

Zoo

Ba Xuyen
11 Green-Wood Cemetery

FLATBUSH AVE.

GOWANUS EXPWY.
SUNSET PARK
Yun Nan Flavour Snack

278 **10**
Pacificana

MCDONALD AVE.

BROOKLYN

1 MILE

Spoonbill and Sugartown, Booksellers −KENT AVE.
Brooklyn Bowl
Artists and Fleas
Blue Bottle Coffee Hotel Le Jolie
WILLIAMSBURG BRIDGE
BERRY ST.
BEDFORD AVE.
BROOKLYN-QUEEN EXPWY.

Brook Farm **7** **8** Union Pool **9**
Fatty 'Cue BROADWAY
−WYTHE AVE.

FORT GREENE PARK
FULTON ST.
Alibi DEKALB AVE.
LAFAYETTE AVE.
Brooklyn Academy of Music **2** **4** No. 7
ATLANTIC AVE.
Southpaw FLATBUSH AVE. Tom's Restaurant **5**
Blue Ribbon Brooklyn
Hotel Le Bleu Brooklyn Museum **6**

NEW JERSEY QUEENS
Statue of Liberty Area of detail
STATEN ISLAND BROOKLYN

East Hampton

On the east end of Long Island, N.Y., the Atlantic Ocean crashes to the shores of the lavish string of villages known as the Hamptons. When New York City's movers and shakers migrate here in the summer for sunning, surfing, fishing, and flirting, the center of the social swirl is historic East Hampton. Lately a raft of luxurious boutiques and restaurants have opened in town. Beloved old hotels and barrooms have been renovated. And celebrities — including Madonna — keep snapping up property in the area.

— BY STEPHANIE ROSENBLOOM

FRIDAY

1 *Social Calendar* 4 p.m.

Want to plunge into the Hamptons social scene? Then your first order of business is to grab the free newspapers and glossy magazines — *Social Life, Hampton Life, Hamptons, Hampton Sheet, Dan's Papers, The East Hampton Star* — and scan them for the weekend's fete, charity event, or oceanfront screening of *Jaws*. You'll find them near the door of many boutiques in East Hampton, but perhaps the most indulgent place to get them is **Scoop du Jour** (35 Newtown Lane; 631-329-4883), the ice cream parlor where waffle cones are stacked with cavity-friendly flavors like cake batter and cotton candy. This is also where you can buy Dreesen's doughnuts, a Hamptons staple since the 1950s. Need a gift for a party host (or yourself)? Shops have sprouted along Main Street, including **Hugo Boss** (No. 46) and **Roberta Freymann** (No. 21).

2 *Pizza Patio* 7 p.m.

It's not just socialites who flee New York for the Hamptons in summer. Manhattan restaurateurs migrate here, too. Among the latest establishments is the Italian standby **Serafina** (104 North Main Street; 631-267-3500; serafinarestaurant.com: $$$). Yellow umbrellas poke up like daffodils from its sidewalk

patio and vine-covered pergola. Fresh pastas and seafood are on the menu, though the brick oven pizzas — in more than two dozen varieties, including pesto — are among the most popular picks. On a typical night, couples canoodle at the bar while well-manicured families stream into the dining room. If your taste leans toward fried seafood, home-made chowder, and frosty drinks, however, head to **Bostwick's Chowder House** (277 Pantigo Road; 631-324-1111; bostwickschowderhouse.com; $$), which has new indoor-outdoor digs.

3 *Water Music* 9 p.m.

Watching boats glide along the horizon is perhaps the simplest and most peaceful of Hamptons pleasures. Happily, a favorite haunt, the **Boathouse** (39 Gann Road; 631-329-3663; easthamptonboathouse.com), has expanded and relocated to a secluded spot overlooking Three Mile Harbor, where Bostwick's was previously located. The open-air decks of this gleaming restaurant are an idyllic perch from which to watch boats dock. But on weekends, as the night progresses, the Boathouse morphs into an indoor-outdoor lounge where the lithe and tanned sip and sway to beats from a D.J.

SATURDAY

4 *Farm Fresh* 10 a.m.

Before men in golf shirts roamed the Hamptons, it was the purview of farmers. Thankfully, there are still some left. Pick up fresh eggs, local produce, and home-baked muffins and scones for breakfast at

OPPOSITE At the Pollock-Krasner House and Study Center visitors don slippers to walk on the paint-splattered floor of Jackson Pollock's studio.

RIGHT Diners in the Boathouse, in a secluded spot overlooking Three Mile Harbor.

Round Swamp Farm (184 Three Mile Harbor Road; 631-324-4438; roundswampfarm.com). Be sure to buy enough for lunch so you can skip the interminable snack bar line at the beach.

5 *Where to Tan* 11 a.m.

Choosing a favorite Hamptons beach is not unlike choosing a favorite child. Still, two beaches were among the U.S. top 10 named in 2010 by Stephen P. Leatherman, director of the Laboratory for Coastal Research at Florida International University. **Coopers Beach** (in Southampton) captured the No. 1 spot, beating out beaches in Florida and California. And **Main Beach** (in East Hampton) took fifth place. Both are wide and clean and — very important — sell food. Many beaches require seasonal parking permits, though visitors can park at Coopers Beach for $40 a day. Parking at Main Beach is $20 a day, but weekdays only; on weekends visitors must walk or ride bikes. (For details, go to the Long Island Convention & Visitors Bureau's Web site, discoverlongisland.com.)

6 *East End Expressionism* 3:30 p.m.

The wetlands and dunes that draw pleasure-seekers today also inspired some of the greatest abstract and landscape artists of our time. Go see why at **LongHouse Reserve** (133 Hands Creek Road; 631-329-3568; longhouse.org), a sprawling but less-visited garden and sculpture park with works by Buckminster Fuller, Dale Chihuly, Willem de Kooning, and Yoko Ono. Founded by the textile designer Jack Lenor Larsen (who still lives there, according to docents), the reserve's nearly 16 acres are open to the public Wednesdays through Saturdays during the summer. Nearby is the **Pollock-Krasner House and Study Center** (830

ABOVE East Hampton's Main Beach.

OPPOSITE A converted storage barn, which Jackson Pollock and Lee Krasner used as their studio, is open to tours at the Pollock-Krasner House and Study Center.

Springs-Fireplace Road; 631-324-4929; pkhouse.org), which Jackson Pollock and Lee Krasner bought for $5,000 in 1946 and turned into their home and studio. Visitors must don padded slippers to enter the barn because the floor is splattered with paint that Pollock dripped and flung for his masterpieces. In fact, some of his paint cans are still there.

7 *Clams and Cocktails* 8 p.m.

Norman Jaffe, the American architect, designed the once popular (and now shuttered) restaurant known as Laundry. The space has a new life as **Race Lane** (31 Race Lane; 631-324-5022; racelanerestaurant.com; $$$) — a sleek yet cozy spot with a tree-shaded patio seemingly engineered for tête-à-têtes over breezy cocktails and clams from the raw bar. Inside, well-heeled couples dine at tables or on couches in the spare, airy space. You'll find seafood dishes like red snapper with saffron and spinach, baked salmon with a ginger glaze over shiitake mushrooms and snow peas, or lobster salad with avocado.

8 *No Velvet Rope* 10 p.m.

The Hamptons nightclub scene has quieted in recent years as action shifts to the tip of Long Island at Montauk, where shabby motels and quaint restaurants are being remade into boho chic establishments. But there are still plenty of pleasures to be had in East Hampton after sunset. The music continues to thump at clubs like Lily Pond and, now, RdV East. Another hot spot is the newly renovated **c/o The Maidstone** (207 Main Street; 631-324-5006; themaidstone.com). The hotel's Living Room restaurant and lounge lure a lively, attractive crowd.

SUNDAY

9 *Morning Runway* 11:30 a.m.

Catch a tennis match or baseball game on flat screens while enjoying panini or frittatas at **CittaNuova** (29 Newtown Lane; 631-324-6300; cittanuova.com; $$$), a Milan-inspired cafe with a facade that peels back to provide indoor-outdoor seating along the village's prime shopping strip. A backyard patio has more tables. The pretty space can

be jammed during events like the World Cup. Should there be no games to hold your attention, people-watching (O.K., fashion-policing) from the outdoor tables will.

10 *Artful Afternoon* 1 p.m.

Many of the artists who settled in the Hamptons exhibited at **Guild Hall** (158 Main Street; 631-324-0806; guildhall.org), the region's celebrated arts center, and current artists still do. Performances are held all summer long.

11 *Behind the Hedges* 2:30 p.m.

Real estate is a blood sport here. And one of the most coveted addresses is Lily Pond Lane.

Take a leisurely drive along the wide road where beyond the hedges you can glimpse houses that belong to the likes of Martha Stewart. Grey Gardens, once the decayed home of Edith Ewing Bouvier Beale and her daughter, can be found where Lily Pond meets West End Road. Along the way you're likely to spot many material girls, but if you are desperately seeking the original, head over to Bridge-hampton, where Madonna owns a horse farm on Mitchell Lane.

THE BASICS

The drive from Manhattan can be lengthy in heavy summer traffic. Try the Long Island Railroad, Hampton Jitney (hamptonjitney.com), or even the Hampton Luxury Liner (hamptonluxuryliner.com). Rent a bicycle once you're there.

c/o The Maidstone
207 Main Street
631-324-5006
themaidstone.com
$$$$
19 modish rooms, beach parking permits, vintage Scandinavian bicycles, and yoga classes.

The 1770 House Restaurant & Inn
143 Main Street
631-324-1770
1770house.com
$$$$
Feels like the home it once was.

The Huntting Inn
94 Main Street
631-324-0410
thepalm.com/Huntting-Inn
$$$-$$$$
A pretty inn that is also home to the popular Palm restaurant.

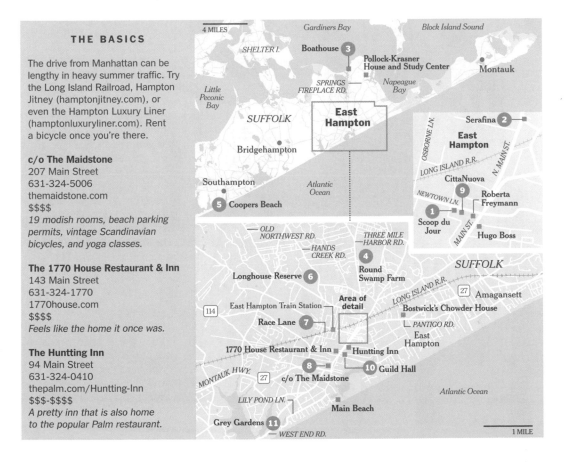

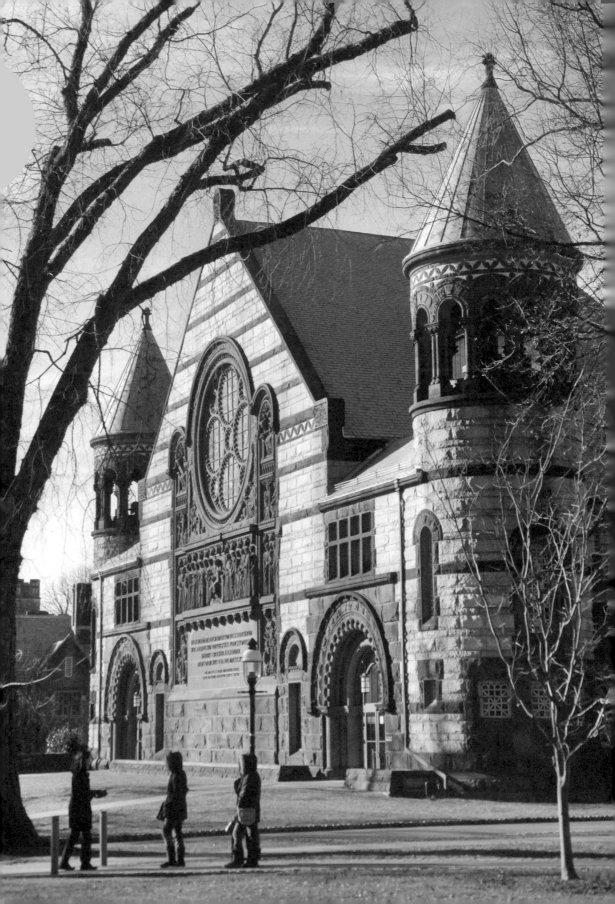

Princeton

"I think of Princeton as being lazy and good-looking and aristocratic — you know, like a spring day," F. Scott Fitzgerald wrote in This Side of Paradise. *Ninety years later, the appraisal still fits. From the century-old wrought-iron FitzRandolph Gate of Princeton University to the sleek rowing shells on sparkling Lake Carnegie, this small New Jersey town retains an air of easygoing noblesse. It is studded with landmarks, from a Revolutionary War battlefield to Albert Einstein's workplace, but nevertheless lives firmly in the present — traditional but not stuffy, charming but not quaint. In the tree-shaded downtown, Colonial-era buildings and high-end spots coexist with jeans-and-corduroy vegetarian hangouts and ice cream shops. And the campus is its own luxurious green city, in the words of Raymond Rhinehart, author of a guide to campus architecture, "a marketplace of ideas, set in a garden." — BY LOUISE TUTELIAN*

FRIDAY

1 *Catch of the Day* 6 p.m.

There's great fishing at the **Blue Point Grill** (258 Nassau Street; 609-921-1211; bluepointgrill.com; $$-$$$). The menu typically lists 20 fish specials, from Barnegat bluefish to a whole Greek bronzini. It's B.Y.O., but not to worry: **Nassau Liquors Grape & Grain** (264 Nassau Street; 609-924-0031) is a handy half-block away.

2 *The Flavor of the Place* 8 p.m.

Get out onto Nassau Street, Princeton's main street, to window-shop the bookstores and boutiques, check out vintage buildings, and peek down side streets at beautifully kept Victorian houses. The red-brick **Bainbridge House** (158 Nassau Street), dating to 1766, is now the Historical Society of Princeton. The Tudor Revival building at 92 Nassau Street, built in 1896, was once a Princeton dormitory.

SATURDAY

3 *Stack 'em Up* 8 a.m.

Get up and go early to **Pj's Pancake House** (154 Nassau Street; 609-924-1353; pancakes.com; $$), Princeton's breakfast nook since 1962, with the initial-carved wooden tables to prove it. Students, young

families, and gray-haired couples rub elbows while plunging their forks into the tender pancakes — butter-milk, blueberry, buckwheat, and more — served with eggs and bacon. Afterward, stroll down to the **Princeton University Store** (114 Nassau Street; 609-921-8500) and pick up a map of the university campus. (Online maps are at princeton.edu.)

4 *Take a Tiger by the Tail* 9 a.m.

The bronze tigers flanking the entrance to Nassau Hall are a fitting invitation to the architec-turally rich Princeton University campus, though their dignity is compromised by the generations of children who have clambered over them. Built in 1756, Nassau Hall survived bombardment in the Revolution and now holds the office of the university president. Alexander Hall has echoed with the words of speakers from William Jennings Bryan to Art Buchwald; Prospect House, deeper into the campus, was Woodrow Wilson's home when he was president of the university. Don't be surprised if a wedding is under way at University Chapel, a Gothic-style landmark. The Frank Gehry-designed Peter B. Lewis math and science library, opened in 2008, adds swooping stainless steel curves to Princeton. The 87,000-square-foot building includes a second-floor "tree house" with 34-foot-high ceilings and clerestory windows framing the trees outside. All over campus,

OPPOSITE Alexander Hall has echoed with the words of speakers from William Jennings Bryan to Art Buchwald.

BELOW The 18th-century Nassau Inn.

look for unusual spires and whimsical gargoyles of cackling monkeys, dinosaurs, and dragons.

5 *Art in the Heart of Campus* 10:30 a.m.

Besides giving Princeton one of the richest endowments of any university in the world, wealthy benefactors have provided it with a wealth of outstanding art at its **Art Museum** (609-258-3788; artmuseum.princeton.edu). Don't rush it — there are more than 60,000 works, and the galleries are spacious, peaceful, blessedly uncrowded — and free. The pre-Columbian and Asian collections are notable, but you can also see Monet's *Water Lilies and Japanese Bridge* and Warhol's *Blue Marilyn*. If you remember reading the 2004 best-selling novel *The Rule of Four*, set on the Princeton campus, picture the student heroes sneaking around these premises in the dark.

6 *Follow the Icons* 12:30 p.m.

Pick up a sandwich on excellent fresh bread at **Witherspoon Bread Company** (74 Witherspoon Street; 609-688-0188; terramomo.com; $) and set out to trace the footsteps of giants. "It's a fine fox hunt, boys!" George Washington is said to have cried to his troops as the British fled from them on Jan. 3, 1777, at **Princeton Battlefield** (500 Mercer Road in neighboring Princetown Township; 609-921-0074; state.nj.us/dep/parksandforests/parks/princeton.html). The victory helped restore faith in the American cause. Check the small museum and picture the troops clashing where students now sunbathe. Back toward town on Mercer Road, turn right onto Olden Lane to reach the **Institute for Advanced Study** (Einstein Drive; 609-734-8000; ias.edu). Einstein used to walk to work there from his house at 112 Mercer Street — sometimes, legend has it, after forgetting to put on his socks. The buildings, still a rarefied haven for distinguished scholars, are closed to the public, but the 500-acre Institute Woods, where violets bloom along the banks of the Stony Brook, is open to the public year-round.

7 *Relativity and Retail* 3 p.m.

Only in Princeton will you find a store that combines an Einstein mini-museum with great deals on woolens. Walk directly to the rear of **Landau of Princeton** (102 Nassau Street; 609-924-3494; landauprinceton.com) to see the Einstein photos, letters, and sketches. Then check out the pop-top mittens made of Alpaca yarn, perfect for texting. Steps away in Palmer Square, dozens of shops sell well-designed and indulgent goods from eye kohls to stemware and sandals. Revive at **The Bent Spoon** ice cream shop (35 Palmer Square West; 609-924-2368; thebentspoon.net), whose owners pledge to use local, organic, and hormone-free ingredients whenever possible in the treats they make fresh every day. Who knew nectarine sorbet could taste so good?

OPPOSITE Princeton University's Peter B. Lewis Library, designed by architect Frank Gehry.

RIGHT A Norman Rockwell mural over the bar at the Nassau Inn's Yankee Doodle Tap Room.

BELOW Bronze tigers guard the entrance to the university's Nassau Hall.

8 *For the Record* 5 p.m.

Since 1980, the **Princeton Record Exchange** (20 South Tulane Street; 609-921-0881; prex.com) has been dispensing used vinyl, CDs, and DVDs at irresistible prices (from $2 for some LPs to under $12 for used DVDs). The store, which is open until 9 p.m., crams 150,000 items onto its floor at any one time.

9 *Sustainable Dining* 8 p.m.

One relaxing choice for dinner is **Mediterra** (29 Hulfish Street; 609-252-9680; terramomo.com; $$$), where wines from 10 countries line the walls; look for paella or locally raised chicken. Locally sourced and sustainable food is the focus at **elements** (163 Bayard Lane; 609-924-0078; elementsprinceton.com; $$$). Golden tilefish, black bass and monkfish are all from area waters.

10 *Brews and Blues* 10 p.m.

You may hear anything from pop to blues to classic rock 'n' roll for a modest cover at **Triumph Brewing Company** (138 Nassau Street; 609-924-7855; triumphbrewing.com), where the crowd is student-heavy but not raucous. A busy bar dispenses hand-crafted beers, and graduate students rub elbows with 40-somethings escaping their teenage children.

SUNDAY

11 *The Tow Path* 11 a.m.

Rent a mountain bike at **Jay's Cycles** (249 Nassau Street, 609-924-7233; jayscycles.com) and cruise southeast on Alexander Street for about a mile and a half until you see Turning Basin Park on the right. You'll be next to the Delaware-Raritan Canal tow path, a level dirt trail that is a delightful place to walk, bike, or jog. If you'd rather be on the

water, you can stow the bike at **Princeton Canoe & Kayak Rental** (483 Alexander Street; 609-452-2403; canoenj.com) and rent a watercraft. Make your way a half-mile up to the Washington Road Bridge and look for impossibly fit young Princetonians sculling under a bright blue spring sky on Lake Carnegie.

ABOVE Regulars can browse the 150,000 or so titles at the Princeton Record Exchange, open since 1980. The store is known for its selection of vinyl.

OPPOSITE Students walk the Princeton University campus, which in the words of Raymond Rhinehart is "a marketplace of ideas, set in a garden."

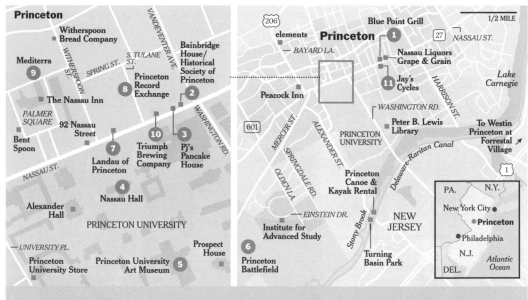

THE BASICS

Princeton is about an hour from New York City by car or New Jersey Transit rail.

The Peacock Inn
20 Bayard Lane
609-924-1707
peacockinn.com

$$-$$$
Boutique hotel in a building dating to 1775. Multimillion-dollar renovation in 2010.

The Nassau Inn
10 Palmer Square East
800-862-7728
nassauinn.com
$$$

In the heart of town, with 18th-century-style furnishings.

Westin Princeton at Forrestal Village
201 Village Boulevard
609-452-7900
westinprinceton.com
$$-$$$
Just outside town.

Cape May

Located at the very southern tip of New Jersey (Garden State Parkway Exit 0), Cape May combines an authentic Victorian past with the present-day ambience of a summer beach town. The entire city of about 3,700 is a National Historic Landmark, and for good reason: there are no fewer than 600 sturdily built Victorian homes and buildings on this 3.5-square mile island. Located on the Atlantic Flyway, Cape May is also an internationally renowned birding hot spot, and devotees cluster there in spring and fall when the birds stop over on their way to distant climes. In summer, another migration takes place, as suntanned masses who don't know a pigeon from a plover descend on this tony resort. — BY LOUISE TUTELIAN

FRIDAY

1 *Bird's Eye View* 4 p.m.

Get the lay of the land by climbing to the top of the 152-year-old **Cape May Lighthouse** (Lighthouse Road, Cape May Point State Park; capemaymac.org; 800-275-4278). At the top, you'll be rewarded for your 199-step trek with a panoramic view of the Cape May Peninsula, and neighboring coastal locations from Wildwood, New Jersey, to the north to — on a clear day — Cape Henlopen, Delaware, to the west. The 157-foot-tall light also offers interpretive exhibits about its history and information on the lives of its former keepers.

2 *Back in Time* 7 p.m.

Tucked in a corner of Congress Hall (251 Beach Avenue; 609-884-8422; congresshall.com; $$), a restored 19th-century grand hotel, the **Blue Pig Tavern** is the place to refuel. Entrees range from its signature seafood pot pie with shrimp, scallops, and crab to four styles of burgers with house-cut fries and slaw. You will be one of a long list of visitors to this space. It was the first tavern in Cape May, a gathering place for whalers in the 1700s.

3 *Kick Back* 9 p.m.

Congress Hall doesn't dwell in the past, however. In its basement is the **Boiler Room Bar**, a nightclub

with bare brick walls and 10 TV monitors so every guest gets a view of the acts that perform nearly every weekend. And yes, it really was the hotel's boiler room.

SATURDAY

4 *On the Wing* 8 a.m.

Cape May is on the Atlantic Flyway, one of the planet's busiest migratory corridors, navigated by hundreds of species in spring and fall. Because of its location amid barrier islands and wetlands, fresh-water and ocean, birds come to rest, eat, and nest. Things are calmer in summer, but there are still plenty of birds to be seen, especially with the help of a good guide. The **Cape May Bird Observatory** (701 East Lake Drive, Cape May Point; 609-884-2736; birdcapemay.org) sponsors naturalist-led walks from 8 to 10 a.m. on Saturdays at Cape May Point State Park on Lighthouse Avenue. Participants can expect to see waterfowl, flycatchers, warblers, piping plovers, and more. The Observatory's Northwoods Center offers free maps for self-guided walks.

5 *Tour a Mansion* 11 a.m.

The **Emlen Physick Estate** (1048 Washington Street; 800-275-4278; capemaymac.org) is a mansion constructed for a Philadelphia physician in the Stick style of the late 1800s. If you are an architecture buff, or even if you're not, take the 45-minute guided tour. Fifteen of the rooms have been restored with historical accuracy, shedding light on how residents lived in the Victorian era, when so many of Cape May's majestic houses were built.

6 *Pick a Panini* 1 p.m.

Skip the Victorian tea sandwiches and head to **Tisha's** (322 Washington Street in the Washington Street Mall; 609-884-9119; tishasfinedining.com; $$) for more contemporary fare. Locals love the restaurant's sandwiches, paninis, and soups, as well as entrees like vegetable salad with grilled shrimp or a bacon bleu burger. The menu changes seasonally.

7 *Beach Bake* 2 p.m.

Hit the beach where the locals do, at the Cove. Located on Beach Avenue at 2nd Street, at the very

OPPOSITE The Cape May lighthouse.

beginning of the Promenade, **Cove Beach** has a lovely view out toward the Lighthouse at Cape May Point. It's an old-school, laid-back spot that's not overly groomed, making it ideal for beach-combing in search of Cape May's plentiful frosted, etched sea glass. From Memorial Day through Labor Day, you'll need a beach pass, available for a small fee at every beach entrance.

8 *Romantic Glow* 6 p.m.

Everyone looks spectacular in the golden light shed from the intricate chandeliers at the **Ebbitt**

Room. Claim a lipstick-red banquette in this intimate space tucked off the lobby of the **Virginia Hotel** (25 Jackson Street; 800-732-4236; virginiahotel.com; $$$) and settle in. The menu changes often, but you might find items like fennel, apple, and celery root salad with blood orange vinaigrette; pomegranate braised short rib; and a decadent milk chocolate caramel tart for dessert.

9 *Curtain Up* 8 p.m.

How many shore towns can boast two professional theater companies? The **Cape May Stage** (Lafayette and Bank Streets; 609-884-1341; capemaystage.com) presents a full season in its 75-seat theater. Productions have included *Say Goodnight, Gracie* by Rupert Holmes, about the legendary George Burns; *The Understudy* by Pulitzer Prize nominee Theresa Rebeck, the-behind-the-scenes tale of a Broadway show; and *Steel Magnolias*, Robert Harling's tale of love among

ABOVE The Virginia Hotel.

LEFT The wildlife refuge at Cape May Point is a rest stop on the migratory path along the Atlantic Seaboard for millions of birds. This guest is a cedar waxwing.

OPPOSITE Birders do some flocking of their own each spring and fall at Cape May.

a band of close friends in the South. At the **East Lynne Theater Company** at First Presbyterian Church (500 Hughes Street; 609-884-5898; eastlynnetheater.org), recent fare has included *He and She* by Rachel Crothers and *The World of Dorothy Parker*, adapted by Gayle Stalhuth.

SUNDAY

10 *The Wheel Thing* 8 a.m.

The boardwalk closes to bicycles at 10 a.m. So get up early to ride its entire length. Many Cape May hotels provide bicycles for their guests — it's bike-friendly on these streets. You can also rent from the conveniently located **Shields Bike Rentals** (11

Gurney Street; 609-898-1818) or the **Village Bicycle Shop** (605 Lafayette Street; 609-884-8500).

11 *Munch Brunch* 10 a.m.

For Sunday brunch, the **Mad Batter** (19 Jackson Street; 609-884-5970; madbatter.com; $$) serves tempting dishes like Chesapeake Bay Benedict with lump crabmeat or orange and almond French toast. Indulge with a pomegranate mimosa — one of six varieties.

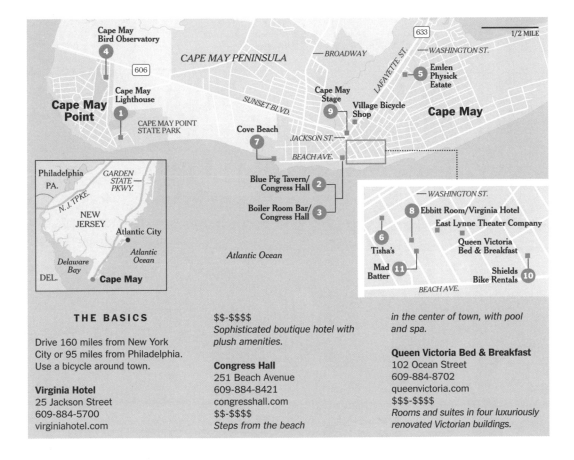

THE BASICS

Drive 160 miles from New York City or 95 miles from Philadelphia. Use a bicycle around town.

Virginia Hotel
25 Jackson Street
609-884-5700
virginiahotel.com

$$-$$$$
Sophisticated boutique hotel with plush amenities.

Congress Hall
251 Beach Avenue
609-884-8421
congresshall.com
$$-$$$$
Steps from the beach

in the center of town, with pool and spa.

Queen Victoria Bed & Breakfast
102 Ocean Street
609-884-8702
queenvictoria.com
$$$-$$$$
Rooms and suites in four luxuriously renovated Victorian buildings.

Philadelphia

The 18th-century city tucked inside Philadelphia, where the United States was born at Independence Hall, swarms all year with curious tourists, history buffs, and children on school trips. Sprawling out from it is the other Philadelphia, firmly rooted in the 21st century and bustling with the activity of a rapidly evolving destination city. Adventurous restaurants reinforce the city's growing culinary reputation, though an obligatory cheese steak still hits the spot. Neighborhoods in transition provide hot spots for shopping and night life, while other areas keep dishing out some old-school Philly "attytood." And traditional leisure-time stops like the Schuylkill riverbanks and the venerable Franklin Institute keep right on drawing them in.

— BY JEFF SCHLEGEL

FRIDAY

1 *Another Go-to Building* 3:30 p.m.

Independence Hall belongs to the ages; **City Hall** (Broad and Market Streets; 215-686-2840; visitphilly.com/history/philadelphia/city-hall) belongs to Philadelphia. This 548-foot-tall 19th-century building is more than just a big hunk of granite interrupting traffic in the heart of the city — it is topped by a 27-ton bronze statue of William Penn, one of 250 statues by Alexander Milne Calder ornamenting the building inside and out. Take the elevator to the top ($5) for 35-mile views from the observation deck.

2 *No Lemon Meringue Pie* 5:30 p.m.

Silk City Diner Bar & Lounge (435 Spring Garden Street; 215-592-8838; silkcityphilly.com) is a twofer with a lower-level nightclub on one side and a traditional diner car on the other with atmospheric, dim red lighting. Grab a counter seat at the diner and choose from a copious selection of bottled beer or a cocktail like the Pink Panther strawberry martini.

OPPOSITE AND RIGHT Philadelphia's massive City Hall is topped by a bronze statue of William Penn weighing 27 tons. Artist Alexander Milne Calder was responsible for the structure's 250-plus statues, including this likeness of Benjamin Franklin (right).

3 *Odd Couple* 7 p.m.

The Chinese-Peruvian fusion at **Chifa** (707 Chestnut Street; 215-925-5555; chifarestaurant.com; $) can kill two cravings with one dish. Chef and owner Jose Garces's fourth Latin-flavored restaurant in town spotlights chifa, a cuisine influenced by Peru's 19th-century Chinese immigrants. Meals start with a bowl of yuca-flour bread balls, a warm, doughy treat dipped in tangy whipped guava butter. The small-plate menu is an amalgam of tastes — the chaufa blends stir-fried rice with a hint of spicy chorizo, topped with sweet soy-glazed scallops. Chupe is a succulent seafood chowder with mussels, shrimp, and purple potatoes.

4 *In a League of Its Own* 10 p.m.

The Big Lebowski meets sleek lounge at **North Bowl** (909 North Second Street; 215-238-2695; northbowlphilly.com), a converted mechanics' garage where segments of original concrete floor and brick wall blend with brightly painted walls, abstract art, and glow-in-the-dark bowling pins. There are 13 lanes of bowling on the first floor, four lanes on the second, and bars on both floors. The soundtrack one night included Blondie and Cuban rhythms; fish tacos and thai beef skewers were on the menu to cure a case of late-night munchies.

SATURDAY

5 *One Man's Labyrinth* 10 a.m.

Some places can't be fully captured by just photos and words. That sums up **Philadelphia's Magic Gardens** (1020-1022 South Street; 215-733-0390; philadelphiasmagicgardens.org), an art center and endearingly bizarre outdoor maze of mortar, bicycle tires, bottles, textiles, artwork, and tchotchkes. The Philadelphia mosaic muralist Isaiah Zagar's magnum opus is a multitextured, multilayered labyrinth that leaves visitors amused, if maybe puzzled. "I think it communicates something, but I don't know what that is," said Mr. Zagar, who frequently roams his creations and obligingly fields questions from visitors.

6 *Slice of Local Color* 11 a.m.

Enticing aromas of homemade sausages, cheeses, and pastries infuse the air along the **Ninth Street Italian Market** (Ninth Street, between Wharton and Fitzwater Streets; phillyitalianmarket.com). Produce vendors ply their wares under green-and-red awnings in front of shops selling Italian specialties and assorted merchandise at this century-old South Philadelphia outdoor market. Hungry? **Lorenzo's Pizza** (Ninth and Christian Streets; 215-922-2540; lorenzospizza.net) is an unpretentious corner shop serving one of the city's best pizza slices. The secret: they don't skimp on spices.

7 *Ben's Place* 1:30 p.m.

Noted for its giant two-story model of a human heart and interactive displays that make it seem more like a theme park than a science museum, the **Franklin Institute** (222 North 20th Street; 215-448-1200; fi.edu) is aptly named for Benjamin Franklin, the city's favorite polymath. Flight simulators, giant locomotives parked indoors, a virtual trip to astronaut world — it's tough to know where to look. The place to start, though, may be on the Web, where you can buy tickets in advance and skip the long lines waiting at the door.

8 *Sewing for Goths* 4 p.m.

Fabric Row (Fourth Street, between South and Catherine Streets) has long been the place to buy a bolt of cloth. Fabric shops still ply their trade there, but they share the street with tattoo parlors and an eclectic mix of retailers in this energetic Queen Village neighborhood. **Armed & Dangerous** (623-625 South Fourth Street; 215-922-4525) sells wares in the "romantic gothic vein," along with a variety of imported Venetian ball masks ($25 to $300). **Bus Stop** (750 South Fourth Street; 215-627-2357;

ABOVE A jogger strikes a *Rocky*-esque pose atop the stairs of the Philadelphia Museum of Art.

OPPOSITE Rowers make their way down the placid Schuylkill River.

busstopboutique.com) specializes in designer shoes from Europe and South America, including the French-designed, Spanish-made Coclico brand and the eco-friendly brand Terra Plana.

9 *Israeli and More* 8 p.m.

Housed in a blocky building in Society Hill and decked out in the dun colors of Jerusalem stone, **Zahav** (237 St. James Place; 215-625-8800; zahavrestaurant.com; $$$) features Israeli recipes and a healthy dose of North African and Middle Eastern fare, too. The ta'yim tasting menu is a good place to start for the uninitiated — first up is a bowl of creamy hummus and a large round of house-baked, earthy flat bread, followed by three small plates and then dessert. The Sabra is flavorful grilled chicken served over fluffy couscous; the salad is a potpourri of eight small dishes that include spicy Moroccan carrots seasoned in cumin and chilies that make your mouth zing.

10 *Down It if You Dare* 10 p.m.

If absinthe is your thing, head to the second-floor lounge at **Time** (1315 Sansom Street; 215-985-4800; timerestaurant.net). It dispenses five versions of the green liqueur, which until recently was banned in the United States. It was the drink of choice among 19th-century Parisian artists, not to mention Ernest Hemingway. If it's not your thing, the downstairs whiskey bar features around 75 scotches and other whiskeys. One late night in the dining room across the foyer, a freewheeling seven-piece jazz band played a raucous gig as some members took breaks in midtune to mingle with the crowd before jumping back in.

SUNDAY

11 *Morning Constitutional* 8:30 a.m.

The best time to hit **Independence National Historic Park** (nps.gov/inde) is first thing in the

morning, ahead of the crowds. Pick up your free tickets (the Visitor Center at 6th and Market Streets opens early) and start with the main attraction, Independence Hall, where lines will soon be longest. Take a quick look at the Liberty Bell through the glass at its dedicated building, and then poke around the restored buildings and inviting lawns.

12 *Riverside* 11 a.m.

Head over to the **Philadelphia Museum of Art** (26th Street and Benjamin Franklin Parkway; 215-763-8100; philamuseum.org), take your picture with the Rocky statue out front, and then walk in to enjoy the collection. From there, walk behind the museum to the **Breakaway Bikes** shed (215-568-6002; breakawaybikes.com) to rent a bike ($10 an hour, helmet and lock included), and ride along the path paralleling the Schuylkill River in Fairmount Park. Look for elegant Victorian-era boathouses built in the heyday of the city's rowing clubs. One of the city's Olympic-level rowers was Grace Kelly's father. Watch today's rowers in their shells as they glide along the river, and take a look at some of the park's sculptures.

ABOVE AND OPPOSITE Philadelphia views from City Hall's observation deck. Above, the downtown skyline, and opposite, the grand Benjamin Franklin Parkway, which cuts through Logan Circle before terminating at the Philadelphia Museum of Art.

THE BASICS

Fly, drive, or take a train on Amtrak's busy Northeast Corridor. Philadelphia is a good walking city, but a car is handy.

The Independent
1234 Locust Street
215-772-1440
theindependenthotel.com
$$
Boutique hotel in a restored building. Some of the 24 rooms have fireplaces.

The Alexander Inn
301 South 12th Street
215-923-3535
alexanderinn.com
$$
Art Deco-inspired touches in 48 designer rooms.

Hotel Palomar
117 South 17th Street
215-563-5006
hotelpalomar-philadelphia.com
$$
Stylish new hotel near City Hall, with 230 rooms.

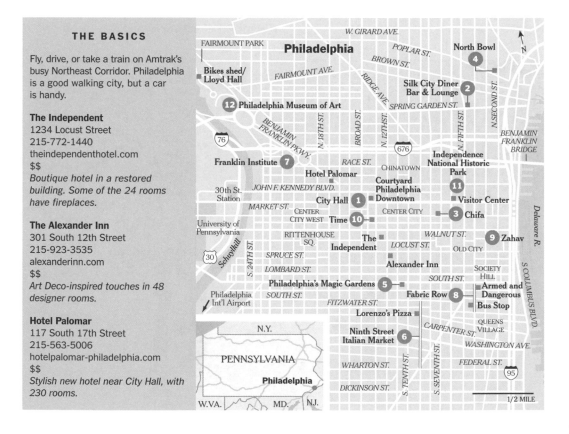

The Brandywine Valley

Only 15 miles from downtown Wilmington, Delaware, the Brandywine Valley is worlds away from the high-rise towers of the city center. Nestled into the northwest corner of Delaware and the southeast section of Pennsylvania, Brandywine, with its historic stone houses and rolling hills, would still look familiar to George Washington, who commanded the Continental Army there in 1777. Later, titans of industry, most notably the du Pont family, built lavish estates that are now open to the public. And artists like Andrew Wyeth made the landscape famous. But the Brandywine Valley is perhaps best enjoyed on horseback or by canoe, following the lazy path of the river, with a picnic and a good bottle of wine from one of the many local vineyards. — BY ANN COLIN HERBST

FRIDAY

1 *Happy Trails* 3:30 p.m.

Brandywine is horse country, but even if you have no equestrian skills, you can still get into the local spirit on an evening trail ride at **Gateway Stables** (949 Merrybell Lane, Kennett Square, Pennsylvania; 610-444-1255; gatewaystables.com). Meander the trails past 200-year-old oaks and enjoy the spectacular scenery of Gateway's 80 wooded acres and meadows skirting the Delaware border. Hourlong excursions for one to four riders are about $40 a person. Helmets are provided; sturdy shoes are recommended. Reservations are required.

2 *Tavern Dining* 5 p.m.

Imbibe some local color at **Buckley's Tavern & Restaurant** in Centreville, Delaware (5812 Kennett Pike/Route 52; 302-656-9776; buckleystavern.org; $$). The building dates to 1817; in the 1930s, the house became a tavern. Choose a pub favorite like fish and chips or look for dinner fare like roasted herb chicken or blackened tuna.

3 *Flowers and Fountains* 7 p.m.

Take advantage of long summer hours to take in the eye-popping horticultural displays at **Longwood Gardens**, Pierre du Pont's former country estate (Route 1, Kennett Square; 610-388-1000; longwoodgardens.org). Longwood's history dates to 1700, when the Peirce family bought the property

from William Penn. In 1906, du Pont bought the land and designed formal rose, wisteria, peony, and conservatory gardens. Italian-style water gardens, topiaries, and a series of fountains light up at night, with music. Admission is $18.

SATURDAY

4 *Wyeths and More* 9:30 a.m.

Housed in a 19th-century grist mill, the **Brandywine River Museum** contains a collection of American illustrations, still lifes, landscapes, and the artwork of three generations of the Wyeth family (Route 1, Chadds Ford, Pennsylvania; 610-388-2700; brandywinemuseum.org). The museum offers vistas of the Brandywine River. Highlights include the original oils by N.C. Wyeth (1882-1945) that were used to illustrate classics like *Treasure Island* and *Robin Hood*. In the Andrew Wyeth Gallery, you may see some of the Helga paintings and works focusing on local subjects like the Kuerner Farm. Also in the museum are works by Albert Bierstadt, Jasper Cropsey, and Asher Durand, as well as a collection of paintings by Jamie Wyeth.

OPPOSITE A Gilbert Stuart portrait of George Washington decorates the dining room of Winterthur, Henry Francis du Pont's country estate.

BELOW A garden picnic at the Chaddsford Winery.

5 *Gather at the River* Noon

You can't visit the Brandywine Valley without spending some time on the Brandywine River. **Wilderness Canoe Trips** (2111 Concord Pike/Route 202, Wilmington; 302-654-2227; wildernesscanoetrips.com) will provide the equipment, and a van puts you in on the Pennsylvania side and picks you up downstream two hours later in Delaware. But don't worry; the river does most of the work, leaving you free to enjoy the view of Brandywine Creek State Park in Delaware, where you might see deer, blue herons, turtles, carp, and bass. Rentals are about $55 for a canoe or tandem kayak, $45 for a one-person kayak. Before heading to the river, pick up a picnic at **Spring Run Natural Foods** (909 East Baltimore Pike, Kennett Square; 610-388-0500; springrunfoods.com), where you can forage an organic, nitrite-free feast.

6 *A Landmark Collection* 4 p.m.

This is du Pont country, and another of the family's contributions is **Winterthur** (5105 Kennett Pike/Route 52, Wilmington, Delaware; 302-888-4600; winterthur.org), Henry Francis du Pont's mansion of 175 rooms decorated in period American furnishings from 1640 to 1860. There are some 85,000 objects, from Chippendale furniture to paintings by Gilbert Stuart, John Singleton Copley, and Charles Willson Peale. The Chinese export porcelain includes 66 pieces from a dinner service once owned by George Washington. The nearly 1,000-acre property has acres of gardens that demonstrate du Pont's naturalistic principles of garden design and can be toured by tram.

7 *Mushrooms and Microbrews* 8 p.m.

Kennett Square bills itself as the Mushroom Capital of the World, and indeed, mushrooms have been a thriving local industry since the late 19th century. Start your evening at the **Half Moon Restaurant & Saloon** (108 West State Street, Kennett Square; 610-444-7232; halfmoonrestaurant.com; $$) with a plate of Chester County exotic mushrooms served with cranberries and walnuts on ciabatta

bread with melted Gorgonzola. If the evening is mild, try one of the bottled Belgian beers in the rooftop garden. (Downstairs at the bar, beers are on tap.) For dinner, you may want to have your mushrooms with an exotic meat like wild boar or kangaroo. For dessert, head to **La Michoacana Homemade Ice Cream** (231 East State Street, Kennett Square; 610-444-2996) for authentic Mexican ice cream, sorbet, and fruit bars in flavors like corn and rice pudding.

SUNDAY

8 *Wyeths' World* 9 a.m.

Members of Brandywine's most famous artistic family have been known to turn up for breakfast at **Hank's Place**, a wood-paneled diner that is a low-key local favorite (at the southwest intersection of Routes 1 and 100, Chadds Ford; 610-388-7061; hanks-place.net; $). Specialty egg dishes are served daily.

9 *An Infamous Day* 10:30 a.m.

Sept. 11, 1777, was a bad day on the Brandywine for George Washington. His troops tried and

ABOVE Mounting for a trail ride from Gateway Stables.

BELOW The conservatory at Longwood Gardens, one of the du Pont family estates in the area that are open to the public for tours.

failed to stop the advancing British, who went on to take Philadelphia. The **Brandywine Battlefield Park** (1491 Baltimore Pike/Route 1, Chadds Ford; 610-459-3342; brandywinebattlefield.org) recalls the story at a visitors' center with a small, low-tech collection of Colonial cannons, sabers, and other artifacts, including Continental currency. Also at the site are the headquarters of Washington and the Marquis de Lafayette, who was only 19 years old when he was wounded at Brandywine.

10 *Out of the Cellar* 1 p.m.

Sniff and sample at **Chaddsford Winery** (632 Baltimore Pike/Route 1, Chadds Ford; 610-388-6221; chaddsford.com), founded in 1982 and based in a

handsome 18th-century barn. The owners offer daily tastings of their wines—pinot noir, chardonnay, merlot, and more. Tour the winemaking and barrel-aging cellars, and for a bit of the Brandywine Valley to savor later, buy a bottle to take home.

ABOVE Buckley's Tavern is in a building dating back to 1817, but the restaurant's menu breaks from traditional fare. If the weather's nice, the front porch and back patio offer outdoor seating; if it's chilly, sit inside by the fire.

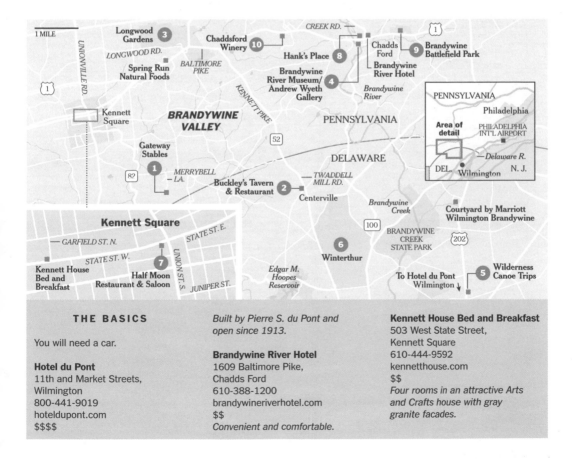

THE BASICS

You will need a car.

Hotel du Pont
11th and Market Streets, Wilmington
800-441-9019
hoteldupont.com
$$$$

Built by Pierre S. du Pont and open since 1913.

Brandywine River Hotel
1609 Baltimore Pike, Chadds Ford
610-388-1200
brandywineriverhotel.com
$$
Convenient and comfortable.

Kennett House Bed and Breakfast
503 West State Street, Kennett Square
610-444-9592
kennetthouse.com
$$
Four rooms in an attractive Arts and Crafts house with gray granite facades.

Baltimore

Baltimore's Inner Harbor, reclaimed from a nadir of rotting piers and warehouses in the 1970s, shines with office towers and hotels, an aquarium and science center, historic ships, and the nearby Camden Yards ballpark. Water taxis connect the Inner Harbor to the row houses, shops, and sometimes rowdy bars of Fell's Point, where the city began. Away from the tourist hubs, urban renewal continues in a more spontaneous form, led by artists in search of cheap rents and warehouse spaces. Once rough neighborhoods have been taken over by studios, galleries, and performance spaces. Crab joints and sports bars share cobblestone streets with fancy cafes and tapas restaurants. And with a little exploration, it's still easy to find the beehive hairdos and wacky museums that fit an old Baltimore nickname, "Charm City." — BY JOSHUA KURLANTZICK

FRIDAY

1 *Into the Woods* 3 p.m.

Though you wouldn't guess it if your only view of Baltimore were from Interstate 95, which passes port terminals and factories spewing smoke, the center of the city conceals a wooded, stream-filled oasis, the **Jones Falls Trail** (baltimorecity.gov). Designed for hiking and biking, it parallels the Jones Falls River and meanders past some of the old mills that once powered Baltimore's economy. It is a rustic and historical look at a sometimes gritty city. Enter at the northern border of Druid Hill Park and head north. Bicycle rentals are at **Light Street Cycles** (1124 Light Street; 410-685-2234; lightstcycles.com).

2 *Crabs and More* 7 p.m.

In a town known for crab cakes and fried fish sandwiches, **Woodberry Kitchen** (2010 Clipper Park Road; 410-464-8000; woodberrykitchen.com; $$$) stands out for its refined local cooking. Set in the Clipper Mill complex, an old foundry that is now an artists' haven, Woodberry serves American comfort food using seasonal and local ingredients,

OPPOSITE The old port city of Baltimore has waterfront enough for Sunday sailors, oceangoing cargo ships, and tourist hordes.

RIGHT The Inner Harbor, where recreation reigns.

like Chesapeake soft-shell crabs served with a spicy tartar sauce or cider-glazed roasted chicken atop a Spanish-style tortilla.

3 *Very Off Broadway* 10 p.m.

For offbeat theater, take a seat at the **Creative Alliance at the Patterson** (3134 Eastern Avenue; 410-276-1651; creativealliance.org), whose stage feels like an old vaudeville house. One night, you might catch burlesque artists stripping down to their pasties; another night, a documentary on Baltimore's decaying schools. The adjacent gallery often features the works of local painters and photographers.

SATURDAY

4 *Underground Cafe* 9 a.m.

Tucked into a basement of an apartment house in the row house neighborhood of Charles Village, near the main campus of Johns Hopkins University, **Carma's Café** (32nd and Saint Paul Streets; 410-243-5200; carmascafe.com; $$) is easy to miss. But neighbors flock to it for buttery cherry-almond scones, fried cheesecake (could a dessert be richer?), frittatas and salads, and innovative coffee drinks like the zamboni, a drinkable version of a snowball.

5 *Sister Act* 11 a.m.

A short walk from Carma's, the **Baltimore Museum of Art** (10 Art Museum Drive; 443-573-1700; artbma.org) has a surprisingly large endowment of post-Impressionist art. The Cone sisters, socialites who lived in Baltimore in the early 20th century, had the foresight to buy thousands of paintings by

the likes of Cézanne, Picasso, and Matisse. They willed the pieces to the museum, for whenever "the status of appreciation of modern art in Baltimore should improve." Apparently it did. Today, the Cone Collection, including Matisse's *Blue Nude* and Gauguin's *Woman of the Mango*, is the heart of the museum. When you're done inside, grab a snack at Gertrude's, the museum's restaurant, and sit at a table in the nearby sculpture garden.

6 *Call It Fell's* 1 p.m.

Explore the patisseries, bars, and galleries of Fell's Point, still a real neighborhood of Baltimore's iconic brick row houses. Start at the open-air plaza at the bottom of Broadway, where skateboarders mix with musicians and couples snuggle on benches. Walk east, along Thames Street, looking over the water. Stop to inhale French pastry at **Bonaparte Breads** (903 South Ann Street; 410-342-4000) before heading on toward Canton, the next waterfront neighborhood, full of restored warehouses turned into shops and condos.

7 *T-shirts Meet Beehives* 4 p.m.

In recent years, the neighborhood of Hampden has gone from working-class to artsy. Packed with galleries and used-clothing stores, Hampden's main drag, a part of 36th Street, called "The Avenue," is where you'll see 20-somethings in stylishly rumpled

vintage jeans sharing cigarettes with "Hons," the nickname for women who wear classic beehive hair-dos. (They're celebrated every June in Baltimore's "Honfest.") For obscure self-published art books and zines, browse through **Atomic Books** (3620 Falls Road; 410-662-4444; atomicbooks.com). Then head to **In Watermelon Sugar** (3555 Chestnut Avenue; 410-662-9090), where you'll find decidedly un-Ikea furniture. You might finish up at **Minás** (815 West 36th Street; 410-732-4258; minasgalleryandboutique.com) for vintage wear, poetry readings, and the work of Baltimore-based artists.

8 *Welcome to Dinner* 7:30 p.m.

Every city needs a neighborhood restaurant that feels like a social club. In Baltimore, that would be **Petit Louis** (4800 Roland Avenue; 410-366-9393; petitlouis.com; $$$), a cozy French bistro in the afflu-ent residential neighborhood of Roland Park. It has the air of a private party, with a host greeting diners by name and the kitchen serving up classic bistro dishes like grilled salmon with asparagus. Don't miss the pommes frites, crispy and sinfully fatty.

9 *Brew Crew* 10 p.m.

There may be tons of bars in Baltimore, but calling the **Brewer's Art** (1106 North Charles Street; 410-547-6925; thebrewersart.com) a bar is like calling crabs just another shellfish. Housed in a classic town house, the pub takes its beers very seriously, pouring everything from Trappist ales from Belgium to local microbrews like Clipper City Pale Ale. The crowd seems just as serious — artists and designers, older couples coming from the symphony, and occa-sional college students looking out of place among the adults.

SUNDAY

10 *The Age of Sail* 10 a.m.

Get a glimpse of authentic maritime history before midday crowds take over at the Inner Harbor. The well-maintained sloop-of-war *Constellation* (410-539-1797; constellation.org), the last all-sail ship built by the Navy and a veteran of the Civil War, is the star of several museum ships at anchor. Before the war, the *Constellation* patrolled the waters off West

Africa to block slave traders. Explore the sleeping quarters, galley, and cannons. Sailing ships once ruled this harbor. Now the craft you see may include paddle boats in the shape of Chessie, the local version of the Loch Ness monster.

11 *Young Artists* Noon

Everyone's got to start somewhere, and for many of Baltimore's top artists, that push came from the **Maryland Institute College of Art** (1300 West Mount Royal Avenue; 410-669 9200; mica.edu). The college, situated in the stately Bolton Hill neighborhood, regularly showcases the work of its promising students and faculty, which is to say the art can be hit or miss. But, as in any treasure hunt, that's part of the fun. If you're hungry, grab a bite at **b** (1501 Bolton Street; 410-383-8600; b-bistro.com; $$), a

simple bistro opened by a brother of Hamid Karzai, the president of Afghanistan. Who says Baltimore's reputation as an inviting spot hasn't gotten around?

OPPOSITE ABOVE A Dalton Ghetti pencil-tip sculpture at the American Visionary Art Museum.

OPPOSITE BELOW The cheese plate at Petit Louis.

ABOVE Cafe Hon anchors "The Avenue" in Hampden, whose pink flamingoes, beehived ladies, and classic cars were made famous through the films of John Waters.

THE BASICS

By car, Baltimore is three and a half hours from New York and less than an hour from Washington, D.C. Amtrak trains are faster. Flights land at Thurgood Marshall BWI Airport. Water taxis serve harborside stops.

Admiral Fell Inn
888 South Broadway
866-583-4162
harbormagic.com
$$$
Eighty rooms in red-brick buildings from the late 18th century.

Hilton Baltimore
401 West Pratt Street
443-573-8700
baltimore.hilton.com
$$$
Downtown, with 757 rooms.

The Inn at Henderson's Wharf
1000 Fell Street
800-522-2088
hendersonswharf.com
$$$
Charm and comfort in an old tobacco factory.

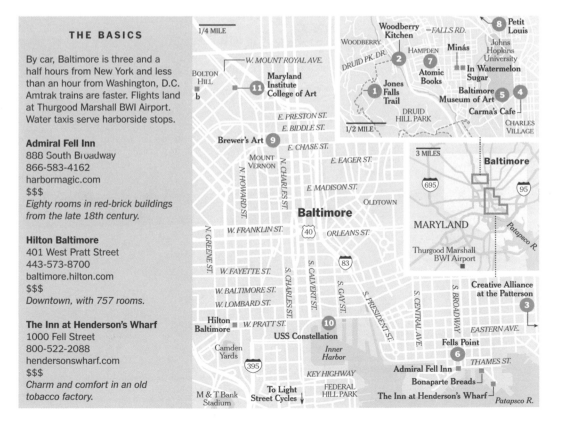

Annapolis

Spring comes to Annapolis, Maryland, on a perfumed cloud of burning wool. Every year at the vernal equinox, boaters in this sailing-mad community on the Chesapeake Bay gather on City Dock to create a bonfire of their winter socks, signaling a bare-toed welcome to the official start of the sailing season. What remains after the smoke clears is a stunningly beautiful village well worth a weekend excursion. Annapolis has undeniable historic importance — it was here that George Washington resigned his commission as commander in chief in 1783, and the city briefly served as the nation's capital. It has been the home of the United States Naval Academy since the academy's founding in 1845. But its charms are not simply academic. It is an architecturally rich, compact town (population about 36,000) made for strolling, where a walk along the waterfront on a sunny afternoon can wipe away the stress of the past work week and where a turn down a small side street can take you back two centuries in time.

— BY STUART EMMRICH

FRIDAY

1 *Sunset on the Dock* 7 p.m.

Start your weekend the way the locals do: with a sunset walk along **City Dock**, in the heart of downtown. Have a quick chat with one of the dozens of sailors getting their small boats ready for a trip out on the water on Saturday. Yachtsmen proudly parade their boats on the finger of water that ends at the dock—so proudly that it has gained the name Ego Alley. Pop into **Storm Bros. Ice Cream Factory** (130 Dock Street; stormbros.com) for a cone or a chocolate malt. Or go across to **Pusser's Carribean Grille** (80 Compromise Street; 410-626-0004; pussersusa.com/locations/annapolis-restaurant) for a beer on its outdoor deck. Like many things in Annapolis, its name has a story. Pusser's was the brand of rum that kept British sailors going on the high seas for hundreds of years.

OPPOSITE The rotunda of Bancroft Hall, the 1.4 million-square-foot dormitory at the United States Naval Academy. All 4,400 midshipmen live in this mammoth building.

RIGHT The exterior of the Academy's chapel. Inside is the crypt of John Paul Jones.

2 *Fusion Infusion* 8 p.m.

The venerable **Middleton Tavern** (2 Market Space; first opened in 1750) is a dinner standby on the dock, often crowded with tourists. For a different experience, walk a few blocks to **Aqua Terra** (164 Main Street; 410-263-1985; aquaterraofannapolis.com; $$-$$$), where fusion cuisine has elbowed its way into the land of clam chowder and crab cakes. The menu changes seasonally, but the emphasis is on sushi, small plates (think potstickers, sliders, and jambalaya) and imaginatively prepared sides for the meats and fish. A well-received newer spot, back at the dock, is **Hell Point Seafood** (12 Dock Street; 410-990-9888; hp-seafood.com; $$-$$$), opened in 2009 by Bob Kinkead, a renowned Washington chef.

3 *Walk Back in Time* 10 p.m.

Take a late evening stroll down **Prince George Street**. Though you will probably want to come back for a daytime view of these spectacular examples of mid-19th-century architecture (Greek Revival town houses, Italianate mansions), there is something particularly evocative about seeing these homes at night, when the streets are empty of cars and tourist-laden horse-drawn carriages, and the vibrantly colored living rooms (deep greens and rich, dark reds) are illuminated by antique lamps.

SATURDAY

4 *Greeting the Day* 8:30 a.m.

Return to the dock, where last night's crowd has been replaced by young families and dog owners

taking their pets out for an early morning walk, and have an al fresco breakfast of a pastry and coffee from **Hard Bean Coffee & Book Sellers** (36 Market Space; 410-263-8770).

5 *18th-Century Splendor* 10 a.m.

One of the most impressive homes in Annapolis is the **William Paca House** (186 Prince George Street; 410-267-7619; annapolis.org), a five-part brick mansion built in 1765 and painstakingly restored two centuries later. Take a walk through the house and then wander through the formal gardens. Afterward, head up to Maryland Avenue, and keep going until you get to the **Maryland State House**. Though the State House can lay claim to being the oldest state legislative building still in use, the tour of the chambers inside can be skipped. Instead, circle around the grounds and take in a sweeping view of the Annapolis skyline from the vantage point of the building's rear balcony.

6 *Picnic on a Campus* 1 p.m.

Stop in at **Re-Sails** (42 Randall Street; 410-263-4982; resails.com) to look over the bags and backpacks made from recycled sails. Then pick up a freshly made gourmet sandwich (prosciutto and provolone, or maybe turkey with brie and apples)

BELOW A carriage navigates the winding streets of downtown Annapolis.

OPPOSITE The showy parade of yachts at the end of downtown's City Dock has earned it the name Ego Alley.

at the **Big Cheese** (47 Randall Street; 410-263-6915; $) and walk up Prince George Street to **St. John's College**, where you can have an impromptu picnic on the campus lawn, with its eye-catching views of the Severn River. St. John's, Annapolis's "other college" (and the older one, dating back to 1696) is a sort of academic antithesis of the Naval Academy. It has no majors, no departments, no written exams, and few lectures; instead, teachers guide students as they read and discuss 130 "great books" by authors as diverse as Plato and Jane Austen. The two schools face off annually in a croquet game that draws as many as 2,000 spectators. St. John's usually wins.

7 *The High Seas* 3 p.m.

Experience the bracing winds off the Chesapeake Bay from the top deck of a sightseeing boat. Forty-minute boat tours of **Annapolis Harbor** (410-268-7601; watermarkcruises.com) leave from the far end of City Dock several times a day in the warm-weather months. Longer cruises, including an all-day journey that takes you to the quaint village of St. Michaels, Maryland, are also available on weekends. A jauntier option is a two-hour schooner cruise (Woodwind Cruises; 410-263-7837; schoonerwoodwind.com).

8 *Dinner and a View* 6:30 p.m.

As the sun begins to set, walk across the **Compromise Street Bridge** to the residential neighborhood of Eastport. Turn left on Severn and then left again on First Street, and walk down to the waterfront. Here, on a small wooden bench overlooking a 10-foot-long strip of sand, you can take in some of the best views of the Naval Academy and of the sailboats coming into harbor after a day out on the sea. Then double back to Severn, and turn right and then left on Third Street for dinner at **O'Learys Seafood Restaurant** (310 Third Street; 410-263-0884; olearysseafood.com; $$$). This elegant establishment is a world away (and twice as expensive) as the chowder houses back at the Annapolis dock. But the snapper, swordfish, mahi-mahi, and their many relatives make it worth the tab.

9 *Variety Show* 8 p.m.

Rams Head On Stage (33 West Street; 410-268-4545; ramsheadtavern.com/annapolis/

onstage.html), a concert venue in the Rams Head Tavern, books nationally known musicians representing genres from acid jazz to pop, rock, R&B, country, and soul. The list of past performers runs from Ladysmith Black Mambazo to Doc Hochman's Mardi Gras Dixieband, with many stops in between. (Check the schedule and consider ordering tickets in advance.)

SUNDAY

10 *Dress Blues* 9:30 a.m.

Early Sunday morning is among the best times to take a tour of the **United States Naval Academy**. The crowds have not yet begun to stream onto the 383-acre campus, and while the chapel (which contains the crypt of John Paul Jones) will not officially be open to visitors until 1 p.m., there is something undeniably stirring about seeing the midshipmen in their dress blues streaming out of church after the Sunday service. Enter the grounds at Gate 1 at Randall and King George Streets; the excellent Armel-Leftwich Visitor Center is just inside. Particularly worth seeing as you tour the grounds: the outsize Bancroft Hall, where all 4,400 midshipmen live; the row of elegant captains' houses on Porter Street; and the riverside walk along Dewey Field.

THE BASICS

Fly into Baltimore-Washington International Airport, drive from Washington, or arrive at City Dock in your boat. Downtown Annapolis is better for walking than for driving.

Historic Inns of Annapolis
58 State Circle
410-263-2641
historicinnsofannapolis.com
$$
Three sister hotels in restored historic buildings. Period touches like wing chairs or four-poster beds.

Marriott Annapolis Waterfront
80 Compromise Street
888-773-0786
annapolismarriott.com
$$$-$$$$
City or Chesapeake Bay waterfront views.

Loews Annapolis Hotel
126 West Street
410-263-7777
loewshotels.com/en/Annapolis-Hotel
$$
Colorful and modern decor, lounge, and spa.

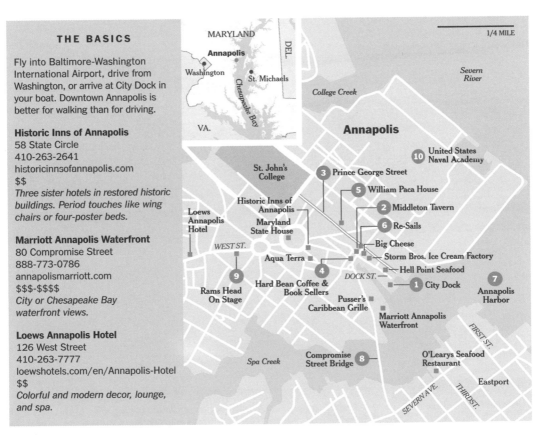

Washington
D.C.

The familiar monuments, symbols, and sites of Washington are American icons no visitor should miss. But there are times on a Washington weekend when it's best to leave the imperial city and spend some time with the people who live here full time. They're not all politicians, but a Washingtonian without some political connection can be hard to find. So stay alert. Someone may be trading insider gossip at the next restaurant table. — BY HELENE COOPER

FRIDAY

1 *House Party* 6 p.m.

Hobnob with the Beltway crowd at **Eighteenth Street Lounge** (1212 18th Street NW; 202-466-3922; eighteenthstreetlounge.com). Enter through the door next to the Mattress Discounters—there's no sign outside—take the stairs, and voila! A multilevel row house, with room after room of velvet couches and fireplaces, awaits you. There's a back deck for spring and summer after-work cocktails, and the crowd is a mix of political activists and Middle Eastern and European World Bank types.

2 *Eat like Oprah* 8 p.m.

Take a taxi to **Capitol Hill**, to **Art and Soul Restaurant** in the Liaison Hotel (415 New Jersey Avenue NW; 202-393-7777; artandsouldc.com; $$$). Oprah Winfrey's former chef, Art Smith, owns this restaurant, and it does a big business in D.C. parties. Yes, you've already had a cocktail, but you're not driving, so be sure to try the margarita at the bar before sitting down to eat. The menu will remind you that Washington is a Southern city. Sprinkled among the more usual listings, like seared ahi tuna and arugula salad, you'll see preparations like "country fried" and "red-eye" and foods like ribs, okra, watermelon pickles, and collard greens. Not to mention the fried green tomatoes.

3 *Freedom Walk* 10 p.m.

With luck, no one in your party wore the five-inch Prada heels tonight, because you're about to walk off that pork chop as you head down the National Mall. Your destination is the **Lincoln Memorial** (nps.gov/linc), with ole Abe backlit at night. Washington's monument row is always best viewed at night,

when the tourists are gone and the romantics are strolling arm in arm. The Lincoln Memorial, long the first destination for African-American visitors to Washington, has often been an emotionally charged spot: think of Marian Anderson's concert in 1939, Martin Luther King's "I Have a Dream" speech, and Election Night 2008, when Illinois learned it was sending another of its sons to Washington. In quieter times it is almost a retreat, as residents and visitors alike come to read the inscription "With malice toward none, with charity for all" and to ponder America the Beautiful.

SATURDAY

4 *Morning Sit-in* 9 a.m.

Breakfast at **Florida Avenue Grill** (1100 Florida Avenue NW; 202-265-1586; floridaavenuegrill.com; $), a soul food institution, is a dip into the past, evoking the feel of lunch counter sit-ins and the civil rights movement. The place has been serving greasy and delicious Southern cooking since 1944. Buttery grits,

OPPOSITE Inside the Capitol Hill Visitor Center, where guests can see the Capitol Dome peering through a large glass ceiling.

BELOW The Lincoln Memorial at night.

Virginia ham, biscuits and gravy, even scrapple—all surrounded by photos of past Washington bigwigs as various as Ron Brown, the former commerce secretary, and Strom Thurmond, the former South Carolina senator.

5 *1600 Pennsylvania* 10 a.m.

We know. It's the ultimate in touristy. But come on, it's the **White House** (1600 Pennsylvania Avenue; 202-456-7041; whitehouse.gov). To schedule a public tour, first you'll need to find nine friends to come with you. Then call your Congressional representative to schedule. (Not sure who? Go to writerep.house.gov.) These self-guided tours—which are allotted on a first-come-first-served basis about one month before

the requested date—allow you to explore the public rooms and the gardens. Sorry, you won't be able to check out the decorating in the first family's private quarters, but you will get to see the East Room, the Diplomatic Reception Room, and the dining room where they have those swanky state dinners.

6 *Hello, Betsy* Noon

No, not that Betsy…there are no star-spangled banners at **Betsy Fisher** (1224 Connecticut Avenue NW; 202-785-1975; betsyfisher.com). This stylish and

ABOVE Ben's Chili Bowl on U Street Northwest, popular by day and an institution late at night.

BELOW The chorus at St. Augustine Roman Catholic Church at 15th and V Streets Northwest, one of the oldest black Catholic churches in the country.

OPPOSITE A view of the Capitol from down the Mall.

funky boutique is port of call for those well-dressed deputies in the White House. The owner, Betsy Fisher Albaugh, always has cocktails and wine on hand to occupy the men who invariably are dragged into the store.

7 *Go Represent* 2 p.m.

It took six years to complete, but the **U.S. Capitol Visitor Center** (Capitol Hill; at the east end of the Mall; 202-225-6827; visitthecapitol.gov) finally opened at the end of 2007. The subterranean center is meant to relieve the bottleneck that used to serve as the entryway for visitors to the Capitol. It does that and more, although some critics say it assumes a life of its own that is too separate from the Capitol itself. See for yourself — you can book a tour via the Web site, or just show up and wander around. The center has a rotating display of historic documents that can range from a ceremonial copy of the 13th Amendment, abolishing slavery, to the speech President George W. Bush delivered to Congress after the Sept. 11 attacks.

8 *Political Dish* 7 p.m.

O.K., enough with the federal touring, it's time to hang out with the real Washingtonians. Head to the always hopping **U Street Corridor**, and plop yourself on a stool at **Local 16** (1602 U Street NW; 202-265-2828; localsixteen.com). There are multiple lounges and, best of all, a roof deck where you can see the city lights while you sip your pre-dinner watermelon martini. Have dinner a few blocks away at **Cork Wine Bar** (1720 14th Street NW; 202-265-2675; corkdc.com; $$), which might have the best fries in town. The menu includes both small and big bites, from marinated olives and cheeses to duck confit and sautéed kale. And for goodness' sake, don't forget those fries! They are tossed with garlic and lemon. In fact, order two helpings.

9 *Smoke-filled Room* 10:30 p.m.

Puff away the rest of your evening at **Chi-Cha** (1624 U Street NW; 202-234-8400; latinconcepts.com/chicha.php), a hookah lounge where you can smoke honey tobacco out of a water pipe and sip late-night cocktails. The eclectic crowd dances to rumba and slow salsa into the wee hours, and there's always a diplomat in a corner couch doing something inappropriate — avert your eyes, enjoy your hookah, and sway to the beat. You could be in Beirut. O.K., let's try that one again. You could be in Marrakesh. Well, maybe Marrakesh with Brazilian music. If you want to keep the night going, stop by **Ben's Chili Bowl** (1213 U Street NW; 202-667-0909; benschilibowl.com), a Washington institution so established that even President Nicolas Sarkozy of France has stopped by for the Chili Half-Smoke hot dogs. He went at noon, but Ben's is busiest in the wee hours.

SUNDAY

10 *River Idyll* 8 a.m.

Washington is known for beautiful mornings along the Potomac River, especially on the water. **Thompson Boat Center** (2900 Virginia Avenue NW; 202-333-9543; thompsonboatcenter.com), just where Georgetown meets Rock Creek Parkway, offers canoe rentals. Paddle up the river, and you might catch a senator (or a Saudi prince) having coffee on the patio of a stately home.

11 *Lift Your Voice* 12:30 p.m.

St. Augustine Roman Catholic Church (1419 V Street NW; 202-265-1470; saintaugustine-dc.org), which calls itself "the Mother Church of Black Catholics in the United States" is one of the oldest black Catholic churches in the country. The 12:30 Sunday Mass combines traditional black spirituals with gospel music. The place rocked with particular fervor after Inauguration Day 2009.

ABOVE Outside the White House, which is off-limits to walk-ins. Group tours are allowed, but they must be arranged a month in advance.

OPPOSITE The Capitol as seen through a window at the Library of Congress.

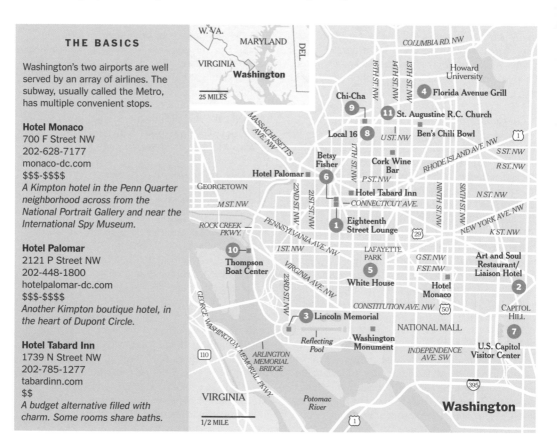

THE BASICS

Washington's two airports are well served by an array of airlines. The subway, usually called the Metro, has multiple convenient stops.

Hotel Monaco
700 F Street NW
202-628-7177
monaco-dc.com
$$$-$$$$
A Kimpton hotel in the Penn Quarter neighborhood across from the National Portrait Gallery and near the International Spy Museum.

Hotel Palomar
2121 P Street NW
202-448-1800
hotelpalomar-dc.com
$$$-$$$$
Another Kimpton boutique hotel, in the heart of Dupont Circle.

Hotel Tabard Inn
1739 N Street NW
202-785-1277
tabardinn.com
$$
A budget alternative filled with charm. Some rooms share baths.

The Laurel Highlands

In the Laurel Highlands of southwestern Pennsylvania, cornfields undulate between forested slopes and rivers spill downward in a rush of whitewater, luring fishermen and rafters. These green hills gave Frank Lloyd Wright the setting for Fallingwater, his cantilevered masterpiece of a house set over a swiftly flowing creek. Nearby, another client hired Wright to design Kentuck Knob, a quirky counterpart. And a bit north in Acme, a Wright ranch house saved from demolition in Illinois arrived in pieces, completing the setting for a Wrightian weekend. Balancing the architectural immersion with a little history and some outdoor adventures creates a memorable experience under the shiny leaves of the mountain laurel.
— BY BETHANY SCHNEIDER AND BARBARA IRELAND

FRIDAY

1 *A Matter of Necessity* 4 p.m.

Everybody has to start somewhere, and George Washington's first battlefield command was in 1754 at what is now **Fort Necessity National Battlefield** (off Route 40 in Farmington; 724-329-5805; nps.gov/fone). The reconstruction of the fort that Washington's forces threw together in their moment of necessity (they were about to be attacked) is terrifying in its meagerness. Sure enough, the French and their Indian allies made mincemeat of the British led by Colonel Washington, then just 22. But other victories came later, and the French and Indian War made Washington's reputation. Rangers evoke the feel of combat in the era when these highlands were virgin forest, delivering dramatic lines like "Half King, Washington's Indian ally, washed his hands in the brains of the French commander."

2 *Dinner Downtown* 7 p.m.

Wash your own hands in something more appropriate as you tidy up for dinner. Find it in the old town center of Uniontown at **Caileigh's** (105 East Fayette Street; 724-437-9463; caileighs.com; $$).

OPPOSITE Frank Lloyd Wright's Fallingwater, the famed masterwork cantilevered over a waterfall in the woods of the Laurel Highlands.

RIGHT The Cucumber Falls at Ohiopyle State Park.

Uniontown was home to coal and steel barons in the boomtown days of this part of Pennsylvania, and Caileigh's occupies one of the era's mansions. As you settle in for dishes like spiced duck or seared grouper topped with Puerto Rican crab, chat with your waiter about General George C. Marshall, father of the Marshall Plan and Uniontown's favorite son.

SATURDAY

3 *The Masterwork* 8:15 a.m.

Arrive in plenty of time for your in-depth tour at **Fallingwater** (724-329-8501; fallingwater.org; tours must be purchased several weeks in advance). You're up early, but it's worth it; this tour, longer than the basic version, allows more time inside the house and more leisure to absorb the complexity of its construction. Projecting airily out over a waterfall on Bear Run Creek, its platforms mimicking the striations of the local rock, the house still looks as strikingly original and eerily perfect for its setting as it did when it was completed in 1939. Instantly famous, it resuscitated the faltering career of its creator, Frank Lloyd Wright, who was then 72. No matter how many times you've seen it, Fallingwater is breathtaking. On one bright May day, a middle-aged visitor from Scotland, dressed in a blue anorak, stood with tears flowing down his cheeks at his first sight of it. The guide assured him this was normal.

4 *Lingering for Lunch* Noon

Fallingwater's inviting grounds, not to mention various vantage points for your perfect photo, will keep you busy until lunchtime, so stay for a sandwich at the cafe. The shopping is good, too. At the Fallingwater Museum Store, even the souvenir mugs are classy.

5 *A Bike in the Forest* 1 p.m.

In Confluence, a tiny, charming town wedged between the tines of three converging rivers, you'll find the gateway to the most beautiful 11 miles of the 150-mile **Great Allegheny Passage** rail trail (atatrail.org), following an old railroad bed. Rent a mountain bike or a recumbent (easy on the body if you're not a regular cyclist) from one of the village outfitters, and glide through the dreamy woodland of **Ohiopyle State Park** (dcnr.state.pa.us/stateparks/parks/ohiopyle.aspx).

6 *Nature's Water Park* 3 p.m.

Cool down in the **Natural Waterslides**, still in the park, just south of Ohiopyle on Route 381. Sit in the stream, and it barrels you across smooth rocks and through a curving sluice, producing an adrenaline rush and maybe a few bruises. Dry off by **Cucumber Falls** around the corner on Route 2019, a bridal veil that splashes into a pool the pale green and rusty red of a glass of Pimm's. When you feel refreshed, cycle back to Confluence and drop off your bike.

7 *Going Usonian* 7:30 p.m.

Make your way over hill and dale to secluded **Polymath Park** (187 Evergreen Lane, Acme; 877-833-7829; polymathpark.com), a quiet, tree-shaded resort whose intriguing business plan centers on architectural preservation. You made your dinner reservations here long ago, so take a little time now to explore the shaded drives and find the **Duncan House**, one of the modest houses that Frank Lloyd Wright designed for the middle class and christened Usonians. Rescued from its original site in Illinois, where it was threatened with teardown, it was moved

to Pennsylvania in thousands of numbered pieces and, after some cliffhanger misadventures, painstakingly reassembled here. The house is vastly more modest than the tour de force of Fallingwater, but it bears the unmistakable marks of Wright's ingenuity. It is available for short-term rentals, so be respectful of the tenants who may be inside and view it from a distance. (Unless, of course, you are the lucky tenant this weekend yourself, in which case you are already well into a uniquely memorable experience.) Wind along the other drives to find three more houses, designed by Wright apprentices and also available as lodging.

8 *Food of the Polymaths* 8 p.m.

The fare runs to entrees like pecan-crusted brook trout and wood-fired filet mignon at **Tree Tops Restaurant** (877-833-7829; $$-$$$) on the Polymath Park grounds. Soak in the atmosphere and share the evening with the other Wright groupies who will have found their way to this quiet spot. If the night is right, you can exchange some stories.

SUNDAY

9 *His Lordship's Getaway* 10 a.m.

Kentuck Knob (723 Kentuck Road, Chalk Hill; 724-329-1901; kentuckknob.com), in another wooded setting, represents the middle ground of your Wright

OPPOSITE ABOVE AND RIGHT Wright's Duncan House, re-assembled in Polymath Park after facing destruction on its original site in Lisle, Illinois, is available for short-term stays.

OPPOSITE BELOW A swivel gun demonstration at Fort Necessity National Battlefield, where Colonel George Washington, just 22 years old, surrendered to the enemy in a battle of the French and Indian War.

weekend: far less spectacular than Fallingwater, but far more so than the Duncan House. A stone-and-cypress hexagon with a balcony ending in a stone prow, it is full of eccentric angles and unexpected viewpoints that add up to the usual Wrightian mastery. Wright designed it as a hillside home for a local ice cream magnate, but the current owner is a British lord who not only lets the public traipse through but also displays his collectibles, from

Claes Oldenburg sculptures to bullets from Custer's Last Stand. Take the tour and then take your time on the grounds.

10 *Tuck It In* 1 p.m.

Locals praise the food at the **Out of the Fire Cafe** (3784 State Route 31, Donegal; 724-593-4200; outofthefirecafe.com; $$), and it's a good spot for a substantial Sunday dinner: an apple-stuffed pork chop with garlic potatoes, perhaps, or pan-seared Scottish salmon with sweet potato and roasted corn hash. Tuck it away, and it should get you all the way back home.

THE BASICS

The Laurel Highlands are southeast of Pittsburgh. The country roads can be confusing. Arm yourself with maps, a GPS unit, and a cellphone.

The Duncan House
187 Evergreen Lane, Acme
877-833-7829
polymathpark.com
$$$$
Designed by Frank Lloyd Wright. Stay overnight and pretend he built it just for you.

Summit Inn Resort
101 Skyline Drive, Farmington
724-438-8594
summitinnresort.com
$$
Porch rockers and mountain views.

Hampton Inn Uniontown
698 West Main Street, Uniontown
724-430-1000
hamptoninn.com
$$
One of several chain options.

Pittsburgh

Pittsburgh has undergone a striking renaissance from a down-and-out smokestack town to a gleaming cultural oasis known for educational and technical prowess. There are great restaurants, excellent shopping, breakthrough galleries, and prestigious museums. The convergence of three rivers and surrounding green hills make a surprisingly pretty urban setting, and with abandoned steel mills long since torn down, more of the natural beauty of this part of Pennsylvania has emerged. If the Pirates are in town, head to the waterfront ballpark. Besides seeing the game, you'll have an excuse to explore downtown and take in the river views.
— BY JEFF SCHLEGEL

FRIDAY

1 *Gridiron and Steel* 4 p.m.

Get to know what makes the city tick at the **Senator John Heinz History Center** (1212 Smallman Street; 412-454-6000; pghhistory.org), which chronicles past and present glories from United States Steel to the Pittsburgh Steelers. This is actually a twofer: the main museum is devoted to everything from the Heinz food empire to the city's polyglot population. The upper two floors are occupied by the Western Pennsylvania Sports Museum.

2 *Waterfall Dining* 7 p.m.

The martini menu changes almost as often at the seasonal specials at **Soba** (5847 Ellsworth Avenue; 412-362-5656; bigburrito.com/soba; $$$), a pan-Asian restaurant with a Victorian exterior and a Zen-like interior that features a two-story wall of cascading water. Scan the menu for dishes like lobster maki and seafood and tandoori-grilled salmon. The wine list is extensive, and the vibe is upscale and trendy, but not in an overbearing way. If you arrive early, grab a special martini, perhaps made with ginger-infused vodka, on the rooftop deck.

3 *Brillo Pad* 10 p.m.

Brillobox (4104 Penn Avenue; 412-621-4900; brillobox.net) feels like an arty bar in New York's East Village — little wonder, considering the 30-something artist couple who own it are former New Yorkers. They came back home to Pittsburgh, they

said, to contribute to the city's growing arts scene, and if the name of their establishment reminds you of Andy Warhol, you're on the right track. Pittsburgh is Warhol's hometown, and the Andy Warhol Museum Downtown holds 12,000 of his works. Brillobox catches some of his adventurous spirit with art film screenings, spoken-word performances, and live music held upstairs in a room decked out in velvet wallpaper and murals. But you can just hang loose in the downstairs bar with its atmospheric red lights and an eclectic jukebox that has Goldfrapp, Patsy Cline, and Snoop Dogg.

SATURDAY

4 *Nosh 'n' Stroll* 10:30 a.m.

By night, the formerly industrial **Strip District** is filled with partygoers bouncing between bars and clubs. But on Saturday mornings, the parallel thoroughfares of Penn Avenue and Smallman Street (roughly between 16th and 26th Streets) are turned into a sprawling outdoor market with international food kiosks that serve Middle Eastern kebabs, Italian sausages, and Greek baklava. Shop for produce, clothing, and vintage knickknacks as accordionists and mariachi bands provide a festive soundtrack. Take a breather with a cup of coffee and a mele, a

OPPOSITE The Mattress Factory on the North Side, home to room-size installations from artists like Yayoi Kusama.

BELOW The Duquesne Incline, a funicular first opened in 1877, takes passengers to Mount Washington for a view of the city.

fruit-filled pastry, at **La Prima Espresso Bar** (205 21st Street; 412-281-1922; laprima.com), where the old men sitting at the outdoor tables look like they've been sipping espresso and playing cards for eternity.

5 *No Beds Here* 1 p.m.

If you're a Warhol fan, don't miss the **Andy Warhol Museum** (117 Sandusky Street; 412-237-8300; warhol.org). For more radical contemporary art, beat a new path in the Mexican War Streets neighborhood to the **Mattress Factory** (500 Sampsonia Way; 412-231-3169; mattress.org). Housed in a former mattress factory, the museum is dedicated to room-size art installations.

6 *Hard-to-Find Items* 3 p.m.

Some of the city's funkiest shopping can be found in the **16:62 Design Zone** (1662designzone.com), which spans the Strip District and Lawrenceville neighborhoods. It has more than 100 locally owned shops that focus on design, home décor, contemporary art, clothing, and architecture. Among the more interesting is the nonprofit **Society for Contemporary Craft** (2100 Smallman Street; 412-261-7003; contemporarycraft.org), a gallery and store that showcases handmade crafts like shiny metal handbags ($300 to $500) and recycled steel cabinets (from $3,500).

7 *Grab the Camera* 6 p.m.

The best views of Pittsburgh are from Mount Washington, and the best way to get there — or at least the most fun — is up the **Duquesne Incline** (1220 Grandview Avenue; 412-381-1665; incline.cc). One of two surviving hillside cable cars from the 1870s, it takes three minutes to climb 800 feet to Grandview

Avenue. There's a neat little history museum at the top that has old newspaper clippings, but the real spectacle is the view of downtown Pittsburgh, where the Allegheny and Monongahela Rivers meet to form the Ohio.

8 *City Under Glass* 7 p.m.

While you're up there, Grandview Avenue is also home to a cliff-hugging restaurant row. For amazing seafood to go with the river views, make reservations for the **Monterey Bay Fish Grotto** (1411 Grandview Avenue; 412-481-4414; montereybayfishgrotto.com; $$$). This tri-level restaurant sits atop a 10-story apartment building. Jackets aren't required, but nice clothes are apropos. Fresh fish is flown in daily, and the menu changes often. On one visit the specials included a charcoal-grilled Atlantic salmon with fresh peppered strawberries in a red-wine sauce.

9 *Off-Downtown Theater* 9 p.m.

Generally regarded as Pittsburgh's most innovative theater company, the **City Theatre** (1300 Bingham Street; 412-431-2489; citytheatrecompany.org) does challenging plays that aren't likely to be staged in the downtown cultural district. Housed in a pair of former churches, it has both a 272-seat mainstage and a more intimate 110-seat theater. After the show, stop in at **Dee's Cafe** (1314 East Carson Street; 412-431-1314;

ABOVE Andy Warhol was from Pittsburgh, and thousands of his works have come to his namesake museum.

RIGHT A table with a view at the Monterey Bay Fish Grotto on Grandview's restaurant row.

deescafe.com), a comfortable, jam-packed dive that is part of what by some counts is the country's longest continuous stretch of bars.

SUNDAY

10 *Brunch and Bric-a-Brac* 11 a.m.

One of city's more unusual brunch spots is the **Zenith** (86 South 26th Street; 412-481-4833; zenithpgh.com; $-$$), a combination art gallery, vintage clothing store, antiques shop, and vegetarian restaurant. For those who can't stomach tofu, brunch includes traditional staples like eggs, pancakes, and French toast. It gets busy, so to avoid the line, get there before it opens at 11.

11 *Brain Food* 12:30 p.m.

The Oakland district teems with intellectual energy from the University of Pittsburgh, Carnegie Mellon University, and several museums. Start out at the Nationality Rooms at the **Cathedral of Learning** (4200 Fifth Avenue; 412-624-6000; pitt.edu/~natrooms), a 42-story Gothic-style tower on the Pittsburgh campus with 27 classrooms, each devoted to a different nationality. Then head over to the renowned **Carnegie Museum of Art** (412-622-3131; cmoa.org) and **Carnegie Natural History Museum** (carnegiemnh.org), both at 4400 Forbes Avenue, for Degas and dinosaurs. Before leaving, pick up a handy walking tour of Oakland and public art in the neighborhood.

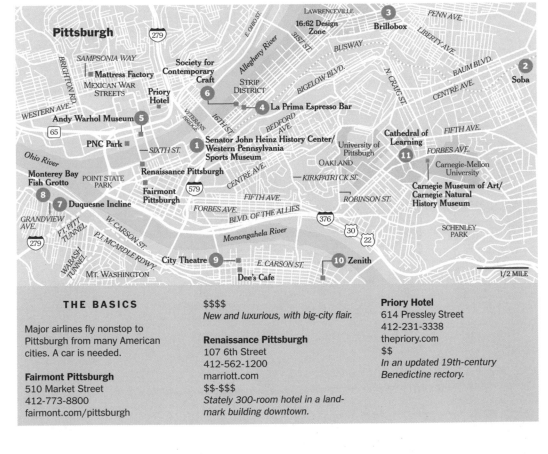

THE BASICS

Major airlines fly nonstop to Pittsburgh from many American cities. A car is needed.

Fairmont Pittsburgh
510 Market Street
412-773-8800
fairmont.com/pittsburgh

$$$$
New and luxurious, with big-city flair.

Renaissance Pittsburgh
107 6th Street
412-562-1200
marriott.com
$$-$$$
Stately 300-room hotel in a landmark building downtown.

Priory Hotel
614 Pressley Street
412-231-3338
thepriory.com
$$
In an updated 19th-century Benedictine rectory.

Buffalo

Prospering where East Coast railroads met Great Lakes cargo, Buffalo, New York, was a rich city around 1900, the same era when dynamic innovators were transforming American architecture. Wealth and vision came together in works by Frank Lloyd Wright, Louis Sullivan, H. H. Richardson, Frederick Law Olmsted, Eliel and Eero Saarinen, and more—arrayed amid blocks of Victorian houses and lavish mansions. When industry eventually collapsed, a shaken and considerably poorer Buffalo slowly realized it had a legacy. Now the city works to preserve its remarkable architectural collection and is eager to show it off. Visit in the months when Buffalo gets a glorious payback for its snowy winters with some of the best summer weather in the country. — BY BARBARA IRELAND

FRIDAY

1 *Lake to River* 2 p.m.

At **Erie Basin Marina** (329 Erie Street), a popular spot with sailors, joggers, and just about everyone else, climb the small observation tower for a view of grain elevators (a Buffalo invention) on the placid Buffalo River, an 1833 lighthouse, and the final expanse of Lake Erie as it narrows to become the Niagara River. The trees a couple of miles across the water are in Canada—British troops came across to burn Buffalo to the ground in the War of 1812, but all is now forgiven. To the north, the river current picks up on the way to Niagara Falls, 15 miles downstream. Climb back down and amble over to **Templeton Landing** (2 Templeton Terrace; 716-852-7337; templetonlanding.com; $$) for a drink and a sandwich on the waterfront patio.

2 *She's the Babe* 4 p.m.

Architectural preservation has achieved the status of a local religion, and the singer Ani DiFranco, a Buffalo native, made a creative contribution with **Babeville** (341 Delaware Avenue; 716-852-3835; babevillebuffalo.com), a towering 1876 red sandstone church adapted into a public event space and the headquarters of her Righteous Babe Records. To

OPPOSITE Daniel Burnham's Ellicott Square Building, one of Buffalo's many architectural gems.

get there, drive north on Delaware Avenue past the massive Art Deco City Hall and the McKinley Monument, a 96-foot-tall marble apology to the president who was assassinated while visiting Buffalo in 1901. Inside Babeville, look over the current show at **Hallwalls** (716-854-1694; hallwalls.org), a contemporary art gallery.

3 *The Temple of Wings* 8 p.m.

Take a table at the **Anchor Bar** (1047 Main Street; 716-886-8920; anchorbar.com; $), where the fame of Buffalo chicken wings began, for a plate of the spicy originals and the tale of their invention by a resourceful cook. Add a salad and some Canadian beer, and stay for live jazz.

SATURDAY

4 *Sullivan and Friends* 9:45 a.m.

See a microcosm of 19th-century American architecture in a downtown walking tour with Preservation Buffalo Niagara (617 Main Street; 716-852-3300; buffalotours.org). Louis Sullivan's 1895 **Guaranty Building** (28 Church Street), 13 stories of intricately molded terra cotta enclosing a steel skeleton, stands across a narrow street from **St. Paul's Cathedral** (128 Pearl Street), designed by Richard Upjohn, the architect of New York City's Trinity Church. Nearby, the Gothic Revival **Erie Community College** (121 Ellicott Street) was built in lavish style as a federal building when the city's friends included President Grover Cleveland, a former Buffalo mayor and briefly the town hangman. Daniel Burnham's elaborate **Ellicott Square Building** (295 Main Street) has been carefully preserved—from the Medusa heads peering out from its roof line perimeter to its refined interior atrium—by its current owner, Carl Paladino, who is better known for his boisterous 2010 campaign for governor of New York.

5 *Olmsted Next Door* Noon

Have a panini at the cafe in the **Albright-Knox Art Gallery** (1285 Elmwood Avenue; 716-882-8700; albrightknox.org) and then take a quick look around, concentrating on mid-20th-century paintings, where the collection is particularly strong. Seymour H.

Knox, a Buffalo banker and heir to part of the F. W. Woolworth fortune, was an early patron of Abstract Expressionists like Willem de Kooning, Mark Rothko, and, especially, Clyfford Still, and he gave the gallery hundreds of their works. Look out from the back portico, past the caryatids sculptured by Augustus Saint-Gaudens, at a view of 350-acre Delaware Park, the "central park" of an extensive system of parks and connecting parkways designed for Buffalo by Frederick Law Olmsted.

6 *Wright Writ Large* 2 p.m.

Frank Lloyd Wright liked nothing more than an open checkbook to work with, and when he designed a home in 1904 for Darwin Martin, a Buffalo business-man, in effect he had one. The result was the **Martin House Complex** (125 Jewett Parkway; 716-856-3858; darwinmartinhouse.org) — a sprawling 15,000-square-foot Prairie-style house filled with art glass and Wright-designed furniture, two smaller houses on the same property, a conservatory, stables, gardens, and a 100-foot-long pergola. A just-completed $50 million restoration has brought it back from long neglect and added an ethereally transparent visitor center designed by Toshiko Mori. Tour the complex, a stunningly beautiful and intricate work of art, and hear the stories. Martin absorbed outrageous cost overruns to give the master a free hand. He became a lifelong friend who bailed Wright out with tens of thousands of dollars in loans that were never repaid. (Their sizable correspondence is at the University at Buffalo.) Wright's obsession with detail extended to designing a dress for Mrs. Wright to wear in the house, but he resisted giving her a closet.

ABOVE A 19th-century grain elevator and a 21st-century marina in the Buffalo harbor.

LEFT The permanent collection at the Albright-Knox Art Gallery includes hundreds of Abstract Expressionist works.

7 *A Little Richardson* 4 p.m.

Back on Elmwood Avenue, drive south, past the **Burchfield-Penney Art Center** (burchfieldpenney.org), a gallery with a collection of eye-poppingly original paintings by the mystically inclined Charles Burchfield. Turn onto Forest Avenue and look behind a graceful screen of trees (another Olmsted landscape) for the majestic, spooky towers of the **H.H. Richardson Complex**. An abandoned mental hospital, it was one of Richardson's earliest and largest buildings in the style now known as Richardsonian Romanesque. Repairs have begun, but full restoration is a long way off.

8 *Retail Break* 4:30 p.m.

Shops are sprinkled along Elmwood Avenue from Bidwell Parkway to West Ferry Street. Browse through jewelry, clothing, and handcrafted curios at **Plum Pudding** (No. 779; 716-881-9748), or pick up a scarf or a Sarah Palin paper doll (her outfits include a moose-antler hat) at **Positively Main Street** (No. 773; 716-882-5858). **Talking Leaves** (No. 951; 716-884-9524; tleavesbooks.com) is a well-stocked independent bookstore. If you're not yet tired of National Historic

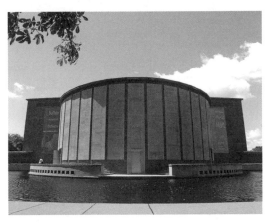

ABOVE A sailboat heads out toward open waters in Lake Erie from the Erie Basin Marina.

RIGHT Kleinhans Music Hall, designed by Eliel and Eero Saarinen, is home to the Buffalo Philharmonic.

Landmarks, drive a few blocks to the 1940 **Kleinhans Music Hall** (370 Pennsylvania Street), where Eliel and Eero Saarinen married upswept lines and near-perfect acoustics. Its carefully shaped wooden interior walls were "as warm as the wood in my violin," Isaac Stern once told an audience there.

9 *The French Style* 8 p.m.

Rue Franklin (341 Franklin Street; 716-852-4416; ruefranklin.com; $$$), whose reputation as Buffalo's best restaurant is rarely challenged, not only serves French wines and updated French food cooked by its French owner, but takes a French-style August vacation. If you're in town during its hiatus, try **Oliver's** (2095 Delaware Avenue; 716-877-9662; oliverscuisine.com; $$$), a favorite since 1936. At either one, expect a well-prepared meal and a relaxing evening.

SUNDAY

10 *Early to Betty's* 9 a.m.

The scones and coffee are great at **Betty's** (370 Virginia Street; 716-362-0633; bettysbuffalo.com; $), but there's more for breakfast, including spinach potato pancakes with bacon or scrambled tofu hash, served in a setting of brick walls and changing work by local artists. Get there early to beat the crowd.

11 *Wright on the Lake* 11:30 a.m.

It's a leisurely drive south along Lake Erie to **Graycliff** (6472 Old Lake Shore Road, Derby; 716-947-9217; graycliffestate.org), the summer house that Frank Lloyd Wright designed in the 1920s for Darwin Martin. The house and its lakeside setting are inspiring, but the story ends sadly here. Martin lost his fortune in the Great Depression, and his family eventually sold or abandoned all of their Wright-designed properties. Remarking on Martin's death in 1935, Wright said he had lost "my best friend."

OPPOSITE Gates Circle, a detail of Buffalo's parks and parkway system designed by Frederick Law Olmsted.

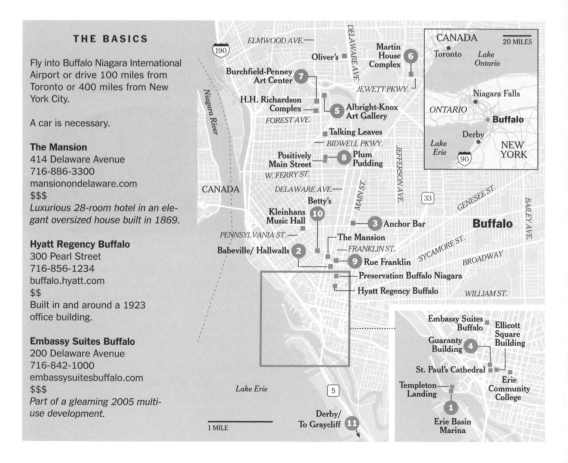

THE BASICS

Fly into Buffalo Niagara International Airport or drive 100 miles from Toronto or 400 miles from New York City.

A car is necessary.

The Mansion
414 Delaware Avenue
716-886-3300
mansionondelaware.com
$$$
Luxurious 28-room hotel in an elegant oversized house built in 1869.

Hyatt Regency Buffalo
300 Pearl Street
716-856-1234
buffalo.hyatt.com
$$
Built in and around a 1923 office building.

Embassy Suites Buffalo
200 Delaware Avenue
716-842-1000
embassysuitesbuffalo.com
$$$
Part of a gleaming 2005 multi-use development.

ELMWOOD AVE.
190
Oliver's
Martin House Complex 6
Burchfield-Penney Art Center 7
JEWETT PKWY.
H.H. Richardson Complex
FOREST AVE.
Albright-Knox Art Gallery 5
Talking Leaves
BIDWELL PKWY.
Positively Main Street
Plum Pudding 8
W. FERRY ST.
CANADA
DELAWARE AVE.
Betty's
Kleinhans Music Hall 10
Anchor Bar 3
Buffalo
PENNSYLVANIA ST.
Babeville/ Hallwalls 2
The Mansion
FRANKLIN ST.
Rue Franklin 9
SYCAMORE ST.
BROADWAY
Preservation Buffalo Niagara
Hyatt Regency Buffalo
WILLIAM ST.
Niagara River
JEFFERSON AVE.
MAIN ST.
33
GENESEE ST.
BAILEY AVE.

CANADA
Toronto
Lake Ontario
20 MILES
Niagara Falls
ONTARIO
Buffalo
Derby
Lake Erie
90
NEW YORK

Lake Erie
5
Derby/ To Graycliff 11
1 MILE

Embassy Suites Buffalo
Ellicott Square Building
Guaranty Building 4
St. Paul's Cathedral
Templeton Landing
Erie Community College
1
Erie Basin Marina

Niagara Falls

At Niagara, the United States is the poor relation and Canada is king. Though they share the famous falls, Nature gave Canada the wide-angle view, and the Canadians' long-term bet on tourism over industry landed most of the visitor comforts on their side of the Niagara River. Yet the story isn't so simple. Casinos, high-rise hotels, and hucksterish come-ons have so proliferated in Niagara Falls, Ontario, that it risks feeling like a tired amusement park. Meanwhile, in Niagara Falls, New York, the visitor who ventures inside the shabby, underfunded state park is surprised to discover vestiges of something like a natural landscape. The party is in Canada. The real feel of the river, in all its awesome power, is more accessible in the United States. So why miss either one? It's an easy border to cross, especially on foot. Hop back and forth to get the best of both Niagaras and see for yourself.
— BY BARBARA IRELAND

FRIDAY

1 *Feet Across the Border* 5 p.m.

Cars sometimes line up for hours to cross the international border at the **Rainbow Bridge**, a few hundred yards downriver from the falls. But on the walkway it's a breeze—a 10-minute stroll for 50 cents in American or Canadian currency (niagarafallsbridges.com). Customs agents at each end are pedestrian-friendly, though you must have your passport. If you're staying on the American side, make your first crossing now. If your hotel is in Canada, wait until tomorrow. Either way, this is one of the most scenic saunters you will ever take.

2 *Brinkmanship* 6 p.m.

Push into the crowds on the riverfront walkway in Canada and see the whole geological spectacle at once. The imposing cascade on the left, 850 feet wide, is the **American Falls**. The supercharged one on the right, nearly half a mile wide, is the **Horseshoe Falls**, often called the Canadian Falls even though

OPPOSITE Niagara Falls State Park offers jaw-dropping up-close views of both the American and Canadian Falls.

RIGHT On the Canadian side of the Falls, Clifton Hill is a funhouse in and of itself.

the international border actually runs through it. Stop at the Horseshoe brink and wait your turn to be doused at the rail by spray from thousands of tons of water plunging down every second. Impressed? This thundering mass is only half of the river's natural flow. The other 50 percent (75 percent in the off-season) is channeled away underground to hydroelectric plants.

3 *Wine and Bacon* 7 p.m.

From the terrace at **Edgewaters Tap & Grill** (6345 Niagara Parkway; 905-356-2217; niagaraparks.com/dining; $$), the tourist hordes below seem far away. Relax and sample one of the Niagara Region wines, like the Inniskillin Riesling. For a casual dinner, try a hearty sandwich made with the high-quality Canadian bacon hard to find south of the border. Afterward, explore shady **Queen Victoria Park**, where gracious landscaping reflects the English style.

4 *Over the Top* 9 p.m.

You want to hate **Clifton Hill**, a garish strip of funhouses, glow-in-the-dark miniature-golf palaces, 4-D theaters, wax museums, and noisy bars. But tackiness on this level cries out to be experienced. So watch a multinational crowd shovel tickets into blinking game machines at the Great Canadian Midway. Observe the story-high monster chomping a hamburger atop the House of Frankenstein. Shop for maple candy and a moose puppet. And climb aboard the **SkyWheel** Ferris wheel (4950 Clifton Hill; cliftonhill.com) for five vertiginous revolutions and a view of the colored lights projected nightly on the falls. (Oh right, there are waterfalls here. Remember?)

SATURDAY

5 *The Central Park* 10 a.m.

Frederick Law Olmsted and Frederic Church were among the 19th-century champions of a radical idea, public parks at Niagara Falls, erasing a clutter of factories and tourist traps (at some locations, visitors had paid to see the falls through a peephole in a fence). The Free Niagara movement succeeded on both sides of the border, and on the American side Olmsted designed landscapes at the crest of both waterfalls and on Goat Island, which separates them. Explore the woods and walkways of the resulting **Niagara Falls State Park** (716-278-1796; niagarafallsstatepark.com) to find what remains of the essential experience of Niagara. For an enticing mix of quiet glades and furious rapids, venture out on the tiny **Three Sisters Islands** above the thunderous Horseshoe.

6 *Wings Optional* 1 p.m.

Buffalo chicken wings were invented just 20 miles away, and the menu at the **Top of the Falls** restaurant (in the state park; 716-278-0337; $$) won't let you forget it. Partake or not; alternatives include salads, burgers, and wraps. Every table has a falls view.

7 *Why the Waterfall?* 2 p.m.

You'll hunt in vain on both sides of the river for a straightforward geological explanation of Niagara Falls. At the **Niagara Gorge Discovery Center** in the state park, look selectively at the displays and ask questions to tease out the basic facts. What's falling is the water of the Great Lakes. The falls are on the move upriver, naturally receding as much as 6 feet a year. There's a giant whirlpool where they took a sharp turn 40 centuries ago. (A Canadian attempt at explaining Niagara, a film called *Niagara's Fury*, niagarasfury.com, is entertaining for children but also not especially informative, mixing cartoon stereotypes with snippets of textbook language.) Outside the Discovery Center, a trail heads toward the deep Niagara Gorge, where hikers get within a few feet of the largest standing waves in North America. Don't bring the kayak: these rapids are Level 6.

8 *The Close-up* 3 p.m.

Many of the contrived attractions at Niagara Falls are overhyped and disappointing. But the **Maid of the Mist** tour boats (maidofthemist.com) have been thrilling customers since 1846. Chug out to the base of the Horseshoe on one of these sturdy craft, struggle to look up 170 feet to the top through the torrents, and you'll grasp the power of what brought you here. Go from the **American dock**. Not only is the wait likely to be shorter than on the Canadian side, but at the end of the ride, you can hang on to your flimsy slicker and take a wet but exhilarating hike to the base of the American Falls.

9 *Culinary Canada* 7 p.m.

AG, the soothing, stylish restaurant in the **Sterling Inn & Spa** (5195 Magdalen Street, Niagara Falls, Ontario; 289-292-0000; sterlingniagara.com; $$$) serves imaginative dishes using seasonal Canadian ingredients, paired with local wines. One

ABOVE The Rainbow Bridge, the international crossing, offers views of the American Falls — and Prospect Point Observation Tower, in the foreground.

BELOW Preparing to be soaked at the Cave of the Winds.

summer menu included basil-and-potato-encrusted Lake Huron trout and pork tenderloin stuffed with macerated Niagara fruit. The desserts are good, too, but if you're not up for one, you can get by on the eye candy of the red, white, and crystal dining room.

SUNDAY

10 *Vineyards Haven* 10 a.m.

Leave the falls behind and drive north along the river in Canada on the lovely **Niagara Parkway**. Beyond placid Queenston, where an American attack was turned back in the War of 1812, the Niagara turns tame, and wineries, peach orchards, manor-like houses, and an inviting bicycle path line the road. The tasting rooms pour chardonnays, pinot noirs, and the regional specialty, ice wine. At **Inniskillin**, (on the Parkway at Line 3; 905-468-9910; inniskillin.com) tours and signboards explain grape-friendly local conditions. **Reif Estate** (15608 Niagara Parkway; 905-468-9463; reifwinery.com) has a gimmicky but pleasant Wine Sensory Garden. **Peller Estates** (just off the parkway at 290 John Street West; peller.com) pairs its vintages with a posh restaurant. Between the reds and whites, stop in at the **Kurtz Orchards Gourmet Marketplace** (16006 Niagara Parkway; 905-468-2937; kurtzorchards.com), where you can munch enough free samples of breads, tapenades, jams, cheeses, and nut butters to take you all the way to dinner.

THE BASICS

By car, Niagara Falls is eight hours from New York City, 90 minutes from Toronto, and 45 minutes from the Buffalo Niagara airport. At the falls, walk and take trolleys and people movers. For exploring, drive a car.

Sterling Inn & Spa
5195 Magdalen Street, Niagara Falls, Ontario
877-783-7772
sterlingniagara.com
$$$
A boutique-hotel oasis at the edge of the tourist maelstrom.

Doubletree Fallsview Resort & Spa
6039 Fallsview Boulevard, Niagara Falls, Ontario
905-358-3817
niagarafallsdoubletree.com
$$
On a hill overlooking the falls.

The Giacomo
222 First Street, Niagara Falls, New York
716-299-0200
thegiacomo.com
$$$
Renovated Art Deco building.

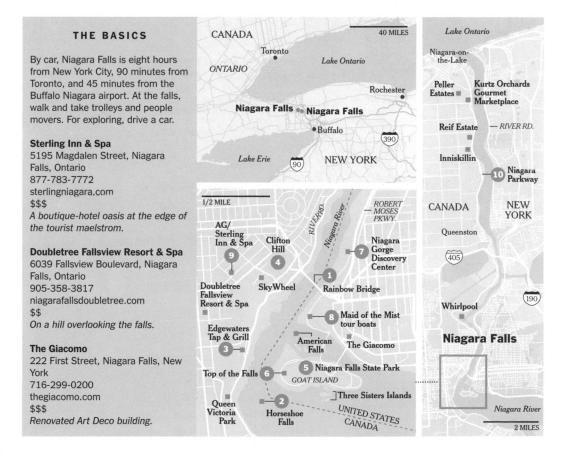

Cooperstown

High culture or sports worship? In Cooperstown, New York, a dilettante's delight of a tree-shaded Victorian town, you can indulge in both. Many of the half-million or so visitors who come each year are bent only on seeing the National Baseball Hall of Fame. But another sizable crowd arrives for the well-regarded Glimmerglass Opera, also an established part of the summer season. And long before anyone had heard of A-Rod or even Babe Ruth, Cooperstown was a pilgrimage site as the home of James Fenimore Cooper, the early-19th-century superstar author whose wildly popular novels, including The Deerslayer *and* The Last of the Mohicans, *put a haze of romance on an upstate New York frontier that had already vanished. So pack your baseball cap and your opera glasses, and come prepared to celebrate your versatility.*

— BY JOHN MOTYKA

FRIDAY

1 *Abner Shopped Here* 4 p.m.

No matter which team you deify, **Main Street**'s shops will provide jerseys, mugs, engraved bats, and logo-imprinted bath rugs. If you also collect baseball cards, you're in heaven. Abner Doubleday, once known as the father of baseball, trod the streets of this preserved downtown before his days as a Civil War general. His baseball connection was eventually exposed as a myth, but by then Cooperstown had become a baseball shrine in its own right. Nearby on Fair Street is a statue of James Fenimore Cooper in Cooper Park, an unlikely oasis of quiet behind the Baseball Hall of Fame.

2 *Get a Glimmer* 6 p.m.

Wander down to **Lakefront Park** for a good look at Lake Otsego, the deep glacial lake that appeared in Cooper's novels as Glimmerglass. He described it as "a broad sheet of water, so placid and limpid that it resembled a bed of pure mountain atmosphere compressed into a setting of hills and woods."

OPPOSITE Collectibles in a Cooperstown shop. Main Street retailers aim to satisfy the baseball fan.

RIGHT The Farmers' Museum, a working replica of 1800s rural life in upstate New York.

Warriors concealed themselves in those woods, and in *The Deerslayer*, an eccentric frontiersman lived on a primitive houseboat on the lake with his spirited daughters. It's less dramatic today, but the park is a good place to sit and watch sailboats drift by.

3 *Take Your Table* 7 p.m.

Back on Main Street, settle in for drinks and dinner at **Alex & Ika** (149 Main Street; 607-547-4070; $$$). The street scene outside may be reminiscent of Fan Day at the stadium, but the food inside is several cuts above the ballpark hot dog. Look for dishes like a star anise confit of duck with lemon grass kaffir-leaf coconut curry.

SATURDAY

4 *Start with Art* 10 a.m.

The neo-Georgian mansion that is now the **Fenimore Art Museum** (5798 State Route 80; 607-547-1400; about $30 for a combination ticket that will also cover your afternoon stops) occupies the former site of James Fenimore Cooper's farmhouse and displays family artifacts including fan mail from the Marquis de Lafayette (Cooper's books quickly made a splash in Europe and by now have been translated into 40 languages). Downstairs is the Thaw Collection of American Indian Art. Exhibits have

included 20th-century Magnum news photography and John Singer Sargent portraits of women.

5 *Literary Perspectives* 11:30 a.m.

From the museum windows, look out at Cooper's view of the lake and imagine him mentally populating its shores with the crack shot Natty Bumppo (the Deerslayer); Natty's Mohican friend Chingachgook and Chingachgook's wife-to-be, Hist; and the Indian enemies who would capture Hist, requiring her rescue. Then, at the museum shop, pick up a copy of *Rural Hours*, by the author's daughter, Susan Fenimore Cooper. This natural history classic, published in 1850, won her belated recognition as America's first great woman nature writer. It preceded *Walden* by four years, and Thoreau referred to it in his journal.

6 *Farm Yes, Factory No* Noon

Drive across the road to the **Farmers' Museum** (5775 Route 80; 607-547-1450; farmersmuseum.org), 29 buildings that function as a working replica of an 1800s farm and town. In the unlikely event that you've never seen a restored village, you may want to return for a full day; otherwise, pick up lunch at one of the cafes and have a quick look around at the cows and chickens, the schoolhouse, and the work of the artisans on staff. The packets for the museum's heirloom seeds are printed on a treadle press. Outside, children ride wooden farm animals on a carousel.

7 *Out with the Crowd* 2 p.m.

You don't have to be a diehard fan to have a good time at the **National Baseball Hall of Fame** (25 Main Street; 888-425-563-3263; baseballhall.org), but memories of childhood days at the ballpark

with Dad, or your own starring role in Little League, will only make it better. The well-presented exhibits take you on a journey from the game's early origins to the current season, and the oak-lined Hall of Fame Gallery honors baseball's greats, from the first five elected in 1936 to the present. See Yogi Berra's catcher's mitt, Hank Aaron's locker, and mementoes of the old Negro League. And that's just the beginning.

8 *Dinner before the Show* 6 p.m.

It's all about the view at the **Blue Mingo Grill**, situated just a couple of miles northwest of town (Sam Smith's Boatyard, 6098 State Highway 80; 607-547-7496; bluemingogrill.com; $$), so reserve a table as close to the lakefront windows as you can. The lemon-grass-marinated lamb or corn-crusted

ABOVE Otsego Lake, the inspiration for the Glimmerglass of James Fenimore Cooper's *The Deerslayer*.

BELOW Shopping for souvenirs on Main Street, near the Baseball Hall of Fame.

shrimp with hot and sweet onions will be perfectly decent, but your principal mission here is to watch the ripples and mellow out before the show. You're on your way to the opera.

9 *High Notes* 8 p.m.

The **Glimmerglass Opera** (7300 Route 80; 607-547-2255; glimmerglass.org), in its striking 900-seat Alice Busch Opera Theater, draws a sophisticated clientele and has a well-earned reputation for quality and variety. Past summer programs have included an American premiere of Handel's *Tolomeo*; a grouping of operas adapted from Shakespeare with the Cole Porter musical *Kiss Me, Kate*, and four operatic takes on the Orpheus story. Every season also includes standard audience-pleasing fare from the likes of Verdi, Puccini, and Rossini. If you arrive early, you'll find a campus of 43 lakeside acres to stroll on.

SUNDAY

10 *Make a Commitment* 10 a.m.

It's time to decide who you really are. Option One: Check for amateur games and take a look around at quaint **Doubleday Field** (Main Street; 607-547-2270), a 9,000-seat stadium. Then go next door to Doubleday Batting Range and while away the morning testing yourself against the same kind of pitching machine used in major-league training. Option Two: Keep stimulating that literary imagination with a drive a few miles north to **Glimmerglass State Park** (1527 Route 31). Just up the hill from the parking lot for Hyde Hall, a 19th-century mansion, find the trail on Mount Wellington and plunge into the woods. You won't see Hist or Susan Cooper, but they'd both be right at home amid the birches and hemlocks.

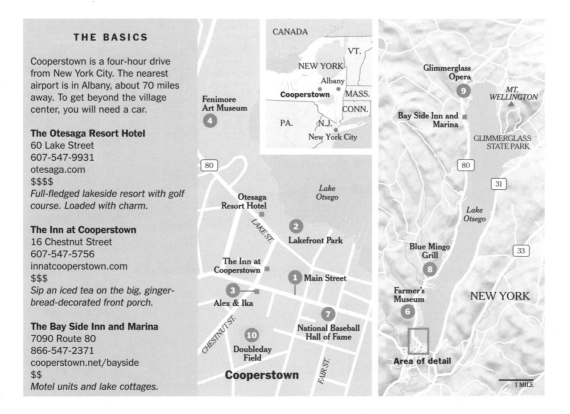

THE BASICS

Cooperstown is a four-hour drive from New York City. The nearest airport is in Albany, about 70 miles away. To get beyond the village center, you will need a car.

The Otesaga Resort Hotel
60 Lake Street
607-547-9931
otesaga.com
$$$$
Full-fledged lakeside resort with golf course. Loaded with charm.

The Inn at Cooperstown
16 Chestnut Street
607-547-5756
innatcooperstown.com
$$$
Sip an iced tea on the big, ginger-bread-decorated front porch.

The Bay Side Inn and Marina
7090 Route 80
866-547-2371
cooperstown.net/bayside
$$
Motel units and lake cottages.

CANADA
VT.
NEW YORK
Albany
Cooperstown · MASS.
CONN.
PA. N.J.
New York City

Fenimore
Art Museum
4

80

Otesaga
Resort Hotel

Lake Otsego

2
Lakefront Park

The Inn at
Cooperstown
3
Alex & Ika

1 Main Street

7
National Baseball
Hall of Fame

10
Doubleday
Field

Cooperstown

Glimmerglass
Opera
9
MT.
WELLINGTON

Bay Side Inn and
Marina

GLIMMERGLASS
STATE PARK

80

31

Lake Otsego

Blue Mingo
Grill
8

33

Farmer's
Museum
6

NEW YORK

Area of detail

1 MILE

New London

Ships have been sailing into the deep harbor of New London, Connecticut, since 1646 — schooners and packet ships, an English armada led by Benedict Arnold, nuclear submarines that glide silently up the Thames River, cresting the water like whales. The town helped shape Eugene O'Neill, who set two of his greatest plays at his family's New London cottage, and as tall ships visit and ferries disgorge cars and passengers from Long Island and Block Island, its salty flavor still feels real. New London's struggles are real, too, evidenced by some empty storefronts. But with huge pots of flowers bedecking lampposts and luxury apartments renting in once-neglected buildings, a new liveliness blends with breathtaking harbor vistas, glimpses of history, and the enduring draw of the sea. — BY MAURA J. CASEY

FRIDAY

1 *Lobster in the Rough* 7 p.m.

A little difficult to find, but worth the persistence, is **Captain Scott's Lobster Dock** (80 Hamilton Street; 860-439-1741; captscotts.com; $), a warm-months-only lobster shack with seating at outdoor picnic tables. It's off Howard Street, nestled between railroad tracks and a sheltered marina. The right choice here is the lobster roll, served cold or hot with drawn butter drizzled over generous chunks of lobster. Order the red potatoes, too, and if you're still hungry, have some ice cream.

2 *Rock around the Clock* 8 p.m.

New London's music scene has become more varied and vibrant in the last several years, with downtown bars hosting bands several nights a week for cover charges under $10. **The Oasis Pub** (16 Bank Street; 860-447-3929; oasisnewlondon.blogspot.com) is the spirited — some would say raucous — center of the local indie rock scene and sometimes hosts touring acts. The **El 'n' Gee Club** (86 Golden Street; myspace.com/thegee860) showcases punk, rock, and metal bands. The Bank Street Café (639 Bank Street; 860-444-1444; bankstreetcafe.com) features original

OPPOSITE Halfway between New York City and Boston, New London is an old New England port town that not only looks the part but still plays it, welcoming craft from pleasure boats to submarines in its deep-water harbor.

music and spotlights blues and country. About a mile or so from downtown is **Stash's Cafe** (95 Pequot Avenue; 860-443-1095; stashs.com), home to alternative rock bands.

SATURDAY

3 *Breakfast with Cannons* 9 a.m.

Sniff the flowers as you order sticky buns, scones, and your caffeine of choice at the **Thames River Greenery/Beanery** (70 State Street; 860-443-6817), a combination flower shop and coffee bar. You won't lack for reading material, either, as the shop opens out into City News, a store that offers more than 100 journals, magazines, and newspapers for sale. Pause at an outside table to watch for ships cruising down below past the Union Railroad Station, which was designed by H. H. Richardson, and listen for Amtrak trains whistling their way through it. Then take your repast to **Fort Trumbull State Park** (90 Walbach Street; 860-444-7591), a massive 19th-century fortification with jaw-dropping views of the Thames (New World pronunciation: Thaymes) and Long Island Sound. There are few prettier places for a picnic and few more pleasant ways to get a sense of New London's history and strategic location than by strolling around the fort, now a state park, inspecting the cannons and ramparts.

4 *Gallery Stroll* 11 a.m.

Small, distinctive galleries dot the downtown area, all within an easy walk. Stop in at **Yah-Ta-Hey Gallery** (279 State Street; 860-443-3204; yahtaheygallery.com) to see Native American art. **Hygienic Art** (81 Bank Street; 860-447-3240; hygienic.ning.com) is a residential art cooperative with rotating exhibits. **The Gallery at Firehouse Square** (239 Bank Street; 860-443-0344; firehousesquare.com) specializes in nautical art.

5 *Choose Your Asia* 1 p.m.

In the time-honored tradition of seaports everywhere, New London attracts a population from far-flung parts of the world, and on State Street, you can choose an inexpensive lunch from several national cuisines. **Bangkok City** and **Little Tokyo** (860-442-6970 and 860-447-2388) serve Thai and Japanese cuisine under the same roof at 123 and 131 State Street. Steps

away, **Northern Indian Restaurant** (150 State Street; 860-437-3978) offers a generous lunch buffet for about $10.

6 *Ah, Dramatists* 2 p.m.

When Eugene O'Neill wrote his detailed set directions for *Long Day's Journey Into Night* and *Ah, Wilderness!* he was recreating the living room and surroundings of **Monte Cristo Cottage** (325 Pequot Avenue; 860-443-5378 extension 285; theoneill.org/prog/monte/montprog.htm), the summer home his family owned from 1884 to 1921, down to the wicker chairs and the wood of the writing desk. This cottage, where the O'Neills loved, suffered, and laughed as the characters do in these autobiographical plays, looks much as it did onstage. Tours run regularly from Memorial Day through Labor Day and by appointment the rest of the year with the exception of O'Neill's birthday, October 16, when the house is usually open for readings from his plays.

7 *A Drink with Eugene* 5 p.m.

O'Neill played on the New London waterfront as a boy and drank there as an adult. To follow in his footsteps, first look over the bronze statue at the foot of State Street based on a picture of him at age 7 sitting on the banks of the Thames River, and then take a seat at the **Dutch Tavern** (23 Green Street; 860-442-3453), legendary as the only remaining New London watering hole that he frequented. The owners are proud that the place, with its tin ceiling and century-old tables, still looks largely as it did in O'Neill's day. This is a basic bar, small and no-frills, but it serves a variety of ales and nonalcoholic drinks. It has been the setting for readings of O'Neill plays, among them, appropriately, *The Iceman Cometh*.

ABOVE Fort Trumbull, forbidding from the water but, once on the grounds, a great place to picnic.

RIGHT The young Eugene O'Neill, in bronze, at the waterfront where he played as a boy.

8 *Pasta and Malbec* 7 p.m.

Relax over dinner at **Tony D's** (92 Huntington Street; 860-443-9900; tonydsrestaurant.com; $$), a family-run New London favorite. Don't expect surprises here, but do count on reliable renditions of the standards, from homemade ravioli to eggplant parmigiana and veal piccata. For dessert, you will of course order cannoli.

9 *Jazz It Up* 8 p.m.

New London music isn't all indie and rock. Several times a month, celebrated and emerging jazz artists like Cyrus Chestnut, Tierney Sutton, and Sophie Milman play at the intimate 120-seat Oasis Room in the **Garde Arts Center**, (325 State Street; 860-444-7373; gardearts.org). And you'll never know what will be playing in the center's 1,450-seat restored vaudeville palace, the **Garde Theater** (built in 1926). On any given week it may be hosting contemporary music, touring Broadway musicals, symphony orchestras, opera, or dance. Its giant movie screen shows contemporary, international, and classic films.

SUNDAY

10 *Wake Up on the Boardwalk* 10 a.m.

A great place for a morning walk or a brisk swim is **Ocean Beach Park** (off Ocean Avenue), established after homes in the area were wiped out by the Great Hurricane of 1938. The park has a wide, sandy beach with a half-mile-long boardwalk, a water slide,

several restaurants, an Olympic-size swimming pool, and, on clear days, sparkling views of Long Island and Fishers Island, New York. When you've worked up an appetite, move on to **Muddy Waters** (42 Bank Street; 860-444-2232; $) for bagels, yogurt, muffins, or a breakfast sandwich with egg, tomato, baby spinach, cheese, and bacon. Don't forget a mug of Mystic Roasters coffee, espresso, or cappuccino.

11 *Shipping News* 1 p.m.

The **Custom House and Maritime Society Museum** (150 Bank Street; 860-447-2501; nlmaritimesociety.org) operates in a building that is also the oldest operating customs house in the United States. An 1833 jewel by Robert Mills, the designer of the Washington Monument, it has vaulted ceilings and a flying staircase. Two doors are made of wood taken from Old Ironsides, the

storied battleship *Constitution*. (When the ship, commissioned in 1797, was being refurbished in the 1830s, some of its original wood was offered for public buildings.) The exhibits include ships' logs from the 1700s and artifacts from the whaling industry that was New London's economic base in the early 1800s. The permanent exhibit "*Amistad*: A True Story of Freedom" tells the story of the escaped slaves who commandeered the schooner *Amistad* in 1839.

ABOVE Its maritime history makes New London a stop for sailing ships like this replica of Henry Hudson's *Half Moon*.

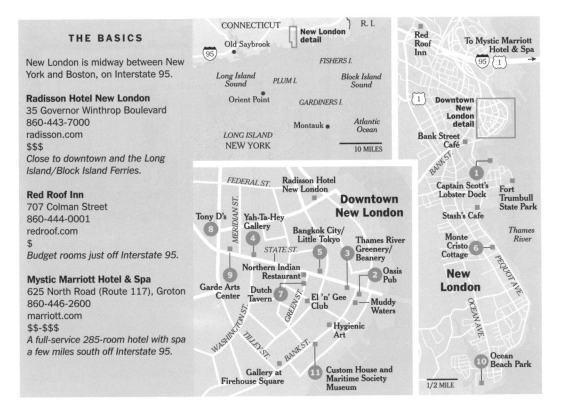

THE BASICS

New London is midway between New York and Boston, on Interstate 95.

Radisson Hotel New London
35 Governor Winthrop Boulevard
860-443-7000
radisson.com
$$$
Close to downtown and the Long Island/Block Island Ferries.

Red Roof Inn
707 Colman Street
860-444-0001
redroof.com
$
Budget rooms just off Interstate 95.

Mystic Marriott Hotel & Spa
625 North Road (Route 117), Groton
860-446-2600
marriott.com
$$-$$$
A full-service 285-room hotel with spa a few miles south off Interstate 95.

CONNECTICUT
New London detail
Old Saybrook
95
R. I.
FISHERS I.
Long Island Sound
PLUM I.
Block Island Sound
Orient Point
GARDINERS I.
Montauk
Atlantic Ocean
LONG ISLAND
NEW YORK
10 MILES

Red Roof Inn
To Mystic Marriott Hotel & Spa
95 1
1 Downtown New London detail
Bank Street Café
BANK ST.
1
Captain Scott's Lobster Dock
Fort Trumbull State Park
Stash's Cafe
Thames River
Monte Cristo Cottage 6
New London
PEQUOT AVE.
OCEAN AVE.
10 Ocean Beach Park
1/2 MILE

FEDERAL ST.
Radisson Hotel New London
MERIDIAN ST.
Tony D's 8
Yah-Ta-Hey Gallery
4
STATE ST.
Bangkok City/ Little Tokyo 5
3
Thames River Greenery/ Beanery
Northern Indian Restaurant
2 Oasis Pub
Garde Arts Center
Dutch Tavern 7
GREEN ST.
El 'n' Gee Club
Muddy Waters
Downtown New London
WASHINGTON ST.
TILLEY ST.
Hygienic Art
BANK ST.
Gallery at Firehouse Square
11 Custom House and Maritime Society Museum
New London

Providence

In its early days, Rhode Island was known as "Rogues' Island," a reference to the willingness of its founder, Roger Williams, to accept every element of society, as well as (more memorably) every religion — a distinct departure from the usual 17th-century custom. A few centuries later, Providence is still a hodgepodge, and a charming one. The revitalized waterfront and gleaming new downtown, including the Dunkin' Donuts Convention Center, complement colonial brick buildings and tidy frame houses spruced up in one of the country's most successful preservation efforts. Ivy League college students, a cutting-edge art school, and top-flight chefs all help define a newly energized city. But Providence still remembers, too, how to feel like a small town. — BY KAREN DEUTSCH

FRIDAY

1 *Espresso in the Air* 5 p.m.

Federal Hill (providencefederalhill.com) offers a different kind of Providence history and vibe, one that owes more to food than to colonial iconoclasts. Stroll down Atwells Avenue, center of the city's Little Italy, where the scent of sopressata drifts overhead. Much of the crowd checking out the food shops and boutiques is under 30, and the neighborhood is gentrifying, but there's still a small old-school contingent that congregates over pepper biscuits and pignoli. An espresso on **Caffe Dolce Vita's** outdoor patio (59 DePasquale Plaza; 401-331-8240; caffedolcevita.com) and a coin toss into the DePasquale Fountain will get you into the mood. This might also be the time to book a gondola ride (**La Gondola**; WaterPlace Park; 401-421-8877; gondolari.com) on the river for another day.

2 *Top Tomato* 8 p.m.

No one questions that **Al Forno** (577 South Main Street; 401-273-9760; alforno.com; $$$) put Providence on the culinary map three decades ago. And while some foodies prefer the town's splashier new kitchens, no one does rustic Italian better than Al Forno's

OPPOSITE A street in the College Hill neighborhood, home to Brown University and the Rhode Island School of Design.

RIGHT Gondola tours are a good fit in a city with three rivers and its own Little Italy.

owners, George Germon and Johanne Killeen. Favorites include handmade bread gnocchi with spicy sausage, crackling grilled pizzas, and homemade ice cream. For those who like things intimate, Germon and Killeen also run a 20-seat Mediterranean tapas restaurant called **Tini** (200 Washington Street, 401-383-2400; thetini.com).

SATURDAY

3 *I'll Have Mine with Lemon* 9 a.m.

Walk under the playful pink-and-green lettering (easy to read isn't the point here) of the sign on **Brickway on Wickenden**'s facade (234 Wickenden Street; 401-751-2477; brickwayonwickenden.com; $) and take a table for coffee and a breakfast hearty enough to satisfy the hungry young Brown University students who might be at the next table. The menu offers the standards — bacon, eggs, omelets — plus some surprises, like the lemon blueberry French toast.

4 *Walking Back in Time* 10:30 a.m.

Stroll out and take a long look at some of the architecture that gives Providence its powerful sense of place. The **Rhode Island Historical Society** (401-331-8575; rihs.org) gives 90-minute walking tours of Benefit Street, a quaint strip that sits on College Hill, austerely overlooking modern condos. Find the former **State House** (150 Benefit Street; 401-222-3103) where, in 1776, Rhode Islanders declared independence two months before the rest of the American colonies. Wander through the **John Brown House Museum** (52 Power Street; 401-273-7507), completed

in 1788 and home to one of the founders of Brown University. Another highlight is the **Providence Athenaeum** (251 Benefit Street; 401-421-6970; providenceathenaeum.org), founded in 1753.

5 *Across the Universe* 1 p.m.

Keep your walking shoes on and turn into the picturesque Brown campus (brown.edu), founded in 1764. Murmur sweet nothings at the rear archway to the **Metcalf Chemistry Building** (190 Thayer Street), a microcosmic whispering gallery for shy romantics. Enjoy the patriotic air at **University Hall** (1 Prospect

Street), where George Washington accepted an honorary degree in 1790. You can also contemplate the fate of H.P. Lovecraft (*Weird Tales, At the Mountains of Madness*), Providence's pulp fiction aficionado and author, who was denied entrance to Brown in the early 20th century after a nervous breakdown prevented his high school graduation.

6 *Shopping Street* 3 p.m.

Ready for a rest? Stop in at one of the cafes on Westminster Street, but don't linger too long. This is shopping country. Women congregate at shops like **Queen of Hearts** (No. 222; 401-421-1471; queenofheartsprovidence.com), which offers one-of-a-kind fashion choices, and the shoe emporium **Modern Love** (No. 220; 401-421-1476). The androgynous **Clover** boutique (No. 233; 401-490-4626; cloverprovidence.com) carries casual knits for her and button-downs for him.

7 *Diner Chic* 7:30 p.m.

Once upon a time, **Nicks on Broadway** (500 Broadway; 401-421-0286; nicksonbroadway.com;

ABOVE *WaterFire*, a river installation by the sculptor Barnaby Evans that comes to shimmering life downtown on Saturday nights from May to October.

LEFT Nicks on Broadway, a diner gone upscale.

$$-$$$) was a classic, hash-slinging diner. Then a local chef snapped up the diner and gave the blue-plate specials a culinary twist. The menu changes, but expect plenty of seafood, including the likes of oysters on the half-shell or pan-roasted striped bass.

8 *Watermark* 9:30 p.m.

In 1994, a Brown alumnus and artist named Barnaby Evans created a sculpture of 100 mini-bonfires that marked the convergence of the Providence, Moshassuck, and Woonasquatucket Rivers in the heart of downtown. The work, *WaterFire* (waterfire.org), continues today, drawing crowds on Saturday evenings between May and October.

9 *Tap Dance* 11 p.m.

Welcome the wee hours at **Local 121** (121 Washington Street; 401-274-2121; local121.com), a restaurant and nightspot in a hotel dating from the 1890s. Young crowds mix with old style as students and artists dance amid the stained-glass and Art Deco décor.

SUNDAY

10 *Graduate's Showing* 10 a.m.

The **RISD Museum** (224 Benefit Street; 401-454-6500; risdmuseum.org) of the Rhode Island School of Design houses 84,000 pieces, from ancient Greek statues to French Impressionist paintings and contemporary sculpture. The permanent collection includes attractive examples of the kind of furniture and interiors that once decorated Providence's colonial houses. But it's safe to expect something more daring as well. Past exhibitions have ranged from eccentric giant glass creations of Dale Chihuly, an RISD graduate, to a show of works made entirely of Styrofoam.

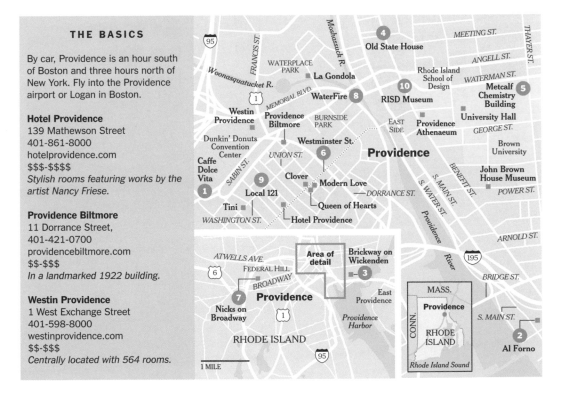

THE BASICS

By car, Providence is an hour south of Boston and three hours north of New York. Fly into the Providence airport or Logan in Boston.

Hotel Providence
139 Mathewson Street
401-861-8000
hotelprovidence.com
$$$-$$$$
Stylish rooms featuring works by the artist Nancy Friese.

Providence Biltmore
11 Dorrance Street,
401-421-0700
providencebiltmore.com
$$-$$$
In a landmarked 1922 building.

Westin Providence
1 West Exchange Street
401-598-8000
westinprovidence.com
$$-$$$
Centrally located with 564 rooms.

Newport

Each summer, two million tourists head to Narragansett Bay to shuffle their way through the Gilded Age trophy homes of Newport, Rhode Island — the lumbering white elephants (or are they overdressed maiden aunts?) perched hip to hip on the city's glittering rocky coastline. You too can explore America's insatiable appetite for... darn nearly everything here, and ponder the freakishness of the wealthy. Glut your senses by driving down Newport's main drag, otherwise known as Bellevue Avenue, a weird bazaar of architectural expression that includes more Versailles references than is probably healthy. If you continue along Ocean Drive, you will note attempts by contemporary architects to be this century's Stanford White (and that is not necessarily a good thing). But keep your eyes on the rugged coast, green parks, and yacht-filled harbor, all cooled on hot summer days by the ocean breeze, and you will remember how all of this got here.
— BY PENELOPE GREEN

FRIDAY

1 *The Cliff Walk* 3 p.m.

Get a jump on the weekend crowd with a Friday-afternoon trip to the Fifth Avenue of nature walks. Newport's famous **Cliff Walk** (cliffwalk.com) runs for three and a half miles along shoreline that makes everyone love an ocean view. It can be jam-packed on the weekends with tourists ogling the backyards of the Bellevue Avenue estates, many of which it slices into. Here is a strategy: Park at Easton's Beach on Memorial Boulevard, just below the Chanler at Cliff Walk hotel. You will find the path entrance right there. Follow the path to the end at Ledge Road (only if you are strong; this will take more than an hour) or to the stone staircase called the 40 Steps (about 20 minutes). Walk up Ledge Road to Bellevue Avenue, make a left, and you will see a bus stop for Newport's trolleys (if you make it only to the 40 Steps, there is a stop at Narragansett and Ochre Point). Take a trolley back

OPPOSITE The Breakers, one of the trophy mansions that typified Newport's golden age and are now open for tour.

RIGHT The 3.5-mile Cliff Walk, where the public enjoys the Gilded Age plutocrats' treasured ocean views.

into town, get off at the Newport Casino, and walk down Memorial Boulevard to your car.

2 *Find Salvation* 7 p.m.

Have drinks and dinner at the **Salvation Restaurant and Bar** (140 Broadway; 401-847-2620; salvationcafe.com; $$), the way the locals do. The tattooed waiters and vaguely Asian-hippie menu remind you that Newport is only 40 miles from the Rhode Island School of Design. On the drinks menu, Tiger Tea is described as "an Arnold Palmer for the amoral set." Dinner can jump from a bamboo basket appetizer with vegetable dumplings and edamame to an entree of hanger steak. Stick around for dessert.

SATURDAY

3 *Eggs at the Dock* 9 a.m.

Take an outdoor table for breakfast at **Belle's Cafe**, at the Newport Shipyard (1 Washington Street; 401-846-6000; newportshipyard.com; $$). The eggy burritos are good, and the yacht-people watching is, too.

4 *A Heart-Shaped World* 10 a.m.

One of Stanford White's prettiest and silliest houses is **Rosecliff** (548 Bellevue Avenue), built for the heiress Tessie Oelrichs in 1902. You can read all about it in *The Architect of Desire*, a hypnotic family memoir about the tragic and emotional legacy of the Gilded Age's favorite architect, written by his great-granddaughter, Suzannah Lessard. (Tessie died alone at Rosecliff in 1926, Lessard wrote, talking to

imaginary guests.) With its heart-shaped double staircase and baby-blue trompe-l'oeil ballroom ceiling, Rosecliff is sweeter and lighter than many of Newport's lavish hulks from the same period. Allow an hour for a tour of the house and a little more time to wander Rosecliff's green lawns, which swoop down to the cliffs. The house is one of 11 properties and landscapes owned by the Preservation Society of Newport County, which runs this and other mansion tours (401-847-1000; newportmansions.org).

5 *Rare Books* Noon

If the crowds haven't gotten to you yet, they soon will. Find an oasis at the **Redwood Library & Athenaeum** (50 Bellevue Avenue; 401-847-0292; redwoodlibrary.org), the oldest lending library in the United States. There's a collection of furniture, sculpture, and paintings, including six portraits signed by Gilbert Stuart. But even more charming is the Original Collection of 750 titles, purchased from England in 1748 by a group of Newport citizens. You may not always be able to just drop in to read them, but a look at the titles is an interesting window on the wide interests of the library's founders—from theology to bloodletting techniques to how to build a privy.

6 *Make Mine Gothic* 1 p.m.

Bannister's and Bowen's wharves, smack in the middle of Newport Harbor, make up ground zero for Newport's seafaring past. They are very scenic and wharfy. But you knew that. What you might not know is that many of the exteriors in a marvelous camp classic, the gothic soap opera *Dark Shadows*, were shot in Newport. Have a salad at the **Black Pearl** (Bannister's Wharf; 401-846-5264; blackpearlnewport.com, $$), which was known as the Blue Whale in *Dark Shadows*.

ABOVE Harborside dining at Bannister's Wharf in the old Narragansett Bay port area, now transformed into a playground for vacationers, sailors, and summer residents.

RIGHT A rock wall along the Cliff Walk.

7 *Teak and Brass* 2 p.m.

Walk down to the **International Yacht Restoration School** (449 Thames Street; 401-848-5777; iyrs.org), which is both a center for restoring classic yachts and a school for history-minded craftsmen learning how to be restorers. There are heartbreakingly beautiful boats everywhere, in all stages of restoration. Make sure you wander through the turn-of-the-century factory building and out to the water, where you will find the school's most ambitious project, a 133-foot schooner, built in 1885, called *Coronet*. To see more, take a water taxi (newportharborshuttle.com) to the affiliated **Museum of Yachting** (moy.org), out on a bay island at Fort Adams State Park. Its exhibitions dovetail with the restoration work, explaining and expanding on what visitors see at the school.

8 *Back to the Wharf* 7 p.m.

Make an evening of it at the **Clarke Cooke House** (Banister's Wharf; clarkecooke.com), a lovely, rambling 18th-century house-turned-restaurant that covers all the bases for high-toned seaside night life. Start with drinks at its Midway Bar, and then, if you were feeling flush enough earlier to make a reservation, have dinner on the third floor at the airy and elegant **Porch** (401-849-2900; $$$), where you can watch the harbor below. Native lobster sautéed out of the shell requires no disassembly. Observe the patrons' variations on the dress code (gentlemen must wear collared shirts) and wait for the dancing at 11 p.m. Or invest a bit less and go down a floor and a half to the Candy Store, where you might try a huge crab cake served on New England brown bread.

SUNDAY

9 *Around the Dunes* 9 a.m.

You will need a salty wind to ruffle your hair today, something brisk and fresh to blow away all that dust and glitter. Head a few miles north out of town to the **Sachuest Wildlife Refuge** (769 Sachuest Point Road, Middletown; 401-847-5511; fws.gov/sachuestpoint). Its 242 acres of salt and freshwater marshes, sea grass, bayberry, and bittersweet and its rocky coastline are welcoming territory for all manner of wildlife, including seals, nesting terns, and harlequin ducks. Travel along the three-mile perimeter trail so you can be constantly on the water.

10 *In the Bay* 11 a.m.

For another perspective on Narragansett Bay, drive out onto the two-mile-long Claiborne Pell Bridge, which soars some 215 feet above the bay, and take the first exit, at Jamestown. This much smaller town is overshadowed by Newport, but its waterfront is worth a visit, with its own galleries, restaurants, and shops. Pick up some provisions, find the dock for the **Jamestown-Newport Ferry** (Conanicut Marina; 20 Narragansett Avenue; jamestownnewportferry.com), and park your car. Then ride the ferry to its first stop, Rose Island, and eat your lunch at the **Rose Island Lighthouse** (401-847-4242; roseisland.org). You'll find yourself in the middle of the bay, with gorgeous views of boats and sparkling water in every direction.

THE BASICS

By car, Newport is three to four hours from New York and an hour from the airport in Providence, Rhode Island.

Drive your car and use the RIPTA public bus system.

The Chanler at Cliff Walk
117 Memorial Boulevard
401-847-1300
thechanler.com
$$$$
Luxury, stunning views, and beautifully decorated rooms.

Hotel Viking
1 Bellevue Avenue
401-847-3300
hotelviking.com
$$$
Recently renovated historic hotel, built in the 1920s.

Sarah Kendall House
47 Washington Street
401-846-7976
sarahkendallhouse.com
$$-$$$
Pleasant Victorian near the southern end of the Point District.

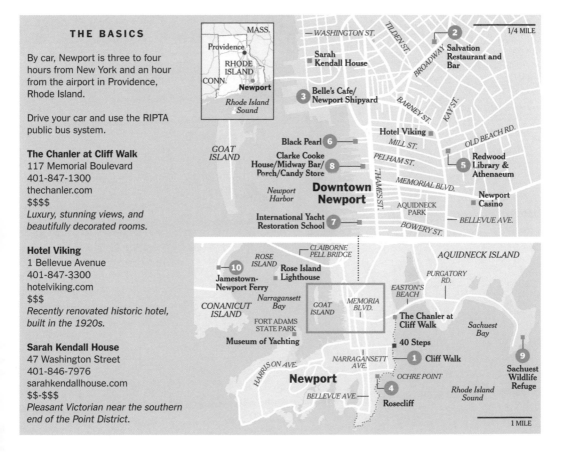

Martha's Vineyard

What is it about presidents (at least Democratic ones) and Martha's Vineyard? The Kennedys have been coming since there were actual vineyards. The Clintons turned up nearly every summer of their White House years, and the Obamas followed. Wealthy A-listers usually hover nearby, hoping for invitations to the same parties where the first families show up. But part of the Vineyard's appeal is its easy way of shrugging off snobbery. Despite its popularity among the presidential set, this island, off Cape Cod in Massachusetts, is still a laid-back place with a lot of mopeds, fish shacks, and nice beaches. Folks here will tell you that the Vineyard is really just an old fishing community — that is, if you don't get stuck behind a motorcade. — DANIELLE PERGAMENT

FRIDAY

1 *Like a Kennedy* 2 p.m.

Martha's Vineyard is prettiest from the water, especially from the deck of a wooden sailboat with an American flag whipping off the stern. If you've ever wanted to know what it feels like to be a Kennedy or star in your own Ralph Lauren ad, you can charter a private sailboat through **Book A Boat** (508-645-2400; bookaboatmv.com). The company will arrange the place, type of boat, and all the particulars. For $50 to $75 a person, book a two-hour tour aboard a 40-foot boat. And don't be alarmed if the crew seems rather young. "I've been sailing here since I was a kid," one 19-year-old captain said reassuringly.

2 *Lobster Worship* 6 p.m.

Lobsters are practically a religion on the island, so it's fitting that some of the freshest are served in a church. On summer Fridays from 4:30 to 7:30 p.m., **Grace Church** in the tree-lined town of Vineyard Haven (Woodlawn Avenue and William Street; 508-693-0332; gracechurchmv.com) sets up picnic tables and sells lobster rolls — fresh, meaty cuts tossed lightly with mayonnaise and served on soft

hot dog buns. Judging by the long lines, the church-supper prices ($15 for lobster roll, chips, and a drink) might be the best deal in town. Sit with fellow worshipers, or take your meal down by the docks for a sunset view of the harbor.

3 *Secret Sweets* 9 p.m.

On summer nights, in a dark parking lot in the busier town of Oak Bluffs, a small crowd lines up at the screen door of the **Martha's Vineyard Gourmet Cafe and Bakery** (508-693-3688; 5 Post Office Square; mvbakery.com), waiting for warm doughnuts right out of the oven. The open secret is known as Back Door Donuts. The doughnuts are soft, sticky, and delicious, though veterans will tell you the apple fritters are superior.

SATURDAY

4 *Egg Rolls and Grandma's Jam* 9 a.m.

Get to the **West Tisbury Farmers' Market** (1067 State Road) when it opens at 9 so you can watch the stalls being set up — and shop before the best produce is picked over. Take your camera along on this expedition: you'll find the Vineyard farmers' market is a colorful scene of wildflowers, organic fruits and vegetables, homemade jams, and, somewhat curiously, a stall selling spicy Vietnamese egg rolls.

5 *Say Baaah* 10:30 a.m.

Martha's Vineyard is like a miniature Ireland — roads wind among bright green pastures where sheep, horses, and cattle graze, and many of the

OPPOSITE The Allen Sheep Farm & Wool Company, where even the livestock has an ocean view.

RIGHT The harbor at Oak Bluffs, a town of boats, beaches, and Victorian gingerbread houses.

farms welcome visitors. The **Allen Farm Sheep & Wool Company** in the bucolic town of Chilmark (421 South Road; 508-645-9064) has been run by the same family since 1762. Take in the views of rolling fields. Buy lamb chops or try on a handmade wool sweater in the gift shop. Those things grazing out front? They're lambs, and they're very friendly.

6 *Fried Goodness* 1 p.m.

It's a picture-perfect beach shack — without the beach. Housed in a tiny, weathered shingle house on a small side street in the old fishing port of Menemsha, the **Bite** (29 Basin Road; 508-645-9239; thebitemenemsha.com; $$) has been serving what many regard as the island's best fried clams, oysters, squid, shrimp, and scallops for more than 20 years. There are only two picnic tables, so bring a couple of icy beers, get a small order of clams, and take the paper bag of crispy deliciousness to the dock and watch the fishermen.

7 *Time in the Sand* 2 p.m.

The nicest beaches on Martha's Vineyard are private; you need a key to get in. But one that's open to the public is **Menemsha Beach**, a lovely stretch of sand just outside of town (ask for directions at the Bite; you're close). It is popular with families, and in the evening, it's a favorite place to watch the sunset. Swim a little, walk a little, or just hang out.

8 *Take a Hike* 4 p.m.

Yes, the Vineyard looks great from the water. But for a less-photographed view of the island's natural beauty, drive inland to **Waskosim's Rock Reservation** (mvlandbank.com), a nature reserve with 185 acres of open fields, wooded trails, and marshes. A modest, mile-long hike takes you to Waskosim's Rock, the boulder that divided the island between the English and Native American Wampanoag tribe 350 years ago. Tempting though it may be, resist climbing the rock — Vineyarders want to make sure it's around for another 350.

9 *State Dinner* 8 p.m.

It may not be as famous as the vegetable garden on Pennsylvania Avenue, but the herb and vegetable patch at the **State Road** restaurant (688 State Road; 508-693-8582; stateroadmv.com; $$) has its admirers. State Road features American cuisine using local ingredients. Inside, the place is simple and sleek — hardwood floors, high ceilings, and Edison bulb chandeliers. Look for the Island Farm to Table Plate, a selection of fingerling potatoes and seasonal vegetables from the restaurant garden, and pan-roasted sea scallops, locally caught, of course.

10 *Night at the Ritz* 11 p.m.

The island isn't known for night life, but your best bet for a nightcap is in the handful of lively bars

along Circuit Avenue in Oak Bluffs. Stop by the **Ritz Café** (4 Circuit Avenue; 508-693-9851), which attracts locals and has live music. Don't be fooled by the name — it's more of a draft beer than an appletini kind of joint.

SUNDAY

11 *Stores by the Seashore* 10 a.m.

There's a lot of good shopping between all those seagull paintings and dancing lobster napkins. In Vineyard Haven, drop by Carly Simon's **Midnight Farm** (18 Water-Cromwell Lane; 508-693-1997; midnightfarm.net) for its eclectic mix of gauzy sundresses, home furnishings, and, at times, signed copies of Simon's CDs. Up the street is **Nochi** (29

Main Street; 508-693-9074; nochimv.com), which sells robes, blankets, and all things cozy. And down the street is **LeRoux at Home** (62 Main Street; 508-693-0030; lerouxkitchen.com), a housewares store with a great selection of kitchen supplies including those dancing lobster napkins.

OPPOSITE The Menemsha Inn.

ABOVE The twice-a-week West Tisbury Farmer's Market attracts farmers and shoppers from all over the island.

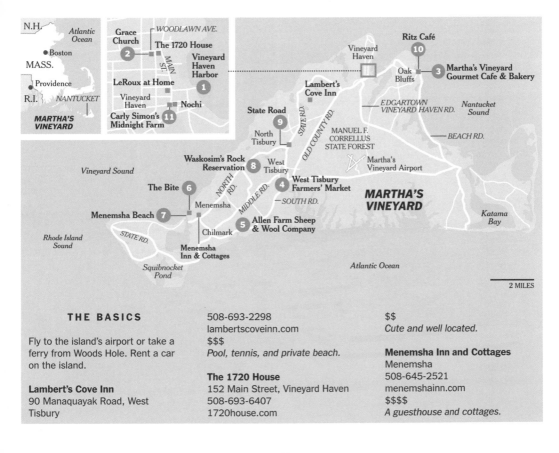

THE BASICS

Fly to the island's airport or take a ferry from Woods Hole. Rent a car on the island.

Lambert's Cove Inn
90 Manaquayak Road, West Tisbury

508-693-2298
lambertscoveinn.com
$$$
Pool, tennis, and private beach.

The 1720 House
152 Main Street, Vineyard Haven
508-693-6407
1720house.com

$$
Cute and well located.

Menemsha Inn and Cottages
Menemsha
508-645-2521
menemshainn.com
$$$$
A guesthouse and cottages.

Nantucket

Near the beginning of Moby-Dick, Ishmael explains why he decided to set sail from Nantucket: "There was a fine, boisterous something about everything connected with that famous old island." Today, more than a century and a half after it was written, that characterization still rings true. Though its downtown cobblestone streets and windswept fringes are now filled with expensive (some say exorbitant) restaurants and elegant cocktail bars, the island still has a swagger. To see it in full swing, linger over pints at one of the many harborside pubs, especially at sundown when sailors and fishing boats return to port.

— BY SARAH GOLD

FRIDAY

1 *Historic Bearings* 3 p.m.

Main Street is lined with 19th-century storefronts and buckled brick sidewalks that seem to require deck shoes. To bone up on island history, visit **Mitchell's Book Corner** (54 Main Street; 508-228-1080; mitchellsbookcorner.com), a venerable four-decade-old bookstore. It has been renovated to include a spacious second floor that hosts weekly readings by local authors like Elin Hilderbrand and the National Book Award winner Nathaniel Philbrick. The beloved Nantucket Room remains, with hundreds of titles about island lore.

2 *Preppy It Up* 5 p.m.

You can still find a bona fide pair of the pinkish chinos called Nantucket Reds at **Murray's Toggery Shop** (62 Main Street; 508-228-0437; nantucketreds.com), and buy sunscreen or fancy bath products at **Nantucket Pharmacy** (45 Main Street; 508-228-0180), another classic of Nantucket shopping. But snappy new boutiques are always opening. One recent addition is **Jack Wills** (11 South Water Street; 508-332-1601; jackwills.com), the first stateside outpost of the British university outfitter, carrying jaunty polos, cable-knit sweaters, and canvas totes in signal-flag colors. Another is **Milly & Grace** (2 Washington

OPPOSITE Yachts rule in Nantucket Harbor, once the refuge of whaling ships.

RIGHT Brant Point Lighthouse in the harbor.

Street; 508-901-5051; millyandgrace.com), which sells bohemian-style caftans and tunics, cashmere sweaters, and embossed-silver jewelry.

3 *Fish of the Moment* 8 p.m.

Dune (20 Broad Street; 508-228-5550; dunenantucket.com; $$$) serves local seafood and produce in an intimate, warmly illuminated space. There are three dining rooms as well as a patio, but you'll need to book ahead. Changing menus have included dishes like flaky pan-roasted halibut fillet and minty spring-pea soup with tender baby shrimps. Stop by the petite quartzite bar on your way out.

4 *Beach Martinis* 10 p.m.

A young, tanned crowd fills the back room of **Galley Beach** (54 Jefferson Avenue; 508-228-9641; galleybeach.net; $$$). A cherished beachside restaurant, it has also become a late-night gathering spot since its 2008 renovation, serving drinks like pomegranate margaritas and the Seaside martini, made with Hendrick's gin and cucumber. By midnight the party spills outside, where tiki torches and sofas line the sand.

SATURDAY

5 *Island Market* 10 a.m.

Started in 2007, the **Nantucket Farmers & Artisans Market** (Cambridge and North Union Streets;

508-228-3399; sustainablenantucket.org) offers the wares of dozens of island farmers and artisans throughout the season and hosts workshops to encourage other would-be island growers and craftsmen. Keep an eye out for handmade quilts, freshly picked blueberries and raspberries, and fresh baked goods.

6 *Surf and Seals* Noon

If you're looking for a day of sand and saltwater and don't mind company, decamp to one of the favorite public swimming beaches, like Cisco Beach in the island's southwest, where strong waves draw surfers. But if you want to see a wilder and more natural Nantucket, drive out to the far west end, where the island tapers to the twin forks of Eel Point and Smith's Point. You'll need to rent a four-by-four—make sure it has a beach-driving permit; if not, you'll have to buy one for $150 at the Nantucket Police Station. You'll also need to reduce the tire pressure to maximize traction and minimize environmental damage. But after bumping along hillocky dune trails, you'll enter onto wide-open, mostly empty shores. There are no amenities to speak of, so bring all the supplies you'll need,

BELOW Traditional weathered wooden shingles are everywhere, even on this luxury hotel, the White Elephant.

including food and water. Oh, and a camera. You might spot gray seals.

7 *Brew with a View* 5 p.m.

An afternoon of salty, sandy fun can leave you pretty thirsty. So it's convenient that the island's fabled west-end watering hole has reopened as **Millie's** (326 Madaket Road; 508-228-8435; milliesnantucket.com). Unlike its predecessor, the Westender, which closed a few years back, Millie's takes full advantage of the sunset location. A glassed-in second-floor bar lets you drink in panoramic vistas along with your Grey Lady or Whale's Tale Pale Ale, both from the Cisco Brewery a few miles down the road.

8 *Baja Style* 8 p.m.

Corazón del Mar (21 South Water Street; 508-228-0815; corazonnantucket.com; $$) has attracted a slavish following. This cozy, tiny papaya-orange den turns out south-of-the-border-inspired dishes like sea-scallop ceviche dressed in chili-citrus aji sauce or soft, Baja-style tacos filled with beer-battered cod, cabbage slaw, and spicy aioli. After dinner, take a stroll along Straight Wharf to **Nantucket Ice Cream** (44 Straight Wharf; 508-332-4949; nantucketicecream.com) for a cone or the house specialty: a sandwich of lemon sugar cookies and blueberry ice cream.

SUNDAY

9 *Sea Saviors* 10 a.m.

More than 700 shipwrecks litter the treacherous shoals and surrounding waters around Nantucket. For a fascinating glimpse into the island's underwater heritage, head to the **Nantucket Shipwreck & Lifesaving Museum** (158 Polpis Road; 508-228-1885; nantucketshipwreck.org). Reopened in 2009 after a $3 million expansion, the museum has vintage surfboats once used to save wreck survivors, child-friendly exhibits on Coast Guard sea dogs, and—most chillingly—grainy black-and-white 1956 film footage of one of the most infamous wrecks, the Italian ship *Andrea Doria*, shown slowly listing into the sea after its collision with a Swedish ocean liner.

10 *Beachside Brunch* Noon

The **Summer House Restaurant** in Siasconset village (17 Ocean Avenue; 508-257-9976; thesummerhouse.com; $$$$) is the island's most civilized spot for lunch, especially at its umbrella-shaded Beachside Bistro. Look for jazzed-up summertime classics like crab cake with corn salsa and tarragon aioli or a warm poached lobster salad with green beans and beurre blanc.

11 *Not Quite Open House* 1 p.m.

The **Bluff Walk** in Siasconset village was once the south shore's most fiercely guarded secret. But though you'll probably share the unmarked path with other visitors these days, a stroll here is still breathtaking. Pick up the trail in the village center (take a right and then a quick left at the end of Front Street) and walk along the high, Atlantic-skirting bluffs, past the backyards of some of the island's stateliest gray-shingled mansions. Erosion has left its mark (the last third of a mile, which used to extend all the way to Sankaty Head lighthouse, is now closed). But just stay on the path, keep your voice down and wear long pants — some residents, whether intentionally or not, let their sections become overgrown.

OPPOSITE ABOVE Windswept and far out to sea, Nantucket is rich in sandy spots for taking the sun.

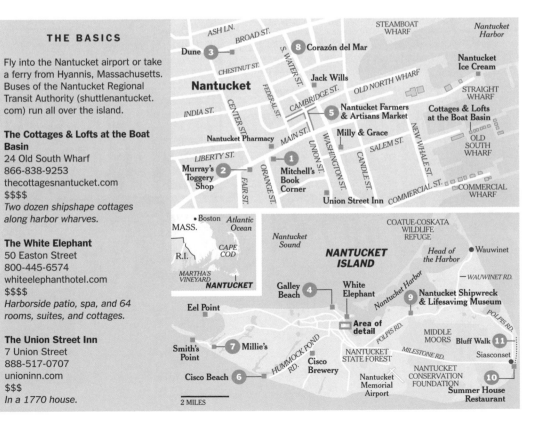

THE BASICS

Fly into the Nantucket airport or take a ferry from Hyannis, Massachusetts. Buses of the Nantucket Regional Transit Authority (shuttlenantucket.com) run all over the island.

The Cottages & Lofts at the Boat Basin
24 Old South Wharf
866-838-9253
thecottagesnantucket.com
$$$$
Two dozen shipshape cottages along harbor wharves.

The White Elephant
50 Easton Street
800-445-6574
whiteelephanthotel.com
$$$$
Harborside patio, spa, and 64 rooms, suites, and cottages.

The Union Street Inn
7 Union Street
888-517-0707
unioninn.com
$$$
In a 1770 house.

ASH LN.
BROAD ST.
STEAMBOAT WHARF
Nantucket Harbor
Dune 3
CHESTNUT ST.
S. WATER ST.
8 Corazón del Mar
Nantucket Ice Cream
Nantucket
FEDERAL ST.
Jack Wills
CAMBRIDGE ST.
OLD NORTH WHARF
STRAIGHT WHARF
INDIA ST.
CENTER ST.
5 Nantucket Farmers & Artisans Market
Cottages & Lofts at the Boat Basin
Nantucket Pharmacy
MAIN ST.
Milly & Grace
NEW WHALE ST.
OLD SOUTH WHARF
LIBERTY ST.
UNION ST.
WASHINGTON ST.
SALEM ST.
1
Murray's 2
Toggery Shop
ORANGE ST.
FAIR ST.
Mitchell's Book Corner
CANDLE ST.
Union Street Inn
COMMERCIAL ST.
COMMERCIAL WHARF

• Boston Atlantic Ocean
MASS.
Nantucket Sound
COATUE-COSKATA WILDLIFE REFUGE
CAPE COD
R.I.
NANTUCKET ISLAND
Head of the Harbor
• Wauwinet
MARTHA'S VINEYARD
NANTUCKET
Galley Beach 4
White Elephant
Nantucket Harbor
WAUWINET RD.
Eel Point
9 Nantucket Shipwreck & Lifesavimg Museum
POLPIS RD.
Area of detail
POLPIS RD.
MIDDLE MOORS
Bluff Walk 11
Smith's Point
7 Millie's
HUMMOCK POND RD.
Cisco Brewery
NANTUCKET STATE FOREST
MILESTONE RD.
Siasconset
Cisco Beach 6
Nantucket Memorial Airport
NANTUCKET CONSERVATION FOUNDATION
10
Summer House Restaurant
2 MILES

Provincetown

Park yourself anywhere on Commercial Street, the bustling main artery of Provincetown, and you will see celebrities, some real (John Waters, Paula Poundstone), some fake (that wasn't Cher). But mostly you will see ordinary people — lesbian, gay, bisexual, transgendered, and none of the above. Of the first 100 obvious couples to walk past Wired Puppy, a coffee-and-Wi-Fi joint, one typical summer night, 28 were female-female, 31 male-male, and 41 male-female. Four hundred years after the Pilgrims arrived here on the Mayflower, water is still Provincetown's raison d'être — it provides the gorgeous scenery and the cod, sole, haddock, clams, lobsters, and oysters that make this a food lover's paradise. The trick, as in any resort town, is to eat at odd hours, which makes it possible to avoid crowds even on weekends. And then exercise. With great places to walk, bike, and swim, Provincetown makes burning calories as much fun as consuming them. — BY FRED A. BERNSTEIN

FRIDAY

1 *On Two Wheels* 4 p.m.

Try to arrive in Provincetown by plane or boat. A car is useless in Provincetown, and besides, you can't really appreciate the place unless you see it as the Pilgrims saw it — on the ground, with the ocean out the front door and a vast bay out the back. Have the taxi driver take you straight to **Ptown Bikes** (42 Bradford Street; 508-487-8735; ptownbikes.com) for a reasonably priced bicycle rental. Then beat the evening crowd with an early trip to **Fanizzi's by the Sea** (539 Commercial Street; 508-487-1964; fanizzisrestaurant.com; $$), where you can find cold beer and the classic fish and chips, lightly battered fried clams, or a local fishermen's platter.

2 *Dune Buggin'* 5:30 p.m.

Time to burn off some of what you just ate. Ride your bike southwest to the end of Commercial Street, turn right at the traffic circle, and pedal till you see the Herring Cove Beach parking lot. At the end of the lot, a small opening in the fence leads to the bike trail into the **Province Lands** (nps.gov/caco). It's a five-foot-wide strip of asphalt that swoops up and down the dunes like a glorious doodle. It's about four miles to **Race Point Beach** — perhaps the town's most

breathtaking stretch of sand. Fill up at the water fountain and return to town in time for sunset.

3 *Night Galleries* 8 p.m.

Park your bike at the **Provincetown Art Association and Museum** (460 Commercial Street; 508-487-1750; paam.org). The town's premier art space, it grew with a smart addition by Machado and Silvetti (the architects of the Getty Villa restoration in Los Angeles). It's open till 10 p.m. (and free) on Friday nights. There are dozens of other galleries in Provincetown, and they, too, are open late on Fridays. Walk through the commercial district and drop in on a few.

4 *Love the Nightlife* 10 p.m.

The **Crown & Anchor** (247 Commercial Street; 508-487-1430; onlyatthecrown.com) offers one-stop shopping for gay entertainment. Arrayed around its courtyard are a disco with laser lights and throbbing speakers, a leather bar with hirsute habitués, a piano bar where everyone knows the lyrics, and more.

OPPOSITE Leave the car at home. Provincetown's main drag, Commercial Street, is best navigated on foot or by bicycle.

BELOW A trail ride down the Beech Forest Trail in the Province Lands area.

When the bars close at 1 a.m., follow the crowd to **Spiritus Pizza** (190 Commercial Street; 508-487-2808; spirituspizza.com; $). Some call it the "sidewalk sale" — the last chance for a hookup — but really it's

ABOVE The West End, at Provincetown Harbor.

BELOW Provincetown is on the East Coast, but its location at the end of curving Cape Cod makes it a good place for watching sunsets, like this one at Herring Cove Beach.

a giant block party. The pizza, with thin crust and more marinara than cheese, is super.

SATURDAY

5 *Window Seat* 10 a.m.

If your hotel doesn't have breakfast, head to **Cafe Heaven** (199 Commercial Street; 508-487-9639; $$) for delicious omelets, homemade granola, and banana pancakes. From behind its big windows, you can peruse the local papers for concert and theater listings.

6 *Stairway after Heaven* 11:30 a.m.

You loved those pancakes. Now work them off. Head to the **Pilgrim Monument**, a gray stone crenellated tower that has looked out over the town and out to sea since 1910 (pilgrim-monument.org). Buy a bottle of water from the machine outside and then start climbing; a mix of stairs and ramps will take you to the top of the 252-foot tower. On a clear day, you can see the tops of Boston's tallest buildings.

7 *The End of Cape Cod* 1 p.m.

Head to **Angel Foods** in the East End (467 Commercial Street; 508-487-6666; angelfoods.com) for takeout — ask for the delicious lobster cakes and a savory curry chicken salad. With lunch in your backpack, ride to the traffic circle at the end of Commercial

Street and lock your bike to the split-rail fence. Walk out onto the breakwater, a 1.2-mile-long line of rocks the size of automobiles. After a spectacular 25-minute trek, you'll find yourself on a deserted beach.

8 *Retail Corridor* 4 p.m.

Time for some shopping. **Wa** (220 Commercial Street; 508-487-6355; waharmony.com) is a shop that looks more like a perfectly curated museum of Asian art and furniture. **Forbidden Fruit** (173 Commercial Street; 508-487-9800; eatmyapple.com) sells unusual home decor items that run from funky to bizarre, including shiny masks with a slightly carnal tone. At **Alice Brock Studio** (69 Commercial Street; 508-487-2127; alicebrock.com), you may meet the proprietor, who sells her artwork here. It's not her first commercial venture—she is the Alice immortalized by Arlo Guthrie in the song *Alice's Restaurant*.

BELOW The view from Cape Cod Bay inland toward Commercial Street and the town center.

9 *Master of Margaritas* 9:30 p.m.

The dinner crowds are thinning; now it's time to eat. Try **Lorraine's** (133 Commercial Street; 508-487-6074; $$), a nouvelle Mexican restaurant where the margarita menu offers a vast selection of tequilas in price ranges from under $10 to closer to $75. Try the crab enchiladas or tuna tacos. Or if you've overdosed on seafood, look for choices like rack of lamb and filet mignon. Vegetarians will survive here, too, with plenty of rice, vegetables, and cheese in Mexican-style combinations.

SUNDAY

10 *Portuguese Breakfast* 10 a.m.

This time, breakfast at **Chach** (73 Shank Painter Road; 508-487-1530; $$), an update on the diner theme with a retro checkered floor and vinyl booths. There are plenty of typical breakfast choices, and this is a good place for Portuguese sweet bread, a nod to the Portuguese fishermen

who once dominated this town. The abundant cod that sustained them are largely fished out, but some of those fishermen's descendants remain, and Provincetown celebrates their traditions with its Portuguese Festival every summer.

11 *The Windblown Shore* 1 p.m.
Take a guided trip by S.U.V. through the **Cape Cod National Seashore** with **Art's Dune Tours** (4 Standish Street; 508-487-1950; artsdunetours.com).

The tour ventures out into the sand dunes on protected lands at the tip of Cape Cod, and will take you past dune shacks where writers and artists like Eugene O'Neill, Jack Kerouac, Tennessee Williams, and Jackson Pollock once spent summers working in near total isolation. The dunes are a magical experience, and the guides are happy to share their knowledge about the people who once lived here and the hardy plants and wildlife that find sustenance in this remote and windy spot.

ABOVE Wa, an Asian-themed shop on Commercial Street.

OPPOSITE Although Provincetown today is anything but austere, the Pilgrim Monument celebrates its Puritan roots.

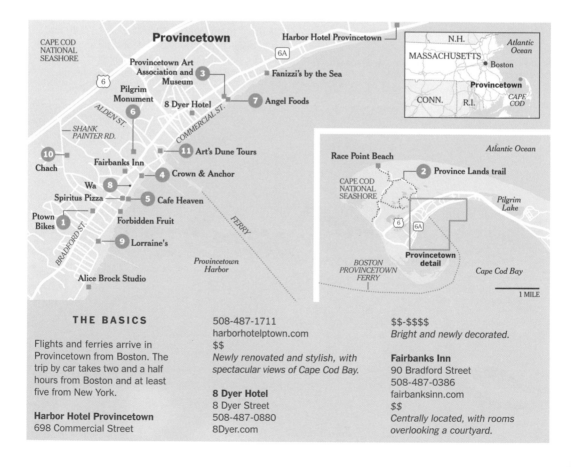

THE BASICS

Flights and ferries arrive in Provincetown from Boston. The trip by car takes two and a half hours from Boston and at least five from New York.

Harbor Hotel Provincetown
698 Commercial Street

508-487-1711
harborhotelptown.com
$$
Newly renovated and stylish, with spectacular views of Cape Cod Bay.

8 Dyer Hotel
8 Dyer Street
508-487-0880
8Dyer.com

$$-$$$$
Bright and newly decorated.

Fairbanks Inn
90 Bradford Street
508-487-0386
fairbanksinn.com
$$
Centrally located, with rooms overlooking a courtyard.

Boston

Boston is known for its bricks and brownstones, but with downtown stretching unimpeded to the water-front after the $15 billion Big Dig, these days it feels like a whole new city. High-tech exuberance, modern parks, and a reclaimed harbor add to the sheen of newness, complementing the youthful energy of the large student population. There's no danger that the city will forget its pivotal role in American history. The Freedom Trail is still there for the walking, and stately colonial houses still invite a stroll in Beacon Hill. But Boston offers some new paths to travel, too.
— BY KATIE ZEZIMA

FRIDAY

1 *Everything Old Is New* 4:30 p.m.

In a city this historic, it's not every day that a new neighborhood is built from scratch. But that is essentially the story with Fan Pier, a former area of industrial blight on the South Boston waterfront being slowly transformed into a hub of fashion, art, and dining. Anchored by the **Institute of Contemporary Art** (100 Northern Avenue; 617-478-3100; icaboston.org), a glass-and-steel museum that seems to hover over the harbor, it is a go-to place for the cool crowd. Shopping's a draw, too: **LouisBoston** (60 Northern Avenue; 617-262-6100; louisboston.com), the high-end store, has a 20,000-square-foot flagship, with a restaurant, next to the museum.

2 *Taste of Dakar* 8 p.m.

There's more on Boston dinner plates than baked beans. As the city becomes more diversified, so do its culinary offerings. Case in point: **Teranga** (1746 Washington Street; 617-266-0003; terangaboston.com; $), a Senegalese restaurant that opened in May 2009 on a busy South End street, far from the well-dressed masses. An elegant space with exposed brick walls and a long banquette, it serves spicy, fragrant dishes like nems, spring rolls stuffed with vermicelli, and thiébou

djeun, a popular West African dish with kingfish, jasmine rice, tomato sauce, carrots, and cabbage.

3 *Hear the Buzz* 10 p.m.

There are plenty of places to catch a show but not so many to hear live music with no cover. The **Beehive** (541 Tremont Street; 617-423-0069; beehiveboston.com), a restaurant where the lights are low and bands are chill, fills the void. Descend the staircase to be closer to the band, or stick to the quieter bar upstairs. Either way, don't leave without catching the intricate, hand-painted bathroom walls.

SATURDAY

4 *Easy as Green* 11 a.m.

Downtown was once defined by an elevated steel highway. Then by the Big Dig, the seemingly never-ending project to sink the roadway underground. After billions of dollars and untold numbers of delays, it is finally home to the **Rose Kennedy Greenway** (rosekennedygreenway.org), a mile-long ribbon of lawns, public art, and much-needed playgrounds snaking along Atlantic Avenue. To explore this emerald oasis, start at South Station and meander toward the North End, stopping to frolic in the fountains or take a spin on the carousel. At **Christopher Columbus Park**, find a spot under a wisteria-covered trellis and watch as boats bob in the harbor and planes take off from Logan Airport. It was worth the wait.

5 *Lobster Bar* 1 p.m.

It's a cliché for a reason: you can't visit Boston, smell a salt breeze, and not want to eat seafood.

OPPOSITE The landmark Custom House Tower, now a Marriott hotel, overlooking the Rose Kennedy Greenway in Boston.

RIGHT Wharf District Park, one of the interconnected public spaces along the Rose Kennedy Greenway.

Steer clear of the waterfront traps and head to **Neptune Oyster** (63 Salem Street; 617-742-3474; neptuneoyster.com; $$$), a tiny spot where Sam Adams-swilling frat boys rub shoulders with fabulous Champagne sippers at the marble bar. The attraction? Why, the lobster roll, a mountain of warm, butter-slicked lobster piled into a soft brioche bun, with a side of crispy skin-on fries.

6 *Couture and Cannolis* 3 p.m.

The North End, Boston's Italian neighborhood, is now as much Milan as manicotti, with boutiques popping up between restaurants and pastry shops. **Acquire** (61 Salem Street; 857-362-7380; acquireboutique.com)

melds vintage and modern housewares; the **Velvet Fly** (28 Parmenter Street; 617-557-4359; thevelvetfly.com) does the same with indie designers and old threads. In the continuing battle between women and the perfect jeans, the ladies win at **In.jean.ius** (441 Hanover Street; 617-523-5326; injeanius.com), where the friendly staff stops at nothing to turn up that perfect pair.

7 *Personalized Libations* 6 p.m.

Tired of forking over $15 for a cocktail that doesn't quite speak to your individual tastes? Then pull up to **Drink** (348 Congress Street; 617-695-1806; drinkfortpoint.com), where mixology becomes personal. Instead of providing menus, bartenders ask patrons about their tastes and liquors of choice, and try to concoct the perfect tincture. The bar is reminiscent of a booze-drenched chemistry lab, and any experiments that don't turn out right can be sent back. You can't go wrong with the Maximilian Affair, a smoky combination of mezcal, St. Germain, Punt e Mes, and lemon juice.

8 *Provence on the Charles* 8 p.m.

Boston raised its culinary game with **Bistro du Midi** (272 Boylston Street; 617-426-7878;

ABOVE AND LEFT The 1909 main building and the Foster + Partners-designed American wing, opened a century later, of the venerable Museum of Fine Arts Boston.

bistrodumidi.com; $$$), run by Robert Sisca, for-
merly the executive sous chef at the renowned New
York restaurant Le Bernardin. Here Sisca has created
a Provençal menu with a focus on local fish. Ask to be
seated upstairs, where businessmen and dolled-up
couples sit in buttery yellow leather chairs and gaze
at unbeatable views of the Public Garden outside.

9 *Local Tallboys* 10:30 p.m.

Tourists flock to the "Cheers" bar at 84 Beacon
Street, made famous by the television series. But
there's an antidote around the corner at **75 Chestnut**
(75 Chestnut Street; 617-227-2175; 75chestnut.com).
Tucked on a romantic side street, this dimly lighted
restaurant feels like a modern take on an old brown-
stone, with tin ceilings and mahogany pillars. For a
younger and cooler scene, check out the **Delux Café**
(100 Chandler Street; 617-338-5258), a reigning temple
of kitsch with walls decorated with records, comic
books, and a bust of Elvis. To get some New England
hipster cred, order a tallboy Narragansett Beer, the
region's answer to Pabst Blue Ribbon.

SUNDAY

10 *Morning Hash* 10 a.m.

Put your sunglasses on and grab an outdoor
seat at the **Woodward**, a restaurant and tavern
at the Ames Hotel (1 Court Street; 617-979-8200;

woodwardatames.com; $$$) that is injecting mini-
malist style into the staid Financial District. Brunch
offers modern New England fare, like lobster and
leek hash, along with great people-watching.

11 *Art and Architects* Noon

Boston has had a first-rate art collection, spread
over its well-known museums, for as long as anyone

TOP The Institute of Contemporary Art in Fan Pier, a
new go-to neighborhood in South Boston. The museum's
glass-and-steel cantilever hovers over the harbor.

ABOVE Custom mixologists at Drink, a South Boston bar.

can remember. Lately, renowned architects have arrived in town to design more display space. The old Fogg Museum, across the Charles River at Harvard, closed to make way for a larger building by Renzo Piano, to open in 2013. Piano also designed new breathing space for the quirky **Isabella Stewart Gardner Museum** (280 The Fenway; 617- 566-1401; gardnermuseum.org), although its masterpieces must remain in the Venetian-style palazzo where Ms. Gardner installed them. To see art and architecture

newly blended at the venerable **Museum of Fine Arts** (465 Huntington Avenue; 617-267-9300; mfa.org), head to its Art of the Americas wing by Foster + Partners, which opened in 2010. The I.M. Pei-designed galleries added in the 1980s are still worth a look, too. Prefer a ballgame to a museum trip? If it's baseball season and the Red Sox are in town, take in a game at **Fenway Park** (4 Yawkey Way; redsox.com), the beloved ballpark that remains right where it was when it opened in 1912.

ABOVE Fenway Park, home of the Boston Red Sox.

OPPOSITE Sailboats in the fleet of Community Boating Inc. on the Charles River Esplanade.

THE BASICS

Fly to Logan Airport or take a high-speed Amtrak train from New York.

Public transporation is plentiful (mbta.com).

The W Boston
100 Stuart Street
617-261-8700
whotels.com/boston
$$$-$$$$
Opened in 2009, with 235 sleek rooms overlooking the Theater District.

The Ames Hotel
1 Court Street
617-979-8100
ameshotel.com
$$$
Also new in 2009. Minimalist rooms and trendy décor.

Newbury Guest House
261 Newbury Street
617-437-7666
newburyguesthouse.com
$$
A brownstone with quaint touches and 32 rooms.

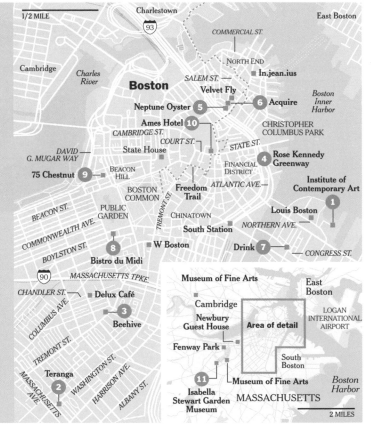

Cambridge

Home of Harvard and the Massachusetts Institute of Technology, with a quarter of its 100,000-plus residents enrolled at one or the other, Cambridge, Massachusetts, has a well-deserved reputation as the country's academic epicenter. The life of the mind comes with plenty of perks: a collection of arty cinemas, a thriving music scene, scads of independent bookshops, and a smorgasbord of international restaurants. Though Harvard Square is the tourist center, other neighborhoods offer visitors respites from both its escalating gentrification and its Ivy League self-regard. The grittier Central Square is home to great clubs and cheap, sophisticated ethnic restaurants, and Inman Square is young and adventurous. — BY POOJA BHATIA

FRIDAY

1 *Pizza cum Laude* 7 p.m.

Locals usually delight in dissing all things Yale, but for some reason they defer to New Haven when it comes to pizza. There's really no need. The patrons lining up for seats at **Emma's** (40 Hampshire Street; 617-864-8534; emmaspizza.com; $) say it slings the best pies in the Northeast, with crackling, wafer-thin crusts; about 30 interesting but not-too-outré toppings; and the ideal crust-sauce-cheese ratio. Design your own pie; one winning combination is goat cheese, basil, thyme-roasted mushrooms, and roasted tomatoes. For some heat, try rosemary sauce, hot cherry peppers, and Italian sweet sausage. Don't overdo it. Your next stop is dessert.

2 *Creativity on Ice* 9 p.m.

Cantabrigians take their ice cream seriously. Many profess to the molto-rich versions at Toscanini's; frozen yogurt lovers lean to BerryLine. But foodies in the know flock to **Christina's** (1255 Cambridge Street; 617-492-7021; christinasicecream.com), where adzuki bean and ginger molasses are among the dozens of flavors and a scoop of khulfi accurately

translates the cardamom-rich Indian treat. Purists, be content: Christina's has good old vanilla, chocolate, and strawberry, too.

3 *Time to Improvise* 10 p.m.

Catch the second set at the dark, intimate **Regattabar** at the Charles Hotel (1 Bennett Street; 617-661-5000; regattabarjazz.com), which has long been the leading jazz spot in town—and some who have said that weren't talking only about Cambridge, but about Boston as well. Fans of jazz, blues, soul, R&B, and world music also venture across the Charles River to Allston to catch their favorites at **Scullers Jazz Club** (400 Soldiers Road; 617-783-0090; scullersjazz.com) in the Doubletree Hotel. Both spots book nationally known musicians.

SATURDAY

4 *Pass the Jam* 10 a.m.

Toast, French or traditional from homemade breads, isn't the only choice at the **Friendly Toast** (1 Kendall Square, Building 200; 617-621-1200; thefriendlytoast.net; $$), a breakfast favorite steps from M.I.T. Eggs in many permutations, pancakes decorated with coconut and chocolate chips, and plain Belgian waffles are all on the extensive menu. If the excesses of last night's student-style dinner were too much, try the fruit salad with granola.

5 *Getting Beyond Euclid* 11 a.m.

At M.I.T., Cambridge's "other" university, numbers are king. They denote classes ("I've got

OPPOSITE An autumn regatta on the Charles River near the campus of Harvard University.

RIGHT A courtyard view of the Frank Gehry-designed Stata Center at the Massachusetts Institute of Technology.

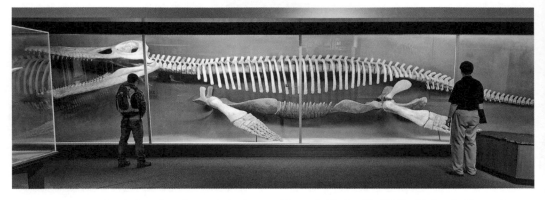

6012" means you're headed to microelectronic devices and circuits) and even majors (8, for instance, is physics), and most buildings on the largely undistinguished campus are known by them. But some recent additions have not only names but also architectural verve. The undergrads living in **Simmons Hall** (229-243 Vassar Street), designed by Steven Holl, say it reminds them of a waffle or sponge, thanks to the 5,500 cut-out windows that give it a porous look. Just down the road is Frank Gehry's fanciful **Stata Center** (32 Vassar Street). Orange brick portions pay humorous homage to M.I.T.'s boxy engineering labs, but they're cut up by aluminum waves, lacking right angles, that resemble the pleats of a skirt or a chef's toque.

6 *Food for Curiosity* Noon

You're at M.I.T., so don't miss the **MIT Museum** (265 Massachusetts Avenue; 617-253-5927; web.mit.edu/museum) 15,000 square feet of inviting ongoing and rotating exhibits that will absorb anyone who likes to ask "Why?" or "How does it work?" Visit Kismet, the sociable robot; step into the nucleus of a cell to watch DNA do its job; and tilt your head to see the shimmering changeability of some of the museum's hundreds of 3-D holograms. Look for gizmos like the

"Remarkable Double Piddler Hydraulic Happening Machine," which uses a strobe light to deconstruct a water stream into individual droplets.

7 *The World in a Square* 3 p.m.

Give Harvard equal time with a walk in Harvard Yard, and then turn your attention to Harvard Square. Chain restaurants call it home these days, but so do quirky street performers, plotting chess masters, texting teenagers, and independent bookstores holding out against the tide of online book buying that has swamped so many of their number. Book lovers should plan to spend some serious time at the **Harvard Book Store** (1256 Massachusetts Avenue; 617-661-1515; harvard.com), which has been around for nearly 80 years and has an outstanding selection of books to suit every interest, as well as a solid used-book section. A half-block away, the **Grolier Poetry Book Shop** (6 Plympton Street; 617-547-4648; grolierpoetrybookshop.org) is a destination for poets and scholars from around the world. If you're looking for Camus or Cervantes in the original language, head to **Schoenhof's Foreign Books** (76A Mount Auburn Street, 617-547-8855; schoenhofs.com).

8 *The View at Dinner* 8 p.m.

The decor alone is reason enough to visit the **Soiree Room** at **UpStairs on the Square** (91 Winthrop Street; 617-864-1933; upstairsonthesquare.com; $$$). Begin your gawking at the leopard-print carpet and work your way up along the walls, painted à la Klimt, to the gilded mirror ceiling. Somehow it all adds up to whimsical charm. The food, like poached Atlantic salmon or lobster bouillabaisse, can be as luxe as the furnishings, but even the humblest dishes are well tended. Tasting menus are both standard and vegetarian.

9 *Nightclub Nightcap* 9:30 p.m.

With Persianesque drapings on its platforms and divans, the **Enormous Room** (567 Massachusetts Avenue; 617-491-5599; enormous.tv) lets you lie down and absorb the atmosphere—that is, if you can find the unlabeled entrance. (Hint: Look for the elephant silhouette.) With a North African vibe and reliable D.J.'s, this bar attracts would-be bohemians—though the high-priced cocktails can require a trust fund. On most Saturday nights the place fills up by 10.

SUNDAY

10 *Riverside* 11 a.m.
Six days a week, cars choke Memorial Drive on the banks of the Charles River. On Sundays from the end of April to mid-November the road closes to cars and fills up with runners, walkers, in-line skaters, and cyclists, all eager to burn off weekend excesses. The

route, punctuated by boathouses, parks, and geese, is lovely in any season, especially when the sun shines and the river sparkles under an azure sky. If you'd like to get out on the river yourself, cross the river to Boston and rent a kayak at **Community Boating** (21 David G. Mugar Way, Boston; 617-523-1038; community-boating.org). Paddle out for some of the best views to be had of both Boston and Cambridge.

OPPOSITE ABOVE The skeleton of a Kronosaurus queenslandicus at the Harvard Natural History Museum.

OPPOSITE BELOW Nightlife at the Enormous Room, where the atmosphere feels bohemian but the cocktail prices might shock a starving artist.

THE BASICS

Cambridge is a 15-minute cab ride from Logan International Airport in Boston. Parking is a nightmare. Plan on plenty of walking.

Hotel Veritas
1 Remington Street
617-520-5000
thehotelveritas.com
$$$
New but intentionally old-looking 31-room hotel just east of Harvard Square. Free passes to a nearby yoga studio and gym.

Charles Hotel
One Bennett Street
617-864-1200
charleshotel.com
$$$
Close to Harvard's quads and the Kennedy School of Government.

Hotel Marlowe
25 Edwin H. Land Boulevard
800-825-7140
hotelmarlowe.com
$$-$$$$
A Kimpton boutique hotel in East Cambridge.

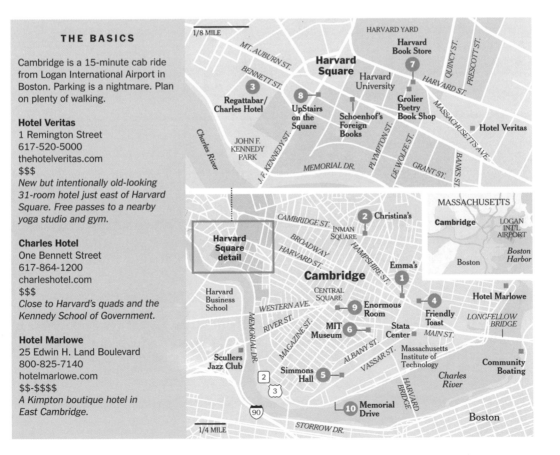

Portsmouth

Driving into town, it is hard to miss the fact that Portsmouth is still a working deep-water port, the seafaring hub of New Hampshire's 18-mile slice of Atlantic coast. But Market Street also leads to a charming downtown filled with eccentric and upscale shops, galleries, and restaurants. That's the Portsmouth paradox: It's a seacoast getaway town without a beach, an escapist retreat with a decidedly real-world spin. It's also scenic. Settled in 1623, Portsmouth grew as a shipbuilding center, making wood-masted ships for the King's Navy. Four fires in the first half of the 1800s led the residents to build with brick, creating a legacy of remarkable 19th-century city architecture including the white-steepled North Church, the town landmark.

— BY DAVID A. KELLY

FRIDAY

1 *Tugboat City* 6 p.m.

A working harbor means tugboats, which in Portsmouth are often docked downtown, along the side of Ceres Street. The blunt-nosed red and black Moran tugs are used to guide ships up and down the swift currents and winding channels of the Piscataqua River. For the tugboat-obsessed (or anyone who likes nautical gifts), a visit to nearby **Tugboat Alley** (47 Bow Street; 603-430-9556; tugboatalley.com) is in order. In addition to everything tugboat, the store offers harbor tours aboard the six-passenger *Tug Alley Too.*

2 *Dinner on the Deck* 7 p.m.

Portsmouth's tugboats also make a great back-drop for an outdoor dinner. Explore the waterfront decks and bars along the back of Bow Street. **Poco's Bow Street Cantina** (37 Bow Street; 603-431-5967; pocosbowstreetcantina.com; $) has a usually packed bar area as well as outdoor seating. The menu mixes Mexico and New England with dishes like lobster quesadilla and lobster salad tacos. The **River House** (53 Bow Street; 603-431-2600; riverhouse53bow.com;

OPPOSITE North Church, on Market Square, is part of Portsmouth's well-kept legacy of 19th-century brick buildings.

RIGHT Despite its name, the Portsmouth Naval Shipyard is just across the Piscataqua River in Kittery, Maine.

$$) serves up casual entrees along with great deck views of the river and the bridge across it to Maine. On a warm summer night, you may have to wait for a table.

3 *Watering Hole* 9 p.m.

For a peek into the past, stop by the **Spring Hill Tavern** (15 Bow Street; 603-431-5222), just below the **Dolphin Striker** restaurant (dolphinstriker.com). At the far end of the low-slung bar is a freshwater spring (now under glass) in an old brick well where the early mariners filled up their freshwater reserves. You can soak up your own refreshments while listening to one of the blues, jazz, and rock bands that play almost every night.

4 *A Bite Before Bed* Midnight

When the bars empty out, Gilley's fills up. It doesn't take long for a line of 20 or 30 people to snake out the door of this moveable 1940 diner, the latest of a series of food trailers here dating to a horse-drawn cart in 1912. **Gilley's PM Lunch** (175 Fleet Street; 603-431-6343; gilleyspmlunch.com) feeds Portsmouth until 2:30 a.m. with fare like hamburgers or kraut dogs, for about $3 each, and chocolate milk.

SATURDAY

5 *Water, Water Everywhere* 10 a.m.

Visiting Portsmouth without going out on the water is almost a sin. Boat trips with **Portsmouth Harbor Cruises** (64 Ceres Street Dock; 603-436-8084; portsmouthharbor.com) go into the harbor and beyond. The Isles of Shoals cruise will take you

to a group of colorfully named islands (Peavey's, Smuttynose) six miles off shore. They were explored by Captain John Smith of Pocahontas fame, and the pirate Blackbeard lurked among them — he is said to have left behind a buried treasure of silver bars.

6 *Island with a View* 1 p.m.

For a nice picnic spot and a good viewpoint toward the Portsmouth Naval Shipyard across the river in Kittery, Maine, drive out to **Peirce Island** (seacoastnh.com/Travel/Scenic_Walks/Peirce_Island/). Park and walk over the causeway to Four Tree Island. Unroll a blanket, unpack a picnic lunch, and watch the big tankers roll in. The shipyard dates to 1800; John Paul Jones's ship, *Ranger*, was built there. These days the yard overhauls, services, and refuels nuclear-powered submarines.

7 *Past and Present* 2 p.m.

Back across the bridge lies **Prescott Park**, a stretch of pretty waterfront that in the late 1800s and early 1900s was home to brothels and bars popular with sailors from the shipyard. These days it fills with crowds for the performances of the Prescott Park Arts Festival (prescottpark.org), featuring musical comedy and concerts in genres from jazz to folk and country. Nearby in **Strawbery Banke** (14 Hancock Street; 603-433-1100; strawberybanke.org), one of the country's most unusual outdoor museums, costumed role-players re-create Portsmouth life from the 1600s to the 20th century. Visitors find themselves chatting with an 18th-century storekeeper and then walking down a few doors to a 1950s living room with Roy Rogers and Dale Evans on the television set.

8 *Life on the Square* 5 p.m.

Market Square and nearby streets are lined with shops and galleries good for browsing and gift buying. For a cappuccino and some people-watching, hunt for an outdoor table at **Breaking New Grounds** (14 Market Square; 603-436-9555), a coffee shop frequented by everyone from business types to artists. At some point your eyes will also be drawn to the brick facade and towering chimneys of the **Portsmouth Athenaeum** (9 Market Square; 603-431-2538; portsmouthathenaeum.org), built in 1805. Inside is one of the oldest private libraries in the United States, a repository of local history including a research library and exhibition gallery that are both open to the public a few days each week.

9 *Brick Bistro* 8 p.m.

Expect to find seasonal ingredients at **Black Trumpet Bistro** (29 Ceres Street; 603-431-0887; blacktrumpetbistro.com; $$-$$$), which pledges that its menu changes every six weeks. The building dates to the early 19th century, with brick walls, hand-hewn beams in the upstairs wine bar, and windows overlooking the river. Contemporary takes on steak and seafood entrees enlist accompaniments like cactus-poblano hashcakes and cipollini onions, and the updated New England desserts may include gingerbread pineapple upside-down cake with mango coulis.

SUNDAY

10 *Next Door Harbor* 10 a.m.

Pick up coffee at the **Works Bakery Cafe** (9 Congress Street; 603-431-4434; worksbakerycafe.com). Then get in the car and drive a few miles down the

BELOW Street music on a hammer dulcimer.

coast to Rye, a part-rural, part-seaside town whose affluent residents have included the writer Dan Brown and Senator Scott Brown of Massachusetts. At **Rye Harbor State Park** (1730 Ocean Boulevard, Rye; 603-436-1552; nhstateparks.org/explore/state-parks/rye-harbor-state-park.aspx), settle on a bench and enjoy the views of the harbor and the Isles of Shoals.

11 *But Did They Drink Mimosas?* Noon

Have a lavish brunch at **Wentworth by the Sea** (588 Wentworth Road, New Castle; 603-422-7322; $$$), a grand Victorian hotel with sea views from the dining room and outdoor deck. A place this old has to have some history, and the Wentworth does. It was already 30 years old when Russian and Japanese

delegates stayed there in 1905, brought together by President Theodore Roosevelt to negotiate the end of the Russo-Japanese War. They cemented their agreement in the Treaty of Portsmouth, and Roosevelt won the Nobel Peace Prize.

OPPOSITE ABOVE Red brick and coffee on Congress Street.

ABOVE Tour boats cruise in the harbor and venture to offshore islands that were once a pirates' hideout.

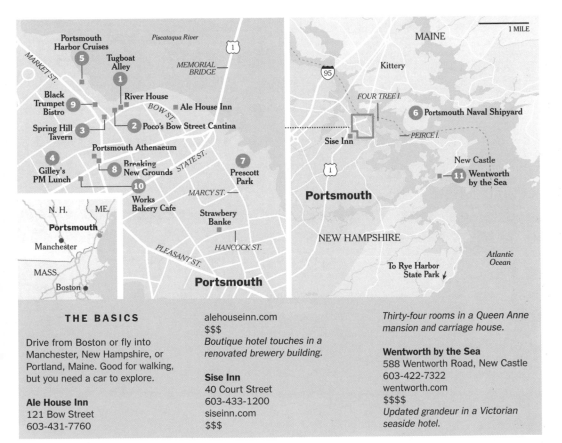

THE BASICS

Drive from Boston or fly into Manchester, New Hampshire, or Portland, Maine. Good for walking, but you need a car to explore.

Ale House Inn
121 Bow Street
603-431-7760

alehouseinn.com
$$$
Boutique hotel touches in a renovated brewery building.

Sise Inn
40 Court Street
603-433-1200
siseinn.com
$$$

Thirty-four rooms in a Queen Anne mansion and carriage house.

Wentworth by the Sea
588 Wentworth Road, New Castle
603-422-7322
wentworth.com
$$$$
Updated grandeur in a Victorian seaside hotel.

Portland
Maine

Portland is known for three L's: lobster, lighthouses, and L.L. Bean (O.K., make that four L's). Here's another: local. In recent years, this city on the coast of Maine has welcomed a wave of locavore restaurants, urban farms, and galleries that feature local artists. Abandoned brick warehouses are being repurposed as eco-friendly boutiques. In the main square, a 19th-century building has been refashioned into a farmers' market. And everywhere you look, this once-sleepy industrial town is showing signs of rejuvenation, usually by keeping things local.
— BY LIONEL BEEHNER

FRIDAY

1 *The Artsy Crowd* 4 p.m.
To see bohemian Portland, stroll down Congress Street, where at least a dozen galleries, studios, and cafes have opened in recent years. David Marshall, a beret-wearing painter who moonlights as a city councilman, is among the artists who exhibit at **Constellation Gallery** (511 Congress Street; 207-409-6617; constellationart.com). An artsy crowd can be found at **Local Sprouts** (649 Congress Street; 207-899-3529; localsproutscooperative.com), an earthy, community-supported cafe as crunchy as it sounds. Down the street is the **Portland Public Library** (5 Monument Square; 207-871-1700; portlandlibrary.com), which has revamped its gallery and added an atrium.

2 *Made in Maine* 7 p.m.
Portland's locavore scene has blossomed in recent years, as evidenced by attention to it on the Food Network. Among the most talked about restaurants is **Farmer's Table** (205 Commercial Street; 207-347-7479; farmerstablemaine.com; $$), which offers nice terrace views of the harbor. The owner and chef, Jeff Landry, gets his vegetables from area gardens and serves dishes like beef short ribs from grass-fed cows reared on a nearby farm. Or try **Caiola's** (58 Pine Street; 207-772-1110; caiolas.com; $$), a locals' favorite serving Mediterranean fare.

3 *Indie Playground* 9 p.m.
Live music anchors Portland's night life. The **State Theatre** (609 Congress Street; 207-956-6000;

statetheatreportland.com), a Depression-era movie house that closed in 2006, reopened as a concert hall in 2010, drawing touring bands like Bright Eyes and Hinder. Music buffs also make their way to the **Port City Music Hall** (504 Congress Street; 207-899-4990; portcitymusichall.com), a club glitzy by Portland standards that even lifts a velvet rope for its V.I.P.'s. A younger, more relaxed crowd flocks to **Space Gallery** (538 Congress Street; 207-828-5600; space538.org), scruffy art space by day and indie rock music spot by night.

SATURDAY

4 *Suburban Bagels* 8:30 a.m.
Across a drawbridge lies South Portland, a city of bungalows with a quiet beach. But the sweetest reason to visit is the **Scratch Baking Co.** (416 Preble Street, South Portland; 207-799-0668; scratchbakingco.com; $), a bakery on Willard Square that sells oven-fresh muffins, scones, and sourdough bagels. Get there before 9 a.m., as the bagels run out fast. Then snag a spot on Willard Beach, a patch of rocky sand with views of the coast.

5 *Free Island* 10 a.m.
The free spirit of **Peaks Island**, part of the archipelago that surrounds Portland, is evident the moment

OPPOSITE Taking in the view from Peaks Island, an easy ferry ride from town and a good place to explore by bicycle.

BELOW The Munjoy Hill neighborhood as seen from the ferry ride to Peaks Island.

you step off the ferry. If no one is manning **Brad and Wyatt's** (115 Island Avenue; 207-766-5631), a bike rental place housed in a dusty shack, drop some money into the honor-system box ($5 an hour). Then cruise the rocky coastline for the stuff of Maine legend: gorgeous lighthouses, osprey swooping off the surf. The island is pleasantly free of McMansions and private beaches. No wonder the natives tried (unsuccessfully) to secede from Portland a few years back.

6 *Marketing* Noon

A collective moan could be heard when the Public Market, a hangar-size hall run by Maine farmers and fishermen, shuttered in 2006. Luckily, some of those same vendors pooled their resources and opened a scaled-back version on Monument Square. Occupying a building from the mid-1800s, the **Public Market House** (28 Monument Square; 207-228-2056; publicmarkethouse.com) is stocked with bread, cheeses, Maine produce, and micro-beer. More recently it expanded into a loft filled with secondhand couches and food stalls, including **Peanut Butter Jelly Time** (207-712-2408; pbjtime.net), which serves variations of one thing, and **Kamasouptra** (207-415-6692; kamasouptra.com), which makes hearty soups like grilled cheese and tomato.

7 *Vintage Maine* 2 p.m.

Search out the most adventurous shops in the maze of stores lining the Old Port, the historic warehouse district. **Madgirl World** (275 Commercial Street; 207-322-3900; madgirlworld.com) is a quirky studio where Meredith Alex recycles skateboards and Barbie dolls into jewelry and funky, eco-friendly dresses; the restroom doubles as a space for monthly art installations. **Ferdinand's** (243 Congress Street; 207-761-2151; ferdinandhomestore.com) carries handmade goods, vintage fashions, novelty cards, and jewelry. When the Old Port palls, drive to Munjoy Hill, a traditional working-class Irish district that now looks more like Notting Hill, with a grassy promenade that overlooks the water. Among

its sophisticated establishments arc **Rosemont Market & Bakery** (88 Congress Street; 207-773-7888; rosemontmarket.com), which sells fresh breads and sandwiches, and **Angela Adams** (273 Congress Street; 207-774-3523; angelaadams.com), a design store that sells perky home furnishings.

8 *Divine Dining* 8 p.m.

Anchovy truffle butter? The foodie scene is old news here. The latest in Portland's dining scene is reclaimed architecture. A rundown gas station was converted into **El Rayo Taqueria** (101 York Street; 207-780-8226; elrayotaqueria.com), a Mexican cafe with yellow picnic tables. And the old Portland Savings Bank became **Sonny's** (83 Exchange Street; 207-772-7774; sonnysportland.com; $$), a Latin-themed restaurant. A fine example of this culinary invasion is **Grace** (15 Chestnut Street; 207-828-4422; restaurantgrace.com), a New American restaurant in an 1850s Gothic Revival-style church. There is something divine about drinking next to the nave, or gorging on goat cheese gnocchi surrounded by stained-glass windows.

9 *Bowl for Kicks* 10 p.m.

The bars along Wharf Street can get pretty fratty. For a more memorable evening, roll across town to **Bayside Bowl** (58 Alder Street; 207-791-2695; baysidebowl.com), a 12-lane bowling alley. Even if bowling isn't your thing, you can knock back a few pints of Shipyard ale at the sleek bar, which draws a mostly young crowd with tattoos and tie-dyed shirts. Or skip the bowling entirely and go to **Novare Res** (4 Canal Plaza; 207-761-2437; novareresbiercafe.com), a festive beer garden with long beechwood tables and more than 300 beers that feels more Munich than Maine.

SUNDAY

10 *The Mail Run* 10 a.m.

Schooner tours and lobster boat rides can be touristy, not to mention pricey. A better way to cruise around scenic Casco Bay is the mail ferry—a courier fleet that hops around five of the islands. The ferry is run by **Casco Bay Lines** (56 Commercial Street; 207-774-7871; cascobaylines.com) and departs twice a

day, seven days a week, from the main ferry terminal. The loop, which costs less than $20, takes three hours, so pack a lunch.

11 *Fermented Fun* 2 p.m.

Mead, or fermented honey, may have gone out of fashion in, oh, the 16th century, but the **Maine Mead Works** (51 Washington Avenue; 207-773-6323; mainemeadworks.com) is bringing it back. The honey winery opened in 2008 in a gritty warehouse on the edge of town and resembles a mad chemist's garage with tanks and tubes everywhere. A few blocks away but in a similar spirit is the **Urban Farm Fermentory** (200 Anderson Street, Bay 4; 207-653-7406; urbanfarmfermentory.com), a producer of cider,

sauerkraut, and other fermented comestibles that offers seminars on topics like pickling and eco-friendly mulching. It's another example of how Portland can't seem to get enough of recycling.

OPPOSITE The Portland Head Lighthouse, south of the city in Cape Elizabeth, is postcard Maine.

ABOVE Cheeses for sale at the Public Market House, a magnet for locavore shoppers on Monument Square.

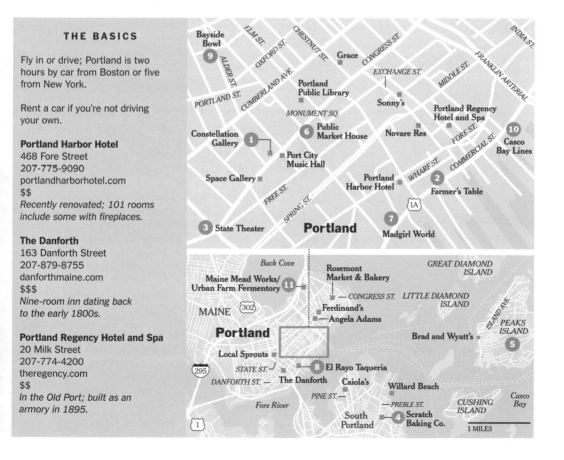

THE BASICS

Fly in or drive; Portland is two hours by car from Boston or five from New York.

Rent a car if you're not driving your own.

Portland Harbor Hotel
468 Fore Street
207-775-9090
portlandharborhotel.com
$$
Recently renovated; 101 rooms include some with fireplaces.

The Danforth
163 Danforth Street
207-879-8755
danforthmaine.com
$$$
Nine-room inn dating back to the early 1800s.

Portland Regency Hotel and Spa
20 Milk Street
207-774-4200
theregency.com
$$
In the Old Port; built as an armory in 1895.

Bar Harbor

Formerly named Eden, Bar Harbor, Maine, may well be the perfect New England tourist town. There are the requisite T-shirt emporiums and fudge shops and homemade-ice cream joints. There are art galleries and chamber music. The architecture consists mainly of grand "cottages" built in the early 20th century by titans of pre-income-tax industry, but they are not about Newportesque excess as much as bygone elegance. Above all else, though, Bar Harbor is special because a few of those early visitors donated their land and pulled the strings to get 40 percent of the incomparably dramatic and beautiful Mount Desert Island, on which Bar Harbor sits, designated as Acadia National Park. Bike, hike, amble, kayak, rock climb, horseback ride, lobster tour, whatever—it's a day tripper's paradise, at least until the leaf peeping ends and the shutters go up around the second week of October.

— BY PAUL SCHNEIDER

FRIDAY

1 *Flickerlight Dining* 8 p.m.

No matter where you're coming from, Bar Harbor is always a little farther away than you estimated. When at last you roll into town, all you really want to do is kick back in an overstuffed chair and eat fresh-baked pizza off a vintage TV table while watching that big hit from Sundance that you missed when it played at home. At **Reel Pizza Cinerama** (33 Kennebec Place; 207-288-3811; reelpizza.net; $$), place your order in the lobby where in a normal movie theater you would be buying popcorn and Junior Mints, and then go into the screening room and stake out a La-Z-Boy. When your number comes up on the screen on the wall, no one minds as you sneak out for your Casino Royale pizza (artichoke hearts, sun-dried tomatoes, and roasted garlic) and another beer.

SATURDAY

2 *Into Wet Air (or Not)* 5 a.m.

Given its extreme eastern location, 1,532-foot **Cadillac Mountain** is said to be the first place in the United States to see the sun rise. But beware, the best-intentioned plans to climb up and greet the dawn may fall victim to classic Maine mist and fog. If so, sleep in until 8 or so and then pick up

a newspaper and wander into **2 Cats** (27 Cottage Street; 207-288-3509; 2catsbarharbor.com; $$) for a breakfast burrito or homemade biscuit and a coffee. With the help of caffeine and newsprint, your personal fog will lift. (Warning to the feline-phobic: yes, you'll see them.)

3 *Here's to You, Mr. Rockefeller* Noon

By 1913 John D. Rockefeller Jr. was already feeling a bit crowded out by all the cars running on his family's gasoline, so he began construction of what became 57 miles of carriage roads that are open only to nonmotorized travelers. Like Mr. R., you want to do your part, so rent bikes at **Acadia Bike** (48 Cottage Street; 800-526-8615; acadiabike.com) and pedal merrily for a couple of hours through the mist along the shore of Eagle Lake, over the granite bridges, and between the dreamy mountains.

4 *Spot of Tea* 2 p.m.

Along the exquisite Park Loop Road, park your bike at the **Jordan Pond House**. By this time,

OPPOSITE AND BELOW Acadia National Park, the creation of a group of early-20th-century preservationists and philanthropists who valued the rocky shores and seascapes of Bar Harbor. Fifty square miles of Mount Desert Island, where Bar Harbor is situated, are in the park.

you'll be ready for its steam-filled popovers and tea (207-276-3316; thejordanpondhouse.com; $$; reservations suggested). The popovers arrive one at a time as you eat them at wooden tables out on the lawn, overlooking the pond and the pair of mountains known as the Bubbles. Afterward, find the bus stop and wait for the free bus that will take you and the bike back to Bar Harbor.

5 *Old Culture, New Culture* 4 p.m.

Back in downtown Bar Harbor, the **Abbe Museum** (26 Mount Desert Street; 207-288-3519; abbemuseum.org) looks back to a Mount Desert culture long preceding the arrival of the Rockefellers. Its displays of artifacts and art from the native peoples who once lived here include masterpieces of Wabanaki quillwork, basketry, and clothing that are almost subversively beautiful in this age of mass production and computer-assisted design.

6 *Sox and Ale* 6 p.m.

Maine, as befitting a state that used to be a part of Massachusetts, is part of the Red Sox nation. The mania is palpable at **Little Anthony's** (131 Cottage Street; 207-288-4700; eatatlittleanthonys.com), where the locals gather. Stop for a pitcher of ale and a few innings. If there are Yankee fans in your party, don't let on.

7 *New England Bistro* 8 p.m.

The locavore sensibility has arrived in Bar Harbor, though it may take looking beyond the obvious tourist-heavy burger joints to find it. At cozy **Mache Bistro** (135 Cottage Street; 207-288-0447; machebistro.com; $$), the owner and chef, Kyle Yarborough, uses ingredients supplied by local farms

and fishermen to create his Maine take on casual French fare. Menus change very frequently, but might include lamb chops and sausage over garlic mashed potatoes or duck breast cassoulet.

SUNDAY

8 *The Beehive* 7:30 a.m.

After loading up on coffee and bagels at **Randonnée Café** (37 Cottage Street, 207-288-9592; randonneecafe.com), drive along Park Loop Road to the Sand Beach parking lot and hike the trail up **Beehive Mountain**. The route is nearly straight up at times, an ascent made possible only by the iron rungs and handrails maintained by the National Park Service. It's not for the faint of heart, but it's short, and on a clear morning you have staggering views out over all the little inlets and islets to yourself. On the way back, take the trail over Gorham Mountain and along the base of the Cadillac Cliffs. It will put you back out on the coast not far from the Thunder Hole, where the air roars its disapproval at being compressed into a cave by the waves. From there

it's an easy walk back to the car and a dip, if you're extremely warm-blooded, at Sand Beach.

9 *Into the Blue* Noon

As you head back to town on the Park Loop Road, stop at the turnoff for Cadillac Mountain and drive up to the summit. Its 360-degree view is more than worth the detour, even if, as is likely, you discover that hundreds of other people feel the same way at exactly the same time.

10 *Put On Your Bib* 1:30 p.m.

As you leave town on Route 3, the time has come at last for lobster. You've turned down all manner of creative crustacean so far ("Uh, what kind of cheese did you say was on that?") because the best way to eat a lobster is with a bib and a cob and a blob of cole slaw. Skip the first lobster pound and any that have tinted-window tour buses parked out front. You could do a lot worse than to get all the way to the **Trenton Bridge Lobster Pound** (1237 Bar Harbor Road; 207-667-2977; trentonbridgelobster.com), just over the bridge in Trenton. After half a century in business, they know how to boil a spider.

OPPOSITE ABOVE A group of kayakers takes a break in a cove on Mount Desert Island's coastline.

OPPOSITE BELOW The Abbe Museum in downtown Bar Harbor.

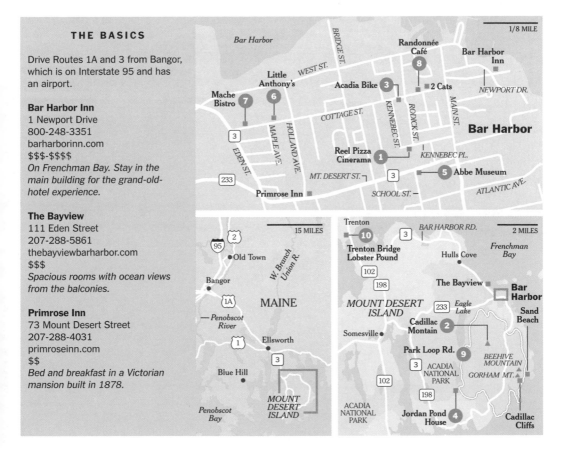

THE BASICS

Drive Routes 1A and 3 from Bangor, which is on Interstate 95 and has an airport.

Bar Harbor Inn
1 Newport Drive
800-248-3351
barharborinn.com
$$$-$$$$
On Frenchman Bay. Stay in the main building for the grand-old-hotel experience.

The Bayview
111 Eden Street
207-288-5861
thebayviewbarharbor.com
$$$
Spacious rooms with ocean views from the balconies.

Primrose Inn
73 Mount Desert Street
207-288-4031
primroseinn.com
$$
Bed and breakfast in a Victorian mansion built in 1878.

Stowe

Envision the idyllic Vermont village: soaring church steeple, covered bridges, no chain stores in sight. That's Stowe, the grande dame of Green Mountain ski towns—which makes it all the more shocking that the ski resort is owned by AIG, the insurance behemoth. That connection helps explain Stowe's $400 million upgrade, with a shiny gondola and a new pedestrian village with a private club and outdoor fire pits galore. But beneath all the modern glitz, Stowe still feels like a quaint place where no one locks the door and folks still dress like Bob Newhart without a hint of irony.
— BY LIONEL BEEHNER

FRIDAY

1 *Maple Flavors* 3 p.m.

On the way into town, stock up on homemade jam from the **Cold Hollow Cider Mill** (3600 Waterbury-Stowe Road; 802-244-8771; coldhollow.com), a farmhouse store that smells like the inside of an 11,000-gallon vat of cider, which just happens to sit in the back. Turn the spigot and help yourself. It goes nicely with the sinfully sweet doughnuts made fresh up front. More provisions wait down the road: the **Cabot Annex Store** (2657 Waterbury-Stowe Road; 802-244-6334) has a smorgasbord of Cheddars — chipotle, horseradish, Tuscan — to sample free.

2 *Old-Time Main Street* 4:30 p.m.

Stroll up Main Street, as folksy as a yellowed New England postcard, past arts-and-crafts shops and century-old inns. **Lackey's** (109 Main Street; 802-253-7624) is an old-fashioned variety store from the mid-1800s with the original wood floor. Or drop by **Shaw's General Store** (54 Main Street; 802-253-4040; heshaw.com) to pick up a rabbit-fur hat or an Icelandic wool sweater. The store dates from the 1890s and still shows off its original wood and tin ceiling.

3 *Vermont Microbrews* 8 p.m.

For good grub at decent prices, head to the **Shed** (1859 Mountain Road; 802-253-4765; $), a casual spot

OPPOSITE The lobby of the new Stowe Mountain Lodge at Spruce Peak.

RIGHT McCarthy's, a popular spot for breakfast.

where shaggy-bearded locals like to name-drop trails over pints of microbrew. The décor is a bit predictable —bumper stickers on the ceiling, deer heads adorned with boas and Mardi Gras beads—but the menu is satisfying, with tasty cheeseburgers and large Cobb salads.

SATURDAY

4 *Irish Send-off* 7 a.m.

Kick off your day at **McCarthy's** (454 Mountain Road; 802-253-8626; $$), a Mel's Diner-like spot where chatty waitresses wink at regulars and out-of-towners alike. Carb-loaded dishes like corned-beef hash, maple-glazed bacon, and honey oatmeal toast draw a packed house. Arrive before 8 a.m. to beat the rush.

5 *Eats, Chutes, and Needles* 8:30 a.m.

Start at **Spruce Peak**'s new base lodge, which has convenient combo lockers, ample parking, and a roomy interior encased in woven timber, before hopping on the still-shiny Over Easy gondola to **Mount Mansfield**. Take another gondola to reach the top, which incidentally is the highest point in Vermont, and feast your eyes on 2,360 vertical feet of powdery terrain. Start off on Gondolier, one of the mountain's signature cruisers with a million well-groomed twists. Once your legs get warmed up, follow the speed demons over to Nosedive, a steep chute that is among the oldest trails in Vermont. For

tree skiing, head to Hayride, a gently sloped glade run with evenly spaced spruces.

6 *Waffle House* Noon

Don't expect a cafeteria with chili bowls and frozen pizzas at the top of Mount Mansfield. This is scenic Vermont, so lunch means a casual sit-down at the **Cliff House** (802-253-3665; $$-$$$), a timber lodge with old wooden tables that serves upscale fare. Favorites include Prince Edward Island mussels, rich lamb stew, and daily crepe specials. Soaring floor-to-cathedral-ceiling windows offer sunny views of Smuggler's Notch and Mount Washington on the horizon. Grab a chocolate-coated waffle on your way out.

7 *Stowe's Better Half* 1:30 p.m.

After lunch, follow the sun over to **Spruce Peak**, the smaller of Stowe's two mountains. Once the neglected stepchild of Mount Mansfield and ignored by groomers, Spruce Peak now has great cruiser trails, new snow-making, and a newish quad chair replacing a creaky lift that took 20 minutes to reach the top. Main Street and Sterling are wide-open cruisers with lots of variety. If you find yourself back on Mount Mansfield, a nice and easy chaser to a long day of skiing is Toll Road, a never-ending trail with gorgeous views.

8 *A Secret Trail* 4 p.m.

Stowe has a lively après ski scene, which begins as early as 2 p.m. on weekends and seems more crowded since the resort did away with its night skiing a few years back. Insiders take the Bruce Trail, a cross-country path that winds its way to the **Matterhorn Bar** (4969 Mountain Road; 802-253-8198; matterhornbar.com). Stuffed with pool tables, a disco ball, and waitresses in trucker hats serving Pabst

ABOVE Snowboarding near the summit of Mount Mansfield, the highest point in Vermont.

RIGHT Spruce Peak at Stowe Mountain Resort.

Blue Ribbon, it is a raucous but civilized place to unwind after a day on the slopes. A wooden patio and sushi bar overlooks a brook, while a cover band plays classic rock up front.

9 *Spruced Up* 8 p.m.

The centerpiece of Spruce Peak is the **Stowe Mountain Lodge**, a six-story compound of exposed timber and stonework. Lamps look like twisted logs, and you're never more than 20 feet from a roaring, if gas-fueled, fireplace. Ascend the staircase to **Solstice** (802-760-4735; stowemountainlodge.com; $$-$$$), whose soaring salmon-toned walls, white-stone fireplaces, and open kitchen make it feel like the great room in an outdoorsy billionaire's house. The New American cuisine uses regional ingredients and has included dishes like Maine lobster risotto and Newfoundland steelhead trout.

10 *My Way or the Highway* 10 p.m.

The **Rusty Nail** (1190 Mountain Road; 802-253-6245; rustynailbar.com; $$) looks right out of the 1980s movie *Road House*. Gritty, crowded, with the stench of stale beer and a beefy tattooed bouncer out front, this popular spot serves up microbrews and martinis while live music keeps the crowds swinging on the sunken dance floor. Check out the outdoors ice bar most weekends.

SUNDAY

11 *Vroom with a View* 10 a.m.

To see Stowe's backcountry up close, jump aboard a snowmobile and glide over 10 heart-racing miles of luge-like twists and turns. Expect gorgeous scenery and occasional scowls from cross-country skiers. Two-hour tours are about $150 per person from **Stowe Snowmobile Tours** (849 South Main Street; 802-253-6221; snowmobilevermont.com).

12 *Sugar-Coated Rubdown* Noon

The smell of wood crackling in the two-way fireplace and a plate of homemade cookies greet guests to the **Topnotch Resort and Spa** (4000 Mountain Road; 802-253-8585; topnotchresort.com; spa entry, $50), where the 35,000-square-foot spa and gym was recently renovated. Kick your feet up by the large indoor pool bedecked in blond wood and sip some mint tea. Or soak in the outdoor hot tub overlooking Mount Mansfield. Even better, swaddle yourself in a terry cloth robe, slap on some June Jacobs facial cream, and tuck into a cozy treatment room for a rubdown with a concoction using — what else? — Vermont maple syrup.

ABOVE Inside Stowe Mercantile, one of the appealing spots for browsing and buying on Main Street.

THE BASICS

The Burlington airport is about an hour away. By car, Stowe is about five hours from New York City.

Stowe Mountain Lodge
7412 Mountain Road
802-253-3560
stowemountainlodge.com
$$$$
The only ski-in, ski-out hotel at the mountain. Marble baths, balconies, fireplaces.

Topnotch Resort and Spa
4000 Mountain Road
802-253-8585
topnotchresort.com
$$$$
The best rooms face the slopes, not the parking lot.

Green Mountain Inn
18 Main Street
802-253-7301
greenmountaininn.com
$$
Book a room in the main lodge, built in 1833.

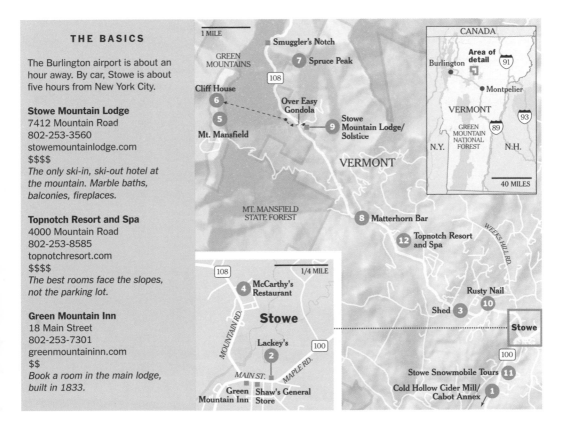

Burlington

It is no surprise that Burlington, Vermont, a city whose biggest exports include the jam band Phish and Ben & Jerry's ice cream, has a hip, socially conscious vibe. But in counterpoint to its worldliness — antiglobalization rallies and fair-trade products abound — Burlington turns a discerning eye to the local. The Lake Champlain shoreline has undergone a renaissance, with gleaming new hotels, bike and sailboat rental shops, and parks with sweeping views of the Adirondack Mountains. In the city's restaurants, local means locavore; urbane menus are filled with heirloom tomatoes and grass-fed beef from (where else?) Vermont. And you're practically required to wash it all down with a local microbrew.
— BY KATIE ZEZIMA

FRIDAY

1 *Stroll, Shop, Snack* 4:30 p.m.

With its eclectic mix of students, activists, artists, families, and professors (the University of Vermont is based here), Burlington offers some interesting people-watching. Take in the sights at the **Church Street Marketplace** (2 Church Street; churchstmarketplace.com), a wide, four-block concourse that is the city's social center and home to more than 100 shops and restaurants. The pace is slow, leisurely, and crowded, so be sure to leave plenty of time to explore. Pop into **Sweet Lady Jane** (40 Church Street; 802-862-5051; sweetladyjane.biz) for funky women's clothes and accessories; **Frog Hollow** (85 Church Street; 802-863-6458; froghollow.org) to check out treasures created by Vermont artists; and **Lake Champlain Chocolates** (65 Church Street; 802-862-5185; lakechamplainchocolates.com), where a hot chocolate doubles as a meal and you'll be hard put to eat just one truffle.

2 *Chic Tables* 7:30 p.m.

Long known as a town for gravy fries, pizza, and other collegiate staples, Burlington has seen a flurry of upscale restaurants opening in recent years. **L'Amante** (126 College Street; 802-863-5200; lamante.com; $$$) helped lead the charge. If one were to take Tuscany and add a splash of Vermont, the result would be this hearty yet crunchy menu. Starters might include squash blossom fritters, and main dishes include items like grilled Vermont quail. It's sleek and low-lit, yet somehow informal, despite an expensive wine list that leans heavily on Italian reds.

3 *Music and Maple Syrup* 10 p.m.

If there are three things that Burlington does well, they are live music, beer, and coffee. **Radio Bean** (8 North Winooski Avenue; 802-660-9346; radiobean.com), a coffee bar with exposed brick walls covered in local artworks, has all three. It's like hearing a band at a friend's party, if your friend lives in a ridiculously cool loft. Try the Five Dollar Shake, a brilliant concoction of stout, espresso, and maple syrup that satisfies your desire to drink beer and stay awake at the same time. And yes, it's $5.

SATURDAY

4 *View from a Bicycle* 9 a.m.

Playing outside, whether on ski slopes, hiking trails, or lakes, is a way of life in Burlington, so it's no surprise that biking is a popular way to get around. Rent a bike at one of the many local shops like **North Star Sports** (100 Main Street; 802-863-3832; northstarsportsvt.com), for about $20 an hour or $30 a day. For those who want to see the city, marked bike lanes make it easy to ride, but its steep hills will have your quads thinking otherwise. Head out along Lake Champlain, however, and the terrain is mostly

OPPOSITE A winter view of the Burlington Community Boathouse and Lake Champlain.

RIGHT The Frog Hollow Gift Shop, an arts center and gallery of Vermont-made arts and crafts.

flat, joining to some 1,100 miles of trails crisscrossing through New York and Canada. Maps are available at champlainbikeways.org.

5 *Weightless Suds* 1 p.m.

Chances are **American Flatbread Burlington Hearth** (115 St. Paul Street; 802-861-2999; americanflatbread.com; $) will be packed with everyone from kids to beer geeks when you get there. But don't panic; just order one of the Zero Gravity house beers—this place specializes in Belgian styles. The crispy flatbreads, baked in a wood-fired hearth, are essentially thin-crust pizzas topped with things like kalamata olives, sweet red peppers, goat cheese, rosemary, and red onions.

6 *Wrecks and Monsters* 3 p.m.

Lake Champlain isn't just what makes Burlington so picturesque. It's also a huge ecosystem that is the home of one of the world's oldest coral reefs (now fossilized) and hundreds of species of fish and plants. The **ECHO Lake Aquarium and Science Center** (at the Leahy Center for Lake Champlain, 1 College Street; 877-324-6386; echovermont.org) explores the scientific, ecological, and cultural and historical importance of the lake with hands-on exhibitions, including the remnants of an old shipwreck and an installation that gives visitors new respect for frogs. Children will enjoy working in a recreated paleontologic dig box, and adults will marvel at the lake's complexity. The center even explores Lake Champlain's biggest mystery: Is Champ a mythical lake monster or real? Try to spot him from the second-floor deck.

7 *No Page Unturned* 5 p.m.

Reading and recycling are cultivated arts in Burlington, and no place combines both better than the **Crow Bookshop** (14 Church Street; 802-862-0848; crowbooks.com). Stroll on the creaky wooden floor and browse a trove of used and rare books as well as publishers' overstocks, ranging from gardening guides to gently used copies of Shakespeare. Let the children explore their part of the store while you hang out on one of the couches and thumb through a stranger's old textbook.

8 *Paris in Vermont* 8 p.m.

In a city where style is inspired more by Birkenstocks than Birkin bags, **Leunig's Bistro** (115 Church Street; 802-863-3759; leunigsbistro.com; $$) offers a welcome dash of French flair. With its cherub lamps, cozy booths, and alfresco dining, it remains a social center. Go for a traditional beef Bourguignon or look for something with a local touch, perhaps maple-and-cardamom-marinated pork loin.

9 *Choose Your Nightlife* 10:30 p.m.

Follow the thumping bass to **Red Square** (136 Church Street; 802-859-8909; redsquarevt.com), a friendly nightclub that draws club kids and music lovers. Live bands usually play the first half of the night or, if the weather permits, on the outdoor patio. Late night is for D.J.'s spinning hip-hop, rock, and reggae to college students in halter tops and T-shirts. For something on the mellower side, head to **Nectar's** (188 Main Street; 802-658-4771; liveatnectars.com), the club where Phish got its start. Not interested in live music? Walk to **Green Room** (86 St. Paul Street; 802-651-9669; greenroomburlington.com) for a nightcap on a cushy sofa.

SUNDAY

10 *Green Eggs or Tofu* 11 a.m.

Prefer tofu in your scramble? Try **Magnolia Bistro** (1 Lawson Lane; 802-846-7446; magnoliabistro.com;

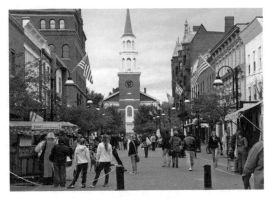

$), where eggs are always interchangeable for tofu and homemade granola is on the menu. For meat eaters, there are choices like an open-faced steak sandwich with Cheddar or tarragon chicken sandwich. Magnolia also claims to be one of Burlington's most environmentally friendly restaurants, which means it must be really, really green. Indeed, everything is recycled, and it's certified by the national Green Restaurant Association.

11 *Could This Be Stonehenge?* 1 p.m.

Not sure of the time? Find out at the **Burlington Earth Clock**, a 43-foot-wide sundial at **Oakledge Park and Beach** (end of Flynn Street) made of slabs of granite from local quarries. Stand in the middle and look toward the mountains; the stones in front of you represent where the sun sets during equinoxes and

solstices. Also in the park is a studio-size treehouse reachable even for kids in wheelchairs. It's an inclusive childhood fantasy come true.

OPPOSITE ABOVE On the popular Burlington Bike Path.

OPPOSITE BELOW The Earth Clock, a 42-foot sundial, shares Oakledge Park with a swimming beach, picnic and recreation spaces, and a wheelchair-accessible treehouse.

ABOVE Church Street Marketplace, the place for shopping, people watching, and decadent hot chocolate.

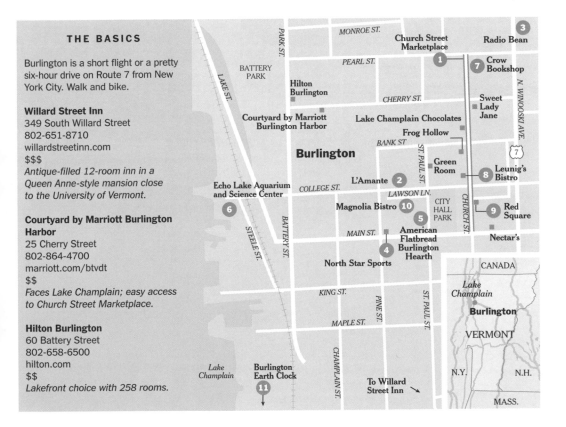

THE BASICS

Burlington is a short flight or a pretty six-hour drive on Route 7 from New York City. Walk and bike.

Willard Street Inn
349 South Willard Street
802-651-8710
willardstreetinn.com
$$$
Antique-filled 12-room inn in a Queen Anne-style mansion close to the University of Vermont.

Courtyard by Marriott Burlington Harbor
25 Cherry Street
802-864-4700
marriott.com/btvdt
$$
Faces Lake Champlain; easy access to Church Street Marketplace.

Hilton Burlington
60 Battery Street
802-658-6500
hilton.com
$$
Lakefront choice with 258 rooms.

Lake Placid

In any trip to Lake Placid, there will be a moment when you catch yourself thinking: Do you believe this little place was the host of two Olympic Games? Not because something so symbolic and global does not fit in a tiny upstate New York village of 3,000, but, more striking, because it will dawn on you that it is the perfect place. While the Olympics have become outsized, intimate Lake Placid retains ties to simpler times, whether 1932, when the Winter Games first came to visit, or 1980, a time remembered fondly by Americans for the Miracle-on-Ice United States hockey team. Still, a visit is less about the Olympics as they were than about life as it was. Lake Placid has the rhythm of a small town, albeit one with the sophistication to have played host to the world, and its pace is spiked by active people who embrace the mountain and lake setting that has attracted visitors for centuries. In the end, at least occasionally, you have to buy into the Olympic motto — Swifter, Higher, Stronger — and just go with it. Oh, and hold on for dear life. — BY BILL PENNINGTON

FRIDAY

1 *A Reason to Scream* 7 p.m.

Park your car in the center of the village, get out and follow the screaming. It will lead you to a three-story ramp next to Mirror Lake. You're here in winter, so buy a ticket to rent a toboggan. (Don't look up.) Climb to the top of this converted ski jump and place your toboggan on the solid-ice runway. (Don't look down.) Someone will push you down the steep chute, and after a few harrowing seconds at 40 miles an hour, you will be flung out across the frozen lake. (Don't get out.) The toboggan often does 360-degree turns before it stops. Then get up and do it again. (Don't forget to scream this time.) You have just experienced the **Lake Placid Toboggan Chute** (Parkside Drive; 518-523-2591; northelba.org/government/park-district/toboggan-chute.html).

OPPOSITE Mirror Lake in Lake Placid on a fall day, before the Adirondack snowfalls and the winter rush.

RIGHT Snow-season downtime in one of the cozy common rooms at the Mirror Lake Inn.

2 *Toast Your Triumph* 8 p.m.

Now that you have been baptized in the ways of the Olympic village, your bravery will be rewarded at the **Lake Placid Pub and Brewery** (813 Mirror Lake Drive; 518-523-3813; lakeplacidpubandbrewery.com), a few steps from the toboggan chute. Its signature Ubu Ale, a dark, smooth brew, will quickly calm your nerves.

3 *Window or Hearth?* 9 p.m.

A short trip up the hill overlooking the village of Lake Placid, on Olympic Drive, is a wonderful way to get the lay of the land, even at night. That frozen patch where your toboggan flew, Mirror Lake, is the dominant feature of the village. (Lake Placid itself is to the north.) This view of the village is best from **Veranda** (1 Olympic Drive; 518-523-3339; lakeplacidcp.com/dining.htm; $$$), where you can warm up at a table by the fire or look out from a table with lake and mountain views. This is the Adirondacks, so order the duck.

SATURDAY

4 *Expanded Slopes* 9 a.m.

Although *Ski Magazine* has called **Whiteface Mountain**, about seven miles from Lake Placid, the best ski area in the Eastern United States, somehow the place remains perhaps the most underrated snow sports destination in North America. People used to say it was too hard and too cold. It is true Whiteface's black diamond runs include the steep trails used

for the 1980 Olympic races, but the mountain has expanded its terrain to soften the harsh edges. There is something good for everyone now at Whiteface, most of all, a speedy — and warm — gondola.

5 *A Bite at the Brown Dog* 2 p.m.

With few lift lines at Whiteface it is easy to pack a whole day's skiing into a few hours, so don't be surprised when you find yourself back in the village in time for a late lunch. The **Brown Dog Cafe and**

Wine Bar (2409 Main Street; 518-523-3036; $$) has sandwiches and salads as well as a selection of red and white wines. It also has a view of Mirror Lake — look, there goes another toboggan.

6 *Where'd You Get That Hat?* 3 p.m.

Lake Placid's Main Street is a door-to-door feast of shops featuring Adirondack-style furniture and outdoor-inspired clothing. Be sure to poke your head into **Where'd You Get That Hat?** (2569 Main Street; 518-523-3101; wheredyougetthathat.com). When you make a purchase of this store's distinctive headgear, and you will, it is guaranteed that people will approach you for the next several months to ask, "Where'd you get that hat?" The appropriate response: "Exactly." Before leaving Main Street, duck into the **Olympic Center** (2634 Main Street; 518-523-1655; whiteface.com/facilities/oc.php), home to the Miracle on Ice hockey rink from 1980. You may be stunned by how small it is. An Olympic museum at the same address has an exhibit devoted to the 1980 team, as well as skating outfits and pink skates from Sonja Henie, the figure-skating darling of the 1932 Olympics.

ABOVE The Olympic speed skating oval, where Eric Heiden won five gold medals in the 1980 Winter Games, is open to the public for skating.

LEFT Whiteface Mountain, where Olympic skiers raced.

7 *Spa Treatment* 5 p.m.

You could rent skates and push yourself around the 400-meter oval where Eric Heiden won his five gold medals, but come on, enough is enough. It's time to pamper those tense toboggan muscles and stretched skiing tendons at the **Spa at the Mirror Lake Inn** (77 Mirror Lake Drive; 518-302-3010; mirrorlakeinn.com). Tranquillity reigns in this sanctuary. Besides, it's really nice to stop and plop into the hot tub.

8 *Critters by Candlelight* 7 p.m.

Stay at the Mirror Lake Inn and take a table at the **View** (518-302-3000; $$$), its tablecloth-and-candlelight restaurant. An eclectic menu ranges to dishes like rutabaga-and-mushroom tournedos, but again, this is winter in the Adirondacks, and you really ought to order game. There's usually some on the menu, perhaps quail or grilled rack of wild boar. If not, you can always make do with the beef.

SUNDAY

9 *Do You Iditarod?* 10 a.m.

Alaska is not the only place to go dog-sledding. Just off Main Street, **Thunder Mountain Dog Sled Tours** (518-891-6239; across from the High Peaks Resort) will have you mushing around Mirror Lake in no time. Watch out for flying toboggans.

10 *Lakefront Lunch* 11 a.m.

A few miles outside the village is the **Lake Placid Lodge** (144 Lodge Way; 518-523-2700; lakeplacidlodge.com), a place both refined and rustic. It is also a place of fine dining. In **Maggie's**

TOP Dogsledding on frozen Mirror Lake.

ABOVE The view from the top of the Lake Placid bobsled run, which was used in the 1932 and 1980 Olympics.

Pub ($$$$), even the burgers on the lunch menu have suggested wine pairings.

11 *Bobsled Finale* 1 p.m.

Now that you are comfortably at ease, it is time to create a lasting memory of Lake Placid. On your way out of town on Route 73, stop at the **Olympic Sports Complex** (220 Bobsled Run Lane; 518-523-4436; whiteface.com/activities/bob.php). Rent a thick, heavy helmet and hire a clear-eyed professional driver and a brakeman who will steer you down the Olympic

bobsled course at 50 or 60 miles an hour. There is much less screaming than at the toboggan run. That may be because you are often sideways or more or less upside down, which for a few seconds turns breathing into a new Olympic sport. All in all, a fitting conclusion to a breathtaking visit.

ABOVE Professional sledders swoosh paying thrill-seekers down the Olympic bobsled run.

OPPOSITE The Follies trail on Whiteface Mountain.

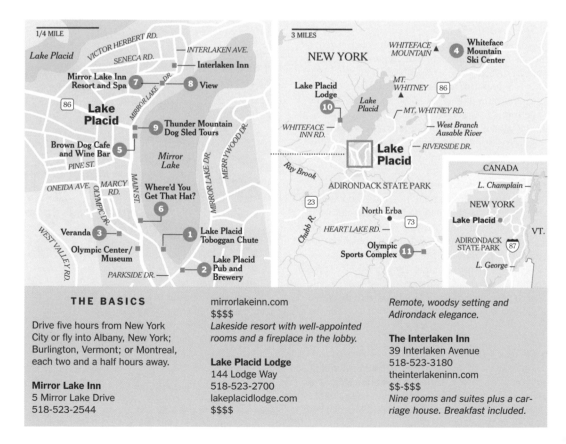

THE BASICS

Drive five hours from New York City or fly into Albany, New York; Burlington, Vermont; or Montreal, each two and a half hours away.

Mirror Lake Inn
5 Mirror Lake Drive
518-523-2544

mirrorlakeinn.com
$$$$
Lakeside resort with well-appointed rooms and a fireplace in the lobby.

Lake Placid Lodge
144 Lodge Way
518-523-2700
lakeplacidlodge.com
$$$$

Remote, woodsy setting and Adirondack elegance.

The Interlaken Inn
39 Interlaken Avenue
518-523-3180
theinterlakeninn.com
$$-$$$
Nine rooms and suites plus a carriage house. Breakfast included.

Toronto

As one of the planet's most diverse cities, Toronto is oddly clean and orderly. Sidewalks are spotless, trolleys run like clockwork, and the locals are polite almost to a fault. That's not to say that Torontonians are dull. Far from it. With a population that is now half foreign-born — fueled by growing numbers of East Indians, Chinese, and Sri Lankans — this city on the shore of Lake Ontario offers a kaleidoscope of world cultures. Sing karaoke in a Vietnamese bar, sip espresso in Little Italy, and catch a new Bollywood release, all in one night. The art and design scenes are thriving, too, and not just on the red carpets of the Toronto International Film Festival, held every September. Industrial zones have been reborn into gallery districts, and dark alleys now lead to designer studios, giving Canada's financial capital an almost disheveled mien. — BY DENNY LEE

FRIDAY

1 *West Enders* 4 p.m.

Toronto's cool scene seems to migrate west along Queen Street West every few years. It started out at Yonge Street, with punk rockers and art students pouring into sweaty clubs. Then, when mainstream stores like the Gap moved in, the scenesters fled west, past Bathurst Street, to a district now called **West Queen West** (westqueenwest.ca), where old appliance stores are still being carved into rough-hewn galleries and hunter-chic boutiques. Start your stroll along Toronto's art mile at Bathurst Street and go west. Raw spaces that showcase young Canadian artists include **Paul Petro Contemporary Art** (980 Queen Street West; 416-979-7874; paulpetro.com).

2 *Designer Meats* 8 p.m.

For a taste of hipsterdom, put on a T-shirt and squeeze into **OddFellows** (936 Queen Street West; 416-534-5244; oddfellows.ca; $$), a boutique-like bistro where the area's beard-and-flannel posse gathers nightly. The corner restaurant is run by Brian Richer and Kei Ng, partners in a maverick design firm,

OPPOSITE Santiago Calatrava's atrium at Brookfield Place has been described as the "crystal cathedral of commerce."

RIGHT Leslieville is packed with cafes and antiques shops.

Castor Design (castordesign.ca), known for elevating mundane materials into clever objects. The menu follows similar sleights of hand. Manly cuts are skillfully turned into Canadian comfort dishes like bison meatloaf and venison burgers. The long communal table, made of polished limestone and random legs, encourages chitchat.

3 *Trend North* 10:30 p.m.

Let the frat boys have College Street. And West Queen West has been overrun lately with 905ers, slang for out-of-towners with suburban area codes. The cool kids, it seems, are now migrating north along Ossington Avenue, which some Toronto bloggers are already calling Next West Queen West. Bookending the district are **Sweaty Betty's** (13 Ossington Avenue; 416-535-6861), a hole-in-the-wall with a brash jukebox, and **Communist's Daughter** (1149 Dundas Street West; 647-435-0103), an understated lounge. A trendy bar crawl is emerging in between, tucked among old Portuguese bakeries and kitchen supply stores.

SATURDAY

4 *Eggs and Egg Chairs* 10:30 a.m.

Brunch is serious business in this town, and discerning eaters are making their way to Leslieville, a once grimy neighborhood in East Toronto now packed with smart-looking cafes and midcentury-modern stores. Get your morning eggs at **Table 17** (782 Queen Street East; 416-519-1851; table17.ca; $$), a country-style French bistro. Afterward, look over well-priced and well-curated antiques shops like

Machine Age Modern (1000 Queen Street East; 416-461-3588; machineagemodern.com), which carries teak dining tables, Georg Jensen clocks, and other vintage modern treasures.

5 *O Calcutta* 2 p.m.

This is a city of minority neighborhoods, from the souvlaki joints in Greektown to the rainbow-hued windows of Gay Village. There are even two Chinatowns. But for color and spice, hop a taxi to Little India. The hilltop district spans just six blocks along Gerrard Street East, but it's jammed with more than a hundred stores and restaurants. Wander the shops and try the food. **Dubai Jewellers** (1407 Gerrard Street East; 416-465-1200) has a dazzling assortment of Indian-designed gold pieces. And for a midday snack, **Udupi Palace** (No. 1460; 416-405-8189; udupipalace.ca) is a bright restaurant that makes delicious dosas, chaats, and other South Indian treats.

6 *Made in Canada* 4 p.m.

Local fashion is disappointing, even in West Queen West. A handsome exception is **Klaxon Howl** (at the rear entrance of 694 Queen Street West; 647-436-6628; klaxonhowl.com), a homegrown men's label that blends vintage military gear with its own rugged work shirts, selvage denim jeans, and waxed cotton jackets. The design scene, on the other hand, is flourishing. For clever housewares, take a slight detour to **Made** (867 Dundas Street West; 416-607-6384; madedesign.ca), a gallery store that represents young product designers with a fresh and playful eye.

7 *Nomadic Tastes* 8 p.m.

A new culinary confidence has taken hold of Toronto. Not only are kitchens updating traditional Canadian fare like charcuterie and wild boar, but young chefs are tapping Toronto's global roots in ways that transcend standard fusion. Asian fusion restaurants like **Madeline's** (601 King Street West; 416-603-2205; susur.com/madelines) are busy. But also making a mark are hot spots like **Nyood** (1096 Queen Street West; 416-466-1888; nyood.ca; $), a pan-Mediterranean restaurant with big chandeliers and frilly molding. Dishes like the Malta braised short ribs are a hit, while tasty cocktails like the berry mojito keep the party going.

8 *Get Wiggy* 11 p.m.

O.K., College Street is not all bad, especially if you're single and in your mid-20s to 30s. A place to start is the unimaginatively named **College Street Bar** (No. 574; 416-533-2417; collegestreetbar.com). The dim space has brick walls, a woodsy patio, and a refreshing microbrew that draws a good-looking crowd of Web designers and writer types. Afterward, you can catch the 1 a.m. drag show at **El Convento Rico** (No. 750; 416-588-7800; elconventorico.com), a low-rent, high-octane club that attracts an exuberant mix of bachelorettes in plastic tiaras and muscular men with high voices.

SUNDAY

9 *Dim Sum Luxe* 11 a.m.

For inventive dim sum you won't find anywhere else, make a beeline for **Lai Wah Heen** (108 Chestnut Street; 416-977-9899; laiwahheen.com; $$$), a white-tablecloth restaurant on the second floor of the Metropolitan Hotel. Expect fanciful creations like

crab dumplings that resemble purple crabs and tofu paired with truffles and mushroom.

10 *Trophy Museum* 1 p.m.

The CN Tower notwithstanding, Toronto has impressive architecture by giants like Ludwig Mies van der Rohe, Santiago Calatrava, and Thom Mayne. But work by its favorite son, Frank Gehry, was missing until 2008, when the **Art Gallery of Ontario** (317 Dundas Street West; 416-979-6648; ago.net) reopened with a bold renovation by Gehry, who grew up just blocks from the century-old museum. He wrapped the original Beaux-Arts structure in sheets of billowing glass and swaths of Douglas fir, and added a spiraling wood staircase that pierces the glass roof to a new contemporary-art wing. It's a stunning homecoming for an architect credited with helping other cities flourish—not that Toronto needs a hand.

OPPOSITE ABOVE Street scene in Toronto.

OPPOSITE BELOW A staircase at Toronto's New City Hall, designed by Finnish architect Viljo Revell.

ABOVE Inside Klaxon Howl in the West Queen West district.

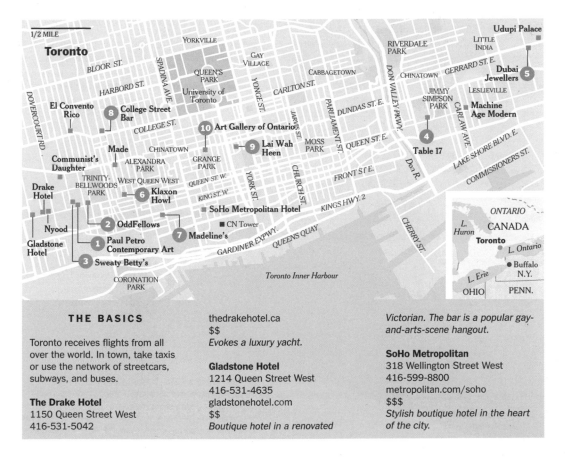

THE BASICS

Toronto receives flights from all over the world. In town, take taxis or use the network of streetcars, subways, and buses.

The Drake Hotel
1150 Queen Street West
416-531-5042
thedrakehotel.ca
$$
Evokes a luxury yacht.

Gladstone Hotel
1214 Queen Street West
416-531-4635
gladstonehotel.com
$$
Boutique hotel in a renovated
Victorian. The bar is a popular gay-
and-arts-scene hangout.

SoHo Metropolitan
318 Wellington Street West
416-599-8800
metropolitan.com/soho
$$$
Stylish boutique hotel in the heart of the city.

Montreal

French or English? One of the beautiful things about Montreal is that you never know in what language you will be greeted. Which brings up a second thing: Maybe it's the good food, the open skies, or the free-spirited students who call this city their campus, but the folks of Montreal are friendly. Ask someone for directions in the Métro, part of the vast Underground City that stays toasty during the winter, and you may end up making drinks plans later. That's not a bad thing, bien sûr. With the city's music-charged night life, slaughterhouse-chic restaurants, and postindustrial revival, it helps to have a guide. — BY DENNY LEE

FRIDAY

1 *Get Wheels* 4:30 p.m.
Public bikes have swept Europe, so leave it to Montreal, "the other Paris," to popularize the concept in North America. When 5,000 gray-and-red Bixi bikes were deployed in 2009, they became an instant hit. Familiarize yourself with the system: it's as easy as swiping a credit card at one of the 400 **Bixi** stations and going for a spin. (Go to bixi.com for details.) It's one of the quickest ways to get around and, at 5 Canadian dollars (about the same in U.S. dollars) for 24 hours, among the cheapest. To find the nearest Bixi station, including a large one on Rue McGill with 20 docks, download one of the many iPhone apps that offer real-time updates on available bikes, including Bixou Lite (free).

2 *Downtown Roll* 5 p.m.
A bike is only as good as the network it's on. And Montreal delivers, with 310-plus miles of bike lanes that crisscross the city, about half of which are physically separated from cars. To see why Montreal was designated a Unesco City of Design in 2006, point your handlebars toward the Lachine Canal, a former industrial waterfront that has been transformed into a lush green belt. The path is dotted with architectural gems like **Habitat 67** (2600, avenue Pierre-Dupuy; habitat67.com), a Brutalist-style experiment in

OPPOSITE The Biosphere, designed by Buckminster Fuller for an exposition in 1967, lives on as a Montreal landmark.

RIGHT Bixi bikes, cheap to rent and ride around town.

modular housing designed by Moshe Safdie. Or pedal along Boulevard de Maisonneuve, which cuts through downtown Montreal, where a 2.1-mile path is named after the late Claire Morissette, a cycling activist.

3 *Québécois Plates* 8 p.m.
Normand Laprise, who pioneered the use of fresh Québécois ingredients at the pricey Toqué!, often praised by critics as the city's best restaurant, opened a midpriced sister restaurant in 2010, **Brasserie t!** (1425, rue Jeanne Mance; 514-282-0808; brasserie-t.com; $$$). Situated at the foot of the Contemporary Art Museum, the brasserie looks like a sleek cargo container. Inside, a contemporary French menu showcases unfussy dishes like grilled flank steak and cod brandade.

4 *Musical Mile* 10 p.m.
The music snobs may have moved on, but it's still impossible to talk about the Mile End district without name-dropping bands like Arcade Fire and the gritty stages that gave them their start. The beloved Green Room closed because of a fire, but upstart bands are still jamming at **Divan Orange** (4234, boulevard St.-Laurent; 514-840-9090; divanorange.org). An alternative, with a bigger stage and sound, is **Il Motore** (179, rue Jean-Talon Ouest; 514-284-0122; ilmotore.ca). To see who's playing, pick up either of the two free art weeklies, *Hour* or *Mirror*.

SATURDAY
5 *Like the Marais* 10 a.m.
While Mile End is still the place to hear bands, its retail scene has cooled off. The action has shifted to

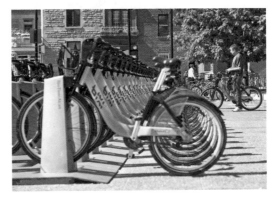

Old Montreal, where historic cobblestones and high foot traffic ensure the survival of indie boutiques. For homegrown designers like Denis Gagnon and Arielle de Pinto, squeeze inside **Reborn** (231, rue St.-Paul Ouest, Suite 100; 514-499-8549; reborn.ws), a small shop with a sharp eye. Down the block is **À Table Tout le Monde** (361, rue St.-Paul Ouest; 514-750-0311; atabletoutlemonde.com), an elegant store that carries

ABOVE Get a glimpse of Moshe Safdie's Habitat 67, an experiment in modular housing, from the Lachine Canal bike path.

BELOW The path along the Lachine Canal is part of a 300-mile system of bicycle routes and lanes in Montreal.

exquisitely crafted ceramics and housewares. And while you're exploring the historic district, drop into **DHC Art** (451, rue St.-Jean; 514-849-3742; dhc-art.org), one of the city's leading contemporary art galleries.

6 *Three Little Pigs* 1 p.m.

Blame it on the poutine and foie gras, but Montreal was early to the nose-to-tail game, with countless meat-centric restaurants around town. But how many can also claim their own organic garden out back? That's one of the surprises at **McKiernan** (2485, rue Notre-Dame Ouest; 514-759-6677; mckiernanbaravin.com: $$), the latest in a mini-empire of restaurants from the same trio behind the much-hyped Joe Beef and Liverpool House, which are next door. Another surprise? McKiernan might look like a farm-stand luncheonette, with checkered wax paper liners and tin baskets, but the food is top flight. Try the porchetta tacos, made with fresh tortillas.

7 *City of Design* 4 p.m.

An inviting strip of design shops has sprung up along Rue Amherst. One of the smallest is also the nicest, **Montreal Modern** (No. 1853; 514-293-7903; mtlmodern.com), which feels like a midcentury modern jewel box. If you like your modern design on a grander scale, the **Musée des Beaux-Arts de Montreal** (1379-80, rue Sherbrooke Ouest; 514-285-2000; mmfa.qc.ca) has a strong collection, along with Old

Masters and contemporary Canadian artists. And the **Canadian Centre for Architecture** (1920, rue Baile; 514-939-7026; cca.qc.ca) holds regular exhibitions on architecture and urbanism in a striking 19th-century mansion with a modern stone addition.

8 *French Bites* 8 p.m.

A neighborhood wine bar that happens to serve terrific food is one of those pleasures that make Paris, well, Paris. That's the vibe at **Buvette Chez Simone** (4869, avenue du Parc; 514-750-6577; buvettechezsimone.com; $$$), an oaky bar in Mile End with sly design touches. The comfy brasserie

ABOVE The dance floor at the Velvet Speakeasy.

BELOW A Jenny Holzer exhibit at DHC Art, one of the city's leading contemporary art galleries. DHC is part of a trendy retail and art scene in cobblestoned Old Montreal.

menu features dishes like a roast chicken served on a carving board with roasted potatoes. If you're hankering for more inventive fare, bike over to **Pullman** (3424, avenue du Parc; 514-288-7779; pullman-mtl.com; $$$), a high-end tapas bar that serves clever plates like venison tartare, foie gras cookies, and olives with candied lemon. The crowd at both restaurants skews young, fashionable, and chatty.

9 *Electronic Artists* 10 p.m.

In another sign of Euro-flair, techno music is huge in Montreal. And one of the coolest parties is thrown by **Neon** (iloveneon.ca), a digital music collective that has showcased a who's who of electronic artists like

Glass Candy and Hudson Mohawke. Many events take place at **Le Belmont sur le Boulevard** (4483, boulevard St.-Laurent; 514-845-8443; lebelmont.com), an intimate club that has a pool table up front and a pulsing sound system in the rear. For a more analog vibe, head to **Velvet Speakeasy** (420, rue St.-Gabriel; velvetspeakeasy.ca), a posh club in the Old Port district.

SUNDAY

10 *Eggs to Go* 11 a.m.

For a delightful brunch served in an old town house with communal tables, look no farther than **Le Cartet** (106, rue McGill; 514-871-8887; lecartet.com; $$). Part cafe, part grocery store, Le Cartet draws young families and professionals with hearty platters of eggs that come with figs, cheese, and salad greens.

On your way out, feel free to stock up on crusty baguettes, French mustards, and picnic cheeses.

11 *Dancing Man* 2 p.m.

If it's sunny, join Montreal's barefoot and pierced crowd at **Piknic Électronik** (piknicelectronik.com), an outdoor rave held on Île Ste.-Hélène during the summer. At Jean-Drapeau Park, follow the slithering beats to *The Man*, a giant sculpture, created by Alexander Calder for the 1967 Expo, which hovers over the dance floor. The leafy island has other architectural ruins from the Expo. Between beats, stroll over to the **Montreal Biosphere** (biosphere.ec.gc.ca), the iconic geodesic dome that still evokes a utopian vision of technology.

OPPOSITE À Table Tout le Monde in Old Montreal.

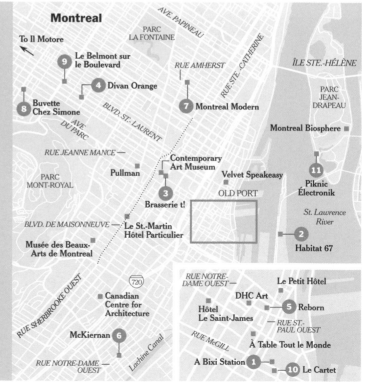

THE BASICS

Multiple airlines serve Montreal. Highways connect to U.S. cities; the drive from New York takes seven hours. Bike, walk, or use the subway.

Le St.-Martin Hôtel Particulier
980, boulevard de Maisonneuve Ouest
514-843-3000
lestmartinmontreal.com
$$$
Luxury in a downtown high-rise.

Le Petit Hôtel
168, rue St.-Paul Ouest
514-940-0360
petithotelmontreal.com
$$
In a 19th-century building in Old Montreal.

Hôtel Le Saint-James
355, rue Saint-Jacques
514-841-3111
hotellestjames.com
$$$$
Grand style in Old Montreal.

Mont Tremblant

One of the oldest ski resorts in North America, with miles of runs in the evergreen-topped Laurentian Mountains, Mont Tremblant, Quebec, seems to have it all. Combining the Canadian charm of a rustic logging town with the Old World flavor of the French Alps, Tremblant is consistently ranked by Ski Magazine *readers as the East's No. 1 resort. Hotels, condos, and bed-and-breakfasts accommodate thousands of skiers, and there are enough restaurants, shops, pools, and spas to keep everyone busy after a day on the slopes. Mont Tremblant is a year-round resort, with golf courses, a casino, and a national park, but it is in winter, when 150 inches of snow keep the ski trails slippery and the rooftops white, that it really comes into its own.* — BY LIONEL BEEHNER

FRIDAY

1 *Sleigh Bells Ring* 4 p.m.

For an action-packed lay of the land, hop on a sleigh ride with the resort's **Activity Center** (Place St. Bernard; 819-681-4848; tremblantactivities.com), which offers hourlong rides for 35 Canadian dollars (despite fluctuating currency rates, the prices usually aren't too different in U.S. dollars). Two beefy Percheron horses — steam wafting from their bodies — pull a rickety yet comfortable sleigh through Quebec's boreal forest, while the tour guide animatedly regales passengers with stories about the "trembling" mountain and may even sing some Québécois folk songs. The trip is like an Alpine safari; the trail is teeming with wildlife, like white-tail deer and red foxes. Bundle up — the mercury often dips below zero. Blankets are provided, and halfway through the ride everyone gulps down some hot cocoa.

2 *Alternative Shopping* 5 p.m.

Skip the resort's pricey boutiques and head to historic St.-Jovite — a village now rechristened Centre-Ville Mont-Tremblant — a 10-minute drive

OPPOSITE The base village at Mont Tremblant, widely considered to be the No. 1 ski resort in eastern North America.

RIGHT The shops of St.-Jovite, now called Centre-Ville Mont-Tremblant, are a 10-minute drive from the mountain.

from the mountain. Explore the shops on Rue St.-Jovite. **Plaisirs de Provence** (No. 814; 819-425-2000; plaisirsdeprovence.com) is a Québécois version of a Pottery Barn, with upscale dishware, cutlery, and chocolate. For handmade golf shoes and high-end ladies' footwear, drop by **Nycole St.-Louis Collections** (No. 822; 819-425-3583; nycolestlouis.com). Folk arts and country antiques are the specialty at **Le Coq Rouge** (No. 821; 819-425-3205).

3 *Poutine Time* 7 p.m.

Foodies will appreciate the Quebec-style fusion cooking at **sEb** (444 Rue St.-Georges; 819-429-6991; resto-seb.com; $$$). A high-end restaurant with a laid-back vibe, it gives comfort food a modern twist. Traditional dishes like rabbit stew or bison strip loin steak are jazzed up with local foie gras or the hefty regional favorite known as poutine, cheese curd with fries and gravy. Sébastien Houle, the young proprietor, cut his culinary teeth as a chef on the yacht of Paul Allen, a cofounder of Microsoft.

4 *Canadian Bandstand* 9 p.m.

Find Tremblant's young partyers at **P'tit Caribou** (125 Chemin de Kandahar; 819-681-4500; ptitcaribou.com), a dive bar in the base village with beer-soaked wooden floors and bar-top dancers. D.J.'s, popcorn, and low prices keep things lively,

and if the exuberance appears particularly youthful, recall that the legal drinking age in Quebec is 18.

SATURDAY

5 *French Breakfast* 7:30 a.m.

Kick off your day with something sweet. **Crêperie Catherine** (113 Chemin de Kandahar; 819-681-4888; creperiecatherine.ca; $$), carved out of a former chalet, is famous among local skiers for its old-fashioned crepes, and the hundreds of chef-themed dolls, teapots, cookie jars, and other tchotchkes that line its walls. Order the house specialty — a crepe with hot and velvety sucre à la crème. Arrive early. Seats here are in demand.

6 *Go North, Young Skier* 8:30 a.m.

Tremblant (819-681-2000; tremblant.ca) is a mountain folded in four parts, with a south, north and soleil (sunny) side and a segment called the Edge. Start the morning on the north side, when there is usually more sun and less wind. Long cruisers like Beauchemin let you find your balance before conquering the fast bumps on Saute-Moutons. After lunch, follow the sun over to the south side. Nansen offers marvelous views largely untainted by condos, while speed demons should hit the steeps of Kandahar. To ski off-piste, take the Telecabine Express gondola to the top and ski down to the Edge

lift, or trek over to the soleil side. Of Tremblant's 94 trails, 15 are glades. If the conditions get icy — this is the East Coast, after all — drop by the cozy Grand Manitou summit restaurant. Or just high-tail it back to your condo's hot tub.

7 *Aprés-Ski Sweets* 3:30 p.m.

Polish off a long day of skiing with a beavertail. Basically it consists of a whole wheat pastry deep-fried, smothered with your choice of maple syrup or Nutella and shaped like, yup, a beaver's tail. Drop by the takeout window at **Queues de Castor** (116 Chemin de Kandahar; 819-681-4678).

8 *Nordic Thaw* 5 p.m.

Landed a few face plants? Pamper those sore muscles at **Le Scandinave** (4280 Montée Ryan; 819-425-5524; scandinave.com), a Nordic-themed spa in a barnlike fortress on the outskirts of town. The spa's rustic-chic motif and thermal waterfalls will

ABOVE Mont Tremblant National Park, vast and just outside town, is laced with waterways and comes alive in summer with canoeing, hiking, and fishing.

OPPOSITE ABOVE AND BELOW Pampering is available indoors and out at Le Scandinave, a Nordic-themed spa. Warm up in a hot bath before plunging into the icy Diable River, or stick to the massages and thermal waterfalls inside.

lull bathers into a state of relaxation. Warm up in a Finnish sauna or Norwegian steam bath before taking a cold plunge in the Diable River out back. Sadly, the 17,000-square-foot spa doesn't offer maple syrup scrubs like some of its competitors. But a Swedish massage will rejuvenate even the sorest of muscles. Take it from two of the owners, who are retired NHL hockey players.

9 *Slopeside Fondue* 7:30 p.m.
 "Have you tried the fondue at La Savoie?" You'll hear that question a lot in Mont Tremblant. In the middle of the base village, **La Savoie** (115 Chemin de Kandahar; 819-681-4573; restaurantlasavoie. com; $$$) has a homey décor befitting a chateau in the Savoy region in the French Alps. The same

goes for the fondue. Tabletop pierrades and raclettes let patrons cook up their own shrimp, chicken, fish, or filet mignon in communal fashion, before dunking the morsels into melted cheeses, red wine, or garlic sauces. Chances are you won't have room for the chocolate fondue.

10 *Hockey-Free Zone* 9:30 p.m.
 Most bars in town, it seems, are just repositories of wall-mounted moose heads and bad cover bands. A welcome exception is **La Diable** (117 Chemin de

Kandahar; 819-681-4546), a low-key microbrasserie that serves up an eclectic array of devil-themed brews like the Extreme Onction — a Belgian Trappist-style ale with 8.5 percent alcohol. La Diable might also be the only mountainside bar without hockey playing on the flat screen.

SUNDAY

11 *Call of the Wild* 8:15 a.m.

Ever wanted to commandeer a caravan of canines through the Canadian wilderness? Pay a visit to

Nordic Adventure Dog Sledding (Place St. Bernard; 819-681-4848; tremblantactivities.com). After a 40-minute bus ride, you arrive at what looks like the setting of a Jack London novel — a secluded camp in the woods surrounded by nothing but Siberian huskies. Above the din of barking dogs, the gregarious guide explains how to steer and how to stop and go ("Hop-hop!" or "Mush!"). Eight harness-linked dogs sprint at breakneck speed. The two-hour ride (about 150 Canadian dollars) winds its way through some challenging terrain, interrupted only by a cabin break for hot chocolate and a prep course in fire-starting.

ABOVE AND OPPOSITE Skiing is the preferred way to play outside, but there are others. One option is dogsledding in Mont Tremblant's reliable fresh snow, with you in the driver's seat. Count on the guide to teach you when to say "Mush!"

THE BASICS

Fly direct to Mont Tremblant from several U.S. and Canadian cities. Most hotels offer airport shuttles, but a rental car is desirable.

Hôtel Quintessence
3004 Chemin de la Chapelle
819-425-3400
hotelquintessence.com
$$$$
Elegance in 30 suites overlooking Tremblant Lake.

Château Beauvallon
6385 Montée Ryan
888-245-4030
chateaubeauvallon.com
$$$
Suites with kitchens, gas fireplaces, and private balconies.

The Crystal Inn
100 Chemin Joseph Thibault
819-681-7775
crystal-inn.com
$$
Colorful, cozy bed-and-breakfast outfitted with crazy murals and a small spa.

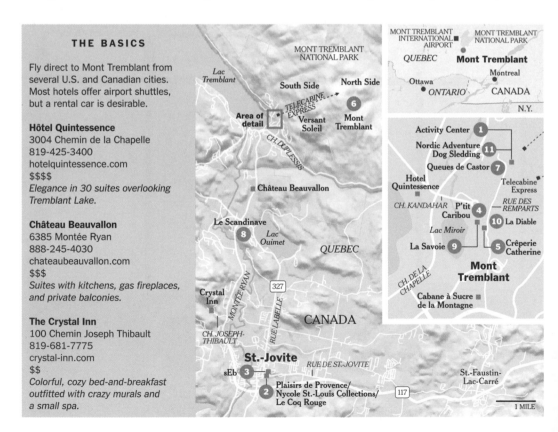

Quebec City

Quebec can give provincialism a good name. Orphaned by mother France, dominated by Britain (after what Québécois still call the Conquest) and then for years by majority-Anglophone Canada, the people of Quebec have followed Voltaire's advice to tend to their own garden. This is especially true of Quebec City, the provincial capital. Proudly dated, lovingly maintained, Quebec City has charm to spare, particularly within the city walls of the Old Town and in the Lower Town tucked between those walls and the St. Lawrence River. The city's French heart is always on its sleeve, and a stroll over the cobblestones leads to patisseries, sidewalk cafes, and a profusion of art galleries. Yet a vast, cold wilderness is the next stop due north, putting game on restaurant menus and a kind of backwoods vigor in the city's spirit. To a Yankee it all seems European. But there is no place like this in Europe; there is nothing else like it in North America, either. And that's reason enough to celebrate.

— BY SCOTT L. MALCOMSON

FRIDAY

1 *Champagne and Cigars* 6 p.m.

It's too late in the day to head out for kayaking on the St. Lawrence River, so go instead to the first-floor **St. Laurent Bar & Lounge** at the **Fairmont Le Château Frontenac** (1, rue des Carrières; 418-692-3861; fairmont.com/frontenac) for Champagne. You're atop the city's cliffs, and this semicircular room has wonderful views of the St. Lawrence. A drink in the château, as it is called (it's that enormous castle-like building, built as a grand hotel for the Canadian Pacific Railway) is always pricey, but luxury can be like that. Even the bar food is classy, running to snacks like assiette of smoked fish. If all this old-money atmosphere makes you crave a Cuban cigar, buy a supply at **Société Cigare** (575, Grande Allée; 418-647-2000), just outside the Old Town walls. It is also a bar (dark wood, low lights, single malts), so it's open most of the time.

2 *Lower Town Update* 8 p.m.

Fast-forward a few decades by finding your way down to St. Roch in the Lower Town, hard up against the cliff. Once a grim commercial district, it has evolved into a hotspot of high-tech businesses,

artists' studios, galleries, shops, and cafés. One of the pioneering restaurants in the transformation was the sleek **Versa** (432, rue du Parvis; 418-523-9995; versarestaurant.com; $$$), which touts its mojitos and boasts that it is the city's only oyster bar. The menu mixes bistro food and more formal entrees like poached swordfish or veal sweetbreads and roasted cheek.

3 *Dancing Feet* 10 p.m.

For a taste of St. Roch nightlife, drop in at **Le Boudoir** (441, rue de l'Église; 418-524-2777; boudoirlounge.com), a bar packed with young professionals. D.J.'s keep things hopping on the weekends, and the sound system boasts 60 speakers. There's dancing on the lower level.

SATURDAY

4 *On the Plains* 10 a.m.

Take a jog or a leisurely walk on the **Plains of Abraham**, an extensive, undulating rectangle on the heights above the St. Lawrence just west of the Frontenac. This is where British invaders led by James Wolfe defeated Louis-Joseph de Montcalm in 1759, the battle that set in motion the decline of French power in North America. Today it is a playground, an urban park (ccbn-nbc.gc.ca) where children race around

OPPOSITE The guards at Quebec's Citadel may look English, but their regiment's official language is French.

BELOW For tourists, walking is the way to get around.

the open spaces, actors stroll by in 18th-century garb, skiers glide in winter, and Paul McCartney gave a free concert in 2008 to mark Quebec City's 400th birthday. For a concrete example of Quebec's mixed historical legacy, stop off at the **Citadel** (1, Côte de la Citadelle; 418-694-2815; lacitadelle.qc.ca), where an officially French-speaking regiment performs an English-style changing of the guard, complete with black bearskin hats, every summer morning at 10.

5 *Market Bounty* Noon

The farmers' market (**Marché du Vieux-Port**; 160, Quai Saint-André, near the old train station; 418-692-2517; marchevieuxport.com) is open year-round. In summer there's an abundance of fresh vegetables and fruits. Even in winter, you can find

local cheeses, meat pies, fish, sausage, baked goods, and foie gras. Look for spruce beer, which George Washington is reported to have served to his troops for medicinal reasons. One taste and you'll see why: it is the poor colonist's retsina.

6 *Provincial Special* 2 p.m.

At least once this weekend you have to eat poutine, the concoction of French fries, cheese curd, and gravy that is close to the French Canadian soul, if not particularly friendly to its heart. Find it at **Buffet de l'Antiquaire** (95, rue St.-Paul; 418-692-2661; $), a Lower Town institution with sidewalk tables in summer. It is a very good, very local diner that serves all kinds of Canadian comfort food and is always worth a visit at breakfast, too.

7 *That Perfect Find* 3 p.m.

Walk out into the rue St.-Paul, a street lined with easygoing antiques shops and art galleries, to poke through Victoriana, country furniture, Art Deco relics, and assorted gewgaws. If you still can't find the right present to take home, take the first

ABOVE The Lower Town along the St. Lawrence River.

LEFT J.A. Moisan, a gourmet grocery store.

OPPOSITE The Château Frontenac is now a Fairmont Hotel.

left up into the Old Town and head for **Artisans du Bas-Canada** (30, côte de la Fabrique; 418-692-2109; artisanscanada.com), which has jewelry made from Canadian diamonds and amber as well as an abundance of Québécois tchotchkes.

8 *Take to the Ramparts* 6 p.m.

Stroll along the ramparts of the Old Town for a stirring view of the St. Lawrence. Quebec City was strategic because of its commanding position on the river just at the point where it begins to widen and grow into the Gulf of St. Lawrence on its way to the Atlantic. Then proceed downhill for a drink at the friendly and cozy **Belley Tavern** (249, rue St.-Paul; 418-692-1694). Or try **Môss** (225, rue St.-Paul; 418-692-0233), a "bistro belge" that has a wide selection of Belgian beers, including several on tap, and many ways of preparing mussels.

9 *Haute Cuisine* 8 p.m.

Most Québécois speak English, but French, even bad French, goes over well. So use yours to ask for directions to the luxury hotel called **Auberge Saint-Antoine** (8, rue St.-Antoine). Its restaurant, **Panache** (418-692-2211; restaurantpanache.com; $$$$), is a point of reference for Quebec City's haute cuisine. Start off with Champagne cocktails, then on to an amuse-bouche and the tasting menu, which moves at a leisurely pace from an appetizer, perhaps foie gras, through seafood and meats that often include venison or other Canadian game, and finally to dessert, all with suitable wines. It is easy to drag this out — in a space that is like a rustic loft with upholstered chairs — for three hours or more. After dinner, make your way through the narrow streets to admire the restored buildings of the Place-Royal at your leisure.

area—was such a hit that the city soon set to work extending it to a length that will eventually reach for six more miles.

SUNDAY

10 *Riverside* 11 a.m.

You've gazed at the St. Lawrence from the heights; now it's time to get close. Join the locals catching the breeze on the **Promenade Samuel de Champlain**, a riverfront strip park that opened in 2008, in time for the city's 400th anniversary celebration. The 1.5-mile-long promenade, on land between the boulevard Champlain and the river—for many years a degraded industrial

11 *One Last Chance* Noon

If you're still in the market for something to take home, check out **J. A. Moisan** (699, rue Saint-Jean; 418-522-0685; jamoisan.com), which claims to be the oldest gourmet grocery store in North America. Should the cheeses, chocolates, pasta, and other fare fail to charm, you'll find a selection of other high-end shops on rue Saint-Jean.

ABOVE AND OPPOSITE Quebec City's charming Old Town.

THE BASICS

Quebec's Old Town is a 30-minute drive from Jean Lesage International Airport. Once in town, plan to walk. To go from Lower to Upper Town, take the funicular.

Fairmont Le Château Frontenac
1, rue des Carrières
418-692-3861
fairmont.com/frontenac
$$$
A classic grand hotel with 618 rooms and river views. Quebec's gold standard.

Hotel Ste.-Anne
32, rue Ste.-Anne
418-694-1455
hotelste-anne.com
$$
Sleek rooms in two adjoining 17th-century stone buildings.

Hotel Le Germain Dominion
126, rue Saint-Pierre
418-692-2224
germaindominion.com
$$
An airy and modern break from the fleurs-de-lis and polished wood of the Old Town.

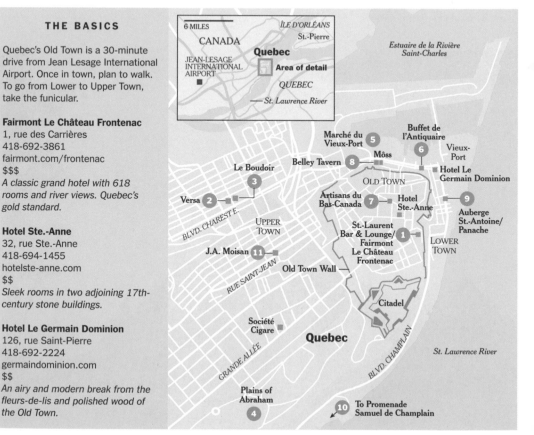

The Bay of Fundy

At Fundy National Park in New Brunswick, the salty ocean air is laced with the scent of pine. The park's smooth lakes and quiet forests alone would be enough to make it one of Canada's favorites. But the real wonder here is a strange natural phenomenon: the sweeping tides of the Bay of Fundy. Residents around the bay say its tides are the highest in the world, and only a bay in far northern Quebec challenges the claim; the Canadian government diplomatically calls it a tie. Highest or not, the Fundy tides are extreme and dramatic, rising at their largest surge by 33 feet and leaving, when they recede, vast tidal flats ready for exploring. Tourists who drive north through New Brunswick on their way to Fundy will be struck by the forests stretching to the horizon and by the comfortable mix of French and English influences that has cashiers and waitresses calling out "Hello bonjour!"

— BY KAREN HOUPPERT

FRIDAY

1 *Park Central* 3 p.m.

The main attraction is **Fundy National Park** (506-887-6000; pc.gc.ca/eng/pn-np/nb/fundy/index.aspx), which covers about 50,000 acres and is laced with trails and sprinkled with campsites that make it a paradise for backpackers. Away from the hub of activity around the park headquarters (and not counting the surprising presence of a nine-hole golf course), there are few tourist services. Get your bearings at the **Visitor Reception Centre**, close to the southeastern park entrance near the gateway town of Alma. Pick up maps, find out about the interpretive programs for the weekend, and most important, check the tide tables.

2 *Fundy Fare* 6 p.m.

Drive into Alma for dinner (there's no dining in the park itself). You'll find lobster with a view at the **Tides Restaurant**, located in the **Parkland Village Inn** (8601 Main Street, Alma; 506-887-2313;

OPPOSITE AND RIGHT Fundy National Park's 68 miles of well-tended trails wind into forests and meadows, past waterfalls and beaver dams. Although spectacular tides, rising 33 feet, are the area's major attraction, the park is also prized for its inland natural beauty.

parklandvillageinn.com; $$), where the dining room overlooks the bay. The choices run to the traditional and hearty, including steaks and various kinds of Atlantic seafood, good for packing it in at the start of an active weekend. Tables at the Tides can fill up fast, so take care to reserve in advance.

3 *Brushwork* 7 p.m.

Fundy's vast, muddy stretches of beach mean that even high tide makes for poor swimming. The water remains shallow for a quarter mile out to sea. The park does its best to compensate, offering visitors a swim in its heated salt-water pool overlooking the bay. But if the Bay of Fundy is not great for swimming, it is a sensuous delight. As evening approaches, stroll along the coastal paths to take it in. At dusk, as the fog rolls in, the hills and cliffs beyond the shore shimmer with the deep green of thousands of pines. The silky-smooth red clay of the tidal flat provides a rich saturation of complementary color. It's like stepping into a Van Gogh.

SATURDAY

4 *Sticky Fingers* 9 a.m.

You could go for the fresh home-baked bread or doughnuts, or come back at lunch for sandwiches and chili, but the star of the show at **Kelly's Bake Shop**

(8587 Main Street, Alma; 506-887-2460) is the sticky bun. Locally renowned and alluring for tourists, the buns keep customers lined up at Kelly's, which sells as many as 3,000 of them on a busy day. They're sweet, flavorful, and enormous. Don't expect to eat more than one.

5 *Reset the Clock* 9:30 a.m.

Venture to one of Alma's two small general stores to pick up provisions for later. Then consult your new clock, the lunar version that announces itself in the Fundy tides. It's important to be at the beach when the mud flats are exposed — that's the experience that draws people here. So plan your day accordingly — not by the numbers on your watch or cellphone, but by the water's flow.

6 *Out to Sea* Low Tide

At low tide the vast intertidal zone is other-worldly: endless red muddy flats, shallow pools and sporadic, massive barnacle-covered boulders that appear to have been randomly dropped into the muddy flatness from an alien spaceship. Beachcombers can walk along the exposed ocean floor, hunting for shells and bits of sea-smoothed glass, for more than half a mile before they reach the water's edge. The impulse to scoop up the clay underfoot and squeeze it through your fingers is hard to suppress. While grown-up travelers seem to enjoy the delightful respite the wet clay of the bare ocean floor provides to tired feet after a hard day of hiking, kids have been known to do full body rolls in the squishy muck. The spot where you're standing will probably be under water again before long, but there's no need to fear. The tide's return is gradual, progressive, and orderly — very Canadian — and nicely nudges you back shoreward with small, gentle, very cold waves.

7 *Into the Woods* High Tide

When the water claims the beach, go hiking. The park's 68 miles of well-tended trails wind deep into forests and flower-strewn meadows, past waterfalls and beaver dams, and even to a covered bridge. By the standards of many busier parks, it is blissfully quiet. Even in August, the prime season, it is possible for hikers to trek the 2.8-mile **Mathews Head** trail along the park's rocky southern shore and not pass a single person. The path offers teasing ocean views from atop cliffs that drop to the sea. And amid the solitude, there is a silence so pervasive that even children grow pensive at the wonder of these head-lands, which feel like the end of the earth.

8 *Shell and Claw* 7 p.m.

Do as the locals do and find a table at the **Harbour View Market & Restaurant** (8598 Main Street, Alma; 506-887-2450; $). You can get your daily ration of shell-fish — in the seafood chowder or a lobster roll — and perhaps pick up some local gossip at the same time.

9 *Nature Theater* 8 p.m.

Don't look for rangers at Fundy National Park — here they are interpreters. The staff is serious about the job of making Fundy accessible, and in summer there is a program almost every night at the **Outdoor Theatre**. You may learn about the wildlife, from moose and bears to flying squirrels. You may hear about the rivers that wash kayakers upstream when the tide comes in, the whales and migratory

birds that thrive offshore, or the area's history — this is Acadia, where French and English cultures clashed and mingled. Expect a multimedia experience, with video, music, comedy, or even drama.

SUNDAY

10 *Water Power* 10 a.m.

For an appropriate last stop, drive about 25 miles north of Alma to Hopewell Cape, where the bay shore is littered with eroded sea stacks known as the **Flowerpot Rocks**. See them from a clifftop trail, and if it's low tide inspect them close up, at the **Hopewell Rocks Ocean Tidal Exploration Site** (Highway 114; 877-734-3429; thehopewellrocks.ca). Resembling pillars or top-heavy mushrooms, some with trees growing on their tops, the rocks are part of a rugged shoreline of caves, tunnels, and misshapen crags, all

of it a testament to the relentless force of the water constantly tugged back and forth against the shore by the Fundy tides.

OPPOSITE ABOVE The world's highest tides (officially tied with those in a more remote Quebec bay) flow out to leave vast flats for exploring.

OPPOSITE BELOW Mathews Head, a high rocky headland on the Fundy coast.

ABOVE A sunrise over Owl's Head, seen from Alma Beach in Fundy National Park.

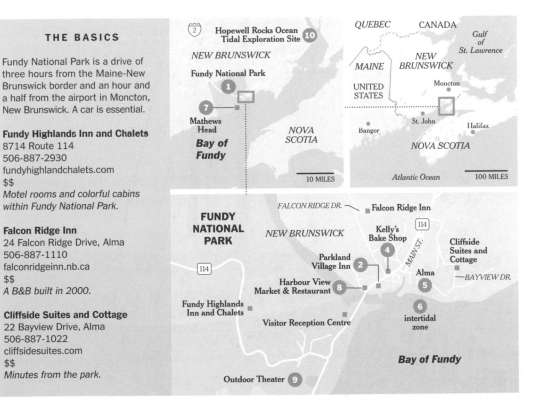

THE BASICS

Fundy National Park is a drive of three hours from the Maine-New Brunswick border and an hour and a half from the airport in Moncton, New Brunswick. A car is essential.

Fundy Highlands Inn and Chalets
8714 Route 114
506-887-2930
fundyhighlandchalets.com
$$
Motel rooms and colorful cabins within Fundy National Park.

Falcon Ridge Inn
24 Falcon Ridge Drive, Alma
506-887-1110
falconridgeinn.nb.ca
$$
A B&B built in 2000.

Cliffside Suites and Cottage
22 Bayview Drive, Alma
506-887-1022
cliffsidesuites.com
$$
Minutes from the park.

Hopewell Rocks Ocean Tidal Exploration Site

NEW BRUNSWICK

Fundy National Park

Mathews Head

Bay of Fundy

NOVA SCOTIA

10 MILES

QUEBEC   CANADA

Gulf of St. Lawrence

MAINE   NEW BRUNSWICK

Moncton

UNITED STATES

Bangor   St. John   Halifax

NOVA SCOTIA

Atlantic Ocean   100 MILES

FALCON RIDGE DR.   Falcon Ridge Inn

FUNDY NATIONAL PARK

NEW BRUNSWICK

Kelly's Bake Shop   114

Cliffside Suites and Cottage

Parkland Village Inn

Alma   BAYVIEW DR.

Harbour View Market & Restaurant

114

Fundy Highlands Inn and Chalets

Visitor Reception Centre

intertidal zone

Bay of Fundy

Outdoor Theater

Halifax

Halifax, Nova Scotia, is a harbor city steeped in maritime history. Founded in 1749 as a British naval and military base, it originally served as a strategic counter to French bases elsewhere in Atlantic Canada—and many years later as an assembly point for shipping convoys during World Wars I and II. Today, Halifax is better known for its lobster, which you can fill up on from morning (lobster eggs Benedict, anyone?) till night and still have enough cash left for a sail around the harbor on a tall ship. A vibrant student population—the city's several universities have thousands of students—gives Halifax a youthful, bohemian feel, too. As a result, it's often compared to that other hilly town on the ocean, San Francisco, but you'll find that Halifax's blend of fair-trade coffee bars, wharfside lobster shacks, and public gardens has a character all its own.

— BY TATIANA BONCOMPAGNI

FRIDAY

1 *A Pint and a Pirate Joke* 5 p.m.

Start the weekend right at the **Alexander Keith's Nova Scotia Brewery** (1496 Lower Water Street; 902-455-1474; keiths.ca). Take the 55-minute tour led by local actors in 19th-century garb, and you'll get not only a primer on the history of Halifax's oldest working brewery—it dates back to the 1820s—but a pint of its finest as well. Find a comfy bench in the brewery's Stag's Head Tavern, where barkeepers have been known to regale the crowd with old pirate jokes and barmaids have burst into song.

2 *Bard of Nova Scotia* 7 p.m.

Shakespeare is so much better in the grass, methinks. Grab a blanket and some cushions and head to **Point Pleasant Park** (Queen Victoria leased it to Halifax around the mid-19th century for one shilling a year, which the city still pays), where the **Shakespeare by the Sea Theater Society** (902-422-0295; shakespearebythesea.ca) stages the Bard's plays. The

OPPOSITE The *Bluenose II*, a replica of the schooner on the back of the Canadian dime, docked on the waterfront. Halifax's natural harbor is one of the world's largest.

RIGHT Firing the noon-day gun at Halifax Citadel.

park overlooks the entrance to Halifax Harbor, so enjoy the sublime views, then arrive for the performance 10 minutes before show time and stake your claim in the grass. A $15 donation is encouraged.

3 *Bring Your Own Shoes* 10 p.m.

For a late meal, a sophisticated spot is the **Economy Shoe Shop** (1663 Argyle Street; 902-423-7463; economyshoeshop.ca; $-$$), a cafe and bar that takes its name from a salvaged neon sign hanging from the side of its building. It is divided into four sections —Shoe, Backstage, Diamond, and Oasis—based on décor. Ask to be seated in Oasis, a comparatively quiet nook in the back of the building. Honor Haligonian tradition by ordering seafood chowder or fish cakes.

SATURDAY

4 *Breakfast on the Commons* 9:30 a.m.

In the 18th century, town authorities set aside more than 200 acres for community cattle grazing and military use. The part that remains, called the Commons, is a municipal complex of sports fields and playgrounds—a great place for a morning jog. But for those who would rather slip into the day more gently, there's **jane's on the common** (2394 Robie Street; 902-431-5683; janesonthecommon.com; $$), which serves a killer brunch from 9:30 a.m. to 2:30 p.m. on weekends. The ricotta pancakes with fresh bananas and Nova Scotia maple syrup are light and

Soupe du jour
Madras Curried Lentil & Vegetable
cup $3.25 bowl $4.25
Rain chasers...
Mimosa (2 oz champagne + OJ) $3.50
Bloody Caesar (1 oz Vodka) $4.50
Austen Apricot Wheat Ale $4.50

The Sweet Hereafter
* Creme Caramel $4.50
* Double Chocolate Torte $5.25
* Coconut Cream in a shortbread crust $4.95
* Bumble Fruit Crisp $4.50
* Passion Fruit Pannacotta $4.95 w/ fresh Banana
* Jost Vidal Ice $9.95 (50 ml bot)

jane's
on the common

ng is like love.
hould be entered into
h abandon or not at all!"
~ Harriet Van Ho

fluffy, the eggs come with sausage or fish, and there's tofu for the vegans.

5 *Antiquing on Agricola* 10:30 a.m.

If you're in the market for well-priced antiques or reproductions, make sure you hit Agricola Street, where a handful of the city's best dealers have set up shop. At **McLellan Antiques & Restoration** (2738 Agricola Street; 902-455-4545; mclellanantiques.com) you'll find furniture including bureaus and cupboards, early pine pieces, and 1920s mahogany. **Finer Things Antiques** (2797 Agricola Street; 902-456-1412; finerthingsantiques.com) is the place to go for nautical antiques like old ship's wheels and compasses.

6 *Sail On* 1 p.m.

No trip to Halifax is complete without a tour around the harbor — considered the second-largest natural harbor anywhere, after Sydney's — in one of the tall ships that dock along the wharf. Sign up for a two-hour sail aboard the **Bluenose II** (1675 Lower Water Street, 902-634-1963; halifaxkiosk.com/Bluenose-II.php), a replica of the schooner that earned its spot on the Canadian dime by collecting numerous racing trophies in the 1920s and '30s. It has a 4,150-square-foot mainsail and a top speed of 16

knots. If the *Bluenose II* isn't in town — its home port is Lunenburg, about 60 miles away, and it travels along the Maritime and New England coasts — sail the harbor aboard the **Silva** (tallshipsilva.com) or the **Mar II** (mtcw.ca/TourSailing.php). Dress warmly; it can get cold on deck.

7 *Remembrance* 5 p.m.

Halifax's role as a busy port city, sometimes complicated by the North Atlantic's infamous fog, has cursed it with a legacy of shipwrecks and catastrophe. The **Maritime Museum of the Atlantic** (1675 Lower Water Street; 902-424-7490; museum.gov.ns.ca/mma/) has moving displays of artifacts from them. One commemorates the disaster most horrific for Halifax. It happened in 1917, when a French ship loaded with explosives collided in the harbor with a Belgian relief ship, resulting in a blast that killed nearly 2,000 people, injured thousands more, and obliterated the north end of the city. The museum also displays an incredibly well-preserved deck chair from the *Titanic*, which sank off the Grand Banks in 1912. Of the 328 bodies recovered from the *Titanic*, 150 are buried in Halifax.

8 *Menu Study* 8 p.m.

Make your way to the neighborhood of Dalhousie University's downtown Sexton campus for dinner at **Chives Canadian Bistro**, (1537 Barrington Street; 902-420-9626; chives.ca/about; $$$). Its imaginative

ABOVE Weekend brunch at jane's on the common.

dishes are made with local and seasonal ingredients, so selections change. Scan the menu for dishes like pan-seared Nova Scotia sea bass or classic coq au vin on egg yolk fettucine.

SUNDAY

9 *The Citadel* 11 a.m.

The best views in the city can be had from the **Halifax Citadel** (5425 Sackville Street; 902-426-5080; pc.gc.ca/lhn-nhs/ns/halifax/index.aspx), a star-shaped fort built on its highest hill. The British built four forts atop the summit, the last of which was completed in 1856, when the United States posed

ABOVE Homage to the original brewmaster at Alexander Keith's Nova Scotia Brewery.

the greatest threat to the harbor and city. Be sure to get there in time for the "noon-day gun" firing of the cannon. Afterward watch pipers and drummers perform in the enormous gravel courtyard.

10 *Last Call for Lobster* 1 p.m.

It wouldn't be right to leave without a taste of sweet Nova Scotia lobster. Snag an umbrella-shaded outdoor table at **Salty's** (1869 Upper Water Street; 902-423-6818; saltys.ca; $$-$$$). Go for a steamed one-and-a-half-pounder and a side of hot sweet-potato fries, and you won't be hungry on the plane going home.

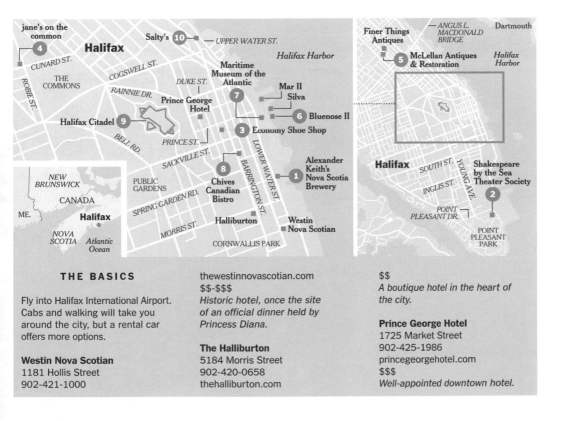

THE BASICS

Fly into Halifax International Airport. Cabs and walking will take you around the city, but a rental car offers more options.

Westin Nova Scotian
1181 Hollis Street
902-421-1000

thewestinnovascotian.com
$$-$$$
Historic hotel, once the site of an official dinner held by Princess Diana.

The Halliburton
5184 Morris Street
902-420-0658
thehalliburton.com

$$
A boutique hotel in the heart of the city.

Prince George Hotel
1725 Market Street
902-425-1986
princegeorgehotel.com
$$$
Well-appointed downtown hotel.

St. John's

Founded in the late 16th century on North America's easternmost edge, St. John's was already a settlement when New York was a mere gleam in the eye of European colonizers. Cod was king then and for centuries afterward, and although now it's the offshore oil industry that brings in cash and confidence, the city has hung onto its unique, quirky character. Brightly colored row houses cascade down toward the harbor, not far from where icebergs, whales, and puffins pass by in summer. George Street is the North Atlantic version of Bourbon Street. And as the capital of the Canadian province of Newfoundland and Labrador, St. John's shares in the region's typical friendliness but keeps its own decidedly Irish twist — many locals speak with the thickest brogues west of Galway. — BY JEFF SCHLEGEL

FRIDAY

1 *It Happened Out There* 3:30 p.m.

An ideal first stop is Signal Hill, a rocky sentinel that overlooks the entrance to the harbor. Before reaching the top, though, visit the **Johnson Geo Centre** (175 Signal Hill Road; 709-737-7880; geocentre.ca), where one exhibit tells the tale of the sinking of the *Titanic* 350 miles off this coast. The ship's radio distress signals were picked up by Newfoundland stations, and St. John's has been a frequent departure point for explorers' trips to the wreck. Shake your head in disbelief as you read about the decision not to equip the ship with enough lifeboats because it would "clutter up the deck." Atop Signal Hill looms **Cabot Tower** (pc.gc.ca/lhn-nhs/nl/signalhill), a castle-like structure next to where Marconi received the first trans-Atlantic wireless message in 1901. At the lookout point, take in a sweeping view.

2 *Cod Tongues, Anyone?* 6 p.m.

Velma's Place (264 Water Street; 709-576-2264; $) specializes in healthy helpings of traditional cuisine. An appetizer of cod tongues with scrunchions, or fat pork, and a meal of baked cod au gratin or fish and

chips made with cod is as Newfoundland as it gets. Home-cooked food is the rule, and the hot turkey sandwich is made with real roast turkey with dark meat, not bland deli meat.

3 *Off Off Off Broadway* 8 p.m.

Take in a play at the newly refurbished **Resource Center for the Arts** in the former Longshoremen's Protective Union Hall (3 Victoria Street; 709-753-4531; rca.nf.ca). The center hosts theater and dance. It is also a venue for art shows ranging from experimental to traditional, particularly promoting emerging artists in Newfoundland and Labrador.

4 *Have a Cow, Man* 10 p.m.

For a post-show treat, visit **Moo-Moo's Ice Cream** (88 Kings Road; 709-753-3046), a boxy building painted a mottled black and white in dairy-cow fashion. The store makes more than 300 flavors of ice cream in its basement factory, and serves them upstairs. Two of the favorites are turtle cheesecake — a mix of cheesecake, Oreo crumbs, and English toffee — and the chocolate-heavy tornado, which is made with Mirage candy bars, a Canadian favorite.

SATURDAY

5 *Coffee and Crumpets* 9 a.m.

Fuel up on an espresso drink or the house brew at **Coffee Matters** (1 Military Road; 709-753-6980;

OPPOSITE St. John's, Newfoundland and Labrador. European ships have used its harbor since the early 1500s.

RIGHT Climb to the top of Signal Hill for sweeping views.

coffeematters.ca; $) in a neat frame building down-town. Hot drinks are the stars here. Besides the usual lattes, macchiato, and house brews, there's a selection of hot chocolates, including banana silk and Aztec. This is a coffee house, but you can settle in for a sit-down breakfast. Besides the usual waffles and eggs, there's the crumpet sandwich. That's egg, sausage, and cheese on—that's right, a crumpet.

6 *Trailing the Puffin* 11 a.m.

After breakfast, drive about half an hour south to **Bay Bulls** (Highway 2 south to Highway 3, which merges into Highway 10 south). **Gatherall's Puffin & Whale Watch** (Northside Road; 709-334-2887; gatheralls.com) is one of the eco-tour operators in town that ferry passengers to the Witless Bay Ecological Reserve, a group of offshore islands that in summer are host to 2.5 million mating seabirds, including about 500,000 puffins. Whales also appear in the bay during their summer migration and, if the currents are right, you might see an iceberg or two floating down from Greenland.

7 *Provincial Culture* 3 p.m.

It's hard to miss the **Rooms** (9 Bonaventure Avenue; 709-757-8000; therooms.ca), a huge museum and art gallery that towers above the city from a hilltop perch. Designed to resemble traditional Newfoundland fishing rooms where

families processed their catch, the Rooms combines the Provincial Museum, the Provincial Art Gallery, and the Provincial Archives under one roof. The spotlight is on artists from Newfoundland and Labrador and elsewhere in Canada. Unofficially, among its best displays is the view of the harbor's meeting with the Atlantic at Signal Hill.

8 *Pews and Stouts* 5 p.m.

The **Ship Pub** (Solomon's Lane at 265 Duckworth Street; 709-753-3870) is a classic watering hole with a laid-back vibe. There are several tables scattered about and a lot of old wood, including church pews set along the walls. It's easy to belly up to the time-worn bar and chat up the barkeepers or the mix of locals ranging from artists to lawyers. "It's just not a pub," one customer said. "It's a living room."

9 *Nouvelle Caribou* 7 p.m.

After a drink or two, it's time for dinner. **Bacalao** — the name means salted codfish — gives Newfoundland and Labrador food an upscale nouvelle Canadian twist (65 Lemarchant Road; 709-579-6565; bacalaocuisine.ca; $$$). There's a salt cod dish of the day, and the caribou medallions may arrive with a sauce of Canadian fruit wine and partridgeberries,

ABOVE Cape Spear's 1955 lighthouse.

a native fruit and local favorite. Vegetarians are not forgotten; look for pasta with locally grown vegetables in season.

10 *Irish Energy* 9 p.m.

Downtown, George Street is party central, a stretch of pedestrian-only mayhem jammed with loud bars, dance spots, and clubs for Irish music, starting around 10:30 p.m. On a Saturday night at **Bridie Molloy's Pub & Eatery** (5 George Street; 709-576-5990), an acoustic trio played to the accompaniment of an Irish step dancer. Over at **O'Reilly's Irish Newfoundland Pub** (15 George Street; 709-722-3735; oreillyspub.com), a band with electric guitars played a more raucous set of Irish-tinged music.

SUNDAY

11 *Is That Europe Yonder?* 10 a.m.

You can't get much farther east in North America than **Cape Spear National Historic Site** (709-772-5367; pc.gc.ca/lhn-nhs/nl/spear/index.aspx). Follow Water Street southwest, turn left on Leslie Street, and find the sign for Cape Spear Drive. The drive passes through rugged terrain until it meets the ocean. There are two lighthouses—the original from 1836 and one built in 1955. You can pick up the **East Coast Trail** (eastcoasttrail.com) at the parking lot and hike south along the high sea cliffs. Imagine the sails of the ships that began arriving here soon after John Cabot found the rich nearby fishing grounds in 1497.

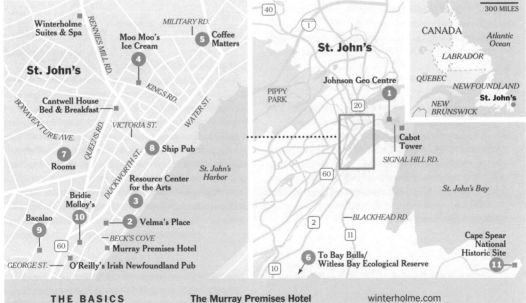

THE BASICS

Direct flights to St. John's leave from Newark, New Jersey; London; and several Canadian cities. By car and ferry, St. John's is about 1,500 miles from either Boston or Montreal. If you're not driving your own car, reserve in advance to rent one at the airport.

The Murray Premises Hotel
5 Beck's Cove
709-738-7773
murraypremiseshotel.com
$$$
Boutique hotel on the harbor.

Winterholme Suites & Spa
79 Rennies Mill Road
709-739-7979

winterholme.com
$$-$$$
In a Queen Anne house.

Cantwell House Bed & Breakfast
25 Queens Road
709-754-8439
cantwellhouse.nf.net
$$
Fabulous view of harbor and city.

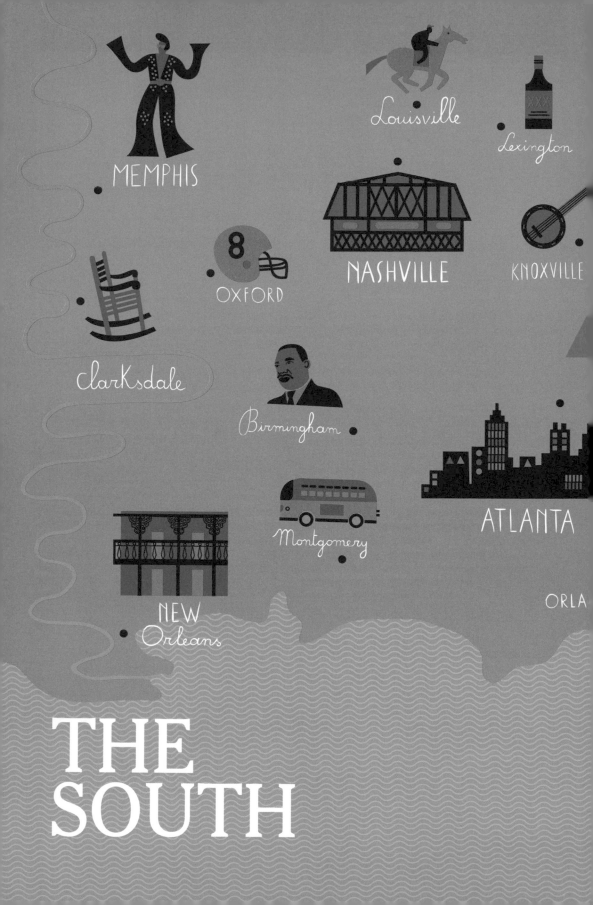

MEMPHIS

Louisville

Lexington

OXFORD

NASHVILLE

KNOXVILLE

ClarKsdale

Birmingham

ATLANTA

Montgomery

ORLA

NEW
Orleans

THE
SOUTH

Charlottesville

Richmond

Williamsburg

inlurg

ASHEVILLE

Raleigh-Durham

VIRGINIA
Beach

charleston

SAVANNAH

St. Simons
Island

CAPE
Canaveral

NAPLES

Palm
Beach

MIAMI

Fort
Lauderdale

Cuban
Miami

South
Beach

the Everglades

KEY WEST

Richmond

As the heart of the old Confederacy, Richmond, Virginia, will always have a claim as the capital of the South, a place to find Southern tradition and a center of Civil War history. But for decades in the late 20th century, it watched with envy as cities like Atlanta and Charlotte leaped ahead economically and culturally. Now Richmond is surging back to life in the present. A building boom in the last few years has seen century-old tobacco warehouses transformed into lofts and art studios. Chefs are setting up kitchens in formerly gritty neighborhoods. And the city's once buttoned-up downtown has life after dusk, thanks to new bars and a performing arts complex, Richmond CenterStage. Without forfeiting all of its Old South personality, Richmond now is a player in the New South, too.

— BY JUSTIN BERGMAN AND LINDSAY MORAN

FRIDAY

1 *Tea and Wisteria* 2 p.m.

For a sense of what makes Richmond Richmond, take a drive in the Fan District, so named because its wisteria- and tree-lined streets spread out like a fan. Park the car and walk along Monument Avenue, one of the loveliest places anywhere for an urban stroll. The monuments are statues — of Robert E. Lee, Stonewall Jackson, J.E.B. Stuart, and Jefferson Davis — sharing space somewhat incongruously with a more recent favorite son, Arthur Ashe Jr., the tennis champion. The stately houses are Queen Anne, Victorian, Tudor, Colonial, Italianate, Greek Revival. To complete the genteel experience, take afternoon tea, with scones and finger sandwiches, in the **Jefferson Hotel** (101 West Franklin Street; 804-788-8000; jeffersonhotel.com), whose grand style dates back to 1895.

2 *Fast Forward* 5 p.m.

Jump into the 21st century in Carytown, where shoppers and people watchers make their way to a half-mile stretch of boutiques, vintage clothing stores, and cafes. This colorful strip is Richmond at its most eclectic, mixing floppy-haired musicians, gay hipsters with pierced eyebrows, and suburban mothers pushing strollers. Check out local T-shirt designs at the **Need Supply Company** (3010 West Cary Street;

804-355-5880; needsupply.com). Examine the retro ball gowns, tiaras, and cigarette cases at **Bygones** (2916 West Cary Street; 804-353-1919; bygonesvintage.com). Or seek Japanese anime, underground graphic novels, and comics at **Chop Suey Books** (2913 West Cary Street; 804-422-8066; chopsueybooks.com).

3 *Fed in Virginia* 8 p.m.

The locavore movement was late in coming to Richmond, but residents have taken to it in a big way at the perpetually packed **Mezzanine** (3433 West Cary Street; 804-353-2186; mezzanine3433.com; $$). Produce, meats, and seafood come from Virginia farmers and fishermen. Check the ever-changing, seven-foot-tall chalkboard menu, and expect dishes like green curry quinoa with gingered bok choy and oyster mushrooms. A downside: the outdoor patio looks out over a pair of glowing golden arches across the street.

4 *Cash Bar* 10 p.m.

Richmonders used to flee downtown for the suburbs come 6 p.m. Now young politicos migrate from the nearby State Capitol to gather at **Bank** (1005 East Main Street; 804-648-3070; bankandvault.com), a century-old bank that's been transformed into a swank night spot, complete with a bar made with the building's original marble, a martini lounge in the old

OPPOSITE The Fan District, a bastion of old Richmond.

BELOW Belle Isle, now an island park accessible by footbridge from the bank of the James River, was used as a prison camp during the Civil War.

president's office, and a cavernous downstairs club, Vault. Eavesdrop at the bar and you might pick up some juicy political gossip.

SATURDAY

5 *Three-Sided War* 10 a.m.

A few diehards still call the Civil War the War of Northern Aggression, but the **American Civil War Center at Historic Tredegar** (500 Tredegar Street; 804-780-1865; tredegar.org) takes a less pro-Southern

ABOVE The American Civil War Center, which tells the story of the war from the three different perspectives of the Union, the South, and the slave population, is in the old Tredegar Gun Foundry.

approach. With interactive displays, it tells the story of the war from three perspectives: those of the Union, the Confederacy, and the slaves. The museum building itself is a giant relic, the old 1861 Tredegar Gun Foundry, a major munitions factory during the war. At the adjacent **Richmond National Battlefield Park** (nps.gov/rich), recorded voices read written wartime accounts by local witnesses, including Garland H. White, a former slave who tells of entering defeated Richmond as a Union soldier and being reunited with his mother, "an aged woman," from whom he had been sold as a small boy.

6 *Battle of the Lunch* Noon

There's a new war being waged at the **Black Sheep** (901 West Marshall Street; 804-648-1300; theblacksheeprva.com; $$), a cozy restaurant with barn-wood wainscoting and church pews for benches. Brave eaters attack two-foot-long subs named after Civil War-era ships in what the menu calls the "War of Northern Ingestion." Served on French baguettes,

NOT IN HOSTILITY TO OTHERS, NOT TO INJURE SEC

the CSS Virginia is topped with fried chicken livers, shredded cabbage, and apples, while the USS Brooklyn has jerk barbecued chicken and banana ketchup. A warning: each behemoth can feed at least two.

7 *Into the Trees* 2 p.m.

Need an adrenaline boost? How about maneuvering through the trees like Tarzan? Across the James River in the Stratford Hills section, instructors at **Riverside Outfitters** (6836 Old Westham Road; 804-560-0068; riversideoutfitters.net) lead expeditions that include zip lines and harnessed walks along limbs 40 feet above the ground. Expect to pay at least $150 for two hours. If you prefer lower altitudes—and prices—stay on the Capitol side of the river and find **Belle Isle** (jamesriverpark.org), an island accessible by footbridge from Tredegar Street. It's crisscrossed with trails and offers views of Richmond's natural urban rapids, where you are likely to see intrepid kayakers. Used as a prison camp in the Civil War, the island once held 8,000 captured Union soldiers.

8 *Haute Home Cookin'* 7 p.m.

The industrial-chic bistro **LuLu's** (21 North 17th Street; 804-343-9771; lu-lusrichmond.com; $$) provides comfort food done right to the polo-shirt-wearing young professionals who have moved into the historic neighborhood of Shockoe Bottom, occupying lofts in renovated tobacco warehouses.

Scan the LuLu's menu for easygoing dishes like chicken and dumplings or a pork chop with grilled macaroni and cheese.

9 *Uptown Music* 9 p.m.

You can stay in Shockoe Bottom for drinks and dancing as its nightclubs begin to fill up. But for a quieter evening, head uptown to the **Camel** (1621 West Broad Street; 804-353-4901; thecamel.org), a venue to catch up-and-coming Southern rock and bluegrass bands, acoustic singer-songwriters, and jazz and funk musicians.

SUNDAY

10 *Havana Breakfast* 10 a.m.

Don't expect to find amazing ethnic food in Richmond—this is fried okra country, not an immigrant town. The one exception is **Kuba Kuba** (1601 Park Avenue; 804-355-8817; kubakuba.info; $-$$), a hole-in-the-wall cafe founded by a Cuban émigré, Manny Mendez. The brunch menu mixes paella and Cuban sandwiches with Huevos Kuba,

ABOVE AND OPPOSITE BELOW Jefferson Davis, gesturing grandly, and General J.E.B. Stuart, astride a cavalry horse, are among the sculpted Southern heroes on Monument Avenue. In the late 20th century this Confederate crowd was joined by a bronze of the tennis star Arthur Ashe.

eggs with Cuban-inflected hash, rice, and cornbread. Richmonders line up here for the straight-out-of-Havana vibe. The waitresses sway to Cuban music, and Kuba Kuba also doubles as a bodega where you can load up on Café Bustelo and Our Lady of Guadalupe candles.

11 *Art Factory* Noon

Once an industrial wasteland, the Manchester neighborhood has emerged as an arts district with loft apartments. The anchor is the former MeadWestvaco packaging plant, now a huge art complex with 75 studios and three galleries. Stroll through the mazelike **Art Works** (320 Hull Street; 804-291-1400; artworksrichmond.com), where artists sell their creations, many for under $200. Then, since you're in the neighborhood, head to **Legend Brewery** (321 West Seventh Street; 804-232-3446; legendbrewing.com; $), for a snack and a local microbrew.

ABOVE Bygones, a retro-inspired store in Carytown, a strip of shops and cafes frequented by an eclectic crowd.

OPPOSITE Sipping in style at afternoon tea in the elegantly appointed Jefferson Hotel.

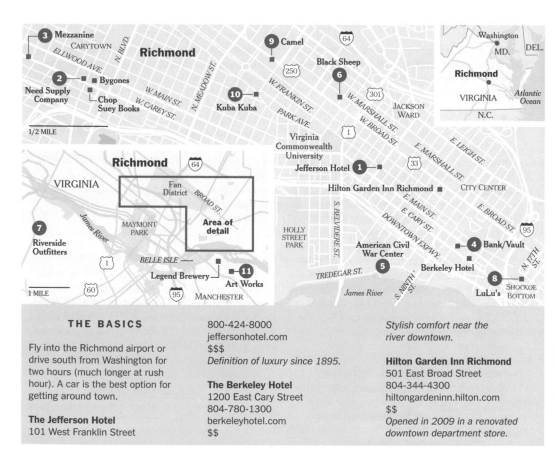

THE BASICS

Fly into the Richmond airport or drive south from Washington for two hours (much longer at rush hour). A car is the best option for getting around town.

The Jefferson Hotel
101 West Franklin Street

800-424-8000
jeffersonhotel.com
$$$
Definition of luxury since 1895.

The Berkeley Hotel
1200 East Cary Street
804-780-1300
berkeleyhotel.com
$$

Stylish comfort near the river downtown.

Hilton Garden Inn Richmond
501 East Broad Street
804-344-4300
hiltongardeninn.hilton.com
$$
Opened in 2009 in a renovated downtown department store.

Charlottesville

As far as Charlottesville is concerned, Thomas Jefferson might still be living on the hill at Monticello. There and at the University of Virginia, which he founded in 1819, he is referred to as "Mr. Jefferson" with a familiarity that suggests he might stroll past, horticulture manual in hand, at any moment. To this day an inordinate number of houses and buildings in the area resemble the back of a nickel. But Jefferson was always at the cutting edge, and the traveler today can share in some of that spirit, too, thanks to the energy emanating from the university he left behind. The active music scene has produced megastars like the Dave Matthews Band and helped to launch the modern roots-rock wave. Local chefs marry grits and fried chicken with international influences. Prize-winning vineyards checker the foothills, a development that Jefferson would have appreciated. He succeeded at nearly everything, but he couldn't coax a decent wine out of Virginia's soil.

— BY JENNIFER TUNG AND JOSHUA KURLANTZICK

FRIDAY

1 *Al Fresco Downtown* 5 p.m.

Walk through the oak-lined downtown mall, where students talk philosophy over coffee and locals gravitate for drinks. You will pass rows of restored brick buildings, street entertainers like mimes and violinists, a central plaza for public art, and al fresco cafes. Stop in just off the main mall at **Feast** (416 West Main Street, Suite H; 434-244-7800; feastvirginia.com), an artisanal cheese shop, charcuterie, and gourmet market that feels as if it could be in Paris.

2 *Old and New* 7 p.m.

Only 10 minutes from downtown Charlottesville, the **Clifton Inn** (1296 Clifton Inn Drive; 434-971-1800; cliftoninn.net; $$$$) sits amid rolling hills and pasture land. Virginia's inns have embarked on a culinary arms race, and the Clifton has kept up. Its restaurant, inside a white-pillared *Gone With*

OPPOSITE Monticello, Thomas Jefferson's home and a conspicuous example of his architectural prowess.

RIGHT The restaurant at the *Gone with the Wind*-style Clifton Inn is worth the drive out of town.

the *Wind*-style Southern mansion, offers a design-your-own tasting menu featuring local ingredients. Reservations are essential. For a more casual dinner, eat in Charlottesville at **C & O** (515 East Water Street; 434-971-7044; candorestaurant.com; $$-$$$), a 110-year-old building that originally served as a railroad stop. Sit in the mezzanine, a candlelit room as dark and narrow as a mine shaft, and order dishes like local organic lamb or house-made chorizo with braised collard greens and purple potato frites.

SATURDAY

3 *The Morning Tour* 8 a.m.

A quiet Saturday morning is a good time to see Jefferson's Academical Village, the central buildings he designed at the University of Virginia. Pick up coffee at **Mudhouse** on the Main Street mall (213 Main Street; 434-984-6833; mudhouse.com), and walk onto the Grounds (Mr. Jefferson never used the word "campus," and neither does anyone else in Charlottesville). Begin at the **Rotunda** (tours, 434-924-7969; virginia.edu/uvatours/rotunda), inspired by the Pantheon in Rome, which sits at the north end of the 225-foot-long Lawn. Flanking the Lawn are the Pavilions, where esteemed professors live, and dorm rooms occupied by high-achieving final-year students ("senior" isn't a word here,

cither). The charming gardens behind the Pavilions, divided by undulating serpentine walls, are the professors' backyards but are open to the public.

4 *Outback* 10 a.m.

For a fascinating detour little known by outsiders, visit the university's **Kluge-Ruhe Aboriginal Art Collection**. John W. Kluge, a billionaire businessman, built perhaps the largest collection of aboriginal art outside Australia and then donated it to the University of Virginia. The free guided tour, every Saturday at 10:30 a.m., is essential to understanding these stark and sometimes inscrutable works of art (400 Worrell Drive, Peter Jefferson Place; 434-244-0234; virginia.edu/kluge-ruhe).

5 *Colonial Fried Chicken* Noon

Let the lady in the bonnet and the big skirt corral you into the lunch line at **Michie Tavern**, an inn that dates back to 1784 (683 Thomas Jefferson Parkway; 434-977-1234; michietavern.com; $$$). Let more women in bonnets pile fried chicken, black-eyed

BELOW Tasting at Barboursville Vineyard. The winery has a notable restaurant and a Jefferson-designed building.

OPPOSITE Comestibles at Feast, a stop on the oak-lined downtown mall near the University of Virginia.

peas, stewed tomatoes, and cornbread onto your pewter-style plate; then eat at a wooden table by the hearth. Once you accept full tourist status, the food is very tasty.

6 *The Back of the Nickel* 1 p.m.

Tours of historical sites are rarely billed as exciting, but Jefferson's home, **Monticello** (434-984-9800; monticello.org), actually causes goose bumps. Jefferson designed the house to invoke classical ideals of reason, proportion, and balance, and sited it on a rise ("Monticello" is from the Italian for "small hill") for a view of distant mountains. After your introduction at the new visitor center, opened in 2009, enter the house and note the elk antlers in the entrance hall, courtesy of Lewis and Clark, and the private library that once housed 6,700 books. Guides point out Jefferson's design innovations, including a dumbwaiter hidden in a fireplace, and offer insight into the unsung lives of the slaves who kept everything going. Monticello lost its spot on the back of the nickel coin for a brief period a few years ago, but Eric Cantor, a Virginia representative and influential House Republican, ushered through legislation to guarantee that after 2006 it would be back to stay.

7 *Country Roads* 5 p.m.

Drive back toward Charlottesville and turn northeast on Route 20 to Barboursville. The drive, through an area called the **Southwest Mountains Rural Historic District**, winds up and down through green farmland sitting in the shadow of the Southwest range. Keep your eyes out for historical marker signs; the area also boasts a rich trove of African-American history (nps.gov/history/nr/travel/journey/sou.htm).

8 *Dining Amid the Ruins* 7 p.m.

There's more of Jefferson (didn't this man ever sleep?) to be seen at the Barboursville Vineyard, where you should have made reservations well before now for dinner at the **Palladio Restaurant** (17655 Winery Road, Barboursville; 540-832-7848; barboursvillewine.net; $$$$). Jefferson designed the main building at the vineyard, which dates back to 1814. There was a fire in the late 1880s, but you can see the ruins of his design. The restaurant

features Northern Italian cooking as well as locally inspired dishes like quail with corn cakes.

9 *Miller Time* 10 p.m.

Every college town needs a few decent bars for grungy bands to play in, but in Charlottesville, you wind up later seeing those bands on MTV. The Dave Matthews Band had its start here back when Matthews tended bar at **Miller's** (109 West Main Street; 434-971-8511; millersdowntown.com). He moved on, but Miller's, a converted drugstore that retains the trappings of an old-time apothecary, is still there. Get there by 10, before the college crowd packs the place, and try to catch the one night of the week when the famed bebop jazz trumpeter and local music professor John D'earth headlines the bill.

SUNDAY

10 *Take a Hike* 10 a.m.

Drive west for 30 minutes on Interstate 64 to **Shenandoah National Park** (Exit 99). By mid-morning the early mist will have lifted. Follow signs to Skyline Drive and the Blue Ridge Parkway. For a vigorous hike, start at the Humpback Gap parking area, six miles south of the Blue Ridge Parkway's northern end. Follow the Appalachian Trail a half-mile south to a challenging spur trail that leads to a breathtaking view of the Shenandoah Valley.

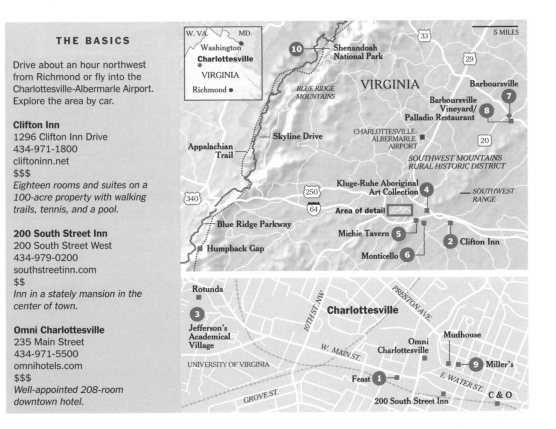

THE BASICS

Drive about an hour northwest from Richmond or fly into the Charlottesville-Albermarle Airport. Explore the area by car.

Clifton Inn
1296 Clifton Inn Drive
434-971-1800
cliftoninn.net
$$$
Eighteen rooms and suites on a 100-acre property with walking trails, tennis, and a pool.

200 South Street Inn
200 South Street West
434-979-0200
southstreetinn.com
$$
Inn in a stately mansion in the center of town.

Omni Charlottesville
235 Main Street
434-971-5500
omnihotels.com
$$$
Well-appointed 208-room downtown hotel.

Williamsburg

Williamsburg, Virginia, with its restored Historic Area of 18th-century buildings, will always be a destination for education-minded families, Revolutionary War buffs, and anyone who likes to imagine life in another time. But Williamsburg can also be a more rounded — and upscale — experience. Local chefs have updated traditional Southern cooking, and the food is often accompanied by high-quality Virginia wines. Among the Colonial homes of Williamsburg's central district, it's possible to have a spa treatment or buy interesting folk art. Of course if you want to see a staging of Patrick Henry's "Give Me Liberty, or Give Me Death!" speech, or stick your head in the stocks, that's still there, too.
— BY JOSHUA KURLANTZICK

FRIDAY

1 *Virginia Vintages* 4 p.m.

Once consigned to the bargain bin of wine shops, Virginia wines now hold their own in global wine competitions, and the **Williamsburg Winery**, a few miles from the colonial district (5800 Wessex Hundred Road; 757-229-0999; williamsburgwinery.com), is one of the largest in the state. Its chardonnays — particularly the fruity, oaky Acte 12 chardonnay — have won much acclaim from critics. Attend a tasting and then head over to the adjacent tavern for a light pre-dinner snack.

2 *Barbecue and Pound Cake* 7 p.m.

Southerners can argue about barbecue with the same spirit they exhibit for college football, and Virginia-style barbecue is certainly worthy of a heated debate. It tends to be smokier and milder than North Carolina's vinegary, tangy version. In the Williamsburg area, **Pierce's Pitt Bar-B-Que** (447 East Rochambeau Drive; 757-565-2955; pierces.com; $$) is a local legend. The smell of smoking meat wafts out of the restaurant and even pervades a nearby stretch of highway. At all times of the day, the parking lot is packed and crowds clamber for barbecue sandwiches and full racks of ribs. Pork rules, but Pierce's also serves chicken, salads, buttery corn bread, and

homemade carrot and lemon pound cakes. (But beware: if you ask for a chicken salad, the waiter may think there's something wrong with you.)

3 *The Neighborhood* 8:30 p.m.

Most visitors to Williamsburg stay in hotels outside the **Historic Area**, but by far the most interesting (though largely unknown) lodging option is to stay in a restored home, tavern, or other structure within the colonial district. Whether or not you're unpacking your suitcase right in the neighborhood, after dinner take a leisurely stroll through the heart of the district, dead quiet once all the tourists have left.

SATURDAY

4 *Back in Time* 10 a.m.

It's best to check out the Colonial buildings and re-enactments in the morning, before the heat and humidity and tourist buses arrive. *Colonial Williamsburg This Week*, a free print publication, contains up-to-date listings of re-enactments, but don't miss the **Governor's Palace**, home to royal governors (and Patrick Henry) and the **Bruton Parish Church** (one of the oldest Episcopal churches in America). And look for re-enactors who are engaged in political debates, which tend to be less stilted than other re-enactments.

OPPOSITE The Wythe House, one of the 18th-century buildings of Williamsburg, a restored colonial-era city.

RIGHT A craft shop at Merchants Square.

5 *The People's Art* Noon

Abby Aldrich Rockefeller was one of the earliest patrons of American folk art, and her collection, housed in the **Abby Aldrich Rockefeller Folk Art Museum** (325 West Francis Street; history.org/history/museums) showcases the immense diversity of the genre. The collection ranges from staid family portraits to whimsical sculptures of watermelons to elegiac paintings of Christ that resemble the works of El Greco. Because folk art is less known than, say, Picasso's, take a docent-guided tour of the collection.

6 *Merchants of Americana* 2 p.m.

More than just a purveyor of cider mugs and souvenir tricorner hats, **Merchants Square**, on the west end of the Colonial District, also serves up unusual—and often pricey—antiques, quilts, silver, and other American crafts. Try the **Nancy Thomas Gallery of Folk Art** (402 West Duke of Gloucester Street; 757-259-1938; nancythomas.com) or **J. Fenton Modern American Crafts** (110 South Henry Street; 757-221-8200; quiltsunlimited.com) for updated interpretations—in jewelry, clothing, and other formats—of the quirky traditions of folk art found in the Rockefeller collection. For lunch, grab a sandwich at the **Cheese Shop** (410 West Duke of Gloucester Street; 757-220-1324; cheeseshopwilliamsburg.com) on the square.

7 *Old-Time Pampering* 5 p.m.

Exhausted from a long day of walking and shopping? A visit to the **Spa of Colonial Williamsburg** (307 South England Street; 800-688-6479; colonialwilliamsburgresort.com/spa) might just be what you need. Right in the Historic Area, the spa serves the usual menu of treatments, but in keeping with the history theme, it also offers a twist: packages based on practices from the early days of American history—for example, an 18th-century treatment with colonial-era herbs like pennyroyal, sage, rosemary, angelica, and juniper berries.

8 *Dinner Update* 7 p.m.

Situated right on Merchants Square, **Fat Canary** (410 West Duke of Gloucester Street; 757-229-3333; fatcanarywilliamsburg.com; $$$) quickly established itself with a departure from the pub-style food and alehouse atmosphere more typical in the heart of Colonial Williamsburg. In a well-designed, Art Deco-influenced dining area, Fat Canary serves nouvelle cuisine that gives local dishes innovative treatment, resulting in combinations like crispy cornmeal oysters with charred tomato or free-range pheasant with polenta, pine nuts, and pancetta. Reservations are essential.

SUNDAY

9 *Take a Drive* 9 a.m.

If you have children along, this is a good day to indulge them with a side trip to the **Busch Gardens** theme park, just three miles east of Williamsburg. But for something more serene, take a drive. You have to go only a few miles outside Colonial Williamsburg, past the mall sprawl, to appreciate the rural character of much of the surrounding area. Head onto the 23-mile-long **Colonial Parkway**, a winding, wooded

ABOVE See the Colonial-era buildings and re-enactments in the morning, before the heat and tourist buses arrive.

BELOW One interesting lodging option is a stay in a restored home, tavern, or other structure.

road connecting three Virginia towns important in history: Williamsburg, Jamestown, and Yorktown. With a low speed limit, it's perfect for a mellow tour, stopping at scenic turnouts to look out at the York and James Rivers.

10 *Bottoms Up* Noon

In colonial times, Williamsburg was known as much for drinking as for debating. Taverns served as meeting places, the perfect setting for wielding influence in the powerful Virginia colony. The restored Historic Area features four working taverns—all serving lunch, dinner, or both—striving to recreate an authentic atmosphere. Most feature workaday fare like sandwiches and local seafood, but the ambience

can't be beat. Try **Chowning's Tavern** (109 East Duke of Gloucester Street; 757-229-2141; $$) for lunch. Its garden tables offer views of Market Square and the Governor's Palace (it does not take reservations). After lunch, it's an easy walk to the lavish **Peyton Randolph House** and other central Colonial homes.

ABOVE At Pierce's Pitt Bar-B-Que, the meat is cooked Virginia-style and the parking lot is always packed. Pork is king, but savor the buttery cornbread, too.

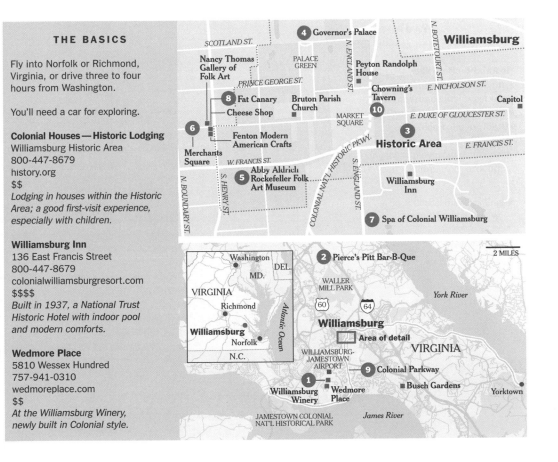

THE BASICS

Fly into Norfolk or Richmond, Virginia, or drive three to four hours from Washington.

You'll need a car for exploring.

Colonial Houses—Historic Lodging
Williamsburg Historic Area
800-447-8679
history.org
$$
Lodging in houses within the Historic Area; a good first-visit experience, especially with children.

Williamsburg Inn
136 East Francis Street
800-447-8679
colonialwilliamsburgresort.com
$$$$
Built in 1937, a National Trust Historic Hotel with indoor pool and modern comforts.

Wedmore Place
5810 Wessex Hundred
757-941-0310
wedmoreplace.com
$$
At the Williamsburg Winery, newly built in Colonial style.

Virginia Beach

In 1607, a group of adventurers landed at Cape Henry, now known as Virginia Beach, but moved on to Jamestown to establish England's first permanent American colony. Four centuries later, Virginia Beach isn't snubbed anymore. It's the largest city in Virginia, home to more than 440,000 people and part of a metropolitan area of 1.6 million that also includes Norfolk and Newport News. Famous for its naval installations and picturesque shorelines, Virginia Beach also has an array of famous residents past and present: the hip-hop stars Missy Elliott, Tim Mosley (a k a Timbaland), and Chad Hugo and Pharrell Williams; the televangelist Pat Robertson; and the legendary psychic Edgar Cayce, who in 1925 was "called" to live in this city, with its gentle climate and lush locale along the Atlantic shore.
— BY LISA RICHMON

FRIDAY

1 *Kiss Off* 4 p.m.

Perch across the street from the Naval Air Station Oceana for a chance to see what the Navy's top fighter jocks are doing with your tax dollars. Look for takeoffs, landings, and — if you're lucky — more. After maneuvers over the ocean, pilots turn their F/A-18 Hornets and Super Hornets back to the base in formation. The lead pilot gives the "kiss off," the signal to peel off and land, and the planes simulate a carrier landing by dropping sharply onto a box painted on the runway. Watch for it from the jet landing observation area at **POW/MIA Flame of Hope Memorial Park** (Oceana Boulevard near the intersection with Bells Road).

2 *Virginia Is for Beach Lovers* 5 p.m.

Virginia Beach is all about its boardwalk, fringed with flowers and outdoor cafes, and its 100-yard-wide beach. Catch the sea breeze and look around. You will see joyful children, preening sun-bathers, and surfer dudes. Each August competitors arrive here for the East Coast Surfing Championship. Fishermen find a second home at the central pier off 15th Street.

OPPOSITE Sand, boardwalk, and city at Virginia Beach.

RIGHT The breakfast menu at Doc Taylor's includes the Heart Attack: eggs with sausage, bacon, and steak.

3 *New Southern Cooking* 7 p.m.

Sushi parlors have sprouted up where once there was only Virginia ham, and the hands-down favorite is **Mizuno Japanese Restaurant** (1860 Laskin Road; 757-422-1200; mizuno-sushi.com; $$), run by Walter Mizuno, a sushi chef born and trained in Tokyo. Look for the tuna tartare and the delicately loaded sashimi salad of octopus, avocado, tuna, seaweed, and fresh greens. For accompaniment, Mizuno offers the largest sake list in the area.

SATURDAY

4 *Magic Morning* 6:30 a.m.

A due east sunrise that lights up the boardwalk from 1st Street to 40th Street is what locals love most about Virginia Beach. The rich coastline means good feeding for dolphins that pop up from the ocean and pelicans that glide along the air current of a wave for miles. Large ships dot the seascape, and broken crockery from centuries-old shipwrecks still washes up on shore.

5 *Sample and Shop* 9 a.m.

Nibble breakfast and pick up picnic food for later at the **Old Beach Farmers Market** (620 19th Street; oldbeachfarmersmarket.com) in the parking lot of Crocs eco-bistro. You will find fresh fruit in season, baked goods, Virginia artisanal cheeses, and boutique organic wines. Then shop for beachwear at the **17th Street Surf Shop** (1612 Pacific Avenue; 757-422-6105; 17thstsurfshop.com), where surfers find denims for their dry off-hours, or at **Meg's Swimwear** (307 Laskin Road; 757-428-7945), known for fitting

swimsuits to women's bodies rather than expecting things to work the other way around.

6 *Where Ocean Meets Bay* Noon

First Landing State Park (2500 Shore Drive; 757-412-2300; dcr.virginia.gov/state_parks/fir.shtml) commemorates the spot where the settlers of 1607 established an elective government before pushing on to Jamestown. Today, it's the most visited park in Virginia, a nearly 3,000-acre paradise for cyclists, hikers, and nature lovers, at the spot where the Atlantic Ocean meets the Chesapeake Bay. Hike some of the nine walking trails, totaling 19 miles, that wind around dunes and ponds surrounded by moss-covered live oak and bald cypress trees.

7 *Aura of Health* 3 p.m.

Edgar Cayce was a farm boy from Kentucky who harnessed his psychic powers to "enter" other people's bodies to diagnose illnesses, which he then treated with what he called readings. He also made general predictions of the future (reportedly he foresaw the stock market crash and World War II) and gained the attention of scientists, medical experts, and President Woodrow Wilson. In 1925 Cayce settled

ABOVE Joyous children, preening sun-bathers, fishermen, and surfer dudes populate the beach. Overhead, fighter jets streak toward Naval Air Station Oceana.

in Virginia Beach and in 1928 he founded the Cayce Hospital, based on his faith-healing principles. It closed two years later, but at the **Association for Research and Enlightenment**, dedicated to Cayce's legacy (215 67th Street, Virginia Beach; 757-428-3588; edgarcayce.org), you can browse the gift shop, buy holistic products, and attend a day spa offering Cayce-based remedies dispensed with the belief that we are all just one session of colon hydrotherapy away from attaining good chi.

8 *Catch of the Night* 7 p.m.

For a great view of the scenery of both the natural and Saturday-night varieties, hit **Catch 31 Fish House and Bar** at the **Hilton Virginia Beach Oceanfront** (3001 Atlantic Avenue, 757-213-3474; catch31.com; $$$). The large glass bar extends outdoors, where it overlooks the boardwalk. Inside, the jam-packed grazing area is flanked by two dining areas offering a large selection of fresh fish. A raw bar features several varieties of oysters.

9 *Reggae Meets Rugelach* 9 p.m.

The **Jewish Mother** (Laskin and First Colonial Roads; 757-622-5915; jewishmother.com) is a deli by day and a restaurant and live-music bar by night. John Hammond, Roomful of Blues, and Dr. John are among the performers who have appeared on its stage; local bands play four or five nights a week.

If you're hungry, the Mother's Son Reuben is a specialty of the house, as is, of course, the chicken soup with matzo balls.

SUNDAY

10 *Eggs on the Veranda* 9 a.m.

In 1949, before Virginia Beach had a proper hospital, there was **Doc Taylor's** home office. Today, it's an all-day breakfast and lunch joint (207 23rd Street; 757-425-1960; doctaylors.com; $-$$), and the big doses of sunlight that pour into its covered porch are just what the doctor ordered. Breakfasts at Doc Taylor's include the Heart Attack (three eggs, bacon, and a strip steak) and the Nurse Ratchett (omelet

with grilled red peppers, portobellos, spinach, and hollandaise). **Tautog's**, the sister cottage next door (No. 205; 757-422-0081; tautogs.com; $$), takes over when Doc Taylor's closes at 5 p.m.

11 *Sea and Be Seen* 11 a.m.

The **Virginia Aquarium and Marine Science Center** (717 General Booth Boulevard; 757-425-3474; virginiaaquarium.com) features a 300,000-gallon tank with sharks and stingrays, a 100,000-gallon Red Sea Aquarium tank, an adjacent salt marsh and woodland preserve, and an IMAX theater. Dolphin-watching tours, led by the center's knowledgeable staff, run daily in summer and on weekends into October (757-437-2628 for reservations).

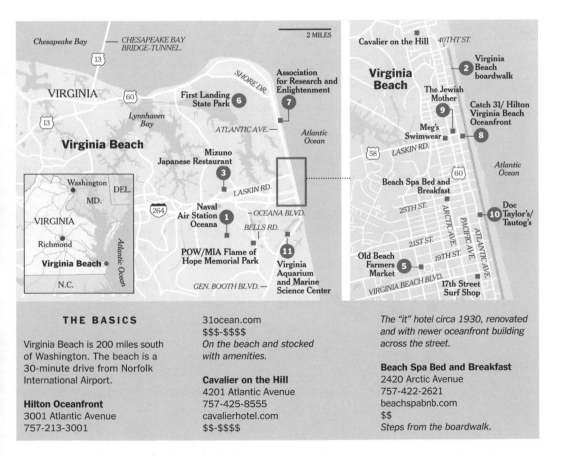

THE BASICS

Virginia Beach is 200 miles south of Washington. The beach is a 30-minute drive from Norfolk International Airport.

Hilton Oceanfront
3001 Atlantic Avenue
757-213-3001

31ocean.com
$$$-$$$$
On the beach and stocked with amenities.

Cavalier on the Hill
4201 Atlantic Avenue
757-425-8555
cavalierhotel.com
$$-$$$$

The "it" hotel circa 1930, renovated and with newer oceanfront building across the street.

Beach Spa Bed and Breakfast
2420 Arctic Avenue
757-422-2621
beachspabnb.com
$$
Steps from the boardwalk.

Raleigh-Durham

Tell North Carolinians you're heading to the Raleigh-Durham area, locally called the Research Triangle or just the Triangle, and they will probably ask, "Which school are you visiting?" Yet the close-knit cities of Raleigh, Durham, and Chapel Hill, North Carolina, are marked by more than college bars and basketball fans. Visitors not bound for Duke (Durham), the University of North Carolina (Chapel Hill), or North Carolina State (Raleigh) come to see buzz-worthy bands, dine on food from farm-worshiping chefs, and explore outdoor art. From its biscuits to its boutiques, the Triangle occupies a happy place between slow-paced Southern charm and urban cool.

— BY J. J. GOODE

FRIDAY

1 *Art Inside Out* 3 p.m.

The collection at the **North Carolina Museum of Art** (2110 Blue Ridge Road, Raleigh; 919-839-6262; ncartmuseum.org) is succinct by major museum standards, and that has its advantages. The lack of tour bus crowds means unfettered access to the museum's Old Masters and contemporary heavyweights like Anselm Kiefer. The real treat is the adjacent Museum Park, more than 164 acres of open fields and woodlands punctuated by environmental art like Cloud Chamber, a stone hut that acts as a camera obscura with a small hole in the roof projecting inverted, otherworldly images of slowly swaying trees on the floor and walls.

2 *Tower of Bauble* 5 p.m.

There's no pigeonholing the eclectic wares in the four-story indie mini-mall collectively known as **Father & Son Antiques** (107 West Hargett Street, Raleigh; 919-832-3030; swankarama.com) and including Southern Swank and 2nd Floor Vintage. The organizing principle, if there is one, might be high design meets kitschy Americana, as the intermingling of vintage disco dresses, Mexican wrestling masks, and Eames aluminum chairs attests.

3 *Upscale Diner* 7 p.m.

Memorable meals abound in the Triangle owing to its high concentration of accomplished, produce-fondling chefs like Ashley Christensen.

She left one of the area's top kitchens to open **Poole's Downtown Diner** (426 South McDowell Street, Raleigh; 919-832-4477; poolesdowntowndiner.com; $-$$) in a space that began as a 1940s pie shop. Diners sitting in the bright-red booths dig into Christensen's low-pretense, high-flavor dishes. You might find a starter of lovably sloppy fried green tomatoes crowned with local pork smoked over cherry wood, or an entree of ground-in-house chuck roll seared in duck fat, topped with cheese, and perched on a slice of grilled brioche.

4 *Cheers to the Chief* 10 p.m.

The owner of the **Raleigh Times Bar** (14 East Hargett Street, Raleigh; 919-833-0999; raleightimesbar.com), Greg Hatem, painstakingly restored the century-old building that once housed the now-defunct *Raleigh Times* and decorated the walls with old clippings, paperboy bags, and other artifacts from the newspaper's heyday. The place was soon packed with patrons choosing from more than 100 beers, including esoteric Belgians and local brews you won't find elsewhere. Barack Obama showed up the day of the state's Democratic primary in 2008, bought a $2 Pabst Blue Ribbon, and left an $18 tip. Anyone not campaigning might make a pricier selection.

OPPOSITE Outdoor entertainment at the Koka Booth Amphitheatre in Cary, a Raleigh suburb.

BELOW Museum Park, 164 acres of woods, fields, and outdoor art adjacent to Raleigh's North Carolina Museum of Art.

SATURDAY

5 *Eco Junk* 10:30 a.m.

The **Scrap Exchange** (548 Foster Street, Durham; 919-688-6960; scrapexchange.org) is a "nonprofit creative reuse center" specializing in industrial discards or, for those not versed in eco-jargon, a bazaar of modestly priced former junk donated by Carolinians and scavenged from local businesses that have included a hosiery mill, a zipper factory, and a parachute plant. Even if you are not one of the giddy artists, teachers, or theater producers who comb for utilitarian treasures, plan to spend at least an hour rummaging in a cool-struck trance through items like test tubes, empty fire extinguishers, and swaths of double-knit polyester.

6 *Taco Time* Noon

Anyone not on a hunt for serious Mexican food might drive past **Taqueria La Vaquita** (2700 Chapel Hill Road, Durham; 919-402-0209; lavaquitanc.com; $), an unassuming freestanding structure with a plastic cow on its roof, just five minutes from Duke University. But if you did, you'd miss tacos made with house-made corn tortillas, uncommonly delicate discs topped with exceptional barbacoa de res (slow-cooked beef) or carnitas (braised-then-fried pork).

7 *River Walk* 2 p.m.

One of the Triangle's charms is that its urban trappings and booming suburbs, like upscale Cary, are so easy to escape. A 10-mile drive from downtown Durham brings you to **Eno River State Park** (6101 Cole Mill Road, Durham; 919-383-1686; ncparks.gov). Its trails progress through swaying pines and follow the river past patches of delicate purple-and-yellow wildflowers and turtles sunning themselves on low branches in the water.

8 *Going for the Whole Hog* 5 p.m.

Small towns and back roads, not cities, have a monopoly on great barbecue. What makes **The Pit** (328 West Davie Street, Raleigh; 919-890-4500; thepit-raleigh.com; $) a striking exception is Ed Mitchell, the legendary master of the eastern North Carolina art form of whole hog cooking. Instead of trekking 100 miles to porcine capitals like Ayden and Lexington, you can dig into pilgrimage-worthy chopped or pulled pork—made from pigs purchased from family farms and cooked for 10 to 14 hours over coals and hickory or oak—just a short stroll from the North Carolina Capitol Building. Your chopped barbecued pork plate comes with two sides and greaseless hush puppies.

9 *Root for the Home Team* 7 p.m.

The Triangle is college basketball country, home to two of the winningest teams—Duke and North Carolina—and some of the most rabid fans in college sports history. But soon after the madness of March, the more tranquil fans of local baseball stream into the **Durham Bulls Athletic Park** (409 Blackwell Street, Durham; 919-687-6500; dbulls.com). The Bulls, founded in 1902 as the Tobacconists, still offer professional baseball at bargain prices.

10 *Big Bands* 10 p.m.

Nirvana played at the **Cat's Cradle** (300 East Main Street, Carrboro; 919-967-9053; catscradle.com)

ABOVE University of North Carolina basketball fans. The excitement rises when the opponent is Duke University.

BELOW Father & Son Antiques in Raleigh.

for the first time in pre-*Nevermind* 1990 to about 100 people. A year later Pearl Jam played to three times as many, filling just half the standing-room-only space. Today the Cradle, just a mile from downtown Chapel Hill, hosts acts you may be hearing more about tomorrow, for low ticket prices that seem more like yesterday.

SUNDAY

11 *Drive-Thru Biscuits* 10 a.m.

There are several places in Chapel Hill that serve a distinguished Southern breakfast for an easy-to-swallow price. Diners linger over gravy-smothered pork chops and eggs at **Mama Dip's** (408 West Rosemary Street; 919-942-5837; mamadips.com) and peerless shrimp and grits at **Crook's Corner** (610 West

Franklin Street; 919-929-7643; crookscorner.com). But for a morning meal on the go that's equally unforgettable, roll up to the drive-through-only **Sunrise Biscuit Kitchen** (1305 East Franklin Street; 919-933-1324; $), where the iced tea is tooth-achingly sweet and the main course is fluffy, buttery, and filled with salty country ham or crisp fried chicken.

ABOVE When college basketball ends, it's time for local baseball fans to stream into Durham Bulls Athletic Park. Professional baseball in Durham dates back to 1902.

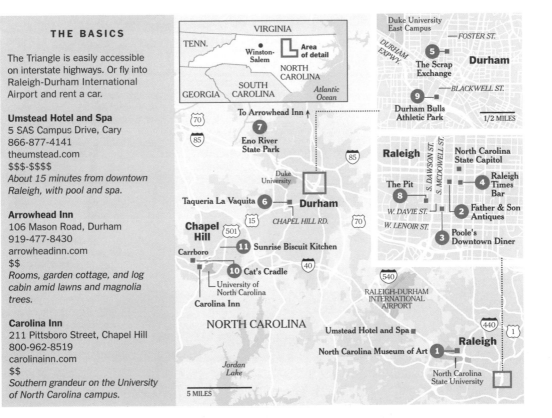

THE BASICS

The Triangle is easily accessible on interstate highways. Or fly into Raleigh-Durham International Airport and rent a car.

Umstead Hotel and Spa
5 SAS Campus Drive, Cary
866-877-4141
theumstead.com
$$$-$$$$
About 15 minutes from downtown Raleigh, with pool and spa.

Arrowhead Inn
106 Mason Road, Durham
919-477-8430
arrowheadinn.com
$$
Rooms, garden cottage, and log cabin amid lawns and magnolia trees.

Carolina Inn
211 Pittsboro Street, Chapel Hill
800-962-8519
carolinainn.com
$$
Southern grandeur on the University of North Carolina campus.

Charleston

Charleston, South Carolina, still has its cannons aimed at Fort Sumter, where the Civil War began. With some of the country's most aggressive historic preservation, it maintains magnolia-and-hibiscus charm on streets lined with Colonial and antebellum mansions. Tours give visitors a glimpse of the lives and language of the African-American people who built the Gullah culture nearby. But a newer and younger Charleston asserts itself, too — in galleries on Broad Street and in a festoonery of restaurants, bars, and boutique bakeries in the design district on upper King Street. Charlestonians, governed by laws of hospitality as incontrovertible as those of gravity, cannot help themselves from sharing their new finds, even if you are "from off," as those who grew up on this once swampy peninsula refer to outsiders.
— BY SHAILA DEWAN

FRIDAY

1 *Meeting Lucinda* 3 p.m.

Embracing the past doesn't always mean being honest about it, but the new Charleston acknowledges both sides of its history. The four-block **Gateway Walk** shares hidden beauty, taking visitors through quiet gardens and past lovely old churches. Enter it from Church Street across from St. Philip's Episcopal Church, and follow the plaques. Next, walk a couple of blocks to see the darker past. In 1856, the city banned outdoor slave markets as out of keeping with its genteel image. Trade moved indoors to places like Ryan's Mart, where the first sale was a 20-year-old woman named Lucinda. The building opened in 2007 as the **Old Slave Mart Museum** (6 Chalmers Street; 843-958-6467; nps.gov/history/nr/travel/charleston). It brings slavery to horrifying life, addressing topics like the stigma attached to slave trading and the ways slaves were dressed, shaved, and fed in preparation for market day.

2 *Lowcountry Cuisine* 7 p.m.

Charleston is the unofficial capital of the swampy coastal Lowcountry in this part of South Carolina. For a taste of its traditional cuisine gone upscale, have dinner at **Cypress Lowcountry Grille** (167 East Bay Street, 843-727-0111; magnolias-blossom-cypress.com; $$$), where the chef, Craig Deihl, makes his own charcuterie

(served with lard biscuits) and pork schnitzel while throwing a bone to value-seeking diners with a prix fixe menu for about $40.

3 *Jazz Refuge* 10 p.m.

Charleston is not particularly known for its night life — the options sometimes come down to one outlandishly named martini versus another (caramel macchiatotini? Charlestoniantini?). But locals with an evening to kill stop by the lounge of the Charleston Grill, a grand ballroom of a restaurant tucked away in a posh hotel, the **Charleston Place** (224 King Street; 843-577-4522; charlestongrill.com). From a glamorous white banquette, you can take in the sophisticated tunes of the Quentin Baxter Ensemble and the very polite antics of practically all of Charleston, from dads and debutantes to Gullah painters. Snack on truffle Parmesan popcorn and a kiwi version of the Pimm's cup.

SATURDAY

4 *Sweetgrass and Crepes* 9 a.m.

The old South finds new takes at the **Charleston Farmers Market** in Marion Square (843-724-7305; charlestonarts.sc), a bustling downtown market where you may find pickled watermelon rind, sweetgrass baskets, and flower arrangements that

OPPOSITE Guided kayaking tours take paddlers into the marshy terrain of South Carolina's Lowcountry.

BELOW Shopping at the Charleston Farmers Market.

make use of old windows. Be prepared to fight your way through the throngs buying their week's supply of groceries or lining up for fresh crepes (charlestoncrepecompany.com).

5 *Shopping Belles* 10 a.m.

King Street has long been the stylish epicenter of Charleston, but it's been invaded by the major chain stores. Take refuge on and around upper King, north of Marion Square, where chic shops and high-concept restaurants coexist with fading emporiums. Pick up a handy one-page guide to parking and neighborhood restaurants at **Blue Bicycle Books** (420 King Street; 843-722-2666; bluebicyclebooks.com). Sample a pastry at the fashionably French **Macaroon Boutique** (45 John Street; 843-577-5441; macaroonboutique.com), and then browse the baffling assortment of odds and ends at **Read Brothers**, established in 1912 (593 King Street; 843-723-7276; readbrothers.com), which now calls itself a stereo and fabric store. For a splurge, head to **Magar Hatworks** (57 Cannon Street; 843-345-4483; magarhatworks.com; call for appointment), a millinery where Leigh Magar makes recherché hats (around $175 to $700) that sell at high-end stores like Barneys New York.

6 *Not Quite Teetotaling* 2 p.m.

Many people spend a lifetime trying to repli-cate Grandma's recipes — not so at **Irvin-House Vineyards** (6775 Bears Bluff Road, 843-559-6867; charlestonwine.com), a scenic vineyard about a 30-minute drive from downtown on sleepy Wadmalaw Island. The owners have spent years trying to make muscadine wine without the syrupy, made-at-home sweetness those words bring to Southerners' minds. A few years ago, the owners took on another iconic Southern taste, iced tea,

ABOVE Leigh Magar, the milliner behind Magar Hatworks.

OPPOSITE Jazz at the Charleston Grill, tucked away in the posh Charleston Place hotel.

blending it with vodka to make Firefly Sweet Tea Vodka, whose authentic lazy-Sunday-afternoon flavor made it a runaway success. After the free Saturday vineyard tour at 2 p.m., you can taste both.

7 *Old Growth* 4 p.m.

On the way back to town, take a short detour to the **Angel Oak**, a tree so large it could whomp 10 Hogwarts willows (3688 Angel Oak Road). The tree, which is thought to be at least 300 to 400 years old, is threatened by plans for a nearby shopping center. It is protected by a fence; the gate closes at 5 p.m.

8 *Fish Camp Supper* 6 p.m.

Before the **Bowens Island Restaurant** burned down in 2006, the humble cinderblock fish camp was covered in decades' worth of graffiti scrawled by loyal customers. Eventually, it reopened in a large, screened-in room on 18-foot stilts, with a nicer deck and a better view of the dolphins playing in Folly Creek (1870 Bowens Island Road, 843-795-2757; bowensislandrestaurant.com; $$). Marker-wielding patrons have wasted no time in trying to cover the new lumber with fresh scrawls. You can try to decipher them as you wait for your roasted oysters and oversize hush puppies. Get here early to avoid the crush.

9 *Georgian Encore* 8 p.m.

When the **Dock Street Theater** (135 Church Street) opened in 1736, the first production had a name only a pre-Revolutionary could love: *The Recruiting Officer.* Luckily, the producers chose a different work, *Flora,* an early English opera, when it reopened in 2010 with all its Georgian splendor restored. Said to be the first building in America built to be a theater, the Dock hosts the Spoleto Festival, the city's artistic crown jewel, in May and June (spoletousa.org) and Charleston Stage (charlestonstage.com), which presents musicals and popular fare, the rest of the year.

SUNDAY

10 *Sticky and Delicious* 9 a.m.

When it opened, **WildFlour Pastry** (73 Spring Street, 843-327-2621; wildflourpastrycharleston.com) created an instant tradition with "sticky bun

Sundays." A steady stream of customers comes through the door in search of this warm, chewy, generously pecanned confection. Those with less of a sweet tooth will be happy with crumbly, fruity, or savory scones or a hardboiled Sea Island egg.

11 *Gardens and Gators* 11 a.m.

Ever since Pat Conroy's novel *Prince of Tides*, Charleston has been known for its mossy Lowcountry terrain as much as for its picturesque history. At **Middleton Place** plantation (4300 Ashley River Road; 800-782-3608; middletonplace.org), one of several plantations within easy reach of downtown, you can get a close-up view of the marsh — or, in winter, of a primeval cypress swamp — on a guided

kayak tour. Alligators, bald eagles, and river otters are among the possible sights, as is the architectural award-winning **Inn at Middleton Place**, where the tours meet (4290 Ashley River Road; 843-628-2879; charlestonkayakcompany.blogspot.com). After your paddle, you can take in domesticated nature on the plantation grounds, billed as the oldest landscaped garden in the country, with twin butterfly lakes, or visit the blacksmith and cooper workshops. Some things in Charleston don't change.

THE BASICS

Multiple airlines fly to Charleston. Walk in the downtown. To explore further, rent a car.

Hampton Inn Charleston-Historic District
345 Meeting Street
843-723-4000
hamptoninn.hilton.com
$$
In a restored warehouse just old enough to be billed as the area's only antebellum hotel.

Battery Carriage House Inn
20 South Battery
843-727-3100
batterycarriagehouse.com
$$
Eleven rooms a stone's throw from White Point Gardens at the Battery. Enjoy breakfast in a shady walled garden reputed to be haunted.

Market Pavilion Hotel
225 East Bay Street
843-723-0500
marketpavilion.com
$$$$
Opulent rooms with mahogany furniture and four-poster beds.

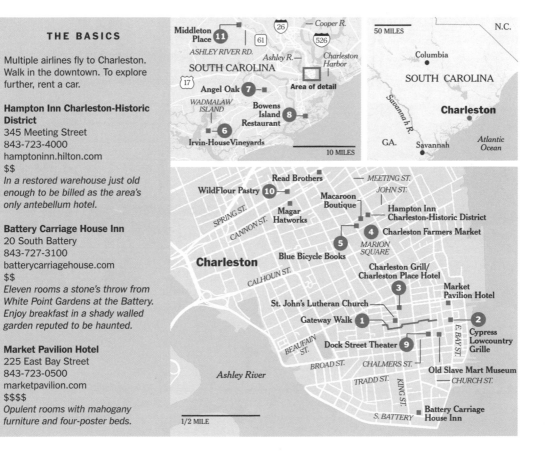

Savannah

Certain things about Savannah never change — it remains one of America's loveliest cities, organized around a grid of 21 squares, where children play, couples wed, and in the evenings lone saxophonists deliver a jazz soundtrack. Live oaks shade the squares; shops and cafes occupy stately old houses; ships still arrive on the Savannah River. But Savannah also has an appetite for the new. A growing emphasis on art has brought both a major expansion of the South's oldest art museum and a lively contemporary scene energized by students and instructors at the booming Savannah College of Art and Design. Civic boosters (thinking technology as well as art) are even trying to reposition the region as Georgia's Creative Coast. And then there is change of another kind: restoration. Before iron-clad protection of the historic district was established, Savannah lost 3 of its 24 squares to developers. Now one of the oldest, Ellis Square, long dominated by a parking lot, has been brought back with restored buildings on its edges and a statue of Savannah's favorite son, the songwriter Johnny Mercer, in its bright new center.
— BY SHAILA DEWAN

FRIDAY

1 *Good and Evil* 3:30 p.m.

You're in the heart of the gracious South, so embrace every cliché from the frilly to the Gothic, with some eccentric characters for good measure. Begin with a tour of the splendid **Mercer Williams House** on Monterey Square (430 Whitaker Street; 912-236-6352; mercerhouse.com; $12.50). It was built in the 1860s for Johnny Mercer's great-grandfather and restored by Jim Williams, the antiques dealer memorialized in a now-classic book, *Midnight in the Garden of Good and Evil.* The stern guide won't dwell on the three murder trials of Mr. Williams, who was acquitted, and guests aren't allowed on the second floor, where Mr. Williams's sister, Dorothy Kingery, still lives. But the guide will offer plenty of detail about the formal

OPPOSITE Savannah, Georgia, in the heart of the gracious South, carefully preserves the elegant houses lining its central grid of oak-shaded squares.

RIGHT The ornate cast-iron fountain in Forsyth Park.

courtyard, the nap-ready veranda, the Continental rococo, and the Edwardian Murano glass.

2 *Georgia on Your Plate* 7 p.m.

Dress up a bit (no flip-flops) for the froufrou milieu of **Elizabeth on 37th** (105 East 37th Street; 912-236-5547; elizabethon37th.net; $$$), a Lowcountry restaurant housed in an early 20th-century mansion where the décor may be prissy but the food is anything but. Expect a seafood-rich menu and what is arguably Savannah's quintessential dining experience. Look for Georgia shrimp, local sea bass, or a pecan crust on the rack of lamb. A seven-course tasting menu is $90 a person.

3 *Creepy Cocktails* 9 p.m.

The city of Savannah began peacefully enough, with a friendship between Tomochichi, the chief of the Yamacraw tribe, and Gen. James Oglethorpe, leader of the British settlers who founded the city in 1733. But then came war, yellow fever, hurricanes, and fires, not to mention pirates and curses — making the city seem, at least to the builders digging around, like one big graveyard. Savannah has turned that sordid history to its advantage: about 30 ghost tours are offered in the city, including a haunted pub crawl. Only one, though, picks you up at your hotel in an open-top hearse, **Hearse Tours** (912-695-1578; hearseghosttours.com; $15). In addition to recounting some of Savannah's most notorious murders, suicides, and deathbed tales, your joke-telling guide might share personal paranormal theories, make everyone scream in unison to spook passersby, or stop for cocktails at favorite haunts. (It's legal to take your julep for a stroll.)

4 *Up-and-Coming* 10 a.m.

Venture out of the historic district to the up-and-coming area called Starland, filled with galleries and studios. Start at **Desotorow** (2427 De Soto Avenue; 912-335-8204; desotorow.org), a non-profit gallery run by current and recent art students, where exhibitions might feature adventurous drawings and collages, doll lamps, or contemporary illustration. Next, make your way up to **Maldoror's** (2418 De Soto Avenue, 912-443-5355; maldorors.com; $), a frame shop with the aura of a Victorian curio cabinet and a print collection to match. Rounding the corner, you'll come to **Back in the Day** (2403 Bull Street; 912-495-9292; backinthedaybakery.com), an old-fashioned bakery that inspires fervent loyalty among locals. Pick up one of the sandwiches, like the Madras curry chicken on ciabatta, and maybe a cupcake, to take with you for lunch.

5 *Picnic with the Dead* Noon

Few cemeteries are more stately and picnic-perfect than **Bonaventure Cemetery** (330 Bonaventure Road), with its 250-year-old live oaks draped with Spanish moss as if perpetually decorated for Halloween. The cemetery, where Conrad Aiken, Johnny Mercer, and other notable residents are buried, looks out over the intracoastal waterway and is a gathering spot for anglers as well as mourners. Find a quiet spot to ponder fate and eat your lunch.

6 *Old Streets, New Museum* 2 p.m.

The battle took years and matched two unlikely adversaries: the **Telfair Museum of Art**, the oldest art museum in the South, which wanted to expand,

ABOVE Elizabeth on 37th serves a seafood-rich menu in a palatial neoclassical-style villa built in 1900.

BELOW Hearse Tours takes visitors to the haunts of Savannah's thriving population of ghosts.

and the powerful Savannah Historic District Board of Review. The result, after intense haggling, was a light-filled building that is as trim as a yacht and has won accolades for its architect, Moshe Safdie. The addition, the **Jepson Center for the Arts** (207 West York Street; 912-790-8800; telfair.org), preserved Savannah's cherished street grid by dividing the structure into two and joining it with two glass bridges while giving the museum much-needed space. The original 19th-century museum (121 Barnard Street) is home to *The Bird Girl*, the now-famous statue that adorns the cover of *Midnight in the Garden*; she was relocated, like a federal witness, from Bonaventure Cemetery for her protection. The museum also operates tours of the nearly 200-year-old **Owens-Thomas House** (124 Abercorn Street). A combination ticket covers all three.

7 *School Fair* 5 p.m.

Shopping in Savannah is increasingly sophisticated, with recent additions like an imposing Marc by Marc Jacobs store on the rapidly gentrifying Broughton Street. But the most interesting retail is at **shopSCAD**, a boutique that sells the creations of the students, faculty, alumni, and staff of the Savannah College of Art and Design (340 Bull Street; 912-525-5180; shopscadonline.com). There is fine art — drawings, paintings, photography, and prints — as well as decorative and wearable items, including

hand-dyed ties by Jen Swearington ($48) and a pendant lamp by Christopher Moulder ($1,150).

8 *Crab Heaven* 7:30 p.m.

Forget about crab cakes, stuffed soft shells, or crabmeat au gratin. Crab is most rewarding when it is pure and unadulterated, served in a pile on newspaper with a can of beer and a blunt instrument for whacking at the shell. That, plus some boiled potatoes and corn, is what you will find at **Desposito's** (3520 Macceo Drive, Thunderbolt; 912-897-9963; $$), an unadorned shack in a onetime fishing village on the outskirts of town. This is not dining; this is working, but the sweet morsels are better than any payday.

9 *Drinking In the Scene* 9:30 p.m.

Many of Savannah's finest bars close early — often when the owners feel like it — so don't wait to start on your drink-by-drink tour. Begin at the **American Legion Post 135**, south of Forsyth Park (1108 Bull Street; 912-233-9277; alpost135.com), a surprisingly shimmery, mirrored space where the clientele is a mix of age and vocation. Proceed to the **Crystal Beer Parlor** (301 West Jones Street; 912-349-4113; crystalbeerparlor.com). On the outside, it's as

ABOVE The no-frills, low-priced Thunderbird Inn plays up its retro ambience.

anonymous as a speakeasy, which it was, but inside, its high-backed booths and colorful hanging lamps are more ice cream than booze. A full menu is available. Wind up at **Planters Tavern** (23 Abercorn Street; 912-232-4286), a noisy, low-ceilinged bar in the basement of the high-dollar Olde Pink House, a dignified restaurant in a 1771 house. With a fireplace on either end of the room, live music, and boisterous locals, it's the place to be.

SUNDAY

10 *Church's Chicken* 11 a.m.

Church and food go together in the South, and they do so especially well at the **Masada Café** (2301

West Bay Street; 912-236-9499), a buffet annex to the United House of Prayer for All People. The church has several locations in Savannah; this one is a mission of sorts, catering to the poor, but the inexpensive, revolving buffet of soul food classics like fried chicken and macaroni and cheese has gained a following among food critics and locals. Get there at 11 a.m. for the Sunday service, where the music and rhythmic hand-clapping surely share some DNA with the "ring shouts" of the Gullah-Geechee people, descendants of slaves who once lived on the nearby barrier islands.

OPPOSITE The ArtZeum inside the Jepson Center for the Arts, an addition to the Telfair Museum of Art.

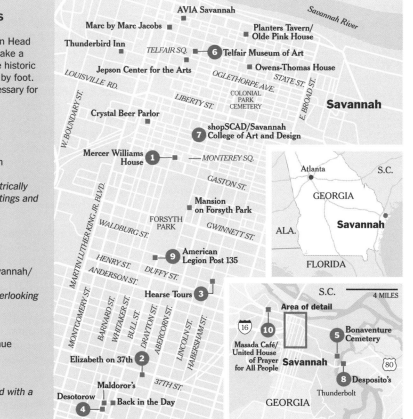

THE BASICS

Fly to the Savannah/Hilton Head International Airport and take a shuttle into Savannah. The historic district is easily traversed by foot. A cab or a car may be necessary for other destinations.

Mansion on Forsyth Park
700 Drayton Street
912-238-5158
mansiononforsythpark.com
$$$
A lavish 1888 home eccentrically decorated with garish paintings and an antique hat collection.

AVIA Savannah
14 Barnard Street
912-233-2116
aviahotels.com/hotels/savannah/
$$$
New, hip boutique hotel overlooking Ellis Square.

Thunderbird Inn
611 West Oglethorpe Avenue
912-232-2661
thethunderbirdinn.com
$$
A no-frills motel refurbished with a vintage flair.

St. Simons Island

The Golden Isles, the barrier islands of Georgia's coast, meld two worlds: the sunny beaches and lollygag pace of island life and the stately Spanish moss-draped grace of the South with antebellum graveyards and ruined plantations. St. Simons, about equidistant between Jacksonville, Fla., and Savannah, Ga., in particular is a literary haunt, home of writers' conferences and a favorite location of authors including Tina McElroy Ansa, whose popular black heroine, Lena McPherson, can see ghosts. Hidden amid the island's resorts and golf courses are remnants of the time when the only residents were Gullah-Geechee people, rice-tenders descended from slaves who speak their own blend of African languages and English. St. Simons, where oak trees turn avenues into tunnels of green, is the hub of the barrier islands, with about 13,000 residents and a bustling strip of restaurants and shops called the Village. — BY SHAILA DEWAN

FRIDAY

1 *On the Pier* 3 p.m.

Start at the **St. Simons Bait & Tackle** shop (121 Mallory Street; 912-634-1888), where you may win a greeting from the African gray parrot, Mr. Byrd (who has his own Facebook page), and rent fishing poles. Walk outside to the pier to try for anything from sheepshead to flounder, or just dangle the line in the water and daydream. A short stroll takes you to the **St. Simons Island Lighthouse**, built in 1872 after Confederates destroyed the original. It is a quaint white structure with a 360-degree observation deck overlooking St. Simons Sound and the mainland. And it gives you some exercise before you embark on a series of buttery, greasy, delicious Southern meals (912-638-4666; saintsimonslighthouse.org; arrive before 4:30 if you want to climb the tower).

2 *Crab Stew and a Beer* 5:30 p.m.

Head north on scenic Highway 17 to experience a true Georgia tradition, the seafood shack. **Hunter's Café** (there's no street address; call 912-832-5771 for

OPPOSITE The Avenue of Oaks at Sea Island resort.

RIGHT A "tree spirit" sculpture by Keith Jennings, one of several scattered around the island.

directions; $) is on a dirt road amid the marinas — or, as they are called here, fish camps — of Shellman Bluff, about a 30-minute drive toward Savannah. (The diners at the next table are likely to be fishermen just returned from a day in the salt marshes.) To the basic shack formula of bright lighting and linoleum floors, Hunter's has added a full bar and a screened porch overlooking the Broro River, but it maintains the customary disdain for any decoration not furnished by a taxidermist. Have the crab stew and fluffy oniony hushpuppies.

3 *Tree Spirits* 9 p.m.

Back on St. Simons, in the commercial district known as the Village, look for the green and yellow awning of **Murphy's Tavern** (415 Mallory Street; 912-638-8966), a favorite haunt of shrimpers, summer residents, and townies. Order a beer, pick someone out and suggest a game of pool. Outside, look for the face of a "tree spirit" carved into a huge old oak tree. A handful of these spirits, sculptures by Keith Jennings, are on public sites scattered around St. Simons; more are hidden away on private property.

SATURDAY

4 *The Breakfast Rush* 9 a.m.

Sit on the front patio and feast on the seafood omelet or the butter pecan French toast at the **4th**

of **May Café** (321 Mallory Street; 912-638-5444; 4thofmay.net; $), a popular Village restaurant named after the common birthday of the three original owners (two were twins). You're early, so you should beat the rush of retirees, young couples, families, tourists, and regulars who descend like gulls for breakfast.

5 *The Little Island* 10:30 a.m.

If you doze off when you hear the phrase "bird-watcher's paradise," just forget about the bird part and catch the boat to **Little St. Simons Island**, a private retreat where you can spend the day lying on the beach and touring the near-pristine live oak and magnolia forest. Two of the resort's main buildings are an old hunting lodge and a stunning cottage made of tabby, a stuccolike material of lime and oyster shells. Family owned, the resort is also family style, which means help yourself to towels, sunscreen, bug spray, and the beer set out in coolers on the porch. Most of the island has been left virtually untouched, and it is possible in one day to observe river otter, dolphins, the endangered greenfly orchid, and bald eagles, as well as roseate spoonbills and a host of other birds. The beach is littered with sand dollars and conch. A day trip is $75 a person and includes lunch, transportation to and from the island, a naturalist-guided tour, and time at the beach. You'll leave from the Hampton River Club Marina (1000 Hampton Point Drive on St. Simons) at 10:30 and will be back by 4:30. Reservations are required (the Lodge on Little St. Simons Island; 912-638-7472; littlessi.com).

6 *Alligator Hazard* 5:30 p.m.

Back on the big island, there's still time for nine holes of golf ($54) at the **King and Prince Golf Course**

ABOVE Christ Church, built by a lumber magnate mourning the death of his wife on their honeymoon.

RIGHT The King and Prince Golf Course, where you might see an alligator eyeing the golfers.

(100 Tabbystone; 912-634-0255; hamptonclub.com), a course that makes full use of the starkly beautiful marsh landscape. Ask to play 10 through 18; four of these holes are on little marsh islands connected by bridges. You'll putt surrounded by a sea of golden grasses that even non-golfers will appreciate. One hole is near an island with a resident alligator.

7 *Upscale Seafood* 8 p.m.

Settle in for drinks and a leisurely dinner at one of the fancy restaurants like **Halyards**, featuring Southern seafood dishes (55 Cinema Lane; 912-638-9100; halyardsrestaurant.com; $$-$$$), or the more traditional **Georgia Sea Grill** (310 Mallory Street; 912-638-1197; $$-$$$).

SUNDAY

8 *Church with a Past* 10 a.m.

It has history, it has literary significance, it has a tragic love story. But the thing to notice at Christ Church, Frederica, built in 1884 by a lumber magnate mourning the death of his wife on their honeymoon, is the thick, lambent lawn, one of the great unnoticed triumphs of Southern horticulture. **Christ Church, Frederica** (6329 Frederica Road; 912-638-8683) was a setting in a novel by Eugenia Price, who is buried in the graveyard there. The oldest grave dates to 1803. Across the street is a wooded garden dedicated

to Charles and John Wesley, who preached on St. Simons in the 1730s as Anglicans; they later returned to England and founded the Methodist Church.

9 *Bicycle-Friendly* 11:30 a.m.

The exclusive **Lodge at Sea Island** (100 Retreat Avenue; 912-638-3611; seaisland.com) is off limits to all but guests and members. But if you go by bike you may be able to sneak a peek of its grounds and the ruins of Retreat Plantation's hospital, where slaves were treated. You'll also experience the island's bicycle-friendly avenues, lined with tremendous 150-year-old oaks. Rent a bike for $15 to $20 a day at **Ocean Motion** (1300 Ocean Boulevard; 912-638-5225) or **Wheel Fun Rentals** (532 Ocean Boulevard; 912-634-0606),

head south following the road around the tip of the island, and make a left on Frederica Road to reach the Avenue of Oaks, which leads to the guard house of the Lodge before it loops back to Frederica Road. You can ask to see the ruins just inside the grounds. If you're ambitious, venture onto the Torras Causeway, which leads to the mainland and has a bike path.

ABOVE Rent a fishing pole and drop in a line.

THE BASICS

Fly into Savannah/Hilton Head International Airport or Jacksonville International Airport. Rent a car for the 90-minute drive from either airport, and then use it to stay mobile.

King and Prince Beach & Golf Resort
201 Arnold Road
912-638-3631
kingandprince.com
$$$-$$$$
A sprawling 75-year-old full-service resort with guest rooms, villas, and cabanas.

The Lodge at Sea Island Resorts
100 Retreat Avenue
866-879-6238
seaisland.com
$$$$
Close to golf courses; 24-hour butler service.

Ocean Inn & Suites
599 Beachview Drive
912-634-2122
oceaninnsuites.com
$-$$
Within walking distance of the Village and the lighthouse.

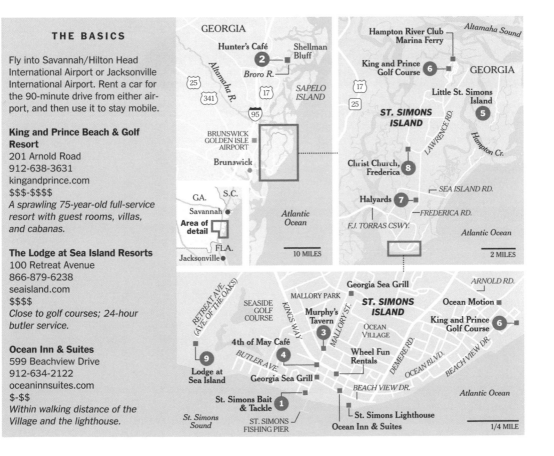

Orlando

People who live in the Orlando area will tell you that there is life here beyond the theme parks, gator farms, and citrus groves. You can't go far without stumbling upon a picturesque lake, and the area abounds with small regional museums like the Zora Neale Hurston National Museum of Fine Arts in nearby Eatonville. Downtown, the new Amway Center, home of the Orlando Magic, has given a boost to the nightlife district on Church Street. And Orlando's many neighborhoods are home to lounge acts, bars, vintage fast-food joints, and brick-paved streets. — BY SHAILA DEWAN

FRIDAY

1 *Plunge In* 2 p.m.

Wakeboarding is to water skiing what snow-boarding is to downhill skiing — in other words, the extreme version of the sport — and Orlando likes to call itself the "wakeboarding capital of the world." At the **Orlando Watersports Complex** (8615 Florida Rock Road; 407-251-3100; orlandowatersports.com), a beginner's cable tow, anchored to poles in the lake, pulls you and your wakeboard around at 17 miles per hour. The patient instructor will give you pointers, and you can watch some of the sport's best-known hot-doggers navigate the ramps and slides.

2 *High Design* 5 p.m.

Just a few miles from downtown Orlando, Winter Park — considered part of the greater Orlando area — is famous for the brick-paved streets of chichi chocolatiers and boutiques along Park Avenue. But across the railroad tracks near Hannibal Square, a coda has popped up with a bent toward high design. Amid the new shops and restaurants, you can find **Rifle Paper Co.** (558 West New England Avenue, Suite 150; 407-622-7679; riflepaperco.com), the fashionable Orlando-based stationer, and the studio and storefront where **Makr Carry Goods** churns out its minimalist leather bags and iPod cases (444 West New England Avenue, Suite 102; 407-284-0192; makr.com).

OPPOSITE Wakeboarding on the advanced cable tow at the Orlando Watersports Complex.

RIGHT The strip-mall location may be uninspiring, but dinner at the Ravenous Pig in Winter Park is worth the trip.

For a taste of local history, visit the **Hannibal Square Heritage Center** (642 West New England Avenue; 407-539-2680; hannibalsquareheritagecenter.org), where a collection of photographs and oral histories document the area's early role as a Reconstruction-era community for freed slaves.

3 *Dress Up, Dress Down* 7 p.m.

From the outside, the **Ravenous Pig** (1234 North Orange Avenue, Winter Park; 407-628-2333; theravenouspig.com; $$$) looks like your average strip-mall restaurant. But with attention to detail like house-made sour mix at the bar and much-in-demand cheese biscuits, James and Julie Petrakis have made their gastropub one of Orlando's most popular gathering spots. The menu, like the restaurant, is dress-up/dress-down, with bar fare like mussels and fries dusted with fennel pollen or more dignified entrees like dry-aged strip steak with wild mushroom bread pudding. Reserve a table or hover in the bar.

4 *Lounge Act* 10 p.m.

If the **Red Fox Lounge** (110 South Orlando Avenue, Winter Park; 407-647-1166) were an amusement park, it might be called ToupeeWorld. This stuck-in-amber hotel bar in a Best Western hotel appeals to a broad cross-section of Orlando, from retirees to young professionals to a drinking club whose members wear identical captain's hats. The main draw is the consummate lounge act. Mark Wayne and Lorna Lambey deliver silky, singalong versions of "Sweet Caroline," "Hava Nagila," and other golden oldies.

SATURDAY

5 *Tiffany Extravaganza* 10 a.m.

Louis Comfort Tiffany's masterpiece was Laurelton Hall, his estate on Long Island, which featured a wisteria blossom window over 30 feet long and a terrace whose columns were crowned in glass daffodils. When the house burned in 1957, Jeanette and Hugh McKean, from Winter Park, rescued those pieces and many more, adding them to what would become the most comprehensive collection of Tiffany glass, jewelry, and ceramics in the world. The collection, including a chapel with a stunning peacock mosaic that was made for the Chicago World's Fair in 1893, is housed in the **Morse Museum of American Art** (445 North Park Avenue, Winter Park; 407-645-5311; morsemuseum.org), where a new wing allows the largest Laurelton Hall pieces, including the daffodil terrace, to be on permanent display.

6 *A Fast-Food Original* Noon

Devotees of American fast food in all its glory will not want to miss the roast beef sandwiches and cherry milkshakes at **Beefy King**, a lunchtime standby for more than four decades (424 North Bumby Avenue; 407-894-2241; beefyking.com; $). Perch on the old-fashioned swivel chairs and admire the vintage logo of a snorting steer, also available on hot pink T-shirts.

7 *Pontoon Tour* 3 p.m.

Orlando is not quite an American Venice, but it does have about 100 lakes, many connected by narrow canals. Despite the alligators, the lakes are prime real estate, and at **Lake Osceola**, you can board a pontoon boat and take an hourlong cruise (**Scenic Boat Tour;** 312 East Morse Boulevard; 407-644-4056; scenicboattours.com) that will provide glimpses of Spanish colonial-style mansions, azalea gardens, stately Rollins College, and moss-laden cypresses. The ride is billed as Florida's longest continuously running tourist attraction, though you are likely to find plenty of locals aboard. The guide will entertain you with celebrity anecdotes, a smattering of history, and a reasonably small number of cheesy jokes. Tours leave on the hour.

8 *Cultural Fusion* 6 p.m.

The city of theme parks does have a studious side, as evidenced in a blossoming neighborhood called College Park, where the streets have names like Harvard and Vassar and where Jack Kerouac wrote *Dharma Bums*. The main commercial drag, Edgewater Drive, is chockablock with local favorites like **K Restaurant** (1710 Edgewater Drive; 407-872-2332; kwinebar.com; $$), where the servers'

ABOVE The Morse Museum of American Art.

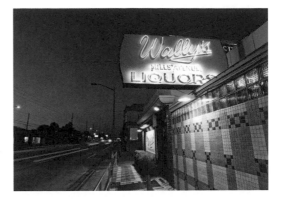

habit of asking for and using your name makes you feel like a regular. With an appetizer of crispy pig's ear on a salad with peanuts and cilantro, the chef gives a nod to Vietnamese flavors that abound in Orlando. At **Infusion Tea** (1600 Edgewater Drive; 407-999-5255; infusionorlando.com; $), choose from dozens of loose teas like Organic Monkey-Picked Oolong to go along with chocolate-coated Cheerios or a cupcake. Or you can choose among the scarves, vintage aprons, and jewelry at the attached artists' collective.

9 *Dive-Bar Hopping* 10 p.m.

Stiff drinks and dive bars are an Orlando staple; much of the night life is centered in the ViMi district, for Virginia Drive and Mills Avenue. Arguably the king of dives is **Wally's Mills Avenue Liquors** (1001 North Mills Avenue; 407-896-6975), with a U-shaped bar and tobacco-stained wallpaper with a motif of naked women. Across the street is the concrete-floored **LMGA**, or Lou's Music, Gaming, and Alcohol (1016 North Mills Avenue; 407-898-0009; myspace.com/unclelousorlando), where the owner,

known as Uncle Lou, wears headphones to block out noise of band concerts. Farther down, **Will's Pub** (1042 North Mills Avenue; 407-898-5070; myspace.com/willspub) has pool tables and indie bands.

SUNDAY

10 *Sweet Potato Hash* 11 a.m.

You never know what will turn up on the improvised brunch menu — a slip of notebook paper with a ballpoint scrawl — at **Stardust Video and Coffee** (1842 East Winter Park Road, 407-623-3393; $), a hub for

ABOVE Wally's, a stop on the dive-bar circuit.

BELOW A Winter Park canal, part of the Orlando area's abundant supply of lakes and connecting waterways.

Orlando's artistic class. Zucchini pancakes, maybe, or vegan sweet potato hash with eggs and (real) bacon. The Web site advertises "bathroom yoga" and "parking lot bingo," but you're more likely to find art installations, an old-fashioned photo booth, and a slew of obscure videos and DVDs for rent on the shelves at the far end of this sunny, airy space. There is a full bar for the performances, screenings, and lectures that unfold here in the later hours.

11 *Fool's Gold, Real Finds* 2 p.m.

Flea markets can offer too many tube socks and T-shirts, while antiques markets can be entirely too stuffy. **Renningers Twin Markets** in Mount Dora (20651 Highway 441; renningers.com), about a 30-minute drive from downtown, puts the thrill back in the hunt. Just past the main entrance, you can turn right and head to a vast antiques barn crammed with treasures like meticulously constructed wooden model ships and 19th-century quilts. Or you can turn left for the flea and farmers' market, where home-grown orchids and leather motorcycle chaps compete for attention. Behind that, there is a field where curio dealers set up tables with all manner of bona fide junk, fool's gold, and the occasional real finds that make it clear why so many thrift aficionados make road trips to Florida.

OPPOSITE The Morse Museum of American Art displays an extensive collection of works by Louis Comfort Tiffany.

THE BASICS

Orlando's busy airport is served by many major airlines.

A car is necessary in Florida's Sunbelt sprawl.

Eō Inn and Spa
227 N. Eola Drive
407-481-8485
eoinn.com
$$
Boutique on swan-infested Lake Eola. Good base for exploring Orlando beyond the theme parks.

Peabody Orlando
9801 International Drive
407-352-4000
peabodyorlando.com
$$-$$$
Luxury accommodations and a famous twice-daily duck parade.

Grand Bohemian Hotel
325 South Orange Avenue
407-313-9000
grandbohemianhotel.com
$$$
Swankiest hotel downtown.

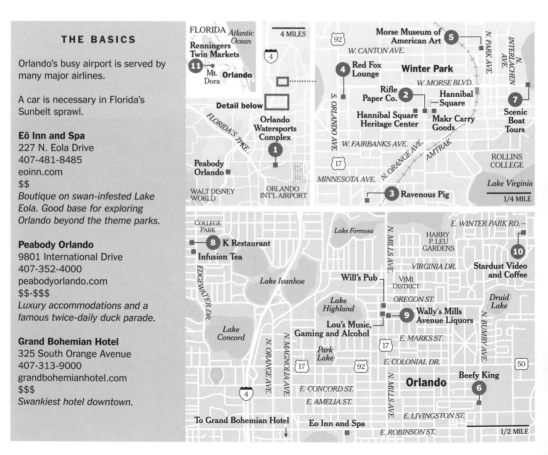

Cape Canaveral

The glory days of the space program, when regular flights to the moon left from Cape Canaveral, are far in the past, but NASA still has a presence, the local area code is still 321, and the Kennedy Space Center remains the conservator of proud national memories. In other ways, this part of Florida is still coming into its own. Cocoa Beach, just south on the long stretch of barrier sand and islands off the state's central Atlantic coast, has been thoroughly discovered, though it still feels almost unspoiled in comparison to the condo-towered shores of South Florida. Canaveral has emerged as a busy cruise port. And there's more to see, from citrus groves and wild protected seashores to one of the country's best surf shops. Feeling hungry? You can dine on fine French cuisine or fresh Florida seafood — or just head to a local souvenir shop for some freeze-dried ice cream, an astronaut favorite.
— BY CHARLES PASSY

FRIDAY

1 *Ocean Outreach* 6 p.m.
The lovably scruffy side of an older Florida reveals itself at the **Cocoa Beach Pier** (401 Meade Avenue, Cocoa Beach; cocoabeachpier.com), a 44-year-old hangout that stretches some 800 feet into the Atlantic Ocean. You come here to drink, dine, or fish — the pier is dotted with stores, bars, and restaurants, both indoors and outdoors — or just take in the expansive view. The pier scene really hops during the Friday-night Boardwalk Bash, when bands perform. Enjoy a cold one and some bar fare (wings, burgers, fish and chips) at **Marlins Good Times Bar & Grill** while listening to the music.

2 *Hang 10, 24/7* 8 p.m.
Who doesn't feel the need to go surfboard shopping on a Friday night? O.K., so maybe you're not ready to plunk down $1,000 to ride the waves in style, but the selections at the justly famous flagship **Ron Jon Surf Shop** (4151 North Atlantic Avenue, Cocoa Beach; 321-799-8888; ronjonsurfshop.com)

OPPOSITE The Rocket Garden at the Kennedy Space Center.

RIGHT Partying comes with a view at the Cocoa Beach Pier, which juts 800 feet out into the Atlantic.

go beyond boards and surfing gear. The two-story, 52,000-square-foot store, which is open 24 hours a day — and claims to be visited by more than two million people annually — also sells beachwear, shot glasses, Polynesian kitsch, and other "why did I buy that?" items. A spirit of endless hooky pervades, as evidenced by the T-shirt for sale that says, "I was on summer vacation for 20 years."

SATURDAY

3 *Breakfast Cubano* 8 a.m.
While Cuban food is most associated with the Miami area, the Canaveral area can lay claim to one of the state's best spots — **Roberto's Little Havana Restaurant** (26 North Orlando Avenue, Cocoa Beach; 321-784-1868; robertoslittlehavana.com; $). It's a downtown Cocoa Beach favorite serving all the Cuban classics, from palomilla steak to fried yuca to flan. But at breakfast time, it's the place to be for an egg-bacon-cheese sandwich, served on soft Cuban bread. Good Cuban coffee, too.

4 *Citrus Stop* 9:30 a.m.
You're a few miles from the Indian River fruit area that is one of Florida's legendary spots for citrus groves. So you'll have to stop for some liquid sunshine. **Policicchio Groves** (5780 North Courtenay Parkway (Route 3); Merritt Island; 321-452-4866;

juicycitrus.com), a family enterprise nearly nine decades old, has an assortment of oranges and grapefruits; the varieties change each month during the winter and the spring-to-early-summer growing seasons. Everything is freshly picked; the groves are across the road. The store will help you pack and ship the bounty.

5 *A Space Odyssey* 10:30 a.m.

Go north on Route 3 and left on NASA Parkway (Route 405) for the **Kennedy Space Center Visitor Complex** (321-449-4444; kennedyspacecenter.com). The complex may vaguely resemble one of Florida's theme parks at first, and the ticket prices suggest something of the kind. But very soon it becomes much more inspiring. Start with a walk through the Rocket Garden, an open-air space that features awe-inspiring Redstone, Atlas, and Titan rockets that date from the days of the Mercury and Gemini missions; you can also squeeze into replicas of the capsules the astronauts used. But that's the appetizer to the space center's main course — a roughly three-hour bus tour that gives you a sense of how big the center truly is (some 140,000 acres, including the surrounding wildlife refuge). Along the way, you'll pass the Vehicle Assembly Building — a structure so cavernous that clouds are said to have formed inside it. The tour's most jaw-dropping stop is the Apollo/Saturn V Center, a huge hangar that contains an actual Saturn V rocket. Take time to look at the individual exhibits about the Apollo program, all presented with extraordinary detail.

6 *Close Encounter* 2:45 p.m.

Now that you've gotten yourself acquainted (or reacquainted) with the space program, it's time to meet a real astronaut. The center's Astronaut Encounter affords an opportunity to do just that. Veterans of the space program, mostly from the shuttle era, give daily 30-minute presentations about their experiences and field questions from the audience. (There are at least three presentations

daily, with one generally at mid-afternoon.) Want a little more face time? For an extra fee, you can sign up for lunch with an astronaut. Among those who have participated in both the encounter and lunch programs are the Apollo 15 astronaut Al Worden and the six-time shuttle veteran Story Musgrave.

7 *Astronaut Memorial* 3:30 p.m.

About two dozen astronauts have died in their attempts to slip "the surly bonds of earth," as the World War II pilot John Gillespie Magee Jr. put it in a poem quoted by President Reagan after the 1986 Challenger disaster. Those men and women are remembered at the center's simple, stark Space Mirror Memorial — a black granite surface in which the names are inscribed. When the light is at the right angle, the names seem to float in space.

8 *Au Côte d'Espace* 7 p.m.

The Cape Canaveral area may not be a citadel of fine dining, but **Café Margaux** (220 Brevard Avenue, Cocoa; 321-639-8343; cafemargaux.com; $$$) is an exception to the rule. This quaint restaurant, set in the tree-lined Cocoa Village district, is proudly French, with a few nods elsewhere. The wine list places equal emphasis on New and Old World vintages.

SUNDAY

9 *Natural Habitat* 10 a.m.

It takes a lot of surrounding land to keep the Kennedy Space Center's launch sites properly isolated. Much of that acreage is encompassed

within the buffer zone that is the **Merritt Island National Wildlife Refuge** (321-861-0667; fws.gov/ merrittisland), a huge, mostly untouched tract that is home to migratory birds and bald eagles. Begin your journey by picking up a map at one of the kiosks near the entrances to the refuge (the small visitor's center may be closed if you're in the wrong season), and then head to the gloriously remote beaches, which are part of the separately managed **Canaveral National Seashore** (321-267-1110; nps.gov/cana). Conclude with a visit to the refuge's Black Point Wildlife Drive — a seven-mile loop that allows you to get close to wildlife, including alligators and egrets, without leaving your car.

10 *In the Realm of the Shrimp* 1 p.m.
    The family-owned **Dixie Crossroads Seafood Restaurant** (1475 Garden Street, Titusville; 321-268-5000; dixiecrossroads.com; $$-$$$) is mostly

about shrimp. It has its own fleet of about 10 full-time commercial shrimpers, which provide the restaurant with its lobsterlike rock shrimp and more firmly textured Royal Red shrimp, among other Florida varieties. (Once you try these, you'll find it hard to go back to garden-variety frozen shrimp.) The shrimp can be had broiled, fried, or steamed. But before you dig in, you'll get to enjoy the corn fritter starters included with every meal. The bustling setting is also a hoot — part Old Florida (wildlife murals and a fish pond), part pure kitsch. You can pose outside with Mr. and Mrs. Rock — cartoonish statues of a rock shrimp family.

OPPOSITE ABOVE Sunrise surfing at the pier.

OPPOSITE BELOW Oranges for the buying at Policicchio Groves. Florida's famous Indian River citrus-growing region is just inland from Cape Canaveral.

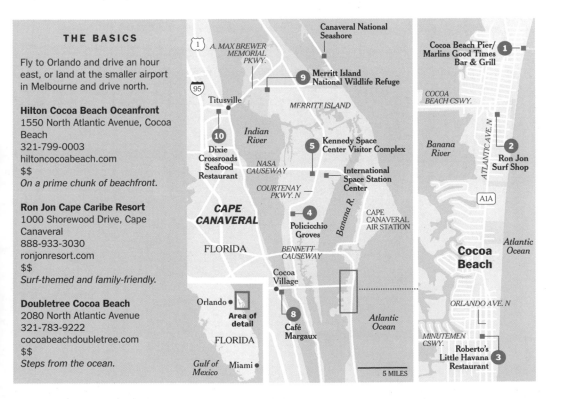

THE BASICS

Fly to Orlando and drive an hour east, or land at the smaller airport in Melbourne and drive north.

Hilton Cocoa Beach Oceanfront
1550 North Atlantic Avenue, Cocoa Beach
321-799-0003
hiltoncocoabeach.com
$$
On a prime chunk of beachfront.

Ron Jon Cape Caribe Resort
1000 Shorewood Drive, Cape Canaveral
888-933-3030
ronjonresort.com
$$
Surf-themed and family-friendly.

Doubletree Cocoa Beach
2080 North Atlantic Avenue
321-783-9222
cocoabeachdoubletree.com
$$
Steps from the ocean.

Palm Beach

The tiny island of Palm Beach, on Florida's southeast coast, boasts some of the country's dreamiest estates, where the staff lives better than many Americans, cashmere sweaters in trademark pastel greens and pinks go for $800, and Rolls-Royces show up at the supermarket with regularity. Some Palm Beachers had to tighten their Gucci belts in the wake of the Bernard Madoff scandal; he selected many of his victims at the local golf club. But judging by the perfectly clipped hedges that envelop the manicured mansions, most residents may be doing with less, but not much less, in a town where more is never quite enough.
— BY GERALDINE FABRIKANT

FRIDAY

1 *The Big Gape* 4 p.m.
   Big money means big house, so rent a nice convertible and stare. For envy-inducing views of these winter palaces, drive south along **South Ocean Boulevard** for about six miles starting at Barton Avenue. Even those obsessed with privacy relish their ocean views (why pay millions for beachfront if you can't enjoy it?), which means the gates and hedges along these mansions are slightly lower than elsewhere in town. You can catch a glimpse of the Mar-a-Lago Club, Donald Trump's former residence and now a private club he owns.

2 *Grande Dame* 6:30 p.m.
   For a sunset cocktail, glide into the **Breakers Hotel** (1 South County Road; 561-655-6611; thebreakers.com), originally built in 1896. So central is its location that the hotel has been rebuilt twice after fires destroyed it. The Seafood Bar has delightful views of the sea. If you prefer upholstered opulence, head for the Tapestry Bar with its two Flemish tapestries and a grand bar built from a mantel from Caxton Hall in London.

3 *Diner's Club* 8:30 p.m.
   Palm Beach dining runs from supremely pretentious to casually simple. Many restaurants survive over decades, and because Palm Beach is a small town, where the same cast shows up frequently, they have the feel of private clubs. The **Palm Beach Grill** (340 Royal Poinciana Way; 561-835-1077; palmbeachgrill.com; $$$) is a darkly wooded, dimly lighted social fixture that is a favorite of the author James Patterson and almost everyone else. If the mobbed dining room is for the island's old guard, the bar seems to attract newcomers: snowbirds deciding whether to move South, city types longing for a slower, more glamorous life, and locals who want to have fun. Don't miss American classics like spare ribs and ice cream sundaes. Book before you fly.

SATURDAY

4 *Empty Beaches* 8 a.m.
   Park on **South Ocean Boulevard** and take a long, languorous walk on the beach. The beaches here are flat, wide, clean, and wonderful in the early morning when there are not many people around.

5 *Early Snowbirds* 9 a.m.
   This may be a party town, but it wakes up early. A clutch of restaurants along Royal Poinciana Way are busy by 8:30 a.m., with diners sitting outside and savoring the sunshine and breakfast. **Testa's**

OPPOSITE The lobby at the Breakers, the iconic Palm Beach hotel where the wealthy have long come to be pampered.

BELOW For drive-by glimpses of the waterfront mansions, head out along South Ocean Boulevard.

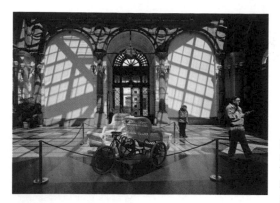

Palm Beach Restaurant (221 Royal Poinciana Way; 561-832-0992; testasrestaurants.com; $$), a sprawling, relaxed space, serves blueberry, pecan, and bran pancakes. Around the corner is **Green's Pharmacy** (151 North County Road; 561-832-4443; $$), which offers breakfast at an old-fashioned lunch counter. Afterward, pick up candy buttons and other long-forgotten stuff.

6 *History Class* 10:30 a.m.

For an authentic sense of Palm Beach in its early days, drop by the **Flagler Museum** (1 Whitehall Way; 561-655-2833; flaglermuseum.us). It was once the home of Henry Morrison Flagler, one of the founders of Standard Oil and the man who brought the railroad to southern Florida. He spent millions in 1902 to build the 55-room house that became a hotel and finally a museum.

7 *Retail Strut* Noon

On Worth Avenue, where every brand that you've seen in *Vogue* has a storefront, the real fun is the crowd: women in green cashmere sweaters walking dogs in matching outfits; elderly gents with bow ties and blazers. But the true gems — Cartier aside — are the smaller, lesser-known stores that have survived by wit and originality. **Maryanna Suzanna** (313 Worth Avenue; 561-833-0204) carries colorful jewelry by Monies and the Italian designer Angela Caputi — some earrings are under $50. Across the street, **Sherry Frankel's Melangerie** (256 Worth Avenue; 561-655-1996) will custom-embroider anything and sells amusing plastic watches for $68. And nearby is **Il Sandalo** (240 Worth Avenue; 561-805-8674; ilsandalo.com), where the shoemaker

ABOVE The Flagler Museum, once the lavish home of Henry Clay Flagler, a founder of Standard Oil. One of the items on display is his private railway car.

RIGHT The Blue Martini in West Palm Beach, the humbler sister town across the Intracoastal Waterway.

Hernan Garcia makes custom sandals starting at around $200. For lunch, head to **Ta-boo** (221 Worth Avenue; 561-835-3500; taboorestaurant.com; $$$), with its British colonial décor, where women swathed in white linen and wearing enormous straw hats pick carefully at the chopped chef's salad.

8 *Gilt Trip* 3:30 p.m.

It's a challenge to fill those sprawling estates with furniture, but there are armies of antiques merchants poised to try. Antiques enthusiasts can start at the elegant French dealer **Cedric Dupont** (820 South Dixie Highway; 561-835-1319; cedricdupontantiques.com) and go all the way south to Southern Boulevard to **The Elephant's Foot** (3800 South Dixie Highway; 561-832-0170; theelephantsfootantiques.com), which has a range of English, French, and Oriental antiques at varying prices. Or for a resale find, try **Circa Who** (531 Northwood Road; 561-655-5224; circawho.com), with faux bamboo, and Old Florida furniture.

9 *Mediterranean Flavor* 8 p.m.

For a casual dinner in the heart of town, head to **Cucina Dell'Arte** (257 Royal Poinciana Way; 561-655-0770; cucinadellarte.com; $$$), which is popular with a younger crowd and is open until 3 a.m. It is decorated in the earth tones and mustards and peaches typical of the Mediterranean and seems

to be busy all day with families, couples, and groups of friends. You can eat outdoors and watch the crowds go by.

10 *Party Time* 10:30 p.m.

There are plenty of multi-carat jewels in Palm Beach, but they are generally worn at private parties. The night life for visitors is casual. Stop in for a drink at the very pretty **Brazilian Court Hotel** (301 Australian Avenue; 561-655-7740; thebraziliancourt.com). You might try a Bikini Martini, with Sagatiba cachaça and passion fruit purée. On Saturdays a small band or D.J. plays in the lobby until 1 a.m., attracting a preppy crowd. Or head across the bridge to **Blue Martini** (CityPlace, 550 South Rosemary Avenue, West Palm Beach; 561-835-8601; bluemartinilounge.com) in a trendy shopping mall, where you can sip a martini and hear the music pour out of B. B. King's Blues Club next door.

SUNDAY

11 *Hit the Trail* 10 a.m.

A flat and easy bike trail hugs the Intracoastal Waterway, which skirts the west side of Palm Beach, and offers fantastic views of the Marina in West Palm Beach. Rent a bike at **Palm Beach Bicycle Trail Shop** (223 Sunrise Avenue; 561-659-4583; palmbeachbicycle.com), which has multispeed bikes. If biking is not your thing, you can jog the route.

ABOVE Palm Beach feels exclusive, but the beach is public. Walk it in the early morning, when few people are out.

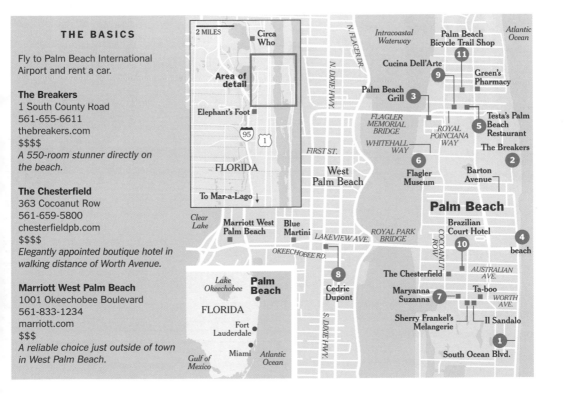

THE BASICS

Fly to Palm Beach International Airport and rent a car.

The Breakers
1 South County Road
561-655-6611
thebreakers.com
$$$$
A 550-room stunner directly on the beach.

The Chesterfield
363 Cocoanut Row
561-659-5800
chesterfieldpb.com
$$$$
Elegantly appointed boutique hotel in walking distance of Worth Avenue.

Marriott West Palm Beach
1001 Okeechobee Boulevard
561-833-1234
marriott.com
$$$
A reliable choice just outside of town in West Palm Beach.

Fort Lauderdale

Fort Lauderdale continues to mature beyond its spring-break days, with posh resorts now rising along the beach. Meanwhile, Las Olas Boulevard, the lively commercial strip that links the beach to downtown, has welcomed an array of new boutiques and restaurants. Sure, a smattering of raucous bars still dot the beach, and the rowdy clubgoers of Himmarshee Village can be three deep in the middle of the week. But at the end of a sunny, water-logged day, this Florida resort town offers a sophisticated evening that doesn't involve neon bikinis and syrupy daiquiris. — BY GERALDINE FABRIKANT

FRIDAY

1 *Seaside Dusk* 5 p.m.

There are a slew of beachfront spots where you can have a drink, watch the clouds roll over the ocean, soak up the sea air, and catch the parade of sun-soaked tourists and residents going home in suits and ties. Two of the more welcoming are **Margarita Cantina Crab and Seafood House** (201 Fort Lauderdale Beach Boulevard; 954-463-7209), where you can sip a chardonnay and listen to the steel band, and the quieter **H2O Café** (101 South Fort Lauderdale Beach Boulevard; 954-414-1024; h2ocafe.net) next door.

2 *Waterfront Wahoo* 7 p.m.

Fort Lauderdale's dining scene is alive and well inland as well as on the water. The **Bimini Boatyard Bar and Grill** (1555 Southeast 17th Street; 954-525-7400; biminiboatyard.com; $$) evokes a New England-style boathouse with its crisp blue and white décor, enormous cathedral ceiling, gleaming oak floors, and portal-style windows. An outdoor bar facing a marina brings in a nautical mix of young and old who dine on fresh seafood like wood-grilled wahoo and yellowtail snapper.

3 *Nice and Cool* 9 p.m.

For a cool nightcap, slide over to **Blue Jean Blues** (3320 Northeast 33rd Street; 954-306-6330;

OPPOSITE Sunrise at Anglin's Pier.

RIGHT The International Swimming Hall of Fame. Among the curious facts to learn inside: Leonardo da Vinci and Benjamin Franklin both experimented with swim fins.

bluejeanblues.net), where you can sit at the bar and listen to live jazz and blues bands. The club has a tiny stage and a dance floor, and the music can go from jazz to Caribbean depending on the evening.

SATURDAY

4 *Dawn Patrol* 8 a.m.

Take an early morning stroll along the wide, white beach. It is open to joggers, walkers, and swimmers and is surprisingly clean. For a leafier, more secluded adventure that is a favorite with resident runners and walkers, try the two-mile loop through the woods in the **Hugh Taylor Birch State Park** (954-468-2791; floridastateparks.org/hughtaylorbirch). Its entrance is only steps from the beach at the intersection of A1A and Sunrise Highway. If you're not a jogger, take a drive through anyway.

5 *Sunny Nosh* 10 a.m.

Finish off the jog at the beachside **Ritz-Carlton** (1 North Fort Lauderdale Beach Boulevard; 954-465-2300; ritzcarlton.com/fortlauderdale). The Ritz-Carlton Hotel Company bought the former St. Regis and put its own stamp on the property. For a relaxed breakfast (served until 11 a.m.), either indoors or out, go to **Via Luna** ($$$), the hotel's restaurant, where you can choose your fare from a buffet with omelets, smoked salmon, cereals, and fruit.

6 *Eccentric Estate* 1 p.m.

Bonnet House (900 North Birch Road; 954-563-5393; bonnethouse.org) was the vacation

night-life scene; one spot to try is the ever-popular **Georgie's Alibi** (2266 Wilton Drive; 954-565-2526; georgiesalibi.com).

home of the artists and art patrons Frederic Bartlett and his wife, Evelyn, whose first husband was the grandson and namesake of the founder of Eli Lilly and Company. They created an eccentric, brightly painted retreat, now a museum — more Caribbean mansion than Florida estate — near a swamp where alligators thrived. Window bars protected the house from the panthers that once roamed the estate and the monkeys that still live there.

7 *Cruising the Pier* 3:30 p.m.

If you want to go a bit off the beaten track, drive up Route A1A to Commercial Boulevard and hang out on **Anglin's Pier**. There is a little shopping area for swim gear, and you can rent a fishing pole. Or just sit and have a coffee.

8 *Crabs or Pizza* 7 p.m.

One of the trendier new restaurants is **Truluck's**, at the Galleria Mall (2584A East Sunrise Boulevard; 954-396-5656; trulucks.com; $$$$). An elegant room with dark woods and red leather upholstery, it adds a bit of glamour to the popular mall and has a busy bar where a piano player entertains all evening. It has a surf-and-turf menu but is perhaps best known for stone crabs. For lighter fare, try **D'Angelo** (4215 North Federal Highway, Oakland Park; 954-561-7300; pizzadangelo.com; $), a modern Tuscan-style restaurant. It attracts a fashion-aware young crowd with its meatball tapas and Napoletana pizzas.

9 *Mall Party* 9 p.m.

It may not be spring break, but you would never know, looking at the huge crowds at the **Blue Martini**, at the Galleria Mall (2432 East Sunrise Boulevard; 954-653-2583; bluemartinilounge.com). But the patrons are decidedly more upscale. By 8 p.m. when the band is playing, the bar is packed with young professionals and snow birds, schmoozing and dancing. A newer place is **SoLita Las Olas** (1032 East Las Olas; 954-357-2616; solitalasolas.com), which has a lively bar. Fort Lauderdale also has a booming gay

10 *Southern Comfort* 11 a.m.

The **Pelican Grand Beach Resort** (2000 North Ocean Boulevard; 954-568-9431; pelicanbeach.com) offers a Sunday brunch with eggs Benedict, rice pilaf, bloody marys, and mimosas. The plantation-style restaurant overlooks the beach, with a big veranda with white wicker tables and rocking chairs that catch the sea breezes.

11 *Super Swimmers* 12:30 p.m.

Water enthusiasts should stop in at the **International Swimming Hall of Fame** (One Hall of Fame Drive; 954-462-6536; ishof.org). Did you know that both Leonardo da Vinci and Benjamin Franklin experimented with swim fins? Or that Polynesian

ABOVE The Bonnet House museum was the vacation home of the artists Frederic and Evelyn Bartlett in the days when panthers roamed the nearby swamps.

BELOW Morning exercise on the beach, with plenty of room for joggers, earlybird swimmers, and martial artists.

swimmers used palm leaves tied to their feet? Those and other nuggets of swimming trivia are lovingly conveyed at this sleek white building on the Intracoastal Waterway.

12 *Las Olas Stroll* 2 p.m.

In an era when shopping in new cities can remind you of every mall back home, Fort Lauderdale has kept its streak of independence: nothing fancy but fun. East Las Olas Boulevard has a rash of one-off stores. **Kumbaya** (No. 1012; 954-768-9004) carries colorful T-shirts and straw bags. **Seldom Seen Gallery** (No. 817; 954-527-7878; seldomseengallery.com) has a riot of wall clocks as well as brightly painted walking sticks. If you want

to take edible gifts home or you can't resist them yourself, drop in at **Kilwin's**, an ice cream, chocolate, and fudge shop (No. 809; 954-523-8338; kilwins. com). Its motto is "Life is uncertain. Eat dessert first." Ponder that over a bag of caramel corn as you explore the rest of the shops.

ABOVE Truluck's, a glamorous dinner spot known for seafood, especially its stone crab.

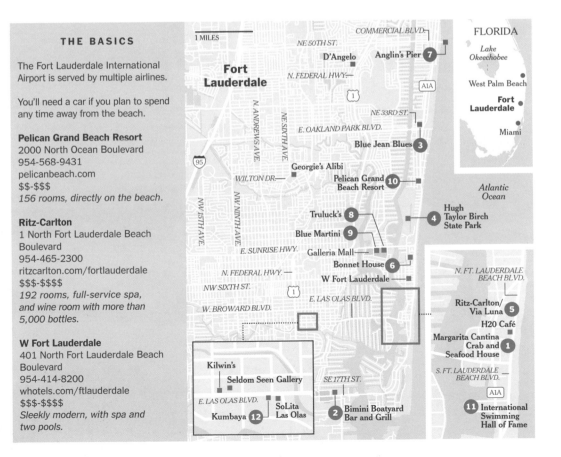

THE BASICS

The Fort Lauderdale International Airport is served by multiple airlines.

You'll need a car if you plan to spend any time away from the beach.

Pelican Grand Beach Resort
2000 North Ocean Boulevard
954-568-9431
pelicanbeach.com
$$-$$$
156 rooms, directly on the beach.

Ritz-Carlton
1 North Fort Lauderdale Beach Boulevard
954-465-2300
ritzcarlton.com/fortlauderdale
$$$-$$$$
192 rooms, full-service spa, and wine room with more than 5,000 bottles.

W Fort Lauderdale
401 North Fort Lauderdale Beach Boulevard
954-414-8200
whotels.com/ftlauderdale
$$$-$$$$
Sleekly modern, with spa and two pools.

1 MILES

FLORIDA

Lake Okeechobee

West Palm Beach

Fort Lauderdale

Miami

Atlantic Ocean

Fort Lauderdale

COMMERCIAL BLVD.
NE 50TH ST.
D'Angelo
Anglin's Pier 7
N. FEDERAL HWY.
A1A
NE 33RD ST.
E. OAKLAND PARK BLVD.
Blue Jean Blues 3
N. ANDREWS AVE.
NE SIXTH AVE.
Georgie's Alibi
WILTON DR.
Pelican Grand Beach Resort 10
Hugh Taylor Birch State Park
Truluck's 8
4
Blue Martini 9
NW NINTH AVE.
NW 15TH AVE.
E. SUNRISE HWY.
Galleria Mall
N. FEDERAL HWY.
Bonnet House 6
N. FT. LAUDERDALE BEACH BLVD.
NW SIXTH ST.
W Fort Lauderdale
E. LAS OLAS BLVD.
W. BROWARD BLVD.
Ritz-Carlton/ Via Luna 5
H20 Café
Margarita Cantina Crab and 1 Seafood House
Kilwin's
Seldom Seen Gallery
SE 17TH ST.
S. FT. LAUDERDALE BEACH BLVD.
E. LAS OLAS BLVD.
SoLita Las Olas
A1A
Kumbaya 12
Bimini Boatyard 2 Bar and Grill
11 International Swimming Hall of Fame

South Beach Miami

South Beach, that trendiest stretch of Miami Beach, Florida, gets a lot of abuse from residents. Too much cologne, critics say; too expensive, too crowded. But like other American meccas of decadence, SoBe still has an irresistible, democratic pull. For everyone from the pale Iowa retiree to the Bentley-driving rapper, it remains the place to strut shamelessly. And even jaded locals still indulge. They may not be taking photos. And perhaps they'll be dressed a bit more casually. But bet on this: They're checking in with the classics and keeping up with the latest trends like everyone else—except they don't need to flaunt it.
— BY DAMIEN CAVE

FRIDAY

1 *On the Boardwalk* 5 p.m.

The beach never gets old. For the timeless South Beach experience, amble along to the wooden boardwalk that extends from 21st to 47th Street before city planners can replace the raised platform with a ground-level path. Take in the views: on one side is the ocean; on the other, the crumbling, yet-to-be-renovated Art Deco hotels that offer a Pompeii-like look back at Miami Beach when diving boards and peach walls still dominated. Then dive into the present at the rooftop pool at the **Gansevoort South** (2377 Collins Avenue; 305-604-1000; gansevoortmiamibeach.com). Sip a SoBe Carnival (cachaça, pineapple juice, and muddled basil) and enjoy the views of either the ocean or the party people.

2 *Music, Not Dancing* 7 p.m.

House. Salsa. Hip-hop. South Beach has many soundtracks, but few musical institutions here are as beloved as the **New World Symphony** (500 17th Street; 305-673-3330; nws.edu), an orchestral academy founded by Michael Tilson Thomas, music director of the San Francisco Symphony. Providing mixed-media extravaganzas one night, free student concerts the next, it manages to be both high-brow

and accessible. You won't find it hard to locate the symphony's new home, designed by Frank Gehry and just a block north of its old location in the Art Deco Lincoln Theater.

3 *Designer Excursion* 9 p.m.

You could follow the herd to **Prime Italian** (101 Ocean Drive; 305-695-8484; primeitalianmiami.com), where Kobe meatballs are a specialty. But lighter, slow-food fare (at better prices) can be found across Biscayne Bay at **Fratelli Lyon** (4141 Northeast Second Avenue; 305-572-2901; fratellilyon.com). Just the fresh cheeses and artisanal olive oil make it worth the trip. Plus, you'll leave with energy to dance. So go straight to the **Florida Room** at Delano (1685 Collins Avenue; 305-674-6152; delano-hotel.com), where on most Fridays Angela Laino belts out funk and soul backed by a band rich with brass.

SATURDAY

4 *Sandy Stretch* 7 a.m.

In the 10-plus years that October Rose (yes, a real person) has offered yoga on South Beach (yogasouthbeach.org), it has become a 365-day-a-year institution. Sometimes there are as many as 20 people near the usual lifeguard stand at Third Street, each donating about $5. All that locust posing will make you hungry, so afterward head to **A La Folie** (516 Espanola Way; 305-538-4484; alafoliecafe.com; $), a hidden French gem, for a butter-sugar crepe with a cappuccino.

OPPOSITE A cruise ship glides past South Pointe, the southern tip of South Beach.

RIGHT Frolicking at the rooftop pool and bar of the Gansevoort South hotel.

5 *Vintage and Vixens* 11 a.m.

Sure, you could buy something new. The malls would love you for it. But why not be both cool and conservationist by going consignment? **Fly Boutique** (650 Lincoln Road; 305-604-8508; flyboutiquevintage.com) is overflowing with few-of-a-kind items, from Emilio Pucci scarves for less than $100 to classic Levi's and even Louis Vuitton luggage large enough for a move to Europe (though the trunk will cost you $1,495). **Beatnix** (1149 Washington Avenue; 305-532-8733; beatnixmiami.com) offers a costume-centric mix, heavy on the polyester. It's also where

South Beach's vixen bartenders buy their get-ups. For $149, Beatnix will make a corset-tutu combo.

6 *Read Your Lunch* 1 p.m.

Miamians sometimes joke that their most popular independent bookseller — **Books and Books** — should be renamed Book and Book because of how little residents read. Regardless, the food and service at its South Beach cafe (927 Lincoln Road; 305-532-3222; booksandbooks.com; $$) are as consistent as Carl Hiaasen's sense of humor. The Key West crab cakes are rich in flavor, but not too heavy, and the homemade cupcakes and Illy espresso might explain why Malcolm Gladwell and other writers spend hours lollygagging at the outdoor tables. Or maybe it really is the books.

7 *Fore!* 3 p.m.

Now it's time for some brawn. Try hitting a large bucket of balls at **Miami Beach Golf Club** (2301 Alton Road; 305-532-3350; miamibeachgolfclub.com). As you hook your drive toward the not-so-distant Atlantic, try to imagine the view in 1923, when the course opened, or during World War II, when the Army rented the course for $1 a day and tossed smoke grenades all over the greens.

LEFT Mac's Club Deuce is a classic dive bar.

8 *Go Gatsby* 8 p.m.

Travel back in time again. First stop, the **Betsy Hotel** (1440 Ocean Drive; 305-531-6100; thebetsyhotel.com), newly renovated to capture an old-fashioned charm that flappers could appreciate — especially in the surrounding sea of neon. The hotel's restaurant, **BLT Steak** (305-673-0044; bltsteak.com; $$$$), part of the upscale steakhouse chain, essentially sits in the lobby. All the better for watching the wealthy and established mix with the young and skimpy. The popovers and aged beef aren't bad either, though prices are best forgotten in a drunken haze.

9 *Highs and Lows* 11 p.m.

Remember when the villains of *Goldfinger* cheated at cards, or when Tony Montana in *Scarface* declared "This is paradise" by the pool? It was at the **Fontainebleau** (4441 Collins Avenue; 305-538-2000;

fontainebleau.com). And after a $1 billion renovation, the FB is back. If you can get past the velvet rope, sashay downstairs into **Liv**, the hotel nightclub where weekends usually include a big celebrity (Jennifer Lopez was one example). If that fails, drink martinis in the lobby, designed by Morris Lapidus, which was also restored. The famous bowtie-tile floors remain, as does the staircase to nowhere, designed solely for grand entrances. Finish the night down to earth, with some cheap beer and pool at **Mac's Club Deuce** (222 14th Street; 305-531-6200), a classic dive bar that draws drunks, drag queens, cops, and traveling executives.

OPPOSITE ABOVE Inside at the Betsy Hotel, renovated but with a charm that flappers could appreciate.

BELOW An early-morning yoga class on the beach with instructor October Rose.

SUNDAY

10 *The Deep End* 9 a.m.

South Pointe Park, at the tip of South Beach, has been treated to a $22 million facelift, and while it looks fantastic, some of the best sights are in the water. The water right off the pier is a great place for snorkeling, surfing, or fishing, with stingrays, bright tropical fish, and lots of colorful locals. You can rent a full snorkeling package for $20 a day at **Tarpoon Dive Center** (300 Alton Road; 305-532-1445; tarpoondivecenter.com).

11 *Soak and Go* Noon

Reliable regeneration can be found with brunch and a good spa cleansing at the **Standard Hotel** (40 Island Avenue; 305-673-1717; standardhotels.com), a 1920s motor lodge that André Balazs turned into a holistic oasis a few years ago. If you don't want to spring for a massage, try the much cheaper alternative of soaking in a scented private tub overlooking Biscayne Bay. Finish up by the pool with an ahi tuna niçoise salad and an Arnold Palmer — that would be half lemonade, half iced tea for all you non-Floridians.

ABOVE The newly refurbished South Pointe Park.

OPPOSITE SoundScape, a park just outside the new Frank Gehry-designed home of the New World Symphony.

THE BASICS

Fly to Miami International Airport and take a cab or shuttle to South Beach. Get around on foot and by cab.

W South Beach
2201 Collins Avenue
305-938-3000
wsouthbeach.com
$$$$
Among the swankiest of several new hotels.

The Gansevoort South
2377 Collins Avenue
305-604-1000
gansevoortmiamibeach.com
$$$$
The enormous pools are a highlight.

The Fontainebleau
4441 Collins Avenue
305-538-2000
fontainebleau.com
$$$$
Recapturing former glory after a $1 billion renovation.

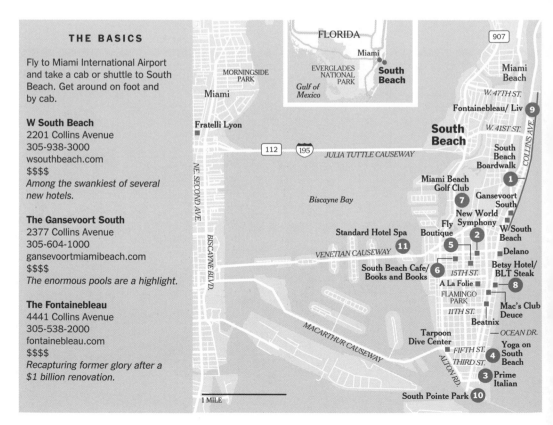

Cuban Miami

Cuban culture is as integral to the colorful fabric of Miami as the palm tree. One could be easily forgiven, in fact, for forgetting that the city's most ubiquitous import from Cuba—the cafecito window, where locals of all persuasions converge to down tiny shots of strong, sugary coffee—has not been a fixture here for as long as the sand or the Florida sun. Other elements play the same tricks on the mind, from minty mojitos to those boxy guayabera shirts, making it a challenge to spend even a few hours in Miami without experiencing at least a hint of its Cuban accent. But it's certainly possible to dig deeper, to be immersed in ways so distilled—through a host of nightclubs, cafes, museums, and galleries—that you could forget that you have not left the United States.
— BY BETH GREENFIELD

FRIDAY

1 *Miami's Ellis Island* 4 p.m.

The **Freedom Tower** (600 Biscayne Boulevard; 305-237-7700), a butter-yellow beacon in downtown Miami, served as an immigration processing center

OPPOSITE Biscayne Bay from the water's edge at Ermita de la Caridad, a shrine to displaced Cubans.

BELOW Watch the cigars being rolled at El Credito Cigar Factory, in the heart of Little Havana.

for more than 400,000 Cubans in the 1960s; today it's a National Historic Landmark that's owned by Miami-Dade College. During special exhibits, which the college holds here regularly (check mdc.edu for a schedule), you can step inside and gaze up at the 40-foot New World Mural, a twice-restored version of the 1925 original, depicting Ponce de Leon and the Tequesta chief standing before a map of the New World. But even if it's closed, the inspiring Spanish Renaissance Revival-style structure is worth a drive-by.

2 *A Banana Republic* 7 p.m.

There's another mural in the family-style dining room at **Islas Canarias** (285 Northwest 27th Avenue; 305-649-0440; islascanariasrestaurant.com; $$) —this one splashy and music-themed, with images of Cuban stars like Celia Cruz and Tito Puente playing in one big fantasy band. But the food is what really sings here; settle in for traditional specialties like Cuban-style pork chops, ropa vieja (shredded, spiced flank steak), or grilled sirloin, all served with the omnipresent sides of rice, yuca, and sweet plantains.

3 *For a Song* 10 p.m.

Have a heart-thumping live-music experience at **Hoy Como Ayer** (2212 Southwest 8th Street; 305-541-2631; hoycomoayer.us), a diminutive club in the legendary Little Havana neighborhood. (The club's name translates to Today as Yesterday.) You'll find a fired-up crowd decked out in suits, guayaberas, and slinky dresses, awaiting Cuban performers like Malena Burke or Amaury Gutierrez and nibbling on tapas of cheese cubes and tostones, served, cleverly, in cigar boxes. If the night is right you'll catch a show by Miami's own exile music queen, Albita Rodríguez, known simply as Albita. During one such performance there, between explosive numbers, she sang a passionate tribute: "Que culpa tengo yo de estas caderas? Que culpa tengo yo de este sabor? Que culpa tengo yo de haber nacido en Cuba?" ("What fault of mine are these hips? What fault of mine is this flavor? What fault of it is mine that I was born in Cuba?") By the end of the song, the entire house had joined in, erupting with extra gusto along with the final chant of "Cuba! Cuba!" punctuated by Albita's fist pumping into the air.

SATURDAY

4 *When Pressed* 9 a.m.

Enriqueta's (186 Northeast 29th Street; 305-573-4681; $), a bright orange family-owned diner, is a festive island on a gritty stretch in the city's Wynwood district. And it offers a delicious, traditional way to start your day — with a plantain omelet, guava empanada, mamey batido (shake), or even a medianoche, a pressed sandwich of roast pork, ham, cheese, and pickles on egg bread. Pair any option, of course, with a steaming café con leche.

5 *Eighth Is Enough* 11 a.m.

Though the majority of Cubans now live elsewhere in the region, Little Havana is still the symbolic heart of Cuban Miami. And the best starting place for an infusion of culture is its slightly scruffy, well-trafficked stretch of Southwest Eighth Street between 17th and 27th Avenues, known as **Calle Ocho**. It's defined by aromatic cigar and coffee shops, a perpetual blare of salsa trumpets wafting from the distance, and the domino and chess games of older men who gather daily in tiny **Maximo Gómez Park**. Explore a dozen or so Latin-art galleries, including **Molina Fine Art** (1634 Southwest 8th Street; 305-642-0444; molinaartgallery.com) and shops like **El Credito Cigar Factory** (1100 Southwest 8th Street; 305-324-0445; elcreditocigars.com), where you can watch cigars being rolled; **Los Pinareños Fruteria** (1334 Southwest 8th Street; 305-285-1135), the place to get a smooth green coconut pierced with a straw; and **El Pub** (1548 Southwest 8th Street; 305-642-9942), decorated with chicken statuary and known for its café con leche. On a nearby stretch of brick sidewalk, a local Walk of Fame pays tribute to entertainment figures including Gloria Estefan and Maria Conchito Alonso.

6 *Where the Past Is Present* 1 p.m.

Around the corner from the Calle Ocho bustle you'll find the small and quiet **Bay of Pigs Museum** (1821 Southwest Ninth Street; 305-649-4719), a cramped collection of memorabilia, writings, and photos honoring the felled 2506 Brigade of 1961. It puts the neighborhood in immediate political context — as does the **Cuban Memorial Boulevard**, a few blocks north on Southwest 13th Avenue, with its 2506 Brigade memorial, a brass relief of Cuba, and a bust of the 19th-century Cuban poet and freedom fighter Jose Martí. A beautiful ceiba tree here receives offerings from Santeria worshipers, its giant roots pressing up out of the earth like rough-skinned dinosaur claws.

7 *Art and Soul* 5 p.m.

For an impressive array of even more visual art, head to nearby Coral Gables, where the airy **Cernuda Arte** (4155 Ponce de Leon Boulevard; 305-461-1050; cernudaarte.com) gallery shows work strictly by Cubans. Its 25-year-old inventory ranges from colonial to modern masters, and exhibits have featured artists like the painter Tomás Sánchez, the mixed-media artist Flora Fong, and the painter César Santos, whose still-life works and intimate portraits resemble striking, brightly lit photographs.

8 *Waterfront Dining* 7 p.m.

Tucked along the edge of the narrow Miami River, **Garcia's** (398 Northwest North River Drive;

ABOVE El Pub in Calle Ocho, decorated with chicken statuary and known for its café con leche.

BELOW Cigars in the final curing process get the once-over at El Credito Cigar Factory.

305-375-0765; garciasmiami.com; $$) is a downtown Miami seafood joint that's a longtime favorite for its super-fresh catches and reasonable prices and for the warm, friendly vibe of the Garcia brothers, fishermen who left Cuba in the late '60s to begin new lives here. Enjoy a plate of grouper, yellow rice, and sweet plantains, plus a glowing view of Miami's skyline.

SUNDAY

9 *A Spiritual Moment* 10 a.m.

Have a contemplative morning on the shores of Biscayne Bay at the **Ermita de la Caridad** (3609 South Miami Avenue, Coconut Grove; 305-854-2404; ermitadelacaridad.org). It's a tepee-shaped shrine to displaced Cubans, with a Catholic chapel featuring a striking sepia mural of exiles' struggles.

10 *New Squeeze* Noon

By now you've most likely realized that mealtimes are a huge part of Cuban culture. Get your last licks at **El Palacio de los Jugos** in West Miami (5721 West Flagler Street; 305-264-8662; $), an unassuming produce-stand–type market that doles out tasty Cuban tamales, grilled pork, and fresh juices from tropical fruits like papaya and mamey. You'll have to elbow your way through the Sunday mobs to snag a spot at one of the few al fresco tables, but it's well worth it — for the food as well as the scene.

THE BASICS

The Miami International Airport is less than 20 minutes from the heart of Little Havana. Explore on foot and by car.

Westin Colonnade
180 Aragon Avenue, Coral Gables
305-441-2600

starwoodhotels.com/westin/coralgables
$$$$
Outdoor heated pool, 24-hour fitness center, in-room massages.

Hotel St. Michel
162 Alcazar Avenue, Coral Gables
305-444-1666
hotelstmichel.com

$$-$$$
Built in 1926; quaint touches.

Hotel Urbano
2500 Brickell Avenue
305-854-2070
hotelurbano.com
$$$
Boutique hotel downtown and close to everything.

The Everglades

Not quite the brackish swamp that many imagine it to be, the vast south Florida wetland known as the Everglades is actually a clear, wide, shallow river that flows like molasses. And living within its million-plus acres are 200 types of fish, 350 species of birds, and 120 different kinds of trees, just for starters, all less than an hour south of Miami. Of course, to see the iridescent-winged purple gallinule, breaching bottlenose dolphins, and still alligators soaking in the sun, you have to be willing to stop and slow down, moving as languidly as the River of Grass itself. Luckily, the availability of ranger programs and self-guided tours means you needn't be an expert hiker or kayaker to get below the surface of this beautiful, tangled landscape. — BY BETH GREENFIELD

FRIDAY

1 *Under the Boardwalk* 2 p.m.

To hang with more creatures than you can count, head into the **Everglades National Park**'s main **Ernest F. Coe** entrance (305-242-7700; nps.gov/ever/planyourvisit/visitorcenters.htm), near Homestead. You'll find winding boardwalks like the Anhinga Trail, named for the majestic water bird that stands with wings stretched wide to dry its black and white feathers in the sun. A stroll will likely reveal several anhingas, plus green and tri-colored herons, red-bellied turtles, double-crested cormorants, and many alligators. Don't miss the striking Pa-hay-okee Overlook, a short and steep walkway that juts out over a dreamily endless field of billowing, wheat-colored sawgrass.

2 *Pleasure Cruise* 4:45 p.m.

Pick up maps at the Coe entrance and then head deeper west in the park to the **Flamingo Visitor Center** (239-695-2945), where a small, quiet tour boat (evergladesnationalparkboattoursflamingo.com) whisks passengers from the close wetlands of the park out into the glimmering, airy expanse of the Florida

Bay. In just under two hours, you'll get a narrated tour, glimpses of elegant water birds (perhaps the great white heron or roseate spoonbill), and a glorious, multicolored sunset over the water.

3 *Search for Tamale* 7:30 p.m.

There's nothing much going on in Homestead, the scruffy town that borders the park's eastern entrance, but a small collection of Mexican restaurants serving tasty eats on North Krome Avenue ensures that you'll at least be well fed. **Casita Tejas** (27 North Krome Avenue, Homestead; 305-248-8224; casitatejas.com; $) offers authentic offerings like beef gorditas, chicken tamales, and chile rellenos in a homey, festive atmosphere.

SATURDAY

4 *Exotic Produce* 8 a.m.

Start your morning off with a thick, fresh-fruit milkshake at **Robert Is Here** (19200 Southwest 344th Street, Homestead; 305-246-1592; robertishere.com), a family-run farm stand offering papayas, star fruits, kumquats, guavas, sapodillas, mameys, and other tropical treats among heaps of fresh oranges and grapefruits.

5 *In the Loop* 10 a.m.

Along the northern rim of the national park you will find the **Shark Valley** entrance (Route 41, Tamiami Trail; 305-221-8776), where a paved loop is traversable by foot, bicycle, or guided tram ride

OPPOSITE Big Cypress National Preserve.

RIGHT Boardwalks in the swamps of Everglades National Park are vantage points for seeing alligators, turtles, and a multicolored profusion of water-loving birds.

and is often host to sleepy crocs or gators. (The Everglades is the only place in the world where alligators, which live in fresh water, and saltwater crocodiles live side by side.) The two-hour tram ride, led by a naturalist, is the best option for coping with the heat and the mosquitoes, which peak here between June and October. It will pause halfway through to let you climb to the top of a 45-foot-high observation deck affording 20-mile wilderness views in all directions.

6 *Swamp Things* 1 p.m.

Just north of the Everglades National Park is the **Big Cypress National Preserve** (nps.gov/bicy) — a tract that narrowly escaped being developed as Miami's international airport in the 1970s. And within its borders lies a novel opportunity for those who prefer to explore this region on foot: ranger-led swamp hikes that set off from the **Oasis Visitor Center** (52105 Tamiami Trail East, Ochopee). "From the highway, all you see is brown and green," noted ranger Corinne Fenner, leading people into the thigh-deep waters of cypress-tree stands. "It's nice to get out into the prairie and notice all the colors."

BELOW Take a ranger-led hike in water that looks surprisingly clean and feels deliciously cool on a hot day.

And the hues you'll see are certainly magical: the butter yellow of the Everglades daisy, bright violet of nettle-leaf velvetberry flowers, electric lime of freshwater sponges, and deep scarlet of a red-bellied woodpecker. The water itself—which collects in a sandy peat and limestone basin, helping silvery bald cypress trees thrive—looks shockingly clear and feels deliciously cool soaking through jeans and sneakers.

7 *Drive-Thru Wilderness* 3:30 p.m.

A Big Cypress driving tour, north of the Gulf Coast canoe launch on the gravel Turner River Road, offers various close-up encounters with wildlife. Along the scenic 17-mile route, you're sure to rub elbows with creeping turtles, nesting ospreys, and clusters of the alligators that like to float lazily in the narrow creeks here, leaving nothing but steely eyes and snouts above water.

8 *Stuffed Animals, Stuffed Belly* 6 p.m.

Not for the faint of heart when it comes to pushing carnivorous limits, the **Rod and Gun Club**, in the small fishing village of Everglades City (200 West Broadway; 239-695-2100; evergladesrodandgun.com; $$), is a handsome, historic riverside inn where you can unwind from your full day of touring with a hearty dinner. Swamp and Turf (steak and frogs legs) and gator nuggets are among the eclectic offerings. Afterward, have a cocktail in the cozy lounge, where you can shoot pool under the eerie double gaze of a gator skin and deer head, both mounted on the wall.

SUNDAY

9 *Paddle Your Own Canoe* 10 a.m.

The southwest edge of the park sits at the precipice of glistening Chokoloskee Bay and the Ten Thousand Islands area—a pristine region of mangroves and sandy keys mostly reachable only by boat via the 99-mile Wilderness Waterway canoe and kayak trail. While experienced paddlers can plunge right into a days-long journey, camping on raised "chickee" platforms or sand spits along the way, beginners are best off joining one of the many shorter, organized trips on more navigable creeks, like the one led weekly by national park naturalists, leaving from the park's **Gulf Coast Visitor Center**

(815 Oyster Bar Lane, Everglades City). "I never get tired of this area," a naturalist, Brian Ettling, said during one such four-hour journey, leading canoeists single file beneath a cathedral of arching mangrove branches. He excitedly pointed out blue herons, jumping mullet fish, and skittish tree crabs. He gave lessons on the hunting habits of swooping turkey vultures, which have a sense of smell rivaling a bloodhound's, and on the hip attributes of screechy red-shouldered hawks: "They're like the local punk rockers. They eat lizards and scream."

10 *Caught on Film* 3 p.m.
On your way back east along the Tamiami Trail, be sure to stop and visit the **Big Cypress Gallery**

(52388 Tamiami Trail, Ochopee; 239-695-2428; clydebutcher.com). Here, photographer Clyde Butcher's large-format, black and white landscapes perfectly capture the romantic essence of this swampland and put your own fresh experiences into striking artistic perspective.

ABOVE Wild beauty at sunset in the Big Cypress National Preserve.

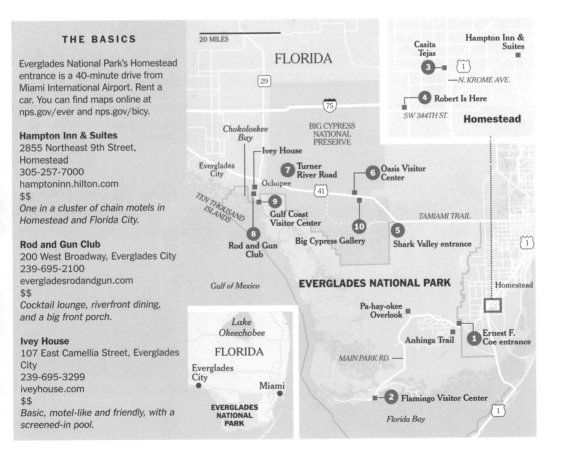

THE BASICS

Everglades National Park's Homestead entrance is a 40-minute drive from Miami International Airport. Rent a car. You can find maps online at nps.gov/ever and nps.gov/bicy.

Hampton Inn & Suites
2855 Northeast 9th Street, Homestead
305-257-7000
hamptoninn.hilton.com
$$
One in a cluster of chain motels in Homestead and Florida City.

Rod and Gun Club
200 West Broadway, Everglades City
239-695-2100
evergladesrodandgun.com
$$
Cocktail lounge, riverfront dining, and a big front porch.

Ivey House
107 East Camellia Street, Everglades City
239-695-3299
iveyhouse.com
$$
Basic, motel-like and friendly, with a screened-in pool.

FLORIDA

Chokoloskee Bay

BIG CYPRESS NATIONAL PRESERVE

Ivey House

Everglades City

Turner River Road

Oasis Visitor Center

Ochopee

Gulf Coast Visitor Center

TEN THOUSAND ISLANDS

Rod and Gun Club

Big Cypress Gallery

Shark Valley entrance

TAMIAMI TRAIL

Gulf of Mexico

EVERGLADES NATIONAL PARK

Homestead

Pa-hay-okee Overlook

Anhinga Trail

Ernest F. Coe entrance

MAIN PARK RD.

Flamingo Visitor Center

Florida Bay

Casita Tejas

Hampton Inn & Suites

N. KROME AVE.

Robert Is Here

SW 344TH ST.

Homestead

Lake Okeechobee

FLORIDA

Everglades City

Miami

EVERGLADES NATIONAL PARK

20 MILES

Key West

Key West, haven to artists and writers, chefs and hippies, is somehow more Caribbean than Floridian. The independent-spirited transplants who inhabit it work hard to keep it that way. One-speed bicycles weave their way through colorful village streets crammed with almost as many chickens as cars. Happy hour blends into dinner. And everything is shaped by the ocean, from the fish market-driven menus and the nautical-inspired art to the dawn gatherings of sunrise worshipers and the tipplers' goodbye waves at sunset. Be careful or you might just catch what islanders call "Keys disease" — a sudden desire to cut ties with home and move there.
— BY SARAH WILDMAN

FRIDAY

1 *Two Wheels Are Enough* 4 p.m.

As any self-respecting bohemian local knows, the best way to get around Key West is on a bicycle. Bike rental businesses offer drop-off service to many hotels. Two reliable companies are **Eaton Bikes** (830 Eaton Street; 305-294-8188; eatonbikes.com) and **Re-Cycle** (5160 Overseas Highway; U.S. 1; 305-292-3336; recyclekw.com). Rentals will be around $20 for the first day and half that for each additional. Orient yourself by biking over to the **Truman Annex**, a palm-lined oasis of calm made up of two-story whitewashed buildings that surrounds the **Little White House** (111 Front Street; 305-294-9911; trumanlittlewhitehouse.com), where Harry Truman spent working vacations.

2 *Cleanse the Palate* 7 p.m.

Key West chefs pride themselves on a culinary philosophy of simple cooking and fresh ingredients. A perfect example is the **Flaming Buoy Filet Co.** (1100 Packer Street; 305-295-7970; theflamingbuoy.com; $$), a nouveau seafood restaurant owned and run by two Cincinnati transplants, Fred Isch and his partner, Scot Forste. The 10 rustic wood tables are hand-painted in orange and yellow; the lights are

OPPOSITE A December day at Casa Marina Resort.

RIGHT A Key West sunset. Many of the growing population of islanders moved in after succumbing to what they call "Keys disease," a visitor's sudden desire to stay for good.

low and the crowd amiable. This is home-cooking, island style, with dishes like black bean soup swirled with Cheddar cheese, sour cream, and cilantro or the fresh catch of the day served with a broccoli cake and tasty mashed potatoes.

3 *Small World* 9 p.m.

You can't bike a block on this island without bumping into a would-be Gauguin wielding a palette and paintbrush. There's an outsize and vibrant arts scene that's evident at places like **Lucky Street Gallery** (1130 Duval Street; 305-294-3973; luckystreetgallery.com) and the **Gallery on Greene** (606 Greene Street; 305-294-1669; galleryongreene.com). For a warm introduction, head to the Armory, a rifle storage house built in 1903 and recently converted into the **Studios of Key West** (600 White Street; 305-296-0458; tskw.org), an airy, art-filled space with rotating exhibitions, evening folk concerts, talks by artists-in-residence, and drop-in art classes. Expect to find your barista there, and the bike rental guy and the woman who will sell you a T-shirt tomorrow. It's a small town.

4 *Mix It Up* 11 p.m.

While Key West night life has long been synonymous with boozy karaoke and mediocre margaritas, watering holes like the tiny **Orchid Bar** (1004 Duval Street; 305-296-9915; orchidkeyinn.com) are quietly moving in a more sophisticated direction. Bartenders there take mixology seriously. Try the St.-Germain 75, with Hendrick's Gin, St.-Germain, fresh lemon

juice, and Champagne. This Deco-cool sliver of a space overlooks an illuminated pool and draws a mellow crew.

SATURDAY

5 *Salute the Sun* 8:15 a.m.

Every morning, a dozen spiritual seekers—an eclectic mix including tattooed artists and elementary-school teachers—assemble at Fort Zachary Taylor State Park for **Yoga on the Beach** (305-296-7352; yogaonbeach.com). Nancy Curran and Don Bartolone, yogis from Massachusetts, teach energetic vinyasa-style yoga in a clearing of pines, facing the sea. The $18 drop-in fee includes state park entrance, muslin dropcloths, and yoga mats.

6 *Imports at Breakfast* 11 a.m.

An island of transplants offers plenty to sample from the world over. Craving France? Stop at **La Crêperie Key West** (300 Petronia Street; 305-517-6799; lacreperiekeywest.com; $$), where Yolande Findlay and Sylvie Le Nouail, both Brittany born, serve crepes in an open kitchen. Start with a savory crepe like ratatouille and then move on to something sweet like red velvet with dark Belgian chocolate, strawberries, and English custard. If you feel more like New York, try **Sarabeth's** (530 Simonton Street; 305-293-8181; sarabethskeywest.com; $), a branch of the popular Manhattan brunch spot.

7 *Island Style* 1 p.m.

Just because islanders pride themselves on being casual, do not assume they don't want to look great. **Bésame Mucho** (315 Petronia Street; 305-294-1928; besamemucho.net) is an old-world general store packed with everything from Belgian linen to Dr. Hauschka skin care, to delicate baubles like tiny beaded pyrite necklaces. Across the street is **Wanderlust kw** (310 Petronia Street; 305-509-7065; wanderlustkw.com), stocked with well-priced dresses and whimsical watercolors of Key West houses by

local artists. For swank décor, check out **Jan George Interior Design** (600 Frances Street; 305-509-8449; jangeorge.com), a furniture shop that carries dreamy stark-white couches from the Italian line Gervasoni. The owners, Jan Oostdyk and his spouse, George Rutgers, landed as tourists from the Netherlands and never left.

8 *Drinks at Sunset* 5 p.m.

Skip the hustle of Mallory Square and work your way through the white-tablecloth dining room to **Louie's Backyard Afterdeck Bar** (700 Waddell Avenue; 305-294-1061; louiesbackyard.com), where a large wood-planked patio faces the ocean and the setting sun. A gregarious crowd of artists and New England snowbirds gathers daily. It's like an outdoor Cheers.

9 *Dining on the Duval* 7 p.m.

Since opening in 2002, the restaurant **Nine One Five** (915 Duval Street; 305-296-0669; 915duval.com; $$$) has gotten high marks for its Asian-inspired seafood and ambience—a large white porch that's great for people-watching. Later the owner, Stuart Kemp, turned the second floor into the Point5 lounge, serving smaller bites like grilled snapper tacos

ABOVE Some of the finds at Bésame Mucho, one of multiple shopping options around town.

BELOW Touring by bicycle with Lloyd's Tropical Bike.

and stick-to-your-ribs mac and cheese to a younger crowd. If you linger after dinner, Point5 becomes a party, with D.J. George spinning funk and soul and the island's gay and straight worlds dancing together under filament lights strung outdoors.

10 *Drag Show* 9 p.m.

Drag shows are part of Key West's patrimony. One favorite performer is Randy Roberts, who has performed as Bette Midler, Cher, and Lady Gaga at **La Te Da** (1125 Duval Street; 305-296-6706; lateda.com). After the show, hoof it down to **Porch** (429 Caroline Street, No. 2; 305-517-6358; theporchkw.com), a wine and artisanal beer bar on the luminous first floor of a Victorian mansion, just off Duval.

SUNDAY

11 *Seaworthy Pursuits* Noon

With all the shopping and eating, it is easy to forget why you're really here: to get off the street and onto the water. **Lazy Dog** (5114 Overseas Highway; 305-295-9898; lazydog.com) offers two- and four-hour kayaking or two-hour paddleboard tours through crystal clear coastal waters and into the deep green waterways of the gnarled mangrove forests. Or if you're just looking to dip a toe in the sea, bike over to Clarence S. Higgs Memorial Beach, a strip of sand by the genial beach bar restaurant **Salute!** (1000 Atlantic Boulevard; 305-292-1117; saluteonthebeach.com), rent a beach chair, and kick back.

THE BASICS

Fly into Key West airport, take a fast ferry from Miami, or drive United States Route 1 through the Florida Keys. In town, rent a bicycle.

Gardens Hotel
526 Angela Street
305-294-2661
gardens.com
$$-$$$$
Seventeen suites spread across an acre of tropical gardens, steps from everything but as quiet as a country inn.

Alexander's Guest House
1118 Fleming Street
305-294-9919
alexanderskeywest.com
$$-$$$
Stylish bed-and-breakfast that attracts a primarily gay and lesbian crowd.

Casa Marina
1500 Ranch Avenue
888-303-5717
casamarinaresort.com
$$$-$$$$
Part of the Waldorf-Astoria Collection.

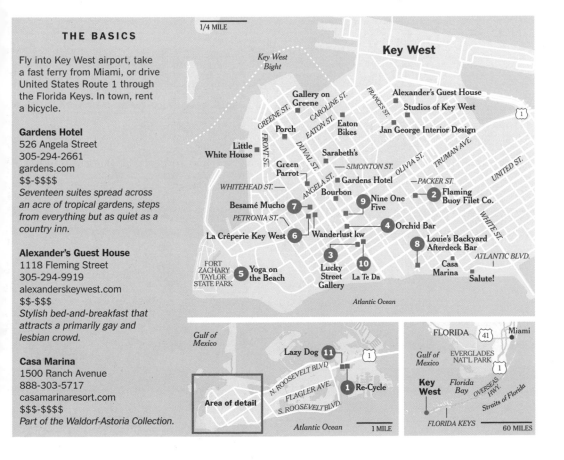

Naples

If you filtered all the glitz out of Miami, you'd get Naples, Florida. This small Gulf-side city has a pleasingly anodyne quality that's worlds away from the cosmopolitan bustle found only a two-hour drive due east, on the Atlantic coast. Affluent Midwesterners, who have adopted Naples as a getaway from nasty Northern weather, bring a certain oh-gosh air to town. Don't be surprised if you keep seeing the same faces over and over — these snowbirds might move at a slower pace than the Miami set, but they get around.
— BY TED LOOS

FRIDAY

1 *Sunset Cocktails* 5 p.m.
Cocktail hour is sacred around these parts. As the sun sets, make your way to **Gumbo Limbo**, the beachfront bar and restaurant at the Ritz-Carlton, Naples (280 Vanderbilt Beach Road; 239-598-3300; ritzcarlton.com/naples). Order a Naples Sunset, a fruity rum drink, and follow the dipping sun as the outdoor deck lights up with tiki torches and the laughter of the polo-shirt-wearing crowd.

2 *Well Seasoned* 8 p.m.
Don't go to Naples expecting molecular gastronomy; restaurants play it conservatively. Among the more exciting spots is **Sea Salt** (1186 Third Street South; 239-434-7258; seasaltnaples.com; $$$), a boisterous place that opened in 2008 and has been praised by magazines like *Esquire* for its devotion to local and organic ingredients. The menu prizes bold flavors over razzle-dazzle: buffalo mozzarella salad, well-marbled Wagyu rib-eye. The chef also has a thing for sprinkles: porcini powder, cinnamon salt, and of course sea salt. The wine list roams the globe, with particular attention to Italy.

3 *Early Night Owls* 10 p.m.
Naples will never be known for its night life. But even here, 20-something fans of bottle service can go to **Vision Night Club** (11901 Tamiami Trail North; 239-591-8383; visionniteclub.com), where three rooms with disco balls and colored lights keep the dance floor moving. A mellower vibe can be found at **Avenue Wine Café** (483 Fifth Avenue South; 239-403-9463; avenuewinecafe.com), where

Colin Estrem, the owner, said he catered to "young professionals, not the rich Naples crowd." Inside, patrons sample from 100 wines and about 70 beers on offer. Outside, cigar aficionados puff away on the patio until the wee hours.

SATURDAY

4 *Modern Art* 10 a.m.
The **Naples Museum of Art** (5833 Pelican Bay Boulevard; 239-597-1900; thephil.org) is a small gem, with a permanent collection that has a strong selection of American modernism (including works by Charles Sheeler and Oscar Bluemner) and Mexican modernism (renowned names like Tamayo and Orozco). The senior-citizen docents are lovingly bossy, and not shy about steering visitors toward what they consider the best views.

5 *Million-Dollar Beach* 11:30 a.m.
When the sun is strong, Neapolitans hit the beach. Don't set up camp near the town pier at Fifth Street South — it's too crowded. Ditto for anything along the northern end — too many hotels. For a spot that's just right, head south toward 18th

OPPOSITE Mosaic tile work by Roberto Burle Marx in the Brazilian Garden at the Naples Botanical Garden.

BELOW When the sun is strong, Neapolitans hit the beach, open to the public even in front of the mansions.

Avenue South, the last downtown street with direct beach access. (Parking can be scarce, so bring a pocketful of quarters and try nearby Gordon Drive.) With flip-flops in hand, a short walk south offers privacy. It also induces real estate envy. Some of Naples's plushest over-the-top mansions are along this stretch of beach, exposed to prying eyes.

6 *Jolly Good* 2 p.m.

A faithful adherence to classic pub fare draws a loyal crowd to the **Jolly Cricket** (720 Fifth Avenue South; 239-304-9460; thejollycricket.com; $$), which opened last year along the city's main drag. Ceiling fans and wicker chairs set the mood. At night there's even a standards-playing pianist, complete with brandy snifter for tips. The kitchen turns out a succulent fish 'n chips served with housemade tartar sauce.

7 *Dress Up* 4 p.m.

Downtown shopping favors women's clothing and accessories. Some of the best shops are concentrated on Third Street South. **Marissa Collections** (No. 1167; 239-263-4333; marissacollections.com), a high-fashion fixture, has added mini-boutiques for Oscar de la Renta and a men's line from the designer Brunello Cucinelli. Another good retail cluster lines Fifth Avenue South. Stop by **Seraphim Boutique** (No. 600, Suite 106; 239-261-8494; seraphimboutique.com), where Tanya Anderson, the owner, specializes in flirty, fun resort wear — the kind of thing you'd pick up on a vacation, like a Luna Luz tie-dyed halter dress.

8 *Sigh and Meditate* 6 p.m.

Until recently, spas weren't as prominent as Naples's luxe reputation would suggest. So the arrival a few years ago of a **Golden Door** spa (475 Seagate Drive; 239-594-6321; goldendoor.com/naples) was a cause for celebration — and a new reason for a trip here. Situated at the Naples Grande Resort, the 16,000-square-foot spa is filled with Asian-inflected details like bamboo groves and teak trim. In addition to

the sauna and whirlpool, there's a meditation labyrinth where you can unwind after an avocado-citrus wrap.

9 *French Provincial* 8 p.m.

A sweet little bistro tucked onto a side street downtown, **Bleu Provence** (1234 Eighth Street South; 239-261-8239; bleuprovencenaples.com; $$$) is done up as a farmhouse dining room and really feels as if you could be in the hills above Nice. Escargot, moules-frites, foie gras, loup de mer, tarte aux oignons — there's plenty of French to go on. After dinner, wander down to the dock to see if the pelicans are still awake.

SUNDAY

10 *Bring a Racquet* 10 a.m.

The thunking of tennis balls is heard everywhere in Naples, but most of the courts are sequestered behind hedges in high-end condo developments. That makes the **Arthur L. Allen Tennis Center** (735 Eighth Street South; 239-213-3060; allentenniscenter.com),

ABOVE Marissa Collections is a 10,000-square-foot bastion of luxury that sells designer fashion.

BELOW The Naples Museum of Art, a small gem with a strong selection of American and Mexican modernism.

in downtown's quiet Cambier Park, all the more inviting. The 12 Har-Tru courts are as well kept as a private club's, but for an affordable fee, anyone can play. There's a sign-up board to help you find pick-up games at your level (blue cards for men, pink ones for ladies).

11 *Lush Vegetation* 1 p.m.

Beaches are great, but a slightly more educational way to experience Naples's balmy climate is found at the dramatically expanded and renovated **Naples Botanical Garden** (4820 Bayshore Drive; 239-643-7275; naplesgarden.org), which focuses on subtropical flora. Lush Caribbean and Brazilian gardens are perfectly manicured, and the Children's

Garden features a tiny herb patch and spraying fountains. The colorful butterfly house draws the most visitors, and as you look for the elusive electric-blue variety, you may run into that well-dressed couple you dined next to the previous evening. Par for the course in Naples.

ABOVE The Children's Garden at the Naples Botanical Garden has a boardwalk, an herb patch, and fountains.

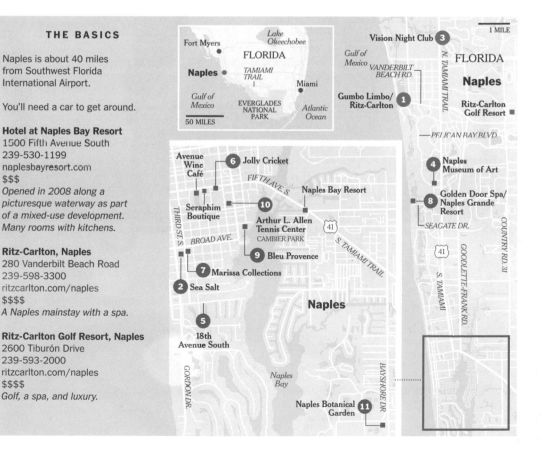

THE BASICS

Naples is about 40 miles from Southwest Florida International Airport.

You'll need a car to get around.

Hotel at Naples Bay Resort
1500 Fifth Avenue South
239-530-1199
naplesbayresort.com
$$$
Opened in 2008 along a picturesque waterway as part of a mixed-use development. Many rooms with kitchens.

Ritz-Carlton, Naples
280 Vanderbilt Beach Road
239-598-3300
ritzcarlton.com/naples
$$$$
A Naples mainstay with a spa.

Ritz-Carlton Golf Resort, Naples
2600 Tiburón Drive
239-593-2000
ritzcarlton.com/naples
$$$$
Golf, a spa, and luxury.

Atlanta

First, don't call it Hotlanta anymore. It's the ATL, the code for the teeming airport that is a fitting emblem for a city so transient it barely recognizes itself, where more than half the adult population is from somewhere else, and where every urban fad, from underground parking to savory ice cream, is embraced. A corporate stronghold, a Southern belle, and a hip-hop capital, Atlanta has wrestled with identity confusion, trying out several slogans in the past few years, from a hip-hop-accompanied "Every Day Is an Opening Day" to a blander "City Lights, Southern Nights." Major civic investments like a grandiose $220 million aquarium, a significant expansion of the High Museum of Art by the architect Renzo Piano, and the purchase of the papers of the Rev. Dr. Martin Luther King Jr. add up to a high tide of enthusiasm, even in a city where optimism is liberally indulged. — BY SHAILA DEWAN

FRIDAY

1 *Tastes of the Town* 5:30 p.m.

Few places can be said to be definitively Atlantan, but the **Colonnade** (1879 Cheshire Bridge Road NE; 404-874-5642; colonnadeatl.com; $) is one: a meat-and-three restaurant with a full bar (rare) and a sizable gay clientele (more rare). The resulting mix is spectacular: black fingernails, Sansabelt trousers, birthday tiaras, Hawaiian shirts, all in a buzzing carpeted dining room with efficiently friendly waiters. When it comes to ordering, stick to the classics: a Bloody Mary to start, fried chicken with yeasty dinner rolls straight from the school cafeteria, and the day's pie.

2 *Old-Time Steps* 7:20 p.m.

Though it sounds vaguely revolutionary, contra dancing is a folk tradition that involves following instructions from a caller, like square-dancing. If the notion of trying this in public gives you qualms, remember that 1) the likelihood of being seen by someone you know is low and 2) the tolerance quotient, at a weekly event where men have been known

OPPOSITE The Atlanta Cyclorama and Civil War Museum. Inside is a panoramic painting of the Battle of Atlanta.

RIGHT Smooth moves at the Golden Glide rink. Roller skating is an integral part of Atlanta hip-hop culture.

to show up wearing skirts to keep cool, is high. Show up at the **Clarkston Community Center** (3701 College Avenue, Clarkston) before 7:20 p.m. for basic lessons by the Chattahoochee County Dancers (770-939-8646; contradance.org), and then, when the dance begins at 8, swing your partner (you can easily find one there) to live old-time bands with names like Jump in the Skillet and Cattywampus. Wear soft-soled shoes, or boogie in your socks.

3 *Where Heads Spin* 10:30 p.m.

Since you're already dizzy, visit the **Sun Dial**, the revolving bar atop the Westin hotel (210 Peachtree Street; 404-589-7506; sundialrestaurant.com), where young Atlantans come for the throwback cool and occasional exhibitions of local art. Sip an Atlanta Hurricane (it's in the colada-daiquiri family and arrives in a souvenir glass) or a chocolate martini as you orient yourself with a glittery panoramic view of downtown, the Georgia Dome, CNN's headquarters, and the Georgia Aquarium.

4 *On a Roll* 11:30 p.m.

Roller-skating is an integral part of hip-hop culture in Atlanta, which is home to OutKast, Usher, and Young Jeezy, among other stars. Beyoncé had her 21st birthday party at the Cascade roller rink here, and Dallas Austin paid homage to the flawless moves of

skate dancers in his film *The ATL*. On Friday nights, the virtuosos descend on **Golden Glide** (2750 Wesley Chapel Road in Decatur, but it's tucked behind a shopping strip; 404-288-7773; atlantarollerskating.com) for adult skate, where posses practice their smooth moves until the wee hours. If you haven't been practicing, skate inside the green line for your own safety. Or just stay on the sideline and gawk.

SATURDAY

5 *Robust Start* Noon

You had a late night, so take your time getting to **Watershed** (406 West Ponce de Leon Avenue, Decatur; 404-378-4900; watershedrestaurant.com; $$), a gas station converted into an airy Southern restaurant. Reservations are recommended, and child-tolerance is required, but the chicken hash with griddle cakes and poached eggs is worth the bother.

6 *A Little Shopping* 1:30 p.m.

After brunch, browse the chic specialty shops near the main square of Decatur, the city-suburb that has won praise for its sensitive take on urban revitalization. One favorite is **Mingei World Arts** (427 Church Street; 404-371-0101; mingeiworldarts.com), an import store with a sense of humor, which offers items like vintage Bollywood posters or baskets woven from telephone wire. For the designer chef there's **Taste** (416 Church Street; 404-370-1863; tastedecatur.com), with two-handed Dumbo cups and vintage-print aprons.

7 *War on Canvas* 3:30 p.m.

When Gen. John A. Logan was considering a run for vice president in the 1880s, he commissioned a political ad in the form of a giant painting of the Battle of Atlanta, in which he for a time commanded the Army of the Tennessee for the Union. The work, billed as the world's largest oil painting, is now housed in **Grant Park**, in a circular room not unlike a planetarium, and viewed from a rotating bank of seats (**Atlanta Cyclorama and Civil War Museum**; 800 Cherokee Avenue; 404-624-1071; bcaatlanta. com). It is accompanied by a taped narration, a good way to get your requisite dose of Civil War history. A diorama was added in the 1930s, which sounds like a terrible idea until you see how seamlessly it blends into the painting, or notice a replica of Clark Gable as a dead Yankee. Leave some time to see the exhibit on the Great Locomotive Chase, a slapstick adventure involving hand cars, cut wires, and engines traveling in reverse.

ABOVE AND OPPOSITE The Martin Luther King Jr. National Historic Site includes King's tomb and exhibits recalling his leadership in the struggle to end racial segregation in the South. Other stops are his boyhood home and the Ebenezer Baptist Church he served as pastor.

8 *Spreading the Sopchoppy* 6 p.m.

    A city where a treasured chef's departure can be front-page news, Atlanta has more than its share of fine restaurants, many of them cavernous, overdesigned colonizations of old industrial buildings. Smaller and friendlier is **Restaurant Eugene** (2277 Peachtree Road; 404-355-0321; restauranteugene.com; $$$), where the staff shares its passions readily and the menu can read like a Southern safari: foie gras on French toast with Sopchoppy brand molasses from Florida; A & J Farms squash blossoms with Anson Mills's grits and Sweetgrass Dairy goat cheese.

9 *Car-Driven Culture* 10 p.m.

    The **Starlight Six Drive-In** (2000 Moreland Avenue SE; 404-627-5786; starlightdrivein.com) — "movies and fun since 1949" — has that Southern-culture-on-the-skids charm, retro with a hint of rockabilly. Sometimes used for campy evenings of B-movies and bands

(check starlightdrivein.com for the schedule), the rest of the time this is just a straight-up, steamy-windowed cinematic experience in a hummocky parking lot. It's not hard to find a decent movie on the schedule, but bring your own refreshments, as the snack bar is paltry.

SUNDAY

10 *Pancakes and Quiet Neighbors* 10 a.m.

    The gruff proprietor of **Ria's Bluebird** (421 Memorial Drive SE; 404-521-3737; riasbluebird.com; $) has the word "hate" tattooed on the nape of her neck. But local residents give her nothing but love, lining up, pleasantly sleep-tousled, on weekend mornings for what some customers say are the world's best pancakes. The light-filled storefront is just right if you feel the need to keep your sun-glasses on in the morning; the floor is made from

wooden wall paneling, creating the illusion of an old barroom. The restaurant is across the street from Atlanta's oldest and loveliest cemetery, **Oakland Cemetery** (248 Oakland Avenue SE; 404-688-2107; oaklandcemetery.com), where Margaret Mitchell, author of *Gone with the Wind*; 25 mayors; and thousands of unidentified Confederate soldiers are buried. In warm weather, guided tours are available on Sunday afternoons.

11 *The King Legacy* 11 a.m.

At the **Martin Luther King Jr. National Historic Site** (450 Auburn Avenue NE; 404-331-6922; nps.gov/malu), you can take a tour of the house where King was born (501 Auburn Avenue NE; reserve

in advance) and, at the visitor center, see his life retraced in photos, print, film, video, and art. If you get an earlier start, you might want to stop by the new Ebenezer Baptist Church, adjacent to the visitor center, for a service. The historic **Old Ebenezer Baptist Church**, where King, his father, and his grandfather preached, is across the street (407 Auburn Avenue NE), no longer used for services but open to view. Inside, in the quiet sanctuary where King's inspiring words once echoed, visitors may find their emotions running high.

OPPOSITE Oakland Cemetery, burial place of 25 Atlanta mayors and Margaret Mitchell, the author of *Gone with the Wind*.

THE BASICS

It is easy to fly nonstop into Hartsfield-Jackson International Airport, a major travel hub.

If you do fly in, rent a car.

Twelve Atlantic Station
361 17th Street NW
404-961-1212
twelvehotels.com
$$$
Full amenities in a bustling Midtown development.

Glenn Hotel
110 Marietta Street N.W.
404-521-2250
glennhotel.com
$$-$$$
Gossamer curtains and a rooftop bar.

Ellis Hotel
176 Peachtree Street N.W.
404-523-5155
ellishotel.com
$$
Functional boutique hotel in a landmark downtown building.

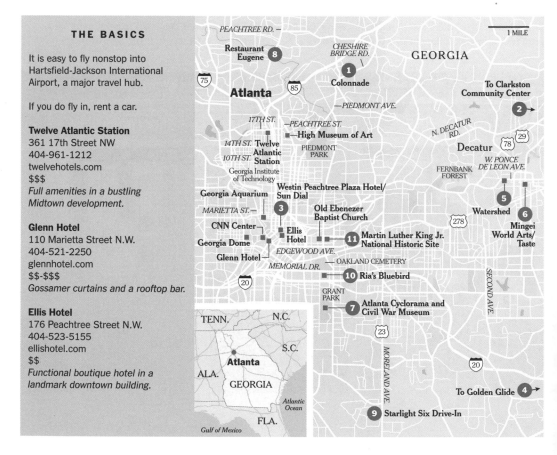

Asheville

Whether it's culture, the great outdoors, or homegrown food and beer, Asheville, North Carolina, takes its pleasures seriously. Playgrounds are equipped with rock-climbing walls. Bumper stickers exhort the locals to buy local. The town is proud of Biltmore, the outsize Vanderbilt mansion, but funds are also being raised for a distinctly more modern kind of museum: tracing the intersection of science and music, and named for Bob Moog, the synthesizer pioneer, who lived in Asheville. All this connoisseurship unfolds, to the benefit of the casual visitor, against the backdrop of the seriously beautiful Blue Ridge Mountains.
— BY SHAILA DEWAN

FRIDAY

1 *Secret (Edible) Garden* 3 p.m.

A small amphitheater, an interactive fountain, and public sculpture adorn the newly redone **Pack Square Park** (packsquarepark.org) at the pink Art Deco-style city hall. But a quick walk away is another, almost secret, park that embodies the scruffy, idealistic side of Asheville: **George Washington Carver Edible Park**. There, the public can graze on apples, chestnuts, and other delectables. To find it, take the outdoor stairway behind Pack's Tavern, go left on Marjorie Street, and cross the pedestrian bridge by the corner of Marjorie and Davidson.

2 *Chai Time* 5 p.m.

Asheville residents love their Indian food, and they are particularly taken with a bright cafe called **Chai Pani** (22 Battery Park Avenue; 828-254-4003; chaipani.net; $) for its fresh, cilantro-strewn takes on Indian street food. For a late-afternoon snack, pop in for a nimbu pani, or salty limeade, and bhel puri, a snack of puffed rice and chickpea noodles in fresh tamarind chutney.

3 *Downtown Drumming* 7 p.m.

There may be 10 onlookers for every drummer at the long-running Friday-night drum circle in triangular **Pritchard Park** (College Street and Patton Avenue) — and there are plenty of drummers. The congas, doumbeks, tambourines, and cowbells provide an ecstatic soundtrack for families, college couples, and dreadlocked nomads. The drum circle is the throbbing heart of downtown, a district of shops, bars, buskers, and street magicians that springs into action as the weekend begins.

4 *Microbrew and a Movie* 9 p.m.

In recent years, Asheville has come to rival Portland, Oregon, as a center for craft beer, and the city has claimed to have more microbreweries per capita — from places like **Green Man Brewery** (greenmanbrewery.com) with its cask-conditioned beers, to the hip **Wedge Brewing Company** (wedgebrewing.com) in the River Arts District. You can try a few on an **Asheville Brews Cruise** tour (brewscruise.com), or linger at the student-friendly **Asheville Pizza and Brewing Company** (675 Merrimon Avenue; 828-254-1281; ashevillebrewing.com), which has a bar, arcade, and cut-rate movie theater. Settle down in front of the large screen with a pint of Rocket Girl or Ninja Porter and a quite respectable pizza (toppings may include Spam, as well as smoked Gouda and artichoke hearts).

SATURDAY

5 *Wood-Fired Breakfast* 9 a.m.

The East-West fusion and wholesome rusticity in Farm and Sparrow's wood-fired pastries

OPPOSITE A class at Black Mountain Yoga. You won't be in Asheville for long before feeling its bohemian spirit.

BELOW Find locally crafted pottery, a western North Carolina specialty, at Curve Studios in the River Arts District.

seem to sum up Asheville. The croissants stuffed with kimchi and an open-faced pear, Gorgonzola, and bee pollen confection are made at the bakery (farmandsparrow.com) in nearby Candler, N.C., and are available at some of Asheville's tailgate markets, a kind of hyper-local version of a farmers' market. The **North Asheville Tailgate Market** (828-712-4644; northashevilletailgatemarket.org), held in a parking lot on the campus of the University of North Carolina at Asheville, is where you'll also find locally made kombucha from Buchi, trout dip from the Sunburst Trout Company, and fresh goat cheese with lavender from Three Graces Dairy.

6 *Mountain Stretch* 10:30 a.m.

Like any bohemian resort worth its coarse-ground Himalayan salt, Asheville has its share of healing arts. Find spa treatments, colonics, and "affordable acupuncture" at the **Thrifty Taoist** in the town of Black Mountain (106 Black Mountain Avenue; 828-713-9185; thriftytaoist.com), about 15 minutes from downtown. **Black Mountain Yoga** offers one-on-one yoga therapy sessions with Martia Rachman and her husband, Brad, a naturopath (120 Broadway Street, Black Mountain; 828-669-2939; blackmountainyoga.com). While you perform stretches and poses, one of the Rachmans will identify problem areas and massage and manipulate stubborn muscles. An hour later, a looser, more relaxed you will emerge from their clutches.

7 *Artists' Utopia* Noon

Short-lived but enormously influential, **Black Mountain College** (blackmountaincollege.org) was evidence of Asheville's pull on the unconventionally creative. John Cage, Merce Cunningham, Buckminster Fuller, and Josef Albers were among the teachers at this oft-re-examined intellectual utopia that closed, after a quarter-century, in the late 1950s. The campus at Lake Eden (375 Lake Eden Road, Black Mountain) is now a Christian boys' camp, but when it is not in session you can still inspect the Bauhaus-inspired main campus building and fading murals by Jean

Charlot. Twice a year, the **Lake Eden Arts Festival** (828-686-8742; theleaf.org) unfolds there.

8 *Robot vs. Mermaid* 2 p.m.

Western North Carolina is known for pottery, and you can find some of the artists themselves at work at **Curve Studios** in the River Arts District (6, 9, and 12 Riverside Drive; 828-388-3526; curvestudiosnc.com). At the showroom-cum-studios, you might find robot vases by Patty Bilbro ($165), a mermaid figurine by Fran Welch ($35), or sophisticated tableware by Akira Satake and Maria Andrade Troya.

9 *Old-Time Architecture* 3 p.m.

On the Obamas' Asheville vacation in 2010, they joined a long line of presidents and celebrities who have stayed at the **Grove Park Inn** (290 Macon Avenue; 800-438-5800; groveparkinn.com), a giant pile of rocks topped by a red roof that looks like melting snow. The inn retains a Craftsman-era grace, despite some remodeling involving a good deal of wood paneling. Take in the splendor of the Great Hall—and a Great Hall Bloody, the definitive bloody mary—accompanied by the local bands that play mostly old-time, Americana, and bluegrass music on Saturday afternoons.

10 *Toast to Literature* 5 p.m.

The **Battery Park Book Exchange and Champagne Bar** (Grove Arcade, 1 Page Avenue; 828-252-0020; batteryparkbookexchange.com) is not a place to find shabby paperbacks. Instead, think never-read leather-bound volumes of Dickens ($435 for a set), an edition of *The Catcher in the Rye* with the carousel horse cover ($200), acres of gardening and art hardbacks, and a glass of fizzy Heidsieck & Co. Monopole ($15). The Mission-style sofas and leather armchairs in book-lined alcoves bring the cozy nook idea to a new level.

11 *Gastro-Dive* 8 p.m.

What are truffles, steak tartare, and imported oysters doing in a cinderblock dive bar amid the cool haunts of West Asheville? One bite of dinner at the **Admiral** (400 Haywood Road; 828-252-2541; theadmiralnc.com) and such questions subside into flavor combinations like balsamic pears with honey cap mushrooms or foie gras with Nutella. When new owners bought the old B&D Bar, renamed it, and installed a gastropub with an ever-changing menu, the Admiral became Asheville's hottest restaurant; reservations recommended. Late on Saturday nights, the tables are cleared away for a crowded and sweaty dance party.

SUNDAY

12 *Treetop Zip* 9 a.m.

Leaf peeping is a serious sport in Asheville — hence the weekly "fall color report" from the local visitor's bureau (exploreasheville.com). Experience the local treetops, whatever the season, from a whole new angle on the three-and-a-half-hour zipline course at **Navitat Canopy Adventures**, about 20 minutes north of town (242 Poverty Branch Road, Barnardsville; 828-626-3700; navitat.com). Wearing a hard hat, you'll be strapped in and hooked up with a series of reassuring clicks for each of the 10 zips, the longest at 1,100 feet. They take you from chestnut oaks to tulip poplars, soaring over valleys with a bird's-eye view that will remind you, once again, of the Blue Ridge bedrock of Asheville's eternal appeal.

OPPOSITE The Friday drum circle at Pritchard Park draws families, college couples, and dreadlocked nomads.

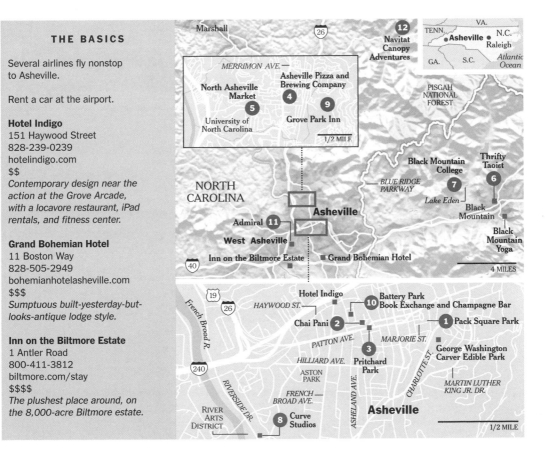

THE BASICS

Several airlines fly nonstop to Asheville.

Rent a car at the airport.

Hotel Indigo
151 Haywood Street
828-239-0239
hotelindigo.com
$$
Contemporary design near the action at the Grove Arcade, with a locavore restaurant, iPad rentals, and fitness center.

Grand Bohemian Hotel
11 Boston Way
828-505-2949
bohemianhotelasheville.com
$$$
Sumptuous built-yesterday-but-looks-antique lodge style.

Inn on the Biltmore Estate
1 Antler Road
800-411-3812
biltmore.com/stay
$$$$
The plushest place around, on the 8,000-acre Biltmore estate.

Gatlinburg

Gatlinburg, Tennessee, the gateway town to Great Smoky Mountains National Park, has a string of garish tourist traps on its congested main street, but no amount of over-the-top hucksterism can spoil its setting, nudged up against the misty blue peaks of the Smokies. The park is spectacular all year, with deep-green canopies in summer, red and gold vistas in fall, and blankets of white in winter. Perhaps the best time to visit is spring, when orchids and violets bloom in its half-million acres of rolling hills, whitewater tumbles on the rivers, festivals spill into the streets of Gatlinburg, and bluegrass twangs in the air.
— BY SARAH TUFF

FRIDAY

1 *United Artists* 3:30 p.m.

One of the greatest achievements by any sorority might be the 1912 founding of the Settlement School by the Pi Beta Phi sisters, who aimed to educate the Appalachian poor. Eventually, it became the **Arrowmont School of Arts and Crafts** (556 Parkway; 865-436-5860; arrowmont.org), a funky, airy studio and gallery in downtown Gatlinburg. (Or, as one online travel forum user wrote, an oasis in a sea of fudge.) It's free and open — with occasional workshops and an adjacent craft shop — until 4:30 p.m. Peer in on artists at work from the catwalk that runs above separate studios, or admire oil paintings, woodwork, and delicate sterling-silver sculptures in the three galleries.

2 *Tourists Trapped* 5 p.m.

Many tourists who travel to Gatlinburg don't know about Great Smoky Mountains National Park. Shocking — but then again there do seem to be quite a lot of distractions along the Parkway, the main drag that leads through town to the park. The **Space Needle** (115 Historic Nature Trail; 865-436-4629; gatlinburgspaceneedle.com) is a 1970 landmark with an elevator that whisks, well, works its way

OPPOSITE Laurel Creek near Cades Cove in Great Smoky Mountains National Park.

RIGHT The Smoky Mountain Trout House, one place in town to eat the favorite local fish.

342 feet up for an open-air, 360-degree view. At **Ripley's Believe It or Not! Museum** (800 Parkway; 865-436-5096; gatlinburg.ripleys.com), you can gawk at attractions like a 6,600-foot gum wrapper chain, shrunken heads, and locusts preserved from an 1860 plague. There's also a haunted house that might actually spook you and, down the road, an aquarium with a walk-through shark lagoon. But nothing as scary as the museum's sushi lint art and 5.5-pound pig hairball.

3 *Tequila Wish, Tortilla Dream* 7:30 p.m.

Hungry? After Ripley's, you're probably not in the mood for sushi — or anything that has to do with a pig. But your appetite will quickly return after a pitcher or two of margaritas on the outdoor deck at **No Way Jose's Cantina** (555 Parkway; 865-430-5673; nowayjosescantina.com; $), a Tex-Mex joint overlooking the Little Pigeon River. Try the deep fried ice cream, adorned with cinnamon, honey, chocolate, and whipped cream. Before you get to that, go for the fajitas. But nothing too spicy — you're hiking tomorrow morning, and servicios are scarce to nonexistent along those Great Smoky trails.

SATURDAY

4 *Stacked in Your Favor* 7 a.m.

If you're staying along the Little Pigeon River, you might rise to the sight of an angler trying to

reel in a trout. An easier way to find breakfast is at one of Gatlinburg's pancake parlors, whose choices might leave you reeling yourself. The **Pancake Pantry** (628 Parkway; 865-436-4724; pancakepantry.com; $), which says it became Tennessee's first pancake house in 1960, now flips 24 varieties, including apricot lemon and Peach Delight. The Pantry will also pack you an inexpensive lunch for the park.

5 *Chasing Waterfalls* 8 a.m.

Drop the pancake fork. Slowly back away from any nearby candy shop. There are more than 800 miles of hiking trails in **Great Smoky Mountains National Park** (nps.gov/grsm) and nearly as many waterfalls. You will have most of the footpaths and falling water all to yourself, perhaps shared with a few of the 31 species of salamanders that slither through the Smokies, an area known for the rich diversity of its critters. **Ramsey Cascades** (off Route 321, past the Greenbrier entrance and ranger station) is a rugged eight-mile round-trip hike that gains about 2,140 feet in altitude. It takes you through the Smokies' largest chunk of old-growth forest — cherry, hemlock, and tulip trees — before arriving at the 90-foot falls and its cooling spray. Another path in the Smokies is the Appalachian Trail; when the through-hikers walking it from Georgia to Maine get to Gatlinburg, they are 200 miles, or about 9 percent, of the way into the trip.

6 *Rapid Transit* 3 p.m.

When Daniel Jennette, a river-rafting guide with **Smoky Mountain Outdoors** (453 Brookside Village Way; 800-771-7238; smokymountainrafting.com), chose Lost Guide as the name for one of the 70 rapids on a 6.5-mile stretch of the upper Big Pigeon River,

he wasn't joking. The Class IV is where most new guides — and you, the rookie rafter — tumble into the drink during a two-hour trip. Your best shot at staying dry (or at least dryish) is to keep paddling, maintain your center of gravity, and stay tough. Be ready for the first Class IV, 30 seconds into the trip, and for the more placid After Shave and Bombs Lake sections, where you can finally kick back for a couple of minutes. For a lazier float, rent inner tubes from Smoky Mountain and ply the Little River, or consider the gentle lower Big Pigeon, where even young children are allowed to go rafting.

7 *Bottoms Up* 6:30 p.m.

The brew master Marty Velas, who helped open the **Smoky Mountain Brewery** (1004 Parkway; 865-436-4200; coppercellar.com) in 1996, knows a thing or two about beer. He has collected some 6,000 bottles, half of which are lined along the exposed beams upstairs in this brewery pub. Try the Mountain Light or, should you need more recovery from the rafting, the more potent Black Bear Ale.

8 *Trout and About* 8 p.m.

Remember that trout that got away, around breakfast time today? Look for its cousin, boned and pan-fried, next door to the Smoky Mountain Brewery at the **Park Grill** (1110 Parkway; 865-436-2300; parkgrillgatlinburg.com; $$). Or satisfy your inner carnivore, if you must, with one of the hefty steaks. Then it's back to the brewery, where the band will start playing around 9:30.

ABOVE Black Bear Ale at the Smoky Mountain Brewery, a place to recover after a day of exploring. Look for hikers who have detoured into town from the Appalachian Trail.

9 *Tennessee Shangri-La* 8 a.m.

About 30 miles into Great Smoky Mountains National Park from Gatlinburg, **Cades Cove** is a cluster of 19th-century cabins, mills, and churches in a wide green valley, now left to the deer, otter, bears, and wild turkeys. At midday, cars clog the 11-mile loop around the cove, but if you get an early start, you can avoid the crush and enjoy the area on a bicycle (nps.gov/grsm/planyourvisit/biking.htm). Things are even better on summer Wednesday and Saturday mornings, when the area is open only to hikers and cyclists until 10 a.m. You can rent bikes at the **Cades Cove Campground Store**

(865-448-9034; cadescove.net). Or hop on a horse at the nearby **Cades Cove Riding Stable** (423-448-6286; cadescovestables.com).

10 *Justly Deserved* Noon

Be sure you don't leave Gatlinburg without stopping by **Desserts & More**, at Sweetpea's Cafe & Antique Lounge (458 Parkway; 865-277-7711; dessertsandmore.com). This is home cooking, from thick chicken-salad sandwiches to fluffy coconut pie and creamy chocolate-chip cheesecake, all made from scratch. Enjoy them with homemade lemonade and flavored iced teas. Slices or entire pies and cakes are available to go — though chances are they won't make it very far.

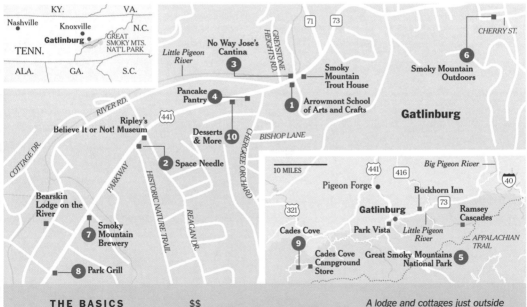

THE BASICS

Rent a car at the Knoxville airport and drive about an hour to Gatlinburg.

Bearskin Lodge on the River
840 River Road
865-430-4330
thebearskinlodge.com

$$
Away from the congested Parkway and relatively quiet. Balconies overlook the Little Pigeon River.

Buckhorn Inn
2140 Tudor Mountain Road
865-436-4668
buckhorninn.com
$$-$$$

A lodge and cottages just outside the center of town; mountain views.

Park Vista
705 Cherokee Orchard Road
865-436-9211
parkvista.com
$$
Recently renovated Doubletree property on a mountaintop site.

Knoxville

Knoxville, Tennessee, is often called "the couch" by the people who live there. It is a place too unassuming to shout about but too comfortable to leave. The city, the third largest in Tennessee behind Nashville and Memphis, is also referred to as Knoxpatch, Knoxvegas, and for those prone to irony and finger pistols, K-town, baby. The truth is, Knoxville, a college town cheerfully ensconced in the foothills of the Great Smoky Mountains and banked against the Tennessee River, has an intrinsically lazy, soulful air about it. The geography is soft, green, and rolling. The climate is gentle, breezy, and bright. Locals tend to be not just friendly — a given in most Southern towns — but chilled out, too. This is not the Old South of magnolias and seersucker so much as a modern Appalachia of roots music, locavore food, folk art, and hillbilly pride. Or, as yet another city moniker aptly puts it, "Austin without the hype." — BY ALLISON GLOCK

FRIDAY

1 *Cultivated Bluegrass* Noon

Knoxville is known for its music — Dolly Parton was discovered here, Hank Williams stopped here

OPPOSITE Sequoyah Hills Park has 87 acres of land with trails for walking, running, and biking, as well as free boat access to the Tennessee River.

BELOW The Sunsphere was built for a 1982 world's fair.

on his last road trip, and most locals know their way around a banjo. The listener-supported station **WDVX-FM**, multiple winner of the national title Bluegrass Station of the Year, hosts the Monday-through-Saturday *Blue Plate Special* show, offering free live music from noon to 1 p.m. (301 South Gay Street; 865-544-1029; wdvx.com). Guests include everyone from Béla Fleck and Ricky Skaggs to the Gypsy jazz band Ameranouche and homegrown Appalachian talent. Bring a bag lunch or pick up an ice-cold cola and some snacks from the old-fashioned mercantile **Mast General Store** (402 South Gay Street; 865-546-1336; mastgeneralstore.com) and take a seat for some down-home music in an unusually intimate setting.

2 *Art for All Y'all* 2 p.m.

Part gallery, part stationery shop, all handmade cool, **Yee-Haw Industries** (413 South Gay Street; 865-522-1812; yeehawindustries.com) is a great spot to idle for an hour or two, soaking up the walls and ceilings blanketed with one-of-a-kind letterpress posters, bags, shirts, calendars, and fine art prints. Stop in and chat with the owner-artists Julie Belcher and Kevin Bradley, who, if you're lucky, will take you upstairs to show you their latest projects, most painstakingly created from carved woodblock, then letterpressed using vintage machinery. The results are distinctive, beautiful, and evocative of the past. If nothing else, pick up some cards. The sets, hand printed on 100 percent recycled stock, are unlike anything you're likely to find at Hallmark.

3 *Meats and Sweets* 5 p.m.

Litton's (2803 Essary Road; 865-687-8788; littonburgers.com; $) is a bit off the beaten path, which doesn't keep it from being standing room only virtually every lunch and dinner. Started in a small back room, the diner-style restaurant, meat market, and bakery has sprawled to fill a warehouse's worth of space. Known for its burgers and desserts, Litton's is not the place to come if cholesterol is a preoccupation. Go for the Thunder Road burger (pimento cheese, sautéed onions, and jalapeño with fries) and a slice of red velvet cake. Lines are long, but pews are available while you wait. Just be sure to sign in on the chalkboard.

ABOVE Inside the restored Tennessee Theatre in the Market Square area, the heart of downtown.

SATURDAY

4 *Green Acres* 8 a.m.

Jog, walk, bike, or paddle at **Sequoyah Hills Park** (1400 Cherokee Boulevard; ci.knoxville.tn.us/parks/sequoyah.asp), an 87-acre sprawl of green lawns, flowering trees, dog paths, and picnic spots on the Tennessee River. Water access is easy, as is parking. For a longer hike, the **Ijams Nature Center** (2915 Island Home Avenue; 865-577-4717; ijams.org), a 160-acre park and wildlife sanctuary, is a 10-minute drive from downtown.

5 *Pioneer Spirit* 11 a.m.

Twenty minutes outside Knoxville will take you to the **Museum of Appalachia** (2819 Andersonville Highway, Clinton; 865-494-7680; museumofappalachia.org). Born of the historian John Rice Irwin's love for the mountain people of Tennessee, the museum encompasses truckloads of Appalachian pioneer artifacts and folk art as well as actual cabins, churches, and outbuildings that were carefully moved from their original locations and reassembled on its expansive grounds. Live music can be heard almost every day thanks to the Porch Musicians Project,

Irwin's effort to expose all guests to "authentic old-time music" and preserve America's aural history. Lunch is available in the cafe. Order the fresh-fried pinto beans and cornbread.

6 *Let Them Eat Cupcakes* 4 p.m.

Cupcake mania has swept the nation. But nowhere is it more deserved than at **MagPies** (846 North Central Street; 865-673-0471; magpiescakes.com), a place whose motto is "all butter all the time." The baker, proprietress, and adequate accordion player Peggy Hambright specializes in "super deluxe flavors" that change every month. (Examples: Chocolate Guinness Stout, Key lime pie, and blackberry buttermilk.) A dozen minis or a six-pack of regulars, the usual units of purchase, may seem like a lot to buy at once, but don't plan on any leftovers.

7 *Say Tomato* 7 p.m.

The nexus for all things hip and happening in town, the vegan-friendly **Tomato Head** (12 Market Square; 865-637-4067; thetomatohead.com; $$), is the place to go for epicurean pizza and unparalleled people watching. The founder, chef, and local foodie icon Mahasti Vafaie makes everything you eat there, including the breads, buns, and salad dressings. Order the No. 8 (pesto-based pizza with Roma tomato and roasted portobello), the Greek salad (heavy on the kalamata olives), and a glass of wine. Sit outside

if you can, where your table overlooks the whole of Market Square—a cheek-by-jowl assortment of cafes, boutiques, galleries, and pubs all with a bustling shared common area.

8 *Square Deal* 8:30 p.m.

Market Square restaurants have outdoor seating, and most evenings find amateur pickers and singers performing in the square, lending the whole space the feeling of a giant impromptu party. Stores worth some après dinner window shopping include **Reruns Consignment Boutique** (2 Market Square; 865-525-9525; rerunsboutique.com) for bargain-priced designer finds and **Bliss** (24 Market Square; 865-329-8868; shopinbliss.com), an everything-but-the-kitchen-sink gift emporium offering apparel, furniture, frames, and flatware.

ABOVE Poster making at Yee-Haw Industries.

BELOW A mural of a London Street in the Crown & Goose English-style pub, where brunch can include Stilton cheese.

9 *Ale Power* 10 p.m.

Amid the Market Square madness sits the **Preservation Pub** (28 Market Square; 865-524-2224; preservationpub.com), a narrow slip of a bar that manages to squeeze quite a few folks and even more beer choices into its cozy confines. There are 20-plus strong ale selections alone (try the Stone Arrogant Bastard or the Orkney Skull Splitter) but know that the bartenders keep an eye on the number of strong ales you down, so as to avoid chaos spilling onto the square—unless it is live music night. Then all bets are off.

SUNDAY

10 *English Eaten Here* 11 a.m.

The Crown & Goose gastropub (123 South Central Street; 865-524-2100; thecrownandgoose.com; $$)

serves a hearty brunch along with whatever soccer match happens to be on TV that day. Sidle up to the huge 19th-century-style bar and sample the eggs Benedict with fried green tomatoes or the Belgian waffles dipped in cider batter and loaded with sweet cream cheese, maple syrup, and fresh fruit. Traditional English fare is also on offer, from a cheese board that includes Stilton to the requisite fish and chips.

11 *Heights and Hoops* 3 p.m.

Before you leave, take the elevator to the top of the **Sunsphere** (810 Clinch Avenue), an architectural leftover from the 1982 World's Fair and a parody victim of *The Simpsons*. The Sunsphere, a 600-ton,

266-foot steel truss topped with a 74-foot gold ball, looks like a Titleist on steroids but offers the best views of the city and the mountains just beyond. The **Women's Basketball Hall of Fame** (700 Hall of Fame Drive; 865-633-9000; wbhof.com) is the home of the world's largest basketball — 30 feet tall, 10 tons, no Sunsphere, but still — and myriad artifacts of early women's basketball from throughout the world, including an original 1901 rulebook. Of course, tributes to Pat Summit, the coach of the hometown University of Tennessee Lady Vols, who has the most victories in Division 1 basketball history (well over 1,000 and counting), rightfully abound.

ABOVE One of the preserved historic buildings moved to the grounds of the Museum of Appalachia, a treasure trove of pioneer artifacts and folk art.

OPPOSITE The exterior of the Crown & Goose.

THE BASICS

Fly in and rent a car.

Hotel St. Oliver
407 Union Avenue
865-521-0050
stoliverhotel.com
$$

Historic inn off Market Square.

Four Points by Sheraton KnoxvilleCumberland House
1109 White Avenue
865-971-4663
starwoodhotels.com/fourpoints/
knoxville
$$

Close to the University of Tennessee campus.

Hilton Knoxville
501 West Church Avenue
865-523-2300
knoxvillehilton.com
$$
Standard Hilton amenities.

Lexington

Miles of low fences line the winding, two-lane roads of the Bluegrass Country around Lexington, Kentucky, and enclose its rolling green horse farms, where magnificent thoroughbreds rest near pristinely painted barns. Now and again, the fences break for a leafy lane leading to an age-old bourbon distillery with doors open for a tour and a tipple. Then they lead away to a quaint 19th-century town, a quintessential country inn, or a serene Shaker village. These magical fences, made of wood or of stones stacked long ago by slaves and Scots-Irish settlers, take you back in time and away in space. But you'll be brought back soon enough by Kentucky's modern hosts serving up Southern charm and distinctly American food and drink. — BY TAYLOR HOLLIDAY

FRIDAY

1 *Horse Fixation* 1:45 p.m.

Lexington, a leisurely university city with preserved antebellum houses, calls itself the horse capital of the world. On thousands of acres of nearby farms, pampered horses graze on the local bluegrass, so called because it blooms a purplish blue. Dip into the horse world at **Kentucky Horse Park** (4089 Iron Works Parkway, Lexington; 859-233-4303; kyhorsepark.com). It may seem at first like merely a giant horsy theme park, but the horse trailers in the parking lot attest to its importance for competitions as well. There are displays on the history of the horse, paeans to winners like Man o' War and Cigar, and a Parade of Breeds (catch it at 2 p.m.). Horse shows and races are frequent — you might catch a steeplechase. And in June, musicians arrive from far and wide for a festival of bluegrass music.

2 *Chefs of the Country* 7 p.m.

Northwest of Lexington, Route 62 cuts a path through lush countryside to charming little Midway, a railroad town of about 1,600 people where trains still run right down the middle of the main street. A gem

of a restaurant, the **Holly Hill Inn** (426 North Winter Street, Midway; 859-846-4732; hollyhillinn.com; $$$), awaits you down a nearby lane, in a house dating to 1839. Ouita Michel, the chef, and her husband, Chris, the sommelier, both graduates of the Culinary Institute of America, serve a four-course prix fixe dinner. Choices on the changing menus have included spoonbread souffle, pork roast with figs and dates, and tile fish with Kentucky red rice.

SATURDAY

3 *Brake for Bourbon* 10 a.m.

The land around Lexington grows more than thoroughbreds. West of the city, you're in bourbon country. Several distillers have banded together to create what they call the Bourbon Trail, so spend a day learning why their product is such a source of Kentucky pride. Stop first in Versailles (pronounce it "ver-SALES"), where the stately limestone **Woodford Reserve** (7855 McCracken Pike; 859-879-1812; woodfordreserve.com) is nestled deep among farms with cupola-topped stables and miles of black-painted board fences. The only product made here is the small-batch Woodford Reserve, but visitors come by the thousands, and you'll see the entire bourbon-making process from mash to bottle. Inhale the smells of whiskey and old wood, and sip a sample.

OPPOSITE A thoroughbred at home amid the black rail fences of the Kentucky Bluegrass Country around Lexington.

RIGHT Woodford Reserve, one of the Kentucky bourbon distilleries where a tour is capped with a sip of the whiskey.

4 *Whiskey Saga* Noon

Bardstown, a city of about 10,000 in the heart of bourbon territory, honors its debt to spirits at the **Oscar Getz Museum of Whiskey History** (114 North Fifth Street; 502-348-2999; whiskeymuseum.com). In the 1790s, Scotch-Irish distillers fleeing George Washington's whiskey tax and the quelling of the subsequent Whiskey Rebellion landed in an area of Virginia then called Bourbon County, which now covers several counties of northeastern Kentucky. They found perfect conditions for their trade, partly because of a layer of limestone that filters iron from the local water, and bourbon whiskey was born. In the museum, examine local artifacts including authentic moonshine stills.

5 *Vary the Stimuli* 1 p.m.

Make a temporary switch from booze to caffeine at **Java Joint** (126 North 3rd Street, Bardstown; 502-350-0883; thejavajoint.homestead.com; $), where you can grab a quick lunch of sandwiches, soup, or salad along with the signature cup of flavorful coffee.

6 *Dip Your Own* 2 p.m.

Meander about 15 miles south on Route 49 to tiny Loretto and enter the red-shuttered, brown-clapboard buildings of **Maker's Mark** (3350 Burks Springs Road; 270-865-2099). The oldest bourbon distillery in the country, dating to 1805, it is well schooled in the rules

of bourbon: the mash must be at least 51 percent corn, barrels for aging must be new and made of charred white oak, alcohol must be at prescribed strengths in the years-long process of transforming grain into whiskey. The tour here shows you the cooker, mash fermentation, the still, aging rackhouses, and hand-bottling. You can dip a finger into a vat of bubbling, fermenting mash to get a taste (like sweetened cereal gone sour), and they'll even let you hand-dip your own souvenir bottle in the trademark red wax.

7 *Jim Beam's Place* 4 p.m.

Drive back north to Bardstown and take Route 245 west to Clermont, the home of **Jim Beam** (149 Happy Hollow Road; 502-543-9877; jimbeam.com), the biggest of the bourbon distillers. Jim Beam doesn't have an extensive tour, but you'll get a good tasting. And from the porch of the Beam family's whitewashed mansion on the hill, you have a perfect view of the vapor-spewing, multibuilding factory, which has turned out millions of bottles of bourbon.

8 *Not a Colonel in Sight* 6 p.m.

For real Kentucky skillet-fried chicken, take a table at **Kurtz** (418 East Stephen Foster Avenue, Bardstown; 502-348-8964; bardstownparkview.com/dining.htm; $$), which has been satisfying hungry Kentuckians for 70 years. The chicken is superb and the fixings are traditional—mashed potatoes,

cornbread, green beans with Kentucky ham. For dessert, ask for the biscuit pudding with bourbon sauce.

9 *Bourbons by the Dozen* 8 p.m.

When you're finished with the day's driving and ready to relax, sample the atmosphere and the libations at a bourbon bar, where knowledgeable bartenders serve Kentucky's favorite drink in dozens of varieties. In Bardstown, there's a classic of the genre at **Old Talbott Tavern** (107 West Stephen Foster Avenue; 502-348-3494; talbotts.com). In Lexington, try **Bluegrass Tavern** (115 Cheapside, Lexington; 859-389-6664) or the **Horse and Barrel Pub** at deSha's Restaurant and Bar (101 North Broadway; 859-259-3771; tavernrestaurantgroup.com).

SUNDAY

10 *Thoroughbreds at Home* 9 a.m.

Taking tourists to the horse farms is a Lexington specialty — the local convention and visitors bureau publishes a list of tour companies and private guides (visitlex.com/idea/horse-farms.php). One good choice is a trip with the women of **Horse Farm Tours** (859-268-2906; horsefarmtours.com), who point out historical buildings in downtown Lexington on the way to a sampling of farms. If decadently luxurious stables and a 10-bedroom mansion at one farm are a reminder that thoroughbreds are a rich person's

hobby, the wholesome young broodmare manager at the next farm, attending to the mares and their wobbly, week-old foals, is proof of how intense the horse-and-human relationship can be. At the stud farm, it's all about bloodlines and breeding techniques. You'll also be whisked to the best seats in the ivy-covered

OPPOSITE Oak barrels at Woodford Reserve. On the tour, you'll see the bourbon-making process from mash to bottle.

TOP Green countryside near Loretto, on one of the winding side roads to explore near Lexington.

ABOVE Whiskey makers migrated to this part of Kentucky, then known as Bourbon County, Virginia, around 1800. Some of their tools are displayed at Maker's Mark distillery.

limestone viewing stand at Keeneland, Lexington's renowned race track — to see, perhaps, some horses in training.

11 *Plain Cooking* 1 p.m.

Drive south from Lexington on Route 68, through gently undulating hills and higher forested bluffs, to **Shaker Village of Pleasant Hill** (3501 Lexington Road, Harrodsburg; 859-734-5411; shakervillageky.org), a preserved home of the plain-living 19th-century Shaker sect. It feels remarkably like the real deal; the most beautiful of its 34 remaining buildings needed only light restoration to return them to the middle 1800s, when the community was at its peak. (Shakerism embraced celibacy and eventually died out.) Have dinner in the spare and lovely Trustees' Office Dining Room restaurant (call for reservations), which cooks with heirloom vegetables from its own garden, and tour the quiet grounds.

ABOVE Maker's Mark, in Loretto, finishes off its bourbon bottles with signature red wax.

OPPOSITE Inside a storage warehouse at the Jim Beam distillery in Clermont.

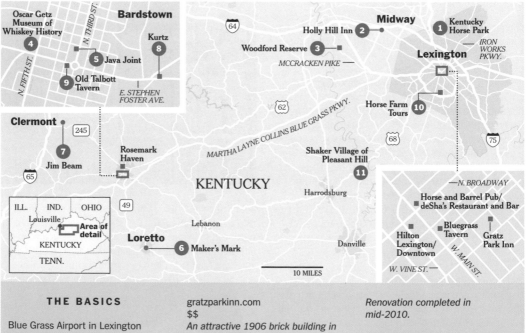

THE BASICS

Blue Grass Airport in Lexington is served by several airlines and rental car companies.

Gratz Park Inn
120 West Second Street, Lexington
859-231-1777
gratzparkinn.com
$$
An attractive 1906 brick building in the Gratz Park Historic District.

Hilton Lexington/Downtown
369 West Vine Street
859-231-9000
lexingtondowntownhotel.com
$$
Renovation completed in mid-2010.

A Rosemark Haven
714 North Third Street, Bardstown
502-348-8218
rosemarkhaven.com
$$
Seven stylish guestrooms in a restored 1830s mansion.

Louisville

Every May, Louisville, Kentucky, bolts into the public eye for 120 seconds — the time it takes to run the Kentucky Derby. But there is more to this courtly city on the Ohio River than the Derby. The last decade has seen a cultural and civic blooming, with new galleries, restaurants, and performance spaces taking their place alongside the city's already robust roster of seductions. Entire neighborhoods — Butchertown, for instance, and East Market — have been reimagined as engines of cultural and culinary expression. Regardless of the changes, Derby City retains its easy charm — a glass of fine bourbon and good conversation aren't hard to find. And for the record, it's pronounced "LOU-uh-vull."
— BY MICHAEL WASHBURN

FRIDAY

1 *Getting Acquainted* 6 p.m.

More than 45 different watering holes line the roughly two miles of the Bardstown Road-Baxter Avenue corridor, from elegant restaurants to sticky-floored dives. Sandwiched among them are cafes, galleries specializing in regional ceramics and woodwork, and shops selling vintage clothing and jewelry, musical instruments, and Louisville-themed curiosities. A welcome addition is the **Holy Grale** (1034 Bardstown Road; 502-459-9939; holygralelouisville.com). Recently opened in a century-old church, this dark, snug tavern with a polished bar running its length offers a selection of fine beers, including 20 rare drafts like the unpasteurized Aecht Schlenkerla Rauchbier Urbock, a dark beer that is surprisingly light despite its smoky, chocolate flavor. The chorizo tacos make a fiery complement.

2 *Bootleggers and Grits* 8:30 p.m.

Jack Fry's (1007 Bardstown Road; 502-452-9244; jackfrys.com; $$$) opened in 1933 as a haven for bootleggers and bookies and has remained a popular dining spot, with its classic Old South atmosphere and original décor. A collection of 1930s-era photographs — including shots of the 1937 flood that devastated

downtown Louisville and prompted development in the eastern, now more affluent, sections of town — adorns the walls, and a discreet jazz trio performs in the corner. These days the restaurant focuses on subtle reinventions of Southern staples: shrimp and grits with red-eye gravy and country ham, for example, or lamb chops in a rosemary natural jus with shiitakes and thyme.

3 *Night Music* 10:30 p.m.

From Will Oldham and Slint to My Morning Jacket, Louisville performers have sent their music echoing around the world. Even if you're not lucky enough to catch Oldham or MMJ in one of their local appearances, with other talent — like Wax Fang, Cheyenne Mize, Seluah, and Joe Manning — you can always find something to spirit you away. **Zanzabar** (2100 South Preston Street; 502-635-9227; zanzabarlouisville.com) offers cheap whiskey for you to sip at its horseshoe-shaped bar while you catch one of the city's (or country's) comers on its intimate stage. Closing time here — and almost everywhere in Louisville — is 4 a.m.

SATURDAY

4 *Art and Comfort Food* 9 a.m.

The East Market District, dubbed NuLu (new Louisville) is perhaps the best of the city's revitalization projects, offering antiques stores and shiny new galleries. The **Zephyr Gallery** (610 East Market Street; 502-585-5646; zephyrgallery.org) and **Swanson Reed Contemporary** (638 East Market Street; 502-589-5466; swansonreedgallery.com) display paintings, videos, and installation work from

OPPOSITE On the track at the Kentucky Derby.

RIGHT The Moonshine Breakfast at Hillbilly Tea.

regional and national artists. Before exploring too far, visit the new **Hillbilly Tea** (120 South First Street; 502-587-7350; hillbillytea.com; $$) for the Moonshine Breakfast: a grilled pork chop with bourbon and sage, herb scrambled eggs, and potatoes. The gettin's good, and the locals know it, so be patient.

5 *Float Like a Butterfly* 11 a.m.

Louisville's greatest son is the greatest: Muhammad Ali. The **Muhammad Ali Center** (144 North Sixth Street; 502-584-9254; alicenter.org) celebrates his singular talent as a fighter and his post-retirement humanitarian efforts, but the curators pulled no punches with the history. Sure, you can try the speed bag, but not before you're immersed in multimedia presentations that contextualize Ali's career within the civil rights struggle. The Ali Center is part of **Museum Row** (museumrowonmain.com), an eclectic confederation of museums and galleries devoted to science, blown glass art, Louisville Slugger baseball bats, historical artifacts (including armor worn by English knights), and more.

6 *Riders Up!* 1:30 p.m.

Churchill Downs (700 Central Avenue; 502-636-4400; churchilldowns.com) demands a visit even if you're not here for the Derby — especially if you're not here for the Derby. During other races in the spring meet, which runs for several months,

a spot on Millionaire's Row costing Diddy and his ilk $68,000 on Derby Day will set you back only $20 when you walk among the mortals; don't worry, the ponies charge just as hard. Adjacent to the Downs, the **Kentucky Derby Museum** (704 Central Avenue; 502-637-7097; derbymuseum.org), open all year, offers an overview of the Run for the Roses and hosts several track tours, including one of the "backside," home to 1,400 thoroughbreds during racing season. After leaving the Downs, visit **Wagner's Pharmacy** (3113 South

ABOVE Reliving the Derby at the Kentucky Derby Museum.

BELOW Churchill Downs, active on more than Derby Day.

OPPOSITE Holy Grale, a stop on the bar strip.

Fourth Street; 502-375-3800; wagnerspharmacy.com), fabled hangout of grooms, jockeys, and sportswriters. Barely changed since 1922, Wagner's lunch counter displays fading photos of legends—two- and four-legged—from Derby history.

7 *Whiskey Row* 6 p.m.

Doc Crows (127 West Main Street; 502-587-1626; doccrows.com; $$) occupies the former Bonnie Bros. distillery, one of Louisville's collection of cast-iron-facade buildings in an area called Whiskey Row. Take a seat in the back room of this 1880s-era gem and enjoy oysters on the half shell with bourbon mignonette or Carolina-style pulled pork. Brett Davis, an owner, one of 112 master sommeliers in the country, prowls about most nights. Ask Brett to select which of the 64 bourbons will go best with your meal.

8 *Broadway on the Ohio* 8 p.m.

Home of the annual spring Humana Festival of New American Plays, one of the nation's foremost new-works festivals, **Actors Theatre of Louisville** (316 West Main Street; 502-584-1205; actorstheatre.org) not only provides a rigorous testing ground for new talent, but shows well-acted plays for most of the year. The festival introduced Pulitzer Prize-winning plays including *Dinner With Friends* and *Crimes of the Heart* and has sent an impressive cadre of graduates on to Broadway. If nothing at Actors Theatre

strikes your fancy, check out the **Kentucky Center for the Arts** (501 West Main Street; 502-562-0100; kentuckycenter.org), which hosts touring productions as well as performances by the Louisville Orchestra and the Louisville Ballet.

9 *Borne Back Ceaselessly* 10:30 p.m.

The college crowd and some of their elders party at Louisville's overwrought, underthought **Fourth Street Live**, an urban mall featuring clubs, bars, and places like T.G.I. Fridays and a Hard Rock Cafe. Take a few steps from that chaos, however, and discover the wonderfully worn **Old Seelbach Bar** (500 Fourth Street; 502-585-3200; seelbachhilton.com). It's rumored that when F. Scott Fitzgerald was a young military officer stationed in Louisville, he would while away the hours at this stately lounge directly off the Seelbach Hotel's grand lobby. The hotel itself has a cameo in the film version of *The Great Gatsby*, but Fitzgerald didn't highlight the bar in his masterpiece, preferring to keep the best for himself. At least that's how the local story goes. Whatever the reason, it's better this way.

SUNDAY

10 *A Walk in the Park* 10 a.m.

Wake up with a jolt from the local favorite **Heine Brothers' Coffee** (1295 Bardstown Road;

502-456-5108; heinebroscoffee.com). This location shares a passageway with one of the last great bookstores, **Carmichael's** (1295 Bardstown Road; 502-456-6950; carmichaelsbookstore.com). Feel free to amble back and forth while you prepare

ABOVE You can try out the punching bag, but the Muhammad Ali Center isn't all about boxing. Multimedia presentations contextualize the life and career of Ali, who grew up in Louisville, within the civil rights struggle.

OPPOSITE At Jack Fry's, a legendary haven for bootleggers and bookies, diners now find a more genteel atmosphere.

for **Cherokee Park**. Opened in 1892, Cherokee was one of Frederick Law Olmsted's last and wildest creations — think Prospect Park in the foothills of Appalachia. Park near Hogan's Fountain and you can explore the nearly 400 acres of trails, hills, and meadows.

11 *Cave Hill* 1 p.m.

Colonel Harland Sanders — yes, that Colonel Sanders — lies alongside local luminaries like George Rogers Clark, the city's founder, at **Cave Hill Cemetery** (701 Baxter Avenue; 502-451-5630; cavehillcemetery.com), a lush Victorian-era graveyard that offers, unsurprisingly, a peaceful respite amid the bustle of the Highlands neighborhood. Before leaving, go native and leave a spork or a packet of ketchup at the Colonel's Doric-columned grave site, a memorial to his fried chicken fame.

THE BASICS

Fly into Louisville International Airport or drive into town on interstate highways 64, 65, or 71.

You will need a car to get around.

21C Museum Hotel
700 West Main Street
502-217-6300
21chotel.com
$$$
A highly rated hotel-art gallery with 9,000 square feet of exhibition space.

The Brown Hotel
335 West Broadway
502-583-1234
brownhotel.com
$$
Grand old hotel open since 1923.

The Seelbach-Hilton
500 Fourth Street
502-585-3200
seelbachhilton.com
$$$$
A Louisville classic.

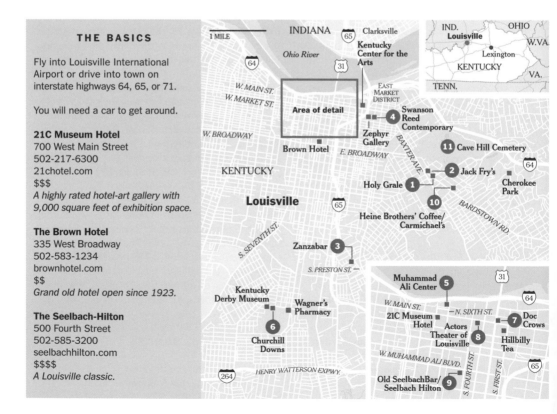

Nashville

Nashville, Tennessee, isn't nicknamed Music City for nothing. Singers, songwriters, and pickers — not to mention their toe-tapping admirers — have been pouring in for decades. This is where country music lives and breathes, but Nashville is a big tent for good music, nurturing generations of musicians playing rock and alt-country, R & B, and even jazz and classical. While it revels in its country roots, there's a new beat in once-sleepy neighborhoods like East Nashville and 12 South that thrive with lively bars, stylish restaurants, and a young, eclectic crop of music makers, churning out everything from bluegrass to punkabilly.
— BY KEITH MULVIHILL AND TAYLOR HOLLIDAY

FRIDAY

1 *Get the Picture* 4 p.m.

For an introduction to downtown, traditionally country music central, stroll along the Cumberland River and over the Shelby Avenue bridge, where the view is superb. Heading uptown along Broadway, don't miss **Hatch Show Print** (316 Broadway; 615-256-2805; hatchshowprint.com), in business since 1879. A letterpress print shop and gallery, it displays and sells handmade copies of gems like "Dolly Parton and Her Family Traveling Band" and "In Person: B.B. King." Down the street, the **Ernest Tubb Record Shop** (417 Broadway; 615-255-7503; etrecordshop.com), where the original honky-tonk hero once broadcast his midnight radio jamboree, carries almost every classic country and bluegrass recording available. And close by is the Ryman Auditorium, the original Grand Ole Opry stage.

2 *Green Cuisine* 7 p.m.

Take a short drive and relax away from downtown's crowds. Earthy hues set a pleasant, unfussy vibe at **Tayst** (2100 21st Avenue South; 615-383-1953; taystrestaurant.com; $$), which bills itself as Nashville's first restaurant to earn certification from the Green Restaurant Association, a nonprofit based in Boston that promotes environmentally friendly

OPPOSITE The Ryman Auditorium downtown.

RIGHT A mural fades downtown, but a younger, dynamic Nashville, rich in new and old music, is only blocks away.

restaurants. Look for seasonal American dishes from local farms; one autumn menu included pork brined with maple syrup served with wild rice, chestnuts, and spicy cranberries. A smartly dressed after-work crowd mingles at the wine bar.

3 *Do the Grapevine* 9:30 p.m.

In the mid-1990s, *The Wildhorse Saloon Dance Show* on the Nashville Network inspired legions of viewers to learn the Boot Scootin' Boogie and the Watermelon Crawl. Today, the sprawling **Wildhorse Saloon** (120 Second Avenue North; 615-902-8200; wildhorsesaloon.com) continues to draw eager crowds. That there are more flip-flops than cowboy boots is a tad disheartening, but the enthusiasm for line dancing doesn't appear to have waned. You don't know how to do a grapevine? No problem. Check the schedule and arrive early for a lesson when an instructor walks everyone through the steps. You'll be kick-ball-change-stomp stomping like a pro.

SATURDAY

4 *Music Box* 10:30 a.m.

Hundreds of country hits were recorded at **Studio B** (1611 Roy Acuff Place), a drab cinderblock building in the historic Music Row district, where RCA legends like Elvis, Roy Orbison, and Dolly Parton sang their hearts out. The unglamorous space looks largely unchanged from when it was shuttered in 1977. Many visiting music fans haven't even heard of the studio let alone realize that it's one of the last vestiges of country music's golden years. The **Country Music**

Hall of Fame (222 Fifth Avenue South; 615-416-2001; countrymusichalloffame.org) offers hourlong tours of the studio. Piano players may be invited to tickle the ivories of the original Steinway grand piano.

5 *Fire Bird* 1 p.m.

"You can't handle it," a woman at **Prince's Hot Chicken Shack** (123 Ewing Drive; 615-226-9442; $), told one group of newbies who tried to order the "medium" spicy fried chicken. This long-revered spot serves four variations of its exceptional dish: mild, medium, hot, and extra hot. Order at your peril. The moist flesh is marinated and enveloped in a spicy rub before it's fried, so the hotness runs deep. Never mind the hole-in-the-wall décor; the savory hellfire is the draw—that, and the terrific sides of baked beans, coleslaw, and oh-so-sweet chess pie.

6 *Popsicles and Fringe* 3 p.m.

Cool off your first-degree burn at **Las Paletas** (2905 12th Avenue South; 615-386-2101), a small storefront that makes popsicles from fresh fruit and vegetables like honeydew, avocado, or hibiscus. Known simply as 12 South, 12th Avenue South is a trendy, tree-lined

BELOW Dolly Parton, Elvis Presley, and Roy Orbison all sang their hearts out for recordings made in Studio B.

OPPOSITE Hatch is a classic maker of country music posters.

neighborhood packed with boutiques, cafes, and bars. You'll also find **Katy K Designs** (2407 12th Avenue South; 615-297-4242; katyk.com), a vintage clothing shop that specializes in country western wear from Johnny Cash black to Dollyesque showstoppers. A clutch of antiques shops including the **Eighth Avenue Antique Mall** (2015 Eighth Avenue South; 615-279-9922) is nearby. If it's indie recordings you crave, gems can be found at **Grimey's New & Preloved Music** (1604 Eighth Avenue South; 615-254-4801; grimeys.com).

7 *Opryland or Not* 7 p.m.

If country is calling, you'll find the sometimes corny, sometimes brilliant, but always endearing Grand Ole Opry most weekends several miles from downtown at **Opryland** (2804 Opryland Drive; 615-871-6779; opry.com). Country legends, has-beens, stars, and wannabes all show up for this broadcast, the world's longest-running radio show. If you want more adventurous live music, hop over to East Nashville, a trendy neighborhood with a bevy of newer venues. Start off at the **Family Wash** (2038 Greenwood Avenue; 615-226-6070; familywash.com; $) where you can dig into tasty shepherd's pie, traditional or veggie. The alt-country, alt-rock, alt-folk acts start at 9 p.m.; the alt-crowd kicks back with locally brewed Yazoo beers. Next, head a few minutes down the road to the **5 Spot** (1006 Forrest Avenue; 615-650-9333; the5spotlive.com), where 20-somethings groove to live rock, country, or rockabilly.

8 *Southern Comfort* 11 p.m.

If your ears need a rest, grab a stool at the **Patterson House** (1711 Division Street; 615-636-7724; thepattersonnashville.com), a trendy mahogany-lined bar. Its creative libations have included a bacon-infused old-fashioned and the Juliet and Romeo, made with gin, rosewater, angostura bitters, mint, and a sliver of cucumber. Dark wood and dim chandeliers make for a seductive backdrop.

SUNDAY

9 *Alt-Brunch* 9 a.m.

The menu may not list Southern good-ole-boy favorites, but there's nothing persnickety about **Marché Artisan Foods** (1000 Main Street; 615-262-1111;

marcheartisanfoods.com; $$) in East Nashville, a bistro and market that fills a former boat showroom. The space has a homey vibe thanks to enticing display cases filled with baked goods, and a few family-size wooden tables. Standouts include the quiche with sausage and provolone.

10 *Horsey Set* 11 a.m.

Before Nashville was known for its music, life here was moved by melodies both sweet and lowdown. Relive those antebellum days at **Belle Meade Plantation** (5025 Harding Pike; 615-356-0501; bellemeadeplantation.com), a 30-acre estate six miles from downtown. The centerpiece is a grand Greek-revival mansion completed in 1853, with a

labyrinth of colorful rooms. In its heyday, the planta-tion was one of the most prosperous and successful thoroughbred farms around. Portraits of muscular stallions grace the walls. In the library, visitors can view the silver-capped hooves of Iroquois, in 1881 the first American horse to win the English Derby. A posh carriage house, sobering slave quarters, and an 18th-century log cabin dot the lush grounds. Nashville's popularity may spring from country hits, but its cultural history offers a whole lot more.

THE BASICS

Several carriers serve the Nashville airport, a 15-minute drive from downtown.

If you're not driving your own car, rent one.

Hermitage Hotel
231 Sixth Avenue North
615-244-3121
thehermitagehotel.com
$$$
An updated Nashville classic. High tea is served in the romantic Beaux-Arts lobby.

Hutton Hotel
1808 West End Avenue
615-340-9333
huttonhotel.com
$$
New, centrally located, smoke-free, and eco-friendly.

Union Station Hotel
1001 Broadway
615-726-1001
unionstationhotelnashville.com
$$
Ultramodern rooms in a former train station.

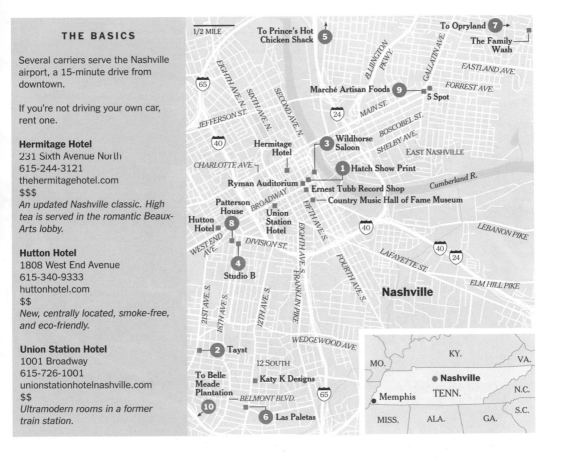

Memphis

You've worn Memphis's cotton, moved to its rhythm, sung its blues. Elvis Presley found his sound in this bluff city; B.B. King took his name, the Beale Street Blues Boy, from its 1940s entertainment district. "Home of the blues," the city now likes to trumpet. "Birthplace of rock 'n' roll." But these cultural revolutions, and the African-American milieu that spawned them, got no respect until Elvis died in 1977 and the city was inundated by grieving fans spending green money. Soon, Memphis began the urban-renewed version of Beale Street — its answer to Bourbon Street, sans the nudie shows — which over the years has become more like frat row. But deep blues do still exist in Memphis. You just have to dig deep to find them. — BY ROBERT GORDON

FRIDAY

1 *Three Little Words* 3 p.m.

Discussions about Memphis barbecue, even among friends, can lead to fisticuffs. Stop at **Payne's** (1762 Lamar Avenue; 901-272-1523; $) on your way in from the airport. It's a former service station, cavernous and spare. In Memphis, barbecue means pork shoulder, pulled from the bone or chopped and served with hot sauce or mild, with a dollop of cole slaw on top. The slaw is essential, as the perfect sandwich — i.e., Payne's — is a matter not only of taste but also of texture. "One chopped hot," you say at the counter, and three little words have never meant so much. The meat is succulent and tender; the mustardy slaw seeps into the tangy sauce. Don't worry. The sandwich isn't big enough to spoil dinner.

2 *It Came from Memphis* 5 p.m.

As Elvis would assure us, the world does indeed look great from inside a '55 Cadillac. See for yourself on Tad Pierson's three-hour **Greatest Hits** tour (901-527-8870; americandreamsafari.com; $200 for a party of one to five people). He picks you up — usually at the Peabody hotel (149 Union Avenue), although other arrangements may be made — in his refurbished Caddy and shows you the opulence and poverty of the city and its famous recording studios: Sun, home to Howling Wolf and Elvis; Stax, where Booker T. and the MG's backed Otis Redding; Hi, where Al Green recorded his sultry hits. In the entrepreneurial spirit of the city that brought you Holiday Inns and self-serve supermarkets, Mr. Pierson also peddles his Memphis Mary, a bloody mary mix with barbecue sauce. Get you some.

3 *You Said You Was High Class* 8:30 p.m.

There's a lot of grease in your future, so tonight it's dine fancy. **Mollie Fontaine** (679 Adams Avenue; 901-524-1886; molliefontainelounge.com; $$-$$$), a stylish bar and restaurant, fills two floors of a Victorian house where the soul songwriter Dan Penn — "Do Right Woman," "Cry Like a Baby" — once had his studio. Songs still float in the air, and patrons are as likely as the local greats — Di Anne Price included — to be playing them on the bar's piano. The menu of small plates mingles eclectic selections like lamb souvlaki and Spanish-style garlic shrimp with upscaled versions of sliders and fish fry.

4 *Nothin' but the Blues* 10:30 p.m.

It would be easy to hit Beale Street (if you do go, look for the soul performers James Govan or FreeWorld), but you came to Memphis for deep blues. Drive to **Wild Bill's** (1580 Vollintine Avenue; 901-726-5473), a storefront juke joint in a crumbling shopping strip. The room is deep and narrow, with snapshots of revelers tacked to the walls. Beer is served in quarts on long community tables, and when the dance floor fills up, folks shake it in the aisles. The band evolves and revolves; these players have backed Albert King and B.B. King, played world tours and dirt-floor hovels, and they'll transport you back in time, a real good time.

SATURDAY

5 *Hot Water Cornbread* 9:30 a.m.

Ease in with a Memphis Mary in your room before facing the harsh sun outside. Then hop the Main Street Trolley (matatransit.com), jumping off at Market Avenue to duck into **Alcenia's** (317 North Main Street; 901-523-0200; alcenias.com; $). B.J. — Alcenia's daughter — hugs everyone, and she usually serves hot water cornbread while you wait for your food.

OPPOSITE Beale Street now courts a party crowd, but deep blues still exist in Memphis.

You can't make a bad choice: options include salmon croquettes, dense pancakes, and sublime fried green tomatoes. Service can be slow, but this morning you're probably not moving too fast anyway.

6 *Soul, Man* 11 a.m.

Last night you lived the music, today you'll learn it. The headset tour at the **Memphis Rock 'n' Soul Museum** (191 Beale Street, in the FedExForum; 901-205-2533; memphisrocknsoul.org) includes original interviews and great music, evoking Memphis as a crossroads that bred new ideas and sounds. Look for an exhibit about Sputnik Monroe, a white wrestler who used his black fan base to integrate the city auditorium in the '50s. Then drive to the **Stax Museum of American Soul Music** (926 East McLemore Avenue; 901-946-2535; staxmuseum.com), an institution of a completely different nature—it has a dance floor, you dig? Stax was a studio and record label from 1957 to 1975, home of Isaac Hayes, Sam & Dave, the Staples Singers, and Albert King. There are more short, fun films than you can absorb in one visit, and you'll exit (into the gift shop) snapping your fingers.

7 *Memphis Soul Stew* 3 p.m.

You're hungry, you're in Soulsville USA—time for some soul food. The **Four Way** (998 Mississippi Boulevard; 901-507-1519; $) has been serving heaping portions for decades. The tender catfish is salted to perfection and fried in a crispy crust; the fried chicken is among the best in the South. Even if you're full, leaving without tasting the lemon meringue pie would be a tragedy.

ABOVE The Rock 'n' Soul Museum evokes Memphis as a crossroads that bred new ideas and sounds.

RIGHT Drinks in the piano bar at Mollie Fontaine, a stylish spot occupying two floors of a Victorian house where the soul songwriter Dan Penn once had his studio.

OPPOSITE The Mississippi River at Memphis.

8 *Find the Vinyl* 4:30 p.m.

There's good record hunting in Memphis—blues, rock 'n' roll, soul, indies. Start at **Goner Records** (2152 Young Avenue; 901-722-0095; goner-records.com) or nearby **Shangri-La Records** (1916 Madison Avenue; 901-274-1916; shangri.com). Both double as indie labels and have achieved national attention with regional artists, including the late garage rocker Jay Reatard, Harlan T. Bobo, and the Grifters. At Goner, look for the mini-shrine to Elvis impersonators. **Audiomania** (1698 Madison Avenue; 901-278-1166) has a deeper jazz and soul collection.

9 *Rollin' on the River* 6 p.m.

Park anywhere on Front Street downtown and take a few steps to the **Riverwalk**, a footpath carved into the bluffs along the Mississippi River. Evenings don't always cool down, but the whiff of magnolia and the sight of a tug pushing a massive load upstream will inspire the Huck Finn in anyone. During May weekends, Memphians throng the riverbank for events—a music festival, a barbecue contest, a symphony (memphisinmay.org).

10 *Night of Many Sounds* 9 p.m.

The cocktail is the concoction at the **Cove** (2559 Broad Avenue; 901-730-0719; thecovememphis.com). Disappear into an overstuffed leatherette booth and float away on the Blue Steel—tequila, just enough curacao to make it glow, and a lemon twist. Catch upcoming locals and some of the better indie bands here, or drift not far to the **Hi-Tone Café** (1913 Poplar Avenue; 901-278-8663; hitonememphis.com), where

higher-profile acts perform. The Hi-Tone is in the location of the former dojo where Elvis got his black belt; there's a photo over the bar. If you want a D.J. who's as likely to play Rufus Thomas as the latest dance hit, sail back downtown to the **Hollywood Disco** (115 Vance Avenue; 901-528-9313; hollywooddisco.com), and put on your b-b-boogie shoes.

SUNDAY

11 *Love, Happiness, Breakfast* 10 a.m.
The soul food on the menu at the **Rev. Al Green's Full Gospel Tabernacle Church** (787 Hale Road; algreenmusic.com/fullgospeltabernacle.html) is purely of the intangible kind. Even though he has a

rejuvenated pop career, the reverend makes it home for more Sundays than he misses. He's as likely to break out into "Take Me to the River" as a psalm. Visitors are welcome, appropriate dress encouraged. Services start at 11:15, but first grab a sweet-potato-pancake breakfast with eggs and grits at the **Arcade Restaurant** (540 South Main Street; 901-526-5757; arcaderestaurant.com; $), across from the train station. In Jim Jarmusch's film *Mystery Train*, Elvis reappears at the Arcade. Keep your eyes open.

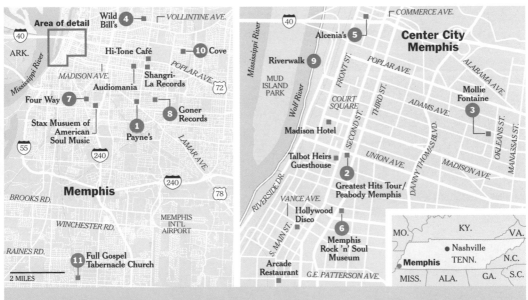

THE BASICS

Memphis International Airport is served by major airlines. About the only transportation worse than taxis in Memphis is the bus service. Rent a car.

The Peabody Memphis
149 Union Avenue
901-529-4000
peabodymemphis.com
$$$
Refurbished grand old downtown hotel, dripping with tradition and known for its resident ducks.

The Talbot Heirs Guesthouse
99 South Second Street
901-527-9772
talbotheirs.com
$$-$$$
One of Memphis's best secrets.

Madison Hotel
79 Madison Avenue
901-333-1200
madisonhotelmemphis.com
$$$
Lots of character.

Clarksdale

For decades, Clarksdale, Mississippi, has been more famous for the musicians who left than for anyone who stayed. The electric blues masters Muddy Waters and John Lee Hooker, the rhythm and blues pioneer Ike Turner and the soul man Sam Cooke are just a few of the refugees who made a hard turn onto Highway 61 north and never looked back. They sought greater opportunity, but also were fleeing poverty and the Jim Crow South. Want and hardship still haunt Clarksdale—those shotgun shacks are not for nostalgic show—but clarksdaletourism.com beckons visitors with a blue guitar and two highway signs that mark the mythic crossroads where, it is said, the bluesman Robert Johnson sold his soul to ol' Scratch in exchange for a few otherworldly guitar licks. Clarksdale's downtown is just a few square blocks—fine for a city of about 20,000—but its legend, as a kiln for shaping the blues, resonates worldwide. (And you never know when you might stumble over the ghost of Tennessee Williams, who spent much of his childhood here.)
— BY ROBERT GORDON

FRIDAY

1 *Blues Highway* 3 p.m.

Unless you pilot a crop duster (like some of the locals), you'll fly into Memphis and rent a car to get to Clarksdale. The drive south will take you through cotton fields and cypress swamps and is dotted with small towns—Lula, Robinsonville, and Tunica. An old diner there, the **Blue & White** (1355 Highway 61 north, Tunica; 662-363-1371; $), serves sublime onion rings in a delicate but crunchy batter, and homemade pies. Allow a leisurely hour and a half for the 75-mile drive. When you find yourself swaying to the soulful sounds of **WROX** (1450 AM and 92.1 FM; wroxradio.com), you're getting close.

2 *Picking Cotton Not Required* 5 p.m.

The **Hopson Plantation** is where the mechanical cotton picker was unveiled in 1941, and it is again on the cutting edge—this time with cultural tourism. The **Shack Up Inn** consists of six former sharecropper shacks, each transformed into a guesthouse that sleeps three or four. Yes, there is indoor plumbing (and kitchenettes). The contrast of the shacks' down-at-the-heels histories and their contemporary

coziness can, at first, feel presumptuous and like a form of exploitation. One guestbook comment read: "Negrophilia: Commodification: Everything but the burden. Thanks!" But the silence and the breeze sneaking through the shacks' open doors make them a profound way to experience the Mississippi Delta. The **Cotton Gin Inn** recently opened on the same site: five hotel rooms built into an old cotton gin building.

3 *The Clarksdale Redemption* 7 p.m.

Just as you've become accustomed to the sense of being somewhere else, step into **Madidi** (164 Delta Avenue; 662-627-7724; madidires.com; $$$), a restaurant and cosmopolitan oasis. Entrees focus on urbane choices like rack of lamb or duck a l'orange, but starters may include regional flavors like frog legs or shrimp and grits. Madidi is partly owned by Morgan Freeman, who lives in nearby Charleston. After dinner, stroll through the small downtown to Freeman's other venture: **Ground Zero Blues Club** (364 Delta Avenue; 662-621-9009; groundzerobluesclub.com). A former cotton warehouse, Ground Zero is Clarksdale's top blues spot. The local favorites include Super Chikan, Jimbo Mathus (former leader of Squirrel Nut Zippers), the Deep Cuts, and Anthony Sherard—tomorrow's bluesman playing today—and his band, Big A and the All Stars.

OPPOSITE The Delta Amusement Blues Cafe serves a conventional breakfast, but its name honors Clarksdale's legacy as home of the blues.

BELOW Authentic blues at the Ground Zero Blues Club.

SATURDAY

4 *Back-Door Museum* 9 a.m.

Breakfast at the **Delta Amusement Blues Cafe** (348 Delta Avenue; 662-624-4040; $) isn't anything you can't get on a grill elsewhere, but the sense of small-town intrigue is straight out of Eudora Welty. You can hear the laughing and cursing over poker and dominos even when the games aren't being played. Walk out the back door to the **Delta Blues Museum** (1 Blues Alley; 662-627-6820; deltabluesmuseum.org). Alluringly low-tech, it delivers not only the music but also the culture that produced it. Located in a former freight depot, the museum houses Muddy Waters's childhood cabin. Step inside and feel the blues falling down like rain. Nearby is **Cat Head Delta Blues & Folk Art** (252 Delta Avenue; 662-624-5992; cathead.biz), a shop stuffed with Southern creations.

5 *My Meal Is Red Hot* 11 a.m.

Robert Johnson sang about them in "They're Red Hot," and you can savor the heritage of Delta hot tamales at **Hicks Tamales & BBQ Shop** (305 South State Street; 662-624-9887). Creamy cornmeal mashes with spicy beef centers, they're simmered for hours inside a cornhusk. Unwrap, eat, then whoop. For barbecue, locals favor **Abe's** (616 North State Street; 662-624-9947) and **Big Jim's** (1700 North State Street), a shack the size of a pickup where a summer treat is the "koolickle": cucumbers steeped in cherry, grape, or strawberry Kool-Aid.

6 *Of Indians and Desire* Noon

Even for those who know Clarksdale well, **Robert Birdsong's tour** ($60 for three hours, custom tours available; 662-624-6051; mississippimojo@yahoo.com) gives the place new life. Standing on the bank of the Sunflower River, where two Indian trading paths met, Birdsong lectures on an 1880 landslide that exposed a tribal burial site, attracting a Smithsonian excavation team. He then ties those events to the town's founder, John Clark, and his daughter Blanche Cutrer, whose homes are nearby. Ms. Cutrer, an eccentric party-giver, fascinated a young neighborhood boy named Tom Williams, who one day became Tennessee and the writer of *A Streetcar Named Desire*. Blanche, of course, remained accustomed to the finer things.

7 *A Fine Mess* 3 p.m.

Hightail it 15 miles north to Friar's Point, a blocklong town that peaked in the early 1900s but has clung to life like morning dew on sweet potato vines. The **North Delta Museum** (700 Second Street; 662-383-2233 or 645-5063), at the base of the curving Mississippi River levee, comes across as the family attic given a rarefied name. Holdings include Civil War and World War I memorabilia and American Indian displays. Across the street is Hirsberg's, an old-time dry-goods store; Robert Johnson played from that bench out front.

8 *Faulkner, Twitty, Crayfish* 6 p.m.

In the middle of somebody's nowhere, you are near an unusual fine-dining experience for anybody. In 1926, an Elks Lodge was built on Moon Lake in Dundee, attracting local gamblers. The place was owned by Tennessee Williams's family and later by relatives of Conway Twitty (who was born in Friar's Point); William Faulkner used to frequent it. Since the mid-70s, it has been **Uncle Henry's Place** (5860 Moon Lake Road; 662-337-2757; unclehenrysplace.com; $$-$$$), run by George Wright, its chef, and his mother, Sarah, the resident historian. The food reflects their Louisiana roots (look for crayfish étouffée), but their talk is local.

9 *Rust Never Sleeps* 9 p.m.

It's a 25-minute drive back to Clarksdale, and time to check in at **Red's** (395 Sunflower Avenue) for some deep local flavor. The outside is strewn with rusted grills. And inside, the live music will push you toward abandon.

SUNDAY

10 *Sunday, Coming Down* 9:30 a.m.

Another comment from the Shack Up Inn guest book: "Great fried shrimp at Ramon's. T-Model Ford at Red's, Wiley and the Checkmates at Ground Zero.

Try fried grits with honey. Learn to take it slower."
Sound advice and, faced with Clarksdale's blue laws,
you don't have much choice. Try breakfast at the
Shady Nook (16774 Highway 61 north; 662-621-1525),
a truck-stop cafeteria on the north side of town.
And be sure to chat with other guests passing through
the shacks' lobby, which is owner Bill Talbot's
living room.

11 *Take Me to the River* 11 a.m.
The **Quapaw Canoe Company** (291 Sunflower
Avenue; 662-627-4070 or 902-7841; island63.com),
named for a regional Indian tribe, does for the
Mississippi River what Robert Birdsong does for the
city. Trips can vary from an outing of a couple hours

to several weeks. John Ruskey, one of Quapaw's
guides, lives in a house once owned by the Wingfields,
where the missus was known for her menagerie of
glass animals; it's also the **Catalpa House** bed-and-
breakfast (110 Catalpa Street; 662-627-5621).

OPPOSITE AND ABOVE The converted sharecropper shacks
of the Shack Up Inn have the comforts their original
occupants lacked, but remain a link to the hardscrabble
life that fostered the deeply emotional Delta blues.

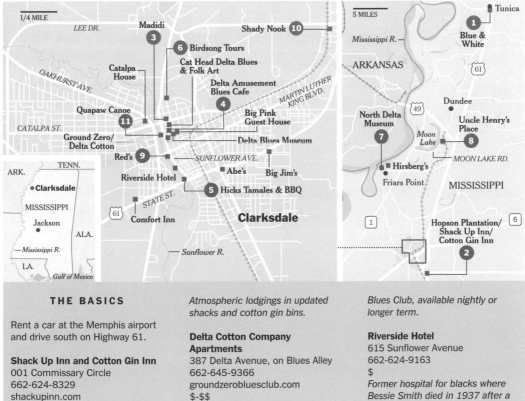

THE BASICS

Rent a car at the Memphis airport
and drive south on Highway 61.

Shack Up Inn and Cotton Gin Inn
001 Commissary Circle
662-624-8329
shackupinn.com
$

*Atmospheric lodgings in updated
shacks and cotton gin bins.*

**Delta Cotton Company
Apartments**
387 Delta Avenue, on Blues Alley
662-645-9366
groundzerobluesclub.com
$-$$
Upstairs from the Ground Zero

*Blues Club, available nightly or
longer term.*

Riverside Hotel
615 Sunflower Avenue
662-624-9163
$
*Former hospital for blacks where
Bessie Smith died in 1937 after a
car accident.*

Oxford

William Faulkner was born over in New Albany. But Oxford, Mississippi, claims him as its own, for he honed fictional Yoknapatawpha County from the people and places of surrounding Lafayette County. Named for Oxford, England, in a successful bid to lure Mississippi's liberal arts university, this town of about 20,000 sprawls out from the courthouse, described in Faulkner's 1951 novel Requiem for a Nun *as "brooding, symbolic, and ponderable, tall as cloud, solid as rock, dominating all." Faulkner still matters here. A majestic bronze statue of him, resting on a bench, pipe in hand, flanks the entrance to City Hall. The local temple of intellect, Square Books, stocks what seems like every blessed thing he wrote. And his home, Rowan Oak, went through a multimillion-dollar refurbishing and is open for tours. Though the courthouse square he knew — ringed by hardware stores and barbershops — is now the domain of boutiques and cigar boîtes, the local underclass of writers, artists, and graduate students remains a vigilant steward of the town's reputation as a velvet ditch for ne'er-do-wells.*
— BY JOHN T. EDGE

FRIDAY

1 *Nobel Blues* 4 p.m.

At the heart of the University of Mississippi campus, on the top floor of the **J. D. Williams Library**, a literary-cultural archive and a blues archive (662-915-7408; olemiss.edu) co-exist. James Meredith, the black man who integrated the campus as a student in 1962, donated his papers to Ole Miss, so you can see the note he received from Rosa Parks in support of his efforts. That is Faulkner's Nobel Prize over in the corner, swaddled in purple velvet. And B. B. King's personal collection is here, too. Thanks to a staff that understands how these collections complement one another, you will also see displays like a signed copy of Elmore Leonard's Mississippi-centered 2002 novel *Tishomingo Blues* alongside a 78-r.p.m. record of the same name, recorded in 1926 by Peg Leg Howell.

2 *Drinking with the Lions* 6 p.m.

Want to stalk a literary lion? The second-story bar at the **City Grocery** restaurant (152 Courthouse Square; 662-232-8080; citygroceryonline.com; $$$) is the place for it. Jack Pendarvis drinks Manhattans

and other fancy-pants cocktails here. Tom Franklin favors Bud Lights. Even if the literati are not around, you can ogle the brass plaques that are nailed to the bar when the owner decides that regulars have earned their stripes. The prime perches are on the balcony overlooking the square; they're scarce, so get here early. When you're ready for dinner, descend the staircase at the back and enter the restaurant, a white-tablecloth affair in a onetime grocery. John Currence, the owner, is a gutsy cook and in the vanguard of new Southern cuisine.

3 *Shot and a Beer* 10 p.m.

Every college town needs a dank beer-and-a-shot bar; the **Blind Pig** (105 North Lamar Boulevard; 662-234-5119) does the job in Oxford. You might see a rocking local band, like Tyler Keith and the Preacher's Kids. Fair warning: Last calls on the weekend are 12:45 on Friday night and 11:45 on Saturday night.

SATURDAY

4 *Ginger Scones and Peacocks* 9 a.m.

The owner of **Bottletree Bakery** (923 Van Buren Avenue; 662-236-5000), Cynthia Gerlach, got her master's in Southern studies from the university's Center for the Study of Southern Culture, writing her thesis on B.F. Perkins, an Alabama painter known for his vividly colored peacocks. After a spell at the low-slung counter, it's hard to tell whether your morning buzz is born of the kinetic images that blanket the walls, the sugary punch of a candied ginger-studded scone, or the coffee that Gerlach imports from her hometown, Portland, Oregon.

5 *Square Stroll* 10 a.m.

Oxonians take pride in their literary heritage. They even elected Richard Howorth, proprietor of three storefront bookshops (squarebooks.com), their mayor for two terms. **Square Books** (160 Courthouse Square; 662-236-2262) is the place for a staggering array of signed firsts; **Off Square Books** (129 Courthouse Square; 662-236-2828) specializes in used

OPPOSITE Rowan Oak, William Faulkner's home. Oxford was thinly disguised as "Jefferson" in Faulkner's fiction.

OXFORD

and remaindered; and **Jr.** (111 Courthouse Square; 662-236-2207) is for, well, juniors. Other square shops worthy of your wallet and eyes are the **Southside Gallery** (150 Courthouse Square; 662-234-9090; southsideartgallery.com), which exhibits photographers like Maude Schuyler Clay; **Amelia** (1006 Van Buren Avenue; 901-355-0311; ameliapresents.com), where craft meets design and intersects with cupcakes; and **Neilson's** (119 Courthouse Square; 662-234-1161; neilsons1839.com), a department store that has been in business since 1839.

6 *Frill Pick Shooting* 1 p.m.

The **Ajax Diner** (118 Courthouse Square; 662-232-8880; ajaxdiner.net; $) fixes plate lunches built around meatloaf, chicken and gravy, fried catfish, and the like, accompanied by sweet potato casserole, mashed potatoes drenched in gravy, and butter beans swimming in a peppery "potlikker." The place is best appreciated on warm spring days when the step-through windows are thrown open. While waiting for lunch, do what the cool kids do: snag a frill-topped toothpick, load it into a plastic straw and send it blowgun-style into the ceiling tiles.

7 *The Grove* 2 p.m.

On seven or eight Saturday afternoons in fall, Oxford is transformed as alumni and adoring fans arrive for Ole Miss football. For hours before the game, they mingle, party, and get pumped up by the

thousands at the **Grove**, ten shady acres on campus. If it's one of the other 45 Saturdays of the year, you might find some serenity in a stroll under those same oak, elm, and magnolia trees. (Enter campus from the east, on University Avenue, and you'll soon see it on your right. For maximum effect, enter under an archway inscribed "Walk of the Champions.") Walk a bit farther, across the University Circle and behind the Lyceum, to find the **Civil Rights Monument**, a bronze statue of Meredith striding onto the campus in 1962.

8 *Visions of Plenty* 4 p.m.

The **Mary Buie collection** of the **University of Mississippi Museum** (University Avenue and North Fifth Street; 662-915-7073; museum.olemiss.edu) is a Grandma's attic showcase of curiosities (rings crafted from peach pits; hair from the tail of Robert E. Lee's horse, Traveler) as well as folk art (Luster Willis, Sultan Rogers) and choice modern art (William Eggleston, William Dunlap). It's also a great air-conditioned break after a campus walk on a hot day.

9 *Country Roads and Eats* 7 p.m.

Time for a drive. Pilot your car southwest about eight miles on Taylor Road, and you will dead-end at the hamlet of Taylor. At the center of a shamble of storefronts stands **Taylor Grocery** (04-A County Road 338, Taylor; 662-236-1716; taylorgrocery.com; $-$$), a restaurant embellished with corrugated tin and

ABOVE The Mary Buie collection ranges from the gowns of belles to hair from the tail of Robert E. Lee's horse.

BELOW A porch-rocker view of Courthouse Square.

graffiti. It may serve the best cornmeal-dusted catfish in this catfish-crazy state. Before you go in for dinner, take a walk around the town, where artists gather and shops and galleries sell their work.

SUNDAY

10 *A Different Kind of Benedict* 10 a.m.

Better known as a bar that books literate rock one night and a hippie jam band the next, **Proud Larry's** (211 South Lamar Boulevard; 662-236-0050; proudlarrys.com; $) emerges from six days of beer and sacrilege to serve late-morning fare to church-goers. Standard-bearers include fat biscuits in sausage gravy and the Larry Benedict, two English muffins

topped with sausage patties and poached eggs and drenched in Tabasco-spiked hollandaise sauce.

11 *Mr. Bill's Place* 12:30 p.m.

Locals once took pride in telling visitors that Rowan Oak (913 Old Taylor Road; 662-234-3284; rowanoak.com), William Faulkner's home on Old Taylor Road, remained much as it was when he died in 1962. His muddy boots and his Underwood typewriter sat where he had left them. But eventually restoration took place. Tours don't start until 1 p.m., but arrive early to wander the grounds, stroll among the cedars that frame the front walk, and peer through the windows at the outline for *A Fable* scrawled on the wall of his study.

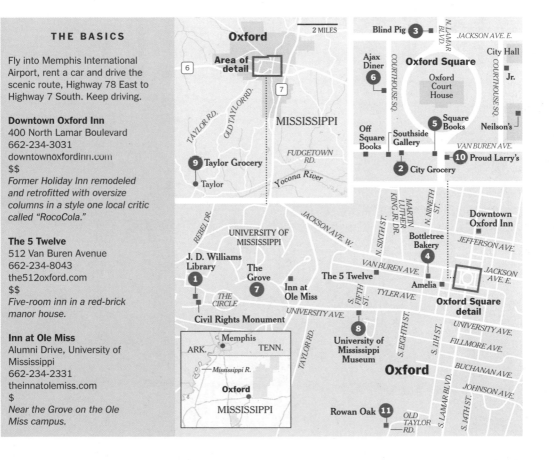

THE BASICS

Fly into Memphis International Airport, rent a car and drive the scenic route, Highway 78 East to Highway 7 South. Keep driving.

Downtown Oxford Inn
400 North Lamar Boulevard
662-234-3031
downtownoxfordinn.com
$$
Former Holiday Inn remodeled and retrofitted with oversize columns in a style one local critic called "RocoCola."

The 5 Twelve
512 Van Buren Avenue
662-234-8043
the512oxford.com
$$
Five-room inn in a red-brick manor house.

Inn at Ole Miss
Alumni Drive, University of Mississippi
662-234-2331
theinnatolemiss.com
$
Near the Grove on the Ole Miss campus.

Birmingham

In the golden days of rail travel, a sign proclaiming "Welcome to Birmingham, the Magic City" greeted passengers arriving at Terminal Station. Although the station is only a memory today, Alabama's largest city still retains a special ability to surprise the uninitiated — particularly for modern visitors who arrive with collective memories of the city's violent civil rights past. That past is certainly memorialized, but the city has plenty more to offer: enticing takes on Southern cuisine, a nationally acclaimed motorsports park, and upscale shopping opportunities.
— BY JIM NOLES

FRIDAY

1 *Standing Tall* 4 p.m.

In 1871, Birmingham was incorporated at the strategic juncture of two rail lines where local deposits of iron and coal would nurture the young city's iron furnaces. The founders' vision was so successful that when the city's Commerce Club was invited to dispatch a symbol of Birmingham to the 1904 World's Fair, it commissioned a cast-iron statue of **Vulcan**, the Roman god of the forge. Today, the impressive statue (1701 Valley View Drive; 205-933-1409; visitvulcan.com) stands in a park atop Red Mountain, offering an unmatched vista of Birmingham's downtown skyline to those who go up to visit it — and providing residents of downtown Homewood, south of the mountain, with a view of Vulcan's massive bare rump.

2 *Not Your Grandma's Grits* 6 p.m.

Highlands Bar & Grill (2011 11th Avenue South; 205-939-1400; highlandsbarandgrill.com; $$$), recognized by the James Beard Foundation as one of the country's best restaurants, owes its reputation to chef and owner Frank Stitt, who deftly combines fresh, rural ingredients and French-inspired technique. The restaurant's stone-ground baked grits, accented with Smoky Mountain-raised country ham, mushrooms, thyme, and Parmesan, have been a local favorite for years. Call ahead for a reservation, but arrive early for a drink at the bar, where fresh oysters on the half-shell whet appetites for entrees like farm-raised lamb with fresh mint and sweet peas.

3 *All Work and All Play* 9 p.m.

The brainchild of Alan Hunter, one of MTV's original V.J.'s, **WorkPlay** (500 23rd Street South; 205-879-4773; workplay.com) is an entertainment complex that includes a live-music venue, a bar packed with a 20-something crowd, a professional sound stage, and even a suite of offices for creative professional types, all on the edge of Birmingham's warehouse district. The bar usually clears out when the live music starts next door, courtesy of acts ranging from the singer-songwriter Neko Case to the Southern rockers the Zac Brown Band. Intimacy is part of the appeal: a mere arm's length separates the musicians from the audience. Check WorkPlay's Web site for scheduled acts and to purchase tickets.

SATURDAY

4 *Continental's Breakfast* 8 a.m.

Just over the crest of Red Mountain, **Continental Bakery** (1909 Cahaba Road; 205-870-5584; birminghammenus.com/chezlulu) greets arrivals to English Village, a small commercial district on the edge of the affluent suburb of Mountain Brook. Order inside the narrow shop, where display cases lined with fresh baguettes, bread, and pastries conjure the ambience of Dijon rather than Dixie. Outside, claim a seat at a sidewalk table, pet a neighbor's dog, and enjoy a butter croissant.

OPPOSITE Vulcan, cast in iron, stands atop Red Mountain. The iron and steel industry built Birmingham.

RIGHT An after-work crowd at Highlands Bar & Grill.

5 *It Takes a Village* 10 a.m.

Just down the hill from English Village, Mountain Brook Village holds tony shops befitting the area's origins as a forested suburban refuge from the soot-spewing smokestacks of early industrial Birmingham. At **Table Matters** (2402 Montevallo Road; 205-879-0125; table-matters.com), shoppers brush shoulders as they search for gifts ranging from William Yeoward crystal to the Good Earth Pottery produced by the Mississippi craftsman Richie Watts. Nearby at **Etc. Jewelry and Accessories** (2726 Cahaba Road; 205-871-6747), husbands seek surreptitious guidance on the latest jewelry from the designer Priyadarshini Himatsingka or handbags from Monica Botkier.

6 *Good Golly Miss Myra* 12:30 p.m.

In any travel article discussing Alabama, you'd expect a reference to barbecue. Here it is. Although every Birmingham resident has a favorite, **Miss Myra's Pit Bar-B-Q** (3278 Cahaba Heights Road; 205-967-6004; missmyrasbbq.com; $) makes any aficionado's short list. The lunch crowd is steady, even into the early afternoon, as fragrant smoke wafts across the parking lot from the wide brick chimney. Inside, the décor of this former convenience store is mostly a celebration of the past glory of the Crimson Tide; a display of porcelain pigs donated by loyal customers offers its own homage to the restaurant's most delectable offerings. Pork and rib sandwiches and plates are available, of course, but Myra Grissom's signature white sauce (a concoction of mayo, pepper and vinegar) works particularly well on her chicken.

7 *A Monument to Injustice* 2 p.m.

Two very different museums offer equally compelling glimpses of Birmingham—one of its past, the other of its future. Across the street from the historic **Sixteenth Street Baptist Church** (site of the infamous bombing that killed four girls in 1963), the **Birmingham Civil Rights Institute** (520 16th Street North; 205-328-9696; bcri.org) tells the story of the civil rights movement in Alabama and beyond and provides a somber reminder of how far the city and the nation have come in four decades. The church itself, still serving a downtown congregation, offers tours Tuesday through Friday, and, by appointment only, on Saturdays (205-251-9402).

8 *Need for Speed* 4 p.m.

Twenty minutes east of town, in the rolling hills along the Cahaba River, the **Barber Vintage Motorsports Museum** (6030 Barber Motorsports Parkway; 205-699-7275; barbermuseum.org) hints at how Birmingham's future reputation might be cast. The museum claims the largest motorcycle collection in North America (more than 900 bikes in total) in an airy five-story display that feels as much like an art museum as a motor pool. The **Barber Motorsports Park** (barbermotorsports.com) is adjacent to the museum. Its creator, George Barber, likens its immaculately groomed grounds to "the Augusta of racetracks."

9 *Front Row Seats* 6 p.m.

Despite his restaurant's name, Chris Hastings, the chef and owner of the **Hot and Hot Fish Club** (2180 11th Court South; 205-933-5474; hotandhotfishclub.com; $$$), quickly recommended the pork-belly appetizer. "It will set your mind free," he said. The dish combined a melt-in-your-mouth fattiness with just the right amount of crispy skin. "I get my pork from Henry

Fudge, up in north Alabama," Hastings added. "The man's a pig genius." Apparently so. Hastings reserved similar enthusiasm for his simple grilled fish, on this partcular visit a pompano that just the day before it was served had been swimming in the Gulf of Mexico. It was served whole on a bed of couscous. Reservations are suggested, as are seats at the chef's counter, where conversation with fellow patrons flows naturally.

SUNDAY

10 *Brunch at the Park* 11 a.m.
  Little Savannah (3811 Clairmont Avenue; 205-591-1119; birminghammenus.com/littlesavannah;

$$), on the edge of the historic Forest Park neighborhood, calls itself a "quaint neighborhood Southern Bistro" — an apt description. Orders of the cranberry-pecan cream cheese-filled French toast and the crab cake with bacon, creamed spinach, and a poached egg threatened to disrupt the peace one Sunday with a lively debate on which selection was better. Reservations recommended.

OPPOSITE ABOVE Half art museum, half motor pool, the Barber Vintage Motorsports Museum has 900 bikes.

OPPOSITE BELOW The Birmingham Civil Rights Institute is a reminder of how far the city has come since the infamous church bombing that killed four girls in 1963.

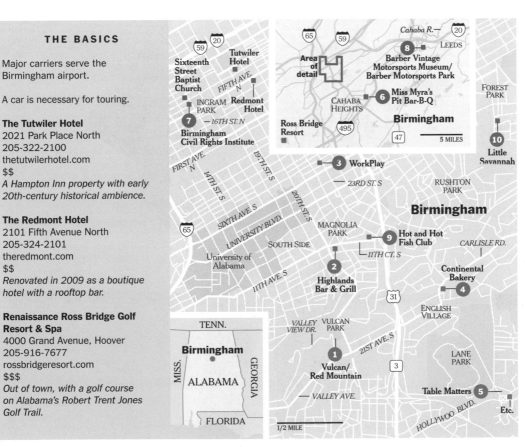

THE BASICS

Major carriers serve the Birmingham airport.

A car is necessary for touring.

The Tutwiler Hotel
2021 Park Place North
205-322-2100
thetutwilerhotel.com
$$
A Hampton Inn property with early 20th-century historical ambience.

The Redmont Hotel
2101 Fifth Avenue North
205-324-2101
theredmont.com
$$
Renovated in 2009 as a boutique hotel with a rooftop bar.

Renaissance Ross Bridge Golf Resort & Spa
4000 Grand Avenue, Hoover
205-916-7677
rossbridgeresort.com
$$$
Out of town, with a golf course on Alabama's Robert Trent Jones Golf Trail.

Montgomery

When the United Daughters of the Confederacy organized a Montgomery branch in 1896, its members named their chapter "Cradle of the Confederacy." Approximately a century later, veterans of the civil rights movement began referring to Alabama, and its capital, Montgomery, in particular, as the "birthplace of the civil rights movement." At a gooseneck bend in the Alabama River, this city of 200,000 delivers on both claims. A spate of museum building and downtown redevelopment now attract cultural tourists, but the transition has not wiped clean the contradictions. Drive south of downtown and, in the shadow of the Martin Luther King Jr. Expressway (Interstate 85), you will pass a sign for Taraland Learning Center. It's just a few blocks west of the intersection of Jefferson Davis and Rosa L. Parks Avenues.

— BY JOHN T. EDGE

FRIDAY

1 *Learning about Hank* 4 p.m.

Hank Williams, who was born near Garland, Alabama, is the city's favorite musical son. And the best place to get a bead on the man who, before his death at the age of 29 in 1953, wrote and recorded standards like "I'll Never Get Out of This World Alive," is the storefront **Hank Williams Museum** (118 Commerce Street; 334-262-3600; thehankwilliamsmuseum.com). View the baby blue Cadillac in which Williams died and artifacts like a selection of toothpicks pulled from one of his suits, a lime-fringed black shirt custom-made by Nudie's Rodeo Tailors, and the saddle he used for riding his horse, Hi-Life.

2 *Alabama Riverside* 8 p.m.

Call for directions to the **Capitol Oyster Bar** at the Montgomery Marina (617 Shady Street; 334-239-8958; capitoloysterbar.com; $), and you're still likely to get lost. But a short trek across a web of freight tracks and through the city's industrial areas brings you to the ideal time-worn perch for a sunset beer. Below are the slips of sailboats and cabin cruisers. In the

OPPOSITE A bronze Hank Williams strums perpetually across from the City Auditorium in Montgomery.

RIGHT The Cross Garden, one man's roadside obsession.

distance, barges ply the Alabama River. Stay for a casual dinner. The menu is simple (fried seafood platters, steak, cheeseburgers), but the setting is lulling and there may be some music.

3 *Jazz Underground* 11 p.m.

Keep the evening going at **Sous La Terre Downtown Underground** (82 Commerce Street; 334-265-2069), a private club set, true to its moniker, in a windowless basement. It usually opens around 11 p.m. and springs to life after midnight when a jazz piano player, Henry Pugh, takes the stage. Guests must apply for membership to enter, but you won't find that much of a barrier. The crowd is friendly and the jazz is the real thing.

SATURDAY

4 *Curbside Eating* 9 a.m.

Open since 1927, downtown's **Montgomery Curb Market** (1004 Madison Avenue; 334-263-6445; montgomeryal.gov/index.aspx?page=648) is an open-air shebang lighted by dangling bulbs and topped by a metal roof. In addition to produce, you'll find a heady array of baked goods. Hungry? Look for homemade sausage and cheese biscuits, fried peach pies, and miniature sweet potato pies.

5 *Old South* 10 a.m.

Dexter Avenue is only six blocks long, but it's the spine of a route from the site of Jefferson Davis's inauguration to the bus stop where Rosa Parks boarded for her fateful journey. Start an Old South morning atop Goat Hill, at the **Alabama State Capitol**

(600 Dexter Avenue; 334-242-3935; sos.state.al.us/
OfficeOfSoS/CapitolTours.aspx), which is ringed
by statuary and monuments that honor, among
others, Dr. J. Marion Sims, who is called the father of
modern gynecology. From the portico, where Davis
took his oath as president of the Confederacy in 1861,
George Wallace proclaimed in 1963, "Segregation
now, segregation tomorrow, segregation forever." On
the northern lawn rises a white marble memorial to
the Confederacy. Detour one street south of Dexter
Avenue and you stand in front of the **First White
House of the Confederacy** (644 Washington Avenue;
334-242-1861; firstwhitehouse.org), the modest — and
now musty — Italianate two-story building that
Davis and his family called home in the aftermath of
secession. The gift shop sells books and souvenirs
including reproduction Confederate money.

6 *All American* 1 p.m.

Take a lunch break from history at **Chris' Hot
Dogs** (138 Dexter Avenue; 334-265-6850;
chrishotdogs.com), which has been selling the
timeless American snack since 1917. The dogs come
mustard-slathered and drenched in chili sauce. Snag
a stool at the worn linoleum counter where some
locals say Hank Williams sat and scribbled lyrics.

7 *New South* 2 p.m.

Advance to the 20th century, starting at the
Civil Rights Memorial (400 Washington Avenue;
splcenter.org/civil-rights-memorial), designed by
Maya Lin and commissioned by the Southern Poverty
Law Center, the group that bankrupted the United
Klans of America. Water emerges from the core of
a circular granite table, washing over the names of
martyrs of the civil rights movement in what might
be interpreted as absolution of the South's sins. Back
on Dexter Avenue, the **Dexter Avenue King Memorial
Baptist Church** (454 Dexter Avenue; 334-263-3970;
dexterkingmemorial.org), where Martin Luther
King Jr. rose to fame as leader of the Montgomery
Improvement Association, stands out in red brick

among the white masonry of state government buildings. Founded by former slaves in 1877, it remains a
church and also gives tours where docents explain
the history. One comment about Vernon Johns, King's
predecessor: "If he had led the movement, we'd all
be dead — he wasn't one to turn the other cheek." The
Rosa L. Parks Library and Museum (252 Montgomery
Street; 334-241-8615; montgomery.troy.edu/rosaparks),
at the spot where in 1955 Parks refused to give up her
seat on a bus to a white passenger, has multimedia
displays and uses special effects to take visitors on a
simulated bus ride back in time.

8 *Pull the Trigger* 7 p.m.

A shotgun restaurant with a bar on the side and
a trophy-size blue marlin arcing across the back wall,
Jubilee Seafood (1057 Woodley Road; 334-262-6224;
jubileeseafoodrestaurant.com; $$-$$$) serves up
dishes like pecan-topped snapper and grilled sea
bass with mushrooms and crabmeat. The Key lime
pie is a comely whorl of citrus and meringue.

SUNDAY

9 *Brimstone in the Pines* 9 a.m.

Drive about 12 miles north on I-65 and a few
miles west on Highway 82 toward Prattville,
and take a left on Autauga County Road 86, also
called Indian Hills Road. At a bend in the two-lane

blacktop, the **Cross Garden** erupts. Constructed as a testimony of Christian faith by W.C. Rice, who died in 2004, this folk art environment, set amid gullies rife with castoff appliances, warns, by way of hundreds of painted crosses, "Hell Is Hot, Hot, Hot!" and recalls Flannery O'Connor's observation that the South was a "Christ-haunted" place.

10 *Country-Fried Brunch* 10:45 a.m.

Wend back into town for an experience closer to the heavenly side. **Martin's Restaurant** (1796 Carter Hill Road; 334-265-1767; martinsrestaurant.org; $$) has been frying chickens and baking coconut meringue pies since 1940. It also does right by collard greens, candied yams, and string beans. But the best is the

simplest: corn muffins crisp and steaming with sweet corn flavor. Plan to arrive soon after they open at 10:45, or you'll spend your Sunday morning in line with the crowds that flock from nearby churches.

OPPOSITE ABOVE The Rosa Parks bus replica.

OPPOSITE BELOW The Civil Rights Monument.

ABOVE The Alabama State Capitol.

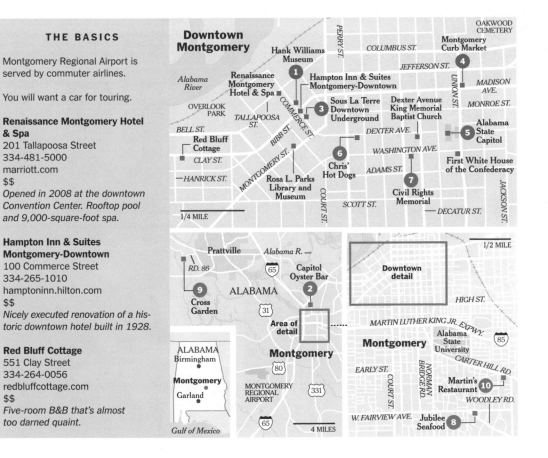

THE BASICS

Montgomery Regional Airport is served by commuter airlines.

You will want a car for touring.

Renaissance Montgomery Hotel & Spa
201 Tallapoosa Street
334-481-5000
marriott.com
$$
Opened in 2008 at the downtown Convention Center. Rooftop pool and 9,000-square-foot spa.

Hampton Inn & Suites Montgomery-Downtown
100 Commerce Street
334-265-1010
hamptoninn.hilton.com
$$
Nicely executed renovation of a historic downtown hotel built in 1928.

Red Bluff Cottage
551 Clay Street
334-264-0056
redbluffcottage.com
$$
Five-room B&B that's almost too darned quaint.

Downtown Montgomery

Hank Williams Museum
Alabama River
Renaissance Montgomery Hotel & Spa
OVERLOOK PARK
BELL ST.
TALLAPOOSA ST.
Red Bluff Cottage
CLAY ST.
HANRICK ST.
COMMERCE ST.
BIBB ST.
MONTGOMERY ST.
Rosa L. Parks Library and Museum
COURT ST.
1/4 MILE

PERRY ST.
COLUMBUS ST.
JEFFERSON ST.
1 Hampton Inn & Suites Montgomery-Downtown
3 Sous La Terre Downtown Underground
Dexter Avenue King Memorial Baptist Church
DEXTER AVE.
6 Chris' Hot Dogs
WASHINGTON AVE.
ADAMS ST.
7 Civil Rights Memorial
SCOTT ST.
DECATUR ST.

OAKWOOD CEMETERY
Montgomery Curb Market
UNION ST.
MADISON AVE.
MONROE ST.
4
Alabama State Capitol
5
First White House of the Confederacy
JACKSON ST.

1/2 MILE
Downtown detail
HIGH ST.

Prattville
Alabama R.
RD. 86
9 Cross Garden
65
ALABAMA
31
Area of detail

65
Capitol Oyster Bar
2

ALABAMA
Birmingham
Montgomery
Garland
Gulf of Mexico

80
MONTGOMERY REGIONAL AIRPORT
331
65
4 MILES

Montgomery
Alabama State University
MARTIN LUTHER KING JR. EXPWY.
85
CARTER HILL RD.
EARLY ST.
NORMAN BRIDGE RD.
COURT ST.
Martin's Restaurant **10**
WOODLEY RD.
W. FAIRVIEW AVE.
Jubilee Seafood **8**

New Orleans

What other city, after being half-drowned and left to starve, foiled by bureaucracy, and attacked by the auto-immune disease of rampant crime, could stagger to its feet to welcome visitors with a platter of oysters on the half shell and a rousing brass band? Within only a couple of years after Hurricane Katrina in 2005, New Orleans was providing streetcar rides and impromptu parades, riverboat calliopes and sidewalk tap dancers. And a few months after the notorious BP oil spill of 2010 blackened the Louisiana coast, the pre-Mardi Gras parades were rolling through New Orleans neighborhoods and the smell of long loaves baking for po' boy sandwiches was still sweetening the air. When chroniclers look back, the city's ability to be itself—a place that embraces sorrow and joy with equal gusto—even in its hardest of times will become part of its legend. — BY SHAILA DEWAN

FRIDAY

1 *Drinks on the Porch* 5 p.m.

New Orleans is a state of mind, one acquired most efficiently with an afternoon cocktail. At the bar of the **Columns** (3811 St. Charles Avenue; 504-899-9308; thecolumns.com), an Italianate mansion turned hotel in the Garden District, what must be the South's most inviting porch flirts with the city's grandest thoroughfare. Have a Campari and soda alfresco or step into the bar, with its ornately painted 16-foot ceiling and a circular settee. Both over the top and the tiniest bit down at the heels, the Columns was the perfect backdrop for *Pretty Baby*, Louis Malle's movie about a turn-of-the-century brothel, even though it is a world away from the former red-light district it was meant to evoke.

2 *Asian Infusion* 7 p.m.

Post-Katrina and post-oil spill, the New Orleans restaurant scene is stronger and more innovative than ever. **Mike's on the Avenue** (628 St. Charles Avenue; 504-523-7600; mikesontheavenue.com; $$$), which

OPPOSITE The French Quarter, New Orleans.

RIGHT The city's Social Aid and Pleasure Clubs not only provide jazz funerals, but parade through New Orleans neighborhoods on Sunday afternoons.

opened in 2010, is one good example, melding Asian and Hawaiian food influences with the flavors of Louisiana. Some of its playful offerings have included a sushi box that includes a Cajun crab roll and duck with shiitake mushrooms, brown rice, and chunks of Cajun ham and andouille sausage.

3 *Jazz and Books* 9 p.m.

In 1768, the French settlers of New Orleans ran an unloved Spanish governor out of town and had a street named after them for their trouble: Frenchmen Street. Today, the street stands in happy rebellion against another takeover: the tourist swarm in the French Quarter on the other side of Esplanade. On Frenchmen, both good music and friendly local people spill out of the clubs and into the streets. For serious jazz head to **Snug Harbor** (626 Frenchmen; 504-949-0696; snugjazz.com), where members of the Marsalis or Neville dynasties make frequent appearances. A more casual, and funkier, atmosphere reigns across the street at the **Spotted Cat** (623 Frenchmen; 206-337-3273; spottedcatmusicclub.com). At **d.b.a.** (618 Frenchmen; 504-942-3731; dbabars.com/dbano), live music coexists with a long list of single-malt Scotches. When your ears need a rest, stop in at **Faubourg Marigny Art & Books** (600 Frenchmen; 504-947-3700; fabonfrenchmen.com), where you can find books about New Orleans, gay and lesbian literature, postcards, and the lowdown on the town from Otis Fennell, the owner, who stays open "as late as it takes."

SATURDAY

4 *The Real Story* 10 a.m.

Much of the history of New Orleans musicians, plus other largely African-American New Orleans traditions like skeleton gangs, jazz parades, and the Mardi Gras Indians with their handmade, proto-Vegas costumes, has been lovingly collected by Sylvester Francis. His **Backstreet Cultural Museum** (1116 St. Claude Avenue; 504-522-4806; backstreetmuseum.org)

ABOVE Casual night life at the Spotted Cat.

BELOW Kermit Ruffins, a New Orleans favorite. Check the listings to see where the top acts are playing.

is tucked inside a former funeral home in the Tremé district. In a city where history is still happening, little shrines like Backstreet are legion and their sole proprietors, like Francis, are oracles.

5 *Potions and Scents* 11 a.m.

The **New Orleans Pharmacy Museum** (514 Chartres Street; 504-565-8027; pharmacymuseum.org) might sound a bit dry, but this 1823 town house is like a concentrated version of the city itself, with exhibits on not only apothecary supplies and soda fountains, but also hangover remedies, voodoo potions, absinthe, opium, and "questionable medical practices." You can also get some good souvenir ideas in the neighborhood. A "rare and intoxicating tobacco" called perique, grown only in a small tract of land in one parish in Louisiana, is available at the nearby **Cigar Factory** (415 Decatur Street; 504-568-1003; cigarfactoryneworleans.com). Vetivert, an earthy scent the museum says was favored by Creole women, can be purchased around the corner at **Hové Parfumeur**, as a perfume, soap, or simply bundles of root (824 Royal Street; 504-525-7827; hoveparfumeur.com).

6 *Eat Your Po' Boy* Noon

New Orleans is called the Crescent City because of the Mississippi River's snaky pinch, which also has made it hard to discern north, south, east, and west.

The custom instead is this: you can go toward the lake, toward the river, upriver or downriver. Starting in Jackson Square, which looks to this day like a Mary Poppins movie set, stroll toward the lake. Go all the way to Rampart Street and turn right. That's downriver. Cross Esplanade, continue one block, and enter the bright orange convenience store. That's heaven. Also known as the **Rampart Street Food Store** (1700 North Rampart Street; 504-944-7777; $). Order the shrimp po' boy on French bread and join all the other people, some still in their bedroom slippers, waiting for their po' boy fix.

7 *After the Flood* 1 p.m.

Katrina couldn't kill New Orleans, but it's a smaller city now, with fewer people living in the lowest coastal neighborhoods. See the hurricane's remaining effects and hear what made the city so vulnerable by taking a seat on the **Gray Line Katrina Tour** (graylineneworleans.com; 504-569-1401; leaving where Toulouse Street meets the river). Guides will explain how levees were breached, tell how the city's residents were affected in the immediate aftermath, and explain the effects of the loss of coastal wetlands.

ABOVE For every renowned restaurant, there is a beloved neighborhood place. This one is Dick and Jenny's.

PAGE 337 Hové Parfumeur carries Creole scent.

You'll also see the port. If three hours on a bus is too much, find one of the many cab drivers with a tour guide license and negotiate a shorter trip.

8 *Local Fare* 6 p.m.

For every Emeril's, Antoine's, or Brennan's in this city of fine dining, there is a beloved neighborhood restaurant where locals will wait hours for a table. At **Dick and Jenny's** (4501 Tchoupitoulas Street; 504-894-9880; dickandjennys.com), in a rambling Uptown barge-board cottage, the dishes might include savory crawfish and andouille cheesecake, pecan-crusted veal sweetbreads, and salmon with Gewürztraminer beurre blanc. They don't take reservations, so settle in on a porch glider with a cocktail and wait.

9 *The Play List* 9 p.m.

Ask New Orleanians about the night's music offerings and chances are they'll rattle them off from memory (if not, pick up a free copy of *Offbeat* magazine). Listen for the city's top acts—the Rebirth Brass Band, the Hot 8, Kermit Ruffins and the Barbecue Swingers, John Boutté, Troy (Trombone Shorty) Andrews. They play at various venues including the **Maple Leaf Bar** (8316 Oak Street; 504-866-9359; mapleleafbar.com), which has a packed dance floor, pressed-tin walls, and a courtyard perfect for brief respites.

SUNDAY

10 *Ambition* 10 a.m.

The thing to love about **Elizabeth's** (601 Gallier Street; 504-944-9272; elizabeths-restaurant.com) is that somebody there tried to make bacon better. The result is praline bacon — a combination of pecan candy and salty pork. The homely little restaurant in the shadow of the Mississippi River levee keeps them coming at breakfast with dishes like strawberry stuffed French toast and Cajun Bubble and Squeak, combining bacon, cabbage, shrimp, poached eggs, and Hollandaise.

11 *Follow the Music* 1 p.m.

New Orleans is a tribal place, made up of Mardi Gras Indian tribes and krewes, and groups known as Social Aid and Pleasure Clubs, originally formed to provide burial insurance. Now the clubs not only provide jazz funerals, but also mount their own parades, known as second lines, that pass through the city's neighborhoods — often from bar to bar — on Sunday afternoons. The Nine Times, the Original Four, the Mahogany Ladies — those are but a few of the clubs that try to one-up one another with color-coded haberdashery and the city's best brass bands. If you have some extra time, get a "route sheet" for the second line (the idea is to follow it, not stand at the side and watch it). To that end, begin asking around early — Sylvester Francis at the Backstreet might let you in on it — or sidle up to your bartender or doorman. Because, as anyone in New Orleans will tell you, the best way to hear a brass band is to dance down the street behind it.

THE BASICS

Fly into Louis Armstrong New Orleans International Airport

Travel on foot and by streetcar.

The Roosevelt New Orleans
123 Baronne Street
therooseveltneworleans.com
504-648-1200
$$$
New Orleans landmark, formerly the Fairmont; renovated after Katrina damage and reopened in 2009.

Olivier House
828 Toulouse Street
504-525-8456
olivierhouse.com
$$
A New Orleans classic with a maze-like series of interior courtyards.

Lookout Inn
833 Poland Avenue
504-947-8188
lookoutneworleans.com
$
Four suites and a saltwater pool.

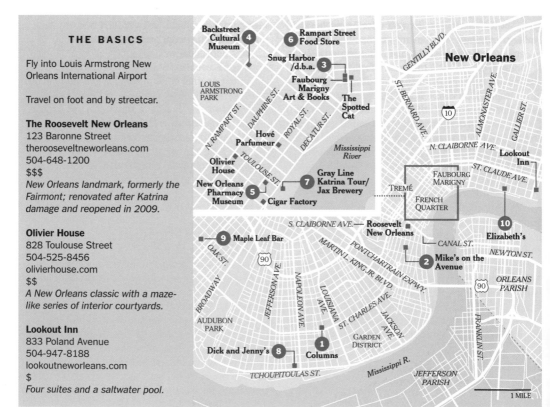

THE MIDWEST

the Black Hills

MINNEAPOLIS
St. Paul

Madis

the Niobrara
River Valley

Iowa's
Mississippi
river

Kansas
City

Fayetteville

St. Louis

uth

MILWAUKEE

traverse
City

Oak Park

Chicago
by Water

Detroit

CHICAGO

cleveland

Indianapolis

Cincinnati

Chicago

All cities have their ups and downs, but Chicago has learned to play to its strengths, adding parks, architectural crowd pleasers, and public art. A solid base of good urban design and buildings gave the city a lot to build from — this is a place where adventurous architecture was already a tradition, despite the inevitable overlay of urban decay. But now Chicago is going forward, too. A raft of improvements in the last decade or so have left it fortified by both 19th- and 20th-century public spaces brimming with 21st-century attractions. — BY FRED A. BERNSTEIN

FRIDAY

1 *Loop the Loop* 3 p.m.

Even if you've been there in the past, a good place to start in Chicago is at the **Chicago Architecture Foundation** (224 South Michigan Avenue; 312-922-3432; caf.architecture.org). The guided downtown walking tour orients newbies to the late 19th- and early 20th-century buildings that first gave Chicago its reputation as a center of great architecture, and several other walking tours will help give you a feeling for the city. If you already know what to look for, get reacquainted with a ride on the "L," the elevated railway that defines the Loop (transitchicago.com). Get on the brown, orange or pink line — it doesn't matter which color, as long as you sit in the first car by the front-view window — and ride around the two-square-mile area. You'll see Bertrand Goldberg's spectacular **Marina City**, with a design inspired by corncobs; the new **Trump International Hotel and Tower**; Frank Gehry's **Pritzker Pavilion** band shell; and Louis Sullivan's **Auditorium Building**, now part of Roosevelt University.

2 *Midway Fare* 8 p.m.

A number of good midprice but high-style restaurants have opened in Chicago in the past few years. A favorite is **Gilt Bar** (230 West Kinzie Street; 312-464-9544; giltbarchicago.com; $$), a casual restaurant in the River North neighborhood that

isn't casual about its cooking. The menu features New American dishes like blackened cauliflower with capers and ricotta gnocchi with sage and brown butter. After dinner, head downstairs to **Curio**, a basement bar with a Prohibition theme. Try the Death's Door Daisy, made with artisanal Wisconsin vodka and Aperol, a blood orange liqueur.

3 *Come On In* 11 p.m.

There are so many clubs on Ontario Street, just north of the loop, that it's sometimes known as Red Bull Row. For a mellower jolt, head to the Uptown neighborhood, to **Big Chicks** (5024 North Sheridan Road; 773-728-5511; bigchicks.com) a gay bar that welcomes everyone. The drinks are cheap, the crowd is friendly, and the décor is appealingly kooky.

SATURDAY

4 *Eggs Plus* 9 a.m.

Couldn't get to dinner at Frontera Grill, the nouvelle Mexican restaurant owned by the celebrity chef Rick Bayless? No worries. Just head over to **Xoco** (65 West Illinois Street; 312-661-1434; rickbayless.com; $), another Bayless restaurant. Breakfast is served till 10 a.m.; expect a line after 8:30. Favorites include scrambled egg empanada with poblano chili, and an open-face torta with soft poached egg, salsa, cheese, cilantro, and black beans.

5 *Off-Label Strip* 11 a.m.

The Magnificent Mile area is filled with flagships (Gucci, Vuitton — you know the list). But there are still some independent stores you won't find at your

OPPOSITE Chicago's urban canyons and the Willis Tower, formerly the Sears Tower.

RIGHT The Pritzker Pavilion and its Frank Gehry-designed band shell, in Millennium Park.

CHICAGO

hometown mall. **Ikram** (873 North Rush Street; 312-587-1000; ikram.com) is the stylish boutique that counts Michelle Obama among its customers, with fashion-forward labels like Jason Wu and Martin Margiela. East Oak Street has a couple of cool shops, including **Sofia** (No. 72; 312-640-0878; sofiavintage.com) and **Colletti Gallery** (No. 102; 312-664-6767; collettigallery.com), with a gorgeous selection of Art Deco and Art Nouveau furniture and objets. It's a short walk from there to the **Museum of Contemporary Art** (220 East Chicago Avenue; 312-280-2660; mcachicago.org).

6 *First Neighborhood* 2 p.m.

Walking around **Hyde Park**, a leafy enclave about seven miles south of the Loop, it's easy to see why Barack and Michelle Obama settled there. Their house, on South Greenwood Avenue between 50th and 51st Streets, is nearly invisible behind Secret Service barricades. But the streets are great for walking, and the beautifully landscaped **University of Chicago** campus is worth exploring for an afternoon.

7 *Livestock Menu* 7 p.m.

Chicago was once the meatpacking capital of the world, and it still knows what to do with meat. Take **Girl & the Goat** (809 West Randolph Street, 312-492-6262; girlandthegoat.com; $$), a much-blogged-about restaurant where the *Top Chef* winner Stephanie Izard takes livestock parts seriously. The often-updated menu has included the likes of lamb ribs with grilled avocado and pistachio piccata, and braised beef tongue with masa and beef vinaigrette. But you don't have to be a carnivore. If you are vegetarian, there is something for you, too—perhaps chickpeas three ways, and for dessert, potato fritters with lemon poached eggplant and Greek yogurt. The soaring dining room, designed by the Chicago design firm 555 International, is warm and modern, with exposed beams, walls of charred cedar, and a large open kitchen.

8 *Funny Bone* 10 p.m.

You won't find big names at the **Red Bar Comedy Club** (in the Ontourage Night Club, 157 West Ontario Street; 773-387-8412; redbarcomedy.com). But a hit-or-miss roster of itinerant comedians will be looking for laughs, including some who heckle the audience in language that Grandma would not consider polite.

SUNDAY

9 *Beautification Brunch* 10 a.m.

Logan Square, about five to six miles northwest of the Loop, is a remnant of Chicago's late-19th-century beautification movement, with a statue of an eagle by Evelyn Longman where two of the grandest boulevards meet. Nearby, **Longman & Eagle** (2657 North Kedzie Avenue; 773-276-7110; longmanandeagle.com; $$) is a rough-edged bar that serves a refined brunch featuring items like a chunky sockeye salmon tartare with pickled mango or a wild boar Sloppy Joe.

10 *Grand Piano* 11 a.m.

Chicago knows how to mix neoclassical architecture with contemporary design, and no place in town does it better than the **Art Institute of Chicago** (111 South Michigan Avenue; 312-443-3600; artinstituteofchicago.org), which opened its celebrated

ABOVE The Girl and the Goat, Chef Stephanie Izard's restaurant on Randolph Street just west of downtown.

BELOW Curio, the basement bar beneath Gilt Bar, has a Prohibition theme and a speakeasy atmosphere.

Modern Wing in 2009. Designed by Renzo Piano, the luminous addition contains a magnificent set of galleries for 1900-1950 European art (Picasso, Giacometti, and Klee are among the big names) and a capacious room for the museum's design collection. Hungry or not, check out **Terzo Piano**, the stunning rooftop restaurant with views of the Pritzker Pavilion in Millennium Park across the street.

11 *Wheels Up* 1 p.m.

From the museum, walk over the pedestrian bridge, also designed by Piano, to Millennium Park, and rent bikes from **Bike and Roll** (312-729-1000; bikechicago.com) for a ride up the shore of Lake Michigan. You'll pass Navy Pier, skyscrapers by

Mies van der Rohe, and hundreds of beach volleyball courts that make this the Malibu of the Midwest on summer and fall weekends. Along the way, you'll see Lincoln Park, with a new pavilion by the Chicago architect Jeanne Gang—another example of how the city is updating its open spaces.

ABOVE At Ikram, a designer boutique, one regular shopper is Michelle Obama.

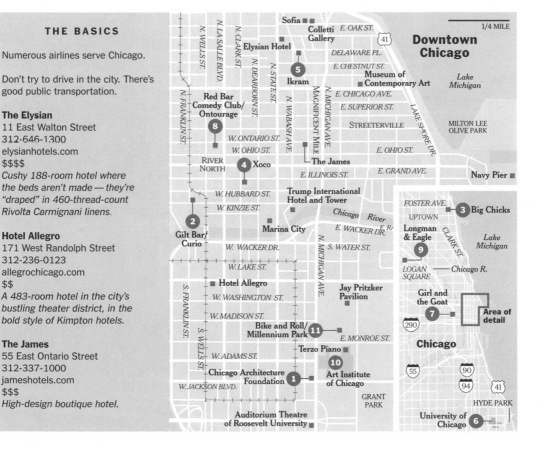

THE BASICS

Numerous airlines serve Chicago.

Don't try to drive in the city. There's good public transportation.

The Elysian
11 East Walton Street
312-646-1300
elysianhotels.com
$$$$
Cushy 188-room hotel where the beds aren't made — they're "draped" in 460-thread-count Rivolta Carmignani linens.

Hotel Allegro
171 West Randolph Street
312-236-0123
allegrochicago.com
$$
A 483-room hotel in the city's bustling theater district, in the bold style of Kimpton hotels.

The James
55 East Ontario Street
312-337-1000
jameshotels.com
$$$
High-design boutique hotel.

Downtown Chicago

Sofia
Colletti Gallery
Elysian Hotel
E. OAK ST.
DELAWARE PL.
E. CHESTNUT ST.
Ikram
Museum of Contemporary Art
Lake Michigan
E. CHICAGO AVE.
Red Bar Comedy Club/ Ontourage
E. SUPERIOR ST.
STREETERVILLE
MILTON LEE OLIVE PARK
W. ONTARIO ST.
W. OHIO ST.
E. OHIO ST.
RIVER NORTH
Xoco
The James
E. ILLINOIS ST.
E. GRAND AVE.
Navy Pier
W. HUBBARD ST.
Trump International Hotel and Tower
W. KINZIE ST.
Chicago River
FOSTER AVE.
Big Chicks
Gilt Bar/ Curio
Marina City
E. WACKER DR.
UPTOWN
Longman & Eagle
Lake Michigan
W. WACKER DR.
S. WATER ST.
W. LAKE ST.
LOGAN SQUARE
Chicago R.
Hotel Allegro
W. WASHINGTON ST.
Jay Pritzker Pavilion
Girl and the Goat
Area of detail
W. MADISON ST.
Bike and Roll/ Millennium Park
E. MONROE ST.
Chicago
Terzo Piano
W. ADAMS ST.
Chicago Architecture Foundation
Art Institute of Chicago
W. JACKSON BLVD.
GRANT PARK
HYDE PARK
Auditorium Theatre of Roosevelt University
University of Chicago

Chicago by Water

Expensive water-view condos and gleaming commercial towers line the Chicago River in downtown Chicago, close to its connection to Lake Michigan. Long ago the river was a polluted dumping ground, but now kayakers ply its waters and tour boats glide along as guides explain some of the wealth of interesting architecture on the banks. For an intimate, easygoing exploration of the river, with stops to look deeper at some of what's close by on land, create your own tour by water taxi. From late spring through fall, two taxi companies operate on the river, running distinct, though partly overlapping, routes. One ventures out into Lake Michigan. The boats operate like buses, following scheduled routes that take you to standard tourist stops. Hop on and off at will, and see the heart of the city from a different point of view.
— BY RUSSELL WORKING

FRIDAY

1 *Know Your River* 3 p.m.

Get your bearings at the **Michigan Avenue Bridge**. Stop on the pedestrian walkway, gaze down the river into the heart of the city and then back the other way toward Lake Michigan. You may spot a water taxi—yellow for Chicago Water Taxi or blue for Shoreline. Inside the ornately decorated stone tower at the southwest corner of the bridge is the **McCormick Tribune Bridgehouse & Chicago River Museum** (376 North Michigan Avenue; bridgehousemuseum.org), where you can see the inner workings of a drawbridge and learn about river history, including the arrival of Jean Baptiste Point du-Sable, a black French pioneer, in the 1780s. At the north end of the bridge, duck down to the lower level and find the **Billy Goat Tavern** (430 North Michigan Avenue; billygoattavern.com), a reporters' watering hole for generations and the inspiration for the *Saturday Night Live* "cheeseburger" sketches with John Belushi as the single-minded counter man.

2 *Down by the Docks* 4 p.m.

Still at the bridge's north end, walk down to water level to see where the taxis leave. For **Chicago Water Taxi** (400 North Michigan Avenue; 312-337-1446; chicagowatertaxi.com for routes and prices), go down the stairs by the **Wrigley Building** and follow the signs to the taxi dock. For **Shoreline Water Taxi** (401 North Michigan Avenue; 312-222-9328; shorelinewatertaxi.com), take the steps down on the northeast side of the bridge. There's no reason to take a water taxi anywhere today, but if you'd like to have the names and histories to go with some of the buildings you'll see on your taxi tour tomorrow, one option is to cross the bridge, walk down the steps on the southern side, and find the dock for the **Chicago Architecture Foundation**'s 90-minute architecture cruise. (To minimize waiting, buy tickets in advance; check caf.architecture.org or go to the foundation's shop at 224 South Michigan Avenue). It's a pleasant, breezy introduction to the heart of the city. Another way to prepare is with a guidebook; a good one is Jennifer Marjorie Bosch's *View From the River: The Chicago Architecture Foundation River Cruise* (Pomegranate Communications).

3 *Mellow Out* 8 p.m.

Relax and plan your strategy for tomorrow over drinks and dinner at **State and Lake** (201 North State Street; 312-239-9400; stateandlakechicago.com; $$), a restaurant that's at least as much about the beverages as the food. The dining choices include comfort food specials, sandwiches and salads, and entrees like steak frites or angel hair pasta and shrimp. Linger over one of the wines or a draft or bottled beer.

SATURDAY

4 *Squint at the Corncobs* 9 a.m.

Return to the Michigan Avenue dock and catch a Chicago Water Taxi headed west. Out on the river, glide along for a while, squinting upward at the skyscrapers in the morning light. There are dozens of landmarks, including the **Marina City** towers at 300 North State Street, designed to resemble corncobs; the sprawling **Merchandise Mart** at North Wells Street, built in 1930; and the **Civic Opera House** on North Wacker Drive, constructed in the Art Deco armchair form and nicknamed Insull's Throne after the tycoon who commissioned it.

OPPOSITE The Merchandise Mart, built in 1930, hulks over the Chicago River, a highway for water taxis.

5 *Waterside* 10 a.m.

Get off at the LaSalle/Clark Street stop and walk across the river on the Clark Street bridge to find the new **Riverwalk** (explorechicago.org). Explore for a while, passing outdoor cafes and kiosks that thrive in the summer season. You're also close here to the area around State and Randolph Streets that is home to several major theaters and the Joffrey Ballet.

6 *Brunch Umbrellas* Noon

A pleasant place for brunch is **Flatwater** (321 North Clark Street, river level; 312-644-0283; flatwater.us; $$), where tables under green umbrellas are lined up close to the river's edge and yachts pull up to dock for lunch. There's also indoor seating, but the river is the real draw here, so why not stay close? (The people watching is good, too.) Check the menu for the crab cakes Benedict. When you're ready to venture out again, return to the LaSalle/Clark Street stop to pick up another taxi and continue west on the river.

7 *Do Look Down* 1:30 p.m.

After the river bends south, alight at the spot near the **Willis Tower** (233 South Wacker Drive; willistower.com), once known as the Sears Tower, where both taxi lines stop. Ride the elevator to the Skydeck (theskydeck.com). Take the dare — venture out onto one of the glass-floored retractable bays to join the other sightseers scaring themselves silly by staring 1,353 feet straight down at the street. Across the river is Union Station, a cavernous rail terminal. Its Beaux-Arts Great Hall has been featured in several films, including *The Untouchables*.

8 *Chinatown* 3:30 p.m.

Continue south on the Chicago Water Taxi to **Ping Tom Memorial Park** (named for a Chinese-American civic leader), and proceed on foot under an ornate gate into **Chinatown**, where you'll find hole-in-the-wall restaurants and stores selling barrels of ginseng or aquariums full of live frogs. Stop

in at the one-room **Dr. Sun Yat-Sen Museum** (2245 South Wentworth Avenue, third floor; 312-842-5462; open until 5 p.m.), dedicated to the revolutionary who played a leading role in overthrowing the Qing Dynasty — the last of the Chinese emperors — in 1911. The photos inside include some from Sun's visit to Chicago at around that time. At **Chinatown Square**, an outdoor mall just south of the park, you'll find stores selling green tea and Chinese cookies, a Chinese newspaper's offices, and your choice of restaurants. If you'd like an early dinner, try **Spring World** (2109 South China Place in Chinatown Square; 312-326-9966; $), which serves the spicy food of Yunnan Province. When you've seen enough, catch a water taxi for the half-hour trip back to Michigan Avenue.

9 *Honky-Tonk Bard* 7 p.m.

There's enough going on at the **Navy Pier** (navypier.com) to keep you busy all weekend. Reach it from the Michigan Avenue dock of the Shoreline Water Taxi. (And as you debark, take note of the schedule; you don't want to miss the last taxi back.) The pier is 50 acres of parks, promenades, restaurants, carnival-like stalls, and souvenir shops, with fireworks on summer Saturday nights. There's also an indoor garden, a stained-glass museum, and the **Chicago Shakespeare Theater** (800 East Grand Avenue; 312-595-5600; chicagoshakes.com), where you might find local fare in addition to the serious drama. A few years ago Second City's *Rod Blagojevich Superstar* had a successful run at the theater, including an appearance by Blagojevich himself, although he was still smarting from the scandal that cost him the Illinois governorship. He recited lines from *Henry V* and invited the cast for dinner, adding, "We'll be serving tarantulas."

ABOVE The Shedd Aquarium and the Adler Planetarium at Grant Park, on Lake Michigan. Get there from downtown on the Shoreline Water Taxi. Both Shoreline and Chicago Water Taxis cater to commuters and tourists alike.

SUNDAY

10 *Feeding the Spirit* 10 a.m.

From either Michigan Avenue or the LaSalle/Clark stop, it's a short walk to the **House of Blues** (329 North Dearborn Street; 312-923-2000; houseofblues.com; $$$), where the Sunday-morning Gospel Brunch includes a buffet with blackened catfish, jambalaya, fried chicken, and omelets, along with exhilarating African-American worship and music.

11 *Lakeside Dinosaurs* Noon

For a nice ride out into Lake Michigan, take the Shoreline taxi to the Navy Pier, change boats, and go to the lakeside museum campus that is home to the **Field Museum, Shedd Aquarium**, and **Adler Planetarium**. All are worth serious time, but for generations of children, the must-see has been the Field's dinosaur skeletons, including a Tyrannosaurus rex found in South Dakota in 1990 and nicknamed Sue.

ABOVE The view from the Chicago River up at the Clark Street Bridge.

THE BASICS

The Chicago River, in the heart of downtown, is the north and west boundary of the Loop.

When you're not on a water taxi, take the "L" (that's "El" to some) or land-bound cabs.

Fairmont Chicago Millennium Park
200 North Columbus Drive
312-565-8000
fairmont.com/chicago
$$
Recently renovated; a short walk to the Michigan Avenue bridge.

Wit Hotel
201 North State Street
312-467-0200
thewithotel.com
$$
A chic, fairly new hotel with a popular rooftop bar.

Hotel Sax
333 North Dearborn Street
312-245-0333
hotelsaxchicago.com
$$
Stylish hotel beneath Marina City towers.

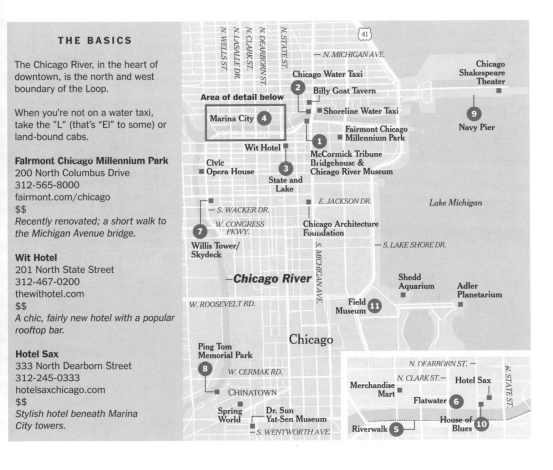

Oak Park

On most weekends, people from all over the world can be seen walking slowly down the streets of Oak Park, Illinois, clutching their maps, guidebooks, audio-tour wands, and cameras. Spotting a celebrity — a house designed by Frank Lloyd Wright — they stop, stare, and snap photographs. Then they move on to the next Wright house amid the historic district's attractive but conventional Victorians. Oak Park, which is the location not only of the home and studio where Wright spent his early career, but of the world's largest collection of his buildings (25), has long attracted design pilgrims. In a weekend there, you will also find galleries, shops, restaurants, and the painstakingly restored childhood home of Ernest Hemingway. And a few miles away in the Hyde Park section of Chicago, another Wright house awaits, one of the master's most renowned.
— BY BETSY RUBINER

FRIDAY

1 *The Son Also Rises* 3 p.m.

Ernest Hemingway was born in Oak Park in 1899 and lived here through high school. Whether Hemingway ever actually described the town as a place of "broad lawns and narrow minds" is in dispute. But you can get a feel for his genteel origins at the **Ernest Hemingway Birthplace Home** (339 North Oak Park Avenue; 708-848-2222; ehfop.org). Just south, at the companion **Ernest Hemingway Museum** (200 North Oak Park Avenue), you can see Hemingway's high school report card (he did well in commercial law, not so well in geometry) and teenage scribblings.

2 *Emerging Artists* 4:30 p.m.

If Oak Park was a good place to create ground-breaking architectural designs and to develop the skills of a landmark novelist, why not for today's generation of creative types? In the **Oak Park Arts District** (Harrison Street between Austin Boulevard and Ridgeland Avenue; oakparkartsdistrict.com), galleries, studios, and shops occupy small store-fronts in a quiet residential neighborhood. Drop in at **Expressions Graphics** (29 Harrison Street; 708-386-3552; expressionsgraphics.org), an artists' cooperative that specializes in prints; at **Prodigy Glassworks** (207 Harrison Street; 708-445-8000;

prodigyglassworks.com), which sells hand-blown and fused glass pieces made by local artists; or at one of the painters' studios. Amid the art spaces are New Age-y offerings like Buddhist meditation, rolfing, and yoga classes.

3 *Carni, Pesce, Paste, Pizze* 6:30 p.m.

Oak Park is a small town, but not too small to have a restaurant with menu headings in Italian. Try out the cuisine at **Mancini's** (1111 Lake Street; 708-445-9700; mancinispizzapastacafe.com; $-$$), an Oak Park fixture since 1976, which serves wine and beer along with its zuppe-to-dolce dinner selections. Don't neglect the gelato.

4 *Reading Up* 8 p.m.

Bone up for a weekend of Frank Lloyd Wright immersion with some selections from the **Book Table** (1045 Lake Street; 708-386-9800; booktable.net), which stocks several titles on the master in its pleasant, book-filled store. Wright's profoundly original and seminal architecture is what assures his continuing fame, but when he was alive, his flamboyant personality garnered more attention. As you pick up some books of your own, you can go serious, with scholarly architectural criticism; local, focusing on Wright in Oak Park; or gossipy, digging into recent books on the architect's sometimes messy, sometimes tragic private life.

OPPOSITE AND BELOW The sanctuary of Unity Temple and the exterior of the Frank Lloyd Wright Home and Studio. Wright designed both structures, and several others in town, during his years as an Oak Park resident.

SATURDAY

5 *The Main Attraction* 10:30 a.m.

Before Frank Lloyd Wright built homes for clients, he field-tested many of his design principles in the house he built for his first wife and their six children. Wright built a compact dark-wood and light-brick New England Shingle-style home in 1889, and in 1898 he added the eye-catching studio addition where he developed his Prairie style. Walking through his rooms during the guided interior tour of what is now the **Frank Lloyd Wright Home and Studio** (951 Chicago Avenue; 708-848-1976; gowright.org), you experience his ideas about space, light, and shelter. You'll also see his signature touches — the art glass, the central hearth, the intimate spaces tucked within the open plan. During a guided walking tour (exteriors only) of other Wright-designed homes nearby, you'll see how his ideas evolved. Arrive early or buy advance tickets online — tours often fill quickly.

6 *On the Avenue* 1:30 p.m.

For over a century, the intersection of Oak Park Avenue and Lake Street has been a lively retail area known by locals as "the Avenue." Stop for lunch at **Winberie's** (151 North Oak Park Avenue; 708-386-2600; winberies.com; $$) in a 1905 Prairie-style commercial building in Scoville Square. It's a bistro with large picture windows, exposed brick walls, and shiny white-and-black tile floors, and it serves a broad selection of sandwiches, salads, and pastas.

7 *The Jewel Box* 3 p.m.

Sitting sternly, almost bunkerlike, on a busy downtown street, **Unity Temple** (875 Lake Street; 708-383-8873; unitytemple.org) is one of Wright's most

influential buildings and is still home to its original Unitarian Universalist congregation. The building resembles three giant children's blocks made of poured concrete. A guided tour leads you through a low, dark cloister and into a stunning high-ceilinged sanctuary filled with light filtered through art-glass windows. The intimate, minutely detailed interior is profoundly calming. Wright called it his "little jewel box."

8 *Try the Thai* 7 p.m.

Rangsan Sutcharit, who once cooked at Arun's, a superb Thai restaurant in Chicago, now cooks simpler and less expensive but still delicious Thai food, combining fresh ingredients and pungent spices, at **Amarind's** (6822 West North Avenue, Chicago; 773-889-9999; amarinds.com; $). It's in a small brick castle-like building on an easy-to-miss corner just over Oak Park's northern border with Chicago. Don't miss the Golden Cup appetizer, delicate flower-shaped pastry cups filled with corn, shrimp, sweet peas, and shiitake mushrooms. The signature entree is spinach noodles with shrimp and crab in a chili sauce.

9 *Roots Music* 9:30 p.m.

A weathered club inside a green wood-frame building, **FitzGerald's** (6615 West Roosevelt Road, Berwyn; 708-788-2118; fitzgeraldsnightclub.com) still looks and feels like a 1920s roadhouse. But it sits back slightly on a commercial strip in Berwyn, just south of Oak Park. One of the best places in the Chicago area to hear live roots music, FitzGerald's has long been host to impressive national and local musicians who play everything from Chicago blues to R&B, jazz, rock, and alternative country. Bands play on a simple raised

ABOVE Frank Lloyd Wright is Oak Park's main claim to fame, but Ernest Hemingway spent time there, too — from birth through high school. His home is open for tour.

RIGHT Spring in an Oak Park city park.

stage for a beer-in-hand crowd gathered on the scuffed wooden dance floor.

SUNDAY

10 *Going Organic* 9 a.m.

The buzz about **Buzz Café** (905 South Lombard Avenue; 708-524-2899; thebuzzcafe.com; $) is that it's a community-minded gathering spot, with plenty of organic and vegetarian choices, in the Harrison Street Arts District. Paintings and drawings by local artists cover the green and purple walls, artists sketch at tables while sitting on brightly painted second-hand chairs, and children and reading groups curl up on comfy sofas in the back. Sunday brunch entrees includes eggs and sausage, pancakes, waffles, and wraps.

11 *Chicago Prairie* 11 a.m.

Wright's Oak Park houses show the development of his style in his first decades as an architect, culminating in his signature Prairie houses. To see the Prairie house in full flower and on a scale that only his wealthiest clients could afford, journey to the Hyde Park neighborhood of Chicago to tour his **Robie House** (5757 South Woodlawn Avenue, Chicago; 312-994-4000; gowright.org). This is a masterpiece, one of the clearest examples anywhere of a building that is fully, from top to bottom and inside and out, an integrated and harmonious work of art.

THE BASICS

Oak Park is a 20-minute drive or train ride from downtown Chicago.

The Chicago area is well served by public transportation.

Carleton of Oak Park
1110 Pleasant Street
708-848-5000
carletonhotel.com
$$
Dated but in a perfect location, with 153 rooms in two buildings.

Harvey House Bed & Breakfast
107 South Scoville Avenue
708-848-6810
harveyhousebb.com
$$$
Five nicely appointed rooms; massage available.

Under the Ginkgo Tree Bed and Breakfast
300 North Kenilworth Avenue
708-524-2327
undertheginkgotreebb.com
$
Four pleasant rooms in a Queen Anne Victorian.

Traverse City

Driving along the fingerlike peninsulas of Grand Traverse Bay, it's easy to see why this part of Michigan calls itself the cherry capital. In spring, dense orchards explode in creamy blossoms, their pink hues like Impressionist smudges against the brilliant blue of Lake Michigan; come July's harvest time, the branches are thick with ruby fruit. But sprouting from the rolling green hillsides between the orchards is evidence of yet another fruitful enterprise—neat rows of vineyards that are drawing oenophiles and casual wine tasters alike. Around Grand Traverse Bay and in its urban center, Traverse City, are ample opportunities to experience both, with plenty of shopping, dining, and historic stop-offs—not to mention more than a hundred miles of sparkling waterfront—along the way.
— BY BETH GREENFIELD

FRIDAY

1 *Cherry Picking* 4 p.m.

Cherries are a prominent theme on Front Street in Traverse City, a pleasantly hip town that is also home to the weeklong summer National Cherry Festival. Amid the galleries, antiques, stores, and shops is the **Cherry Stop** boutique (211 East Front Street; 231-929-3990; cherrystop.com), stocked with cherry pie, cherry-pepper jam, cherry-scented candles, cherry-chipotle sauce, cherry body lotion, cherry cookbooks, and aprons bearing bold cherry prints. For cherry ice cream, choose **Kilwin's** (231-946-2403; 129 East Front Street; kilwins.com), which also proffers fat slabs of fudge.

2 *Creative Reuse* 6 p.m.

Another constellation of shops worth exploring resides in an unlikely place: within the Victorian Italianate brick walls of the former Northern Michigan Asylum for the Insane, founded in 1885 and redeveloped over the past few years into the retail and residential **Village at Grand Traverse Commons**. A slightly eerie vibe remains on the sprawling grounds, but inside the buildings you'll find a labyrinth of cool and quirky spots like **Creation**

Pharm (800 Cottageview Drive, Suite 45; 231-929-1100; creationpharm.com), with homemade soaps; **Gallery Fifty** (800 Cottageview Drive, Suite 50; 231-932-0775; galleryfifty.com), showing mixed-media works by local artists; and **Left Foot Charley** (806 Red Drive, Suite 100; 231-995-0500; leftfootcharley.com), an urban winery offering tastes of its Rieslings, pinot blancs, pinot grigios, and Gewurztraminers.

3 *Notes from the Underground* 7:30 p.m.

Settle in for dinner at **Trattoria Stella** (830 Cottageview Drive, Suite G-01; 231-929-8989; stellatc.com; $$–$$$), located in the surprisingly romantic former asylum cellar. Its contemporary Italian menu has a local focus, offering dishes like baked lasagna with roasted squash and shiitake mushrooms—not to mention an extensive wine list.

SATURDAY

4 *Protein Fix* 9 a.m.

Slide into a booth at the **Omelette Shoppe** (1209 East Front Street; 231-946-0590; omeletteshoppe.com; $), where options for the signature breakfast range from simple (western, Greek) to over-the-top (Chicken Fajita, with chicken, pepper, onions, avocado, cheese, and sour cream).

5 *Sip Sliding Away* 11 a.m.

Head due north out of the city onto the **Old Mission Peninsula**, a 22-mile strip that's narrow enough in stretches to let you drive up its spine while taking in bay views in both directions. Its length is a stretch of gently rolling hills, maple syrup stands, red barns, B&Bs, and cherry orchards—as well as several wineries, including the **Chateau Grand Traverse** (12239 Center Road; 231-223-7355; cgtwines.com) and **Chateau Chantal** (15900 Rue de Vin; 800-969-4009; chateauchantal.com), both of which have guest houses with rooms overlooking the vineyards. All offer daily tastings of their Rieslings and pinot noirs and, naturally, some version or other of a cloying cherry port.

6 *Lunch with a View* 1 p.m.

The **Old Mission General Store** (18250 Mission Road; 231-223-4310; oldmissiongeneralstore.com), should not be missed. It opened in a wigwam in

1839 as the first trading post between Detroit and Mackinac Island. Jim Richards, a former actor, now runs the place, his days onstage and in soap operas still evident in his booming voice and jaunty derby (it's a store rule that all the male workers wear period hats). There are creaky wood floors, big barrels of peanuts, an antique Victrola, and a heavy, ancient telephone whose receiver Richards picks up when it ding-a-lings — plus modern additions like store-made cherry salsa, steaming cups of chai, and fat Italian sandwiches. Order a couple and take them to the peninsula's northern tip for a picnic at a latitude of almost exactly 45 degrees north, halfway between the Equator and the North Pole. Stroll onto wide, muddy flats and peer out to the bay or back inland, where a clutch of furry pine trees hugs a tiny white church, a squat 1870 lighthouse, and the **Hesler Log House**, an 1856 residence constructed from hand-hewn pines and hemlocks and restored for visitors, complete with a faux cherry pie on a windowsill.

7 *Sweet and Dry* 2 p.m.

Loop back down Old Mission and then up the longer and wider **Leelanau Peninsula**, exploring winding country roads and precious little towns like **Suttons Bay**, with a neat row of restaurants and boutiques, and blink-and-you'll-miss-it **Lake Leelanau**. And certainly keep up the vino theme; Leelanau's 18 wineries include both the large **Black Star Farms** (10844 East Revold Road, Suttons Bay; 231-944-1270; blackstarfarms.com), where visitors sample pinot noir, brandy, and cheeses in a sun-drenched tasting room, and many smaller

ABOVE Farming with a view on the Leelenau Peninsula.

RIGHT You'll find an artists' community in Leland, where the prime attraction is Fishtown, a Lilliputian commercial-fishing post. Worn wooden docks and ramshackle structures hold shops and studios.

OPPOSITE Cherries on the tree near Traverse City.

vintners. "Go off a side road and through the woods and you'll find a vineyard here, a vineyard there, hundreds of acres of new vineyards," said Joel Goldberg, editor of the Detroit-based online consumer guide MichWine.com, who spoke between sips at the small **Chateau Fontaine** (2290 South French Road, Lake Leelanau; 231-256-0000; chateaufontaine.com).

8 *Fish Tales* 4 p.m.

You'll find an artists' community in **Leland**, where the prime attraction is **Fishtown**, a Lilliputian commercial-fishing post. Its worn wooden docks and ramshackle structures hold tiny clothing shops, a sunny pottery studio, and seafood stores like **Carlson's**, which sells fresh and smoked fish (205 West River; 231-256-9801). Fishing boats, both working and tourist, come and go, as do the Manitou Islands ferries, carrying gear-laden campers and hikers.

9 *Gone the Sun* 6 p.m.

This peninsula's tip, **Northport**, has a lighthouse, too — the red-roofed and climbable **Grand Traverse Lighthouse**, whose interior has been restored to its 1920s style. It's in the 1,300-acre **Leelanau State Park** (leelanaustatepark.com), with hiking paths and a leafy campground. The park fronts Lake Michigan, stretching out west toward Wisconsin, where you'll glimpse the perfect sunset to wind up your day.

10 *From Lake and Garden* 8 p.m.

From there, head back to the Old Mission Peninsula and the bayfront **Boathouse Restaurant**

(14039 Peninsula Drive, Traverse City; 231-223-4030; boathouseonwestbay.com; $$–$$$), where the chef prepares French-infused local-seasonal meals including creative takes on pan-seared lake perch. The choice of wines will make your head spin before you've had a sip.

SUNDAY

11 *Farewell Song* 11 a.m.

Ten minutes northeast of Traverse City, the quirky **Music House Museum** (7377 Route 31 North, Acme; 231-938-9300; musichouse.org) in a converted 1908 barn houses a collection of automatic musical instruments including a 1924 Wurlitzer theater organ,

a gorgeous 1917 Estey pipe organ, and an 18-foot-high Mortier dance organ from Belgium, hand-carved out of rosewood in 1922 and sounding like a full, festive band. A walnut and gold-leaf reproducing piano plays rolls remade from those created by George Gershwin. "This is exactly how he played *Rhapsody in Blue,* " explained a museum guide, Jack Pechur. And for nearly five minutes the keyboard dipped and heaved, ghostlike, through the piece, filling the soaring space with romantic sounds.

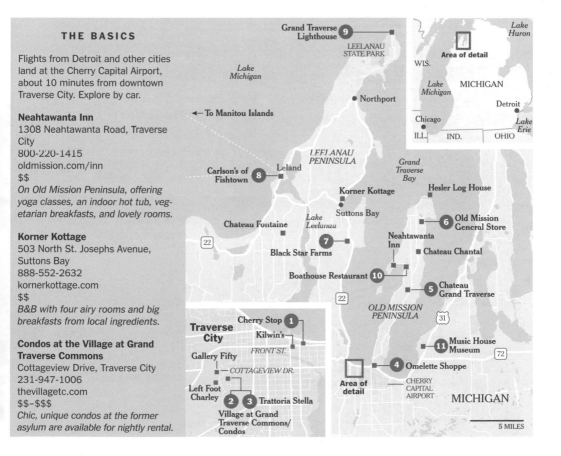

THE BASICS

Flights from Detroit and other cities land at the Cherry Capital Airport, about 10 minutes from downtown Traverse City. Explore by car.

Neahtawanta Inn
1308 Neahtawanta Road, Traverse City
800-220-1415
oldmission.com/inn
$$
On Old Mission Peninsula, offering yoga classes, an indoor hot tub, vegetarian breakfasts, and lovely rooms.

Korner Kottage
503 North St. Josephs Avenue, Suttons Bay
888-552-2632
kornerkottage.com
$$
B&B with four airy rooms and big breakfasts from local ingredients.

Condos at the Village at Grand Traverse Commons
Cottageview Drive, Traverse City
231-947-1006
thevillagetc.com
$$–$$$
Chic, unique condos at the former asylum are available for nightly rental.

Detroit

Eminem celebrated Detroit, Michigan, in a slick Super Bowl commercial. Glenn Beck denigrated it by comparing it to Hiroshima. To visit Detroit these days is to experience both ends of that spectrum — a once great metropolis worn down by decades of corruption and economic woes, and a city fueled by newfound hope and enthusiasm as it painstakingly rebuilds itself. Edgy cafes and shops cater to young artists and professionals moving into downtown loft spaces. Established restaurants, museums, and musical venues recapture the storied past. You may have to work a little to find the best of Detroit, but it's worth it.
— BY JENNIFER CONLIN

FRIDAY

1 *Groove Time* 2 p.m.

Get into the beat of Detroit immediately with a visit to the **Motown Historical Museum** (2648 West Grand Boulevard; 313-875-2264; motownmuseum.com), where the tour guides are nearly as entertaining as the artists who first recorded their songs here at Berry Gordy Jr.'s recording studio, Hitsville USA, in the early 1960s. The memorabilia ranges from Marvelettes album covers to the Jackson Five's psychedelic bell bottoms. You can't help but sing the tunes of Marvin Gaye, Stevie Wonder, Diana Ross, Smokey Robinson, the Four Tops, and the Temptations as you wander into Studio A, where it all began.

2 *French Flavor* 5 p.m.

Though it is easy to forget this city's French colonial roots, at **Good Girls Go to Paris Crepes** (15

East Kirby Street, Suite 115; 877-727-4727; goodgirlsgotopariscrepes.com; $), Le Détroit feels alive and well in a setting of dark red walls and classic French movie posters. Try a Celeste (Brie, dried cranberries, and roast beef) or a Claire (chicken, broccoli, and Cotswold cheese), and leave room for an ooh-la-la dessert crepe. After dinner, stroll over to the elegant **Detroit Institute of Arts** (5200 Woodward Avenue; 313-833-7900; dia.org), which stays open until 10 p.m. on Fridays. There are works by Picasso and van Gogh, but the don't-miss is Diego Rivera's *Detroit Industry* fresco cycle from the 1930s.

3 *Cool Cat Cafe* 10 p.m.

Don't let the abandoned buildings or strip joint across the street keep you from **Café D'Mongo's** (1439 Griswold Street; cafedmongos.com), a wonderfully eccentric speakeasy that feels more like a private party than a bustling bar. The owner, Larry Mongo, is like a funky Mr. Rogers who knows everyone in the neighborhood and beyond, from the young "creative class" that frequents his establishment to the glamorous sixty-something women sipping dark cocktails at the bar. Live jazz and country music play on alternating Friday nights. Café D'Mongo's is open only on Fridays and occasionally, if the owner feels like it, the last Saturday of each month.

SATURDAY

4 *To Market* 8 a.m.

The six-block **Eastern Market** (2934 Russell Street; 313-833-9300; detroiteasternmarket.com), founded in 1891, is home to Detroit foodies with more than 250 vendors selling everything from fruits and vegetables to Michigan maple syrup and artisanal breads. This is also a great area for antiques and bric-a-brac. Try **Marketplace Antiques Gallery** (2047 Gratiot Avenue; 313-567-8250) or **Eastern Market Antiques** (2530 Market Street; 313-259-0600;

OPPOSITE The GM Renaissance Center downtown.

LEFT Hitsville USA, now the Motown Historical Museum. Wander into Studio A, where it all began for the likes of Marvin Gaye, Stevie Wonder, and Diana Ross.

easternmarketantiques.com). And if you have not sufficiently grazed your way through the market, stop in at the **Russell St. Deli** (2465 Russell Street; 313-567-2900; russellstreetdeli.com; $) for breakfast. The delicious raisin bread French toast is even better slathered with toasted pecans or fresh fruit.

5 *T Man* 10 a.m.

While Detroit has no shortage of historic homes and museums honoring the car industry, the **Model T Automotive Heritage Complex** (461 Piquette Avenue; 313-872-8759; tplex.org), the birthplace of the Model T Ford, stands out. This was Henry Ford's first factory, and it appears much as it did when it opened in 1904.

See various fully restored Model T's and visit the "secret experimental room" where Ford invented the car that would take motoring to the masses.

6 *Fire Up Your Belly* Noon

Located in Corktown, across the street from one of the saddest yet most historic landmarks in Detroit — the now abandoned Michigan Central Station — **Slows Bar B Q** (2138 Michigan Avenue; 313-962-9828; slowsbarbq.com; $$) is single-handedly revitalizing this area of the city with its baby back ribs, pulled pork, beef brisket, and chicken wings, as well as its charitable donations to local shelters, hospitals, and schools. Inside, the place is comfortable, with salvaged lumber, exposed brick walls, and a wrap-around bar. Outside, there may be a line, but Slows makes it worth taking a place at the end. What's more, waiting gives you a chance to dream up interesting development ideas for the haunting rail building in the distance.

7 *A Matinee Moment* 2 p.m.

The one thing not missing in this city is theaters — and they are housed in pristinely restored historic buildings. While away the afternoon with a performance in one of their classy interiors. On one weekend, matinee choices included a comedy at the intimate **Gem Theatre** (333 Madison Avenue; gemtheatre.com), a dance troupe at the

breathtakingly renovated **Detroit Opera House** (1526 Broadway; motopera.org), a Broadway musical at the **Fisher Theatre** (3011 West Grand Boulevard; broadwayindetroit.com), a children's show at the former movie palace the **Fox Theatre**, (2211 Woodward Avenue; olympiaentertainment.com), and a concert at **Music Hall** (350 Madison Avenue; musichall.org).

8 *Cheap and Cheerful* 6 p.m.

By far the best happy hour deal in town, and the crowds prove it, is at **Roast**, a modern brasserie located on the ground floor of the newly renovated Westin Book Cadillac Hotel (1128 Washington Boulevard; 313-961-2500; roastdetroit.com; $). Sidle up to the polished bar, settle onto a comfortable padded stool, and start ordering. You'll find beer, wine, and cocktails, and the bar food includes burgers, macaroni and cheese, and huge paper cones of hot fries.

9 *Jazz It Up* 9 p.m.

Cliff Bell's (2030 Park Avenue; 313-961-2543; cliffbells.com; $$) is one of the oldest and most famous supper clubs in Detroit (it originally opened in 1935), and after years of meticulous renovations, it is once again the place to be on a weekend night. Amid its Art Deco features, vaulted ceilings, mahogany bar, and mirrored walls, to say nothing of the sounds of the jazz ensembles performing each night, entering Cliff Bell's is like walking into a Fred Astaire film. With a

cocktail menu divided into two categories — Slippers (Dirty Detroit Martini, Gypsy Kiss) and Swizzlers (The Cliff Bell, Cumberland Cup) — food could easily be forgotten, but should not be. The menu ranges from filet mignon to shrimp and grits.

SUNDAY

10 *Art after Porridge* 10 a.m.

Atlas Global Bistro (3111 Woodward Avenue; 313-831-2241; atlasglobalbistro.com; $$) is located in the old Addison Hotel in the Brush Park district of Detroit and serves memorable brunch food — a duck and goat cheese omelet, for example, or wild rice porridge. When you're ready to move on, travel just up the street to the **Museum of Contemporary Art Detroit** (4454 Woodward Ave.; 313-832-6622; mocadetroit.org), housed in a former auto dealership. Exhibits explore emerging ideas in the contemporary art world, and the museum's store serves as a meeting

OPPOSITE ABOVE A survivor from 1911 at the Model T Automotive Heritage Complex, the birthplace of the Model T Ford. The building was Henry Ford's first factory and appears much as it did when it opened in 1904.

OPPOSITE BELOW Good Girls Go to Paris Crepes.

ABOVE The Detroit Opera House.

place for students at the neighboring College for Creative Studies.

11 *Potter's Paradise* 1 p.m.

Truly unique to Detroit is **Pewabic Pottery** (10125 East Jefferson Avenue; 313-626-2000; pewabic.org), a type of tile and vessel ware in unique glazes founded by ceramicist Mary Stratton during the Arts and Crafts movement in 1903. A National Historic Landmark, the building is now a production facility, museum,

and educational center with a store where eager fans, including Martha Stewart, still flock to buy ceramics. Take home a classic Pewabic tile, perhaps an acorn or a dragonfly.

ABOVE The Museum of Contemporary Art Detroit explores emerging art in a former auto dealership.

OPPOSITE The Italian Garden Room at the elegantly restored Book Cadillac Hotel, now a Westin.

THE BASICS

Detroit's airport receives flights from around the world. Walk and use taxis, which are cheap and plentiful.

Westin Book Cadillac Detroit
1114 Washington Boulevard
313-442-1600
bookcadillacwestin.com
$$
Landmark hotel built in 1924 and reopened in 2009 after a $200 million renovation.

Inn on Ferry Street
84 East Ferry Street
313-871-6000
innonferrystreetdetroit.com
$$
Four historic homes and two carriage houses connected as a charming inn.

Detroit Marriott at the Renaissance Center
400 Renaissance Drive
313-568-8000
marriott.com
$$
A 1,298-room skyscraper hotel at General Motors headquarters.

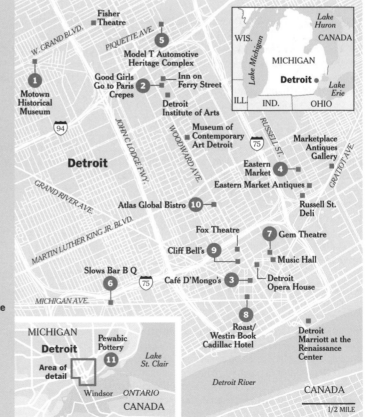

Cleveland

"You Gotta Be Tough" was a popular T-shirt slogan worn by Clevelanders during the 1970s, a grim period marked by industrial decline, large-scale population flight, and an urban environment so toxic that the Cuyahoga River actually caught on fire. These days it still helps to be at least a little tough; a fiercely blue-collar ethos endures in this part of Ohio. But instead of abandoning the city, local entrepreneurs and bohemian dreamers alike are sinking roots; opening a wave of funky boutiques, offbeat art galleries, and sophisticated restaurants; and injecting fresh life into previously rusted-out spaces. Spend the weekend and catch the vibrant spirit. — BRETT SOKOL

FRIDAY

1 *Hello, Cleveland!* 3 p.m.

Staring at platform shoes worn by Keith Moon or at Elvis Presley's white jumpsuit hardly evokes the visceral excitement of rock music, let alone its rich history, but the **Rock and Roll Hall of Fame and Museum** (751 Erieside Avenue; 216-781-7625; rockhall.com) has a wealth of interactive exhibits in addition to its displays of the goofier fashion choices of rock stardom. There's a fascinating look at the genre's initial 1950s heyday, as well as the hysteria that greeted it — preachers and politicians warning of everything from incipient Communist subversion to wanton sexuality.

2 *Iron Chef, Polish Comfort* 7 p.m.

Cleveland's restaurant of popular distinction is **Lolita** (900 Literary Road; 216-771-5652; lolabistro.com; $$$), where the owner, *Iron Chef America* regular Michael Symon, offers creative spins on Mediterranean favorites like duck prosciutto pizza and crispy chicken livers with polenta, wild mushrooms, and pancetta. (Reservations are recommended.) More traditional comfort food is at **Sokolowski's University Inn** (1201 University Road; 216-771-9236; sokolowskis.com; $), a beloved stop for classic Polish dishes since 1923.

OPPOSITE The Cleveland Museum of Art in the culture-saturated University Circle district.

RIGHT At the Velvet Tango Room, the bitters are house-made and the cocktails are precisely mixed.

Even if you're unswayed by Anthony Bourdain's description of the smoked kielbasa as "artery busting" (from him, a compliment) at least swing by for the view from the parking lot — a panorama encompassing Cleveland old and new, from the stadiums dotting the downtown skyline to the smoking factories and oddly beautiful slag heaps on the riverside below.

3 *Classic Cocktails* 10 p.m.

Discerning drinkers head for the **Velvet Tango Room** (2095 Columbus Road; 216-241-8869; velvettangoroom.com), inside a one-time Prohibition-era speakeasy and seemingly little changed: the bitters are house-made, and the bartenders pride themselves on effortlessly mixing a perfect Bourbon Daisy or Rangpur Gimlet. Yes, as their menu explains, you can order a chocolate-tini — "But we die a little bit every time."

SATURDAY

4 *Farm-Fresh* 10 a.m.

Start your day at the **West Side Market** (1979 West 25th Street; 216-664-3387; westsidemarket.com), where many of the city's chefs go to stock their own kitchens. Browse over stalls where 100 vendors sell meat, cheese, fruit, vegetables, and baked goods, or just pull up a chair at **Crêpes De Luxe**'s counter (crepesdeluxe.com; $) for a savory Montréal (filled with smoked brisket and Emmental cheese) or the Elvis homage Le Roi (bananas, peanut butter, and chocolate).

5 *From Steel to Stylish* Noon

The steelworkers who once filled the Tremont neighborhood's low-slung houses and ornately topped churches have largely vanished. A new breed of resident has moved in along with a wealth of upscale restaurants, galleries, and artisanal shops. Inside **Lilly Handmade Chocolates** (761 Starkweather Avenue; 216-771-3333; lillytremont.com), you can join the throngs practically drooling over the mounds of freshly made truffles. Or grab a glass at the wine bar inside **Visible Voice Books** (1023 Kenilworth Avenue; 216-961-0084; visiblevoicebooks.com), which features scores of small-press titles, many by local authors.

6 *Some Still Like Canvas* 3 p.m.

For more than 20 years the **William Busta Gallery** (2731 Prospect Avenue; 216-298-9071; williambustagallery.com) has remained a conceptual-art-free zone—video installations included. "With video, it takes 15 minutes to see how bad somebody really is," said Mr. Busta, the gallery's owner. "With painting, you can spot talent right away." And that's predominantly what he exhibits, with a focus on exciting homegrown figures like Don Harvey and Matthew Kolodziej. In the nearby Warehouse District, **Shaheen Modern & Contemporary Art** (740 West Superior Avenue, Suite 101; 216-830-8888; shaheengallery.com) casts a wider geographic net with solo exhibits from New York-based artists.

7 *Paris on Lake Erie* 6 p.m.

A much talked-about spot is **L'Albatros** (11401 Bellflower Road; 216-791-7880; albatrosbrasserie.com; $$), run by the chef Zachary Bruell. Set inside a 19th-century carriage house on the campus of Case Western Reserve University, this inviting brasserie serves impeccably executed French specialties like chicken liver and foie gras mousseline, a niçoise salad, and cassoulet.

8 *Ballroom Blitz* 8 p.m.

The polka bands are long gone from the **Beachland Ballroom** (15711 Waterloo Road; 216-383-1124; beachlandballroom.com), replaced by an eclectic mix of rock groups. But by running a place that's as much a clubhouse as a concert venue, the co-owners Cindy Barber and Mark Leddy have retained plenty of this former Croatian social hall's old-school character. Beachland books national bands and favorite local acts. Mr. Leddy, formerly an antiques dealer, still hunts down finds for the This Way Out Vintage Shoppe in the basement.

ABOVE The Rock and Roll Hall of Fame, repository of John Lennon's "Sgt. Pepper" suit and Michael Jackson's glove.

BELOW Home cooks and chefs both stock their kitchens at the West Side Market, a good stop for Saturday morning.

SUNDAY

9 *Beets, Then Beats* 10 a.m.

One of the few restaurants in town where requesting the vegan option won't elicit a raised eyebrow, **Tommy's** (1824 Coventry Road; 216-321-7757; tommyscoventry.com; $) has been serving tofu since 1972, when the surrounding Coventry Village, in Cleveland Heights, was a hippie oasis. The bloom is off that countercultural rose, but the delicious falafel and thick milkshakes endure. The time warp continues through a doorway leading into **Mac's Backs** bookstore (No. 1820; 216-321-2665; macsbacks.com), a good place to find out-of-print poetry from Cleveland post-Beat writers like d.a. levy, T. L. Kryss, and rjs.

10 *Free Impressionists* Noon

For decades, the University Circle district has housed many of the city's cultural jewels, including Severance Hall, the majestic Georgian residence of the Cleveland Orchestra; the Cleveland Institute of Art Cinematheque, one of the country's best repertory movie theaters; and the lush 285-acre Lake View Cemetery. At the **Cleveland Museum of Art** (11150 East Boulevard; 216-421-7340; clemusart.com), already famed for its collection of Old Masters and kid-friendly armor, the opening of the Rafael Viñoly-designed East Wing has put the spotlight on more modern fare, from one of Monet's Water Lilies paintings to current work. A further enticement: admission to the museum's permanent collection is absolutely free.

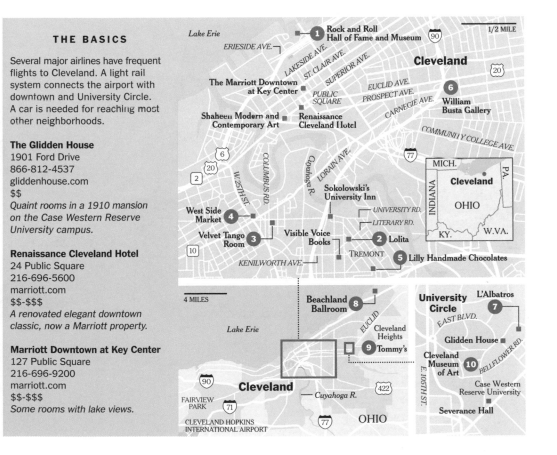

THE BASICS

Several major airlines have frequent flights to Cleveland. A light rail system connects the airport with downtown and University Circle. A car is needed for reaching most other neighborhoods.

The Glidden House
1901 Ford Drive
866-812-4537
gliddenhouse.com
$$
Quaint rooms in a 1910 mansion on the Case Western Reserve University campus.

Renaissance Cleveland Hotel
24 Public Square
216-696-5600
marriott.com
$$-$$$
A renovated elegant downtown classic, now a Marriott property.

Marriott Downtown at Key Center
127 Public Square
216-696-9200
marriott.com
$$-$$$
Some rooms with lake views.

Cincinnati

With the quiet momentum of a work in progress, Cincinnati, Ohio, is finding an artsy swagger, infused with a casual combination of Midwest and Southern charm. The city center, for decades rich with cultural and performing arts venues, now offers a renovated Fountain Square area and a gleaming new baseball stadium with views of the Ohio River. Transformations are taking place in surrounding areas and across the river in the neighboring Kentucky cities of Newport and Covington — with cool music venues, funky shopping outlets, and smart culinary options. While it looks to the future, the city also honors its historic role in the antislavery movement with its National Underground Railroad Freedom Center. — BY KASSIE BRACKEN

FRIDAY

1 *Tranquility and Eternity* 4 p.m.

A graveyard may not be the most obvious place to start a trip, but **Spring Grove Cemetery and Arboretum** (4521 Spring Grove Avenue; 513-681-7526; springgrove.org/sg/arboretum/arboretum.shtm) is not your average resting place. The arboretum, designed in 1845 as a place for botanical experiments, features 1,200 types of plants artfully arranged around mausoleums and tranquil ponds. Roman- and Greek-inspired monuments bear the names of many of Cincinnati's most prominent families, including the Procters and the Gambles, whose business, begun in the 1830s, still dominates Cincinnati. Admission and parking are free, and the office provides printed guides and information about the plant collection.

2 *Where Hipsters Roam* 6 p.m.

The Northside district has blossomed into a casually hip destination for shopping and night life, particularly along Hamilton Avenue. Vinyl gets ample real estate at **Shake It Records** (4156 Hamilton Avenue; 513-591-0123; shakeitrecords.com), a music store specializing in independent labels; if you can't find a title among the 40,000 they carry, the owners will track it down for you. For a bite, locals swear by **Melt**

Eclectic Deli (4165 Hamilton Avenue; 513-681-6358; meltcincy.com; $), a quirky restaurant friendly to vegans and carnivores alike. Order the Joan of Arc sandwich, with blue cheese and caramelized onions atop roast beef, or the hummus-laden Helen of Troy, and retreat to the patio.

3 *Local Bands, Local Beer* 9 p.m.

Saunter next door to find 20-somethings in skinny jeans mingling with 30-somethings in flip-flops at **Northside Tavern** (4163 Hamilton Avenue; 513-542-3603; northside-tavern.com), a prime spot for live music. Sip a pint of Cincinnati's own Christian Moerlein beer and listen to jazz, blues, and acoustic rock acts in the intimate front bar. Or head to the back room, where the best local bands take the larger stage. Wind down with a crowd heavy with artists and musicians at the **Comet** (4579 Hamilton Avenue; 513-541-8900; cometbar.com), a noirish dive bar with an impossibly cool selection on its jukebox and top-notch burritos to satisfy any late-night cravings.

SATURDAY

4 *The Aerobic Arabesque* 9:30 a.m.

The fiberglass pigs in tutus that greet you outside the **Cincinnati Ballet** (1555 Central Parkway; 513-621-5219) might indicate otherwise, but don't be fooled: the Ballet's Open Adult Division program (cballet.org/academy/adult) is a great place to get lean. Start your Saturday with a beginning ballet class (90 minutes, under $20), as a company member steers novices through basic movements. More experienced dancers might try the one-hour Rhythm

OPPOSITE The John A. Roebling Suspension Bridge over the Ohio River connects Cincinnati to its Kentucky suburbs.

RIGHT The revitalized Over-the-Rhine neighborhood.

and Motion class, which combines hip-hop, modern, and African dance. Regulars know the moves, so pick a spot in the back and prepare to sweat.

5 *A Bridge to Brunch* 11:30 a.m.

If John Roebling's Suspension Bridge looks familiar, you might be thinking of his more famous design in New York. (Cincinnati's version opened in 1867, almost two decades before the Brooklyn Bridge.) It's a pedestrian-friendly span over the Ohio River, providing terrific views of the skyline. Cross into Covington, Kentucky, and walk a few blocks to the **Keystone Bar & Grill** (313 Greenup Street; 859-261-6777; keystonebar.com; $-$$), where alcohol-fueled partying gives way to brunch on weekend mornings and the menu runs heavily to gravy. You'll be well fueled for the walk back.

6 *Tracing a Legacy* 2 p.m.

The **National Underground Railroad Freedom Center** (50 East Freedom Way; 513-333-7500; freedomcenter.org) is a dynamic testament to Cincinnati's place in the antislavery movement. Multimedia presentations, art displays, and interactive timelines trace the history of the global slave trade as well as 21st-century human trafficking. Leave time for the genealogy center, where volunteers assist individuals with detailed family searches.

7 *Sin City, Updated* 5 p.m.

For decades, Cincinnatians scoffed at their Kentucky neighbors, but that has been changing in the last few years, especially with the revitalization of Newport, a waterfront and historic housing district. Stroll to **York St. Café** (738 York Street, entrance

ABOVE Spring Grove Cemetery and Arboretum.

RIGHT Northside, an area for shopping and night life.

OPPOSITE The National Underground Railroad Freedom Center. Cincinnati was a stop for many who escaped slavery.

on Eighth Street; 859-261-9675; yorkstonline.com; $$), an 1880s-era apothecary transformed into a three-story restaurant, music, and art space, where wood shelves are stocked with kitschy memorabilia. Browse a bit before scanning the menu for bistro fare like a Mediterranean board (an array of shareable appetizers) or a delicate fresh halibut with spinach and artichoke. Leave room for the excellent homemade desserts, including the strawberry buttermilk cake.

8 *Stage to Stage* 7 p.m.

Cincinnati Playhouse in the Park (962 Mount Adams Circle; 513-421-3888; cincyplay.com), which has been producing plays for five decades, offers splendid vistas of Mount Adams and a solid theatergoing experience. A lesser-known but equally engaging option can be found at the **University of Cincinnati College-Conservatory of Music** (Corry Boulevard; 513-556-4183; ccm.uc.edu/theatre). Students dreaming of Lincoln Center perform in full-scale productions of serious drama and opera. Check the online calendar for showtimes and locations.

9 *Ballroom Bliss* 10 p.m.

Head back to Newport's Third Street and its bars and clubs. A standout, **Southgate House**, is set in an 1814 Victorian mansion that resembles a haunted fraternity (24 East Third Street, Newport; 859-431-2201; southgatehouse.com). It hosts local and national acts dabbling in everything from bluegrass to death metal. On a typical Saturday night, music fans of all ages and sensibilities roam the three venues: an intimate parlor room, a laid-back lounge, and a ballroom with a capacity of 600.

10 *Neighborhood Reborn* 10 a.m.

As the epicenter of 19th-century German immigrant society, the neighborhood known as Over-the-Rhine once teemed with breweries, theaters, and social halls. Though it fell into disrepair and parts remain rough around the edges, an $80 million revitalization effort has slowly brought back visitors. Walk down Main Street between 12th and 15th Streets to find local artists' galleries and the **Iris BookCafe** (1331 Main Street; 513-381-2665), a serene rare-book shop with an outdoor sculpture garden. A few blocks away, Vine Street between Central Parkway and 13th Street offers new boutiques including the craft shop **MiCA 12/v** (1201 Vine Street; 513-421-3500; shopmica.com), which specializes in

contemporary designers like Jonathan Adler and Kenneth Wingard.

11 *Designs to Take Home* 1 p.m.

Before heading home, find inspiring décor at **HighStreet** (1401 Reading Road; 513-723-1901; highstreetcincinnati.com), a spacious and sleek design store. The owners have carefully composed a cosmopolitan mix of textiles, clothing, and jewelry by New York and London designers as well as local artists, showcased in a creatively appointed space. A free cup of red flower tea makes it all the more inviting.

THE BASICS

Fly into Cincinnati/Northern Kentucky International Airport, a 25-minute drive from downtown. A rental car is recommended.

Hilton Cincinnati Netherland Plaza
35 West Fifth Street
513-421-9100
hilton.com
$$
561 renovated rooms in a landmark building, the Art Deco Carew Tower.

The Westin Cincinnati
21 East Fifth Street
513-621-7700
starwoodhotels.com
$$
Downtown with views of Fountain Square from many rooms.

Cincinnatian Hotel
601 Vine Street
513-381-3000
cincinnatianhotel.com
$$
Updated rooms in a classic hotel dating to 1882.

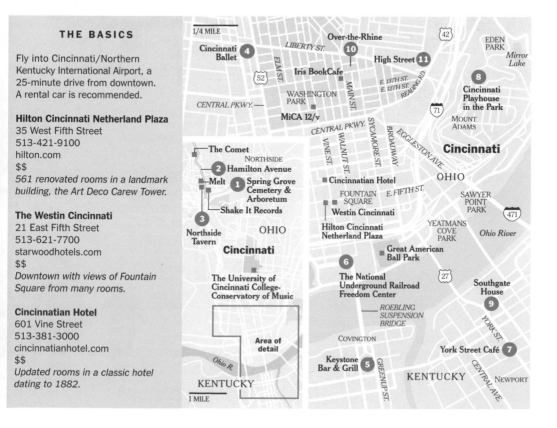

Indianapolis

For years, Indianapolis, Indiana, bore the stigma of nicknames like Nap Town and Indiana No Place. But then construction and development downtown seemed to wake the city up, and today, a thriving cultural scene and the multiethnic influences of immigrant populations mix with Hoosier hospitality and charm. And there are still the old Indianapolis standbys, like the hearty Midwestern food; the many classical monuments and fountains, laid out using elements of Pierre L'Enfant's plan for Washington and built partly by Freemasons; and of course, the Indianapolis Motor Speedway, home of the Indy 500. — BY JOHN HOLL

FRIDAY

1 *A Cocktail with That Scotch* 6:30 p.m.

Start with a drink downtown at one of the city's oldest restaurants, **St. Elmo Steak House** (127 South Illinois Street; 317-635-0636; stelmos.com; $$$), where for more than a century patrons have sidled up to the tiger oak bar—first used in the 1893 Chicago World's Fair—for martinis and single malts. Settle in under the gaze of the Indiana celebrities whose photos adorn the walls (David Letterman, Larry Bird) and try St. Elmo's not-for-the-faint-of-heart signature dish: the shrimp cocktail. The jumbo shrimp are served smothered in horseradish cocktail sauce made every hour to ensure freshness and a proper sinus assault. If you can see through the tears in your eyes, you'll probably notice one of the tuxedoed bartenders having a quiet chuckle at your expense.

2 *New Indiana* 7 p.m.

While downtown has been rejuvenating itself with new development, areas out toward the suburbs have been transformed by immigration, with Pakistanis, Salvadorans, Burmese, and an assortment of other groups mingling comfortably. To see a bit of what this melting pot has brought to Indianapolis dining, drive a few miles to **Abyssinia** (5352 West 38th Street, in the Honey Creek Plaza; 317-299-0608; $), an Ethiopian restaurant decorated with Haile Selassie portraits

and Ethiopia tourism posters. The authentic, well-cooked cuisine incorporates lots of lentils as well as goat in berbere sauce, house-made injera bread, and sambusas, the Ethiopian version of samosas. The place draws Africans, Indians, vegans, and plenty of longtime Indianans who like a culinary adventure.

3 *Blues and Bands* 10:30 p.m.

Indianapolis has had a blues scene for generations, and it's still alive and kickin' at the **Slippery Noodle Inn** (372 South Meridian Street; 317-631-6974; slipperynoodle.com). Housed in a two-story building constructed as a bar and roadhouse around 1850, the Noodle attracts a lively crowd (including, back in the day, the Dillinger Gang) and nationally known blues musicians like Country Joe McDonald and Ronnie Earl. But it's the local bands that make the place rock, so hoist a pint of the Indiana-brewed Upland IPA and groove on the dance floor to the thumping bass.

SATURDAY

4 *Monumental Efforts* 10 a.m.

Start a walking tour in the heart of downtown at the neoclassical **Soldiers and Sailors Monument** (1 Monument Circle; 317-232-7615), a 284-foot tall obelisk dating back to 1902. Look over the Civil War museum in the base and then take the elevator or brave the 330 stairs to the top. Back on the ground, it's a short walk down West Market Street to the **Indiana Statehouse**, a suitably domed and columned structure built in 1888.

OPPOSITE The Canal Walk in downtown Indianapolis.

RIGHT Take the dare and order the super-spicy horseradish shrimp cocktail at the century-old St. Elmo Steak House.

A few blocks north is the **Freemasons' Scottish Rite Cathedral** (650 North Meridian Street; 800-489-3579; aasr-indy.org), actually a meeting hall, not a church. It's a tour de force of ornate decoration with a 212-foot tower, 54 bells, a 2,500-pound gilded bronze chandelier, cavernous oak-paneled halls, and stained-glass windows. If it's open (Monday through Friday and the third Saturday of each month), take an hourlong guided tour.

5 *Duckpins* Noon

Order a salad to keep it light at the **Smokehouse on Shelby** (317-685-1959; $) in the 1928 **Fountain Square Theatre Building** (1105 Prospect Street; fountainsquareindy.com), so that you can follow up with a chocolate malt or a strawberry soda from the restored 1950s soda fountain, rescued from a defunct Woolworth's. Then rent a lane and some shoes at one of the two duckpin bowling alleys in the building. The one upstairs still uses the original 1930s equipment. Downstairs has 50s-vintage bowling.

6 *White River Junction* 3 p.m.

Stroll along the canal and through the green spaces of **White River State Park** (801 West Washington Street; 317-233-2434; inwhiteriver.wrsp.in.gov) on the city's west side. You can take your pick of several museums and the Indianapolis Zoo, but a more unusual destination here is the headquarters

of the National Collegiate Athletic Association. The **N.C.A.A. Hall of Champions** (317-916-4255; ncaahallofchampions.org) has displays on 23 men's and women's sports, a theater showing memorable college sports moments, and interactive simulators that take you on a virtual trip into a game.

7 *Hoosier Heartland* 6 p.m.

For a real taste of Hoosier country (Indianans wear the Hoosier nickname proudly), grab some hors d'oeuvres and a bottle of wine and drive about 40 minutes northeast of the city, past farmland and cornfields, till you come to **Bonge's Tavern** (9830 West 280 North, Perkinsville; 765-734-1625; bongestavern.com; $$), a country roadhouse that opened in 1934. The restaurant does not take reservations for fewer than 10 people, so arrive early and be ready to wait 90 minutes or more. Part of the Bonge's experience is chatting with other patrons while sitting on rocking chairs on the enclosed porch, maybe sharing some of the wine and snacks you so thoughtfully brought. Once inside, order the Perkinsville Pork, a juicy, pounded-flat, parmesan-crusted loin that is worth waiting for.

8 *Basketball Bar* 10 p.m.

High school basketball is practically a religion in Indiana, and there is no more famous team than the 1954 squad from small Milan High School. They won the statewide championship on a final shot by

Bobby Plump, who quickly became a folk hero. The story formed the basis for the 1986 film *Hoosiers*. Today, Plump and his family operate a bar, **Plump's Last Shot** (6416 Cornell Avenue; 317-257-5867; plumpslastshot.com), a hoops-memorabilia-filled hangout in the Broad Ripple neighborhood and the perfect place to catch a game on TV.

SUNDAY

9 *Start Your Engines* Noon

Naturally you want to get a look at the **Indianapolis Motor Speedway** (4790 West 16th Street; 317-492-6784; indianapolismotorspeedway.com), home of the Indianapolis 500. The **Hall of Fame Museum** within the

racetrack grounds displays vintage race cars, trophies, and more than two dozen cars that won the race, including the very first winner (in 1911), a Marmon Wasp. The narrated bus ride around the fabled oval may be the closest you ever come to racing in the old Brickyard, but unfortunately the driver never gets above 30 miles an hour. You will get up-close views of the famed racing pagoda, Gasoline Alley, and the last remaining strip of the track's original brick surface, 36 inches wide, which now serves as the start/finish line.

OPPOSITE The first winner of the Indianapolis 500, on display at the Indianapolis Motor Speedway.

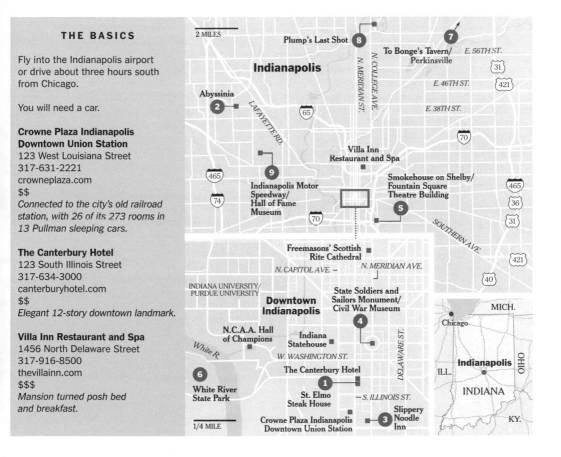

THE BASICS

Fly into the Indianapolis airport or drive about three hours south from Chicago.

You will need a car.

Crowne Plaza Indianapolis Downtown Union Station
123 West Louisiana Street
317-631-2221
crowneplaza.com
$$
Connected to the city's old railroad station, with 26 of its 273 rooms in 13 Pullman sleeping cars.

The Canterbury Hotel
123 South Illinois Street
317-634-3000
canterburyhotel.com
$$
Elegant 12-story downtown landmark.

Villa Inn Restaurant and Spa
1456 North Delaware Street
317-916-8500
thevillainn.com
$$$
Mansion turned posh bed and breakfast.

2 MILES

Plump's Last Shot **8**

7

Indianapolis

To Bonge's Tavern/ E. 56TH ST.
Perkinsville
31

N. MERIDIAN ST.
N. COLLEGE AVE.

E. 46TH ST.
421

Abyssinia
2

LAFAYETTE RD.

65

E. 38TH ST.

70

465

Villa Inn Restaurant and Spa

9

74

Indianapolis Motor Speedway/ Hall of Fame Museum

70

Smokehouse on Shelby/ Fountain Square Theatre Building

5

465

36

SOUTHERN AVE.

31

Freemasons' Scottish Rite Cathedral

N. CAPITOL AVE. –

N. MERIDIAN AVE.

421

40

INDIANA UNIVERSITY/ PURDUE UNIVERSITY

Downtown Indianapolis

State Soldiers and Sailors Monument/ Civil War Museum

4

MICH.

Chicago

N.C.A.A. Hall of Champions

White R.

Indiana Statehouse

W. WASHINGTON ST.

DELAWARE ST.

ILL.

Indianapolis

OHIO

6

White River State Park

The Canterbury Hotel

1

St. Elmo Steak House

– S. ILLINOIS ST.

INDIANA

Slippery Noodle Inn

3

KY.

1/4 MILE

Crowne Plaza Indianapolis Downtown Union Station

Iowa's Mississippi River

"For 60 years the foreign tourist has steamed up and down the river between St. Louis and New Orleans ... believing he had seen all of the river that was worth seeing or that had anything to see," Mark Twain lamented in Life on the Mississippi. *The visitors were missing an "amazing region" to the north, he wrote. They were missing "extraordinary sunsets" and "enchanting scenery." They were missing Iowa. Today, tourists do find Iowa's Mississippi riverfront, thanks partly to modern confections like riverboat casinos and a water park resort, but much of this shore still feels undiscovered. Set out for a weekend car trip on quiet back roads, and you'll find the real life of the Mississippi amid green hilltops and fields, in small villages and busy cities, and on the wide river itself.*
— BY BETSY RUBINER

FRIDAY

1 *Skimming the River* 4 p.m.

Start your Mississippi River explorations in Davenport, about 1,775 miles upstream from the Gulf of Mexico. With no flood wall (though there are perennial arguments about whether to build one), downtown Davenport has a feeling of intimacy with the river, and you can get even closer on the **Channel Cat Water Taxi** (foot of Mound Street at the river; 309-788-3360; qcchannelcat.com) a small ferry with several stops. From its benches you may see blocks-long grain barges, speedboats, 19th-century riverbank mansions, or egrets on small wooded islands.

2 *Field of Dreams* 7 p.m.

One of the best points to enjoy Davenport's unusual eye-level river view is **Modern Woodmen Park** (209 South Gaines Street; 563-322-6348; riverbandits.com), the riverfront minor-league baseball field. If the River Bandits are playing at home, have some hot dogs or cheese steak as you take in a game. (There's also a tiki bar.) The park has a small cornfield where, when the stalks are

OPPOSITE Mississippi River farm country along Highway 52 in Iowa.

RIGHT Try on a riverboat gambler's vest at the River Junction Trade Company, which makes old West gear.

high enough, the Bandits emerge at game time like the ghostly players in *Field of Dreams*, which was filmed in Iowa. If it's not a game night, seek a more substantial dinner at **Front Street Brewery** (208 East River Drive; 563-322-1569; frontstreetbrew.com; $). Look on the menu for walleye, a favorite Midwestern native fish.

SATURDAY

3 *A River Still Traveled* 10 a.m.

Drive down to the levee at **Le Claire** to see a nicely preserved example of the craft used for traveling the river in Twain's day — the *Lone Star*, an 1860s sternwheel steamboat in dry dock at the **Buffalo Bill Museum** (199 North Front Street; 563-289-5580; buffalobillmuseumleclaire.com). Nearby, S.U.V.'s towing today's pleasure boats pull up to a launching ramp, disgorging day trippers toting kids, coolers, and life jackets. After the families have sped off, you may see them again, picnicking on an island. A block from the river, along Cody Road — named, as is the museum, for Le Claire's favorite son, William Cody — inviting shops and restaurants rejuvenate old brick storefronts.

4 *From the Heights* Noon

You're passing some of the world's most expensive farmland — fertile valley acreage conveniently close to river transportation on the grain barges — as you head north on Routes 67 and 52 to Bellevue. The town lives up to its name with sweeping views from the high bluffs at **Bellevue State Park** (24668 Highway 52; 563-872-4019; iowadnr.gov). A display in the park's

nature center recalls an early industry in these river towns: making buttons from mussel shells. In the pretty riverside downtown, check out the pizza at **2nd Street Station** (116 South 2nd Street; 563-872-5410) and stop for a look at **Lock and Dam No. 12** (Route 52 at Franklin Street). Locks are a common feature on the Upper Mississippi, where tugs push as many as 15 barges at a time, carrying as much freight as 870 tractor trailers or a 225-car train.

5 *Luxembourgers* 2:30 p.m.

Stop for a quick glance around tiny **St. Donatus**, where one of America's rarer ethnic groups, immigrants from Luxembourg, arrived in the 1800s and built limestone and stucco buildings. For some classic Iowa landscape (not waterscape), walk up the Way of the Cross path behind the Catholic church and look across the valley at patches of hay and corn quilting the hills. You may smell hogs. Or is it cattle?

6 *Gawk at the Gar* 3 p.m.

Spend some time in **Dubuque**, Davenport's rival Iowa river city. At the **National Mississippi River Museum and Aquarium** (350 East Third Street; 563-557-9545; rivermuseum.com), a Smithsonian affiliate, huge blue catfish, gar, and paddlefish swim in a 30,000-gallon tank, a boardwalk goes through reclaimed wetlands inhabited by herons and bald eagles, and a model shows havoc caused by a 1965

flood. Downtown, Dubuque feels like an old factory town, with Victorian mansions (several converted into inns), brick row houses flush to the street, and many a corner tap and church. Ride the **Fenelon Place Elevator** (512 Fenelon Place), a funicular that makes a steep climb to a bluff top where Wisconsin and Illinois are visible across the river.

7 *American Pie* 6 p.m.

Follow Highway 52 and the County Route C9Y, the Balltown Road, through a peaceful valley up and up onto a ridge with panoramic views worthy of a painting by Grant Wood (an Iowan): wide open sky, a lone pheasant in a field, alternating rows of crops, grazing cows, and tidy farms with stone houses, weathered red barns, and blue silos. Your goal is **Balltown**, which has 73 residents and one famous restaurant, **Breitbach's** (563 Balltown Road, Route C9Y; 563-552-2220; breitbachscountrydining.com; $-$$). It has been open since 1852 and is justly famed for its fried chicken, barbecued ribs, and fresh pie.

ABOVE Riverside baseball in Davenport.

OPPOSITE ABOVE The Fenelon Place Elevator in Dubuque climbs a steep bluff to a panoramic river view.

OPPOSITE BELOW Lock and Dam No. 12 spanning the river at Bellevue.

SUNDAY

8 *A "T" Too Far* 10 a.m.

Forty miles north of Dubuque, Highway 52 brings you to the river at **Guttenberg**, a lovely town settled by German immigrants in the 1840s and named after the inventor of moveable type, Johannes Gutenberg. (Word has it that an early typographical error accounts for the extra T.) Admire the downtown's well-preserved pre-Civil War-era limestone buildings and stroll at mile-long **Ingleside Park**. A few miles farther on, stop at **McGregor**, where boaters hang out by the marina and locals eat bratwurst and drink beer on riverview restaurant decks. Try on a riverboat gambler's vest or a feathered Victorian hat at the **River Junction Trade Company** (312 Main Street, McGregor; 866-259-9172; riverjunction.com), which makes reproductions of Old West gear, sometimes selling to Hollywood production companies.

9 *Pike's Other Peak* 11 a.m.

Even if you're getting weary of river panoramas, stop at **Pikes Peak State Park** (32264 Pikes Peak Road, McGregor; 563-873-2341; iowadnr.gov) to see one from the highest bluff on the Mississippi. Like Pikes Peak in Colorado, this spot is named for the explorer Zebulon Pike. Scouting for federal fort locations in 1805, Pike thought this peak was an ideal spot, and although the fort ended up across the river in Wisconsin, you can understand his reasoning. Look out at a swirl of green forested islands and mud-brown river pools. To the north, suspension bridges connect to Wisconsin. To the south, the Wisconsin River empties out at the place where in 1673 the

explorers Jacques Marquette and Louis Joliet first saw the Mississippi.

10 *Mound Builders* 1 p.m.

At **Effigy Mounds National Monument** (151 Highway 76, Harpers Ferry; 563-873-3491; nps.gov/efmo), 2,526 acres of grounds are dotted with mysterious prehistoric burial and ceremonial mounds, some as old as 2,500 years. The Indians of the Upper Midwest built large numbers of mounds shaped

like animals, most often bears and birds that lived along the Mississippi. Why they were built and who was meant to see them — since the best views are from the sky — remains unknown. Take the two-mile Fire Point Trail up a 360-foot bluff, through forests and past mounds. At the top, a clearing reveals a Mississippi that seems wild — with forested banks and islands, a soupy marsh, and hawks soaring above a bluff — until out of nowhere a speedboat zips by, breaking the silence.

ABOVE A houseboat anchored near McGregor.

OPPOSITE Success in the form of a smallmouth bass, pulled from the Mississippi at McGregor.

THE BASICS

The Mississippi River is a three-hour drive west from Chicago. The Quad City International Airport serves Davenport.

Hotel Blackhawk
200 East 3rd Street, Davenport
563-322-5000
hotelblackhawk.com
$$
Stylishly decorated landmark hotel, reopened in 2010 after extensive renovation.

Hotel Julien Dubuque
563-556-4200
200 Main Street, Dubuque
hoteljuliendubuque.com
$$
Modern boutique decorating, pool, and spa in a hotel with history dating back to Lincoln's day.

The Landing
703 South River Park Drive, Guttenberg
563-252-1615
thelanding615.com
$
Rooms and suites in a renovated stone riverfront warehouse.

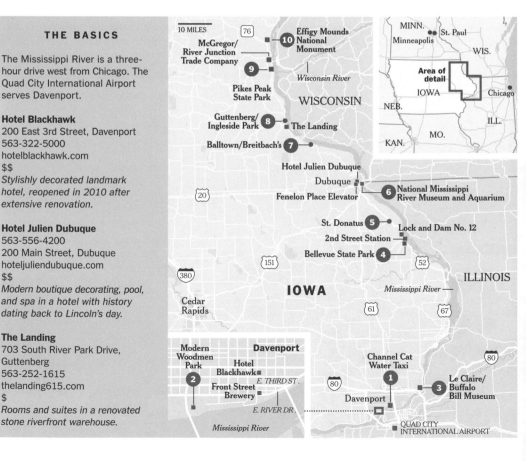

St. Louis

St. Louis, Missouri, is more than just a Gateway to the West. It's a lively destination in its own right, full of inviting neighborhoods, some coming out of a long decline and revitalized by public art, varied night life, and restaurants that draw on the bounty of surrounding farmland and rivers. The famous arch, of course, is still there, along with plenty of 19th-century architecture and an eye-opening amount of green space. Add to that a mix of Midwestern sensibility and Southern charm, and you've got plenty of reason to stay a while. — BY DAN SALTZSTEIN

FRIDAY

1 *Out in the Open* 4 p.m.

The new jewel of downtown St. Louis is **Citygarden** (citygardenstl.org), a sculpture park the city opened in 2009, framed by the old courthouse on one side and the Gateway Arch on the other. The oversize public art, by boldface-name artists like Mark di Suvero and Keith Haring, is terrific, but the real genius of the garden's layout is that it reflects the landscape of the St. Louis area: an arcing wall of local limestone, for instance, echoes the bends of the Mississippi and Missouri Rivers, which join just north of town.

2 *Up in the Sky* 6 p.m.

If you've never been to the top of the 630-foot **Gateway Arch** (gatewayarch.com), the four-minute ride up in a uniquely designed tram system is a must. And even if you have, it's worth reminding yourself that yes, that water down there is the Mississippi River, and that city spreading out beyond it is where a lot of optimistic Easterners slogged their first miles into the west. Eero Saarinen designed the arch, made of stainless steel, and it was completed in 1965. Besides providing a helicopter-height view, it's an elegantly simple artwork that endures.

3 *Soulard Soul* 8 p.m.

Historic Soulard (pronounced SOO-lard) is one of those neighborhoods experiencing a renaissance, thanks in part to several new quality restaurants. **Franco** (1535 South Eighth Street; 314-436-2500; eatatfranco.com; $$), an industrial-chic bistro that opened in 2007 next to the locally famous Soulard

farmers' market, serves soulful takes on French bistro fare, like country-fried frogs' legs in a red wine gravy and grilled Missouri rainbow trout in a crayfish and Cognac cream sauce.

4 *Analog Underground* 10 p.m.

Frederick's Music Lounge, a beloved St. Louis dive bar, is gone, but its legendary owner, Fred Boettcher Jr., a k a Fred Friction, has a new club beneath the restaurant Iron Barley. Follow signs for **FSFU — Fred's Six Feet Under** (5510 Virginia Avenue; 314-351-4500; ironbarley.com). Music venues don't get much more intimate; the band might take up a third of the total space. Drinks are cheap, and the tunes, courtesy of local bands like the Sins of the Pioneers, with their brand of New Orleans R&B, are as unpretentious as the crowd.

SATURDAY

5 *Cupcakes and Blooms* 9 a.m.

In the leafy neighborhood of Shaw, stately architecture mixes with hip spots like **SweetArt** (2203 South 39th Street; 314-771-4278; sweetartstl.com), a mom-and-pop bakery where you can eat a virtuous vegan breakfast topped off by a light-as-air cupcake.

OPPOSITE St. Louis's signature, the Gateway Arch designed by Eero Saarinen. Take the tram to the top, and you'll be riding up 630 feet on an elegant work of art.

BELOW The Missouri Botanical Garden.

Shaw is named for Henry Shaw, a botanist and philanthropist whose crowning achievement is the **Missouri Botanical Garden** (4344 Shaw Boulevard; 314-577-5100; mobot.org). Founded in 1859, it is billed as the oldest continuously operating botanical garden in the nation. It covers an impressive 79 acres and includes a large Japanese garden and Henry Shaw's 1850 estate home, as well as his (slightly creepy) mausoleum.

6 *Taste of Memphis* 1 p.m.

St. Louis-style ribs are found on menus across the country, but it's a Memphis-style joint (think slow-smoked meats, easy on the sauce) that seems to be the consensus favorite for barbecue in town. Just survey the best-of awards that decorate the walls at **Pappy's Smokehouse** (3106 Olive Street; 314-535-4340; pappyssmokehouse.com; $-$$). Crowds line up for heaping plates of meat and sides, served in an unassuming space (while you wait, take a peek at the smoker parked out back on a side street). The ribs and pulled pork are pretty good, but the winners might be the sides — bright and tangy slaw and deep-fried corn on the cob.

7 *Green Day* 3 p.m.

St. Louis boasts 105 city-run parks, but none rivals **Forest Park** (stlouis.missouri.org/citygov/parks/forestpark), which covers more than 1,200 acres smack in the heart of the city. It opened in 1876, but it was the 1904 World's Fair that made it a world-class public space, spawning comely buildings like the Palace of Fine Art, which now houses the Saint Louis Art Museum. In 2002, a $3.5 million renovation of the Jewel Box, a towering, contemporary-looking greenhouse dating back to 1936, gave it an extra sheen. Rent a bike from the visitor's center (314-367-7275; $35 a day) and just meander.

8 *Midwest Bounty* 8 p.m.

Locavore fever has hit St. Louis. Leading the pack may be **Local Harvest Cafe and Catering** (3137 Morgan Ford Road; 314-772-8815; localharvestcafe.com; $$$), a mellow spot in the Tower Grove neighborhood that's a spinoff of an organic grocery store across the street. A chalkboard menu lists all the local products featured that day, including items like honey and peanut butter. On Saturday nights the chef creates a four-course menu based on what's fresh at the farms and markets that morning. One menu included a light vegetarian cassoulet with beer pairings from local producers like Tin Mill Brewery.

9 *Royale Treatment* 10 p.m.

Tower Grove is also home to a handful of fine watering holes, including the **Royale** (3132 South Kingshighway Blvd.; 314-772-3600; theroyale.com), where an Art Deco-style bar of blond wood and glass is accompanied by old photos of political leaders (John F. Kennedy, Martin Luther King Jr., the late Missouri governor Mel Carnahan). But it's the extensive cocktail list, with drinks named after city neighborhoods (like the Carondelet Sazerac), and a backyard patio that keep the aficionados coming.

SUNDAY

10 *The Home Team* 10 a.m.

Take a number for one of the small, worn wooden tables at **Winslow's Home** (7211 Delmar Boulevard;

BELOW The Saint Louis Art Museum occupies a building from the 1904 World's Fair.

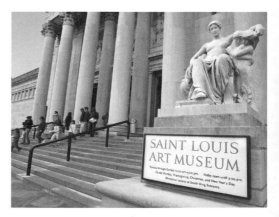

314-725-7559; winslowshome.com; $). It's more than just a pleasant place for brunch; it doubles as a general store that carries groceries, dry goods, and kitchen items like stainless steel olive oil dispensers. When it's time to order, try the brioche French toast with caramelized bananas. It's worth the wait.

11 *Art Class* Noon

Washington University gets high marks for its academics. But the campus, with its rolling green hills and grand halls, is also home to terrific contemporary art. See its collection at the **Mildred Lane Kemper Art Museum** (1 Brookings Drive; 314-935-4523; kemperartmuseum.wustl.edu). Designed by the Pritzker Prize-winning architect Fumihiko Maki, it's charmingly cramped and vaguely organized by theme — so you'll find a Jackson Pollock cheek

by jowl with a 19th-century portrait of Daniel Boone. You'll also find ambitious contemporary art exhibitions curated by Wash U faculty. Like much of St. Louis, the Kemper may not be flashy, but it's full of gems.

OPPOSITE ABOVE Oversize public art finds space at Citygarden, a downtown sculpture park.

ABOVE The extensive cocktail list at the Royale in the Tower Grove area features drinks — the Carondelet Sazerac, for one — that are named after city neighborhoods.

THE BASICS

Lambert International Airport is served by major airlines. For getting around in town, it's best to have a car.

Moonrise Hotel
6177 Delmar Boulevard
314-721-1111
moonrisehotel.com
$$
Pleasant boutique vibe and a central location.

Four Seasons St. Louis
999 North 2nd Street
314-881-5800
fourseasons.com/stlouis
$$$-$$$$
Part of a striking riverside complex that also includes a casino.

St. Louis Union Station Marriott
1820 Market Street
314-621-5262
www.marriott.com
$$
In the grand old downtown railroad station.

Fayetteville

A fast-growing college town in the Ozark foothills, Fayetteville, Arkansas, is flush with youth, character, and natural beauty—especially evident in spring, when the redbuds and dogwoods are in bloom. Hike the lush, forested trails that braid the area. Stroll through the leafy campus and holler "Wooooooooooo, Pig! Sooie!" at the 72,000-seat Reynolds Razorback Stadium at the University of Arkansas (but beware: hotels are probably already booked for the next football season). Soak up the atmosphere that entranced a young Bill Clinton. Then wind your way down lively Dickson Street, a former strip of dive bars that has gotten a good scrubbing. — BY JULIE BESONEN

FRIDAY

1 *George's on My Mind* 5:30 p.m.

Introspection is unthinkable at the boisterous **George's Majestic Lounge** (519 West Dickson Street; 479-442-4226; georgesmajesticlounge.com). Neither majestic nor a lounge, this wood-detailed beer garden with a retractable roof has anchored the Dickson Street music scene for four decades. There's always live music during the Friday happy hour. You might see the revered Cate Brothers, a soulful hometown band known for '70s hits like "Union Man," inspiring everyone to cut loose on the dance floor in broad daylight.

2 *Notes from Underground* 7 p.m.

Right off the late 19th-century town square is **Hugo's** (25 1/2 North Block Avenue; 479-521-7585; hugosfayetteville.com; $), a speakeasy-like basement bistro open since 1977 and overburdened with antique mirrors, vintage portraits, and commemorative presidential plates. Young families and spirited students aren't shy when it comes to tackling the juicy bleu-moon burger, catfish po' boy sandwich, baskets of fries, and homemade pecan pie. And there is a respectable beer selection as well.

3 *Live from the Living Room* 8 p.m.

When you're invited into someone's house for a concert and served coffee and cookies during intermission, it's a cozy, one-of-a-kind evening. Mike Shirkey, host of *The Pickin' Post* on KUAF public radio, frequently presents established folk

and bluegrass musicians, like Al and Emily Cantrell and Stacey Earle, on a stage in the club-size living room of an old wood-frame house very near Hugo's. Called **GoodFolk Productions** (229 North Block Avenue, 479-521-1812; goodfolk.org), it's almost as intimate as someone singing softly in your ear.

SATURDAY

4 *Market on the Square* 10 a.m.

Plenty of towns have farmers' markets, but the one looping around Fayetteville's **Downtown Square** (479-237-2910; fayettevillefarmersmarket.org) is uncommonly engaging. On one corner you might see a harpist and fiddler, on another a banjo player keeping time with a young country clogger whose hip attire and hairdo would not be out of place in Lower Manhattan. The homegrown produce for sale is not typical either: sheriff leeks, mediana spinach, and baby greens with edible flowers. Find the square at Block, Mountain, and Center Streets and East Avenue.

5 *Young Love* 11 a.m.

In 1975, on a salary of $16,450, Bill Clinton, a young University of Arkansas law professor, rashly bought a brick bungalow in Fayetteville for $20,500. Why? Because his elusive girlfriend, Hillary Rodham,

OPPOSITE The Tea Table Rocks in Ozark National Forest, east of Fayetteville.

BELOW The house where Bill and Hillary Clinton married and lived is now a museum with the wedding dress on view.

had made a passing remark on how pretty it was while he was driving her to the airport. When she returned to town, according to his autobiography, *My Life*, he said: "Remember that little house you liked so much? I bought it. You have to marry me now, because I can't live there alone." The ceremony was in the living room, and a reproduction of the bride's Victorian-style lace wedding dress is on display there today. So is early campaign memorabilia. The rest is history, and the house is now the **Clinton House Museum** (930 West Clinton Drive; 877-245-6445; clintonhousemuseum.org).

6 *Pick Up the Red Phone* 12:30 p.m.

Sink your teeth into the smoky, meaty, glazed rack of ribs at **Penguin Ed's B & B Bar-B-Q** (230 South East Avenue; 479-521-3663; penguineds.com; $$), and find rapture. Sides include fare like baked beans, home fries, and macaroni and cheese, but green vegetables are not unknown here. You can also get broccoli or a salad — even a garden burger. Penguin Ed's is in a cedar-lined shack with a tarred roof, and it has stuck with a tradition of having customers call in their orders from red phones at each table.

7 *Objets d'Ozark* 1:30 p.m.

Tired of traveling to regional arts-and-crafts shows to sell their work, several Ozark artists formed a collective and opened **Heartwood Gallery** (428 South Government Avenue; 479-444-0888; heartwoodgallery.org) several years ago. Imaginative jewelry, crazily colorful knit caps, striking watercolors, pottery, and handblown glass are some of the things you may be tempted to take home from the mountains.

ABOVE Hike rugged trails and explore caves at Devil's Den State Park, 25 miles south of Fayetteville.

RIGHT At the farmers' market, find the familiar and the unexpected: tulips and clog dancers, leeks and a harpist.

8 *Library Envy* 2 p.m.

You will need a card if you want to check out a book, but the **Fayetteville Public Library** (401 West Mountain Street; 479-571-2222; faylib.org) is worth checking out for its own sake. Through its sweeping windows you will find unparalleled views of the mountainous landscape. There's also free wireless, a cafe, a serene reading room, a genealogical collection, supercomfy chairs, and a lot of children's programs.

9 *Bivouac on a Mountainside* 4 p.m.

The only Confederate cemetery in Arkansas (500 East Rock Street) didn't open until 1873. The 622 well-ordered and mostly unmarked graves belong to Confederate soldiers who were originally buried where they fell, at nearby battlefields and roadsides or in lonely hollows. Eight years after the war ended, locals were paid $1.40 to $2.50 for each body exhumed and delivered for reburial. It was a tidy sum back then, and though most people probably took the task seriously, historians today are skeptical about some of the remains in the quiet glade on East Mountain.

10 *A Taste of Arkansas* 7 p.m.

Drive about 15 minutes from Fayetteville to Johnson, Arkansas, for sophisticated food in an airy setting at **James at the Mill** (3906 Greathouse Springs Road, Johnson; 479-443-1400; jamesatthemill.com;

$$-$$$$), on the grounds of the Inn at the Mill. The chef, Miles James, blends regional influences with contemporary cuisine, producing hybrid dishes like hickory-grilled pork tenderloin with goat cheese potato galette. The building, designed by the architect James Lambeth, is light-filled, elegant, and filled with interesting touches like the tall, varnished sycamore tree sunk in the bilevel dining room's foundation, its branches reaching to the ceiling.

exploring at **Devil's Den State Park** (Route 170, West Fork; 479-761-3325; mountainstateparks.com/devils-den), 25 miles south of Fayetteville. Or drive out on Routes 412 and 21 to the Ozark National Forest (fs.usda.gov/osfnf), where scenic trails reach forests, lakes, caves, and unusual rock formations.

SUNDAY

11 *Mountaineering* 11 a.m.

Venture deeper into the Ozarks with a drive out of town. Spooky sandstone caves are open for

ABOVE The Heartwood Gallery, a collective where Ozark artists sell their work.

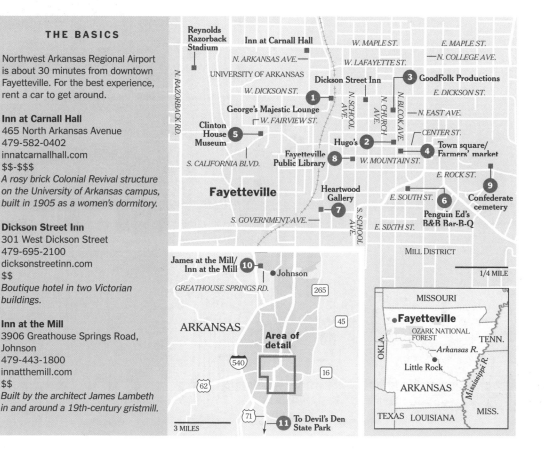

THE BASICS

Northwest Arkansas Regional Airport is about 30 minutes from downtown Fayetteville. For the best experience, rent a car to get around.

Inn at Carnall Hall
465 North Arkansas Avenue
479-582-0402
innatcarnallhall.com
$$-$$$
A rosy brick Colonial Revival structure on the University of Arkansas campus, built in 1905 as a women's dormitory.

Dickson Street Inn
301 West Dickson Street
479-695-2100
dicksonstreetinn.com
$$
Boutique hotel in two Victorian buildings.

Inn at the Mill
3906 Greathouse Springs Road, Johnson
479-443-1800
innatthemill.com
$$
Built by the architect James Lambeth in and around a 19th-century gristmill.

Kansas City

Kansas City, Missouri, is known for its barbecue, bebop, and easy-does-it Midwestern charm. Still a jazz mecca, the place where Charlie Parker, Lester Young, and Count Basie all got their start, it also has a newer and broader cultural richness. A decade-long effort to revitalize the downtown includes construction of the Kauffman Center for the Performing Arts, giving a sleek new home to the symphony, opera, and ballet. Yet while this metropolis on the Missouri River is no backwater, don't expect high polish. The city's best asset may be the unvarnished grit traceable all the way back to its days as the jumping-off point to the West on the Santa Fe Trail. — BY CHARLY WILDER

FRIDAY

1 *Crossroads Redefined* 4 p.m.

Industrial stagnation and suburban exodus in the 1960s left the Crossroads neighborhood nearly deserted. But now it is the **Crossroads Arts District** (kccrossroads.org), home to fashionable lofts in buildings like the former Western Auto offices, and to some 70 galleries. Two pioneering mainstays are **Sherry Leedy Contemporary Art** (2004 Baltimore Avenue; 816-221-2626; sherryleedy.com), which specializes in midcareer artists like Jun Kaneko, and the **Byron C. Cohen Gallery** (2020 Baltimore Avenue, Suite 1N; 816-421-5665; byroncohengallery.com), representing several artists from China. If it's the first Friday of the month, many galleries hold open houses until about 9 p.m.

2 *Sauce It Up* 7 p.m.

Debates over the best barbecue rouse as much passion here as religion or politics. Some swear by the old guard like Gates Bar-B-Q (gatesbbq.com) and Arthur Bryant's (arthurbryantsbbq.com), both of which have multiple branches. Others make the quick trip across the state line into Kansas City, Kansas, to a relative newcomer, **Oklahoma Joe's** (3002 West 47th Avenue; 913-722-3366; oklahomajoesbbq.com; $). It serves up pulled pork and beef brisket piled high on white bread, in a sauce that may just be the perfect amalgam of sweet, smoke, and vinegar.

OPPOSITE Kansas City's Crossroads district.

3 *Indie Scene* 11 p.m.

If the city's indie music scene hasn't garnered the same hype as those in other Midwestern cities like Minneapolis or Omaha, it's not for lack of guts or artistry. Homegrown bands like Ssion, a gender-bending art-punk music collective that has built a following with over-the-top live shows, cut their teeth in downtown galleries and dives. Hear up-and-comers at the **Record Bar** (1020 Westport Road; 816-753-5207; therecordbar.com) and the **Brick** (1727 McGee Street; 816-421-1634; thebrickkcmo.com). One of the newer spots is the **Czar Bar** (1531 Grand Boulevard; 816-221-2244; czarbar.com), owned by John Hulston, who also runs Anodyne Records, which counts the Meat Puppets, the BellRays, and Architects among its better-known acts.

SATURDAY

4 *Park Life* 10 a.m.

Kansas City is said to have more fountains than any other city except Rome. (This is difficult to prove, but with about 200 of them, it certainly has a good claim.) One of the loveliest can be found at **Jacob L. Loose Park** (51st Street and Wornall Road), a Civil War site, where the Laura Conyers Smith Fountain, made of Italian stone, is encircled by thousands of roses in some 150 varieties. The park is popular with picnicking families and bongo-playing teenagers on furlough from the suburbs.

5 *Contemporary Greens* Noon

If last night's barbecue has you yearning for a salad, head to **Café Sebastienne**, an airy, glass-covered restaurant at the **Kemper Museum of Contemporary Art** (4420 Warwick Boulevard; 816-561-7740; kemperart.org/cafe; $$). Seasonal greens come with cucumber, red onion, grape tomatoes, sheep's milk cheese, and grilled pita. After lunch, pop inside for a quick look at the Kemper's small but diverse collection of modern and contemporary works by artists like Dale Chihuly and Louise Bourgeois, whose gigantic iron spider sculpture looms over the front lawn.

6 *Art in a Cube* 1:30 p.m.

In 2007, the **Nelson-Atkins Museum of Art** (4525 Oak Street; 816-751-1278; nelson-atkins.org)

was thrust into the national spotlight when it opened a new wing designed by Steven Holl. The Bloch Building — which holds contemporary art, photography, and special exhibitions — consists of five translucent glass blocks that create what Nicolai Ouroussoff, the architecture critic of *The New York Times*, described as "a work of haunting power." The museum's suite of American Indian galleries shows an assemblage of about 200 works from more than 68 tribes.

7 *18th Street Couture* 4 p.m.

The Crossroads cultural awakening extends beyond art and into fashion. Three boutiques carrying the work of up-and-coming designers occupy a former film storage unit on West 18th Street. Peregrine Honig and Danielle Meister hand-pick lingerie and swimwear to carry at their shop, **Birdies** (116 West 18th Street; 816-842-2473; birdiespanties.com). Kelly Allen selects a quirky cross-section of locally designed clothing and accessories at **Spool** (122 West 18th Street; 816-842-0228). And **Peggy Noland** (124 West 18th Street; 816-221-7652; peggynoland.com) sells creations on the border of art and fashion in a shop that has often changed decor, at one time resembling the interior of a cloud, at another covered floor-to-ceiling with stuffed animals.

8 *Midwest Tapas* 7 p.m.

Stay in the Crossroads to sample modern Mediterranean-style tapas at **Extra Virgin** (1900 Main Street; 816-842-2205; extravirginkc.com; $$-$$$),

whose chef and owner is Kansas City's culinary titan, Michael Smith. The fare is more playful and adventurous than in his formal restaurant (called simply Michael Smith) next door. And if the loud, euro-chic décor, replete with a floor-to-ceiling *La Dolce Vita* mural, seems to be trying a little too hard, the crowd of unbuttoned professionals enjoying inspired dishes like crispy pork belly with green romesco and chick pea fries doesn't seem to mind. The menu is diverse, as is the wine list.

9 *'Round Midnight* 10 p.m.

The flashy new **Kansas City Power and Light District** (1100 Walnut Street; 816-842-1045; powerandlightdistrict.com) offers a wide range of bars, restaurants, and clubs that can feel like an open-air fraternity party. A smarter alternative can be found in the West Bottoms, an industrial neighborhood that draws a more urbane crowd. The **R Bar** (1617 Genessee Street; 816-471-1777; rbarkc.com) features live jazz and bluegrass, as well as old-time cocktails like Moscow mules and mint juleps. When midnight strikes, head to the **Mutual Musicians Foundation** (1823 Highland Avenue; 816-471-5212; thefoundationjamson.org). The legendary haunt opened in 1917, and public jam sessions are held every Saturday until around 6 a.m. For a small cover, you can catch impromptu sets by some of the city's undiscovered musicians in the same room where Charlie Parker had a cymbal thrown at him in 1937.

SUNDAY

10 *Viva Brunch* 10 a.m.

As any resident will tell you, Mexican food is a big deal here. One of the most authentic spots is **Ortega's**

ABOVE The Bloch Building, designed by Steven Holl, at the Nelson-Atkins Museum of Art.

Restaurant (2646 Belleview Avenue; 816-531-5415; ortegas.synthasite.com; $), tucked in the back of a mom-and-pop grocery store in midtown. On Sundays, its huevos rancheros draws a lively mix of churchgoing families and hung-over art students.

11 *Homage to the Greats* 11 a.m.

The **American Jazz Museum** and **Negro Leagues Baseball Museum** (1616 East 18th Street; 816-474-8463 and 816-221-1920; americanjazzmuseum.com and nlbm.com) share a building in the 18th and Vine Historic District, once the heart of the city's African-American shopping area. The jazz museum, with listening stations to bring the music to life, pays tribute to legendary jazz stars including Charlie

Parker, Louis Armstrong, Duke Ellington, and Ella Fitzgerald. The baseball museum is dedicated to the leagues where black stars like Satchel Paige, Josh Gibson, and Kansas City's own Buck O'Neil played until the integration of Major League Baseball in 1947. It was in Kansas City in 1920 that the first of them, the National Negro League, was founded.

ABOVE Sunday morning at Ortega's Restaurant.

THE BASICS

Several airlines serve Kansas City.

In town, you will want a car.

The Raphael
325 Ward Parkway
816-756-3800
raphaelkc.com
$$
Recently renovated bargain, with black marble bathrooms and flat-screen televisions.

Q Hotel + Spa
560 Westport Road
816-931-0001
theqhotel.com
$$
Eco-conscious hotel in the historic Westport district.

Hilton President Kansas City
1329 Baltimore Avenue
816-221-9490
hilton.com
$$
Downtown landmark built in 1926, redone in 2005.

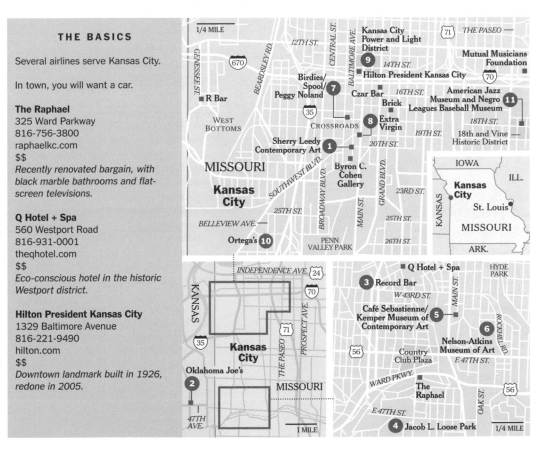

The Niobrara River Valley

To the uninitiated, Nebraska conjures a certain image: a treeless prairie steamrolled pancake-flat, stretching to the horizon. But tucked in a north-central patch of the state is the Niobrara River Valley, filled with a surprising collection of conifers and hardwoods, 200-foot sandstone bluffs, and spring-fed waterfalls. The Niobrara starts in eastern Wyoming and flows across Nebraska for more than 400 miles, emptying into the Missouri River. Seventy-six miles, starting just east of Valentine, are designated as national scenic river (nps.gov/niob). The rapids are mostly riffles, and the water is knee-deep in most spots, inviting a journey by canoe. And although a good float on the river is the center of your trip, there is more to see on land nearby. — BY HELEN OLSSON

FRIDAY

1 *Spurs and Saddles* 2 p.m.

In Valentine (population 2,820), red hearts are painted on the sidewalks and ranchers in cowboy hats roll down Main Street in dusty pickups. Browse the jeans, chaps, hats, ropes, and saddles at **Young's Western Wear** (143 North Main Street; 402-376-1281), purveyor of all things cowboy. Young's also stocks 5,000 pairs of cowboy boots, in snakeskin, elephant, stingray, ostrich, and — if you must — cow leather. Take time to stop by your float trip outfitter to make sure your reservations are in order for tomorrow. A handful of outfitters in Valentine rent canoes, kayaks, and giant inner tubes and can shuttle you or your car from point to point. One is **Little Outlaw** (1005 East Highway 20; 800-238-1867; outlawcanoe.com). If you canoe or kayak, you can run 22 miles from the Fort Niobrara Refuge to Rocky Ford in a day. A lazy float in a tube takes twice as long, so tubers might get only as far as Smith Falls by day's end.

2 *Under the Waterfall* 3:30 p.m.

Drive 23 miles south on Highway 97 through the Sandhills, past grazing cattle, massive spools of rolled hay, and spinning windmills, to **Snake River Falls**. (This Snake River is a tributary of the Niobrara.) Descend the trail through sumac and yucca to the base and crawl behind the 54-foot-wide falls to marvel at the gushing torrent inches away. Look for the cliff swallows' mud nests clinging to the limestone cliffs around the falls.

3 *Caribbean Meets Prairie* 5:30 p.m.

Three miles down Highway 97 is **Merritt Reservoir** (402-376-2969; outdoornebraska.ne.gov/parks.asp), a deep emerald lake rimmed by white sand beaches. Bury your toes in the warm sugar sand and look for the tiny tracks of sand toads. Anglers pull walleyes, crappies, and wide-mouth bass from the depths, and jet skiers trace arcs on the surface. When you're ready for dinner, find your way to the **Merritt Trading Post and Resort** (merritttradingpost.com), the only development at the lake, and its **Waters Edge** restaurant (402-376-1878; $$). Or stop for beef tenderloin or fresh walleye at the **Prairie Club** (402-376-1361; theprairieclub.com), a swanky golf course and country club that opened in 2010. It's 15 miles north of the reservoir on Highway 97.

4 *Yes, It's the Milky Way* 9 p.m.

Because of its remote location, the **Merritt Reservoir** is a prime spot for stargazing. "On a clear

OPPOSITE Floating on the Niobrara near Valentine, Nebraska. The river flows through Nebraska for 400 miles.

RIGHT An elk in the Valentine National Wildlife Refuge, in the Nebraska Sandhills.

moonless night, no kidding, it's so bright the Milky Way casts a shadow," said John Bauer, owner of the Merritt Trading Post and Resort. In late July or early August, amateur astronomers gather here for the annual Nebraska Star Party. They camp on the beach and crane their necks staring into the cosmos. If you're camping at the reservoir, you can gaze until sunrise. Otherwise, get back on the road by 10 or so and let the stars light your way back to Valentine.

SATURDAY

5 *Downriver with a Paddle* 9 a.m.

Grab sandwiches from Henderson's IGA or Scotty's Ranchland, Valentine's local grocers. (There's also a Subway in town.) Meet your outfitter at Cornell Bridge in the **Fort Niobrara National Wildlife Refuge**. Whatever your craft of choice — canoe, kayak, or inner tube — this is where you'll put in and float away on the shallow Niobrara. Over the eons, the Niobrara (pronounced nigh-oh-BRAH-rah) has cut more than 400 feet through a series of rock formations, pinkish-red, chalky white, and gray. Drifting in it is not unlike floating through an enormous block of Neopolitan ice cream. Beach your craft whenever you like and go for a swim or take a walk on shore. On the banks, wade through cold streams and search for small waterfalls tucked in side canyons. A recent National Park Service study found more than 230 falls, most only a few feet

high, tumbling into the river along a 35-mile stretch in this part of the Niobrara.

6 *In the Mist* Noon

Twelve miles down river, just past Allen Bridge, watch for signs along the riverbank for **Smith Falls State Park**. Stop to eat the picnic lunch you packed this morning. Stretch your legs with a short hike to the Smith Falls, Nebraska's tallest. Follow the trail across the steel truss Verdigre Bridge and up a winding boardwalk to the falls, where water plunges 63 feet over a bell-shaped rock. Surrounded by moss and mist, red cedar and bur oak, you'd be surprised to find that just a quick hike will take you to the dry, windswept Sandhills Prairie. The cool, moist environment in the river valley not only nurtures these familiar trees, but has preserved ancient species, like the giant paper birch that died out in the rest of Nebraska as the climate grew hotter and drier thousands of years ago. Animal life thrives here too: turkey vultures ride the thermals, sandpipers perch on sandbars, dragonflies dart above the water's surface.

ABOVE Stars, trailing across the sky in a time-lapse photograph, at the Merritt Reservoir, a lake south of Valentine. The remote reservoir is a prime stargazing spot.

OPPOSITE Sunset at the Merritt Reservoir.

7 *Floating Party Zone* 1:30 p.m.

By now, you are probably passing flotillas of summertime tubers from Iowa, Missouri, Kansas, and Nebraska — young things in bikinis and shorts, broiling in the sun and imbibing mightily. As bald eagles soar overhead, hip-hop may be thumping from boom boxes. Stuart Schneider, a park ranger, patrolled the river one late summer day, passing out mesh bags for empties. "On a busy Saturday, we can get 3,000 people," he said. "My favorite time on the river is the fall," he added. "The water is clear, there are no bugs, and the leaves can be spectacular." And, of course, the students will be back in school.

8 *Time to Take Out* 4:30 p.m.

Having paddled 22 miles, you can take out at **Rocky Ford**, where your outfitter will retrieve you and your canoe and shuttle you back to your car. Beyond Rocky Ford, there are Class III and IV rapids. Unless you have a death wish, exit here.

9 *Meat Eater's Paradise* 7 p.m.

Back in Valentine, reward yourself with a big aged Nebraska steak at **Jordan's** (404 East Highway 20; 402-376-1255). You're in cattle country after all. (Thursdays are livestock auction day in Valentine, where the buyers sit 10 deep on bleachers.) Of course, there isn't a menu in town that doesn't have chicken-fried steak. Jordan's is no exception.

SUNDAY

10 *Fuel Up* 10 a.m.

Have breakfast in Valentine at the **Bunkhouse Restaurant & Saloon** (109 East Highway 20; 402-376-1609; $). Under various names and owners, the Bunkhouse building has been serving grub since the 1940s. Slide into a booth and load up with a sirloin steak and eggs (when in Rome, you know...) or a stack of Joe's pancakes. Try a side order of Indian fry bread with powdered sugar or honey.

Rest assured the window you gaze out won't have the unseemly imprint of Valentine's infamous "Butt Bandit." The man who, for more than a year, left greasy prints of his nether regions on the windows of Valentine businesses was arrested in 2008.

11 *Birder's Paradise* 11 a.m.

Twenty miles south of Valentine, you'll find the **Valentine National Wildlife Refuge** (fws.gov/valentine). Where the Ogallala Aquifer nears the surface, bright blue lakes and marshes sparkle like jewels in the green grass. Hundreds of bird species

have been sighted here: sharp-tailed grouse, blue-winged teal, long-billed curlews. Just beyond the park's main headquarters, a trail mowed through the grass rises up to a rusting fire tower. From that perch, gaze at the Sandhills, which spread out like a turbulent sea in a hundred shades of green, blue and gold. It's time to reflect that the only pancake you've seen in Nebraska came with syrup and a generous pat of butter.

ABOVE A view of West Long Lake in the Valentine National Wildlife Refuge.

OPPOSITE Snake River Falls near the Merritt Reservoir. The rolling hills and waterfalls of the Niobrara Valley and land nearby are a surprise to outsiders who imagine Nebraska as filled with flat prairies.

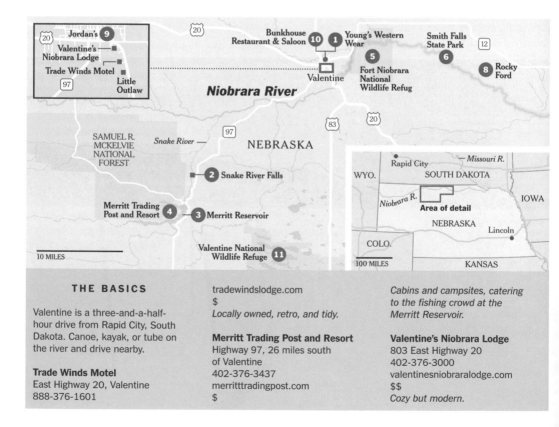

THE BASICS

Valentine is a three-and-a-half-hour drive from Rapid City, South Dakota. Canoe, kayak, or tube on the river and drive nearby.

Trade Winds Motel
East Highway 20, Valentine
888-376-1601

tradewindslodge.com
$
Locally owned, retro, and tidy.

Merritt Trading Post and Resort
Highway 97, 26 miles south
of Valentine
402-376-3437
merritttradingpost.com
$

Cabins and campsites, catering to the fishing crowd at the Merritt Reservoir.

Valentine's Niobrara Lodge
803 East Highway 20
402-376-3000
valentinesniobraralodge.com
$$
Cozy but modern.

The Black Hills

Everything may, as they say, be big in Texas, but everything is positively monumental in the southwest corner of South Dakota, in and around the Black Hills. The caves are unusually cavernous, the badlands especially bad; the archaeological sites turn up mammoths. Giant faces gaze from more than one mountain. Drive through this sometimes hilly, sometimes flat, sometimes grassy, sometimes downright lunar landscape, and it will seem that every crossroad has a sign pointing to an outsize attraction, a national monument, or some other officially remembered site. — BY PAUL SCHNEIDER

FRIDAY

1 *Old Men of the Mountain* 3 p.m.

Begin at **Mount Rushmore National Memorial** (1300 Highway 244, Keystone; 605-574-3171; nps.gov/moru). Never mind that Teddy Roosevelt doesn't altogether fit in the group, or that the former republican solemnity of the place has been woefully squandered by the addition of imperial arches and

OPPOSITE The face of Crazy Horse, an Oglala Lakota chief, at the Crazy Horse Memorial, which has been gradually emerging from a granite mountain since 1948.

BELOW Sunset falls on Badlands National Park, an arid wilderness of singular beauty.

triumphal gewgaws at the entrance. And never mind if you are re-enacting a childhood visit to the place. A visit to Abe and the boys is a fitting start to your zigzagging tour through country where communal gawking and commemoration are de rigueur.

2 *Would Crazy Horse Approve?* 5 p.m.

Just outside Custer, appropriately, is the **Crazy Horse Memorial** (Avenue of the Chiefs, Crazy Horse; 605-673-4681; crazyhorsememorial.org), which when completed, its builders say, will be the largest sculpture on the planet. All of the presidential men on Rushmore would fit on the head of Crazy Horse, an Oglala Lakota chief, which has gradually been emerging from a granite mountain since 1948. The memorial already has what must be one of the world's largest interpretive centers, with all of the requisite snack and souvenir opportunities. The nonprofit, family-run place is somehow unnerving, as much a monument to monument makers and monument marketers as to the man who, with Sitting Bull, defeated George Armstrong Custer at the Little Bighorn. What Crazy Horse, who never permitted a photograph of himself to be taken, would have thought of laser shows projected on his graven image is anybody's guess, but Buffalo Bill Cody would have eaten it up.

3 *Comfort Food* 7 p.m.

Drive into the town of **Hot Springs** and take a quick walk around its eye-catching downtown of carved pink sandstone buildings. Yes, there really are hot springs here, once visited as healing waters and today marketed more as a theme park for children (evansplunge.com). Don't linger too long before finding your way to the **All Star Grill & Pub** (310 South Chicago Street; 605-745-7827; $) for burgers and hot roast beef sandwiches — restaurants close early out here.

SATURDAY

4 *Platters and Provisions* 8 a.m.

You're setting out for a long day of exploring, so have a hearty breakfast at **Dale's Family Restaurant** (745 Battle Mountain Avenue, Hot Springs; 605-745-3028; $), where you can expect hefty portions, standard eggs-and-bacon fare, and a cheerful local

crowd. Before leaving town, pick up some snacks and water. When hunger strikes again, you may be far from the nearest restaurant.

5 *Boys Will Be Boys* 9 a.m.

Even nature seems to be in the business of turning out stone memorials to fallen behemoths. On the southern outskirts of Hot Springs, a mass grave for mammoths is slowly emerging out of an ancient sink hole called the **Mammoth Site** (1800 U.S. 18 Bypass, Hot Springs; 605-745-6017; mammothsite.com). The effect is intensely sculptural: a mass of femurs and fibulas, skulls and tusks, backbones and pelvises, some just beginning to show in bas relief, some nearly freed from the surrounding matrix, some displayed behind glass. A few other animals have turned up in the hole, but it's mostly mammoths that ventured in and couldn't get out. And of those, nearly all seem to have been young males, the population most inclined, some mammoth experts have theorized, to risk-taking behavior.

6 *The Underground* 11 a.m.

Crystal lovers may prefer nearby Jewel Cave National Monument, which is one of the world's largest cavern systems, but **Wind Cave National Park** (nps.gov/wica; visitor center on Route 285 eleven miles north of Hot Springs) is only marginally less labyrinthine, with 134 miles of mapped passages. It is also where Crazy Horse and his fellow Lakota believed a trickster spirit first convinced humans into coming above ground sometime back at the beginning of the world, which seems more in keeping with your monumental mission. Take along a jacket (it's chilly down there), and choose the tour that descends through the natural entrance rather than the elevator.

7 *Slow Roads* 2 p.m.

Take your time for an afternoon meander through some of the most beautiful parts of the Black Hills. Travel north on Route 87 through **Custer State Park** (custerstatepark.info) and turn right, toward Keystone, on Route 16A, which will take you through an improbable number of hairpin turns and one-lane tunnels in turreted mountains. For more of the same, check out the more crowded Route 87, the renowned **Needles Highway**. Either way, when you're ready to re-emerge, make your way north to Rapid City.

8 *Buffalo and a Nice Red* 8 p.m.

The **Corn Exchange** (727 Main Street, Rapid City; 605-343-5070; cornexchange.com; $$) has gained impressive national attention for its well-prepared food, which it describes as New Heartland Cuisine,

ABOVE Mount Rushmore National Memorial. The presidential heads are 60 feet high, with 20-foot noses.

and for its wine list. Relax over dinner (you should make a reservation) and scan the menu for the Buffalo Bolognese.

SUNDAY

9 *Not So Bad* 10 a.m.

The baddest parts of **Badlands National Park**—desiccated, vaguely Martian landscapes formed by erosion—aren't the whole story. Find an alternative on the **Sage Creek Rim Road** (in a convertible if you were smart enough to rent one), which overlooks rolling grasslands that stretch to the horizon. To get to it, leave I-90 at Exit 131, drive south on Route 240, which loops west just before the town called

Interior, and turn left at the sign a few miles past the Pinnacles Overlook. Stop at the Sage Creek primitive campground, where you can just walk off into the wide-open wilderness in whatever direction suits your fancy, following buffalo trails and creek beds.

10 *Quench It* 1 p.m.

Continue on the rim road to the intersection with Route 44 at the minuscule town of Scenic. Route 44 will take you scenically from here back to Rapid City, but stop in first at the **Old Longhorn Saloon** (101 Main Street, Scenic; 605-993-6133; $), the best place to get a cold beer in the middle of nowhere anywhere. Why should the folks with Harleys and halter tops have it all to themselves?

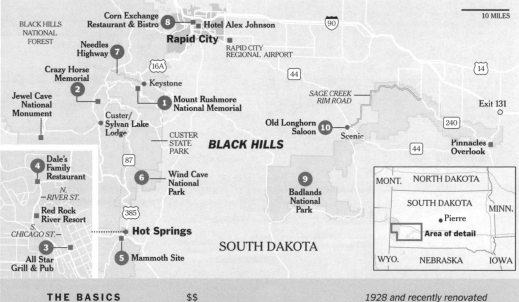

THE BASICS

Major airlines serve the Rapid City Regional Airport. Rent a car.

Red Rock River Resort
603 North River Street, Hot Springs
605-745-4400
redrockriverresort.com

$$
Spa hotel in a small historic downtown of sandstone buildings.

Hotel Alex Johnson
523 Sixth Street, Rapid City
605-342-1210
alexjohnson.com
$$
A Rapid City landmark, open since

1928 and recently renovated with 21st-century amenities.

Sylvan Lake Lodge
24572 Highway 87, Custer
605-574-2561
custerresorts.com
$$
Rustic hotel operated by Custer State Park.

Minneapolis-St. Paul

Minnesotans take pride in their humility, but make an exception when it comes to showing folks around. And they have a lot to show. There is a depth of cultural amenities to Minneapolis and its not-so-twin city St. Paul that will surprise a first-time visitor. And please remember, when they ask you at the coffee shop, "How you doing, today?" they really want to know.
— BY DAVID CARR

FRIDAY

1 *By the Falls of Minnehaha* 5 p.m.

On a hot summer day, there is convenient and diverting respite at **Minnehaha Falls Park** (4825 Minnehaha Avenue South; 612-230-6400; minneapolisparks.org). Don't go there expecting Niagara; rather, you'll find a quaint urban park with both landscaped and wild elements, a surprisingly good seafood restaurant (Sea Salt Eatery) and, of course, the 53-foot falls that inspired Henry Wadsworth Longfellow to write *The Song of Hiawatha*. Now, Longfellow never actually saw the falls — he was inspired by the writing of others — but why put such a fine point on it?

2 *Intermission with a View* 7 p.m.

Many cities in the middle of the country chirp reflexively about their "great theater," but Minneapolis lives up to its rhetoric with strong independent companies. Among them is the **Guthrie Theater** (818 South Second Street; 612-377-2224; guthrietheater.org), a first-rate repertory theater with a new facility featuring a cantilevered bridge to nowhere. Step out and you can see all the way to the city's industrial northeast. Inside, you can take in a well-acted play.

3 *To the Warehouses* 8 p.m.

People are of two minds about Minneapolis's warehouse district. There are those who live for the street-filling frolic of a Friday night, and many who would drive miles to avoid it. A point for the former is the **112 Eatery** (112 North Third Street; 612-343-7696; 112eatery.com; $$), where you can avoid the mob by going to the upstairs bar for the tagliatelle with foie gras meatballs. Afterward, liquid diversions can commence. Start at the **Monte Carlo** (219 Third Avenue North; 612-333-5900). Lawyers, politicos, and media types congregate here amid a mind-boggling, and potentially mind-bending, array of alcohol. Move on to **Lee's Liquor Lounge** (101 Glenwood Avenue; 612-338-9491; leesliquorlounge.com), just west of downtown, where Trailer Trash may be playing. You can face-plant at the nearby and artful Chambers hotel, or just have a nightcap on the rooftop then cab back to your own hotel.

SATURDAY

4 *You Going to Eat That?* 10 a.m.

Tell room service to keep it quiet when they deliver coffee. Or if you are feeling ambitious, go to **Al's Breakfast** in Dinkytown (413 14th Avenue Southeast; 612-331-9991), hard by the east-bank campus of the University of Minnesota. Wait against the wall for one of 14 stools while eyeing the food of the patron whose stool you are coveting. Minnesota is a friendly place, but don't ask for a bite of his blueberry pancakes. Order the hash browns and forswear ever eating so-called home fries again.

OPPOSITE The Guthrie Theater in Minneapolis.

RIGHT Claes Oldenburg and Coosje van Bruggen's giant sculpture called *Spoonbridge and Cherry* sits in the center of the Walker Art Center's sculpture garden in Minneapolis.

5 *Necklace of Blue* 11:30 a.m.

So many lakes right in the city, but which one is for you? If you wear socks with sandals and think walking is a sport, **Lake Harriet** is for you. If you are prone to nudity and like swimming at night, then it's Hidden Beach at Cedar Lake. The rest of us can go to **Lake Calhoun**. Wheels of any kind, most commonly rollerblades, take you around it, but why not go to the boathouse and get a canoe? Avoid the sailboats and windsurfers by paddling under the bridge into Lake of the Isles, which is sort of swampy to walk around, but lovely from the water.

6 *Spoon Feeding* 2:30 p.m.

The **Walker Art Center** (1750 Hennepin Avenue; 612-375-7600; walkerart.org) has one of the best contemporary art collections between the coasts, but why not stay outside for a little artist-designed mini-golf? At the sculpture garden, one might be tempted to climb into the giant spoon by Claes Oldenburg and Coosje van Bruggen. Don't. Motion detectors were installed after locals decided to memorialize their love with nocturnal visits. **Café Lurcat** (1624 Harmon Place; 612-486-5500; cafelurcat.com; $$), across the walking bridge, has excellent small plates.

7 *Ambulatory Retail* 4:30 p.m.

Shopping in Minnesota is usually reductively assigned to the Mall of America, but there is a strollable necklace of stores along Grand Avenue in St. Paul where down-home and style make nice. **Bibelot** (No. 1082; 651-222-0321; bibelotshops.com) has been featuring cool local stuff for four decades, and **Cooks of Crocus Hill** (No. 877; 651-228-1333;

ABOVE Cooks of Crocus Hill on Grand Avenue in St. Paul.

RIGHT 20.21, a Wolfgang Puck restaurant inside the Walker Art Center in downtown Minneapolis.

OPPOSITE You can walk or bike at Lake Calhoun, but why not go to the boathouse and get a canoe?

cooksofcrocushill.com) is the foodie perennial that just won't quit. If you get hungry or thirsty, you can always walk in to **Dixie's on Grand** (No. 695; 651-222-7345; dixiesongrand.com) for some Southern-inspired fare.

8 *The North Star* 7 p.m.

As in many urban areas, the ineffable epicenter of cool migrates on a schedule known only to a select few. In Minneapolis, the indigenous tribe of artists, musicians, and wannabes have forsaken Uptown for Northeast, where trendy restaurants and bars have taken root. **Brasa Rotisserie** (600 East Hennepin Avenue; 612-379-3030; brasa.us) is a new-ish favorite where precious food localism comes without a dear price. Another is **331 Club** (331 13th Avenue Northeast; 612-331-1746; 331club.com), with a neighborhood vibe even a visitor can't miss. Yes, you should try the Hot Polack, a mix of jalapeños, kraut, and bratwurst. And anyone who knows Minneapolis will ask if you visited **Nye's Polonaise Room** (112 East Hennepin Avenue; 612-379-2021; nyespolonaise.com) to sample its wondrously cheesy piano bar and slamming polka.

9 *Here Comes a Regular* 11 p.m.

The Replacements may not drink anymore at the **CC Club** (2600 Lyndale Avenue South; 612-874-7226;

myspace.com/theccclub). And Tom Arnold was 86'ed for the last time a while ago. But the venerable club remains a nexus for the city's down and dirty rock scene. Plus, there's a killer juke box and no live music to try to talk over.

SUNDAY

10 *Over the River* 9 a.m.

Head over the river and check out St. Paul's **City Hall** (15 Kellogg Boulevard West; stpaul.gov), where *Vision of Peace*, a 60-ton onyx statue, towers over a lobby done in black Zigzag Moderne. And try to grab a booth at **Mickey's Diner** (36 Seventh Street West; 651-222-5633; mickeysdiningcar.com).

11 *A Historic Visit* Noon

Historic museums in fairly young places like Minnesota can be dreary, but not so at the **Minnesota History Center** (345 Kellogg Boulevard West, St. Paul; 651-259-3000; mnhs.org/historycenter). Get some metaphorical manure on your boots by visiting the Grainland/Boxcar exhibit. After all the eating you've done, it's worth finding out what happens inside those big elevators that tower over middle America. The hokey charms of so-called Minnesota Nice loom large.

THE BASICS

Take light rail or drive from the airport to downtown.

There are cabs, but you will want a car to get beyond downtown.

Le Méridien Chambers Minneapolis
901 Hennepin Avenue
612-767-6900
chambersminneapolis.com
$$-$$$
Gorgeous, beautifully designed hotel with good food, lovely rooms, and a wonderful lounge.

Renaissance Hotel
225 Third Avenue South
612-375-1700
thedepotminneapolis.com
$$
Retrofitted in the historic Depot.

hotel340
340 Cedar Street, St. Paul
651-280-4120
hotel340.com
$$
Comfortable modern rooms in a lavishly detailed 1917 landmark building.

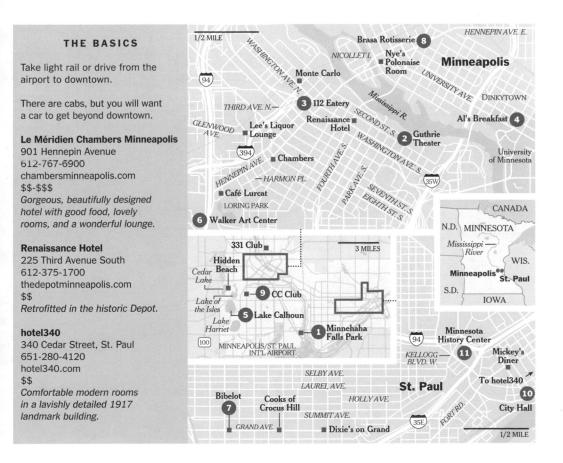

Duluth

Believe it. Minnesota bakes in the summer. And when temperatures hit the 90s, many Minnesotans head for Duluth, a port city on the westernmost tip of Lake Superior that is cooled to comfort by lakeshore breezes. Built into bluffs overlooking this largest of the Great Lakes, Duluth has long been the port gateway to Minnesota's Iron Range. Today, the spacious Victorian mansions built by mining and lumber barons are bed-and-breakfasts or museums. (The city may be better known as the childhood of Bob Dylan.) And the development of Canal Park, once an abandoned warehouse district, has given Duluth a vibrant waterfront of shops, bars, and restaurants.
— BY PAT BORZI

FRIDAY

1 *Lakefront Ramble* 5 p.m.

Acquaint yourself with **Canal Park** and the harbor by strolling the **Lakewalk**, a three-mile path along the Lake Superior shore. Whether you go the whole way or only part of it, rest your feet and enjoy the view from the deck of the **Sunset Grill** in the **Fitger's Brewery Complex** (600 East Superior Street; 218-722-8826; fitgers.com), a mile from Canal Park. A big brewery from 1859 until 1972, Fitger's was converted into shops, restaurants, and a luxury hotel and now houses a microbrewery. It's a great place to have a drink and watch the hulking ore boats inch in and out of the harbor. Too tired to walk back? Hop the Port Town Trolley, which serves Canal Park and the downtown hotels until about 7 p.m. in summer.

2 *What, No Ping?* 7 p.m.

They use real wooden bats in the Northwoods League, whose 12 teams of collegians serve as the Upper Midwest's answer to the Cape Cod Baseball League. The Duluth Huskies play at cozy **Wade Municipal Stadium** (101 North 35th Avenue West; 218-786-9909), a Works Projects Administration relic that opened in 1941. Tickets are cheap, and families have a great time.

OPPOSITE The former Fitger's Brewery Complex now holds shops, restaurants, a hotel, and a microbrewery.

RIGHT The Lake Superior Railroad Museum.

3 *The Lake Superior Sound* 10:30 p.m.

Some longtime Duluth residents say the local music scene isn't what it used to be. That may be, but Duluth offers plenty of late-night options. For one of the best combinations of music and food, hit **Pizza Lucé** (11 East Superior Street; 218-727-7400; pizzaluce.com; $$), where local and out-of-town bands play often and which serves delectable pizzas, pasta, and hot hoagies until 2:30 a.m. on weekends.

SATURDAY

4 *Breakfast at Mom's* 10 a.m.

Few places in Duluth do breakfast as well as the **Amazing Grace Bakery Café** (394 South Lake Avenue; 218-723-0075; amazinggraceduluth.com; $), in the basement of the **DeWitt-Seitz Marketplace** in Canal Park. The funky interior is a hoot. If your mother ever had plastic tablecloths with designs of oranges, apples, and peaches on them, she'd love this place. Try French toast, muffins, or scones.

5 *Mansion with a Past* 11:30 a.m.

Of all the captains of industry who once called Duluth home, Chester A. Congdon was one of the richest. **Glensheen** (3300 London Road; 218-726-8910; glensheen.org), his baronial 39-room lakefront mansion on almost eight acres, was completed in 1908. The basic tour of the main house's lower floors takes about an hour. An expanded tour includes the Arts and Crafts collection on the third floor. At one time tour guides were discouraged from discussing

the double murder committed at the estate in 1977. An intruder smothered the 83-year-old heiress to the Congdon family fortune with a pink satin pillow and beat her night nurse to death with a candlestick holder. Most guides now mention the crime, but you may not hear about it unless you ask.

6 *A View from the Wall* 2 p.m.

Grandma's Saloon & Grill (522 Lake Avenue South; 218-727-4192; grandmasrestaurants.com/retail.htm) is a popular Canal Park destination. Its deck overlooks the century-old Aerial Lift Bridge, where the roadway rises in one piece to let ore and grain boats pass. But it's more fun to grab a single-scoop waffle cone at **Grandma's Ice Cream Boxcar**, the grill's ice cream and soda stand across the parking lot, and join the crowd along the canal wall and watch these huge vessels go by. Wave to the deckhands — they'll wave back — but don't be the one who jumps when the ship sounds its horn.

7 *The Iron Boats* 3:30 p.m.

The doomed ore freighter *Edmund Fitzgerald*, sunk in a storm on Lake Superior in 1975 and immortalized in song by Gordon Lightfoot, departed from Superior, Wisconsin, across the harbor from Duluth. To get a sense of proportion, tour the immense **William A. Irvin**, a 610-foot retired laker that is still 110 feet shorter than the Fitzgerald. The flagship of U.S. Steel's Great Lakes Fleet from 1938

to 1978, the *Irvin* (350 Harbor Drive; 218-722-5573; decc.org) is named for the former U.S. Steel president who occasionally sailed on it himself. The tour takes you through the engine room, the immense hold that could handle up to 14,000 tons of iron ore and coal, and the officers' and crew's quarters. Note the contrast of the stark crew's rooms with the stunning walnut-paneled staterooms for big-shot passengers.

8 *Tequila Sunset* 6 p.m.

Scoring a table at its elevated deck is the tough part at **Little Angie's Cantina** (11 East Buchanan Street; 218-727-6117; grandmasrestaurants.com/littleangies; $$), Canal Park's best spot for people-watching. Once you've done that, you can choose from Angie's 60-plus brands of tequila. Its margaritas come in three sizes. The largest, the 45-ounce mucho, goes well with almost anything on the menu.

9 *Ironman Gelato* 8 p.m.

Sometimes the iron ore didn't make it out of Duluth, and one relic of those days is **Clyde Iron Works** (2920 West Michigan Street; 218-727-1150; clydeparkduluth.com), once a foundry complex that turned out heavy equipment for logging and construction. Today it's a cavernous space that

ABOVE AND BELOW Glensheen, a baronial mansion on the Lake Superior waterfront, belonged to Chester A. Congdon, one of Duluth's captains of industry. If your tour guide doesn't bring it up, ask about the double murder committed at the estate in 1977.

holds a restaurant, bakery, and events hall. Catch some live music or at least dig into a homemade baked dessert or gelato.

SUNDAY

10 *Railway History* 10 a.m.

Hop the trolley to the Depot, also known as the **Lake Superior Railroad Museum** (506 West Michigan Street; 218-727-8025; lsrm.org), and relive Duluth's rich railroad history. Beneath the former Union Depot, which in its heyday handled seven railroads and up to 50 trains a day, lies one of the country's most extensive collections of old locomotives, coaches, and other equipment. The admission price also gets you into the

rest of the St. Louis County Heritage and Arts Center, which includes a children's museum and a gallery.

11 *Just an Embryo* Noon

The **Electric Fetus** (12 East Superior Street; 218-722-9970; electricfetus.com) is a record shop as eccentric as its name suggests. If you absolutely have to get your toddler a Dead Kennedys T-shirt, this is the place to find it. The original Fetus opened in Minneapolis in 1968, and in many ways this branch remains stuck in time: for starters, the store smells like incense. The Fetus is known for offering CD's across every genre, and even if you don't buy anything on your way out of town, you should get a laugh out of looking at the buttons and headshop merchandise.

THE BASICS

Fly into Duluth International Airport or drive two and a half hours from Minneapolis.

You will need a car to venture beyond downtown and Canal Park.

South Pier Inn on the Canal
701 South Lake Avenue
218-786-9007
southpierinn.com
$$-$$$
Near the lift bridge on the Duluth Harbor canal. Designed for water views and built in 2002.

Suites Hotel at Waterfront Plaza
325 Lake Avenue South
218-727-4663
thesuitesduluth.com
$$
Former home of Marshall-Wells, once billed as the world's largest hardware distributor.

Sheraton Duluth
301 East Superior Street
218-733-5660
sheraton.com/duluth
$$
Downtown hotel built in 2007.

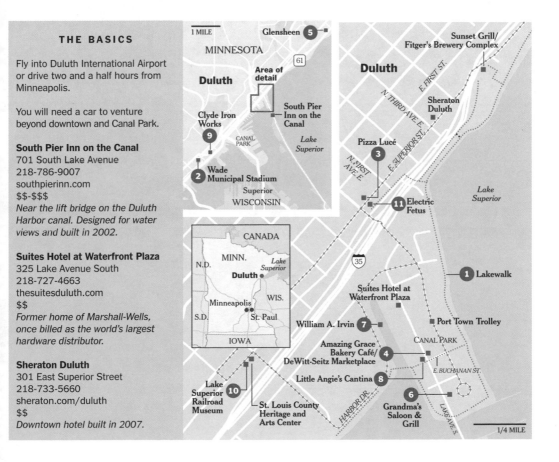

Madison

Madison, Wisconsin, a liberal college town that doubles as the capital of a politically complicated state, pulls its disparate elements together into a spirited reality all its own, a funky amalgam of hard-partying students, socially conscious activists, sports fans, outdoor warriors, politicos from both sides of the aisle, artists, foodies, and more. Long pigeonholed as a hotbed for frat parties and activism, Madison has a vibrant but much more tempered side brimming with arts, culture, and food. In a city with so many types to keep happy, it's impossible not to find something that suits your fancy. — BY KATIE ZEZIMA

FRIDAY

1 *Glimpse of Gridiron* 3 p.m.

University of Wisconsin football inspires obsession, drawing pilgrims even in the off-season to **Camp Randall Stadium** (1440 Monroe Street; 608-263-5645; uwbadgers.com/facilities). Groups of 10 to 75 can reserve free tours that take them onto the field and inside locker rooms and luxury boxes. If you can't find nine friends to go along, you may be able to latch on with a scheduled group; in either case, you must call at least two weeks in advance. Otherwise, peek at the field from a window in the apparel store at the stadium, **Bucky's Locker Room** (inside Gate 1; 608-256-9499), while you're picking up your Badgers cap. Or forget football and explore the **Allen Centennial Gardens** (620 Babcock Drive; allencentennialgardens.org), 2.5 acres of flowers and plants from daylily-lined path to a French garden with shrubs trimmed in the shape of fleurs-de-lis.

2 *Beer and Water* 6 p.m.

Drink in views of Lake Mendota, one of the lakes that give Madison its miles of waterfront, along with your pint at the **Memorial Union Terrace** at the **University of Wisconsin** (800 Langdon Street; 608-265-3000; union.wisc.edu/terrace), an outdoor

four-tiered space with candy-colored chairs, a lakefront path, and live music in the warm months.

3 *Prairie Provisions* 8 p.m.

Madison's culinary scene pulls diners in two very different directions: far from the prairie with dozens of ethnic restaurants and right back to it with an emphasis on the bounty of Wisconsin farms. Expect to see Wisconsin grass-fed beef and house-made pasta on the menu at **Harvest** (21 North Pinckney Street; 608-255-6075; harvest-restaurant.com; $$$). It offers sophisticated seasonal dishes and an extensive wine list in a soothing setting of soft lighting and buttery yellow walls.

SATURDAY

4 *Biking among Badgers* 9 a.m.

Centered on an isthmus between Lakes Mendota and Monona and surrounded by conservation land, Madison is a haven for outdoors types and one of the most bicycle-friendly cities in the country. For some easy exploring, join the biking crowd by picking up a rental at **Machinery Row Bicycles** (601 Williamson Street; 608-442-5974; machineryrowbicycles.com), which sits on the bike path around Monona. Ride around the lake or head over to the 1,260-acre **University of Wisconsin Arboretum** (1207 Seminole Highway; 608-263-7888; uwarboretum.org).

OPPOSITE Badgers loyalists during a football game at the University of Wisconsin in Madison.

RIGHT Late afternoon at Memorial Union Terrace on the University of Wisconsin campus.

5 *The Architect* 1 p.m.

These days Wisconsin wants you to know it was the first and favorite home of Frank Lloyd Wright, but in his lifetime it wasn't so sure. Wright's vision for a sprawling lakeside civic center was rejected in 1938 by one planning-commission vote. In the 1990s, the design was resurrected and Madison built **Monona Terrace** (1 John Nolen Drive; 608-261-4000; mononaterrace.com; tours daily at 1 p.m.). Its open design and tinted windows reflect the water below, and its roof garden and cafe offer the city's best water view. One group that did appreciate Wright was the congregation that hired him to design the **Unitarian Meeting House** (900 University Bay Drive; 608-233-9774; fusmadison.org), completed in 1951. Take a formal tour or look from outside. The church's bold design is unmistakable Wright. The building is a triangle, symbolizing hands clasped in prayer.

6 *Make Mine Cheesy* 3 p.m.

The Old Fashioned (23 North Pinckney Street; 608-310-4545; theoldfashioned.com) serves the food that "makes Wisconsin so Wisconsin," so it's no surprise that an entire section of the menu is devoted to cheese. The bar and restaurant is reminiscent of a late-19th-century saloon filled with Grandma's antiques, but with an updated flair. The cheese curds are a must for sampling, as is the spicy bloody mary.

7 *Where the Shoppers Are* 4 p.m.

Stroll State Street, which links the Capitol with the university. It's a pedestrian thoroughfare brimming with boutiques, restaurants, museums, and bars. Check out **Anthology** (No. 218; 608-204-2644; anthology.typepad.com), a whimsical boutique filled with colorful crafts; the **Soap Opera** (No. 319; 800-251-7627; thesoapopera.com), a fragrant repository of soaps, lotions, and potions; and **B-Side**

Records (No. 436; 608-255-1977; b-sidemadison.com), a trove of vintage vinyl and CDs and a showcase for many of the city's bands.

8 *Andes Express* 8 p.m.

Inka Heritage (602 South Park Street; 608-310-4282; inkaheritagerestaurant.com; $$) is one of Madison's culinary bright spots, and not just because of its fluorescent walls and lively art. Diners are transported to Peru via dishes like fire-roasted beef heart, grilled Peruvian trout, and fried yucca. The wine list includes several selections from Chile and Argentina.

9 *Swing Time* 10:30 p.m.

Madison is a late-night kind of town, especially for fans of live music. Check out a show at the **High Noon Saloon** (701A East Washington Avenue; 608-268-1122; high-noon.com), a large, Western-tinged club with a balcony for catbird views of bands. The club is operated by the former owner of Madison's once beloved O'Cayz Corral, which was destroyed by fire in 2001.

SUNDAY

10 *Double Comfort Score* 10 a.m.

Any restaurant that spells out its name in large Scrabble tiles near the front door is bound to have a

RIGHT B-Side Records, one of the shopping options on State Street, which links the university and the State Capitol.

funky-nerdy-vibe. **Lazy Jane's Cafe and Bakery** (1358 Williamson Street; 608-257-5263; $) becomes crowded and loud but exudes the coziness that comes with a lazy Sunday poring over the newspaper or catching up with an old friend. The food is similarly comfortable, with scones, frittata, grilled cheese sandwiches, and a seitan scramble filled with peppers, onions, and mushrooms that is good enough to impress an avowed meat eater.

11 *Easy Paddling* 11:30 a.m.

Lakes Monona and Mendota are usually the first choices for fun on the water in Madison, but tiny **Lake Wingra**, tucked south of the university arboretum and the Henry Vilas Zoo, is a quieter option. Rent a canoe,

kayak, rowboat, or paddle boat at **Wingra Boats** (824 Knickerbocker Street; 608-233-5332; wingraboats.com), and glide away.

OPPOSITE ABOVE A tour group in Camp Randall Stadium.

ABOVE The Old Fashioned, where the furniture suggests a raid on Grandma's parlor, serves the food that "makes Wisconsin so Wisconsin." Try the cheese curds.

THE BASICS

Drive three hours from Chicago or fly into Dane County Airport and rent a car.

Doubletree Madison
525 West Johnson Street
608-251-5511
doubletreemadison.com
$$
Between the university and Capitol Square; offers airport shuttle service.

Dahlmann Campus Inn
601 Langdon Street
608-257-4391
thecampusinn.com
$$
A touch of boutique refinement in the heart of the campus

Arbor House
3402 Monroe Street
608-238-2981
arbor-house.com
$$
Proudly green, with a native-plant garden and an environmental resource center.

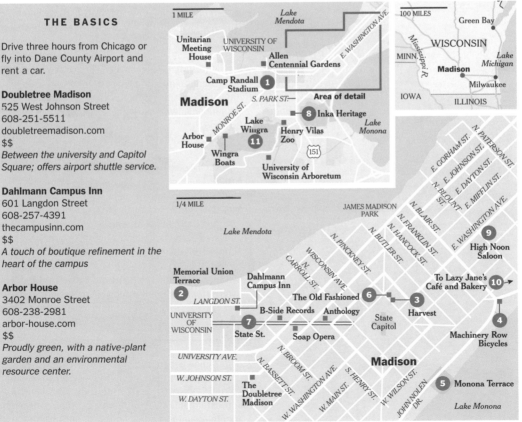

Milwaukee

There's plenty about modern-day Milwaukee, Wisconsin, that would be unrecognizable to Laverne and Shirley from the sitcom set in the late '50s and '60s. Oh, the area still appreciates its beer and bratwurst: delis carry a mind-boggling variety of sausage, and bars are known to have 50-plus brands of brew. But Milwaukee also has 95 miles of bike lanes, lush parks lacing the shores of Lake Michigan, and a revitalized riverfront where sophisticated shops coexist within sight of the city's industrial past. Modern Milwaukee is defined less by the Rust Belt than by its lively downtown and a signature museum so architecturally striking that it competes for attention with the art it holds. — MAURA J. CASEY

FRIDAY

1 *Hog Heaven* 4 p.m.

Roar on over to the **Harley-Davidson Museum** (400 Canal Street; 877-436-8738; h-dmuseum.com), which celebrates the 1903 birth of the signature product of Milwaukee residents William Harley and Arthur Davidson, and the American icon it has become. The Harley-Davidson Museum has 138 motorcycles on display, including the company's first two models, from 1903 and 1905, a 1920 Sport model marketed to women, and the 1932 Servi-Car used for commercial deliveries and credited with keeping the company solvent during the Great Depression. Harley-Davidson has been setting aside at least one motorcycle every year since 1915, and the resulting collection tells the story of a machine, America, and the open road in the 20th century — an absorbing tale whether or not you ride.

2 *Snake Chasers* 6 p.m.

There's more to Milwaukee than beer, but beer undeniably helped build the city. At one point in the 19th century, 150 breweries flourished here, some established by German immigrants whose names were Pabst, Miller, and Schlitz. So to better appreciate all that history and perhaps take a sip yourself, tour the **Lakefront Brewery** (1872 North Commerce Street;

OPPOSITE Inside the Quadracci Pavilion, designed by Santiago Calatrava, at the Milwaukee Art Museum.

RIGHT The Harley-Davidson Museum.

414-372-8800; lakefrontbrewery.com), housed in a century-old former utility building with soaring, 30-foot-high ceilings. You'll learn about how beer is made and taste a few of Lakefront's winning brews, including the Snake Chaser, an Irish-style stout made in honor of St. Patrick's Day. The guides are very funny, so for the laughs alone, it's worth the trip.

3 *Slavic Feast* 8 p.m.

For authentic Eastern European flavors, you can't do better than **Three Brothers Bar and Restaurant** (2414 South St. Clair Street; 414-481-7530; 3brothersrestaurant.com; $$), a Milwaukee institution that has been serving Serbian cuisine since 1954. Where else could you order roast suckling pig with rice and vegetables, served with home-pickled cabbage? Or a chicken paprikash followed by an incredibly light seven-layer walnut torte? The dining room has the unpretentious feel of a neighborhood tavern.

SATURDAY

4 *A Ward Updated* 10 a.m.

Many cities have warehouse districts that have become revitalized; Milwaukee has the **Historic Third Ward** (historicthirdward.org), made up of the blocks between the Milwaukee River and Jackson Street. A century ago, this was a manufacturing center. Now it is a magnet for shoppers, with old brick warehouses converted into boutiques and restaurants. For distinctive fashions, search no farther than **Five Hearts Boutique** (153 North Milwaukee Street;

414-727-4622; shopfivehearts.com). And for an eclectic and international array of home furnishings and artifacts, linger in **Embelezar** (241 North Broadway; 414-224-7644), whose name is Portuguese for, fittingly enough, "to embellish and adorn."

5 *Sausage and Cheese* Noon

Before finding a spot to hang out in one of the city's lovely waterfront parks, pack a picnic on Old World Third Street, the center of German life in 19th-century Milwaukee. The **Wisconsin Cheese Mart** (215 West Highland Avenue; 888-482-7700; wisconsincheesemart.com), which opened in 1938, sells hundreds of varieties of cheese. A few doors down is **Usingers** (1030 North Old World Third Street; 800-558-9998; usinger.com), sausage makers since 1880. There are 70 varieties, including a lean summer sausage.

6 *Spreading Wings* 1:30 p.m.

The **Milwaukee Art Museum** (700 North Art Museum Drive; 414-224-3200; mam.org) may have opened in 1888, but the eye-catching Quadracci Pavilion, designed by Santiago Calatrava and opened in 2001, has become a symbol of modern Milwaukee. With its movable wings expanded to their full, 217-foot span, the building looks either like a large white bird landing on Lake Michigan or the tail of a white whale emerging from the water. There's art, too: extensive collections of folk, central European and Germanic, and post-1960 contemporary.

7 *Find Your Title* 4 p.m.

The first floor of the **Renaissance Book Shop** (834 North Plankinton Avenue; 414-271-6850), in a century-old former furniture store, looks like a book collector's attic, with boxes of used books lining the floor. But it's more organized than it looks, with about half a million books parceled among dozens of categories (Animal Husbandry, Theater Practices and Problems) spread across three floors and a basement. When you're finished shopping, move on

to the west side of the Wells Street Bridge for a look at the Bronzie Fonzie, a life-size statue of the Fonz, the iconic television character from *Happy Days*. It's a favorite spot for a photograph, so smile and remember: two thumbs up for the camera.

8 *Popover Delight* 7 p.m.

If you need to give your arteries a rest, try some lighter fare at **Coast** (931 East Wisconsin Avenue; 414-727-5555; coastrestaurant.com; $$$), an elegant fish and seafood restaurant. Look for baked local walleye served on a cedar plank with roasted red potatoes and haricots verts. The warm popovers are to die for. If you are ready to throw your cholesterol numbers to the wind, try a dessert, perhaps the Praline Pyramid: layers of pecans, meringue wafers, Grand Marnier butter cream, and chocolate ganache glaze.

9 *Blues in the Night* 9:30 p.m.

East Brady Street, which stretches for about eight blocks from Lake Michigan to the Milwaukee River, was a hippie hangout in the 1960s. Today, its well-preserved buildings and 19th-century Victorian homes are a backdrop to one of the city's liveliest neighborhoods. During the day, boutiques and small stores draw shoppers. At night, restaurants and bars keep the street lively. A good spot for music is the **Up and Under Pub** (1216 East Brady Street; 414-276-2677; theupandunderpub.com), which proclaims itself the

ABOVE Lake Michigan and the Milwaukee skyline.

BELOW Lakefront Brewery, a modern heir of Milwaukee's beermaking tradition.

blues capital of Milwaukee. With high ceilings, an antique bar and a couple of dozen beers on tap, it offers live blues, rock, and reggae until 2 a.m. There's usually a $5 cover. If you'd rather avoid alcohol, **Rochambo Coffee and Tea House** down the street (1317 East Brady Street; 414-291-0095; rochambo.com) offers dozens of teas and stays open until midnight.

SUNDAY

10 *Lakeside Brunch* 10 a.m.

The Knick (1030 East Juneau Avenue; 414-272-0011; theknickrestaurant.com; $$) is busy and breezy on Sunday mornings, with an outdoor patio near Lake Michigan overlooking Veterans Park. For a memorable breakfast, try the crab hash, a mixture of crabmeat,

onions, and hash browns topped with two eggs, or the banana pecan pancakes, dripping with whiskey butter and served with maple syrup.

11 *Wisconsin Tropics* 1 p.m.

Rain or shine, the **Mitchell Park Horticultural Conservatory** (524 South Layton Boulevard; 414-649-9830; countyparks.com) offers perennial respite. Affectionately known as the Domes, the conservatory is housed in three 85-foot-high, beehive-shaped buildings with different climates: the Floral Dome has more than 150 floral displays; the Arid Dome mimics the desert, with an oasis-like pool surrounded by cactuses; and the Tropical Dome has 1,200 rain-forest plants, tropical birds flying overhead and a 30-foot waterfall.

MIDWEST

THE BASICS

Fly to the Milwaukee airport and rent a car or drive two hours north from Chicago.

Pfister Hotel
424 East Wisconsin Avenue
800-472-4403
thepfisterhotel.com
$$$
A throwback to Victorian elegance within walking distance of the waterfront.

Iron Horse Hotel
500 West Florida Street
888-543-4766
theironhorsehotel.com
$$$-$$$$
Recent transformation of a 100-year-old warehouse.

Hotel Metro
411 East Mason Street
414-272-1937
hotelmetro.com
$$$
Serenely chic boutique hotel.

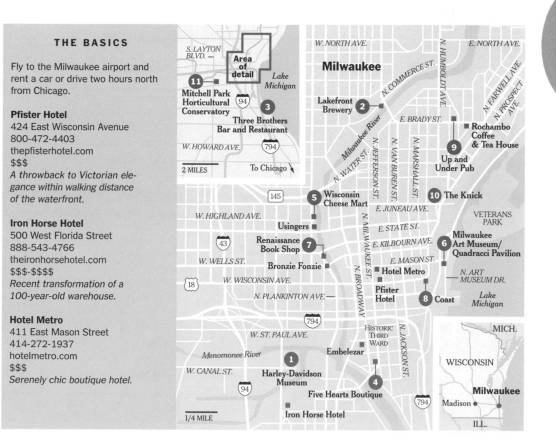

PARK CITY

Salt lake City

MOAB

TELLURIDE

the Grand Canyon

SEDONA

SCOTTSDALE

phoenix

tucson

VAIL

Denver ●

THE SOUTH WEST

Aspen

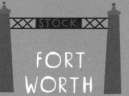

Leadville

Oklahoma City ●

Santa Fe

STOCK

FORT WORTH ● ●

Dallas

SAN ANTONIO

AUSTIN

Houston

Phoenix

With one of the fastest growth rates in the United States, Phoenix, Arizona, seemed to come out of nowhere to rank in the first years of the 21st century as the nation's fifth-largest city. Although the go-go trend came to a crashing halt when the housing bubble collapsed in 2008 and 2009, the city hasn't lost its appeal. The southern Arizona heat makes it an inferno in the summer, but the other nine months of the year are gorgeous and sunny. That means that three-fourths of the time, Phoenix, with its resorts, restaurants, contemporary shops, Southwest culture, and desert and mountain landscape, is perfect for exploring.
— BY RANDAL C. ARCHIBOLD AND AMY SILVERMAN

FRIDAY

1 *One Man's Castle* 3 p.m.

All sorts of people, some of them rich and famous, once flocked to Phoenix for health reasons, at least before smog became a big problem. But perhaps none was stranger than Boyce Luther Gulley, an architect from Seattle, who arrived in 1930 to recover from tuberculosis and, while he was at it, built a "castle" largely from found objects. The **Mystery Castle** (800 East Mineral Road; 602-268-1581), a trippy monument to Gulley's imagination, is adorned with all sorts of stuff, including tree branches for chairs, crooked windows, and Indian artifacts.

2 *Tacos and Mariachi* 6 p.m.

The border is just three hours away by car and more than a third of the city's residents are Latino, so Mexican food rules. Phoenicians argue over the best restaurants, but it is hard to top **Garcia's Las Avenidas** (2212 North 35th Avenue; 602-272-5584; garciasmexicanfood.com; $), a family-run restaurant known for its traditional menu and cavernous setting. A mariachi band often drifts from table to table, belting out ballads. No, the menu is not daring, but the plates come heaping with home-style favorites like tacos and enchiladas that won't damage the wallet. The juicy carnitas de puerco are worth a try.

OPPOSITE Saguaros at the Desert Botanical Garden.

RIGHT Phoenix sprawls out below a lookout point at South Mountain Park.

3 *Hollywood in Phoenix* 9 p.m.

The juggernaut of downtown construction in the frenetic days of the real estate boom—projects included a convention center expansion, a hotel, and condominiums—spared a few jewels, including the historic **Hotel San Carlos** (202 North Central Avenue; 602-253-4121; hotelsancarlos.com). Hollywood stars like Mae West and Marilyn Monroe stayed in this 1928 Italian Renaissance-style landmark, which still exudes an air of European refinement. Have a drink in the **Ghost Lounge**. The name is a reference to apparitions said to haunt the hotel, but it also feels right as homage to the bygone era that the place recalls.

SATURDAY

4 *Up Close at Camelback* 8 a.m.

Camelback Mountain sits in the middle of metropolitan Phoenix, and the Echo Canyon Trail in the **Echo Canyon Recreation Area** (phoenix.gov/recreation/rec/parks/preserves/index.html) is its most renowned hike. Locals call it the Scenic Stairmaster, and they'll warn you that this is no dawdle—the hike is 1.2 miles, and about 1,200 feet up, one way. On a clear day, you can see the Salt River Pima-Maricopa Indian Community to the east and Piestewa Peak (formerly known as Squaw Peak) to the west. You might also see cottontail rabbits, rattlesnakes, coyotes—and unfortunate hikers who didn't bring enough water (prepare yourself with a large bottle). For more child-friendly hiking, try some of the many miles of trails at **South Mountain Park** (phoenixasap.com/south-mountain-park.html), which

at 16,000 acres is sometimes called the world's largest municipal park.

5 *Hiker's Reward* 11 a.m.

Gaze up at the mountain you just conquered from a patio table at **La Grande Orange Grocery** (4410 North 40th Street; 602-840-7777; lagrandeorangegrocery.com; $). You'll fit in at this little fine-foods market and cafe whether you've showered post-hike or not. Look on the menu for the Jersey Girl Omelet made with pastrami

ABOVE Seclusion at the Royal Palms Resort.

BELOW Camelback Mountain rises up beyond the cactus at the Desert Botanical Garden.

and roasted potatoes. Or go vegetarian—there are plenty of good choices.

6 *Hiker's Rejuvenation* Noon

Step into the lobby of the **Arizona Biltmore Resort & Spa** (2400 East Missouri Avenue; 800-950-0086; arizonabiltmore.com) to appreciate the Frank Lloyd Wright-inspired architecture fully. Even on the hottest day, you'll instantly feel cooled by the structure of Biltmore Block, precast concrete blocks that make up the high-ceilinged main building. The Biltmore welcomes nonguests at its spa, so wrap yourself in a thick terry robe and head to a treatment room. (Reservations recommended.) Shopaholics may want to stick around afterward to seek out **Biltmore Fashion Park** (2502 East Camelback Road; 602-955-8400; shopbiltmore.com), a largely open-air mall stocked with high-end stores.

7 *Art Spaces* 2 p.m.

A cluster of galleries, boutiques, and restaurants in rehabilitated bungalows and old commercial buildings along once-forlorn Roosevelt Street have led to the area's christening as **CenPho**, the central Phoenix art district. Examine the local and regional contemporary art at **Modified Arts** (407 East Roosevelt Street; 602-462-5516; modifiedarts.org) and adventurous pieces at **eye lounge** (419 East Roosevelt Street; 602-430-1490; eyelounge.com).

Take a look at **monOrchid** (214 East Roosevelt Street; 602-253-0339; monorchid.com), which does double duty as an art space and a wedding venue. And walk around the corner to the front of **MADE Art Boutique** (922 North Fifth Street; 602-256-6233; madephx.com), which carries books, ceramics, craft items, and jewelry.

8 *The Original Residents* 3:30 p.m.

American Indian culture runs deep here, with several active tribes and reservations in the region. Just about all of them have contributed displays or materials to the **Heard Museum** (2301 North Central Avenue; 602-252-8848; heard.org), renowned for its collection of Native American art. The museum shop is also a great place to buy gifts.

9 *Eat the Unexpected* 7 p.m.

Phoenicians love a good meal as much as the next city slicker, and many flock to **Binkley's** (6920 East Cave Creek Road, Cave Creek; 480-437-1072;

binkleysrestaurant.com; $$$), where topflight contemporary American cuisine with a slight French influence can be enjoyed in golf shirt and shorts. Allow extra time to get there: it is 35 miles north of downtown Phoenix and traffic can be unforgiving. The mini-mall location may seem uninviting, but the chef, Kevin Binkley, is full of surprises. Examples: lobster bisque made with tangerines; black sea bream with daikon, pak choi, grapes, Fresno chile, and cilantro.

ABOVE The Mystery Castle, built by an eccentric architect using rocks, tree branches, and whatever was handy.

BELOW The pool at the Arizona Biltmore Resort.

and the servers wear "Alice eyes" makeup. Need we say more?

10 *Remember Alice?* 10 p.m.

For a drink and a few helpings of eccentricity, drop in at **Alice Cooperstown** (101 East Jackson Street; 602-253-7337; alicecooperstown.com), named after the shock rocker and Phoenix resident Alice Cooper. You may find a live band or a boxing match,

ABOVE Alice Cooperstown, named for a favorite son.

OPPOSITE The Hotel San Carlos, built in 1928.

11 *Urban Desert* 10 a.m.

Driving through central Phoenix, you're more likely to see imported pine trees than saguaros, the giant native cactuses. The **Desert Botanical Garden** (1201 North Galvin Parkway; 480-941-1225; dbg.org) is the perfect place to get your dose of desert life without ever leaving a brick pathway. Spread across 50 acres in Papago Park, the garden is an oasis of towering cacti, aromatic flowers, and surprisingly verdant plants in the middle of the urban grid.

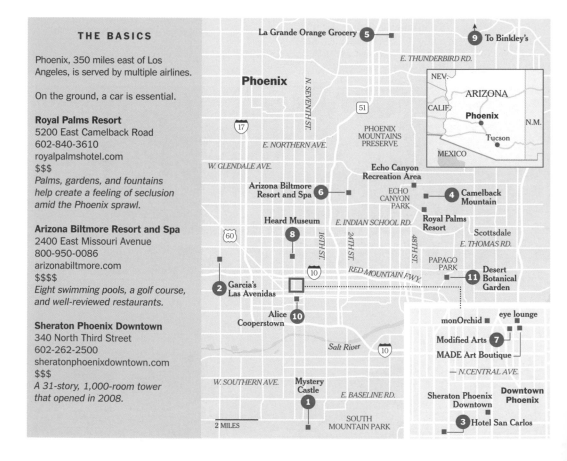

THE BASICS

Phoenix, 350 miles east of Los Angeles, is served by multiple airlines.

On the ground, a car is essential.

Royal Palms Resort
5200 East Camelback Road
602-840-3610
royalpalmshotel.com
$$$
Palms, gardens, and fountains help create a feeling of seclusion amid the Phoenix sprawl.

Arizona Biltmore Resort and Spa
2400 East Missouri Avenue
800-950-0086
arizonabiltmore.com
$$$$
Eight swimming pools, a golf course, and well-reviewed restaurants.

Sheraton Phoenix Downtown
340 North Third Street
602-262-2500
sheratonphoenixdowntown.com
$$$
A 31-story, 1,000-room tower that opened in 2008.

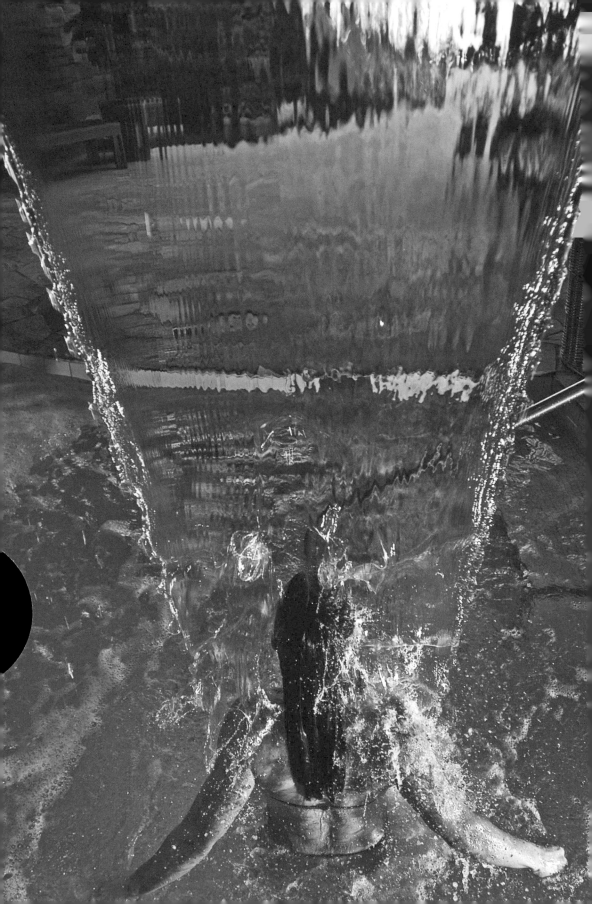

Scottsdale

It might be tempting a curse from the golf gods to enter the Scottsdale city limits without a set of clubs. But it's easy to spend a full weekend here far from the fairways. Just east of Phoenix, Scottsdale was once home to the Hohokam Indians; the town was founded in the 1880s by Winfield Scott, an Army chaplain who bought land to farm sweet potatoes. Today, Scottsdale is associated less with farming than with Frank Lloyd Wright, massage therapists, affluent second-home owners, and posh resorts. Wright's influence can be seen in much of the city's architecture as well as in his own Arizona headquarters, Taliesin West. Golf, if you wish. Or eat, explore, and then float in an infinity pool, contemplating your next cocktail.
— BY JENNIFER STEINHAUER

FRIDAY

1 *Enchilada Central* 7:30 p.m.

Much of Scottsdale may look as if it sprang up yesterday, but there are a few vestiges here and there of an earlier era. **Los Olivos** (7328 East Second Street; 480-946-2256; losolivosrestaurant.com; $), one of the oldest restaurants in the original area known now as Old Town, is still family run and has a personality all its own; the building itself looks like a piece of folk art, with a sculpture of a Mayan head rising from the roof. Inside, there's a lively central dining and bar area and a Blue Room that risks aquamarine overload. The food is solid Tex-Mex.

2 *Exotic Vintages* 10 p.m.

Kazimierz World Wine Bar (7137 East Stetson Drive; 480-946-3004; kazbar.net), known as the Kaz Bar, has all the trappings of hipness — no sign over the door (which is in the back), sofas, and a crowd of varying ages and sexual orientations. There are wines from dozens of nations available — yes, this is the place to find that elusive Thracian Valley merlot from Bulgaria. Expect live music or a D.J., too. Cavelike and dimly lit, Kaz Bar makes for good people watching.

OPPOSITE Spa splashing at the Fairmont Princess.

RIGHT The Old Town Farmers' Market, where local growers show off what a watered desert can provide.

SATURDAY

3 *A Plan over Pancakes* 9 a.m.

The coffee is strong and the banana buttermilk pancakes are yummy at **Cafe ZuZu** in the Hotel Valley Ho (6850 East Main Street; 480-248-2000; hotelvalleyho.com; $). Sit in the supermodern chairs or comfy booths and plot potential misadventures.

4 *Desert Produce* 10 a.m.

For a sense of how irrigation can make a desert bloom, mingle with the locals shopping at the **Old Town Farmers Market** (Brown Avenue and 1st Street; arizonafarmersmarkets.com). Along with the Arizona oranges and vegetables, expect a variety of other artisan and homemade products vying for your attention: apricot walnut bread, vegan desserts, barbecue sauce, bee pollen, cherry pepper relish, organic cider, tamales, hot doughnuts, and more.

5 *A Bit of the Old West* 11 a.m.

Stay in Old Town (roughly Second Street to Fourth Street, north to south; Scottsdale Road to Drinkwater Boulevard, west to east) for a stroll and a little browsing. There are scores of galleries displaying everything from works of the masters to American Indian jewelry to large contemporary paintings by local artists. You'll also find questionable Western-themed statuary, store names with puns (Coyo-T's), and the obligatory wind chimes and

dried chili peppers lilting and listing in the breeze. Check out **Mexican Imports** (3933 North Brown Avenue; 480-945-6476) for all the South of the Border kitsch you've always wanted. Of interest nearby is **Guidon Books** (7117 East Main Street; 480-945-8811; guidon.com), which specializes in out-of-print Western Americana and Civil War volumes.

6 *Then a Taste of the East* 1 p.m.

While you are in the neighborhood, do as the local residents do and hit **Malee's Thai Bistro** (7131 East Main Street; 480-947-6042; maleesthaibistro.com; $), a softly lighted room that muffles the sun-drenched action outside. The best bets are the tofu spinach pot stickers, Evil Jungle Princess (a pile of chicken doused in coconut cream with mushrooms and fresh mint), and the reliable pad Thai.

7 *There's Always the Rub* 3 p.m.

The ways to get pummeled, peeled, and rubbed in Scottsdale are endless, and there seems to be an almost Constitutional obligation to submit. From the shoulder rubs at the most commonplace hair salons to the aquatic watsu massage at the gorgeous **Sanctuary Camelback Mountain Resort & Spa** (5700 East McDonald Drive; 480-948-2100; sanctuaryoncamelback.com), there is something for every (reasonably generous) budget. Right in the middle is the **VH Spa for Vitality and Health** at the Hotel Valley Ho (hotelvalleyho.com), where the Back, Neck, Shoulders massage was heaven.

8 *Serenity, Inside and Out* 7 p.m.

Start dinner right at **Elements** (at the Sanctuary resort; elementsrestaurant.com; $$$) by angling for just the right seat on the patio at the Jade Bar, where you can watch the sunset while eavesdropping on first-daters as you munch on wasabi-covered peanuts. This moment is best paired with an Asian pear cucumber and ginger martini or a glass of sparkling rose. You will want to ask for a window booth inside the restaurant, where the chef cooks up seasonal fare as you take in Paradise Valley. The view is really the main course, but there have been some standout offerings on the changing menu, like grilled salmon, carrot and millet pot stickers, or a diabolical banana fluffernutter sundae. The Zen-like setting with stone and fireplaces is serene.

9 *Find the Party* 10 p.m.

Get a look at a Vegas-minded side of Scottsdale in one of the nightclubs near the W Scottsdale Hotel on East Camelback Road. **Axis-Radius** (7340 East

Indian Plaza; 480-970-1112; axis-radius.com) is a hot spot that draws young singles and aims to keep them dancing. The nearby **Pussycat Lounge** (4426 North Saddlebag Trail; 480-481-3100; pclaz.com), deals in density, packing partiers and their drinks into a small space. The **Suede Restaurant and Lounge** (7333 East Indian Plaza; 480-970-6969; suedeaz.com) seems to be aiming for a slightly more relaxing vibe.

SUNDAY

10 *The Architect's Place* 10:30 a.m.

Do not miss **Taliesin West**, the international headquarters for the Frank Lloyd Wright Foundation and the winter campus for the Frank Lloyd Wright

School of Architecture (12621 Frank Lloyd Wright Boulevard; 480-860-2700; franklloydwright.org). Troubled by poor health, Wright took up half-year residence in this 600-acre "camp" in 1937, and the complex was built by apprentices. Take the 90-minute tour, which takes you through the living quarters, working areas, and outdoor spaces that incorporate indigenous materials and organic forms. Then there's all that Asian art.

OPPOSITE ABOVE Taliesin West, built by Frank Lloyd Wright as a community of architects and apprentices.

OPPOSITE BELOW The rooftop pool at the Willow Stream Spa in the Fairmont Princess.

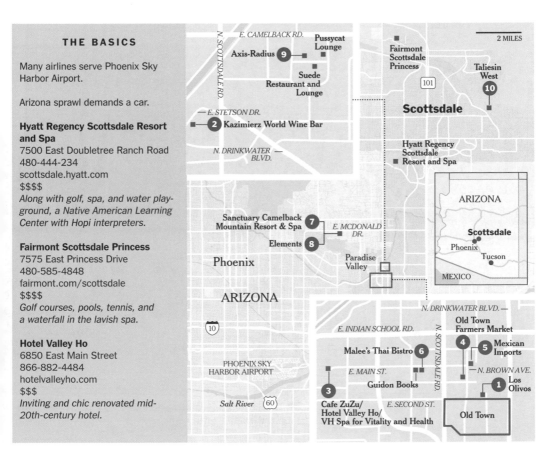

THE BASICS

Many airlines serve Phoenix Sky Harbor Airport.

Arizona sprawl demands a car.

Hyatt Regency Scottsdale Resort and Spa
7500 East Doubletree Ranch Road
480-444-234
scottsdale.hyatt.com
$$$$
Along with golf, spa, and water playground, a Native American Learning Center with Hopi interpreters.

Fairmont Scottsdale Princess
7575 East Princess Drive
480-585-4848
fairmont.com/scottsdale
$$$$
Golf courses, pools, tennis, and a waterfall in the lavish spa.

Hotel Valley Ho
6850 East Main Street
866-882-4484
hotelvalleyho.com
$$$
Inviting and chic renovated mid-20th-century hotel.

Tucson

Tucson, Arizona, has worked hard to shed its reputa-
tion as a tanning salon for retirees and snowbirds.
To complement its natural beauty — a national park
in its midst and mountains on four sides — the city
has poured hundreds of millions of dollars into its
downtown during the last decade. In lieu of adding
strip malls and high-rises, older buildings were saved
and retooled as movie houses and museums. And with
a deep-rooted Hispanic community, tides of Mexican
immigrants, and students from the University of
Arizona who never left after graduation, the city has
a youthful and multicultural glow.
— RICHARD B. WOODWARD

FRIDAY

1 *Jet Age Graveyard* 4 p.m.

Tucson's bone-dry climate is easy on all kinds
of metal bodies. The city is a hunting ground for
used-car buyers as well as home to one of the world's
largest airplane graveyards. A sample of the 4,000
or so stranded military and civilian aircraft can be
viewed by driving along the fence on Kolb Road by
the Davis-Monthan Air Force Base. For a closer look,
the **Pima Air & Space Museum** (6000 East Valencia
Road; 520-574-0462; pimaair.org) offers tours with
frighteningly knowledgeable guides who can run down
all the specs on the SR-71 "Blackbird" spy plane.

2 *Hear That Whistle Blow* 6 p.m.

The Southern Pacific railroad reached Tucson
in 1880, and the moaning whistle of freight and
passenger trains can still be heard day and night.
For a front-row seat to the passing leviathans, head
Maynard's Market and Kitchen (400 North Toole
Avenue; 520-545-0577; maynardsmarkettucson.com;
$$). Less than 50 feet from the tracks, this dark and
handsome former depot attracts an upscale crowd
that comes for the extensive choice of wines (from
the store next door) and the reasonably priced menu.
Meat eaters enjoy the 14-ounce dry-aged New York

strip, and vegetarians the roast garlic and wild
mushroom stone-baked pizza. But just as inviting are
the sights and sounds of the rattling plates and glasses.

3 *Tucson Nights* 8 p.m.

Tucson has a jumping band scene on weekends,
a sleepier one the other five days. On warm nights,
the noise of music pumps through the open doors of
restaurants and bars along Congress Street. The center
of the action is often the historic **Rialto Theater** (318
East Congress Street; 520-740-1000; rialtotheatre.com).
A nonprofit showcase vital to downtown's renewal, it
books major acts but has no stylistic agenda.

SATURDAY

4 *Roadrunner* 9 a.m.

When the summer sun isn't blazing, Tucsonians
head outdoors. A prime destination is the **Saguaro
National Park** (3693 South Old Spanish Trail;
520-733-5153; nps.gov/sagu), which embraces the city
on two sides. To walk among fields of multi-armed
cactus giants, drive west about a half-hour along a
snaking road. Look for an unmarked parking lot a
few hundred feet beyond the Arizona-Sonora Desert
Museum. This is the start of the **King Canyon Trail**
(saguaronationalpark.com/favorite-trails.html),
put in by the Civilian Conservation Corps in the
1930s and the path for a refreshing morning hike. A
covered picnic area is at mile 0.9. Fitter types can
proceed 2.6 miles to Wasson Peak, highest point in
the Tucson Mountains.

OPPOSITE Saguaro National Park, a favorite Tucson play-
ground when the summer sun isn't blazing.

RIGHT Terror remembered: a cold war artifact, the top of a
missile, at the Titan Missile Museum outside Tucson.

5 *Modern Mexican* Noon

Tucson thinks highly of its Mexican restaurants, and one place that it can justly be proud of is **Cafe Poca Cosa** (110 East Pennington Street; 520-622-6400; cafepocacosatucson.com; $$$). Don't be put off by its location (in an ugly office building) or the décor (a vain attempt to import some glam L.A. style). The place has attracted national attention for a novel take on Mexican cuisine, which emphasizes fresh and regional. Try the daily sampler (El Plato Poca Cosa) of three dishes chosen by the chef. Expect an exotic mole and perhaps a zinger like a vegetarian tamale with pineapple salsa. Dinner reservations are essential for weekends.

6 *Picture This* 1:30 p.m.

One of the most impressive collections of 20th-century North American photographs can be found at the **Center for Creative Photography** (1030 North Olive Road; 520-621-7970; creativephotography.org), in a hard-to-find building on the University of Arizona campus. Containing the archives of Ansel Adams, Edward Weston, Garry Winogrand, W. Eugene Smith, and more than 40 other eminent photographers, it also runs a first-rate exhibition program.

7 *The Buy and Buy* 3:30 p.m.

Phoenix-style shopping has arrived at **La Encantada**, a mall in the foothills of the Santa Catalinas, with Tiffany and Louis Vuitton (2905 East Skyline Drive, at Campbell Avenue.; 520-615-2561; laencantadashoppingcenter.com). North of downtown at the **Plaza Palomino** (2970 North Swan Road), local merchants carry more idiosyncratic items like funky handmade jewelry and crafts.

8 *Eyes on the Desert Sky* 5 p.m.

The surrounding mountains are heavenly for stargazing. The **Kitt Peak National Observatory** (Tohono O'odham Reservation; 520-318-8726; noao.edu), about 90 minutes southwest of the city and 6,900 feet above sea level, says it has more optical research telescopes

than anywhere in the world. Aside from serving professional astronomers, it also has generous offerings for amateurs. One of these, the Nightly Observing Program, begins an hour before sunset and lasts four hours. An expert will show you how to use star charts and identify constellations and will give you a peek through one of the mammoth instruments. (Dinner is a deli sandwich; remember to wear warm clothing.) Reserving a month in advance is recommended, but you may get lucky and find an opening the same day.

9 *More Cosmos* 11 p.m.

For a nightcap, head to the boisterous **Club Congress** (311 East Congress Street; 520-622-8848; hotelcongress.com/club), on the ground floor of the Hotel Congress with five bar areas that offer steeply discounted drinks after 10 p.m. Live bands often have crowds of dancers spilling out into the lobby of the hotel. Finish the night at **Plush** (340 East 6th Street; 520-798-1298; plushtucson.com), where the acts are less polished but the drinks are almost as cheap and just as strong.

SUNDAY

10 *Early Bird* 9 a.m.

The **Epic Cafe** (745 North Fourth Avenue; 520-624-6844; epic-cafe.com; $) is a happening spot

ABOVE The control room at the Titan Missile Museum.

BELOW The Kitt Peak National Observatory. For nighttime stargazing, reserve well in advance.

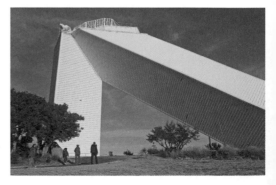

at almost any hour. This neighborhood hub on the corner of University Boulevard is open from 6 a.m. to midnight and serves an eclectic menu of sandwiches, sweets, and drinks to a clientele of laptop-toting would-be intellectuals and dog owners who jam the sidewalk tables. Grab a cup of the excellent coffee and a vegan seed cookie. If it tastes like delicious bird food, that's because it is.

11 *Missile America* 10 a.m.

For a terrifying yet educational reminder of the cold war, drive about 30 minutes south of downtown on Interstate 19 to the **Titan Missile Museum** (1580 West Duval Mine Road, Sahuarita; 520-625-7736; titanmissilemuseum.org). The nuclear silo housed

a single intercontinental ballistic missile equipped with a warhead 700 times more powerful than the Hiroshima bomb. The museum tour lasts an hour. Much of it is underground, behind eight-foot-thick blast walls, and it ends with a peek at the 103-foot weapon, with its warhead removed.

ABOVE At Maynard's Market and Kitchen, in a former depot, glasses rattle as trains go by less than 50 feet away.

THE BASICS

Fly to Tucson, or for often-cheaper rates, land in Phoenix and drive two hours.

A car is essential for touring.

Ritz-Carlton, Dove Mountain
15000 North Secret Springs Drive
520-572-3000
ritzcarlton.com/dovemountain
$$$$
New, with Jack Nicklaus golf course and luxurious spa.

Arizona Inn
2200 East Elm Street
520-325-1541
arizonainn.com
$$$
The granddaddy of Tucson luxury hotels and still family-owned.

Best Western Royal Sun Inn & Suites
1015 North Stone Avenue
520-622-8871
bwroyalsun.com
$$
A good choice for budget travelers.

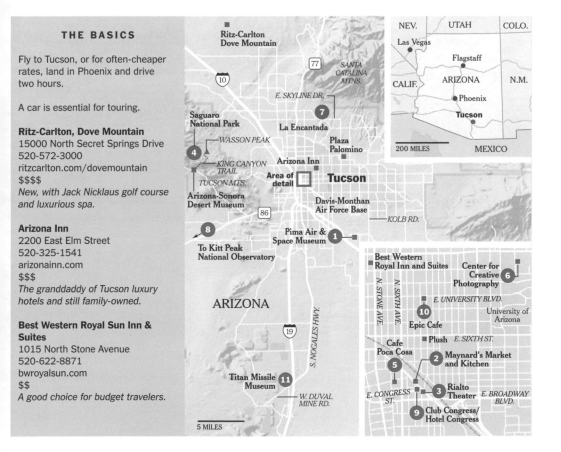

Sedona

Ask five people to sum up Sedona, Arizona, and you'll probably get five wildly different responses. Art lovers exclaim over the galleries specializing in Southwestern tableaus. Shopaholics rave about boutiques selling Western duds and American Indian jewelry. Pessimists rue the rash of T-shirt shops, while enlightenment-seekers wax spiritual about the "vortexes." And outdoor enthusiasts rhapsodize about hiking among red rock spires and ancient Indian ruins. All of this is great news for visitors, who can sample it all in a quirky city that some call the most beautiful place in the United States.
— BY KERIDWEN CORNELIUS

FRIDAY

1 *Red Rock Rover* 4 p.m.

Sedona's cinematic red rocks have been zipping across your windshield like scenes from a Hollywood western as you've driven toward town. Now it's your turn to ride off into the sunset. Turn up Airport Road to Airport Saddleback — you want the tiny parking lot on the left, not the chockablock Airport Vista farther up the road. Slip on hiking boots and hit the **Airport Loop Trail** for close encounters with the towering crimson sandstones: Bell Rock, Courthouse Butte, Coffee Pot Rock, and the Cockscombe. It's a 90-minute ramble, but if your energy flags, just turn back and scramble up Overlook Point, a good spot to watch paprika-red sunsets.

2 *Shopping for Dinner* 7 p.m.

It's hard to find authentic Southwestern food in Sedona, but there are good restaurants. One is **René at Tlaquepaque** (336 State Route 179; 928-282-9255; rene-sedona.com; $$$), where the dishes are mainstream — filet mignon, rack of lamb, duck with wild rice — but the quality is reliable. It's in the **Tlaquepaque Arts & Crafts Village** (tlaq.com), a Spanish-colonial-style shopping arcade with fountains and muscular sycamores. The shops and galleries are worth a look. Peek in the window of Kuivato Glass Gallery, which sells glass sculptures and jewelry.

3 *Wine by the Fire* 9:30 p.m.

Sedona isn't known for its night life. Most bars, in fact, shut down at 10 p.m. For a little art to go with your nightcap, swing by **Hundred Rox** inside the **Amara Resort and Spa** (310 North Highway 89A; 928-340-8900; amararesort.com). Sample a cocktail or a boutique shiraz from a 200-strong wine list as you examine a collection of paintings and sculptures culled from local galleries. The outdoor fire pit is just as picturesque.

SATURDAY

4 *Break an Egg* 9 a.m.

Kick-start your day in classic Sedona fashion with breakfast at the **Coffee Pot Restaurant** (2050 West Highway 89A; 928-282-6626; coffeepotsedona.com; $), which serves 101 "famous" omelets. Locals and tourists pack this kitschy joint, so you may have to browse the gift shop for jewelry and coffee mugs while waiting for a table. But once you're seated, the friendly waitresses are swift and might even leave the coffeepot on your table for convenient refills. Overwhelmed by the omelet choices? Try the hearty huevos rancheros, smothered in green chili. If you have kids, dare them to order the peanut butter, jelly, and banana omelet.

OPPOSITE The red sandstone rocks of Sedona.

BELOW The Chapel of the Holy Cross sits atop one of Sedona's famous vortexes, revered as sites of psychic energy.

5 *Sunsets, Pottery, and Frames* 10 a.m.

Galleries dot the city. The biggest of them is **Exposures International** (561 State Route 179; 928-282-1125; exposuresfineart.com), a sprawling space overflowing with paintings, sculpture, jewelry, and more. Check out Bill Worrell's prehistoric-art-inspired sculptures. Other interesting galleries can be found at **Hozho Center**, including **Lanning Gallery** (431 State Route 179; 928-282-6865; lanninggallery.com), which specializes in contemporary art. To learn more about the local art scene, visit the **Sedona Arts Center** (15 Art Barn Road; 928-282-3865; sedonaartscenter.com), a nonprofit gallery that holds exhibits and poetry readings.

ABOVE Rust-colored cliffs, shaded by oxidation of their iron-laced stone, tower above Enchantment Resort.

BELOW Earth Wisdom tours explore local history, geology, American Indian culture, and vortexes.

OPPOSITE Oak Creek, the gentle stream running through the valley that cradles Sedona.

6 *A Creek Runs Through It* 1 p.m.

Sedona is cradled in a fragrant riparian valley through which Oak Creek gently runs. Weather permitting, dine creekside at **L'Auberge de Sedona** (301 L'Auberge Lane; 928-282-1667; lauberge.com; $$$), a contemporary American restaurant with a stone patio perched at the water's edge. Indulge in grilled salmon or a tenderloin salad. Cottonwoods rustle, the creek burbles, and ducks waddle between the linen-draped tables.

7 *Spirited Away* 2:30 p.m.

You can't get far in Sedona without hearing about the vortexes, places where the earth supposedly radiates psychic energy. Believers claim that they induce everything from heightened energy to tear-inducing spiritual enlightenment. Whether you're a skeptic or believer, a guided tour of the vortexes by **Earth Wisdom Jeep Tours** (293 North Highway 89A; 928-282-4714; earthwisdomjeeptours.com) is definitely scenic. If vortexes aren't your thing, go

anyway. This tour also explores the area's history, geology, and American Indian culture, and there are other tours to choose from. You'll learn how the rocks became rust-colored: add a dash of iron, let it oxidize for several million years and voilà!

8 *Cactus on the Rocks* 6 p.m.

A prickly pear margarita — made from a local cactus — is the must-drink cocktail in Sedona, and one of the best spots to try it is the terrace at **Tii Gavo** at **Enchantment Resort** (525 Boynton Canyon Road; 928-282-2900; enchantmentresort.com). Tii Gavo means gathering place in the Havasupai Indian language, and in this restaurant well-heeled spa-lovers rub elbows with hikers fresh off the trail. Afterward, move inside to the **Yavapai Dining Room** (928-204-6000; $$$; reservations required for nonguests). The restaurant, with its American Indian pottery and views of Boynton Canyon, is no stranger to Sedona's celebrity visitors. The wine

list is extensive and far-ranging, but consider one of the local Echo Canyon reds.

9 *A Galaxy Far, Far Away* 9:30 p.m.

Thanks to strict ordinances on light pollution, the dark skies over Sedona are ideal for stargazing (or U.F.O. spotting). Take a cosmic journey with **Evening Sky Tours** (866-701-0398; eveningskytours.com). You'll be led by an astronomer who can point out those elusive constellations as well as an eyeful of spiral galaxies and the rings of Saturn.

SUNDAY

10 *Rock Your World* 6 a.m.

Soar over Sedona valley in a hot air balloon at sunrise for jaw-dropping views of rose-tinted buttes. **Northern Light Balloon Expeditions** (928-282-2274; northernlightballoon.com) offers three- to four-hour trips that include a Champagne breakfast picnic in a

remote spot (about $200). If you prefer to stay earthbound, pack your own picnic and set out on the 3.6-mile **Broken Arrow Trail**. Buy a Red Rock Day Pass for $5; it allows entry to a number of natural areas and is available at most hotels and convenience stores. Hike along red rocks stained with desert varnish, weave through cypress forests, and climb up a doughlike outcropping for commanding views of Casner Canyon.

11 *Morning Spiritual* 10 a.m.

Peek inside the **Chapel of the Holy Cross** (780 Chapel Road; 928-282-4069; chapeloftheholycross.com),

a modernist icon that looks like a concrete spaceship jutting out of the craggy boulders. Designed in 1932 by Marguerite Brunswig Staude (but not built until 1956), the chapel is sandwiched between soaring concrete walls that bookend a gigantic glass window with a 90-foot-tall cross. Prayer services are held on Monday evenings, so don't worry about interrupting when you make your visit this morning. The chapel affords spectacular photo ops and another chance to have a psychic moment. The chapel sits on — you guessed it — a vortex.

ABOVE Inside Tlaquepaque Arts & Crafts Village, a Spanish-colonial style shopping arcade.

OPPOSITE Poolside relaxing at Mii Amo Spa is part of the outdoor desert ambience at the Enchantment Resort.

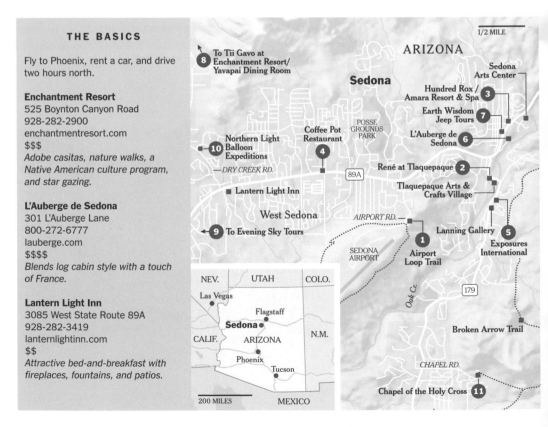

THE BASICS

Fly to Phoenix, rent a car, and drive two hours north.

Enchantment Resort
525 Boynton Canyon Road
928-282-2900
enchantmentresort.com
$$$
Adobe casitas, nature walks, a Native American culture program, and star gazing.

L'Auberge de Sedona
301 L'Auberge Lane
800-272-6777
lauberge.com
$$$$
Blends log cabin style with a touch of France.

Lantern Light Inn
3085 West State Route 89A
928-282-3419
lanternlightinn.com
$$
Attractive bed-and-breakfast with fireplaces, fountains, and patios.

1/2 MILE

To Tii Gavo at Enchantment Resort/ Yavapai Dining Room **8**

ARIZONA

Sedona

Sedona

Sedona Arts Center

Hundred Rox / Amara Resort & Spa **3**

Earth Wisdom Jeep Tours **7**

Coffee Pot Restaurant

POSSE GROUNDS PARK

L'Auberge de Sedona **6**

Northern Light Balloon Expeditions **10**

—DRY CREEK RD.

4

89A

René at Tlaquepaque **2**

Tlaquepaque Arts & Crafts Village

Lantern Light Inn

West Sedona

AIRPORT RD.—

Lanning Gallery **5**

To Evening Sky Tours **9**

SEDONA AIRPORT

Airport Loop Trail **1**

Exposures International

NEV. UTAH COLO.

Las Vegas

Flagstaff

Sedona

CALIF. ARIZONA N.M.

Phoenix
Tucson

Oak Cr.

179

Broken Arrow Trail

CHAPEL RD.

Chapel of the Holy Cross **11**

200 MILES MEXICO

The Grand Canyon

More than a mile deep at its most majestic, the Grand Canyon can still drop the most jaded of jaws. The sun sparkling across the exposed rock, the delicate curl of the Colorado River, the birds chirping in the pinyon pines — and then a bus grinds past you on a hunt for the best postcards in the park. Yes, the Grand Canyon is big in every way, including the category of tourist trap. Over four million people visit this remote corner of Arizona each year, and the experience can be a bit death-by-gift-shop if you don't plan ahead — a necessity even if crowds and kitsch are your thing. During peak season, May through September, hotel rooms sell out months in advance, ditto for those mule rides, and certain rafting trips can be a year-long wait or more. Ah, wilderness!
— BY BROOKS BARNES

FRIDAY

1 *The Main Event* 5 p.m.

Save the best for last? Not on this trip. After driving the 81 miles from Flagstaff, Arizona, the destination where most air travelers land, head to **El Tovar Hotel** (Grand Canyon Village; 928-638-2631, extension 6380; grandcanyonlodges.com) The historic lodge, purposely built at such an angle that guests must leave their rooms to see more than a glimpse of the splendor, features one of the easiest access points to the canyon rim. Stretch your legs with a walk along the eastern portion of the 13-mile **Rim Trail**, which may leave you out of breath at 7,000 feet above sea level. Resist the temptation to go off the trail; park officials say about one person a year falls and dies and others are injured.

2 *Eat Hearty, Folks* 7:30 p.m.

El Tovar may look familiar — the exterior of the hotel had a cameo in *Vacation*, the 1983 road-trip movie. Clark Griswold, a k a, Chevy Chase, pulls up in his pea-green station wagon and robs the front desk. He should have at least eaten dinner first. The restaurant at El Tovar (928-638-2631, extension 6432; $$$) is by far the best in the area. As twin fireplaces blaze, relax with an Arizona Sunrise (orange juice, tequila, and grenadine) and take in the wall-mounted Hopi and Navajo weavings. For dinner, start with a house salad with pinyon vinaigrette and then choose between the venison rib chops and beef tenderloin with wild shrimp for the main course.

3 *Star Struck* 10 p.m.

If dinner got a bit pricey, take comfort in a free show afterward. Because there is so little pollution here — the nearest cities, Phoenix and Las Vegas, are both 200 miles or more away — the night sky is crowded with stars. Pick up one of the free constellation-finder brochures in the lobby of El Tovar and gaze away. Bonus points for anybody who can spot the Lesser Watersnake.

SATURDAY

4 *Sunrise Sonata* 5 a.m.

The canyon's multiple layers of exposed rock are glorious in the morning light; download the soundtrack to *2001: A Space Odyssey* as a dawn complement — the combination heightens the experience even further. Take a morning run or walk along the Rim Trail heading west, and keep your

OPPOSITE A lookout point along the Rim Trail at Grand Canyon National Park.

RIGHT The lobby at Bright Angel Lodge, one of the places to stay in the park.

eyes peeled for woodpeckers making their morning rounds. Don't bother trying to make it to Hermit's Rest, a 1914 stone building named for a 19th-century French-Canadian prospector who had a roughly built homestead in the area. These days, it's—you guessed it—a gift shop and snack bar.

5 *Hop On* 10 a.m.

Those famous mules? Buy the postcard. The animals smell, walk narrow ledges carved into the canyon wall, and come with a daunting list of rules. (Reads one brochure: "Each rider must not weigh more than 200 pounds, fully dressed, and, yes, we do weigh everyone!") Join the modern age and tour the canyon aboard an Eco-Star helicopter, an energy-efficient model built with more viewing windows. There are several tour companies that offer flights, but **Maverick Helicopters** (Grand Canyon National Airport on Highway 64; 928-638-2622; maverickhelicopter.com/canyon.php) has a new fleet and friendly service. The tours are personal—seven passengers maximum —and are priced according to the length of the trip, with the longest being about 45 minutes at $235 per person. Ask the pilot to point out the Tower of Ra, a soaring butte named for the Egyptian sun god.

6 *Pack a Picnic* Noon

The nearest town and the location of the heliport, Tusayan, Arizona, is a disappointing collection of fast-food restaurants, motels, and souvenir shops. Get out of Dodge and pick up lunch at the deli counter tucked inside the general store at **Market Plaza** (located a mile or two inside the park gates; 928-638-2262). It's nothing fancy—pastrami sandwiches and the like—but it will at least save you from an order of junk food.

7 *Desert View* 1 p.m.

Hitting this tourist hotspot at midday will keep you clear of the throngs that assemble for sunrise and sunset. The view is still stupendous. From the historic **Desert View Watchtower** (26 miles past Market Plaza on Highway 64 East; scienceviews.com/parks/watchtower.html), constructed in 1932, you can see the Painted Desert, a broad area of badlands where wind and rain have exposed stratified layers of minerals, which glow in hues of violet, red, and gold. Park rangers give daily talks about the area's cultural history.

8 *Play Archaeologist* 3 p.m.

Outdoorsy types will want to do another hike —more power to them. For those who have had enough of the canyon for one day, another of this area's cultural treasures still waits to be explored. About 800 years ago, **Wupatki Pueblo** (about 34 miles north of Flagstaff on Highway 89; 928-679-2365; nps.gov/wupa) was a flourishing home base for the

Sinagua, Kayenta Anasazi, and Cohonina peoples. The remnants of 100 rooms remain, including a space that archaeologists identified as a ball court, similar to those found in pre-Columbian cultures.

9 *Who Screams?* 5:30 p.m.

If heights aren't your thing, relax: You've made it through the hard part of the Grand Canyon. Regroup after the drive back to civilization (or what passes for it here) with ice cream cones on the patio at **Bright Angel Lodge** (about two blocks west of El Tovar; 928-638-2631; grandcanyonlodges.com), which features an old-fashioned soda fountain. It no longer carries Grand Canyon Crunch — the coffee ice cream with caramel swirls and chocolate chip chunks was too expensive to manufacture in limited quantities — but try a strawberry shake. Inside the rustic motel is a newsstand, one of the few in the park.

10 *Dinner and a Dance* 7 p.m.

Apart from the dining room at El Tovar, Grand Canyon food can be alarmingly bad. But walk inside the Bright Angel Lodge and give the **Arizona Room** ($$) a whirl. The dishes are a mouthful in name — chili-crusted, pan-seared wild salmon with fresh melon salsa and pinyon black bean rice pilaf, for example — if not exactly in quality. After dinner, hang out around the stone fireplace in the lobby. With any luck, you will catch one of the randomly presented Hopi dancing demonstrations.

OPPOSITE The Wukoki Pueblo at the Wupatki National Monument near Flagstaff.

BELOW The Desert View Watchtower, built in 1932 and modeled after ancient towers of the Puebloan peoples.

SUNDAY

11 *Wild Side* 10 a.m.

Kaibab National Forest, 1.6 million acres of ponderosa pine that surrounds the Grand Canyon, is a destination on its own for nature lovers and camping enthusiasts. After saying goodbye to the world's most famous hole in the ground, stop on the way back to Flagstaff to explore the **Kendrick Park Watchable Wildlife Trail** (Highway 180, about 20

miles north of Flagstaff; wildlifeviewingareas.com). Elk, badgers, western bluebirds, and red-tailed hawks are relatively easy to see, along with short-horned lizards and a variety of other forest creatures. The Grand Canyon area is also home to scorpions, tarantulas, rattlesnakes, and Gila monsters — but those are (mostly) confined to the canyon itself.

ABOVE A Navajo hoop dancer performing in costume at the canyon's South Rim.

OPPOSITE Mule trains take tourists bumping down into the canyon along the Bright Angel Trail. Other sightseeing options include helicopter rides and rigorous hikes.

THE BASICS

Numerous airlines fly to Flagstaff, Arizona. Rent a car at the airport.

El Tovar Hotel
Off Village Loop in Grand Canyon Village
888-297-2757
grandcanyonlodges.com/
el-tovar-409.html
$$
By far the most upscale lodging in the area, centrally located and recently renovated.

Bright Angel Lodge & Cabins
Near El Tovar
888-297-2757
grandcanyonlodges.com/
bright-angel-lodge-408.html
$$
A cabin-style motel built in the 1930s that is bare bones but surprisingly comfortable.

Red Feather Lodge
106 North Highway 64
866-561-2425
redfeatherlodge.com
$$
As good a motel as any of the many in the Tusayan area.

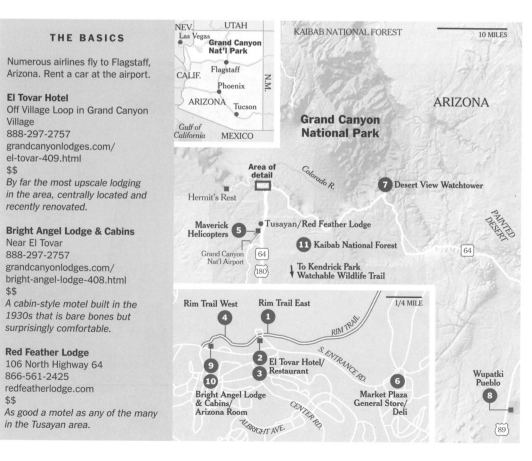

Salt Lake City

Sprawling and rapidly growing, Salt Lake City, Utah, is more complicated and cosmopolitan than most outsiders know. It's also more beautiful. Situated directly below the towering Wasatch Front, the city has a spectacular natural backdrop, beautiful 1900s neighborhoods, and one of the nation's most inviting college campuses at the University of Utah. Salt Lake City is still the headquarters of the Mormon church and the place to go to see Mormon monuments. But it also has hip restaurants, a budding film scene (a spillover effect from the Sundance Film Festival in nearby Park City), a fresh crop of art galleries and boutiques, and an open-door stance toward refugees and immigrants that has brought a variety of newcomers to town. There's also a new partying spirit in town since Utah liquor laws were normalized in 2009, allowing patrons to simply walk into a bar and order a drink.
— BY JAIME GROSS AND CHRIS DIXON

FRIDAY

1 *Creative Souvenirs* 4 p.m.

With its relatively affordable rents and do-it-yourself ethos, Salt Lake City is a bastion of creativity. To survey the design scene, stop by **Frosty Darling** (177 East Broadway; 801-532-4790; frostydarling.com), a whimsical gift shop stocked with retro candy and handmade clothing, accessories, and house wares by the owner, Gentry Blackburn, and other Utah designers. **Signed & Numbered** (2105 East 2100 South; 801-596-2093; signed-numbered.com) specializes in limited-edition, hand-pulled art prints and concert posters. And at **Salt Lake Citizen** (210 East 400 South; 801-363-3619), in the atrium of the Main Library building, you'll find street-inspired clothing and accessories from 40 city designers. One season's selection included embroidered jeans and jewelry made of laser-cut acrylic.

2 *Utah Farms* 7 p.m.

Chain restaurants used to dominate in Salt Lake City, but today intimate spots are popping up, run by young chefs inspired by the bounty of local organic farmers and artisanal purveyors. **Pago** (878 South 900 East; 801-532-0777; pagoslc.com; $$$), a bustling neighborhood joint housed in a squat 1910 brick building, spotlights local organic products in dishes

like steak with heirloom fingerling potatoes and local arugula. The rustic candle-lit dining room seats just 50. **Forage** (370 East 900 South; 801-708-7834; foragerestaurant.com; $$$), serves wildly creative dishes like vanilla-scented diver scallops paired with smoked beluga lentils.

3 *Open City* 9 p.m.

Raise a glass to celebrate the repeal of liquor laws that until 2009 required bars to operate as private clubs and collect membership fees. **The Red Door** (57 West 200 South; 801-363-6030; behindthereddoor.com) has dim lighting, a great martini list and kitschy revolution décor — yes, that's a Che Guevara mural on the wall. **Squatters Pub Brewery** (147 West Broadway; 801-363-2739; squatters.com) serves high-gravity beers from the award-winning brewmaster Jenny Talley, like the 6 percent alcohol India Pale Ale. And **Club Jam** (751 North 300 West; 801-891-1162; jamslc.com) is a friendly gay bar with a house party feel and impromptu barbecues on the back patio.

SATURDAY

4 *Botanical Bliss* 9 a.m.

The **Red Butte Garden**, nestled in the foothills above the University of Utah campus (300 Wakara

OPPOSITE The Salt Lake City Public Library, designed by Moshe Safdie.

BELOW Pago, one in a crop of new restaurants.

Way; 801-585-0556; redbuttegarden.org), has a rose garden, 3.5 miles of walking trails, and morning yoga in the fragrance garden. For a wake-up hike, ask the front desk for directions to the Living Room, a lookout point named for the flat orange rocks that resemble couches. Sit back and absorb the expansive views of the valley, mountains, and the Great Salt Lake.

5 *City Structure* 11 a.m.

Chart your own architecture tour. The city's **Main Library** (210 East 400 South; 801-524-8200; slcpl.lib.ut.us), a curving glass structure built in 2003 and designed by the architect Moshe Safdie, has fireplaces on every floor and a rooftop garden with views of the city and the Wasatch Mountains. For older buildings, wander the **Marmalade Historic District**, home to many original pioneer homes from the 19th century, or go on a walking tour with the **Utah Heritage Foundation** (801-533-0858; utahheritagefoundation.com).

6 *Diverse Palate* 1 p.m.

Salt Lake City has growing contingents of Latinos, Pacific Islanders (particularly Samoan and Tongan), and refugees from Tibet, Bosnia, and Somalia. One place to taste this kind of imported flavor is **Himalayan Kitchen** (360 South State Street; 801-328-2077; himalayankitchen.com; $$), a down-home dining room with turmeric-yellow walls and red tablecloth tables, where you might find Nepali goat curry or Himalayan momos, steamed chicken dumplings served with sesame seed sauce.

7 *Gimme Sugar* 3 p.m.

The **Sugarhouse District** is known for its one-of-a-kind shops and pedestrian-friendly mini-neighborhoods that are near the intersections of 900 East and 900 South (which locals call 9th and 9th), and 1500 East and 1500 South (15th and 15th). Highlights include the **Tea Grotto** (2030 South 900 East; 801-466-8255; teagrotto.com), a funky teahouse that specializes in fair-trade and loose-leaf teas, and

the charming **King's English Bookshop** (1511 South 1500 East; 801-484-9100; kingsenglish.com), a creaky old house filled with books and cozy reading nooks.

8 *Italian Hour* 7 p.m.

Salt Lake City has plenty of appealing Italian restaurants, but the most romantic may be **Fresco Italian Cafe** (1513 South 1500 East; 801-486-1300; frescoitaliancafe.com; $$), an intimate 14-table restaurant tucked off the main drag in a 1920s cottage. The menu is small but spot-on, with simple northern Italian dishes with a twist. The butternut squash ravioli, for example, was served with a splash of reduced apple cider and micro-planed hazelnuts. There's a roaring fire, candlelight, and, in the summer, dining on the brick patio.

9 *Live From Utah* 9 p.m.

As the only sizable city between Denver and Northern California, Salt Lake City gets many touring bands passing through. Hear established and up-and-coming acts at places like the **Urban Lounge** (241 South 500 East; 801-746-0557; theurbanloungeslc.com) and **Kilby Court** (741 South Kilby Court; 801-364-3538; kilbycourt.com). If you want to make your own sweet

ABOVE A light rail trolley system runs through downtown past Temple Square and Mormon monuments.

BELOW The University of Utah's Red Butte Garden and Arboretum has 3.5 miles of walking trails.

music, stop by **Keys on Main** (242 South Main Street; 801-363-3638; keysonmain.com), a piano bar where the audience sings along.

SUNDAY

10 *Voices on High* 9 a.m.

Almost every Sunday morning the 360 volunteer members of the Mormon Tabernacle Choir sing at the **Mormon Tabernacle** in Temple Square (801-240-4150; mormontabernaclechoir.org). The egg-shaped hall, with its 150-foot roof span, is an acoustical marvel (tour guides are fond of dropping a pin on the stage to demonstrate just how well sound carries), and the nearly 12,000-pipe organ is among the largest in the

world. You can join the live audience at the concert broadcast from 9:30 to 10 a.m., but you need to be in your seat by 9:15. Admission is free.

11 *Mormon Central* 10:30 a.m.

You're inside **Temple Square**, Utah's No. 1 tourist attraction, so drop in at one of the visitors' centers (visittemplesquare.com) and then take a look around. If you're not a confirmed Mormon, you won't be allowed inside the main temple, but you can get an idea of the interior by visiting the smaller Assembly Hall, built in 1880 with granite left over from construction of the temple. The square is 35 acres, the epicenter of the Mormon Church, and its monumental scale is a spectacle in itself.

THE BASICS

Most major domestic airlines fly into Salt Lake City.

There's a light rail system downtown, but you'll still want a car.

Grand America Hotel
555 South Main Street
800-621-4505
grandamerica.com
$$
Lives up to its name with afternoon tea and 775 palatial rooms with Italian marble bathrooms.

The Inn on the Hill
225 North State Street
801-328-1466
inn-on-the-hill.com
$$
Twelve guest rooms in a 1909 English-style manor with Tiffany windows.

Hotel Monaco
15 West 200 South
800-805-1801
monaco-saltlakecity.com
$$
Downtown, with 225 whimsical rooms.

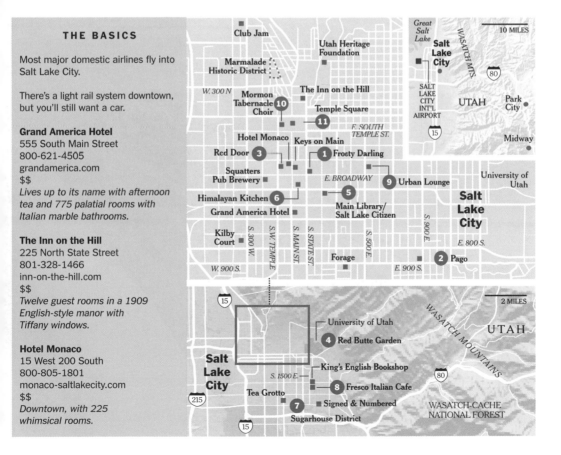

Park City

With a year-round population of about 7,500, Park City, Utah, is a small town, but it is far from remote. Downtown trails off quickly and mountains rise up behind it, but those same mountains fill the town with skiers in winter. Main Street is achingly picturesque under a confectioner's sifting of Utah's famous light snow, but it can also be jammed with smoking S.U.V.'s. Over the past few years, thanks to several factors — the 2002 Winter Olympics; the Sundance Film Festival, held here every winter; a growing realization among wealthy skiing baby boomers that this former silver-mining town is "in Utah but not of Utah" — the area boomed with unbridled second-home development near the ski areas. The upside of that change is an infusion of ambitious new hoteliers and chefs in Park City proper, injecting new life and urban sophistication.
— BY CHRISTOPHER SOLOMON

FRIDAY

1 *Stroll the Snowy Strip* 5:30 p.m.
A pleasure of visiting Park City is bundling up as the sky assumes that special mercury light of a winter's twilight in the mountains and walking the four-block historic **Main Street**, with its brightly painted 19th-century storefronts. True, many of the storefronts are filled with ski-town schlock — T-shirts, pricey shards of quartz with contemplative wolves painted on them, and mural-size photo clichés of yellow aspen groves. But the pleasure here is what Italians call la passeggiata: the stroll.

2 *A Gastronomic Empire* 6 p.m.
If Park City has a restaurant empire, it is Bill White Enterprises, which owns several places in town. One of them is the much-recommended **Wahso** (577 Main Street; 435-615-0300; wahso.com; $$$), where the atmosphere suggests Shanghai of the 1930s. For something more in keeping with the Western theme, try White's **Chimayo** (368 Main Street; 435-649-6222; chimayorestaurant.com; $$$),

which serves high-end Southwest fare. There are a dozen kinds of tequila to sample, and you may find elk on the menu, accompanied by a quesadilla.

3 *Hit the Deck* 10 p.m.
Once full of saloons and brothels, Park City doesn't lack for places to kick up your boot heels. The smoke-free, loungelike **Sidecar** (333 Main Street; 435-645-7468; sidecarbar.com) attracts a real mix of patrons who fill the place on weekends to hear live music and enjoy the heated outdoor deck that overlooks Main Street. The place also serves thin-crust pizza from when the lifts close until 1 a.m.

SATURDAY

4 *Wheels Down, Tips Up* 9 a.m.
Most weekend warriors are only starting to realize just how accessible Utah's skiing is. **Park City Mountain Resort**, the **Canyons Resort** (four miles from Park City), and **Deer Valley Resort** (one mile from downtown) are all about a half-hour drive from the Salt Lake City airport, where about 150 flights arrive by noon daily. That means an early-rising flier from the East can be skiing by noon and ambitious Westerners even sooner. Beat the crowd with an early start.

5 *Haute Slopes* 1:30 p.m.
Deer Valley Resort wisely takes a page from European resorts, which know the importance of eating well on the slopes. Reserve a place at the **Royal Street Café** at the midmountain **Silver Lake Lodge** (435-645-6724; deervalley.com; $$), where the usual

OPPOSITE For a yank to the adrenal glands, take a turn on the bobsled run at the Utah Olympic Park.

RIGHT Park City's 7,500 residents make room for crowds in ski season and during the Sundance Film Festival.

uninspired burgers and nachos have been replaced by fare like crayfish bisque, grilled tuna tacos, and roasted game hen-and-shiitake mushroom pot pie. At Park City resort, pop out of your bindings at the base of the town lift and walk to a booth at cherry-paneled **Butcher's Chop House & Bar** (751 Main Street; 435-647-0040; butcherschophouse.com; $$) for polenta-crusted calamari or a half-pound Kobe cheeseburger.

6 *Ski and Shoot* 3 p.m.

Of the many sports that haven't captivated Americans, few baffle like the biathlon, a mixture of Nordic skiing and gunplay. One reason it hasn't been embraced is that there are few places to try it. At **Soldier Hollow** (25 Soldier Hollow Lane, Midway; 435-654-2002; soldierhollow.com), amateurs can try it out. This was the venue for the 2002 Olympics cross-country skiing and biathlon and is about a 25-minute drive south of Park City. No experience is necessary. Programs range from one-hour introductions to

two-hour shooting sessions with air rifles with timed competitions and all-day gear rentals for the groomed trails.

7 *Splashdown* 4:30 p.m.

Scoot five miles north on the way back to Park City to the **Homestead Resort** (700 North Homestead Road, Midway; 800-327-7220; homesteadresort.com), where you can soak in the **Crater**, a 55-foot-tall beehive-shaped limestone rock that nature has filled with Caribbean-blue, 90- to 96-degree mineral water. Even in snow season, it offers swimming, snorkeling, and scuba diving. Reservations are required.

8 *Shrimp and Saketini* 8 p.m.

Shabu (442 Main Street; 435-645-7253; shabupc.com; $$$) exemplifies the changes in Park City. The executive chef and co-owner, Robert Valaika, who opened Nobu Matsuhisa's restaurant in Aspen and studied under Charlie Trotter in Chicago, came to Park City about four years ago hoping to strike out on his own; he opened Shabu with his brother, Kevin. The Asian cuisine — including the Japanese hot pot dish called shabu shabu, is very popular with locals.

9 *Mayoral Bandwagon* 10:30 p.m.

If you haven't left all of your energy on the slopes, take in the **Spur Bar and Grill** (352 Main Street; 435-615-1618; thespurbarandgrill.com). It generally attracts an older crowd (the leather bar chairs and fireplace are one giveaway), but the no-smoking policy means visiting athletes gravitate there, too — not to mention Park City's mayor, Dana Williams, and his Motherlode Canyon Band. Live music on weekends ranges from blues to bluegrass.

SUNDAY

10 *Stoke the Furnace* 9 a.m.

You've got a big day ahead of you and perhaps a hangover to bury after forgetting how quickly alcohol hits you at 7,000 feet. Start it at a Park City institution, the **Eating Establishment** (317 Main Street; 435-649-8284; theeatingestablishment.net; $$), with a tall glass of fresh-squeezed orange juice and a plate of eggs, potatoes, ham, and toast. After this, you can check eating off your to-do list for a while.

11 *Take a Slide* 11 a.m.

For another yank to the adrenal glands, try banging around the inside of a bobsled at 80 miles an hour. For about $200, at the **Utah Olympic Park** (435-658-4200; utaholympiclegacy.com/programs/

comet-bobsled-rides) just outside town, sliders 16 and older can climb behind an experienced driver and run the Olympic bobsled track, including a 40-story drop in just under a minute and up to five G's of force. Reservations are recommended. For younger kids, or for adults who would like much cheaper thrills, try the Alpine Coaster at the main base area of **Park City Mountain Resort** (1345 Lowell Avenue; 435-649-8111; parkcitymountain.com). It's nearly 4,000 feet of bends, bumps, and curves through naked aspens in a toboggan that's secured to a metal track.

OPPOSITE ABOVE Main Street is achingly picturesque but can also be jammed with smoking S.U.V.'s.

OPPOSITE BELOW On the mountain after a confectioner's sifting of Utah's famous light snow.

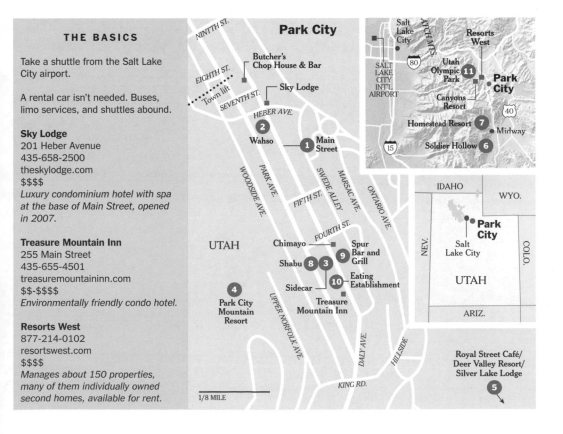

THE BASICS

Take a shuttle from the Salt Lake City airport.

A rental car isn't needed. Buses, limo services, and shuttles abound.

Sky Lodge
201 Heber Avenue
435-658-2500
theskylodge.com
$$$$
Luxury condominium hotel with spa at the base of Main Street, opened in 2007.

Treasure Mountain Inn
255 Main Street
435-655-4501
treasuremountaininn.com
$$-$$$$
Environmentally friendly condo hotel.

Resorts West
877-214-0102
resortswest.com
$$$$
Manages about 150 properties, many of them individually owned second homes, available for rent.

Park City

NINTH ST.
EIGHTH ST.
SEVENTH ST.
Town lift
Butcher's Chop House & Bar
Sky Lodge
HEBER AVE.
2
Wahso
1 Main Street
WOODSIDE AVE.
PARK AVE.
SWEDE ALLEY
MARSAC AVE.
ONTARIO AVE.
FIFTH ST.
FOURTH ST.
Chimayo
Shabu 8 3
9 Spur Bar and Grill
Sidecar
10 Eating Establishment
4
Park City Mountain Resort
UPPER NORFOLK AVE.
Treasure Mountain Inn
DALY AVE.
HILLSIDE
KING RD.
1/8 MILE

Salt Lake City
WASATCH MTS.
Resorts West
SALT LAKE CITY INT'L AIRPORT
80
Utah Olympic Park 11
Canyons Resort
Park City
40
Homestead Resort 7
Midway
15
Soldier Hollow 6

IDAHO
WYO.
Park City
NEV.
Salt Lake City
UTAH
COLO.
ARIZ.

Royal Street Café/ Deer Valley Resort/ Silver Lake Lodge
5

Moab

It's hard not to become a dime-store philosopher in Moab, Utah. With its dipping green valleys and great red rocks piercing the wide blue sky, this tiny Utah town can be a heady study in perspective. One minute you're sipping coffee on Main Street, tucked safely between the wild, barren Canyonlands National Park and the magnificent stony surrealism of Arches National Park. A short drive later, you're thousands of dizzying feet above civilization, the wind whipping you senseless. The startling beauty of this terrain is enough to leave even the most seasoned traveler frozen in the sand, blinking in disbelief.
— BY CINDY PRICE

FRIDAY

1 *A Delicate Balance* 3 p.m.

You can look at a million photos of the **Delicate Arch** (and you will), but nothing prepares you for the real deal. At **Arches National Park** (Highway 191; 435-719-2299; nps.gov/arch), take the mile-and-a-half hike up steep, uneven slick rock to hit the landmark just before sunset (bring a flashlight and plenty of water). The arch doesn't come into view until the last second, and when it does, it's unforgettable. Perched on the brink of an enormous sandstone bowl, you can edge your way around and stand beneath the massive arch for a picture, but be forewarned — though the ground there is wider than a big-city sidewalk, the combination of steep dropoff, gusty wind, and gleaming sun makes for a dizzying few seconds.

2 *The Barroom Floor* 8 p.m.

It's no Las Vegas, but Moab can kick it. Swing by **La Hacienda** (North Main Street; 435-259-6319; $), a townie favorite, for tasty fried fish tacos. Then hit **World Famous Woody's Tavern** (221 South Main Street; myspace.com/worldfamouswoodystavern), where everyone from local hipsters to vacationing Dutch couples pull on cold drafts. Some say the floor is painted to cover up bloodstains from brawls,

OPPOSITE The Delicate Arch, perched on the brink of an enormous sandstone bowl at Arches National Park.

After a uranium mining bust in the 1980s, Moab reinvented itself as an outdoor recreation spot.

but don't be put off — aside from foosball, Woody's is fairly docile these days.

SATURDAY

3 *Rough Riders* 8:30 a.m.

There are gentler ways to take in the lay of the land, but some scenic tours are just too tame. At the **Moab Adventure Center** (225 South Main Street; 435-259-7019; moabadventurecenter.com), you can book a Hummer Safari — a guide does the driving — that will take you in and out of rock canyons and up rough and steep sandstone hills (don't think about what it's going to be like coming down). Moab is also popular with mountain bikers — if that's your thing, check out **Moab Cyclery** (391 Main Street; 435-259-7423; moabcyclery.com) or another local bike outfitter for rentals and day trips.

4 *Old School* 12:30 p.m.

In a town where scenery looms large, it's easy to drive past the unassuming **Milt's Stop & Eat** (356 South 400 East; 435-259-7424; miltsstopandeat.com; $). But this little diner, which has been doling out fresh chili and shakes since 1954, comes through where it counts. Pull up to the counter and order a mouthwatering double bacon cheeseburger. It's a greasy-spoon chef-d'oeuvre, with aged-beef patties and thick slices of smoked bacon. A creamy chocolate malt will have you cursing the advent of frozen yogurt.

5 *Hole Sweet Hole* 1:30 p.m.

In 1945, Albert Christensen built his wife, Gladys, the home of their dreams — in the middle of a rock. Part kitsch memorial, part love story, **Hole N'' the Rock** (11037 South Highway 191; 435-686-2250; theholeintherock.com) is surely a tourist trap, but a heartwarming one. Even the steady drone of the

gum-smacking guide on your tour can't dispel the sheer marvel of this 5,000-square-foot testament to one man's obsession. It took Albert 12 years to hand-drill the place, and Gladys another eight to give it a woman's touch. Each room is lovingly preserved with knick-knacks or Albert's taxidermy. Outside, wander over to the inexplicable but equally delightful petting zoo filled with llamas, emus, and wallabies.

6 *Main Street* 3:30 p.m.

Like most small towns with attitude, Moab has a main street that's pretty darn cute. Start your walk with an iced coffee and a fresh slice of quiche at **EklectiCafé** (352 North Main Street; 435-259-6896; $). For a quick lesson on local topography, check out the area relief map at the **Museum of Moab** (118 East Center Street; 435-259-7985; moabmuseum.org). The artifacts on display include dinosaur bones and tracks, ancient pottery, mining tools, and a proud pioneer's piano — all part of the Moab story.

ABOVE Main Street and its rugged backdrop.

BELOW Heading for a cold draft at Woody's Tavern.

OPPOSITE ABOVE A heartwarming tourist trap.

OPPOSITE BELOW A sunset over Moab.

7 *World's Biggest Stage Set* 6 p.m.

Head out of town, hang a right at Scenic Byway 128, drive 18 miles, and take a right on La Sal Mountain Road toward Castle Valley. The pretty, winding route leads to **Castle Rock** — a dead ringer for Disney's Big Thunder Mountain Railroad and the star of old Chevrolet commercials. Turn around at Castleton Tower and drop into **Red Cliffs Lodge** (Mile Post 14, Highway 128; 435-259-2002; redcliffslodge.com) for a free wine tasting at the **Castle Creek Winery**. Afterward, check out the **Movie Museum** in the basement — a small homage to the many films shot in Moab, including *Rio Grande* and *Indiana Jones and the Last Crusade*.

8 *Local Brew* 8 p.m.

You've tasted the wine. Now sample the ale. The **Moab Brewery** (686 South Main Street; 435-259-6333; themoabbrewery.com; $) has a variety of hearty brews, plus its own homemade root beer. The dinner menu has plenty of beef and chicken, including barbecue, balanced by a cheese-heavy "Very Veggie" section and a promise that the frying is done in zero-trans-fat oil.

SUNDAY

9 *Dawn on the Cliffs* 7 a.m.

There are few reasons to endorse waking up at 7 on a Sunday, but a sunrise at Dead Horse Point passes the test. Hit the **Wicked Brew Drive Thru** (132 North Main Street; 435-259-0021; wickedbrewmoab.com) for an espresso-laced eye opener, and then take the winding drive up Route 313 to the 2,000-foot vantage point at **Dead Horse Point State Park** (435-259-2614;

utah.com/stateparks/dead_horse.htm). Watch the sun break over the vast, beautiful Canyonlands. To the west, look for Shafer Trail, the dusty road where Thelma and Louise sealed their fate in the 1991 Ridley Scott film.

10 *Rapid Observations* 10:30 a.m.

In the '70s, before Moab became known as the mountain-biking capital of the world, whitewater rafting was the big buzz. **Red River Adventures** (1140 South Main Street; 435-259-4046; redriveradventures.com)

offers trips that take it easy through Class II and III rapids, and others that go for Class IV. If you'd rather try a different form of sightseeing, the company also offers rock climbing and horseback trips.

ABOVE Scenery looms large for Moab, tucked between Canyonlands and Arches National Parks.

OPPOSITE Cycling along Scenic Byway 128 outside of town. The local terrain is legendary among mountain bikers, and outfitters in Moab will provide bicycles and gear.

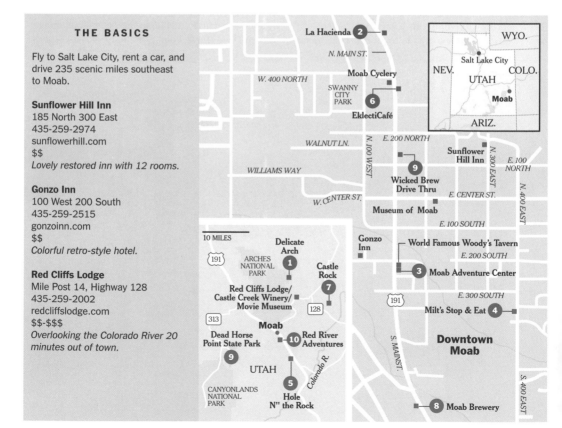

THE BASICS

Fly to Salt Lake City, rent a car, and drive 235 scenic miles southeast to Moab.

Sunflower Hill Inn
185 North 300 East
435-259-2974
sunflowerhill.com
$$
Lovely restored inn with 12 rooms.

Gonzo Inn
100 West 200 South
435-259-2515
gonzoinn.com
$$
Colorful retro-style hotel.

Red Cliffs Lodge
Mile Post 14, Highway 128
435-259-2002
redcliffslodge.com
$$-$$$
Overlooking the Colorado River 20 minutes out of town.

Denver

Denver, Colorado, is a city in a constant state of reinvention, having, in the last decade alone, greatly expanded its cultural institutions, asserted itself in the political discourse by hosting the 2008 Democratic convention, and — despite the challenge presented to chefs by its elevation — embraced a new foodie culture. It was no small point of pride for the energized Mile High City that its increasingly diverse population has been growing, reversing an exodus of families to the suburbs. Visiting some of its recently refurbished attractions, especially the now bustling LoDo district, it's hard to escape the feeling of a modern gold rush.
— BY ERIC WILSON

FRIDAY

1 *Vertical Mile* 1 p.m.
  Walk across Civic Center Park to the steps of the imposingly gray state **Capitol**, a dead ringer for the one in Washington except that it's a study in Colorado granite instead of white marble. Ascend the west side to find the spot, around the 13th step, that is exactly 5,280 feet above sea level. The gold marker makes it official: Denver deserves its altitudinal nickname.

2 *Change to Believe In* 2 p.m.
  Remember those pennies imprinted with a "D" that you found in your childhood coin-collecting phase? Now is your chance to visit the **Denver Mint** (320 West Colfax Avenue; 303-405-4761; usmint.gov) and see where they came from. You'll get some history along with an explanation of how coins are made, but won't see much of the actual production. Reservations are highly recommended (usmint.gov/mint_tours). Just about everything in your pockets is forbidden, so dress as you would for the airport.

3 *The Urban Outdoors* 4 p.m.
  Coloradans are passionate about the outdoors, even in the city. Denver has more than 100 miles of pedestrian and bicycle paths, and you can get to one of the most popular, the **Cherry Creek Path**, right downtown. Hop on the MallRide, a free bus service along 16th Street, at the Civic Center. Hop off at Larimer Street and walk a couple of blocks southwest on Larimer to find the steps down to the creek level. Take the path north, staying alert for

occasional glimpses of the snow-capped Rockies, and arrive at **Confluence Park**, where the creek meets the South Platte River. This is the historic center of Denver, the spot where the city had its start. Continue on the path until you've had enough, and then return.

4 *Where's the Beef?* 7 p.m.
  There's no getting around Denver's culinary specialty, red meat, the starring attraction at Old West-themed grill joints all over town. Count the Wild West species represented in the form of taxidermy on the walls (or on the menu) of **Buckhorn Exchange**, billed as Denver's oldest restaurant (1000 Osage Street; 303-534-9505; buckhornexchange.com; $$$). Here, steak can be ordered by the pound. Another option is to drive to the **Fort**, 18 miles southwest in Morrison (19192 Highway 8; 303-697-4771; thefort.com; $$$), where 80,000 buffalo entrees are served annually in what appears to be a 1960s rendition of the Alamo. The food and service may be as wooden as the décor, but seldom is heard a discouraging word, as the music is turned up real loud.

SATURDAY

5 *The Old Glass Ceiling* 10 a.m.
  One of Denver's most famous homes belonged to a backwoods social climber who set out in the 1880s

OPPOSITE The Denver Art Museum's new Hamilton building, designed by Daniel Libeskind.

BELOW Dining at Rioja in Larimer Square, near where gold was first discovered in Colorado in the 1850s.

to land herself a rich husband and a big house on what was then called Pennsylvania Avenue. (Now it's Pennsylvania Street.) Margaret Tobin Brown, later mythologized as Molly Brown, was a suffragette who survived the sinking of the *Titanic* and ran for United States Senate, unsuccessfully, years before women won the right to vote. Certain spurned trailblazers might find solace in a tour of her Victorian mansion (**Molly Brown House Museum**, 1340 Pennsylvania Street; 303-832-4092; mollybrown.org). They might even be inspired to stand on the front porch like Debbie Reynolds in the 1964 *The Unsinkable Molly Brown* and holler, "Pennsylvania Avenue, I'll admit you gave me a nose full of splinters, but it's all good wood from the very best doors!"

6 *Meet the Artist* 1 p.m.

Denver has a wealth of remarkable galleries, concentrated in Lower Downtown (LoDo) and also along Santa Fe Drive. For novices, one of the most accessible is **Artists on Santa Fe** (747 Santa Fe Drive; 303-573-5903; artistsonsantafe.com), a warren of studios where sculptors and painters in residence will personally explain their work. Wander down the street and you'll find many more.

7 *How the West Was Worn* 4 p.m.

Let's say you have an image problem. Some people, misguided as they may be, think you are an elitist. Now, that's nothing that can't be fixed with a little fashion makeover at **Rockmount Ranch Wear** (1626 Wazee Street; 303-629-7777; rockmount.com), a LoDo shop famous in these parts for introducing the snap button to the western shirt, making it easier

ABOVE The Victorian trophy home of the "unsinkable" *Titanic* survivor, Molly Brown.

RIGHT Dead animals on the walls and red meat on the plate — that's the Buckhorn Exchange, Denver's oldest restaurant.

OPPOSITE The gallery strip on Denver's Santa Fe Drive.

for cowboys to ride the range or re-enact scenes from *Brokeback Mountain*. (Yep, Jack and Ennis were Rockmount customers.) The store — and an accompanying museum — have the fascinating feel of a ghost town relic, with a lasso-rope logo and dusty displays, but the shirts have modern-day prices.

8 *All That Glitters* 8 p.m.

The best of Denver night life can be found in LoDo, around where gold was first discovered in Colorado in the 1850s. Now the closest thing to gold around here is more likely to come in a bottle of Cuervo. At **Rioja**, for example, you can precede your pasta or grilled salmon dinner with the likes of the Loca Hot, made with Fresno pepper-infused tequila, plus Agavero (tequila liqueur), orange, and lime (1431 Larimer Street; 303-820-2282; riojadenver.com; $$-$$$). It's a short walk from here to a wine bar, Crú, and a Champagne bar, Corridor 44. Given the intensified effects of alcohol at high altitudes, you might want to head underground to **Lannie's Clocktower Cabaret**, the local singer Lannie Garrett's place in the basement of the D&F Tower (16th Street and Arapahoe Street; 303-293-0075; lannies.com). Be warned: the raunchy burlesque shows late on Saturday nights may involve some sort of spanking or drag acts.

SUNDAY

9 *Juxtapositions* 10 a.m.

The **Denver Art Museum**'s jutting addition, designed by Daniel Libeskind, looks like an Imperial

Cruiser from *Star Wars*, and once you are inside, the vertigo-inducing floor plan will make you long to get your feet back on earth (100 West 14th Avenue; 720-865-5000; denverartmuseum.org). But the museum's juxtaposition of the work of contemporary art stars with American Indian artifacts is oddly compelling. And if you happen to be having trouble giving up smoking, be sure to look for Damien Hirst's *Party Time* installation, an ashtray the size of a kiddie pool filled with thousands of burned cigarette butts. Dive right in.

10 *Horizontal Mile* 1 p.m.

    The **Mile High Flea Market** could just as well be named the Mile Wide Flea Market, given that its hundreds of tightly packed, pastel-colored stalls cover 80 acres of pavement (I-76 and 88th Avenue; milehighmarketplace.com). Browse through T-shirts, watermelons, antiques, fishing tackle, jewelry, and as many other kinds of merchandise as you can take. You can also sample delicious street fare, like corn on the cob rolled in a tray of butter, Parmesan, and seasoning salt. And if you're man enough, try a chelada, a stomach-churning brew of Clamato juice and Budweiser.

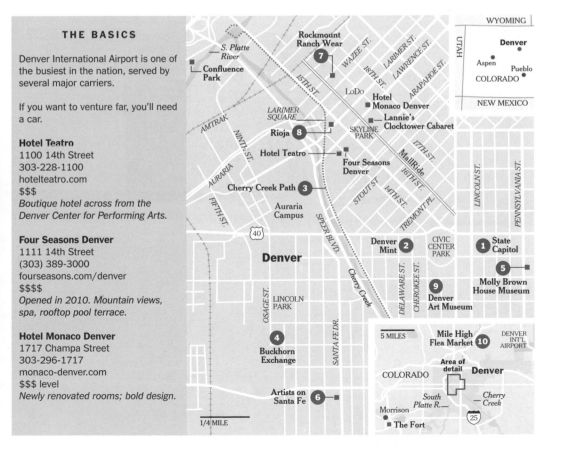

THE BASICS

Denver International Airport is one of the busiest in the nation, served by several major carriers.

If you want to venture far, you'll need a car.

Hotel Teatro
1100 14th Street
303-228-1100
hotelteatro.com
$$$
Boutique hotel across from the Denver Center for Performing Arts.

Four Seasons Denver
1111 14th Street
(303) 389-3000
fourseasons.com/denver
$$$$
Opened in 2010. Mountain views, spa, rooftop pool terrace.

Hotel Monaco Denver
1717 Champa Street
303-296-1717
monaco-denver.com
$$$ level
Newly renovated rooms; bold design.

463

Leadville

Leadville, Colorado, is a rugged mining town perched at a lung-searing 10,152 feet. Victorian buildings cram Harrison Avenue, the main street in its 70-block historic district. Gold and silver made this a boomtown in the 1800s; a molybdenum mine operated until the 1980s. When the mineral-based economy collapsed, Leadville persevered by retooling itself as a tourist destination. Today mountain bikers and horseback riders hit the trails, and anglers pull rainbows from high mountain lakes. Intrepid hikers scale Mounts Elbert and Massive, the 14,000-foot peaks that dominate the skyline. But most tourists are drawn simply by the Western authenticity that gives the place a unique charm. "Leadville's got character," said Chris Albers, a transplant from South Dakota who owns a bicycle store and a coffee shop in town. "It's not just another slick pop-up ski town." — BY HELEN OLSSON

FRIDAY

1 *Streets of Gold* 4 p.m.

Pick up maps for walking and driving tours at the **Leadville Chamber of Commerce** (809 Harrison Avenue; 888-532-3845; leadvilleusa.com), and set out to get acquainted. The walking tour guides you around Harrison Avenue, where the legacy of the golden era can still be seen. Start at the Tabor Opera House, built in 1879 by Horace Tabor, a silver magnate. Climb onto the stage where Oscar Wilde once performed—and where live horses galloped on a treadmill during a production of *Ben-Hur*. Another stop is Western Hardware, now an antiques store jam-packed with relics and replicas, including brothel tokens for $3 apiece. Wander off the tour route onto the town's back alleys and side streets, which are peppered with sagging outhouses, boarded-up barns, and half-painted churches with broken stained glass windows.

2 *Pasta Pig-Out* 6 p.m.

Linger over a glass of Bolla Valpolicella at **Zichittella's** (422 Harrison Avenue; 719-486-1298; $$). While you wait for homemade meatballs simmered in marinara, gaze at the trompe l'oeil ceiling of clouds above. A rooster, the restaurant's icon, is hidden in the cumulonimbus. Near the bar, Plexiglass covers the 12-foot deep, brick-lined cistern built in 1879. Italian lessons are piped into the bathrooms so you can learn handy phrases like, "Ho capelli ricci," which means, "I have curly hair."

3 *Down at the Saloon* 8 p.m.

Post tiramisu, head across the street to the **Silver Dollar Saloon** (315 Harrison Avenue; 719-486-9914) for a Budweiser longneck. Before you duck in, look up at the building's intricate bracketed cornice, painted green and yellow. Inside, slide into a booth or shoot pool on the 1930s pool table while listening to Johnny Cash on the juke box. Belly up next to locals in jeans and cowboy hats in the original Brunswick back bar, which has diamond dust mirrors and ornately carved columns of white oak.

SATURDAY

4 *Coffee Couch* 8:30 a.m.

Stop in at **Provin' Grounds Coffee & Bakery** (508 Harrison Avenue; 719-486-0797), Chris Albers's hip coffee shop, located in yet another historic building, this one a brick Victorian painted bright green. Plop onto the couch next to locals sipping lattes and pecking on laptops. Have your cup of Joe with a blueberry crisp or buttermilk scone made from scratch.

5 *The Stone You Chew* 9 a.m.

At the **National Mining Hall of Fame and Museum** (120 West Ninth Street; 719-486-1229;

OPPOSITE Old mining shacks, a Leadville legacy.

BELOW Old West antiques pack Western Hardware on Harrison Avenue. One interesting find was brothel tokens.

mininghalloffame.org), marvel at a model of the ice castle Leadville constructed out of 5,000 tons of ice in 1896. For rockhounds, there's a 2,155-pound hunk of galena, icelike logs of selenite, chunks of polished malachite. Here you will learn that the sparkle in your eye shadow comes from mica and the dust on your chewing gum is limestone.

6 *Ballad of Baby Doe* 10:30 a.m.

During the brutal winter of 1935, Baby Doe Tabor, the second wife of Horace Tabor, was found frozen to death in the cabin at the **Matchless Mine** (East 7th Street; 719-486-1229; matchlessmine.com), where she had lived as a recluse for 35 years. Tour the mine and hear their riches-to-rags story. She was a bodacious, round-eyed beauty; he was a silver magnate who spent lavishly: a $90,000 diamond necklace; diamond-studded diaper pins; 100 peacocks to strut on their mansion grounds in Denver. When the price of silver crashed in 1893, they were left penniless. Alongside the cabin are the mining buildings that once produced the millions.

7 *Thin-Air Pizza* 12:30 p.m.

Tucked on a side street, in an 1800s log cabin painted royal blue, purple, green, and red, **High Mountain Pies** (115 West 4th Street; 719-486-5555; $$) serves up pizzas, calzones, and subs. Slinging dough behind the bar is Dru Pashley, 28, a wiry runner who can tell you about the notorious Leadville 100 — every summer, he joins the other ultramarathoners running 100 miles of rocky trail in the thin air. (T-shirts for sale in Leadville riff on the milk campaign: "Got Oxygen?")

8 *Ride the Rails* 2 p.m.

Rumble on a scenic passenger train along the old South Park rails, where freight cars once hauled ore from the Climax mine. The **Leadville, Colorado & Southern** passenger train (326 East Seventh Street; 866-386-3936; leadville-train.com) runs trips twice daily in summer. The train starts in downtown Leadville and follows the headwaters of the Arkansas River as it meanders through fields of sagebrush. It chugs toward the Continental Divide through aspen and lodgepole forests and past old mining structures. In July and August, there are special tours for viewing wildflowers.

9 *Head for the Hills* 5 p.m.

The best way to appreciate Leadville's mining pedigree is to explore the mining district firsthand. Walk, or jog, on the 11.6-mile **Mineral Belt Trail** (mineralbelttrail.com), a paved path that circum-navigates Leadville and its adjacent mining district. Bikers, inline skaters, and skateboarders use the trail, rolling by a landscape dotted with rusting ore carts, slumping wooden shacks, and old head frames and hoists. Next to a tailings pond filled with water the color of boiled beets, a superfluous sign warns, "No Swimming."

10 *Margarita with a View* 7 p.m.

Leave Harrison Street behind for the **Grill** (715 Elm Street; 719-486-9930; grillbarcafe.com), a family-owned New Mexican-style Mexican restaurant in a

ABOVE Peaks above town rise to 14,000 feet.

BELOW Twin Lakes, a former stagecoach stop, is the gateway to the ruins of the once-glittering Interlaken resort.

peachy-pink stucco building at the outskirts of town. Every fall, ten tons of Anaheim chiles from Pueblo, Colorado, are harvested and fire-roasted for the Grill's kitchen. Sit on the patio and enjoy the gardens and the mountain views. The chicken sopapillas are enormous, and the house margaritas are served by the liter.

SUNDAY

11 *Ghost Resort* 11 a.m.

Drive south from Leadville 20 miles to the tiny town of Twin Lakes. An 1879 stagecoach stop and brothel for miners heading over Independence Pass to Aspen, it's now a ramshackle collection of dirt roads,

sloping 1800s shacks, and log cabins. Columbines grow among the weeds. Rent a boat at **Twin Lakes Canoe & Kayak** (719-251-9961; coloradovacation.com/outdoors/twinlakerentals). The outfit is run by Johnny Gwaltney, a k a Johnny Canoe, who wears purple-tinted glasses and a giant silver belt buckle, and calls himself a "hikerneck" — a cross between a hippie, a biker, and a redneck. Paddle half an hour across Twin Lakes to the abandoned Interlaken resort, where Denver's upper crust vacationed in the 1880s. Of the handful of buildings, including a hexagonal six-stall privy that once featured leather seats, only Dexter Cabin has been restored. Inside, explore rooms decorated in eight different imported woods and climb a steep ladder to a cupola overlooking the lake.

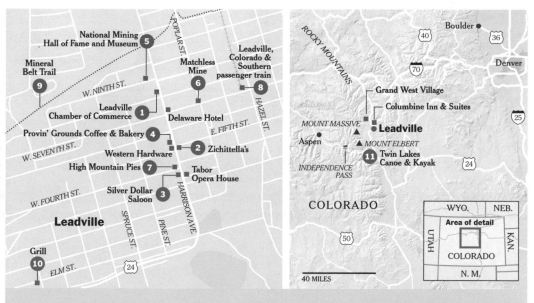

THE BASICS

Leadville is served by airports in Denver, 125 miles away, and Vail, 63 miles away. A car is essential.

Delaware Hotel
700 Harrison Avenue
800-748-2004
delawarehotel.com

$$
Built in 1886 and jammed with antiques. Everything has a price (stuffed mountain goat: $5,000).

Grand West Village
99 Grand West Drive
800-691-3999
grandwest.com
$$

Plush cabins tucked in the woods just north of town.

Columbine Inn & Suites
2019 North Poplar Street
800-954-1110
columbineinn.com
$-$$
Clean, serviceable rooms at budget prices.

Vail

Vail is not the most glamorous of Colorado's ski towns. It does not have the charm of Telluride. Nor does it exude the glitz of Aspen. Even Breckenridge, arguably, has better night life. But the one thing that Vail does have is great snow: some 5,300 skiable acres with a seven-mile-long mountain face, 193 trails, and not one but seven bowls. That hasn't stopped Vail, the United States' largest ski resort by area, from polishing its base village. As part of an upgrade, many of Vail's boxy, 1970s-style facades and outdated streetscapes have been refreshed in the past few years with a modern Bavarian look. Skiers now check into new boutique hotels with ski valets, get pine-scented massages at Zen-channeling spas, and warm themselves by outdoor fire pits.
— BY ELAINE GLUSAC

FRIDAY

1 *Nordic at Dusk* 3:30 p.m.

You don't need to be on the slopes to appreciate the Southern Rockies, 10,000-plus-foot-tall peaks that edge narrow Vail Valley, cut by clear mountain streams that flow in winter's deep freeze. While it's still daylight, explore this winter wonderland on cross-country skis. At the **Vail Nordic Center** (1778 Vail Valley Drive; 970-476-8366; vailnordiccenter.com), trails loop across wooden bridges, gentle pine stands, and snow-blanketed golf fairways.

2 *Western Chic* 5:30 p.m.

Like the mountainside chalets that share a modern rustic look — beamed ceilings, cathedral windows, stone decks — so, too, does the local fashion, which could be described as upscale cowboy. Get into the spirit at **Gorsuch** (263 East Gore Creek Drive; 970-476-2294; gorsuch.com), a luxe store with von Trapp-gone-Vail looks for her (crystal-studded cashmere hats), him (Johann Gottfried suede jackets), and home (Megeve crystal-etched wineglasses). Nearby is **Axel's** (201 Gore Creek Drive; 970-476-7625; axelsltd.com), which carries British tweed sportcoats, shearling coats, and oversized etched belt buckles.

OPPOSITE Après-ski afterglow in Vail.

RIGHT Known for its abundant snow, Vail has 5,300 skiable acres as well as space for pursuits like snowshoeing.

For that rugged cowboy swagger, step into **Kemo Sabe** (230 Bridge Street; 970-479-7474; kemosabe.com), known for its handmade Lucchese cowboy boots.

3 *Colorado Cuisine* 7 p.m.

Eating in Vail is not cheap. But that doesn't stop foodies from packing into **Restaurant Kelly Liken** (12 Vail Road; 970-479-0175; kellyliken.com; $$$-$$$$) for innovative regional fare. Menu items have included a rich elk carpaccio with mustard aioli, roast Colorado rack of lamb with mushroom bread pudding, and locally farmed bass with candied kumquats.

4 *Night Crawl* 9 p.m.

The party starts early in Vail—après-ski cocktails are at 4 p.m., which may explain why the town seems to shut down after dinner. A rollicking exception is the **Red Lion** (304 Bridge Street; 970-476-7676; theredlion.com), a dive bar packed with high-top tables. The entertainment tradition here includes performances by a guitarist and co-owner, Phil Long, that have included Bob Dylan covers, corny jokes, and Elton John sing-a-longs. If you're still wired, walk down the street to the candlelit **Samana Lounge** (228 Bridge Street; 970-476-3433; samanalounge.com), where 20-something snowboarders and South American lift operators pulse to the grooves of visiting D.J.'s.

SATURDAY

5 *Healthy Starter* 7:30 a.m.

Skiing at Vail takes lots of calories, so don't skip breakfast. For a civilized start, make your way to

Terra Bistro (352 East Meadow Drive; 970-476-6836; vailmountainlodge.com; $$), a sophisticated loft-style restaurant in the Vail Mountain Spa and Lodge that serves a delightful organic breakfast. Try the seven-grain hot cereal or cage-free scrambled eggs with potatoes and greens. If your objective is to get an early start, don't sit by the windows, where the snowy street scene induces lingering over cups of locally roasted coffee.

6 *Pick a Bowl* 8:30 a.m.

Skiing Vail's legendary back bowls requires a game plan, not only because of the travel time, which can run upwards of 30 minutes without traffic, but to avoid the morning crush. Aim to catch one of the first lifts to get atop the mountain ridge before everyone else. Expert skiers can claim first tracks on the extreme terrain at Sun Down Bowl, one of several south-facing slopes that make up the so-called backside of Vail Mountain. Try its aptly named neighbor Sun Up Bowl for the softest snow this time of day. Though most of the backside bowls are expert only, intermediate skiers are welcome at China Bowl, a gentler basin with wide-open expanses and panoramic views. Staying ahead of the crowds, push on to Blue Sky Basin, one ridge to the south. Hit the effervescent Champagne Glade before everybody else does.

7 *Unbuckle and Refuel* Noon

Relive your morning conquests at Two Elk Restaurant (970-754-4560; $$), Vail's flagship restaurant atop China Bowl. During lunch, skiers from the mountain's front and back sides meet here to unbuckle their boots and loosen their belts. Although the restaurant has 1,200 seats — all bordered by

ABOVE The lobby at the Arrabelle at Vail Square, a hotel in Lionshead, one of three base villages.

RIGHT Skating at Vail Square in Lionshead, on the rink near the Centre V restaurant.

massive timber-framed windows that overlook the Colorado Rockies — plan on getting there before 12:15 p.m. (alternatively, after 1:30 p.m.), or you'll be left standing. Service may be cafeteria style, but the fare is upscale. Dishes one chilly afternoon included chicken posole soup, buffalo chili, and portobello mushroom sandwiches.

8 *Long-Distance Cruising* 1:30 p.m.

Continue conquering the mountain in contrarian fashion, and skiing where the masses aren't. Now that the back bowls are brimming, point your skis toward Vail's front side, carved with many stamina-testing runs. By midafternoon, hit the four-mile-long Riva Ridge cruiser, the resort's longest trail.

9 *Muscle Relaxer* 4:30 p.m.

As the sun begins to dip and your muscles begin to tire, make your way to the Lionshead, one of Vail's three base villages, and check into the RockResorts Spa at the Arrabelle at Vail Square (675 Lionshead Place; 970-754-7754; arrabelle.rockresorts.com). You'll find separate men's and women's lounges, each with a steam room, a sauna, and a whirlpool. Treatments are mountain-themed: massages with pine-infused oils, body wraps incorporating wildflower essences. Therapists will even treat seriously sore muscles with an ice pack filled with mountain snow.

10 *High and Low* 7:30 p.m.

Still aching for more pampering? Stick around the Arrabelle for dinner at Centre V (970-754-7700;

$$$), a white-tablecloth restaurant that resembles a cozy Lyonnaise brasserie, with vaulted ceilings and a zinc bar. Indulge in French classics like steak frites and duck confit. Reservations recommended. But if you're hankering for more action—and to see Vail's scragglier, less effete side—drive eight miles to the **Minturn Saloon** (146 North Main Street; 970-827-5954; minturnsaloon.com; $$). This knotty-pine and antler-adorned place serves Tex-Mex dishes like chicken burritos as well as hunters' favorites like grilled quail.

SUNDAY

11 *A Walk in the Woods* 9:30 a.m.

In a ski town that lives and breathes sports, Olympic-caliber athletes are the real celebrities. So if you're planning to go snowshoeing, there's no better guide than Ellen Miller, the first North American woman to reach the summit of Mount Everest from

both the north and south sides. Miller teaches a 90-minute Mountain Divas class at the **Vail Athletic Club** (352 East Meadow Drive; 970-476-7960; vailmountainlodge.com), which takes a crunchy cult of triathletes and trail racers on a valley trek through towering aspen forests, past trout-filled streams, and under snowy pine boughs. Unlike skiing, snowshoeing requires no special skills. Beginners, finally, are welcome.

ABOVE Belt buckles at Axel's, one of many shops in Vail that can supply the ingredients for an upscale cowboy look. Other stores carry luxe furnishings for your chalet.

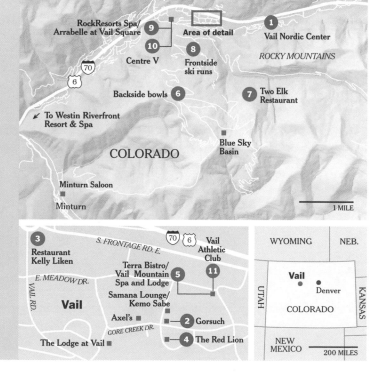

THE BASICS

From Vail/Eagle County Airport, downtown Vail is a 35-mile drive along I-70. To get around, you will want a car.

Arrabelle at Vail Square
675 Lionshead Place
970-754-7777
arrabelle.rockresorts.com
$$$$
At the base of the Eagle Bahn Gondola. In-room fireplaces.

Westin Riverfront Resort & Spa
126 Riverfront Lane, Avon
866-949-1616
westin.com/riverfrontavon
$$$
A gondola zips guests to Beaver Creek, Vail's sister resort.

The Lodge at Vail
174 East Gore Creek Drive
970-476-5011
lodgeatvail.rockresorts.com
$$$
The best rooms face the ski runs.

Aspen

At times Aspen, Colorado, verges on parody. Scoring reservations at the restaurant du jour requires the will of a tenacious personal assistant. Lines waiting to hand over black American Express cards for $1,000 Moncler jackets rival the ones for the Silver Queen gondola. Yet behind the mirrored aviator sunglasses is a culture devoted to the mountain's transcendent beauty and perpetual sporting life: skiing, boarding, hiking, snowshoeing, fly-fishing. Aspen is an international playground that remains a small town, one where it doesn't matter how much money you have, it matters how you handle a bump run.
— BY MARY BILLARD

FRIDAY

1 *Après Someone Else's Skiing* 5 p.m.

With alpenglow illuminating the Wheeler Opera House (1889) and the Elks Building dome (1891), saunter through this 19th-century Victorian mining town while enjoying the crisp mountain air and window shopping at stores like Fendi (fur flip-flops?). Though you didn't earn it, join the après ski action at the **39 Degrees Lounge** in the **Sky Hotel** (709 East Durant Avenue; 970-925-6760; theskyhotel.com), where a young, windburned crowd gathers by a crackling fire in wool hats to watch Teton Gravity

OPPOSITE Working the moguls at Aspen Highlands, with the Maroon Bells peaks in the background.

BELOW Cloud Nine Bistro, a good spot for lunch, is 100 yards below the Cloud Nine chair.

Research movies on flat-screen TVs. The footage of death-defying flips is a perfect way to get revved up. So are the drinks, including the Ménage à Trois, a mixologist's triumph combining vodka, double shots of espresso, and coffee beans.

2 *Chill over Chili* 7:30 p.m.

In the Roaring Fork Valley, billionaires aspire to be locals. Trade the *Us Weekly* setting for a more traditional down-home scene: the red-and-white-checked tablecloth décor at **Little Annie's Eating House** (517 East Hyman Avenue; 970-925-1098; littleannies.com; $$), an Aspen mainstay since 1972. Thick homemade soups, juicy burgers, and hearty chili are on the menu, as well as fresh trout. Everything goes with Fat Tire or Sunshine beer.

3 *Fresh Musical Tracks* 10 p.m.

Aspen offers a wide variety of night life in a few tightly packed streets, from South American frat-boy types playing pool at **Eric's Bar** (315 East Hyman Avenue; 970-920-1488; ericsbaraspen.com), to the fun-fur-wearing Euros at the members-only Caribou Club (caribouclub.com). But for live music go to the **Belly Up Aspen** (450 South Galena Street; 970-544-9800; bellyupaspen.com), formerly the Double Diamond. Ben Harper, the Flaming Lips, Ice-T, Stone Temple Pilots, and Dwight Yoakam have all played this 450-seat club.

SATURDAY

4 *Sunblock, Advil, Small Talk* 8 a.m.

To forestall the slight headache that may come with the high altitude (or a hangover), make a pit stop at **Carl's Pharmacy** (306 East Main Street; 970-925-3273) for a dose of small-town friendliness. Stocked with everything from hand warmers to wine, and open from 9 a.m. to 9 p.m., it is a place to trade gossip and feel at home. Even the out-of-town customers are Mayberry polite. And if you're buying a knee brace or reading glasses, someone will commiserate.

5 *Think about Seizing the Day* 8:30 a.m.

As you wait for the sun to soften up the snow from the overnight freeze, fuel up at **Paradise**

Bakery (320 South Galena Street; 970-925-7585; paradisebakery.com). Fresh muffins and something delicious from the coffee family are ready to be enjoyed while you sit on one of the outside benches facing the mountain. Read *The Aspen Times* and *The Aspen Daily News*, whose slogan is "If you don't want it printed, don't let it happen." Far from being resort boosters, the newspapers report on community concerns like seasonal workers and affordable housing and always have letters to the editor complaining about nearly everything. A town of millionaires shows its hippie heritage by still raging against the machine.

6 *Follow the Sun* 10 a.m.

Start with the legendary Ajax. The east-facing black runs — Walsh's or Kristi or the section called the Dumps — are best in the morning sun. **Bonnie's** (970-544-6252; $-$$) above Lift 3 is a must for lunch. Avoid the crowds by going before noon or after 1:30, and grab a spot on the deck. The staff makes everything from scratch, including the pizza dough. Look for warming choices like chicken artichoke chili pesto pizza and white-bean chili. The strudel is made with apples from a Colorado orchard, and it's best with fresh schlag. While some prefer the reserved seating of the members-only Aspen Mountain Club, there are plenty of captains of industry, Hollywood players, and members of the House of Saud carrying cafeteria trays. After lunch, hit the west-facing Face of Bell when the afternoon sun lights up the bumps and trees.

7 *Après Schussing, Shopping* 4 p.m.

Aspen has been called, and sometimes not so lovingly, Rodeo Drive East. The one global fashion temple to check out is **Prada** (312 South Galena Street; 970-925-7001), not only for its sleek

RIGHT Jogging past a Lamborghini. Behind the glitz and glamour, Aspen hides a real town of full-time residents.

clothes, but also for the shop's rustic-chic modern mountain design of luxurious woods and stone. People frequently ask the name of the architect (Roberto Baciocchi of Arezzo, Italy). Then head to **Performance Ski** (408 South Hunter Street; 970-925-8657), where the co-owner Lee Keating and the latest crop of snowboard dudes will give you honest answers on how those Prada pants actually fit. A very pleasant place to curl up in an old leather club chair is **Explore Booksellers and Bistro** (221 East Main Street; 970-925-5336; explorebooksellers. com), a warren of book-laden rooms, a vegetarian restaurant, and a coffeehouse. For housewares, head to **Amen Wardy Home** (520 East Durant Avenue; 970-920-7700; amenwardy.com). The merchandise is so unusual (whimsical house gifts to fur blankets for a few thousand dollars), that it's worth shipping home.

8 *Spa Decadence* 6 p.m.

To take care of those aching muscles, hobble over to the 15,000-square-foot **Remède Spa** at the **St. Regis Resort** (315 East Dean Street; 970-920-6783; remede.com). It's pricey, but worth it. All treatments end with something that sounds a little zany but is actually relaxing: a stop at a cozy parlor where white-robed spagoers lie on chaise longues and strap on air masks, inhaling oxygen infused with fresh fruit essences. Prosecco and chocolates are also provided.

9 *Did You Reserve Last Month?* 8 p.m.

The ski trails are never that crowded, even during school holidays, but trying to get a table for six at a hot Aspen restaurant is brutal. Two newcomers worth speed-dialing are out-of-towners with Italian cuisine. New York's famed **Il Mulino** (501 East Dean Street; 970-205-1000; ilmulino.com/aspen; $$$-$$$$) has old-school Italian pastas, fresh fish, and flirtatious waiters. Miami export **Casa Tua** (403 South Galena Street; 970-920-7277; $$$-$$$$) goes for a feel of an Italian Alps chalet.

SUNDAY

10 *Morning Tuneup* 8 a.m.

Stretch your muscles with a pre-ski yoga or pilates class at **O2Aspen** (500 West Main Street; 970-925-4002; 02aspen.com), in a beautifully renovated Victorian house. Drop-in classes are about $20. A small

boutique has everything from cashmere sweaters in the $500 range to more moderately priced workout wear.

11 *Bragging Rights* 10 a.m.

The cool kids tackle the Highland Bowl. It is not served by any lifts, and it takes anywhere from 20 minutes to an hour to climb 750 feet to its 12,392-foot-high summit with a fearsome 45-degree pitch. The really cool kids do circuits of two or three laps. Slightly tamer is Deep Temerity, a 180-acre bowl that gives expert skiers an additional 1,000-foot drop. Lunch at the aptly named **Cloud Nine Alpine Bistro** (970-544-3063) 100 yards below the Cloud Nine chair, with an old ski-hut feel and views of the Maroon Bells.

OPPOSITE ABOVE Downtown Aspen at dusk.

THE BASICS

The Aspen airport connects to Denver and a few other mostly Western cities. Or fly to Vail or Denver and take a car or shuttle. In town, use the buses.

Hotel Jerome
30 East Main Street
970-920-1000
hoteljerome.com
$$$$
Beautiful bones; built in 1889.

Annabelle Inn
232 West Main Street
970-925-3822
annabelleinn.com
$$$
Thirty-five rooms and two hot tubs.

Limelight Lodge
355 South Monarch Street
970-925-3025
limelightlodge.com
$$$$
In the shadow of Ajax Mountain.

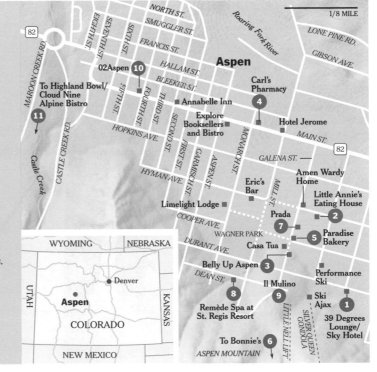

Telluride

Telluride almost begs comparisons with Aspen. A Colorado mining town affixed to a world-class ski resort; rugged locals brushing elbows with the occasional celebrity; white-tablecloth restaurants serving up foie gras next to taco dives. "It's like Aspen was back in the '70s, but less pretentious," said Bo Bedford, a self-described Aspen refugee and a manager at the New Sheridan Hotel. "It hasn't gone Hollywood yet." There is, of course, a certain star-studded film festival. And Telluride does count Jerry Seinfeld and Tom Cruise among its regulars. Yet the town stays true to its hardscrabble roots. Dogs roam off-leash, folks rummage for freebies at a so-called Free Box, and residents zip up in flannel instead of fur coats. — BY LIONEL BEEHNER

FRIDAY

1 *Das Boot* 4 p.m.

Ski shops are often staffed by workers straight out of *Bill and Ted's Excellent Adventure*. Not **Boot Doctors** (650 Mountain Village Boulevard; 970-728-8954; bootdoctors.com), where Bob Gleason and his team of "surgeons" run a kind of operating room for your ill-fitting equipment. But don't expect a sterile ward — it looks more like a torture chamber, with pinchers and clawlike tools to stretch, squeeze, and custom-shape any size boots (prices range from about $20 for a boot stretch to $175 for a custom-molded sole).

2 *Broadway Meets Opry* 6 p.m.

Film and theater buffs will take comfort in Telluride's abundance of preserved art-house theaters. Take the intricately stenciled balcony and the maple floors of the **Sheridan Opera House** (110 North Oak Street; 970-728-6363; sheridanoperahouse.com), which dates from 1913. Part '30s vaudeville, part Grand Ole Opry, the stage has been graced with everything from Broadway musicals to bluegrass bands. It is also the hub of the Telluride Film Festival, which brings crowds to town each September.

3 *High Steaks* 8:30 p.m.

If the **New Sheridan** feels like the kind of joint with a secret poker game going on in a smoky backroom, well, that's because it is. (H. Norman Schwarzkopf

is said to be among the regulars.) But the real draw of this Victorian hotel is its newly refurbished **Chop House Restaurant** (233 West Colorado Avenue; 970-728-9100; newsheridan.com; $$$), which serves large platters of prime steaks. Like the hotel, which was reopened in 2008 after extensive renovations, the musty dining room has been spiffed up with plush booths and crystal chandeliers. After dinner, sneak away next door (there's a secret passage in the back) to the New Sheridan bar, which looks much as it did in 1895 — with its crackling fire and carved mahogany bar — but has added a billiard room in back and, yup, a poker table.

SATURDAY

4 *Biscuits and Gravy* 7:30 a.m.

With its red-checkered tablecloths and folksy service, **Maggie's Bakery** (300 West Colorado Avenue; 970-728-3334; $) holds its own against any ski-town greasy spoon. Start the day with a healthy-size biscuit and gravy.

5 *Gold Rush* 9 a.m.

Telluride feels as though it belongs in the Alps — with its 2,000-plus acres of backcountry-like terrain and above-the-tree-line chutes, European-style chalets, and snowy peaks framed by boxy

OPPOSITE Snow-carpeted trails roll past wide meadows and frozen waterfalls in the pocket of southwest Colorado around Telluride.

BELOW Alpino Vino has the feel of an Italian chalet.

canyons and craggy rock formations. Throw in thin crowds and short lift lines, and what's not to like? To warm up, take the Prospect Bowl Express over to Madison or Magnolia — gentle runs that weave through trees below the gaze of Bald Mountain. Or hop on the Gold Hill Express lift to find the mountain's newer expert terrain: Revelation Bowl. Hang a left off the top of the Revelation Lift to the Gold Hill Chutes (Nos. 2 to 5), said to be some of the steepest terrain in North America.

6 *Wine and Cheese* Noon

Telluride does not believe in summit cafeterias, at least not the traditional kind with long tables for diners and deep fryers in the kitchen. Its hilltop restaurants come the size of tree forts. Case in point is **Alpino Vino** (970-708-1120; $$), a spot just off the Gold Hill Express Lift that resembles a chalet airlifted from the Italian Alps. Diners in ski helmets huddle around cherry-wood tables and a roaring

fireplace, sipping Tuscan reds, while neatly groomed waiters bring plates of cured meats and fine cheeses. Arrive by noon, as this place fills up fast. For more casual grub, swing by **Giuseppe's** (970-728-7503; $) at the top of Lift 9, which stacks two shelves of Tabasco sauce and a refrigerator full of Fat Tire beer to go with home-style dishes like chicken and chorizo gumbo. After lunch, glide down See Forever, a long, winding trail that snakes all the way back to the village. Detour to Lift 9 if you want to burn off a few more calories.

7 *Full Pint or Halfpipe?* 5:30 p.m.

A free gondola links the historic town of Telluride with the faux-European base area known as Mountain Village. Just before sunset, hop off at the gondola's midstation, situated atop a ridge. For a civilized drink without cover bands, you'll find **Allred's** (970-728-7474; allredsrestaurant.com), a rustic-chic lodge with craft beers on tap. Grab a window seat for sunset views of the San Juan Mountains. Shaun White wannabes, however, will want to continue down to a new terrain park with an 18-foot-high halfpipe. Illuminated by klieg lights until 8 p.m., it is one of Colorado's few half-pipes where you can flip a McTwist under the stars.

8 *No Vegans* 8 p.m.

Carnivores should feel at home in Telluride. At some spots, steak knives look like machetes

ABOVE Downtown Telluride. Butch Cassidy robbed his first bank on Main Street in 1889.

OPPOSITE ABOVE The Gold Hill Chutes, some of the steepest terrain open to skiers in North America.

OPPOSITE BELOW A terrain park with an 18-foot-high half-pipe is illuminated by klieg lights.

and the beef is said to come from Ralph Lauren's nearby ranch. For tasty Colorado lamb chops, try the **Palmyra Restaurant** (136 Country Club Drive; 970-728-6800; thepeaksresort.com; $$$). Opened in 2009 at the Peaks Resort & Spa in Mountain Village, the glass-walled restaurant has dazzling fire features and romantic valley views. Or, for hearty grub you might find at a firehouse, head into town and loosen your belt at **Oak** (250 W. San Juan Avenue; 970-728-3985; $), a no-frills joint with old wooden tables and a counter where you can order Texas-style barbecued spareribs and breaded-to-order fried chicken.

9 *Getting High* 10 p.m.

If the high altitude and lack of oxygen leave you winded — and they probably will — pull up a bar stool at the **Bubble Lounge** (200 West Colorado Avenue; 970-728-9653; telluridebubblelounge.com), a grungy bar that serves craft beers, Champagne,

and, yes, oxygen. Choose from two dozen scents (cherry and lemon grass, among others) served in bubbling beakers that light up like DayGlo bulbs and look like something in a mad scientist's lab.

SUNDAY

10 *Stomping Grounds* 10 a.m.

The snow-carpeted trails that roll past wide meadows and frozen waterfalls in this pocket of southwest Colorado are ideal for snowshoeing. Stock up on snacks and water before riding to the top of Lift 10, where you'll find a warming teepee run by **Eco Adventures** (565 Mountain Village Boulevard; 970-728-7300). Eco offers guided snowshoe tours,

with ecological lessons thrown in, for under $50, including equipment.

11 *Outlaw Tour* 2 p.m.

Did you know that Butch Cassidy robbed his first bank on Main Street in 1889? Or that the town's red-light district once had 29 bordellos? These and other historical tidbits give Telluride an added sense of place that's missing from newer, corporate-run resorts. For an entertaining tour, contact **Ashley Boling** (970-728-6639; ashleyboling@gmail.com),

a D.J., actor, and self-appointed guide who offers 90-minute tours that are encyclopedic and long on stories ($20 a person; by reservation only). You may see him walking around town in his cowboy hat and red bandanna, guiding little knots of tourists and stopping every few minutes to say hello to friends — unless it's a powder day, in which case Telluride turns into a ghost town.

ABOVE The Bubble Lounge serves craft beers, organic wines, and oxygen. Telluride's altitude is 8,750 feet.

OPPOSITE Grab a window seat at Allred's for sunset views of the San Juan Mountains.

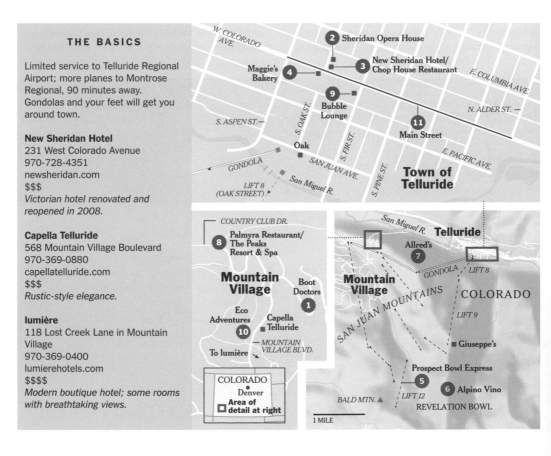

THE BASICS

Limited service to Telluride Regional Airport; more planes to Montrose Regional, 90 minutes away. Gondolas and your feet will get you around town.

New Sheridan Hotel
231 West Colorado Avenue
970-728-4351
newsheridan.com
$$$
Victorian hotel renovated and reopened in 2008.

Capella Telluride
568 Mountain Village Boulevard
970-369-0880
capellatelluride.com
$$$
Rustic-style elegance.

lumière
118 Lost Creek Lane in Mountain Village
970-369-0400
lumierehotels.com
$$$$
Modern boutique hotel; some rooms with breathtaking views.

Santa Fe

The Plaza, the heart of old Santa Fe, New Mexico, hasn't changed much since the Spanish settled here 400 years ago, and it's possible to focus a trip entirely on the historic town center, where Native American handicrafts are for sale on every corner. But surrounding it is an increasingly cosmopolitan city. The rest of Santa Fe now offers groovy contemporary art spaces, hot Asian restaurants, and a park designed by a pair of trailblazing architects. Santa Fe is worth loving not just for what it was, but for what it is.
— BY FRED A. BERNSTEIN

FRIDAY

1 *Public Space* 5 p.m.

For a beautifully curated introduction to Santa Fe, visit the **New Mexico History Museum** (113 Lincoln Avenue; 505-476-5200; nmhistorymuseum.org), which opened in 2009 and includes a gripping display about Los Alamos, where the Manhattan Project was conducted in secret during World War II. A large courtyard with ancient walls and shady trees separates the museum from the Palace of the Governors (palaceofthegovernors.org), the Spanish seat of government in the early 1600s and now a small museum of Colonial and Native American history. The two-museum complex is free on Fridays from 5 to 8 p.m.

2 *White Walls and Wine* 7 p.m.

You'd have to be crazy to pay for a glass of white wine on Fridays. Canyon Road, which angles up from the center of town, has more than 100 galleries, and there are openings every Friday night. According to canyonroadarts.com, the largest category is contemporary representational (think brightly colored paintings of the desert). Check out **Eight Modern** (231 Delgado Street; 505-995-0231; eightmodern.net), where you'll find the geometric scrap-metal constructions of the Santa Fe artist Ted Larsen. The backyard sculpture garden is a great place to marvel at New Mexico's amazingly clear sky and savor its piñon-infused air before heading to dinner.

3 *Ahi Moment* 9 p.m.

Martín Rios is a hometown boy made good. Born in Mexico and raised in Santa Fe, he apprenticed at the Eldorado Hotel and the Inn of the Anasazi — two local stalwarts — and made a brief appearance on *Iron Chef* before opening his own place, **Restaurant Martín** (526 Galisteo Street; 505-820-0919; restaurantmartinsantafe.com; $$), in 2009. The main draw is the food — dishes like ahi tuna tartare and duck breast with smoked bacon polenta and Marcona almonds offer hints of the Southwest, with a dash of global aspiration. But the homey décor makes you want to stick around even after finishing the bittersweet chocolate truffle cake.

SATURDAY

4 *Spice Market* 10 a.m.

The **Santa Fe Farmers' Market** (1607 Paseo de Peralta; 505-983-4098; santafefarmersmarket.com) dates back a half-century, but it stepped up a notch when it moved to a permanent building in 2008. Everything sold here, including dried chilies, yogurt, and grass-fed meats, is produced in northern New Mexico. The market is part of a bustling district that includes the new Railyard Park by the architect Frederic Schwartz and the landscape architect Ken Smith, both Manhattanites whose taste is anything but quaint. As you wander around, be on the lookout for the **Rail Runner** (nmrailrunner.com), a gleaming new passenger train scheduled to pull in from Albuquerque at 11:08 a.m.

OPPOSITE The Sangre de Cristo Mountains form a backdrop for residences designed by Ricardo Legorreta.

BELOW Don Gaspar Avenue in downtown Santa Fe.

5 *Sustainable Salads* Noon

Santa Fe residents care—as you learned roaming the Farmers' Market—where their food comes from. No wonder **Vinaigrette** (709 Don Cubero Alley; 505-820-9205; vinaigretteonline.com; $$) was an immediate hit when it opened in 2008. The brightly colored cafe has a menu based on organic greens grown in the nearby town of Nambé. Choose a base—Caesar, Cobb, and Greek are possibilities—then add diver scallops or hibiscus-cured duck confit. Add a glass of wine for a satisfying meal.

6 *Riding the Spur* 2 p.m.

Thanks to Santa Fe's sometimes depressing sprawl, it's getting harder and harder to find wide-open spaces. But drive (or bike) to the corner of

Galisteo Street and West Rodeo Road, where there's a small parking lot. Then begin pedaling due south, in the direction of Lamy (about 12 miles away). What starts as an asphalt path morphs into a dirt bike trail that swerves around a 19th-century rail spur. There are some pretty steep hills, but they're short, and the momentum from a downhill is usually enough to handle the next uphill. (If only life were like that!) The scenery is always gorgeous, especially in late afternoon, when the sun is low in the sky. **Mellow Velo** (621 Old Santa Fe Trail; 505-995-8356; mellowvelo.com) rents mountain bikes.

7 *Tapas With Strangers* 7 p.m.

La Boca (72 West Marcy Street; 505-982-3433; labocasf.com; $$) is one of downtown Santa Fe's most popular new restaurants—thanks to its contemporary tapas, plus larger dishes like cannelloni filled with crab, scallop, and Manchego. You'll find yourself sharing tips on what to order—and even forkfuls of delicious eats—with strangers.

8 *Reggae for All Ages* 10 p.m.

Santa Fe isn't a night-life town, but **Milagro 139** (139 West San Francisco Street; 505-995-0139; milagro139.com) is helping to change that. A building that had housed a coffee shop was recently converted to a restaurant that becomes a club on Friday and Saturday nights. There's no cover, and the drinks,

including a house margarita called Beginner's Luck, are delicious. A visit one summer evening coincided with performances by Rubixzu, a local band that performed a blend of reggae and Latin hip-hop to a diverse crowd, aged 9 to 90. For a trendier vibe, head to **Meow Wolf** (1800 Second Street; 505-204-4651; meowwolf.com), an alternative art space that is often open late during special exhibitions, or check its Web site for other parties hosted by Meow Wolf artists.

SUNDAY

9 *Free-Range Peacocks* 10 a.m.

For a big breakfast and an early start, drive south on Cerrillos Road about 10 miles past the Interstate, until you see a handwritten cardboard sign that reads, "Pine wood stove pellets sold here." You have arrived at the **San Marcos Café** (3877 State Road 14; 505-471-9298; $$). Dozens of peacocks, turkeys, and hens roam the property (which also houses a feed store), providing an Old MacDonald-like backdrop

for crowd-pleasers like eggs San Marcos, a cheese omelet in a bath of guacamole, beans, and salsa.

10 *Kitsch to Contemporary* Noon

If you ever thought that item you found at a roadside stand was one of a kind, **Jackalope** (2820

OPPOSITE ABOVE The Rail Runner train connects Santa Fe to Albuquerque.

OPPOSITE BELOW Desert, mountains, and Santa Fe.

ABOVE A touch of night life at Milagro 139.

BELOW The Santa Fe Farmers' Market. Everything sold at its stalls, including dried chilies, yogurt, and grass-fed meat, is produced in northern New Mexico.

Cerrillos Road; 505-471-8539; jackalope.com), a sprawling indoor-outdoor flea market, will disabuse you of that notion. There are hundreds of everything —look for items like punched-copper switch plates and tote bags that depict Michelle Obama smiling

ABOVE Revel in kitsch at the Jackalope, a sprawling indoor-outdoor flea market.

OPPOSITE Outside the San Marcos Café.

on a swing. If you need to shake off the kitsch, head to **SITE Santa Fe** (1606 Paseo De Peralta; 505-989-1199; sitesantafe.org), a contemporary art space.

11 *Bring Your Own Adobe* 1 p.m.

It's difficult to spend time in Santa Fe without thinking about buying a home (or second home) here. So check out **Zocalo** (Avenida Rincon; 505-986-0667; zocalosantafe.com), a striking development by the Mexican architect Ricardo Legorreta. He is known for crisp geometry and super-bright colors—a welcome sight in this city of browns and terra cottas. You don't really have to be in the mood to buy. Consider this real estate voyeurism, combined with a crash course in contemporary architecture.

THE BASICS

Santa Fe has a tiny airport with limited service. Most visitors fly into Albuquerque and drive about an hour to Santa Fe.

Hotel St. Francis
210 Don Gaspar Avenue
505-983-5700
hotelstfrancis.com
$$
Billed as the oldest hotel in Santa Fe. Fully renovated in 2009.

The El Rey Inn
1862 Cerrillos Road
505-982-1931
elreyinnsantafe.com
$$
Retro-chic 1930s-style motel with nicely furnished rooms.

Hilton Santa Fe Golf Resort & Spa
20 Buffalo Thunder Trail
505-455-5555
buffalothunderresort.com
$$
Part of a new casino complex 15 minutes north of town.

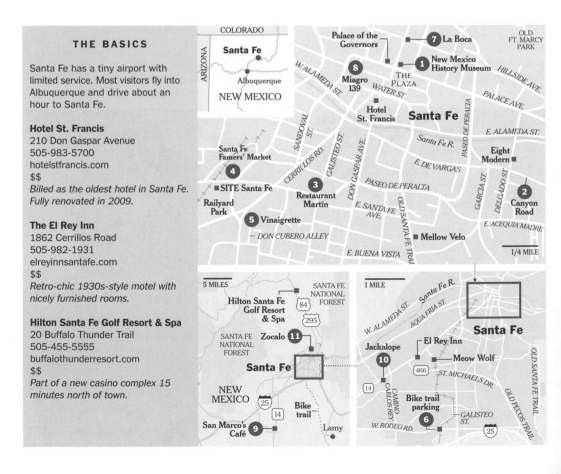

Oklahoma City

It shouldn't take more than a day for the song — who doesn't know that song? — to clear your head. Yes, a constant wind does seem to come sweepin' down the plain (more accurately, the red-dirt prairie). But amid the grand urban projects, gleaming museums, and air of new sophistication in today's Oklahoma City, the only folks yelling "Ayipioeeay" are likely to be visitors. Hints of what's behind the revitalization pop up everywhere: oil rigs, even on the State Capitol grounds. Even so, newcomers to town might wonder at first where they are. A generally flat cityscape, friendly hellos, and Chicago-style downtown architecture suggest the Midwest. Jazz, blues bars, and barbecue joints speak of the South. But the wide vistas and the American Indian shops (Oklahoma has 38 sovereign tribes), pickups, and cowboy hats tell another story: this is the West.
— BY FINN-OLAF JONES

FRIDAY

1 *Bricks and Bronzes* 4 p.m.

The Oklahoma River waterfront has come alive since 1999, when a canal was completed to attract visitors. In the lively Bricktown district, old warehouses now hold restaurants, clubs, and shops. Catch the bold spirit by checking out the monumental commemoration of the great Land Run of 1889, when 10,000 people rushed into town on a single day. A series of bronze statues, the larger-than-life-size work of the sculptor Paul Moore, show pioneers, horses, and wagons charging into the fray. Nearby, duck inside for a look at some of the 300 banjos in the **American Banjo Museum** (9 East Sheridan Avenue; 405-604-2793; americanbanjomuseum.com), ranging from lavishly decorated Jazz Age beauties to replicas of slaves' homemade instruments.

2 *Wasabi on the Range* 7 p.m.

If you're in the mood for steak, you will never have far to look in Oklahoma City. But even if you're not, have dinner at the **Mantel Wine Bar & Bistro** (201 East Sheridan Avenue; 405-236-8040; themantelokc.com; $$). The menu honors the regional theme with several beef entrees, but also offers interesting alternatives like duck breast with cranberry port wine sauce or wasabi-encrusted tuna.

3 *You'll Never Bowl Alone* 9 p.m.

Check out the night life in Bricktown, where taxi boats ferry merrymakers to the teeming homegrown jazz and blues joints. One of the livelier spots is **RedPin** (200 South Oklahoma Avenue; 405-702-8880; bowlredpin.com), a 10-lane bowling alley masquerading as a nightclub. Rent some hip-looking high-top bowling shoes, grab a beer or a pomegranate martini, and bowl the night away.

SATURDAY

4 *Feed Your Inner Cowboy* 11 a.m.

South of the river, the century-old Oklahoma National Stockyards are still used for enormous cattle auctions several times a week, but there's another kind of show one block farther up at **Cattlemen's Steakhouse** (1309 South Agnew Avenue; 405-236-0416; cattlemensrestaurant.com; $$). Long lines form for lunch and dinner (no reservations taken), so try breakfast. "Usually it's just the old-timers that want this," a waitress said when one

OPPOSITE Taxi boats on the canal in Bricktown, a happening Oklahoma City neighborhood.

RIGHT Oil has been good to Oklahoma, and derricks appear all over town, even on the grounds of the State Capitol.

out-of-towner succumbed to curiosity and ordered the calf brains. For the record, it looks like oatmeal, has a slight livery aftertaste, and isn't half bad. But wash it down with a couple of mugs of hot coffee and a plate of eggs and magnificently aged and tenderized steak.

5 *Dress Your Inner Cowboy* 12:30 p.m.

Cross the street to **Langston's Western Wear** (2224 Exchange Avenue; 405-235-9536; langstons.com) for your dungarees and boots, and then wander into the **National Saddlery Company** (1400 South Agnew Avenue; 405-239-2104; nationalsaddlery.com) for a hand-tooled saddle — prices run from about $1,500 for a base model to $30,000 for a masterpiece with silver trimmings. Down the street, **Shorty's Caboy Hattery** (1206 South Agnew Avenue; 405-232-4287; shortyshattery.com) will supply you with a custom-made cattleman's hat described by Mike Nunn, who manned the counter one day, as "the only hat that will stay on your head in Oklahoma wind." On the next block, **Oklahoma Native Art and Jewelry** (1316 South Agnew Avenue; 405-604-9800) carries a broad variety of items from Oklahoma's tribes. White pottery pieces with horse hairs burned onto their surfaces in Jackson Pollock-like swirling patterns are

ABOVE The memorial to victims of the 1995 bombing.

made by the store's owner, Yolanda White Antelope. Her son, Mario Badillo, creates silver jewelry.

6 *Where the West Is Found* 2 p.m.

James Earle Fraser's famous 18-foot statue of an American Indian slumped on his horse, *The End of the Trail*, greets you in the lobby of the **National Cowboy and Western Heritage Museum** (1700 Northeast 63rd Street; 405-478-2250; nationalcowboymuseum.org). Beware. You may think you can cover it in a couple of hours, but a whole day could be too little to reach the end of this trail. Exhibits in tentlike pavilions around a central courtyard cover everything about cowboys from their roots in Africa and England to how they operate on contemporary corporate ranches. Examine a replica of a turn-of-the-century cattle town; guns including John Wayne's impressive personal arsenal; and Western art including works by Frederic Remington, Albert Bierstadt, and Charles M. Russell.

7 *Cosmopolitans* 7 p.m.

The city's new economy has attracted a whole new class of settler, business types from world financial capitals, usually male and accompanied by stylish spouses. Find them — and a pre-dinner cocktail — in the noirish-cool **Lobby Bar** (4322 North Western Avenue; 405-604-4650; willrogerslobbybar.com) in the newly renovated Will Rogers Theater, which looms over an affluent corridor of North Western

Avenue. The street continues up to Tara-sized mansions dotting Nichols Hills, on the way passing establishments like **French Cowgirl** (4514 North Western Avenue; 405-604-4696), which sells tooled cellphone holders to match your saddle. For dinner, drive a few blocks to the **Coach House** (6437 Avondale Drive; 405-842-1000; thecoachhouseokc.com; $$-$$$), where the name of many an entree includes words borrowed from the French.

8 *Dances With Bulls* 10 p.m.

Find friends fast at **Cowboys OKC**, formerly Club Rodeo (2301 South Meridian Avenue; 405-686-1191; cowboysokc.com). Modern cowgirls and cowboys of every age group and shape can be found hootin' and hollerin' at this acre-sized honky-tonk south of downtown near the airport. Fellow carousers will help you figure out the dance moves to go with country sounds. The mood may turn real cowpokey when dance-floor lights go dark to be replaced by spotlights on a tennis-court-sized rodeo ring, where revelers migrate with their beers to watch hopefuls try to hang onto bucking bulls for longer than eight

ABOVE Shorty's Caboy Hattery. The cattleman's hat, they'll tell you at Shorty's, is the only kind that will stay on your head in an Oklahoma wind.

BELOW Downtown Oklahoma City.

that now covers the site, a gently flowing reflecting pool and two massive gates preside over 168 empty bronze chairs—one for each victim, the 19 smaller ones denoting children. Absorb the quiet, and the message.

seconds. The loudest cheers have been known to go to the orneriest bulls.

SUNDAY

9 *The Memorial* 10 a.m.

All longtime residents of Oklahoma City seem to know exactly where they were at 9:02 a.m. on April 19, 1995, when Timothy McVeigh detonated an explosives-filled truck beneath the Alfred P. Murrah Federal Building, killing 168 people and damaging 312 surrounding buildings. At the **Oklahoma City National Memorial** (620 North Harvey Avenue; 405-235-3313; oklahomacitynationalmemorial.org)

10 *Under Glass* 11 a.m.

The **Oklahoma City Museum of Art** (415 Couch Drive; 405-236-3100; okcmoa.com) boasts the world's most comprehensive collection of glass sculptures by Dale Chihuly, starting with the 55-foot-tall centerpiece at the front door. Savor the mesmerizing play of light, color, and fantastic shapes, a fitting goodbye to a town that never seems shy about grabbing your attention.

ABOVE Sunset over the Oklahoma River.

OPPOSITE *The End of the Trail*, by James Earle Fraser, at the National Cowboy and Western Heritage Museum.

THE BASICS

Fly into Will Rogers World Airport.

Rent a car to get around.

The Colcord
15 North Robinson Avenue
405-601-4300
colcordhotel.com
$$
Spacious and stylish rooms in a converted 1910 office building.

Skirvin Hilton
1 Park Avenue
405-272-3040
skirvinhilton.com
$$
Oklahoma City's grand hotel.

Waterford Marriott
6300 Waterford Boulevard
405-848-4782
marriott.com
$$
Well appointed and stocked with amenities.

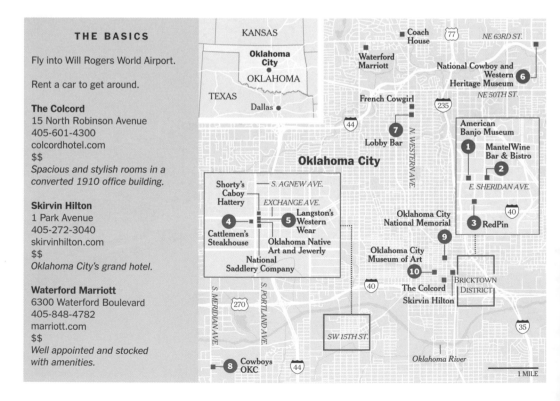

Dallas

Dallas may not be a world-class city, but it's pulling out all the stops to get there. Rich with oil money, it has pumped millions of dollars into civic projects, including the AT&T Performing Arts Center, a recent addition to the 68-acre Arts District. Meanwhile, glamorous subterranean bars and edgy Asian restaurants are giving the city a cosmopolitan aura. But when it comes to entertainment, its No. 1 attraction is still the Cowboys, now in their new, $1.2 billion football stadium featuring one of the largest retractable roofs and high-definition televisions in the world.
— BY LUISITA LOPEZ TORREGROSA

FRIDAY

1 *Architecture Park* 4 p.m.

See what Dallas is happily showing off these days. Go on a walking tour of the **Dallas Arts District** (artsdistrict.org), a 19-block area straddling downtown office skyscrapers and uptown luxury hotels. A prime attraction of the district is the **Performing Arts Center** (2403 Flora Street; 214-954-9925; dallasperformingarts.org), a four-venue complex for music, opera, theater, and dance in a parklike setting. A drum-shaped opera house was designed by Norman Foster and a cube-shaped theater is by Rem Koolhaas. To take it all in, find a bench at the **Nasher Sculpture Center** (2001 Flora Street; 214-242-5100; nashersculpturecenter.org), a museum designed by Renzo Piano with a lush garden that features works from a collection including Rodin, Henry Moore, and George Segal.

2 *Trend-Setter Cocktails* 7:30 p.m.

Size up the city's trend setters and assorted poseurs in their alligator boots and butter-soft tailored jackets at the **Rattlesnake Bar**, a plush lounge with mahogany-paneled walls and chocolate-brown leather sofas at the **Ritz-Carlton, Dallas** (2121 McKinney Avenue; 214-922-4848; ritzcarlton.com/dallas). Order the Dean's Margarita with organic

OPPOSITE Towers of downtown Dallas from the rooftop pool at the Joule hotel.

RIGHT Size up the city's trend setters and assorted poseurs in their alligator boots at the Rattlesnake Bar.

agave nectar, nibble on spring rolls with achiote pulled pork, and watch heads turn whenever a posse of lanky blondes in skinny jeans and designer heels sidles up to the bar.

3 *Southwest Supreme* 8 p.m.

Not so long ago, Dallas was a culinary wasteland, save for its famous barbecue. But in recent years, celebrity chefs like Nobu Matsuhisa, Tom Colicchio, and Charlie Palmer have planted their flags here, joining a fresh crop of hometown talent. At the top is **Fearing's** (2121 McKinney Avenue; 214-922-4848; fearingsrestaurant.com; $$$$), a casual but chic restaurant in the Ritz-Carlton that serves imaginative Southwest-rooted cuisine. Opened in 2007, Fearing's gained national acclaim at the time: Zagat named it No. 1 in domestic hotel dining, and Frank Bruni, the restaurant critic for *The New York Times*, called it one of the country's top 10 new restaurants outside of New York. Expect dishes like lobster coconut bisque and wood-grilled Australian lamb chops on pecorino polenta.

4 *Party High* 10:30 p.m.

There are still men's clubs, honky-tonks, and jukebox joints in Dallas, but the city's night life has gotten decidedly sleeker and flashier, with velvet-roped discos and bottle-service lounges. If you want a stellar view of the stars and the city's bright lights, go to

the rooftop bar of the **Joule** hotel (1530 Main Street; 214-748-1300; luxurycollection.com/joule). It features bedlike sofas and cocoonlike chairs arrayed along a slender, cantilevered swimming pool that juts out 10 stories above the sidewalk. Or, for an even better view, go to **FiveSixty**, Wolfgang Puck's Asian-style restaurant in the glowing ball atop the 560-feet-high **Reunion Tower** (300 Reunion Boulevard; 214-741-5560; wolfgangpuck.com). The rotating bar, which serves a dozen kinds of sake, offers magnificent views of a

ABOVE The Dallas Museum of Art, a city mainstay.

BELOW Forty Five Ten, the epitome of chic Dallas boutiques. The prices are shocking, but it's worth a visit.

skyline edged in colorful lights and the suburban sprawl beyond.

SATURDAY

5 *Morning Glory* 10 a.m.
  Need a breath of fresh air after a late night out? Head to the **Katy Trail** (entrance at Knox Street at Abbott Avenue; 214-303-1180; katytraildallas.org), a 3.5-mile greenway that winds through the city's wooded parks and urban neighborhoods. Built along old railroad tracks, the trail is a favorite of young and old, bikers and runners, stroller-pushing parents and dog walkers.

6 *Slower Food* Noon
  Chicken-fried everything may be a staple in Texas, but in Dallas organic salads and other light fare are just as popular. A trendy spot is **Rise No. 1** (5360 West Lovers Lane; 214-366-9900; risesouffle.com; $$), a charming bistro with a grass-green facade that serves up wonderful soufflés — a slow-paced antidote to Dallas's manic drive-and-shop lifestyle. Try the truffle-infused mushroom soufflé with a glass of dry white.

7 *Retail Overload* 2 p.m.
  Shopping is a sport here, and there are more stores than just Neiman Marcus. For slow-paced window

shopping, stroll around **Inwood Village** (West Lovers Lane and Inwood Road; inwoodvillage.com), a landmark 1949 shopping center with an eclectic range of signature stores. Retail highlights include **Rich Hippie** (5350 West Lovers Lane, No. 127; 214-358-1968; richhippie.com) for retro and avant-garde clothing like a finely tooled pink leather jacket. Next door is **Haute Baby** (5350 West Lovers Lane, No. 128; 214-357-3068; hautebabydallas.com) for cute toddler wear. But perhaps the chicest boutique is **Forty Five Ten** (4510 McKinney Avenue; 214-559-4510; fortyfiveten.com). The prices are shocking but it's worth a visit. One shopper's finds included a vintage trolley case by Globe-Trotter and an iron vase by the Texan artist Jan Barboglio.

8 *Mex-Mex* 8:30 p.m.

One of the most popular Dallas spots for original Mexican fare is **La Duni Latin Cafe** (4620 McKinney Avenue; 214-520-7300; laduni.com; $$), which offers terrific dishes like tacos de picanha (beef loin strips on tortillas). For more inventive cuisine, try **Trece: Mexican Kitchen & Tequila Lounge** (4513 Travis Street; 214-780-1900; trecerestaurant.com; $$). The

formal dining room, dressed in cream, cacao, and sepia colors, invites celebration. Kick things off with a flavored caipirinha or a mojito before tucking into entrees like chipotle braised short ribs or vegetarian chile relleno.

9 *Cool Kids* 11:30 p.m.

Once a ramshackle district, the historic Cedar Springs neighborhood has a new energy, with gay-friendly discos, curio shops, burger bars, boutiques, and galleries. To mingle with the neighborhood's varied stripes, hit **J. R.'s Bar & Grill** (3923 Cedar Springs Road; 214-528-1004; partyattheblock.com), a cavernous club with brick walls, a tin ceiling, and a scuffed dance floor that draws gays, straights,

ABOVE Dallas Cowboys Stadium, the focus of most of the city's energy on home-game Sundays.

RIGHT Try authentic Mexican fare at La Duni Latin Cafe.

middle-aged couples, midnight cowboys, frat boys, and young ladies with thick makeup. Nothing gets going before midnight, when the pub crawlers and night lizards come out to play.

SUNDAY

10 *Sports Madness* 11:30 a.m.

If it's Sunday in Dallas, do as the locals do and hit a sports bar. There are dozens in town, if not

hundreds, but a favorite is the **McKinney Avenue Tavern** (2822 McKinney Avenue; 214-969-1984; mckinneyavenuetavern.com), affectionately nicknamed the Mat. There is a carved-wood bar with two dozen or so rickety tables fronting the 30-odd television screens that show nothing but sports, day and night. When the Cowboys play, the joint is bedlam. Rule No. 1: Go early, stay late.

ABOVE The Morton H. Meyerson Symphony Center in the 19-block Arts District.

OPPOSITE Fearing's, a chic, casual restaurant with imaginative Southwest-rooted cuisine. Celebrity chefs have planted their flags in Dallas, joining a fresh crop of hometown talent.

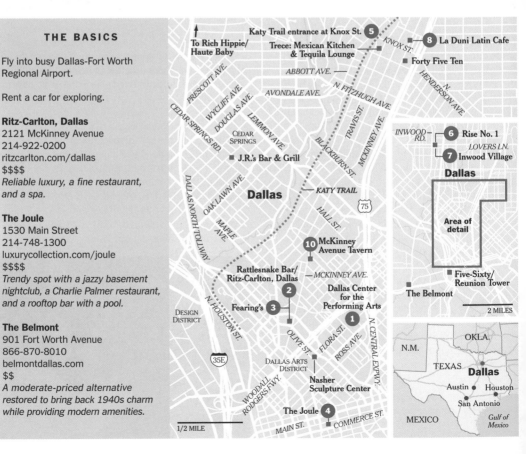

THE BASICS

Fly into busy Dallas-Fort Worth Regional Airport.

Rent a car for exploring.

Ritz-Carlton, Dallas
2121 McKinney Avenue
214-922-0200
ritzcarlton.com/dallas
$$$$
Reliable luxury, a fine restaurant, and a spa.

The Joule
1530 Main Street
214-748-1300
luxurycollection.com/joule
$$$$
Trendy spot with a jazzy basement nightclub, a Charlie Palmer restaurant, and a rooftop bar with a pool.

The Belmont
901 Fort Worth Avenue
866-870-8010
belmontdallas.com
$$
A moderate-priced alternative restored to bring back 1940s charm while providing modern amenities.

Fort Worth

How much art can you look at in one weekend? Of all American cities that might pose this dilemma, Fort Worth, Texas, traditionally a cow town overshadowed by neighboring Dallas, might be the least expected. But with oil-wealthy patrons eager to build its cultural endowment with sought-after artworks and interesting contemporary architecture to hold them, Fort Worth has become a place to go for art immersion. If you fear museum fatigue, take heart. The city's public art galleries don't overwhelm; they're on a uniformly intimate scale. And there's enough cowboy spirit left in town to give you a break from high culture whenever you want to take one. — BY RICHARD B. WOODWARD

FRIDAY

1 *Sundance* 5 p.m.

Fort Worth is dominated by a few families, none mightier than the billionaire Bass clan, famous for giving generously to George W. Bush's campaigns and for revitalizing the north end of the city. See some of their handiwork in **Sundance Square** (sundancesquare.com). Starting with two square blocks they bought in 1978, it has expanded to more than 35 square blocks dominated by a pair of Brutalist skyscrapers designed by Paul Rudolph in the '70s and now holding the headquarters of the Bass businesses. David Schwarz, the family's favorite architect, has contributed buildings in the Texas Deco style (blending Art Deco with state symbols like the star), including Bass Performance Hall, a home to opera, symphony, touring Broadway shows, and the quadrennial piano competition begun by and named after a local hero, Van Cliburn.

2 *Romance of the West* 6 p.m.

At the **Sid Richardson Museum** in the square (309 Main Street; 817-332-6554; sidrichardsonmuseum.org), take your time looking at the 38 oil paintings by Frederic Remington and Charles Russell. The museum displays only a tiny sample of the romantic taste of Sid Richardson, a millionaire oilman and Bass relative

who collected work on Indian and cowboy themes. If you'd like a different take on Western tradition, take a 10-minute drive to the **National Cowgirl Museum and Hall of Fame** (1720 Gendy Street; 817-336-4475; cowgirl.net), which celebrates Western women, from ranchers to celebrity pop stars.

3 *Saloon Chef* 7 p.m.

Chef Tim Love's **Lonesome Dove Western Bistro** (2406 North Main Street; 817-740-8810; lonesomedovebistro.com; $$$), near Fort Worth's traditional economic heart, the Stockyards, is a very modern pairing of *Iron Chef* cooking and cowboy chic. The decor is reminiscent of an Old West saloon, with a long bar and a tin ceiling, and the staff may be wearing cowboy hats. It's hard to say what the cattle drivers who used to come through Fort Worth would make of the cuisine, including dishes like a chili-rubbed pork chop with Yukon Gold-Swiss Chard Gratin and crispy onions, or beef tenderloin stuffed with garlic and accompanied by plaid hash and a Syrah demi-glace.

SATURDAY

4 *Breakfast for All* 9 a.m.

Don't be dismayed if there's a long line at the **Paris Coffee Shop** (704 West Magnolia Avenue; 817-335-2041; pariscoffeeshop.net; $). It seats more than 100, so tables turn over quickly. A Fort Worth institution since the Depression era, it seems to cater to everyone in town. Who could resist a place that offers green tea as well as cheese grits and has ads on the menu for everything from music lessons to bail bondsmen?

OPPOSITE *High Desert Princess*, by Mehl Lawson, outside the National Cowgirl Museum and Hall of Fame.

RIGHT Breakfast at the Paris Coffee Shop.

5 *Art of America* 10 a.m.

This is your day for serious art appreciation in the **Cultural District**, about five miles west of Sundance. Start at the **Amon Carter Museum of American Art** (3501 Camp Bowie Boulevard; 817-738-1933; cartermuseum.org). Carter, who made his fortune in newspapers and radio, was a Fort Worth booster who hated Dallas so much he reportedly carried his lunch when forced to visit, to keep from spending money there. His bequest financed what is now one of the leading collections of American art in the country, especially strong in Western paintings, 19th-century photographs, and Remington sculptures. The museum's original 1961 building by Philip Johnson was expanded in the late '90s.

6 *Art and Water* Noon

The **Modern Art Museum of Fort Worth** (3200 Darnell Street; 817-738-9215; the modern.org) has been an island of tranquility since it opened a new building in 2002. The architect, Tadao Ando, oriented the building around a shallow pool so that several of the wings extend outward and seem to float on the water. Have brunch at its **Café Modern** (817-840-2157; thecafemodern.com; $$), which attempts to serve dishes worthy of the setting—consider the Moroccan chicken salad or mushroom goat cheese crepes. Then explore the galleries, arrayed with a select group of postwar and contemporary works—usual suspects like Jackson Pollock and Dan Flavin, as well as rarities in American museums, like the German Minimalist sculptor Ulrich Rückriem. Whether in the sunlit bays beside the water, where you may find a lead floor piece by Carl Andre, or in a cul-de-sac where a wooden ladder-like sculpture by Martin Puryear reaches between floors, the building is still very much the star.

7 *Art and Light* 3 p.m.

The **Kimbell Art Museum** (3333 Camp Bowie Boulevard; 817-332-8451; kimbellart.org) provides an unrivaled museum experience combining first-rate architecture and first-rate art. From the street, the 1972 building, designed by Louis I. Kahn, offers a plain travertine exterior that will not prepare you for the

soaring harmonies inside. To step into the lobby is to enter a Romanesque church of a museum. Long slits and diffusing louvers in the barrel-vaulted ceiling allow the light to both cut spaces dramatically and softly spill over them. The collections, from all periods and places, are noteworthy for both aesthetic quality and historical depth. An 11th-century Cambodian statue of Siva is less a representative object than a stunningly beautiful one. European paintings — with masterpieces by Bellini, Mantegna, Caravaggio, Velázquez, de la Tour, Goya, Cézanne — are mostly presented without glass.

8 *Steak and Wine* 7 p.m.

You're not finished yet with cowboy-inspired cooking. **Reata** (310 Houston Street; 817-336-1009; reata.net; $$$) is Texas big, spread over several floors of an old building in the heart of Sundance Square. The fourth-floor bar has a panoramic skyline view. Reata's entrees run to steaks and chops, its wine list is extensive, and its desserts are tempting and calorie-laden.

9 *Hang with the Herd* 9 p.m.

Billy Bob's Texas (2520 Rodeo Plaza; 817-624-7117; billybobstexas.com), housed in a former cattle barn and touted as the world's largest honky-tonk, should be visited at least once, and perhaps only once. Walk around and select your entertainment option:

play pool or the 25-cent slot machines, watch live bull riding in a ring or sports on TV, eat barbecue or popcorn, shop for cowboy hats, try your luck at outmoded carnival games, drink at any of 32 bars, or dance and listen to country music on the two musical stages. A few hours at Billy Bob's may not measure up to an afternoon viewing Fort Worth's art collections. But as you merge with the herd (capacity is

ABOVE AND OPPOSITE ABOVE The Modern Art Museum of Fort Worth, an island of tranquility that invites contemplation of both the architecture and the artworks.

BELOW AND OPPOSITE BELOW Pool playing and bull riding at Billy Bob's, an outsize honky-tonk in a former cattle barn. It can entertain 6,000 Texans at a time.

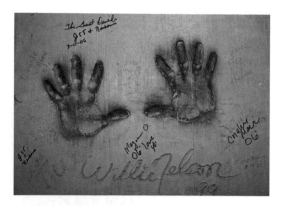

817-871-7686; fwbg.org), home to more than 2,500 species of native and exotic plants that flourish in its 23 specialty gardens. A favorite, the Japanese Garden, is a treat for the senses with koi-filled pools, stonework, and waterfalls. If it's springtime, expect flowering trees and migrating birds—perhaps, if you're lucky, a tree full of cedar waxwings on their way north.

more than 6,000), sipping bourbon and watching the gliding two-steppers on the dance floor, it feels like a much more authentic and less imported experience—much more like Texas.

SUNDAY

10 *Texans Also Garden* 11 a.m.
Spend some peaceful hours at the **Fort Worth Botanic Garden** (3220 Botanic Garden Boulevard;

ABOVE Country musicians' handprints on the walls at Billy Bob's are Fort Worth's answer to movie stars' footprints in concrete in Hollywood. These were made by Willie Nelson.

OPPOSITE Texas exuberance on the dance floor.

THE BASICS

Fly into Dallas/Fort Worth International Airport.

Rent a car to get around.

Renaissance Worthington
200 Main Street
817-870-1000
marriott.com
$$$
In Sundance Square, with 474 rooms and 30 suites at a variety of prices.

The Ashton
610 Main Street
817-332-0100
theashtonhotel.com
$$
Attractive boutique hotel with 39 rooms.

Omni Fort Worth
1300 Houston Street
817-535-6664
omnihotels.com
$$$
Opened in 2009; skyline views and a rooftop garden.

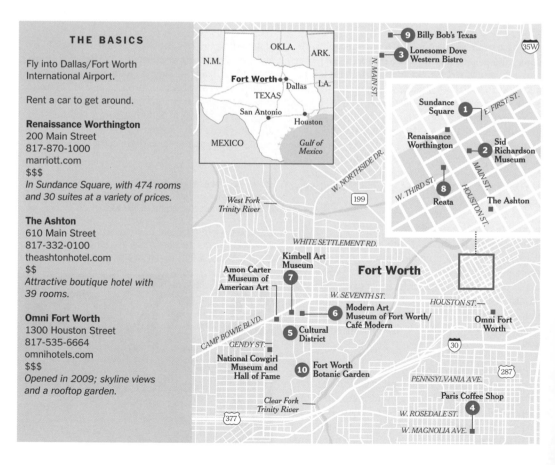

Houston

A snarl of superhighways and skyscrapers, Houston is easily dismissed as a corporate campus — home to Fortune 500 giants like Halliburton and Waste Management and a company formerly known as Enron. Its generic towers sprawl to the horizon. The Johnson Space Center, where the world's eyes were fixed as NASA directed the moon landing from its control center, is 25 miles south of downtown. But this Texas megalopolis has been inching back to its urban core. Cool art galleries have sprung up in once blighted neighborhoods. Midcentury modern buildings have been saved and restored. And former factories have been turned into buzzing restaurants and bars.
— BY DENNY LEE

FRIDAY

1 *Park It Downtown* 5:30 p.m.

Houston may be a sea of office towers, but this subtropical city is also surprisingly green. Hundreds of parks carpet the city, and one of the newest, a 12-acre park called **Discovery Green** (discoverygreen.com), is quickly becoming the heart of the city's still sleepy downtown. Opened in 2008, the park serves as a true public space; elderly couples stroll around the artificial lake as toddlers roll down grassy knolls. For sunset cocktails, follow the area's young professionals to the **Grove** (1611 Lamar Street; 713-337-7321; thegrovehouston.com), a modern restaurant inside the park, which offers treehouse-like views of the skyline.

2 *Gulf of Tex-Mex* 8 p.m.

The city's young chefs are working overtime to step out of the shadow of Texas barbecue. Among the most feted these days is Bryan Caswell, the chef and owner of **Reef** (2600 Travis Street; 713-526-8282; reefhouston.com; $$), a seafood restaurant with a Southern twist. Housed in a former car dealership with soaring windows and ceilings, the restaurant creates a dramatic space for winning dishes like

roasted grouper with corn pudding and grilled peach. The dining room hums with an eclectic crowd — men in white suits eating ceviche, couples on dates, well-dressed families celebrating birthdays.

3 *Slice of Austin* 10 p.m.

Sports bars and mega-clubs fuel much of the city's night life, but a clutch of down-to-earth bars can be found along the tree-lined streets of Montrose. **Poison Girl** (1641 Westheimer Road; 713-527-9929) has pinball machines, a long shelf of whiskeys and a dirt-packed backyard jammed with 20-somethings in vintage Wranglers and Keds. Down the street is **Anvil Bar and Refuge** (1424 Westheimer Road; 713-523-1622; anvilhouston.com), which styles itself as a classic cocktail bar, though it can feel like a meat market on weekends. A handful of gay bars are also nearby, including the oldie but still rowdy **611 Hyde Park Pub** (611 Hyde Park Boulevard; 713-526-7070).

SATURDAY

4 *Drilling for Art* 11 a.m.

With all those petrodollars sloshing around, it's no surprise that contemporary art has an eager benefactor in Houston. The grande dame is still the **Menil Collection** (1515 Sul Ross Street; 713-525-9400; menil.org), opened in 1987 to house the

OPPOSITE The Chapel of St. Basil, designed by Philip Johnson, is part of Houston's remarkable collection of midcentury modern architecture.

RIGHT A downtown view from the Grove restaurant.

collection of Dominique de Menil, an heiress to an oil-equipment fortune. Blue-chip galleries include the **Devin Borden Hiram Butler Gallery** (4520 Blossom Street; 713-863-7097; dbhbg.com) and the **Sicardi Gallery** (2246 Richmond Avenue; 713-529-1313; sicardi.com). Scrappy artists, meanwhile, have carved out studios in downtown warehouses. Some of their work can be seen at the **Station Museum** (1502 Alabama Street; 713-529-6900; stationmuseum. com), which showcases emerging artists inside a big metal shed.

5 *Global Grills* 1:30 p.m.

While the city's sizable Vietnamese community is now scattered, traces of Little Saigon still remain in Midtown, a mixed-use neighborhood dotted with banh mi joints. A retro-favorite is **Cali Sandwich** (3030 Travis Street; 713-520-0710; $), a ho-hum cafeteria with 1970s-style vertical blinds and prices to match: the freshly made sandwiches include barbecue pork. If you're hankering for genuine Texas BBQ, drive north to **Pizzitola's Bar-B-Cue** (1703 Shepherd Drive;

713-227-2283; pizzitolas.com; $). It may not be as packed as Goode's barbecue empire, but Pizzitola's is the real deal, judging by the wood pits that have been charring ribs out back for 70-plus years.

6 *Pottery to Pinball* 3 p.m.

Malls rule in Houston—the biggest, the Galleria, offers 2.4 million square feet of brand names. Off-brand shopping requires a bit more driving. For one-of-a-kind home furnishings, head to **Found** (2422 Bartlett Street; No. 5; 713-522-9191; foundforthehome.com), which takes old industrial objects like hay feeders and turns them into architectural objets. **Sloan/Hall** (2620 Westheimer Road; 713-942-0202; sloanhall.com) carries an odd array of art books, bath products, and pottery—some by Texas artisans. **Peel** (4411 Montrose Boulevard, Suite 400; 713-520-8122; peelgallery.org) blurs the line between art gallery and jewelry boutique. And **Flashback Funtiques** (1627 Westheimer Road; 713-522-7900; flashbackfuntiques.net) is a trove of Lone Star Americana, like old pinball machines and gas pumps.

7 *Southwestern Redux* 7:30 p.m.

Robert Del Grande is considered culinary royalty here, credited with pioneering Southwestern cuisine in the 1980s. So when his restaurant of 29 years, Café Annie, closed in 2009, there was a collective grumble. The hunger was soon sated: he opened **RDG + Bar Annie** (1800 Post Oak Boulevard; 713-840-1111; rdgbarannie.com; $$-$$$), a multiplex of a restaurant with bars, lounges, and dining rooms that attracts a glamorous crowd that seems to favor short party dresses, shiny handbags, and aggressive amounts of gold. The menu is similarly bold and brash, with dishes like lobster meatballs with a rémoulade sauce and grilled rib-eye steak with a smoked Cheddar sauce.

ABOVE Brick-and-stone tradition at Rice University.

LEFT Sloan/Hall, a clever independent store on Westheimer Road.

8 *Two Dives* 10 p.m.

A party corridor has formed along Washington Avenue. A favorite among nearby bobos is **Max's Wine Dive** (4720 Washington Avenue; 713-880-8737; maxswinedive.com), with its long, inexpensive wine list. Seeking a different cast of characters? Night owls find the unmarked door that leads to **Marfreless** (2006 Peden Street; 713-528-0083; marfrelessbar.com), whose dark corners are popular with canoodling couples.

SUNDAY

9 *Bottomless Mimosas* 10 a.m.

A cafe tucked inside a nursery (it's called Thompson + Hanson) may sound precious, but so what? **Tiny Boxwood's** (3614 West Alabama Street; 713-622-4224; tinyboxwoods.com; $$) does a fantastic Sunday brunch. Situated close to the posh River Oaks neighborhood, the sun-washed dining room and vine-covered patio draw a handsome and self-assured crowd that mingles easily around a communal table. Chalkboard specials include leafy salads and a delicious breakfast pizza made with pancetta, goat cheese, and an egg, baked sunny side up in a wood oven. Pick up a cactus on the way out.

10 *Modernist Drive-By* Noon

Despite Houston's lack of zoning (or maybe because of it), the city has a remarkable collection of midcentury modern homes and office towers

ABOVE For one-of-a-kind home furnishings, head to Found, which turns old industrial objects into home décor items.

BELOW The Brochstein Pavilion at Rice University.

together your own architectural tour with **Houston Mod** (houstonmod.org), a preservation group that maintains a resourceful Web site with Google maps and photos.

—some well maintained, others verging on collapse. Landmarks include the gridlike campus for the University of St. Thomas, designed by Philip Johnson. But many more are unknown, like the eerily abandoned **Central Square** building in downtown (2100 Travis Street) or the brawny **Willowick** tower, now condos, in River Oaks (2200 Willowick Road). Piece

ABOVE Cooling off at the Discovery Green park.

OPPOSITE Rice University balances its academic rigor with a richly decorated main campus.

11 *Glass Houses* 2 p.m.

The skyline goes up, up, up every year. But notable architecture also takes place near the ground. The campus at **Rice University**—a neo-Byzantine maze of rose-hued brick and cloisters—got a new glass heart in 2008, when the **Brochstein Pavilion** (rice.edu/brochstein) opened near the central quad. A Kubrick-esque box with floor-to-ceiling windows, it houses a cafe and media lounge, and has a fine-mesh trellis that extends like a mathematical plane in space. The structure is only one story, but it feels much taller—proof that not everything in Houston has to be big.

THE BASICS

Fly in and rent a car.

Hotel Zaza Houston
5701 Main Street
713-526-1991
hotelzazahouston.com
$$
Playful design and polished service in the lively Museum District.

Aloft Houston by the Galleria
5415 Westheimer Road
713-622-7010
alofthouston.com
$$
New with a pool and gym, in the Uptown district.

Hotel Icon
220 Main Street
713-224-4266
hotelicon.com
$$
A mix of boutique and classic hotel style.

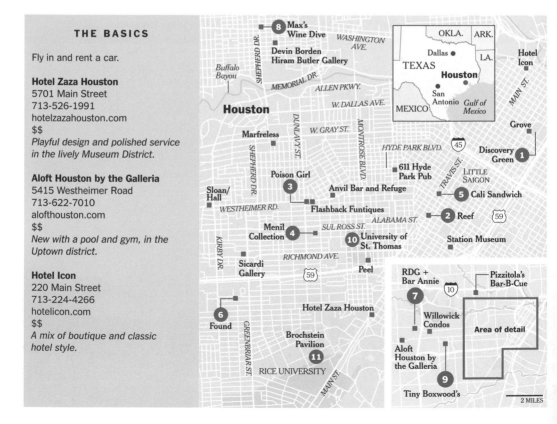

Austin

The unofficial motto of Austin, Texas, "Keep Austin Weird," blares from bumper stickers on BMWs and jalopies alike, on T-shirts worn by joggers along Lady Bird Lake, and in the windows of locally owned, chain-defying shops and restaurants. A college town known for its liberal leanings and rich music scene, Austin asserts its independent spirit in a largely conservative state. It clings to its tolerance of eccentricity in the face of rapid development including high-tech flagships and fleets of new high-rise condos downtown. And while its openhearted citizens, with their colorful bungalows and tattoos, continue to do their part, it has little to fear from encroachment of the staid and ordinary. As one local put it: "As long as Austinites keep decorating their bodies and cars, we're going to be fine." — BY JAIME GROSS

FRIDAY

1 *Dress the Part* 4 p.m.

If you forgot to pack your Western wear, make a beeline for **Heritage Boot** (1200 South Congress Avenue; 512-326-8577; heritageboot.com), where Jerome Ryan and his team of "boot elves" fashion fanciful boots out of exotic leathers like shark and caiman alligator, using vintage 1930s to '60s patterns. With colorful stitching, hand-tooling, and puffy inlays, they are instant collectors' items — priced from a few hundred dollars to around $2,000. For a less expensive route to the Texas look, stop by **Cream Vintage** (2532 Guadalupe Street; 512-474-8787; creamvintage.com) for vintage Western shirts and weathered concert tees, customized to your dimensions by an on-site tailor.

2 *Saucy Platters* 6:30 p.m.

Barbecue is a local sport, and there are a lot of competing choices. For a classic pit experience — meaning you can smell the smoke and sauce as soon as you pull into the state-fair-size parking lot — drive 25 miles southwest to the **Salt Lick** (18300 Farm to Market Road 1826, Driftwood; 512-858-4959; saltlickbbq.com; $$), settle in at a communal picnic table, and order the all-you-can-eat platter, piled high with brisket, ribs, and sausage. If you prefer to stay in downtown Austin, check out **Lambert's Downtown Barbecue** (401 West Second Street; 512-494-1500; lambertsaustin.com; $$). Carved out of a brick-walled

general store that dates from 1873, it is raising the bar (and provoking outrage among purists) with its newfangled "fancy barbecue" — think brown-sugar-and-coffee-rubbed brisket and maple-and-coriander-encrusted pork ribs.

3 *Fine Home for Fine Arts* 8 p.m.

Just off the south shore of Lady Bird Lake (named for Lady Bird Johnson, the former first lady) is the **Long Center for the Performing Arts** (701 West Riverside Drive; 512-457-5100; thelongcenter.org), opened in 2008 after an epic $80 million fund-raising effort. It has one of the largest, most acoustically perfect stages in Texas, home to the Austin Symphony, Austin Lyric Opera, and Ballet Austin. There's also a smaller black box theater spotlighting local musicians, improv troupes, and theater companies. Even if you don't attend a performance, it is worth stopping by for a glimpse of the glittering skyline views from the building's front terrace.

SATURDAY

4 *Start It Right with Tacos* 9 a.m.

Forget the oatmeal. In this town, morning means breakfast tacos, filled with scrambled eggs, potatoes, bacon, beans, and jalapenos in whichever combination you choose. Try them at **Tamale House** (5003 Airport Boulevard, also known as East 50th

OPPOSITE Cycling the Veloway in bluebonnet season.

BELOW Get your custom cowboy boots, crafted in traditional patterns, at Heritage Boot.

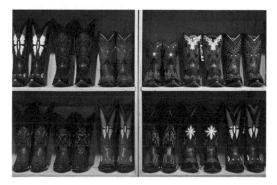

LEFT Austin is a music town with statuary to match. The blues guitarist Stevie Ray Vaughan stands at Lady Bird Lake.

Street; 512-453-9842; $). It doesn't get more authentic, and it doesn't get more Austin.

5 *Bicycle Friendly* 10 a.m.

Explore the city at a leisurely pace by renting a bicycle from **Mellow Johnny's Bike Shop** (400 Nueces Street; 512-473-0222; mellowjohnnys.com), opened by Lance Armstrong, a native son, in 2008. In addition to selling and renting bikes, the shop stocks accessories like wicker baskets, messenger bags, and colorful racing jerseys. If you ask, staff members will chart an appealing route along Austin's 20 miles of urban hike-and-bike trails. A favorite is the **Veloway** (ci.austin.tx.us/parks/trails.htm), where cyclists roll past blooming bluebonnets in the spring.

6 *Munch and Browse* 2 p.m.

Some of Austin's best lunch food is dished out of Airstreams and food trucks by both amateur and professional chefs. You can look for a list on austinfoodcarts.com, or just be on the lookout as you explore South Congress, an appealing neighborhood for shopping or just window shopping. Find rare and collectible vinyl, from 99 cents to $1,000, at **Friends of Sound** (1704 South Congress Avenue; 512-447-1000; friendsofsound.com), down an alley off the main drag. Quirky souvenirs, like a duck decoy or beaver top hat, abound at **Uncommon Objects** (1512 South Congress Avenue; 512-442-4000; uncommonobjects.com), a sprawling emporium with a flea market aesthetic and a giant pink jackalope out front.

7 *Bats!* 7:30 p.m.

From early spring through late fall, the **Congress Avenue Bridge** hosts a Halloween-worthy spectacle: at dusk, more than a million Mexican free-tailed bats pour out from under the bridge and head east to scavenge for insects (austincityguide.com/content/congress-bridge-bats-austin.asp). The best spot for viewing the exodus is from the park at the southeastern end of the bridge, so you can see their flitting forms backlit by the glowing sky. To hear an estimate of the bats' flight time on a particular evening, dial the bat hot line (512-416-5700, extension 3636), operated by *The Austin American-Statesman.*

8 *French Connection* 8:30 p.m.

There's something almost Felliniesque about driving down a dark road lined with industrial warehouses and stumbling onto **Justine's** (4710 East Fifth Street; 512-385-2900; justines1937.com; $$), a pitch-perfect French bistro. Outside, a family plays pétanque on the driveway; inside, groups of friends and couples sit on Thonet chairs at candlelit cast-iron-and-marble cafe tables as a turntable plays old jazz and reggae tunes. With atmosphere this good, the meal — Parisian comfort food, and delicious — is just a bonus.

9 *Performance Anxiety* 10 p.m.

The sheer quantity and variety of music in Austin on any given night can be daunting. Step One: consult Billsmap.com, which lists gigs everywhere in the city, highlights recommendations, and includes links to previous performances on YouTube. Two spots that reliably deliver a good time are the **Broken Spoke**, an old-time honky-tonk dance hall (3201 South Lamar Boulevard; 512-442-6189; brokenspokeaustintx.com), and the retro red-walled **Continental Club** (1315 South Congress Avenue; 512-441-2444; continentalclub.com), which dates from 1957 and has roots, blues, rockabilly, and country music.

SUNDAY

10 *Take a Dip* 10 a.m.

Wake up with a bracing swim in the natural, spring-fed **Barton Springs Pool** (2101 Barton Springs Road; 512-476-9044; ci.austin.tx.us/parks/bartonsprings.htm), a three-acre dammed pool that maintains a steady 68-degree temperature year-round. There's sunbathing (sometimes topless) on the grassy slopes, a springy diving board, and century-old pecan trees lining the banks. Afterward, park yourself out on the patio at **Perla's Seafood & Oyster Bar** (1400 South Congress Avenue; 512-291-7300; perlasaustin.com; $$) for a decadent lobster omelet and an oyster shooter spiked with rum and honeydew.

11 *Wildflower Country* 1 p.m.

Texas is proud of its masses of wildflowers, and you can find out why at the **Lady Bird Johnson Wildflower Preserve** (4801 La Crosse Avenue; 512-232-0100; wildflower.org), a University of Texas research center that is also a public botanical garden and spa. If you have more days to spend near Austin, or even if it has to wait until next time, follow the wild-flower lovers southwest out of town into the beloved Hill Country. A region of rolling limestone hills, bloom-filled meadows, and dozens of wineries, it's the perfect next Texas stop, whether it's bluebonnet season or not.

OPPOSITE BELOW Saturday night at the Broken Spoke.

THE BASICS

Austin is served by major airlines and interstate highways. You will need a car or bicycle to explore the city.

Hotel Saint Cecilia
112 Academy Drive
512-852-2400
hotelsaintcecilia.com
$$$
Bungalows and five rooms in a Victorian house in South Congress. Amenities include a turntable in every room and vinyl records to play on them.

Hotel San José
1316 South Congress Avenue
512-852-2350
sanjosehotel.com
$$
Forty airy rooms simply adorned with Indian bedspreads and framed vintage concert posters.

Kimber Modern Hotel
110 The Circle
512-912-1046
kimbermodern.com
$$$
Six stylish rooms open to a patio shaded by a giant live oak.

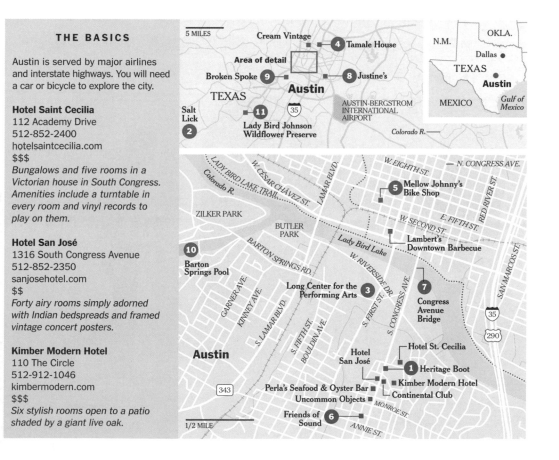

San Antonio

San Antonio, the United States' seventh-largest city, features a threesome of popular attractions: the River Walk (a meandering canal lined with restaurants and bars), Market Square (said to be the largest Mexican-style market outside of Mexico), and the Alamo (no explanation necessary). Beyond those obvious tourist stops, this old city also offers excellent Chicano art, 19th-century-style shopping, church music that goes way beyond hymns, and plenty of that famous Texas hospitality.
— BY DAN SALTZSTEIN

FRIDAY

1 *Shopping as It Was* 3 p.m.

La Villita historic district (South Alamo Street at East Nueva Street; lavillita.com), just off the River Walk, still feels like the little village it once was but is now crammed with artisanal shops, many of which are housed in lovely mid-19th-century buildings. The **Casa Clasal Copper Gallery** (Building No. 400; 210-271-3856; lavillita.com/copper) sells everything copper; a gorgeous set of hammered ewers started at about $40. **Alice Knight** (No. 1700; 210-930-5527; lavillita.com/aliceknight) sells Knight's playful and sometimes goofy paintings, as well as her delicate handmade-paper masks (from about $20). On one shopping day the artist's husband, Jack, was running the store. Is he an artist as well? "She lets me paint the edges," he said.

2 *Italy Comes to Texas* 5:30 p.m.

Five-thirty? What is this, the early-bird special? No, it's **Il Sogno Osteria** (Pearl Brewery Complex, 200 East Grayson Street; 210-212-4843; $$), and since it doesn't take reservations, the crowds line up early. The restaurant is Andrew Weissman's wildly successful Italian follow-up to his popular, now closed La Rêve. The industrial-chic space fills up with families and couples, some barside, gazing at the wood-burning oven in the open kitchen. Antipasti

OPPOSITE Early morning at the Alamo, before the day's onslaught of eager tourist crowds.

RIGHT Museo Alameda, a Smithsonian affiliate, displays Latino and Chicano art.

included an addictive white bean purée, and the lasagna with wild mushrooms was a satisfying pasta option. The Nutella tart, a holdover from La Rêve, is achingly decadent.

3 *More Salsa* 9 p.m.

South Alamo Street, a short but colorful jumble of galleries, shops, and restaurants, is the main strip of the Southtown neighborhood, a diverse and welcoming pocket that's cherished by many locals. Let the beat and the warm bodies pull you into **Rosario's Café y Cantina** (910 South Alamo Street, 210-223-1806; rosariossa.com), a festive Mexican restaurant that pulsates with live salsa music and energetic dancing on Friday nights, especially on each month's First Friday, when the neighborhood sponsors a street fair of art and music. In a town famous for its margaritas, Rosario's are among the tastiest.

SATURDAY

4 *Brewery without Beer* 9:30 a.m.

Starting your Saturday at a brewery? Not to worry. Though it produced beer for over a century, **Pearl Brewery** (200 East Grayson Street; 210-212-7260; pearlbrewery.com) closed in 2001 and after an elaborate renovation reopened as a mixed-use complex. In addition to a few restaurants (Il Sogno included) and a branch of the Culinary Institute of America, there are a growing number of shops, including **Melissa Guerra** (210-293-3983; melissaguerra.com), a kitchenware store owned by the cookbook author, and the **Twig**

Book Shop (210-826-6411; thetwig.booksense.com), an airy spot that offers a nice variety of best sellers and Texas-themed publications. There is also a Saturday-morning farmers' market (pearlfarmersmarket.com) with local vendors selling cheeses, salsa, herbs, nuts, baked goods, and all kinds of produce. Stroll and savor the aromas.

5 *Burgers with Conscience* Noon

Don't oversample at the market, because one of the more unusual dining places in town is a few minutes away in the Five Points neighborhood. **The Cove** (606 West Cypress Street; 210-227-2683; thecove.us; $) is a restaurant, car wash, coin laundry, and music spot. Its sloppy and satisfying Texas Burger (with refried beans, chips, grilled onion, avocado, and salsa) won mention in *Texas Monthly*. The Cove is also notable for its dedication to S.O.L. — sustainable, organic, local — ingredients, and it practices what it preaches with dishes like grilled tilapia tacos or a salad of roasted organic beets, goat cheese, and walnuts.

6 *Spirit of the Smithsonian* 2 p.m.

San Antonio has a broad visual art scene that ranges from contemporary to folk, with a special concentration on Latino work. There's a First Friday art walk (southtown.net); nonprofit centers like **Artpace** (artpace.org); and quality museums like the San Antonio Museum of Art and the Witte Museum. But it's **Museo Alameda** (101 South Santa Rosa Avenue; 210-299-4300; thealameda.org) that was chosen as the first official satellite of the Smithsonian. Alameda's hot-pink exterior belies the straightforward presentations of Latino and Chicano art inside.

ABOVE Creative decorating on the River Walk, the beloved pathway that snakes for four miles through downtown.

RIGHT The Cove, in the Five Points neighborhood, has an updated spin on familiar foods like hamburgers and tacos.

7 *Her Name Is Rio* 5 p.m.

After the Alamo, the most popular attraction in town is probably the **River Walk**, a four-mile stretch of paths that snakes through downtown along the canals (thesanantonioriverwalk.com). Sure, it's touristy, but if you avoid the often overpriced restaurants and bars that line it, a stroll can be lovely, particularly as the sun sets and hanging lights illuminate picturesque bridges.

8 *Eating Up North* 7 p.m.

To satisfy a Tex-Mex craving, head out of town to the Far North area, where you'll see the full extent of San Antonio's sprawl. Amid miles of highway loops, malls, and planned communities, find family-friendly **Aldaco's Stone Oak** (20079 Stone Oak Parkway; 210-494-0561; aldacos-stoneoak.com; $$), which serves up big portions in a large, noisy space. A patio looks toward Texas Hill Country. After your shrimp enchiladas, follow the green glow at Plaza Ciel, a nearby strip mall, to the **Green Lantern** (20626 Stone Oak Parkway; 210-497-3722), San Antonio's contribution to the speakeasy trend. There's no sign, but the low-lighted room and old-school drinks attract young professionals. Order something from the classics list, like a well-made Sazerac.

SUNDAY

9 *The Tourist's Mission* 10 a.m.

If you're a first-timer in San Antonio, or you just love the story of the Texans who fought to the death and want to hear it again, Sunday morning

RIGHT Mexican-American nostalgia in a Museo Alameda gift shop, inspired by a fondly remembered local botanica.

can be a good time to hit the **Alamo** (Alamo Plaza; thealamo.org). You won't lack for company — 2.5 million people a year visit this holiest of Texas civic shrines — and the parking may cost you. But the old walls are still there, and admission is free.

10 *Brisket Brunch* Noon

Texas' most beloved barbecue is served about an hour north in Hill Country, but the **Smokehouse** (3306 Roland Avenue; 210-333-9548; thesmokehousesa.com; $) represents San Antonio proudly. You'll smell the proof from the parking lot: this is the real deal. Friendly staff members work the 40-foot-long mesquite-wood pits. Order a sandwich or a platter

by the pound, including the succulent, charred-on-the-outside brisket.

11 *For the Birds* 2 p.m.

Walk off those calories at **Brackenridge Park** (3910 North St. Mary's Street), a 340-plus-acre green space on the west side of town. The park's sunken Japanese Tea Garden offers a bit of serenity, while the bustling **San Antonio Zoo** (sazoo-aq.org) is particularly child-friendly, with a Lori Landing aviary where visitors can feed, and play with, brightly colored lorikeets. A different sort of Texas hospitality, but an entertaining one for sure.

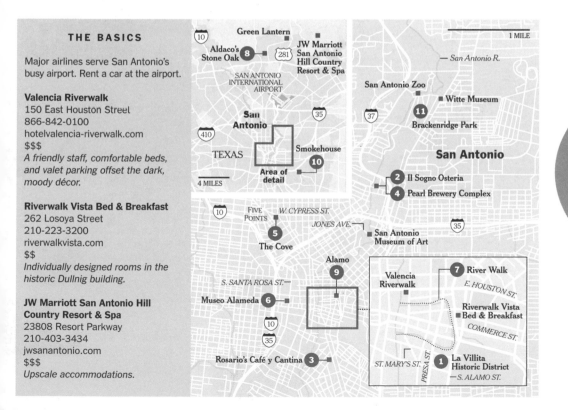

THE BASICS

Major airlines serve San Antonio's busy airport. Rent a car at the airport.

Valencia Riverwalk
150 East Houston Street
866-842-0100
hotelvalencia-riverwalk.com
$$$
A friendly staff, comfortable beds, and valet parking offset the dark, moody décor.

Riverwalk Vista Bed & Breakfast
262 Losoya Street
210-223-3200
riverwalkvista.com
$$
Individually designed rooms in the historic Dullnig building.

JW Marriott San Antonio Hill Country Resort & Spa
23808 Resort Parkway
210-403-3434
jwsanantonio.com
$$$
Upscale accommodations.

Green Lantern
10
Aldaco's
Stone Oak 8 281
JW Marriott
San Antonio
Hill Country
Resort & Spa
SAN ANTONIO
INTERNATIONAL
AIRPORT
**San
Antonio**
410
35
TEXAS
Smokehouse
10
4 MILES
Area of
detail
1 MILE
— San Antonio R.
San Antonio Zoo
■ Witte Museum
37
11
Brackenridge Park
San Antonio
2 Il Sogno Osteria
4 Pearl Brewery Complex

10
FIVE
POINTS
W. CYPRESS ST.
JONES AVE.
5
The Cove
Alamo
9
S. SANTA ROSA ST.
Museo Alameda 6
10
35
Rosario's Café y Cantina 3
San Antonio
Museum of Art
35
Valencia
Riverwalk
7 River Walk
E. HOUSTON ST.
Riverwalk Vista
■ Bed & Breakfast
COMMERCE ST.
ST. MARY'S ST.
PRESA ST.
1 La Villita
Historic District
— S. ALAMO ST.

SOUTHWEST

Los Angeles

Angelenos like to challenge visitors by quipping, "It's a great place to live but I wouldn't want to visit here." Granted, it's tough to decide what to see and do in a city that encompasses 470 square miles. Fortunately, there is always an under-the-radar restaurant, a funky theater, or a splashy store to discover. And you never have to leave the iconic landmarks behind.
— BY LOUISE TUTELIAN

FRIDAY

1 *Stop and Shop* 4 p.m.

The hilly Los Feliz area, just northeast of Hollywood, is an old neighborhood reborn with a hip veneer. A walk along North Vermont Avenue turns up an intriguing trove of vintage clothes, handmade jewelry, antique textiles, books, and much more. **New High (M)Art** (1720 North Vermont Avenue; 323-638-0271; newhighmart.com), an industrial-style space filled with world music and the faint perfume of incense, stocks an eclectic mix. For sale one afternoon were a vintage French army camo jacket and a necklace made from hand-painted leather flags. **Skylight Books** (1818 North Vermont Avenue; 323-660-1175; skylightbooks.com) caters to the many artists, writers, musicians, and actors in the neighborhood — and anyone else who loves a carefully curated arts bookstore. Browse the stacks and you'll see a monograph on Richard Meier next to a tome on *Mad* magazine posters. And don't step on Franny, the resident cat.

2 *Friendly Fare* 6 p.m.

Little Dom's (2128 Hillhurst Avenue; 323-661-0055; littledoms.com; $$-$$$) is the best of homey and hip, a bar/bistro with an inventive menu. The fare is mostly Italian-American, but since executive chef Brandon Boudet hails from New Orleans, there's a dash of the South as well. Pappardelle with house-made sausage? No problem. But Boudet also serves up a succulent fried oyster sandwich with hot sauce mayo, y'all.

OPPOSITE For a lovely walk in west Los Angeles that visitors hardly ever take, stroll among the Venice canals.

RIGHT At the Griffith Park Observatory, stargazers line up for a peek at celestial sights like the rings of Saturn.

3 *Bright Lights, Big City* 8 p.m.

Get the big picture at the **Griffith Park Observatory** (2800 East Observatory Avenue; 213-473-0800; griffithobservatory.org), with its view of the entire Los Angeles basin. Visitors line up for a peek into a massive Zeiss telescope with a 12-inch reflector that reveals celestial sights like the rings of Saturn. The Samuel Oschin Planetarium shows employ laser digital projection and state-of-the-art sound. A show about the brilliant aurora borealis — accompanied by Wagner's *Ride of the Valkyries* — is a cosmic experience.

4 *Alive and Swingin'* 10 p.m.

Featured in the movie *Swingers,* with Vince Vaughn and Jon Favreau, the **Dresden** (1760 North Vermont Avenue; 323-665-4294; thedresden.com/lounge.html) is a welcome throwback to an earlier era, with its upscale 1960s rec room décor and stellar bartenders. You're here to see Marty and Elayne, jazz musicians who also perform pop, standards, and the occasional show tune, with a changing array of guest artists, on Friday and Saturday nights in the lounge. The crowd is a cocktail shaker of twenty-somethings on dates, middle-aged couples with friends, and college kids. Somehow, it all goes down very smoothly.

SATURDAY

5 *From Canyon to Canyon* 10 a.m.

Joni Mitchell doesn't live here anymore, but Laurel Canyon retains its '70s image as a self-

contained artistic enclave (albeit a more expensive one now). Its social hub is the **Canyon Country Store** (2108 Laurel Canyon Boulevard; 323-654-8091), a grocery/deli/liquor store marked by a flower power-style sign that pays homage to its hippie roots. Sip organic oak-roasted espresso at the Canyon Coffee Cart, buy a picnic lunch and head for the high road — Mulholland Drive. The serpentine road follows the ridgeline of the Santa Monica Mountains, and every curve delivers a spectacular vista of the San Fernando Valley and beyond. Drop down into **Franklin Canyon Park** (2600 Franklin Canyon Drive;

310-858-7272; lamountains.com/parks), 605 acres of chaparral, grasslands, and oak woodlands with miles of hiking grounds. Heavenly Pond is a particularly appealing picnic spot.

6 *The Hills of Beverly* 1 p.m.

The stores range from Gap to Gucci, but you don't need deep pockets to enjoy Beverly Hills. **Prada** (343 North Rodeo Drive; 310-278-8661), designed by Rem Koolhaas, delivers a jolt of architectural electricity. The 50-foot entrance is wide open to the street, with no door (and no name, either). A staircase peopled with mannequins ascends mysteriously. On the top level, faux security scanners double as video monitors and luggage-carousel-style shelves hold merchandise. At the **Paley Center for Media** (465 North Beverly Drive; 310-786-1091; paleycenter.org/visit-visitla), enter your own private TVland. At the center's library, anyone can screen segments of classic TV and radio shows, from *The Three Stooges* to *Seinfeld* as well as documentaries and specials. When it's time to cool your heels, head for the **Beverly Canon**

ABOVE Skylight Books in Los Feliz, just northeast of Hollywood, caters to writers, artists, musicians, and actors.

LEFT The crowd at the Dresden, where Marty and Elayne perform on weekends, is a cocktail shaker of 20-somethings on dates, clumps of middle-aged friends, and college kids.

Gardens (241 North Canon Drive), a public park masquerading as a private Italian-style garden. Adjacent to the Montage Hotel, the Gardens have plenty of benches, tables, and chairs, and a large Baroque fountain adding a splashing soundtrack.

7 *Full Exposure* 4 p.m.

The incongruous setting of corporate high-rises is home to the under-appreciated **Annenberg Space for Photography** (2000 Avenue of the Stars; 310-403-3000; annenbergspaceforphotography.org), an oasis of images. One enthralling group show was by nature photographers shooting under Arctic oceans, on a volcano, and deep within Florida swamps. Another featured photographs by Herb Ritts, Mary Ellen Mark, Chuck Close, and other documentarians of beauty and style. The space itself is open and airy, with an iris-like design on the ceiling to represent the aperture of a lens.

8 *Unleashed* 6 p.m.

Don't knock it till you've tried it. Only a restaurant unequivocally named **Animal** (435 North Fairfax Avenue; 323-782-9225; animalrestaurant.com; $$-$$$) can sell diners on dishes like pig ear with chili, lime, and a fried egg, or rabbit legs with mustard and bacon. Or something else if inspiration strikes: the menu doesn't get printed until a half-hour before opening. The place is nondescript with no name on the storefront (it's four doors up from Canter's Deli), but once you've tried the fat pork-belly sliders with crunchy slaw on a buttery brioche bun, you'll beat a path there again.

9 *The Silent Treatment* 8 p.m.

Dedicated to finding, screening, and conserving unusual films (can you say, *"Killer Klowns from Outer Space"*?), the 120-seat **Silent Movie Theater** (611 North Fairfax Avenue; 434-655-2510; cinefamily.org) is like a quirky film class held in a club. Where else can you claim a well-worn couch and pour a cocktail from a punch bowl while waiting for show time? Insider tip: Regulars bring their own bottles of wine.

SUNDAY

10 *Breakfast by the Beach* 10 a.m.

Berries and Brussels sprouts abound at the **Santa Monica Farmer's Market** (2640 Main Street; Santa Monica; 310-458-8712; smgov.net) but there are also 10 stands where local restaurateurs sell dishes prepared on the spot. Among the best are Arcadie's sweet or savory crepes, Carbon Grill's hefty burritos, and the Victorian's custom omelets.

ABOVE Basking poolside at the eco-chic Palomar boutique hotel on Wilshire Boulevard, near the University of California at Los Angeles.

A live band might be playing any genre from jazz to zydeco. Finish up with a scone from the Rockenwagner bakery stand and munch it on the beach, only a block away.

11 *Secret Gardens* 1 p.m.

One of the loveliest walks in west Los Angeles is one visitors hardly ever take: a stroll among the **Venice canals**. The developer Abbott Kinney dug miles of canals in 1905 to create his vision of a

Venice in America. The decades took their toll, but the remaining canals were drained and refurbished in 1993. The surrounding neighborhood is now on the National Register of Historic Places. Charming footpaths crisscross the canals as ducks splash underneath. On the banks, mansions stand next to small bungalows. Residents pull kayaks and canoes up to their homes. It's quiet, serene, and hidden. Hollywood? Where's that?

ABOVE Spindly palms and an evening sky in Los Feliz.

OPPOSITE Within its expanse of 470 square miles, Los Angeles has room for places that can feel remote, like this trail in the Santa Monica Mountains.

THE BASICS

Fly into Los Angeles, Burbank, or Long Beach. You can't get by without a car — preferably one with a GPS.

The Farmer's Daughter Hotel
115 South Fairfax Avenue
323-937-3930

farmersdaughterhotel.com
$$
Cool country-hipster hotel in shopping nirvana.

The Avalon Hotel
9400 West Olympic Boulevard
310-277-5221
theavalonbeverlyhills.com
$$-$$$

Luxe spa style a walk away from Beverly Hills sites.

The Palomar
10740 Wilshire Boulevard
310-475-8711
$$-$$$
Eco-chic boutique hotel close to the University of California at Los Angeles.

Downtown Los Angeles

The sprawl, the scale, all that freeway time — for many, Los Angeles is an acquired taste. But not downtown. New York-like in its density and mishmash, the long-blighted center has become an accessible, pedestrian-friendly destination in recent years; Angelenos walk around en masse, using their actual legs. The immense L.A. Live entertainment complex is largely responsible for this comeback, but the studiously vintage bars and imaginative restaurants that seem to open every other day are also part of the revival. Skid Row and the drifts of homeless camps haven't vanished altogether, and the grittiness still varies by block. But this part of town is alive again, in ways that make sense even to an outsider.
— BY CHRIS COLIN

FRIDAY

1 *Do the Crawl* 4 p.m.

The Downtown Art Walk — a party-in-the-streets bonanza that draws thousands of revelers the second Thursday of every month — is one way to experience the area's robust art scene. But you can do your own art walk anytime, and you should. Lured by low rents, a number of impressive galleries have found a home here, many of them on Chung King Road, a pedestrian alley strung with lanterns in Chinatown. For starters: **The Box** (No. 977; 213-625-1747; theboxla.com), **Jancar Gallery** (No. 961; 213-625-2522; jancargallery.com), **Charlie James Gallery** (975 Chung King Road; 213-687-0844; cjamesgallery.com), and **Sabina Lee Gallery**

(No. 971; 213-620-9404; sabinaleegallery.com). The shows are intimate and occasionally provocative, featuring a broad array of contemporary artists: William Powhida, Orly Cogan, and others. Most galleries stay open till 6 p.m.; Jancar closes at 5 on Fridays.

2 *The City at Its Brightest* 7:30 p.m.

Whether you're catching a Lakers game, touring the Grammy Museum, or attending a concert at the Nokia Theater, there is always something splashy to do at the 27-acre, $2.5 billion sports and entertainment behemoth that is **L.A. Live** (800 West Olympic Boulevard; 213-763-5483; lalive.com). Just strolling the Tokyo-ish Nokia Plaza — 20,000 square feet of LED signage — is diverting. An array of restaurants and bars is clustered at the periphery, but many visitors prefer just to stroll around this giant pedestrian zone, trying to take it all in.

3 *A Late, Great Bite* 10 p.m.

The Gorbals (501 South Spring Street; 213-488-3408; thegorbalsla.com; $$) is one of the more fantastic — and odd — downtown dining options. The chef and owner, a previous *Top Chef* winner, is part Scottish and part Israeli, and his hybrid concoctions are terrific. On one visit, banh mi poutine merged Quebec and Vietnam in ways criminally neglected until now. Bacon-wrapped matzo balls, anyone? The restaurant is tucked into the lobby of the old Alexandria Hotel, a well-worn but charming landmark where Bogart, Chaplin, and Garbo once roamed the halls.

SATURDAY

4 *On the Nickel* 9 a.m.

The maple bacon doughnut is a stand-out on the breakfast menu at the new but ageless **Nickel Diner** (524 South Main Street; 213-623-8301; nickeldiner.com; $). The rest is mostly well-executed diner food. What's

OPPOSITE Broadway in downtown Los Angeles, a pedestrian-friendly destination rebounding from 20th-century decline.

LEFT Fabric in the Fashion District, a 100-block mix of wholesale-only shops and designer retail discounts.

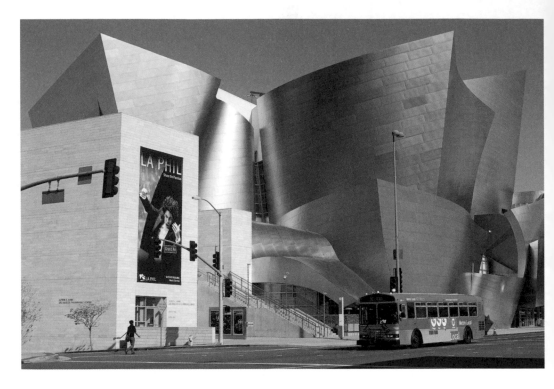

remarkable is the location—until recently, this block was one of Skid Row's most notorious. It's a testament to downtown's revival that the intersection of Main and Fifth (hence "Nickel") is now home to a place where people line up for tables.

5 *Nice Threads* 10:30 a.m.

The 100-block **Fashion District** mixes high and low seamlessly. Though many shops sell wholesale only, you can still find a wide selection of deeply discounted designer clothes, fabric, and accessories. The jumbled shops and warehouses at Ninth and Los Angeles Streets are a good place to start (feel free to bargain). And don't miss the rowdier **Santee Alley** (thesanteealley.com), where cheap meets weird in a thoroughly Los Angeles way. In this chaotic open-air bazaar, energetic vendors hawk the impressive (perfect knock-off handbags) and the odd (toy frogs emblazoned with gang insignias). For a more organized Fashion District expedition, Christine

Silvestri of Urban Shopping Adventures (213-683-9715; urbanshoppingadventures.com) leads three-hour romps, tailored to your particular agenda and with an insider's radar for the best finds. The tours cost $36 a person, with a minimum of two people.

6 *Accessible Architecture* 1 p.m.

The arrival of the conductor Gustavo Dudamel at the Los Angeles Philharmonic has brought new crowds to the symphony, but the **Walt Disney Concert Hall** (111 South Grand Avenue; 323-850-2000; laphil.com) —Frank Gehry's deconstructivist celebration of all that is big, curvy, and shiny—deserves a visit even without a ticket. Bring a picnic and wind your way along the semi-hidden outer staircase up to an excellent city vista and rooftop garden oasis. Free guided tours and self-guided audio tours are available most days. Check first (musiccenter.org/visit/tours.html) for schedules.

7 *Lazy Bones* 7 p.m.

Since 2010, **Lazy Ox Canteen** (241 South San Pedro Street; 213-626-5299; lazyoxcanteen.com; $$-$$$) in Little Tokyo has been the kind of tucked-away gastropub people love to insist is the city's best. Casual and buzzing, the bistro has a long menu featuring adventurous delicacies, from trotters to crispy pigs' ears to lamb neck hash. It's hard to pin the cuisine to a specific origin, but a penchant for bold, meat-centric comfort food is evident. Get several small plates.

ABOVE Find the outdoor stairway on Frank Gehry's Walt Disney Concert Hall and climb its curves to a rooftop garden.

OPPOSITE ABOVE Drinks at Seven Grand, one of the retro bars inspired by downtown's colorful history.

OPPOSITE BELOW The Nickel Diner, a busy spot in a revived area that not so long ago was part of Skid Row.

8 *Pick a Show, Any Show* 8:30 p.m.

If you're downtown for a performance, chances are it's a sprawling affair at L.A. Live. But a handful of smaller settings offer funkier alternatives. The **Redcat Theater** (631 West Second Street; 213-237-2800; redcat.org) plays host to all manner of experimental performances — one Saturday in winter featured theater, dance, puppetry, and live music from a Slovene-Latvian art collaboration. **Club Mayan** (1038 South Hill Street; 213-746-4287; clubmayan.com), an ornate old dance club most nights, occasionally hosts mad events like Lucha VaVoom, which combines burlesque and Mexican wrestling. And the **Smell** (247 South Main Street; thesmell.org), a likably grimy, volunteer-run space, hosts very small bands circled by swaying teenagers.

9 *Drink as if It's Illegal* 10:30 p.m.

Was Los Angeles a hoot during Prohibition? No need to guess, thanks to a slew of meticulously old-timey new bars that exploit the wonderful history of old Los Angeles. From upscale speakeasy (the **Varnish**; 118 East Sixth Street; 213-622-9999; thevarnishbar.com) to converted power plant-chic (the **Edison**; 108 West Second Street; 213-613-0000; edisondowntown.com) to an old bank vault (the **Crocker Club**; 453 South Spring Street; 213-239-9099; crockerclub.com), these spiffy places do set decoration as only Los Angeles can. And fussily delicious artisanal cocktails are as plentiful as you'd imagine. The well-scrubbed will also enjoy the swanky **Seven Grand** (515 West Seventh Street; 213-614-0737; sevengrand.la), while the well-scuffed may feel more at home at **La Cita Bar** (336 South Hill Street; 213-687-7111; lacitabar.com).

SUNDAY

10 *Diamond in the Rough* 9 a.m.

The **Bamboo Plaza** isn't as elegant as its name, but on the second floor of this run-down little Chinatown mall is the **Empress Pavilion** (988 North Hill Street,

ABOVE If an art piece is much older than the first baby boomer, you're not likely to find it in the Museum of Contemporary Art, which is rich in works by Rothko, Oldenburg, Lichtenstein, and Rauschenberg.

OPPOSITE Skyscrapers aglow in the downtown heart of sprawling Los Angeles.

suite 201; 213-617-9898; empresspavilion.com; $$), a dim sum mecca that's lured Angelenos since well before the downtown revival. The vast dining room holds all the appeal of a hotel conference room, but that only underscores the focus on the shrimp har gow, the pork buns, and dozens of other specialties. There will be crowds.

11 *Big Art* 11 a.m.

That rare breed who has gone from gallery owner to director of a significant art institution, Jeffrey Deitch has thrilled (and vexed) critics since taking over the esteemed **Museum of Contemporary Art**. Come see for yourself what he's done with the place, and its renowned collection, including works by Rothko, Oldenburg, Lichtenstein, and Rauschenberg. The museum is spread over three locations; downtown is the main one (250 South Grand Avenue; 213-626-6222; moca.org).

THE BASICS

Flights to Los Angeles are easy to book from anywhere. Walking works better than it used to, but you may still want a car.

Ritz-Carlton
900 West Olympic Boulevard
213-743-8800
lalive.com/stay/ritzcarlton
$$$$
Half of a gleaming new two-hotel complex rising above L.A. Live.

JW Marriott
900 West Olympic Boulevard
213-765-8600
lalive.com/stay/jwmarriott
$$
The other half of the same hotel complex.

Figueroa Hotel
939 South Figueroa Street
213-627-8971
figueroahotel.com
$$
Moroccan-themed.

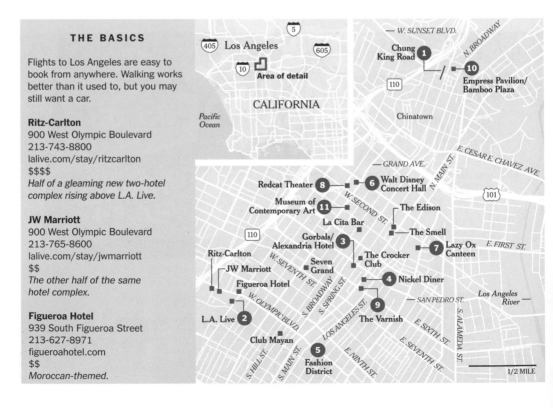

Hollywood

Hollywood is one of those rare places that live up to their stereotypes, right down to the sign. But with minimal effort, it can offer a whole lot more. This pedestrian-friendly district represents both Los Angeles's past, with icons like the Capitol Records building, and the city's future — multi-ethnic, vertical, dense. A recent renaissance means there are now million-dollar condos, trendy restaurants, celebrity watering holes, and a world-class movie theater. But there are still tattoo parlors, sex shops, and homelessness. Tying it all together is the Hollywood Walk of Fame, where it is hard not to be at least momentarily tickled (Hello, Mister Rogers) or merely confused (Who the heck was that?). It remains a place that only Los Angeles could produce.

— BY JENNIFER STEINHAUER

FRIDAY

1 *Costume Change* 4 p.m.

Before you unpack your bags, prepare to fill them up. Hollywood is awash in vintage clothing stores, many of them filled with remnants from television and movie sets past. **Golyester** (136 South La Brea Avenue; 323-931-1339) has amazingly preserved purses, negligees ($278 was the price for one two-piece Christian Dior number), evening gowns (including, on one visit, a white leather dress with fur trim) and more. Of special interest are the shoes — finds like gold sling-backs, emerald stilettos, or elegant Herbert Levine pumps. Down the street is **The Way We Wore** (334 South La Brea Avenue; 323-937-0878; thewaywewore.com) with more vintage treasures. Between them is **Cafe Midi** (148 South La Brea Avenue; 323-939-9860; cafemidi.com), where you can have a cappuccino and take in the Moroccan ceramic bowls and candles in the adjacent store.

2 *Planet Thai* 7:30 p.m.

There are upscale bistros and giant tuna rolls aplenty in the neighborhood, but Los Angelenos love Hollywood for Thai food. Reasonable minds can quibble over the best, which tends to be high on authentic flair, low on atmosphere, and budget-priced. Good examples are the **Sapp Coffee Shop** (5183 Hollywood Boulevard; 323-665-1035) and **Ruen Pair** (5257 Hollywood Boulevard; 323-466-0153). For

a slightly more upscale ambience, check out **Bulan Thai Vegetarian Kitchen** (7168 Melrose Avenue; 323-857-1882; bulanthai.com), a chic spot that's hot with the yoga crowd. Look for menu items like busabu pumpkin, jungle curry, and tum kha.

3 *The New Rat Pack* 10 p.m.

O.K., it might feel like you're traipsing through a cliché, but check out **Teddy's** (7000 Hollywood Boulevard; 323-466-7000; hollywoodroosevelt.com) anyway. Located inside the Hollywood Roosevelt Hotel, the lounge long had a reputation for being as loud and exclusive as possible. These days it has a slightly more diplomatic, if not exactly proletarian, door policy. Celebrity sightings are still common, and the slightly sinister look of the place makes for good sipping.

SATURDAY

4 *Is That TomKat?* 8:30 a.m.

Los Angeles is a morning town, so get going at **Square One Dining** (4854 Fountain Avenue; 323-661-1109; squareonedining.com; $$), a cheerful local spot that focuses on farmers' market produce. Order some French toast with banana citrus caramel or the transporting pressed egg sandwich with tomato

OPPOSITE Amoeba Music on Sunset Boulevard, where new and used CDs and DVDs are found by the mile and you might catch a live performance.

BELOW Across the city to the Hollywood sign.

and arugula. Stare at the Scientology headquarters across the street, among the more relevant fixtures in Hollywood, and try and see who is going in and coming out of its parking structure.

5 *Open House* 11 a.m.

Many a native Angeleno knows not of **Barnsdall Art Park** (4800 Hollywood Boulevard; 323-644-6269; barnsdallartpark.com), a public space donated to the city by the eccentric Aline Barnsdall in 1927. Beyond having one of the best views of the Hollywood sign and grass upon which to sit (a rare thing in Los Angeles), the site is home to the **Los Angeles Municipal Art Gallery**, a theater, and the **Hollyhock House** (323-644-6269; hollyhockhouse.net), Frank Lloyd Wright's first Los Angeles project. Tours of the house begin at 12:30 p.m. Wednesday through Sunday.

6 *Food (and Music) for the Soul* 2 p.m.

You thought you went to Hollywood to eat raw food? That's West Hollywood. Before your afternoon walking tour, load up on carbs at **Roscoe's House of Chicken and Waffles** (1514 North Gower Street; 323-466-7453; roscoeschickenandwaffles.com; $-$$). The beloved soul food chain is known for its half chicken smothered with gravy and served with two waffles. From Roscoe's, it's a fast walk to **Amoeba Records** (6400 Sunset Boulevard; 323-245-6400; amoeba.com), one of the last great independent record stores in the country, where new and used CDs and DVDs are found by the mile. There are also live in-store performances (with a special emphasis on up-and-coming Los Angeles bands).

7 *High-Tech Movie* 5 p.m.

Keep walking. Now you are headed to the **ArcLight Cinema** (6360 West Sunset Boulevard; 323-464-1478; arclightcinemas.com), which has one of the best projection and sound systems in the country, plus comfy chairs. Catch the latest popcorn flick, obscure retrospective, or independent picture with every serious cinema buff in town.

8 *Peru in Hollywood* 8 p.m.

Turn the corner on North Vine, and end up in a tiny spot where the spare décor is made up of small replicas of Lima's famous balcones, or balconies. Known for its ceviches, **Los Balcones del Peru** (1360 North Vine Street; 323-871-9600; $) is a charming restaurant, next to a psychic and across from a KFC, where families, couples, and guys who prefer a place on one of the tiger-patterned bar stools all feed. Start with chicha morada (a fruit drink made with corn water), then hit the lomo saltado, or beef sautéed with onions, or tacu tacu con mariscos, which is refried Peruvian beans with shrimp.

9 *Dark Nights* 11 p.m.

End the evening at the **Woods** (1533 North La Brea Avenue; 323-876-6612; vintagebargroup.com/thewoods.html), which, as the name implies, has an outdoorsy theme. The sleek bar has lots of cedar and elk antler chandeliers hanging from the star-encrusted ceiling. As you scope out the young crowd and peruse the juke box, have one of the signature mint juleps or a seasonal drink like the pumpkin pie shot.

SUNDAY

10 *Celebrity Dog Walkers* 9:30 a.m.

Two blocks north of Hollywood Boulevard is one of the most scenic, unusual urban parks in the country, **Runyon Canyon**. The 130-acre park offers

OPPOSITE A smoggy day on the Runyon Canyon trail.

ABOVE Roscoe's House of Chicken and Waffles keeps its soul-food promise: gravy and waffles come with the chicken.

BELOW Between shows at the ArcLight Cinema.

steep, invigorating hikes with views of the San Fernando Valley, the Pacific, Catalina Island (on clear days), and the Griffith Observatory. The area is popular with dog owners (including celebrities), who take advantage of the leash-free policy. Mixed in among the wild chaparral are the crumbling estates of Carman Runyon, a coal magnate who used the property for hunting, and George Huntington Hartford II, heir to the A&P fortune. Parking can be tricky, so enter from the north, off Mulholland. You'll find a parking lot and start the hike going downhill.

11 *Walk This Way* Noon

You can't leave Hollywood without strolling down Hollywood Boulevard on the **Hollywood Walk of Fame** (hollywoodchamber.net). Take in the hundreds of stars embedded in the sidewalks, just to see how many you recognize. While so doing, stop at **Lucky Devil's** (6613 Hollywood Boulevard; 323-465-8259; luckydevils-la.com) for a caramel pecan sundae waffle. It will make you remember Hollywood with fondness.

ABOVE The Cinerama Dome at the ArcLight complex.

OPPOSITE Check out what's playing at the ArcLight, where you can join serious cinema buffs for the latest popcorn flick, obscure retrospective, or indie.

THE BASICS

Fly into Los Angeles, Long Beach, Ontario, or Burbank.

You can get by without a car.

The Hollywood Roosevelt
7000 Hollywood Boulevard
800-950-7667
hollywoodroosevelt.com
$$$
Can be loud, but historic as a favorite of stars in Hollywood's early days. All the night life you'll ever want.

Hollywood Hills Hotel
1999 North Sycamore Avenue
323-874-5089
hollywoodhillshotel.com
$$
A neighborhood bargain.

The Redbury @ Hollywood and Vine
1717 Vine Street
323-962-1717
theredbury.com
$$$-$$$$
Chic new boutique hotel at a famous corner.

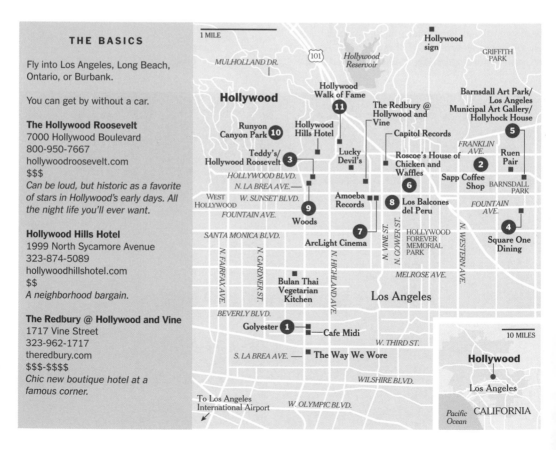

Pasadena

Nestled in the San Gabriel Valley just 10 miles northeast of Los Angeles, Pasadena harbors a distinct, if at times chauvinistic, sense of individual self. Its old-money past continues to flourish in the form of grand mansions and a vast array of museums and gardens, many underwritten by prominent local families. And newer money has helped transform Old Pasadena, in decline for many years, into an energetic shopping and dining destination, with quirky shops and new restaurants. But it is the expansive outdoors, mountain views, and fine climate (except in August, when you could fry a hot dog at the Rose Bowl) that still make Pasadena, the famed City of Roses, a shining jewel of Southern California and an enduring object of jealousy. — BY JENNIFER STEINHAUER

FRIDAY

1 *Dream House* 3 p.m.

Real estate envy is an epidemic in Pasadena, and few homes are more desirable than the **Gamble House** (4 Westmoreland Place; 626-793-3334; gamblehouse.org). While the tour guides can reinforce a certain preciousness, there is no denying the allure of this Craftsman-style home, constructed in 1908 for David and Mary Gamble of the Procter & Gamble Company by the architects Charles Sumner Greene and Henry Mather Greene. To protect the floors, flat shoes are required for the tour, which lasts for an hour. But they'll give you a pair of slippers if you're wearing your Jimmy Choos.

2 *Rose Bowl* 4:30 p.m.

Well, you're here, so why not see where it all happens each winter? You can tool around the Rose Bowl grounds, jog, enjoy the gardens, and imagine you are a rose queen—or one of the many whose efforts add up to the 80,000 hours needed to put together the **Tournament of Roses** (391 South Orange Grove Boulevard; 626-449-4100; tournamentofroses.com).

3 *Burritoville* 6:30 p.m.

There's a depressing number of fast-food restaurants in town, serving the same grub found in any American mall. But one standout is **El Toreo Cafe** (21 South Fair Oaks Avenue; 626-793-2577; $), a hole-in-the-wall that serves terrific and inexpensive

Mexican food. Try the carnitas burritos and chile verde, with large helpings and authentic flair.

4 *Retail Hop* 8:30 p.m.

Many stores in Old Pasadena stay open late. Skip the chains-o-plenty and make your way down Colorado Boulevard, the central corridor, and its side streets. Among the finds: **Distant Lands Travel Bookstore and Outfitters** (20 South Raymond Avenue; 626-449-3220; distantlands.com), which sells travel paraphernalia like Africa maps and packing kits; **Elisa B.** (12 Douglas Alley; 626-792-4746; elisab.com), where the sales staff will get you out of your mom jeans; and **Lula Mae** (100 North Fair Oaks Avenue; 626-304-9996; lulamae.com) for candles and weird gifts like bride-and-groom maracas. End the evening by having some peanut butter or malaga gelato at **Tutti Gelati** (62 West Union Street; 626-440-9800; tuttigelati.com).

SATURDAY

5 *Morning Sweets* 9 a.m.

All good vacation days begin with hot chocolate, so follow the California Institute of Technology students to

OPPOSITE The Japanese garden at the Huntington Library, Art Collections, and Botanical Gardens.

BELOW Changing shoes outside the Rose Bowl.

Euro Pane (950 East Colorado Boulevard; 626-577-1828) and order a hot cup of the chocolaty goodness, along with fresh breads and flaky croissants, which are first-rate. A counter filled with children's books helps keep the young ones entertained.

6 *Fun Under the Sun* 10 a.m.

While children's museums often induce an instant throbbing in the temple — and an urge to reach for a hand sanitizer — a happy exception is **Kidspace Children's Museum** (480 North Arroyo Boulevard; 626-449-9144; kidspacemuseum.org), an active museum where adults can chill with a book under the sun while the kids ride tricycles, check out the dig site, and climb around the mini-model of the city's Arroyo Seco canyon, where it actually "rains" from time to time. The Splash Dance Fountain is a winner.

7 *Order the Obvious* 1 p.m.

No day in Pasadena should pass without a stop at **Pie 'n Burger** (913 East California Boulevard; 626-795-1123; pienburger.com; $), a local institution since 1963. Go ahead and have a chicken pot pie, which is beyond decent, or some pancakes if you're feeling all vegan about it, but honestly, the burger is the way to go. It is a juicy concoction served up in old-school paper liners, with the requisite Thousand Island dressing on the bun. Finish the whole thing

off with a sublime slice of banana cream or cherry pie. Just don't tarry — there are bound to be large groups of folks waiting to get their hands on burgers, too.

8 *Master Class* 3 p.m.

Even if you're feeling a bit tired, there is something oddly relaxing about the **Norton Simon Museum of Art** (411 West Colorado Boulevard; 626-449-6840; nortonsimon.org). There's Degas's *Little Dancer Aged 14*, Van Gogh's *Portrait of a Peasant*, Diego Rivera's *The Flower Vendor*. Natural light streams in from skylights, and a sensible layout makes this a pleasant place to while away the afternoon — not to mention examining the star collection of Western paintings and sculpture from the 14th to 20th centuries. Don't skip the South Asian art downstairs, especially the Buddha Shakyamuni, which sits majestically outdoors. The guided audio tours are quite good.

9 *Solid Italian* 7 p.m.

After a day of cultural and sun soaking, nestle into **Gale's Restaurant** (452 South Fair Oaks Avenue; 626-432-6705; galesrestaurant.com; $$$). A totally local spot, it offers remarkably solid fare just down the road from all the hubbub. Couples, families, and friends who seem to have just finished a day outdoors snuggle amid the brick walls and small wooden tables, drinking wine from slightly cheesy Brighton goblets. Start it off with some warm roasted olives or a steamed artichoke and then move on to the country-style Tuscan steak or caprese salad. For dessert skip the leaden cheesecake and go instead for the poppy seed cake, which is uncommonly tasty.

SUNDAY

10 *Garden Party* 10:30 a.m.

An entire day barely covers a corner of the **Huntington Library, Art Collections, and Botanical Gardens** (1151 Oxford Road, San Marino; 626-405-2100; huntington.org). There are 120 acres of gardens, an enormous library of rare manuscripts and books,

and three permanent art galleries featuring British and French artists of the 18th and 19th centuries. Here is a good plan for a morning: Take a quick run through the exhibit of American silver. Ooh and ahh. Then pick one of the gardens to tour. The Desert garden, with its bizarre-looking cactuses and lunarlike landscapes, is a winner, though the Japanese and Jungle gardens are close rivals. Top it off at the Children's garden, where interactive exhibits can get kids dirty, which pleases everyone but the one stuck changing all the wet shirts. Stay for tea; there's no dress code in the tea room.

OPPOSITE The Gamble House, designed by Charles Sumner Greene and Henry Mather Greene for members of a founding family of Procter & Gamble.

THE BASICS

The closest airport is Burbank, about 15 miles away.

You will need a car.

Langham Huntington Hotel and Spa Pasadena
1401 South Oak Knoll Avenue
626-568-3900
pasadena.langhamhotels.com
$$$
Sits majestically at the foothills of the San Gabriel Mountains and has an 11,000-square-foot spa.

Courtyard by Marriott
180 North Fair Oaks Avenue
626-403-7600
marriott.com
$$$
Pretty much the only bet in Old Pasadena and a good one at that.

Westin Pasadena
191 North Los Robles Avenue
626-792-2727
westin.com
$$$
Heated rooftop pool, beautiful views, and a Kids Club.

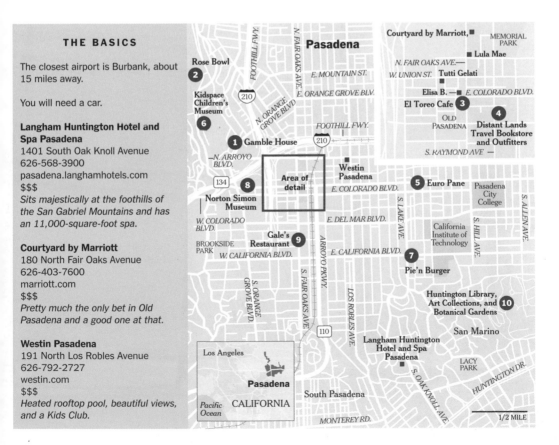

Santa Monica

When Los Angelenos think of the perfect beach town, they think of Santa Monica. With its classic amusement pier, glittering bay, and surfers bobbing on swells, it certainly looks the part. But take a short walk inland, and there's a town asserting its unique identity: eight square miles and about 100,000 people surrounded by districts of the City of Los Angeles, but stubbornly remaining a separate city. Within its borders, a well-preserved Mission-style bungalow sits around the corner from a steel performance space by Frank Gehry. Shops sell goods ranging from vintage Parisian wedding gowns to a whimsical map made entirely out of license plates. To make the most of your time here, enjoy the games and famed carousel of the Santa Monica Pier and then step back from the beach to sample the city's variety the way Santa Monicans themselves do.

— BY FRED A. BERNSTEIN AND LOUISE TUTELIAN

FRIDAY

1 *First, the Beach* 4 p.m.

For a sense of the setting that made Santa Monica, take a stroll in **Palisades Park** (Ocean Avenue at Santa Monica Boulevard; smgov.net/parks),

OPPOSITE Palisades Park, overlooking the Pacific Ocean.

BELOW The Isaac Milbank House, designed by the firm that did Grauman's Chinese Theater, is one of the Craftsman-style houses on Adelaide Drive designated as city landmarks.

an iconic strip of land with manicured lawns and swaying palm trees. Take in the sun and breeze, and wander off on one of the sinuous paths overlooking the beach and Santa Monica pier.

2 *Oyster Shack* 6 p.m.

You're at the sea, so why not enjoy all that it has to offer? The **Blue Plate Oysterette** (1355 Ocean Avenue; 310-576-3474; blueplatesantamonica.com; $$), one of the dozen or so Santa Monica restaurants that face the ocean, may be the most ocean-y, with its raw bar and daily specials like pan-seared rainbow trout. The casual blue-and-white restaurant, with a tin-pressed ceiling and blackboard menus, draws a chic, flip-flop-wearing crowd.

3 *The View That Moves* 8 p.m.

At sunset, the most thrilling view in town is at the beach, from the top of the solar-powered, 130-foot-high Pacific Wheel, the Ferris wheel at the **Santa Monica Pier**. Yes, it's touristy, and yes, it might be crowded, but it is, after all, the city's iconic symbol. As you glide upward, watching the entire city of Santa Monica, and far beyond, slide into view, the whole scene will be bathed in the sunset-colored glow. If you prefer a view that's not mobile, head south into Venice to the rooftop lounge of the **Hotel Erwin** (1697 Pacific Avenue; 310-452-1111; hotelerwin.com), where the banquettes seem to hang over the beach. Gaze at a Santa Monica panorama while sipping a pricey but interesting cocktail like the Venice Vixen, made with pear-flavored Grey Goose, St-Germain elderflower liqueur, and Graham Beck sparkling rosé. You can reserve a table through the hotel's Web site.

SATURDAY

4 *Duck for Breakfast* 8 a.m.

The lines spill out the door, so arrive early at **Huckleberry Bakery and Café** (1014 Wilshire Boulevard; 310-451-2311; huckleberrycafe.com; $$). Breakfast favorites include green eggs and ham, made with pesto and prosciutto, and duck hash with sunny-side-up eggs. The cheerful room — which feels like a large country bakery with pale wood tables and colorful accents — is tended by equally cheerful employees.

5 *Into the Mountains* 9 a.m.

The Backbone Trail, a 69-mile system, roughly follows the crest of the Santa Monica Mountains north from **Will Rogers State Historic Park** just north of Santa Monica (1501 Will Rogers State Park Road, off West Sunset Boulevard, Pacific Palisades; 310-454-8212; nps.gov/samo/planyourvisit/backbonetrail.htm). Hikers can take an easy, sage-scented, two-mile loop from the parking lot at Will Rogers up to Inspiration Point, a sensational overlook of Santa Monica Bay from the Palos Verdes Peninsula to Point Dume in Malibu. Do it on a clear day, and you'll see Catalina Island and the white dots of sails. Behind are the slopes of the Santa Monica Mountains, and in the distance, the high-rises of downtown Los Angeles. Up here, the muted chattering of birds and the hum of insects are the only sounds.

6 *Builders and Shoppers* Noon

Back in northern Santa Monica, natural sights give way to architectural ones. Two houses designated as city landmarks are the Craftsman-style **Isaac Milbank House** (236 Adelaide Drive) — designed by the same firm that did Grauman's Chinese Theater in Hollywood — and the stucco **Worrel House** (710 Adelaide Drive), which was built in the mid-1920s and has been described as a "Pueblo-Revival Maya fantasy." Some of the city's best shopping is nearby on Montana Avenue, known for upscale clothes, home décor, crafts, jewelry, and art. At **Every Picture Tells A Story** (No. 1333; 310-451-2700; everypicture. com), part children's bookstore and part gallery, the specialty is original works by the likes of Maurice Sendak and Dr. Seuss. **Rooms & Gardens** (No. 1311-A; 310-451-5154; roomsandgardens.com) sells furniture, antiques, and accessories like pillows fashioned from an antique Indian sari.

7 *Art at the Trolley Stop* 3 p.m.

The local art scene heated up in 2010 with the arrival of **L&M Arts**, Los Angeles (660 Venice Boulevard, Venice; 310-821-6400; lmgallery.com), a branch of the blue-chip New York gallery. Find its space in a former power station and check what's showing. From there, it's a short drive to **Bergamot Station** (2525 Michigan Avenue; 310-453-7535; bergamotstation.com), a complex of art galleries built on the site of a former trolley-line stop — hence its name. A highlight is the **Santa Monica Museum of Art** (310-586-6488; smmoa.org), a museum with rotating exhibits.

8 *Bistro Evenings* 8 p.m.

There are lots of stylish hotels in Santa Monica, and some of them offer very good food. Case in point is **Fig** (101 Wilshire Boulevard; 310-319-3111; figsantamonica.com; $$$), a contemporary American bistro at the Fairmont Miramar Hotel. The menu features seasonal ingredients and dishes like a halibut "chop" or snap peas with mint. There is seating indoors, in an elegant room with starburst mirrors, as well as on the terrace, with views of the ocean through the lush gardens. The huge Moreton Bay fig tree, from which the restaurant gets its name, will make you feel like climbing.

9 *Disco Nights* 11 p.m.

Santa Monica may be known for sunshine, but there's plenty to do after dark. For a taste of the local night life, head to **Zanzibar** (1301 Fifth Street; 310-451-2221; zanzibarlive.com), a cavernous club that manages to be both cozy and contemporary. It is also the rare venue that seems able to please young and old — you could imagine Joni Mitchell on the dance floor with her grandkids. The D.J.'s play a mix of hip-hop, R&B, and top 40. Even the décor has crossover appeal; hanging from the ceiling are perforated copper lanterns (for a vaguely African feeling) and disco balls.

SUNDAY

10 *No Wet Suit Needed* 10 a.m.

Even in warm weather, the waters of Southern California can be frigid. For a more comfortable swim, duck into the **Annenberg Community Beach House** (415 Pacific Coast Highway; 310-458-4904; annenbergbeachhouse.com), a sleek public facility that opened in 2010. The pool is spectacular, and

you can buy a day pass for a reasonable price. If it's the off-season, head to the public but country-club-stylish **Santa Monica Swim Center** (2225 16th Street; 310-458-8700; smgov.net/aquatics), where the adult and children's pools are kept at 79 and 85 degrees, respectively.

11 *Sunday Retail* Noon

Amid the sneaker stores and used book shops of artsy Main Street, in the Ocean Park neighborhood, look for the Frank Gehry-designed steel boxes of **Edgemar** (2415-2449 Main Street; edgemarcenter.org), which house retail tenants and a performance space around an open courtyard. Gehry's retail footprint in Santa Monica has shrunk since his **Santa Monica Place**, designed in 1980, was replaced by a new version (395 Santa Monica Place; santamonicaplace.com)

in 2010. The glassy new open-air complex spreads across 500,000 square feet and three stories. The retailers' names may not be surprising, but it's the mall, this is California, and you can count on finding shoppers there.

OPPOSITE Ocean-view dining at Santa Monica Place, a glassy new open-air version of a California shopping mall.

ABOVE At sunset, the best view in town is at the beach, from the top of the solar-powered, 130-foot-high Pacific Wheel, the Ferris wheel at the Santa Monica Pier.

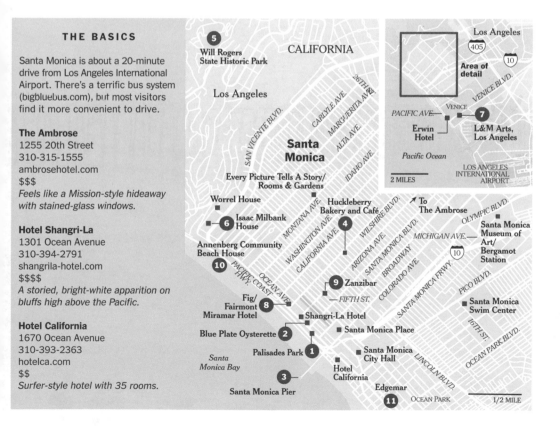

THE BASICS

Santa Monica is about a 20-minute drive from Los Angeles International Airport. There's a terrific bus system (bigbluebus.com), but most visitors find it more convenient to drive.

The Ambrose
1255 20th Street
310-315-1555
ambrosehotel.com
$$$
Feels like a Mission-style hideaway with stained-glass windows.

Hotel Shangri-La
1301 Ocean Avenue
310-394-2791
shangrila-hotel.com
$$$$
A storied, bright-white apparition on bluffs high above the Pacific.

Hotel California
1670 Ocean Avenue
310-393-2363
hotelca.com
$$
Surfer-style hotel with 35 rooms.

Malibu

Locals call it "the Bu"—a laid-back, celebrity-filled strip of a city that sparkles in the collective consciousness as a sun-drenched state of mind. With the busy Pacific Coast Highway running through and no discernible center of town, some of the best of Malibu, which has around 13,000 residents, can disappear in a drive-by. The staggering natural beauty of the sea and mountains is obvious, but pull off the road and stay awhile, and you'll find more: a world-class art museum, local wines, top-notch restaurants, and chic shops.
— BY LOUISE TUTELIAN

FRIDAY

1 *The Wind, the Waves...* 5 p.m.

What's so appealing about Malibu's little slice of coast? Visit **Point Dume State Preserve** (Birdview Avenue and Cliffside Drive; 818-880-0363; parks.ca.gov), and you'll see. A modest walk to the top of this coastal bluff rewards you with a sweeping view of the entire Santa Monica Bay, the inland Santa Monica Mountains, and, on a clear day, Catalina Island. A boardwalk just below the summit leads to a platform for watching swooping pelicans and crashing waves. To feel the sand between your toes, drive down Birdview Avenue to Westward Beach Road and park at the very end of the lot on your left. You'll be looking at Westward Beach, a gem that most visitors miss. Strike a yoga pose. Sigh at will.

2 *Chasing the Sunset* 7 p.m.

Little known fact: Most of Malibu faces south, not west. That means sitting down at just any seaside restaurant at dusk won't guarantee seeing a sunset over the water. But the aptly named **Sunset Restaurant** (6800 Westward Beach Road; 310-589-1007; thesunsetrestaurant.com) is a sure bet, with just the right orientation. Claim a white leather banquette, order a carafe of wine and a tasting plate of cheeses, and settle in for the light show.

3 *Shore Dinner* 9 p.m.

If you're going to spot a celebrity, chances are it will be at **Nobu Malibu** (3835 Cross Creek Road, in the Malibu Country Mart; 310-317-9140; nobumatsuhisa.com; $$$), one of the famed chef Nobu Matsuhisa's many restaurants. The sushi is

sublime, and the entrees measure up. Reservations are essential. The front room is convivial but noisy; the subtly lighted back room is quieter.

SATURDAY

4 *Walk the Pier* 9 a.m.

The 780-foot long **Malibu Pier** (23000 Pacific Coast Highway; 888-310-7437; malibupiersportfishing.com) is the most recognizable (and, arguably, only) landmark in town. Take a morning stroll out to the end, chat with the fishermen, and watch surfers paddle out. You'll be walking on a piece of Malibu history. The pier was originally built in 1905 as a loading dock for construction material, and it was a lookout during World War II. It crops up in numerous movies and TV shows.

5 *Ancient Art* 10 a.m.

The **Getty Villa** (17985 Pacific Coast Highway; 310-440-7300; getty.edu) is just over the city's southern border in Pacific Palisades, but no matter: it shouldn't be missed. The museum, built by J. Paul Getty in the 1970s to resemble a first-century Roman country house, contains Greek, Roman, and Etruscan vessels, gems and statuary, some dating back to 6500 B.C. On the second floor is a rare life-size Greek

OPPOSITE Beach and pier at Malibu, the little slice of Pacific coast that celebrities like to call their own.

BELOW Kai Sanson, a surfing instructor, initiates students into the ways of the waves.

bronze, *Statue of a Victorious Youth*, a prize of the museum. In the outside peristyle gardens, watch the sun glint off bronze statues at the 220-foot-long reflecting pool. Admission is free, but parking is limited, so car reservations are required.

6 *Magic Carpet Tile* 1 p.m.

Even many longtime Angelenos don't know about the **Adamson House** (23200 Pacific Coast Highway; 310-456-8432; adamsonhouse.org), a 1930 Spanish Colonial Revival residence that's a showplace of exquisite ceramic tile from Malibu Potteries, which closed in 1932. Overlooking Surfrider Beach with a view of Malibu Pier, the house belonged to a member of the Rindge family, last owners of the Malibu Spanish land grant. Take a tour and watch for the Persian "carpet" constructed entirely from intricately patterned pieces of tile. Other highlights: a stunning star-shaped fountain and a bathroom tiled top to bottom in an ocean pattern, with ceramic galleons poised in perpetuity on pointy whitecaps in a sea of blue.

7 *Vino on the Green* 4 p.m.

The drive to **Malibu Wines** (31740 Mulholland Highway; 818-865-0605; malibuwines.com) along the serpentine roads of the Santa Monica Mountains is almost as much fun as tipping a glass once you get there. Set on a serene green lawn, the tasting room is really a covered outdoor stone and wood counter. Sidle up and choose a flight of four styles. Or buy a bottle and lounge at one of the tables. (Tip: Regulars request the horseshoes or bocce ball set at the counter.) And don't miss the collection of vintage pickup trucks spread around the property.

8 *Farm to Table* 7 p.m.

Terra (21337 Pacific Coast Highway; 310-456-1221; terrarestaurantla.com; $$$), in the building that was once the original Malibu jail, is an intimate gathering place serving organic meats and nonfarmed fish, with most produce grown in its own gardens. Choose from the menu of the season; past diners have been

delighted to find dishes like oven-roasted organic baby beets or pounded filet mignon with Terra Farms arugula. In warm weather, French doors open to a spacious patio decorated with thousands of fragments of broken Malibu Potteries tile, the better to ward off evil spirits.

SUNDAY

9 *Ride the Surf* 10 a.m.

Surf shops offering lessons and board rentals line the Pacific Coast Highway (P.C.H. in local lingo), but Kai Sanson of **Zuma Surf and Swim Training** (949-742-1086; zsstraining.com) takes his fun seriously. Sanson, a Malibu native, will size you up with a glance and gear the instruction to your skills. Lessons for two are $90 a person. His tales of growing up in Malibu are free. Locals also give high marks to **Malibu Makos Surf Club** (310-317-1229; malibumakos.com).

10 *Brunch in Style (or Not)* Noon

Put on your oversize sunglasses if you're going to **Geoffrey's Malibu** (27400 Pacific Coast Highway; 310-457-1519; geoffreysmalibu.com; $$$). Geoffrey's (pronounced Joffreys) is the hot meeting spot for the

ABOVE A beach view from the bluff at Point Dume. Sweeping vistas here take in Santa Monica Bay, the Santa Monica Mountains, and, on a clear day, Catalina Island.

BELOW Tasting the reds at Malibu Wines.

well-heeled with a hankering for a shiitake mushroom omelet or lobster Cobb salad. Its Richard Neutra-designed building overlooks the Pacific, and every table has an ocean view. If you just want to kick back with *The Malibu Times*, head to **Coogie's Beach Café** (23750 Pacific Coast Highway in the Malibu Colony Plaza; 310-317-1444; coogies.malibu.menuclub.com; $$) and carbo-load with Coogie's French Toast: bagels dipped in egg whites with cinnamon sugar and served with peanut butter and bananas.

11 *Shop Like a Star* 2 p.m.

Whether it's diamonds or designer jeans you're after, the open-air **Malibu Country Mart** (3835 Cross Creek Road; malibucountrymart.com) is the place

to cruise for them. Its more than 50 retail stores and restaurants include Ralph Lauren, Juicy Couture, and Malibu Rock Star jewelry. In an adjacent space is luxe **Malibu Lumber Yard** shopping complex (themalibulumberyard.com), with stores like Alice + Olivia and Tory Burch.

ABOVE The Getty Villa museum, built by J. Paul Getty to resemble a first-century Roman country house.

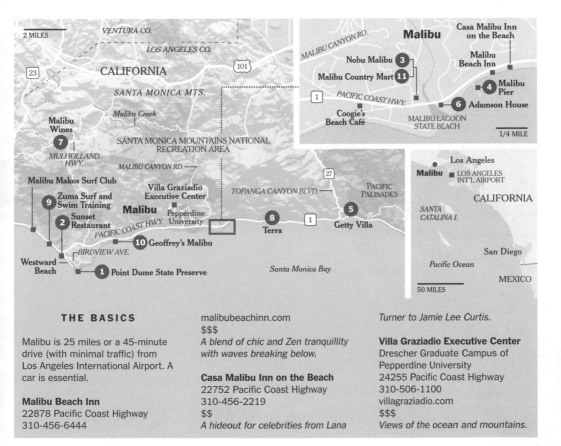

THE BASICS

Malibu is 25 miles or a 45-minute drive (with minimal traffic) from Los Angeles International Airport. A car is essential.

Malibu Beach Inn
22878 Pacific Coast Highway
310-456-6444

malibubeachinn.com
$$$
A blend of chic and Zen tranquillity with waves breaking below.

Casa Malibu Inn on the Beach
22752 Pacific Coast Highway
310-456-2219
$$
A hideout for celebrities from Lana

Turner to Jamie Lee Curtis.

Villa Graziadio Executive Center
Drescher Graduate Campus of Pepperdine University
24255 Pacific Coast Highway
310-506-1100
villagraziadio.com
$$$
Views of the ocean and mountains.

Santa Barbara

Santa Barbara may be tiny — its 90,000 residents could be seated in the Los Angeles Coliseum — but it packs Oprah-like cachet. Indeed, the queen of daytime TV and other A-listers have made this former outpost of Spain's American dominions their second home. Posh hotels, seven-figure mansions, and trendy boutiques have opened along the so-called American Riviera, catering to members of the Hollywood set who drive up every weekend to frolic among the languorous palms and suntanned celebrities. But don't let the crush of Ferraris and Prada fool you. With its perpetually blue skies and taco stands, Santa Barbara remains a laid-back town where the star attraction is still the beach.
— BY FINN-OLAF JONES

FRIDAY

1 *Lingering Glow* 5 p.m.
Santa Barbara's main beaches face southeast, but you can still catch the Pacific sunset by driving along Cliff Drive until it takes you to secluded **Hendry's Beach**. Hemmed by vertiginous cliffs that turn deep orange as the sun sets, the beach is popular with locals, surfers, and dolphins. Order a rum punch at the **Boathouse at Hendry's Beach** (2981 Cliff Drive; 805-898-2628; boathousesb.com), where you can still feel the warmth of the sun (or is it the fire pit?) long after it has set.

2 *Making Friends* 8 p.m.
Fresh California cuisine is the rule in this region of outstanding vineyards, luscious orchards, and right-off-the-boat seafood. Some of the freshest is at **Brophy Brothers Restaurant and Clam Bar** (119 Harbor Way; 805-966-4418; brophybros.com; $$$), which overlooks the harbor. Sit at the long communal table and strike up a conversation with your new friends. The night I was there, I was offered a job by a local developer. While I didn't take the job, I did sample the clam chowder ("The best in town," I was told about five times), followed by a terrific grilled swordfish

with artichoke sauce. Hmmm, what was that starting salary again?

SATURDAY

3 *Bike to Brunch* 10 a.m.
Rent a bike at **Wheel Fun Rentals** (23 East Cabrillo Boulevard; 805-966-2282; wheelfunrentals.com) and roll along the ocean to the **East Beach Grill** (1118 East Cabrillo Boulevard; 805-965-8805; $), a greasy but bright breakfast institution popular with surfers, cyclists, and skaters, who swear by its banana wheat germ pancakes with eggs and bacon.

4 *Sacred Mission* 11:30 a.m.
It's hard not to feel awed when driving up the hill to **Mission Santa Barbara** (2201 Laguna Street; 805-682-4713; sbmission.org), a 1786 landmark with ocher-colored columns that is known as the Queen of the 21 original Spanish missions built along the California coastline. Escape the crowds by wandering outside the flower-scented Sacred Garden. If there's a docent around, ask if you can see the glazed terra-cotta sculpture of St. Barbara watching over Mary and Jesus. A masterpiece from 1522, it was discovered three years ago in a storage room that was being cleaned out. It is now installed in an alcove in the garden's private portico.

OPPOSITE A Santa Barbara sunset at Hendry's Beach.

RIGHT La Super Rica, pronounced by Julia Child to be the best of several good places in Santa Barbara to get a fresh and authentic homemade taco.

5 *Taco Heaven* 1 p.m.

Locals argue endlessly about the city's best taco joint. Julia Child threw her weight behind **La Super Rica** (622 North Milpas Street; 805-963-4940; $), ensuring perpetual lines for its homemade tortillas filled with everything from pork and cheese to spicy ground beans. **Lilly's** (310 Chapala Street; 805-966-9180; $), a tiny spot in the center of town run by the ever-welcoming Sepulveda family, serves up tacos filled with anything from pork to beef eye. And **Palapa** (4123 State Street; 805-683-3074; www.palapa.biz; $) adds fresh seafood to the equation in its cheery patio just north of downtown, where the grilled sole tacos are fresh and light. Try all three places and join the debate.

6 *Paper Chase* 3 p.m.

Walt Disney's original will. A letter by Galileo. Lincoln's second Emancipation Proclamation (the 13th Amendment). The **Karpeles Manuscript Library and Museum** (21 West Anapamu Street; 805-962-5322; www.rain.org/karpeles; free) was started by David

Karpeles, a local real estate tycoon, and has one of the world's largest private manuscript collections. If this whets your appetite for collecting, wander seven blocks to **Randall House Rare Books** (835 Laguna Street; 805-963-1909; www.randallhouserarebooks.com), where the ancient tomes and rare documents have included a signed calling card from Robert E. Lee ($4,500) and the first official map of the State of California ($27,500).

7 *Shop Like the Stars* 5 p.m.

The main shopping drag, State Street, is filled with the usual chain stores like Abercrombie & Fitch. The consumerist cognoscenti head for the hills, to the Platinum Card district of **Montecito**,

ABOVE AND OPPOSITE Three views of Mission Santa Barbara, known as the Queen of the 21 original Spanish missions built along the California coast. Escape the crowds by wandering outside in the flower-scented Sacred Garden.

RIGHT A guest room at San Ysidro Ranch, the longtime celebrity hangout where J.F.K. and Jackie honeymooned.

where you'll find local designers and one-off items along the eucalyptus-lined Coast Village Road. Highlights include **Dressed** (No. 1253; 805-565-1253; dressedonline.com), a small boutique that counts Teri Hatcher and Britney Spears among the fans of its resortwear look, which might include an earthy necklace made of bamboo coral ($733) by a local jeweler, Corrina Gordon. Next door, **Angel** (No. 1221; 805-565-1599; wendyfoster.com) sells casual sportswear with a youthful vibe and hot accessories like tie-dyed hair ties. Across the street, **Lewis & Clark** (No. 1286; 805-969-7177) sells funky curios like colorful Guatemalan altar figures (from about $110), a local favorite given the city's Franciscan roots.

8 *Celebrity Dining* 8 p.m.

J.F.K. and Jackie honeymooned there, Hollywood luminaries like Groucho Marx were regulars, and in 2007 the **San Ysidro Ranch** reopened after a $150 million renovation by a new owner, the Beanie Babies creator Ty Warner. Warner added an enormous terrace, a 4,000-bottle wine cellar, and a lot of buzz by redoing the **Stonehouse** restaurant (900 San Ysidro Lane; 800-368-6788; www.sanysidroranch.com/dine1.cfm; $$$$). Expect to see the T-shirt-with-blazer set sitting around an open fire while dining on dishes like warm mushroom salad, juniper-dusted venison loin, and fresh pastries. Take a post-dinner stroll

around the terraced gardens where many of the ingredients were grown.

9 *Glamorous State* 11 p.m.

State Street heats up after 11 o'clock as college students and moneyed folk from the glittering hills descend to its bars and nightclubs. **Wildcat Lounge** (15 West Ortega Street; 805-962-7970; www.wildcatlounge.com), a retro bar with red-vinyl banquettes, is the place to mingle with the university crowd and local bohos grooving to house music. Cater-corner is **Tonic** (634 State Street; 805-897-1800; www.tonicsb.com), an airy dance club that draws students in chinos and recent graduates in designer T-shirts to its cabanas. The international set heads to **Eos Lounge** (500 Anacapa Street; 805-564-2410; www.eoslounge.com) to dance to world music in a tree-shaded patio that looks like Mykonos on the Pacific.

SUNDAY

10 *Paging Moby-Dick* 10 a.m.

From December to February, some 30,000 gray whales migrate from Alaska to Baja California through a five-mile gap among the Channel Islands, a cluster of rocky isles 20 or so miles off the coast. Catch the commute — and breaching whales — from the decks of the **Condor Express**, a high-speed catamaran that makes daily whale-watching trips (301 West Cabrillo Boulevard; 805-882-0088; www.condorcruises.com;

$94). Porpoises, sea lions, and the occasional killer whale join in on the fun.

11 *Crimson Tide* 3 p.m.

The vineyards of central California gained prominence from the movie *Sideways*, but few can match the vistas at the **Coastal Winery** (217 Stearns Wharf; 805-966-6624; www.coastalwinery.com). It features an airy tasting room where you can tap your inner Miles Raymond and for $15 compare seven wines, including cabs, pinots, and chards, while marveling at amazing views of the Pacific.

OPPOSITE Mission Santa Barbara dates to 1786.

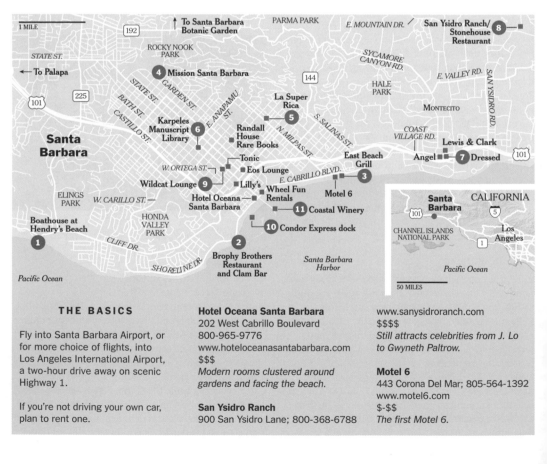

THE BASICS

Fly into Santa Barbara Airport, or for more choice of flights, into Los Angeles International Airport, a two-hour drive away on scenic Highway 1.

If you're not driving your own car, plan to rent one.

Hotel Oceana Santa Barbara
202 West Cabrillo Boulevard
800-965-9776
www.hoteloceanasantabarbara.com
$$$
Modern rooms clustered around gardens and facing the beach.

San Ysidro Ranch
900 San Ysidro Lane; 800-368-6788

www.sanysidroranch.com
$$$$
Still attracts celebrities from J. Lo to Gwyneth Paltrow.

Motel 6
443 Corona Del Mar; 805-564-1392
www.motel6.com
$-$$
The first Motel 6.

San Diego

If San Diego feels half empty, that's because it is. At any given time, swarms of residents have decamped a few miles south to Mexico or a few miles north to upscale resort towns. Also, the Navy is the area's largest employer, so a sizable chunk is presumably floating around on aircraft carriers somewhere. Is it any wonder, then, that the town leans so heavily on big tourist attractions (Shamu, the zoo)? A deeper look, however, will reveal San Diego's personality. A necklace of quirky, sun-kissed neighborhoods rings downtown, from surfer hangouts like Pacific Beach to gentrifying neighborhoods like University Heights. Restaurants are flourishing, too. There is even an emphasis on preserving history, which, for Southern California, is a headline in itself. — BY BROOKS BARNES

FRIDAY

1 *Ease On Down* 5 p.m.

There's no better indoctrination to San Diego's laid-back style than a stroll along the Embarcadero, a two-mile stretch of downtown waterfront where a gentle sea breeze will lull you into a zombie-like state in no time. The decommissioned aircraft carrier *Midway* sits nearby and can be admired from Tuna Harbor Park, a shady nook next to the touristy but tasty **Fish Market** restaurant (750 North Harbor Drive; 619-232-3474; thefishmarket.com; $$). Warning: Skip Seaport Village, a shopping plaza on the board-walk, unless you're into pushy pedicab drivers and shops that sell obnoxious T-shirts.

2 *Gaslamp Glamour* 7:30 p.m.

Much energy and money have been spent gussying up the Gaslamp Quarter, a 16-block down-town neighborhood that was once an archetype of urban blight. The jumble of frat bars is still rather depressing, but several boutique hotels have opened attractive lounges and restaurants. Avoid the W with its hipper-than-thou staff and head to the sleek but comfy **Andaz San Diego** (formerly called the Ivy; 600 F Street; 619-814-1000; sandiego.andaz.hyatt.com).

OPPOSITE AND RIGHT Eye catchers in a Navy Town: *Unconditional Surrender*, by Seward Johnson, and the decommissioned aircraft carrier *Midway*, now a museum, occupying space along the San Diego Embarcadero.

Hollywood bigwigs roost there when attending Comic-Con, the annual comic-book convention and movie marketing extravaganza in July. The hotel's restaurant, **Quarter Kitchen** ($$$) woos with a sophisticated menu and modern décor.

3 *Culture Clash* 10 p.m.

How adventurous are you feeling? If the answer is not very, then perhaps top off the night with a sashay through the Andaz's multilevel Ivy nightclub. For the stronger at heart, there is the Casbah, as in "Rock the…." Conjuring the 1982 hit from the English punk rockers Clash, the **Casbah** (2501 Kettner Boulevard; 619-232-4355; casbahmusic.com) is a venerable, if a tad dingy, music club where Nirvana, the Smashing Pumpkins, and the Lemonheads cultivated an audience. Don't be frightened by the phone number (listed on the Web site as 232-HELL). The club also features more mainstream acts à la Alanis Morissette.

SATURDAY

4 *Pacific Xanadu* 8:30 a.m.

No visit to San Diego is complete without taking in **Balboa Park** (1549 El Prado; 619-239-0512; balboapark.org), the 1,200-acre public park that is home to the Old Globe theater, a gargantuan out-door pipe organ, and a half-dozen major museums. A morning walk or jog along the park's central thoroughfare is a perfect way to experience it. If some of those Spanish Baroque Revival buildings look familiar, it's because they starred as Xanadu, the over-the-top estate in *Citizen Kane*.

5 *California Past* 10 a.m.

Tucked in an easy-to-miss enclave just north of downtown, **Old Town** (oldtownsandiego.org) offers a peek into what life was like in San Diego when agave plants still outnumbered people. Start at the **Old Town Mexican Café** (2489 San Diego Avenue; 619-297-4330; oldtownmexcafe.com), where the "tortilla ladies," visible through giant windows, can be seen frantically hand-rolling corn and flour tortillas, some 7,000 on a busy day, the restaurant says. Don't stop to eat: those tortillas are better seen than tasted. Rather, wander into the **Old Town San Diego State Historic Park** (parks.ca.gov/?page_ID=663) to explore exhibits like the 143-year-old Mason Street School, a one-room shack decorated with pictures of schoolmarms past. Shops scattered around the Old Town grounds sell the wares of local crafts makers. Large glazed ceramic tiles (usually between $100 and $200) are big sellers.

6 *Taco Treat* Noon

This is a desert, after all, and the sun can be exhausting. Recharge at **Casa de Reyes** (2754 Calhoun Street; 619-220-5040; fiestadereyes.com; $), a traditional Mexican restaurant at the Fiesta de Reyes. Decorated in a theme reminiscent of Spanish haciendas, this open-air but breezy restaurant provides a festive atmosphere with folkloric dancers and a mariachi band. Try the tacos, preferably stuffed with crispy-edged carnitas.

7 *Beach Bound* 1:30 p.m.

There are dozens of beaches, but none are more authentic than Ocean Beach, a funky surfers' haven that has stayed frozen in time because of strict zoning rules from the 1970s. Wander through the stuffed-to-the-rafters **Ocean Beach Antique Mall** (4926 Newport Avenue; 619-223-6170; antiquesinsandiego.com). The

ABOVE The Pacific from Sunset Cliffs.

RIGHT You could ride, but walking is also a nice way to make your way down the central thoroughfare of Balboa Park.

sidewalk along Newport Avenue, the main drag, is an attraction in itself. As part of a business district improvement effort, the community sells inscribed sidewalk tiles to anybody with $130 and a printable message. The results are oddly touching. ("Jeff Loves Rosie.") O.B. is a locals' favorite, so you might feel conspicuous without a surfboard or bare feet. Just call everyone dude and you'll be fine.

8 *Salty Sea Air* 4 p.m.

Just south of the Ocean Beach Pier is a recently constructed concrete path that leads to one of Southern California's most spectacular stretches of shoreline. **Sunset Cliffs** (sandiego.gov/park-and-recreation/parks/shoreline/sunset.shtml) spans 68 acres. Stretch out on the grass, fly a kite (as many locals do), or explore the bluffs and tidal pools.

9 *Dinner at a Diner* 6:30 p.m.

You've sampled one of San Diego's pricier restaurants; now go the other way and check out one of the diners that locals gush over. **Hash House a Go Go** (3628 Fifth Avenue; 619-298-4646; hashhouseagogo.com; $$) promises "twisted farm food." It's mobbed at breakfast and lunch but more manageable at dinner. Menu items run from ultra-familiar (salmon with garlic potatoes; chicken pot pie) to the wacky (macaroni and cheese with a duck skewer).

10 *The Fox Rocks* 9 p.m.

If the Regal Beagle, the pub from the 1970s TV sitcom *Three's Company*, ever had a twin, the **Red Fox Steak House** (2223 El Cajon Boulevard; 619-297-1313) would be it. Except that the Red Fox is also a piano

bar. Dimly lighted and with red Naugahyde booths, its lounge attracts a diverse crowd from hipsters to elderly couples. Everybody sings along after a couple of drinks. Give the adjacent dining room a peek; the room was originally built in 1642 in England but was dismantled and shipped to California in 1926 by the actress Marion Davies, who used it as part of a summer home.

SUNDAY

11 *If They Build It* 10 a.m.

Tour the hot and dusty San Diego Zoo if you must. The preferable option, especially for families with younger children, is **Legoland** (One Legoland Drive, Carlsbad; 760-918-5346; legoland.com). No lines, immaculate grounds, and a surprising lack of pressure to buy souvenirs. This is an amusement park? Come before the masses discover it (annual attendance is about a million compared with nearly four million for the zoo). The 128-acre park focuses on interactive educational attractions like the Lost Kingdom Adventure, a ride themed around recovering hidden treasure in 1920s Egypt. For Lego fans — admit it, they're not just for kids — the park features a cavernous store that sells hard-to-find sets as well as little colored bricks in bulk.

ABOVE Strolling the Embarcadero. As the sculpture suggests, fish is often on the menu at the waterfront restaurants.

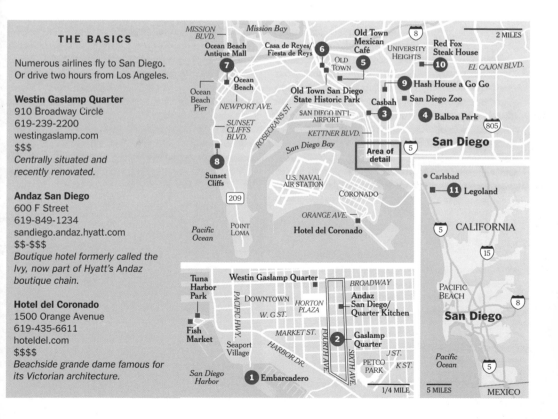

THE BASICS

Numerous airlines fly to San Diego. Or drive two hours from Los Angeles.

Westin Gaslamp Quarter
910 Broadway Circle
619-239-2200
westingaslamp.com
$$$
Centrally situated and recently renovated.

Andaz San Diego
600 F Street
619-849-1234
sandiego.andaz.hyatt.com
$$-$$$
Boutique hotel formerly called the Ivy, now part of Hyatt's Andaz boutique chain.

Hotel del Coronado
1500 Orange Avenue
619-435-6611
hoteldel.com
$$$$
Beachside grande dame famous for its Victorian architecture.

Palm Springs

Palm Springs was once the miles-from-Hollywood getaway that Malibu is now: a place for '60s movers and shakers to eat, drink, and sunbathe poolside while they awaited calls from studio execs. Today, after some hard-earned changes, this California desert town nestled in the Coachella Valley is becoming a destination for laid-back cool once again. The revival of modernism that inspired makeovers of its midcentury hotels, restaurants, and shops brought a revival of style, and the desert sun has never lost its appeal. Now Palm Springs attracts visitors just as happy climbing canyons as sipping cocktails on a lounge chair amid the design and architectural treasures of the past.
— BY ERICA CERULO

FRIDAY

1 *Cruising on Two Wheels* 4 p.m.

Because of its modest size, Palm Springs can easily become familiar over a couple days, or even a few hours. Start your trip with a self-guided bike tour. **Big Wheel Tours** (760-802-2236; bwbtours.com) rents bicycles and can arrange bike and hiking tours. Free maps are available at the **Palm Springs Visitors Center** (777 North Palm Canyon Drive; 760-778-8418; palm-springs.org). To scope out the dramatic terrain and local hot spots, pedal the Downtown Loop, which can be done in less than an hour, or the 10-mile Citywide Loop that takes you past the Moorten Botanical Gardens.

2 *Austria and Beyond* 7 p.m.

At **Johannes** (196 South Indian Canyon Drive; 760-778-0017; johannesrestaurants.com; $$$), the chef Johannes Bacher bills the food as modern Austrian, combining classic Central European special-ties like spaetzle and sauerkraut with decidedly borrowed ingredients and flavors, ranging from polenta to wasabi. But one of the best dishes is also the most traditional: a heaping plate of Wiener schnitzel with parsley potatoes, cucumber salad, and cranberry compote.

OPPOSITE Indian Canyons, a natural oasis on the Agua Caliente Indian Reservation just outside Palm Springs.

RIGHT The Kaufmann House, designed by Richard Neutra.

3 *Partying Poolside* 9:30 p.m.

Back when Frank Sinatra held raucous shindigs at his Twin Palms home, Palm Springs was known for its party scene. These days, the best drinking establishments are in hotels. The white stucco exterior of the **Colony Palms Hotel** (572 North Indian Canyon Drive; 760-969-1800; colonypalmshotel.com) conceals a welcoming hideaway with stone walkways, towering palms, and, when needed, patio heaters. At the buzzing restaurant **Purple Palm**, ask to be seated by the pool and order a plate of Humboldt Fog chèvre, organic honey, and local dates with your drink to top off the night.

SATURDAY

4 *Modernist America* 9:30 a.m.

Along with the moneyed 20th-century tourists came eye-catching buildings: hotels, commercial spaces, and vacation homes. Next to a hopping Starbucks on the main drag sits one of the city's oldest architectural touchstones: a concrete bell tower salvaged from the long-gone Oasis Hotel, which was designed by Lloyd Wright (son of Frank) in 1924. This spot is also where Robert Imber, the often seersucker-clad architectural guru and one-man show behind **PS Modern Tours** (760-318-6118; psmoderntours@aol.com), starts his three-hour excursions, which provide a survey of the city's key structures with a focus on the midcentury sweet spot. Design enthusiasts can catch glimpses of the iconic Albert Frey-designed Tramway Gas Station, Richard Neutra's 1946 Kaufmann Desert House, and the mass-produced but stunning Alexander homes

that your guide identifies by pointing out the four key components — "garage, breezeway, windows, wall" — in their various arrangements. Reserve well in advance.

5 *Chic Cheek* 1 p.m.

The wait for brunch at **Cheeky's** (622 North Palm Canyon Drive; 760-327-7595; cheekysps.com; $$) should be a tip-off: the bright, streamlined space, which feels airlifted from L.A. — in a good way — is popular. The standard eggs and waffles are spiced up with ingredients like beet relish, homemade herbed ricotta, and sour cherry compote.

6 *Used Goods* 3 p.m.

Stroll **Palm Canyon Drive**, a strip that's terrific for high-end vintage shopping, if a little dangerous for those who quickly reach for their credit cards. Among the many stores that focus on better-with-age décor, just a few have mastered the art of curating. At **a La MOD** (768 North Palm Canyon Drive; 760-327-0707; alamod768.com), nearly 70 percent of the merchandise, which is heavy on Lucite and lighting, is sourced locally, according to the shop's owners. Across the street, **Modern Way** (745 North Palm Canyon Drive; 760-320-5455; psmodernway.com) stocks an eclectic collection of larger pieces like Arthur Elrod couches, Verner Panton cone chairs, and Hans Olsen dining sets. For something you can actually take home, head

down to **Bon Vivant** in the **Palm Canyon Galleria** (457 North Palm Canyon Drive, No. 3; 760-534-3197; gmcb.com) where the store's charming proprietors make you feel like a genuine collector for purchasing an $18 engraved brass vase or a $5 tie clip.

7 *Stay Silly* 5 p.m.

At the **Palm Springs Yacht Club**, at the **Parker Palm Springs** hotel (4200 East Palm Canyon Drive; 760-770-5000; theparkerpalmsprings.com), standard spa offerings like deep-tissue rubdowns and wrinkle-fighting facials come with a playful attitude of retro irony. The pampering is real. Expect to pay high-end prices (some treatment packages are well over $300) but go away feeling refreshed and maybe — is it possible? — a little younger.

8 *Friend of the House* 8 p.m.

Most of the favored area restaurants have an old-school vibe: tuxedoed waiters, a headwaiter who has worked there since opening day, and steak-and-lobster specialties. Though **Copley's** (621 North Palm Canyon Drive; 760-327-9555; copleyspalmsprings.com; $$$) might not have the culinary history of nearby Melvyn's Restaurant and Lounge, which opened as an inn in 1935, it has a different sort of storied past — it is housed in what was once Cary Grant's estate. It also has food that incorporates 21st-century flavors (one spring menu included dishes like a duck and artichoke salad with goat cheese, edamame, and litchi).

9 *Toasting Friends* 11 p.m.

The cocktail craze has made its way to the desert, and the guys manning the bar at the cavernous **Amigo Room** at the Ace Hotel (701 East Palm Canyon Drive; 760-325-9900; acehotel.com/palmsprings) are leading

ABOVE Palm trees line a highway entering town.

LEFT Residential architecture of the mid-20th century distinguishes Palm Springs. This example is the Kaufmann House exterior.

the way. In addition to measuring, shaking and pouring classic concoctions like the margarita, they offer more offbeat options like the Figa (fig-infused vodka with Earl Grey and honey tangerine) that reek of late-night innovation. The cool but mellow vibe—supplemented by décor featuring burgundy leather booths and glass tables with inlaid pesos—will keep you ordering.

SUNDAY

10 *Get Close with Cactus* 9 a.m.

Those looking for an early-morning calorie burn might prefer the uphill battles of Gastin or Araby Trail, but a hike through **Tahquitz Canyon** (500 West Mesquite Avenue; 760-416-7044; tahquitzcanyon.com),

part of the natural oasis area called Indian Canyons, offers a leisurely alternative. A small entrance fee gets you access to a 1.8-mile loop and the sights and smells that come with it: desert plants, lizards aplenty and a stunning, 60-foot waterfall. Take a two-hour ranger-led tour or explore the trail at your own pace. You'll see arid desert and cool, palm-lined gorges.

ABOVE Hiking at Tahquitz Canyon.

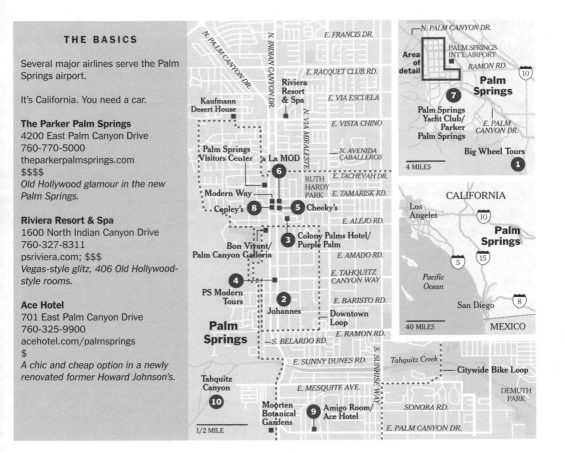

THE BASICS

Several major airlines serve the Palm Springs airport.

It's California. You need a car.

The Parker Palm Springs
4200 East Palm Canyon Drive
760-770-5000
theparkerpalmsprings.com
$$$$
Old Hollywood glamour in the new Palm Springs.

Riviera Resort & Spa
1600 North Indian Canyon Drive
760-327-8311
psriviera.com; $$$
Vegas-style glitz, 406 Old Hollywood-style rooms.

Ace Hotel
701 East Palm Canyon Drive
760-325-9900
acehotel.com/palmsprings
$
A chic and cheap option in a newly renovated former Howard Johnson's.

Map labels:

N. PALM CANYON DR.
N. INDIAN CANYON DR.
E. FRANCIS DR.
N. PALM CANYON DR.
Area of detail
PALM SPRINGS INT'L AIRPORT
RAMON RD.
Palm Springs
10
E. RACQUET CLUB RD.
Riviera Resort & Spa
E. VIA ESCUELA
Kaufmann Desert House
N. VIA MIRALESTE
E. VISTA CHINO
Palm Springs Yacht Club/ Parker Palm Springs
7
E. PALM CANYON DR.
Palm Springs Visitors Center
La MOD
N. AVENIDA CABALLEROS
Big Wheel Tours
1
4 MILES
6
RUTH HARDY PARK
E. TACHEVAH DR.
E. TAMARISK RD.
Modern Way
Copley's 8
5 Cheeky's
E. ALEJO RD.
Los Angeles
10
CALIFORNIA
Bon Vivant/ Palm Canyon Galleria
3 Colony Palms Hotel/ Purple Palm
E. AMADO RD.
Palm Springs
5 15
E. TAHQUITZ CANYON WAY
Pacific Ocean
PS Modern Tours
4
2 Johannes
E. BARISTO RD.
Downtown Loop
San Diego
8
Palm Springs
E. RAMON RD.
S. BELARDO RD.
40 MILES
MEXICO
E. SUNNY DUNES RD.
S. SUNRISE WAY
Tahquitz Creek
Citywide Bike Loop
Tahquitz Canyon
E. MESQUITE AVE.
DEMUTH PARK
10
Moorten Botanical Gardens
9 Amigo Room/ Ace Hotel
SONORA RD.
1/2 MILE
E. PALM CANYON DR.

Las Vegas

The Las Vegas Strip grew fast in the first decade of the millennium, with new hotels, resorts, and entertainment palaces jockeying for attention. Even when hard times hit in the global recession, the building continued — two massive casino-hotel-retail projects, already on the way, opened their doors in 2010 although hotel rooms were empty all over town and the suburbs were hollowing out in the housing bust. The city was humbled, but that didn't stop its business people from hatching plans for new diversions, from a giant Ferris wheel to a gourmet vegan menu at the Wynn. Regardless of economic cycles, Las Vegas is never boring. And in the end, nothing beats a stroll along the Strip for a strong dose of America writ large and bright. — BY RANDAL C. ARCHIBOLD

FRIDAY

1 *Protein Palace* 7:30 p.m.

Start modestly. Guy Savoy at Caesars Palace and Alex at Wynn are among the higher-end restaurants in town, but look for a satisfying meal and a quick table without reservations at **Burger Bar in Mandalay Place** (3930 Las Vegas Boulevard; 702-632-9364; mandalaybay.com; $$-$$$$). It is a slightly upscale spot — you could pay $60 for a hamburger composed of ingredients like Kobe beef, sautéed foie gras, and Madeira sauce, among other delectable possibilities. But you don't have to. The restaurant lets you build your own burger using a cornucopia of ingredients, and most of them aren't so pricey. Then there's the Creamy Cheesecake Burger for dessert.

2 *Sgt. Pepper Does Vegas* 10:30 p.m.

Showtime. The pervasive **Cirque du Soleil** performances — half a dozen or more at different hotels — and the mammoth ads everywhere make Cirque something like the Starbucks of the entertainment circuit here. One of its extravaganzas, *Love*,

OPPOSITE The Las Vegas Strip, where ostentation can never be overdone.

RIGHT At the Mix Lounge in the THEhotel, part of the Mandalay Bay hotel and casino complex, the drinks may be expensive but the view takes in a lot of glitter.

a surrealistic, acrobatic take on the music of the Beatles (at the Mirage, 3400 Las Vegas Boulevard South), created a Vegas version of Beatlemania. It mixes snippets from original recordings and film clips with intriguing lights and shadows and, of course, a lot of oddly clad people floating and flipping around on wires, cords, and other devices. Somewhere in there lurks a story. Tickets for all of the Cirque shows are available at cirquedusoleil.com.

SATURDAY

3 *A Taste of Napa on the Strip* 9 a.m.

Try **Bouchon at the Venetian** (3355 Las Vegas Boulevard South; 702-414-6200; venetian.com; $$) for a French-themed breakfast in a Venice-themed hotel and resort. The restaurant is owned by the chef Thomas Keller, who made his name with the French Laundry in Napa Valley. A word to the wise: there are no reservations at breakfast, so if it looks like a long wait, ask for a seat at the bar. You get the full menu and often faster service. On one visit, custardy French toast arrived in a blink, as did a croque-madame with an eagle's nest of fries.

4 *Vegas at Tiffany's* 10 a.m.

If you've never experienced a shopping center designed by David Libeskind, here's your chance.

At **Crystals at CityCenter** (3720 South Las Vegas Boulevard; crystalsatcitycenter.com), retailers purvey their wares inside what looks like — yes — a cluster of gigantic crystals. Here you can find Tiffany's, Prada, Cartier, Fendi, Versace, and others of their kind, along with a Wolfgang Puck pizzeria, together in one eye-popping setting. It's one element of the huge new CityCenter development, a set of gleaming towers you won't be able to overlook. A smaller, somewhat less pricey collection of new shops is in the Strip's other giant new development, the Cosmopolitan. You don't have to buy to appreciate the spectacle.

5 *The Demi-Eiffel* 1 p.m.

To drink in views of the Strip, many people head to the **Stratosphere Tower**, a 1,149-foot spire (2000 Las Vegas Boulevard South; 702-380-7711; stratospherehotel.com) that has a fine restaurant near the top. But the center of the strip offers an appealing alternative, the **Eiffel Tower** of the **Paris Las Vegas** hotel (3655 Las Vegas Boulevard South; 702-946-7000; parislasvegas.com). It's as close to the real thing as, well, the New York-New York hotel and casino is to that little burg on the Hudson. But at 460 feet, less than half as tall as the original, you see the

Strip and surrounding mountains plus a bonus bird's-eye view of the periodic ultrafountain show outside the Bellagio. It is even more entrancing at night.

6 *Tea and Crustaceans* 2:30 p.m.

A lot of hotel restaurants these days offer afternoon tea. The **Petrossian Bar** at the Bellagio (3600 Las Vegas Boulevard South; 702-693-7111; bellagio.com; $$$) is typical, and it's a lot more than finger sandwiches and crumpets. Expect Maine lobster, pico de gallo, and caviar served open-faced on a brioche. Get a seat outside the main room to watch the parade of people stream through the lobby.

7 *Luck Be a Lady* 4 p.m.

Oh, yeah. Gambling. The new casinos beckon, but consider the slightly older **Wynn Las Vegas** (3131 Las Vegas Boulevard South; 702-770-7000; wynnlasvegas.com), particularly the elbow-to-elbow poker room. Riding the burst of intense interest in the game, several hotel casinos have made more room for pokerphiles. Even if you don't play, just watching the action and checking out the Runyonesque characters who come and go is entertainment enough. And just a few steps away, right in the hotel, is a luxury car dealership, Penske-Wynn Ferrari/Maserati (penskewynn.com). There's a fee just to walk inside, but that shouldn't even make you blink, what with all your poker winnings.

8 *That Old-Time Linguine* 7 p.m.

Get some distance from the Strip's hurly-burly. The **Bootlegger Bistro** (7700 Las Vegas Boulevard South; 702-736-4939; bootleggerlasvegas.com; $$-$$$), an old-fashioned Italian restaurant, dates to 1949, making it practically prehistoric in Las Vegas years. It sits beyond the southern glut of Strip hotels, but it's worth the trip. Its dimly lighted interior of cherry red and dark wood, along with all the celebrity photographs on the walls, evokes the ancient, loungy Vegas. Most nights include live music, sometimes with big-name musicians taking a break from their gigs in the arenas farther north. The house special is seafood del diavolo.

9 *Luck on the Lanes* 9 p.m.

You can catch some live jazz in the **Rocks Lounge** of the new-not-so-long-ago **Red Rock Casino, Resort & Spa** (11011 West Charleston Boulevard; 702-797-7777; redrocklasvegas.com), but when you tire of the shows, there's another option here: go bowling at **Red Rock Lanes** (redrocklanes.com). A luxury bowling center (that's its own description), it has 72 lanes, LCD scoring monitors, lounge service, and Saturday-night cosmic bowling, featuring light-show effects, fog machines, glow-in-the-dark alleys and balls, and pounding music to enjoy it all by.

ABOVE A performance of Cirque du Soleil's Beatles-based show at the Mirage.

BELOW Blackjack tables at the Cosmopolitan. Gambling is still at the heart of it all.

SUNDAY

10 *Desert Respite* 11 a.m.

A one-hour drive from Las Vegas, at the northern end of Lake Mead, is **Valley of Fire State Park** (Interstate 15, Exit 75, Overton; 702-397-2088; parks.nv.gov/vf.htm). Its name comes from the red sandstone formations, but if you travel there in summer you might think otherwise. The rest of the year, it makes for a pleasant trip, with plenty of trails and majestic desert scenery. The open expanses of desert, pocked with otherworldly, towering rock formations, recall Martian landscapes as photographed by NASA. Arch Rock and Poodle Rock are particularly captivating and are accessible from main roads or trails. Beware, or join, the Trekkies: Silica Dome off Fire Creek Road was the setting for the planet where James T. Kirk fell to his death in *Star Trek: Generations*. Mourners still beam themselves there.

ABOVE Valley of Fire State Park, near Lake Mead.

OPPOSITE A downsized Eiffel Tower and Arc de Triomphe at the Paris Las Vegas hotel.

THE BASICS

Las Vegas is a four-hour drive from Los Angeles. Its airport is served by the major airlines. At the Strip, walk or use taxis, buses, and the monorail. Elsewhere, drive a car.

The Cosmopolitan
3708 Las Vegas Boulevard South
702-215-5500
cosmopolitanlasvegas.com
$$$
In a new multibillion-dollar development, with hotel interiors designed by David Rockwell.

Aria Resort and Casino
3730 Las Vegas Boulevard South, in CityCenter
702-590-7111
arialasvegas.com
$$$
In CityCenter, new in 2009, with 4,000 rooms and every amenity (some with extra fees).

Luxor
3900 Las Vegas Boulevard South
702-262-4444
luxor.com
$$
Bargain-hunters could do worse.

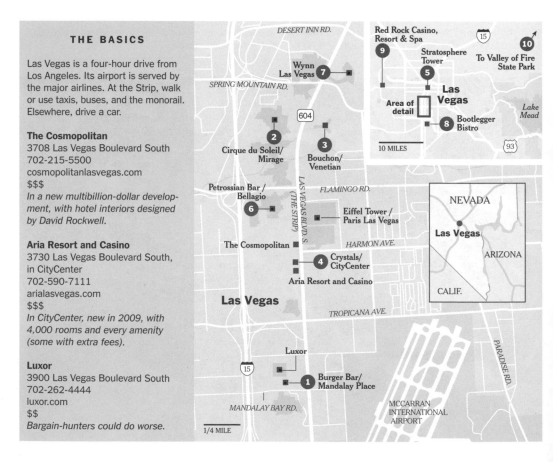

Death Valley

Although Death Valley remains starkly dramatic, electricity, the automobile, and a reliable water supply have conspired to rob it of its terror. It is not what you would call a "pleasant" place, but it is a spectacularly beautiful one, containing typical and unusual Southwestern features in its manageable sprawl. (Death Valley National Park is nearly as large as Connecticut.) It can be hellishly hot in summer — the record is 134 degrees — and ice closes roads in the winter. But in spring and fall, the weather is cooperative. Drive up from Los Angeles, and you will begin by passing through Antelope Valley — where in early spring psychedelic California poppies may blanket the hills — and from there into the unexciting town of Mojave, once a center for borax shipments coming out of the valley. From this point on, things become really interesting. — BY MARK BITTMAN

FRIDAY

1 *Steep Descent* 5 p.m.

As you drive north up Interstate 395 toward **Death Valley National Park** (nps.gov/deva), you will see the Sierra Nevada and Mount Whitney, at nearly 15,000 feet the tallest peak in the contiguous United States, to the west, and a series of far smaller ranges to the east. But at **Olancha**, as you veer eastward on Highway 190, the landscape suddenly takes on an eerie air. Ahead is a barren, deep-orange mountain range, and to the right and left are salt plains, former lakes that shimmer in the late-afternoon light. This is Saline Valley, and it leads to the Argus Range, where a massive red-rocked canyon gapes below the road. Ahead lies a wide, stark valley, which turns out to be not Death Valley but Panamint Valley, and in any other part of the country it would be striking enough. Here, however, there is still the Panamint Range to cross and, after a climb to 5,000 feet, the steep descent begins; it will end at sea level on the floor of Death Valley.

2 *Overnight Oasis* 8 p.m.

Death Valley bares its geologic soul at every turn, and you will soon discover the kinds of details that make the desert delightful: the toughest plant life in the world, well-camouflaged wildlife, and a stunning array of rocks and minerals. If winter has been "wet" (that is, if rain has fallen at more than the usual

pace of two inches a year), spring brings carpets of wildflowers. Head to **Stovepipe Wells**, one of several oases in the park. You'll find a general store, a ranger station that is sometimes open, and **Stovepipe Wells Village**, a serviceable hotel. Dinner at the **Toll Road Restaurant** (760-786-2387; escapetodeathvalley.com; $$) includes some vegetarian options. Drinks are at the **Badwater Saloon**.

SATURDAY

3 *Multiple Sunrises* 6:30 a.m.

Dawn walks are guaranteed to be cool, and a stroll or hike in a canyon will give you several sunrises as the sun peeks above and dips below the upper reaches of the steep walls. **Mosaic Canyon**, in the foothills of Tucki Mountain, is just up the road and through a long alluvial fan. As in many of the park's canyons, you can drive right to the entrance and within minutes find near-pristine isolation. Here, the passage between the steep walls narrows to just a few feet, and you will immediately be engulfed by formations of mosaic and smooth, swirling, multicolored marble.

4 *Sculpted Sand* 10 a.m.

On the road to **Furnace Creek** are the valley's most accessible sand dunes. These look best (and

OPPOSITE A view of eroded hills from Zabriskie Point in Death Valley National Park.

BELOW A bullet-pocked backcountry road sign.

are at their coolest, of course), when the shadows are still long. For kids, the dunes will be the highlight of the trip, but their texture and beauty will excite everyone. Be prepared to become sandy as you wander barefoot, especially if it is breezy. Carry water. You can visit the original Stovepipe Well near here and, back on the road, you will pass Devil's Cornfield, an expanse of arrowweed whose dried stems at first glance resemble bundles of cornstalks.

5 *A History of Borax* Noon

The **Visitor Center & Museum** at Furnace Creek boasts a super collection of material about the area as well as exhibitions that will answer your rapidly accumulating questions about borax. (Should this not be enough, nearby are a borax museum with an impressive collection of machinery and wagons of 20-mule-team fame, and the semi-preserved Harmony Borax Works. Like it or not, chances are you will leave Death Valley a borax expert.) The human history of the valley is outlined here too, from its original known inhabitants, the Shoshones, to the unfortunate 49ers who stumbled into and named the valley while looking for a shortcut to the gold fields.

6 *The High and the Low* 1 p.m.

Have lunch at the **49'er Café** in the Ranch at Furnace Creek (furnacecreekresort.com; $$), which serves standard fare of salads, burgers, and pasta.

(In general, the food in Death Valley is not as bad as you might fear.) Then get directions for the 45-mile round trip down a dead-end road to the mile-high **Dante's View**, from which you can see both the highest (Mount Whitney) and lowest (Badwater, nearly 300 feet below sea level) points in the Lower 48.

7 *Panoramic Palette* 3 p.m.

Late in the afternoon is the best time to see central Death Valley's best-known and most beautiful spots: **Zabriskie Point** and the **Artist's Drive**. The former, thanks to the fame brought by the film of the same name, has a large parking lot and paved walkway to its top. From here there are panoramic views of the gently rounded golden hills nearby, a relatively friendly landscape compared with the stark, darkly colored Panamints in the background. Just down the road is the car-friendly visual highlight, **Artist's Palette**. These vast, multicolored hills, dominated by pink, green, and lavender, virtually pulsate in the soft light of late afternoon and early evening.

8 *Moonlight* 6 p.m.

Have a drink in the quietly tasteful lobby of the **Inn at Furnace Cree**k (furnacecreekresort.com) and then amble down to the **Wrangler Steakhouse** ($$$) at the Furnace Creek Ranch for dinner. Despite the name, steak is not the only option. If you're adventure-some — especially if there is a full moon — this is a

great time to tackle Golden Canyon. Otherwise, you will be tired enough to sleep, and there is plenty to do in the morning.

SUNDAY

9 *Stroll the Canyons* 7 a.m.

Golden Canyon is nestled among the hills seen from Zabriskie Point. Seventy-five years ago it was such a popular destination that a road was built through it. Now it is an easy hike — a stroll, really — that you can enjoy for a quarter of a mile or so, wandering in and out of the lovely side canyons, or take for a mile and a half, until you gain an open

OPPOSITE A campfire glowing against a black desert sky.

ABOVE A scene from Saline Road.

BELOW Hot springs at Saline Valley.

view of the red rocks of the **Red Cathedral** next to the yellow flank of Manley Beacon (you will see the Cathedral almost as soon as you get into the canyon).

10 *Option 1: Easy Exit* 9 a.m.

If you take the southern route out of the park, make a quick stop to gaze again at Artist's Drive, this time from the **Devil's Golf Course**, where the ground is a compacted mass of pure salt and mud. You can walk on it, but be careful: the crystals are sharp enough to cut you if you fall. A few miles down the road is **Badwater**, the lowest point in Death Valley (and the country), a terrifying expanse of salt fields and salt water, and a bitter disappointment to early travelers. Exit the park at Shoshone, and stop for a burger and a

root beer float at the **Crowbar Cafe & Saloon** (Highway 127, Shoshone; 760-852-4123; $$).

11 *Option 2: Rugged Detour* 9 a.m.

If you have time and a four-wheel drive vehicle, you may want to detour to the **Saline Valley Warm Springs**, a countercultural hangout since free spirits planted palms and built soaking tubs on its three levels of natural hot springs in the 1960s. The park took over in the '90s, but the "clothing optional" ethos

still thrives, and a private group (salinepreservation. org) works with the park service. Stock up on fuel and supplies, and then, still just inside the park, turn north off Highway 190 onto a dirt road down into the valley. (It has traditionally been marked by a bullet-perforated "Road Closed" sign left from a long-ago winter.) Wrestle the washboard road for 53 miles. At the end, you'll find a mellow, relaxing scene and friendly people—often including families—bound by a love of the desert and its wide-open spaces.

ABOVE Remains of a tram line that hauled salt.

OPPOSITE The salt flats at Badwater Pool, the lowest point in the United States.

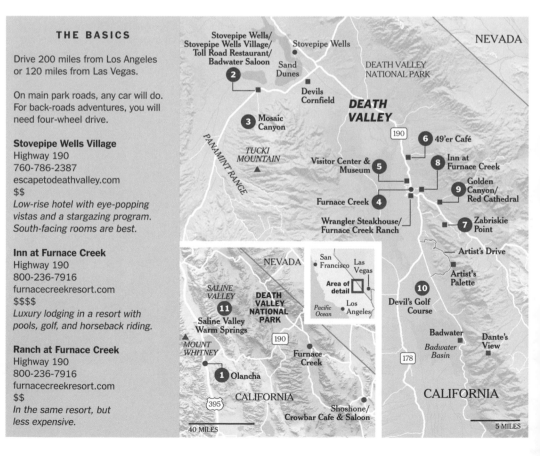

THE BASICS

Drive 200 miles from Los Angeles or 120 miles from Las Vegas.

On main park roads, any car will do. For back-roads adventures, you will need four-wheel drive.

Stovepipe Wells Village
Highway 190
760-786-2387
escapetodeathvalley.com
$$
Low-rise hotel with eye-popping vistas and a stargazing program. South-facing rooms are best.

Inn at Furnace Creek
Highway 190
800-236-7916
furnacecreekresort.com
$$$$
Luxury lodging in a resort with pools, golf, and horseback riding.

Ranch at Furnace Creek
Highway 190
800-236-7916
furnacecreekresort.com
$$
In the same resort, but less expensive.

Mammoth Lakes

For over half a century, winter recreation-seekers from Southern California have flocked to this secluded corner of California's Sierra Nevada mountains. It's easy to see why. Despite the 8,000-foot altitude, Mammoth Lakes' sprawl of splashy condos and strip malls has a distinct Los Angeles feeling. But the surrounding frozen lakes and granite peaks, immortalized by the photographer Ansel Adams, are decidedly un-Los Angeles, and can hold their own with any landscape in Colorado or Canada. Now, with more flights to its airport and a flurry of new après-ski offerings, Mammoth is hoping to draw skiers from beyond California.
— BY LIONEL BEEHNER

FRIDAY

1 *Siberian Spa* 4 p.m.

Imagine a vast white expanse of what looks like frozen Siberian tundra, dotted with natural hot springs and surrounded by soaring peaks. **Hilltop Hot Spring** is popular with locals, but you can join in, too. There are no formal signs or footpaths — just follow the S.U.V.'s past the airport five minutes east of Mammoth Lakes and enjoy a steaming soak, free of charge. For more privacy, cross the road to **Wild Willy's**, a more secluded spring, which requires a 20-minute trek and a pair of snowshoes.

2 *By the Fireplace* 7 p.m.

On the other side of town is **Tamarack Lodge and Resort** (163 Twin Lakes Road, off Lake Mary Road; 760-934-2442; tamaracklodge.com). A rustic log cabin with bark-wood ceiling fixtures and 1920s-era fireplace, it also happens to have an impressive wine collection and an excellent chef: Frederic Pierrel. The intimate **Lakefront Restaurant** ($$$) serves up hearty dishes like a combination platter of elk medallions, grilled quail, and pork marinated in wine on a bed of spicy mashed potatoes. Before being seated, have a mulled wine or hot cider by the fire.

SATURDAY

3 *Pancakes and Biscuits* 6:30 a.m.

Before hitting the slopes, fill up on pancakes and black-and-white memorabilia at the **Stove** (644 Old Mammoth Road; 760-934-2821; $$), a cozy spot with long wooden booths and old pictures of cattle ranchers on its walls. For over 40 years, the Stove has served hearty meals like the Sierra Sunrise, a heap of fried potatoes, peppers, onions, and ham topped with eggs and cheese. On your way out, pick up a homemade pie — apple, apricot, cherry. Get there early. The place fills up fast.

4 *Black Tie Skiing* 7:30 a.m.

Experts from **Black Tie Ski Rentals** (760-934-7009; blacktieskis.com) will come to your condo and fit you for skis or snowboards. And if the boots don't feel snug by midday, they will meet you on the slopes and exchange your gear, or switch your snowboard for a pair of skis.

5 *Fresh Tracks* 8 a.m.

With over 3,500 acres of trails, Mammoth has more variable terrain than most mountains (mammothmountain.com). There are three lodges: Eagle, Canyon, and Main. Skiers in search of soft powder and fresh-groomed runs start on Eagle and follow the sun over to Main or the backside of the mountain (to avoid lift lines, reverse the order). Or take the gondola from Main to the summit, 11,053 feet above sea level, where you can find a relaxing spot for hot cocoa. Marvel at the daredevils who ski

OPPOSITE Imagine a vast white expanse dotted with natural hot springs and surrounded by soaring peaks.

BELOW Outside of ski season, there's always fishing in the cold mountain lakes.

off Hangman's Hollow. Or brave the steep and icy chutes of Dave's Run or Scotty's. A safer alternative is Santiago, off the summit's less crowded backside, which offers scattered glades as well as gorgeous views of the Minarets, a majestic series of jagged granite peaks.

6 *South of the Border* Noon

Lunch on Mammoth typically involves Mexican fare. If you can't find the new Roving Mammoth, a bright orange snowcat that doubles as a food cart, serving up burritos — you can even track the snowcat's whereabouts on Twitter — there are pulled-pork nachos at the **Mill Cafe** (760-934-0675; $$), a festive après-ski spot at the base of Chair 2 (in true California fashion, its entrance is scattered with beach chairs). Or, for overflowing plates of nachos and fish tacos, head to the **Yodler** (10001 Minaret Road; 760-934-2571; $$), a Swiss-style chalet off the Main Lodge. **Gomez's** (100 Canyon Boulevard; 760-924-2693; gomezs.com; $), a Mexican place with over 200 tequilas and fittingly mammoth margaritas, relocated to a spot in the middle of the village last year.

7 *Art Park* 1 p.m.

Take Chair 10 up to ski down a few wide-open runs like Easy Rider or Solitude that stay powdery throughout the day. Or try Quicksilver, a well-groomed trail with gently sloped glades and variable terrain.

Snowboarders should head to the new terrain **Art Park**, which made its debut in December and showcases funky artworks affixed to its rails and steel structures. Mammoth also recently opened the Stomping Grounds, a terrain park packed with jumps, jibs and an Acrobag — which resembles a giant blue moon bounce — to practice flips. Nonsnowboarders should take the newly carved Village Ski Back Trail, a scenic path that meanders past pine trees and the backyards of condos, linking the mountain with the village.

8 *Growlers and Pastries* 4 p.m.

Thankfully, après-ski at Mammoth does not involve bad cover bands. If anything, it revolves around its eponymous microbrew. Insiders make their way to a warehouse converted a few years back into a beer-tasting room for the **Mammoth Brewing Company** (94 Berner Street; 760-934-7141; mammothbrewingco.com). Still in ski gear, they

ABOVE Nighttime options have expanded as Mammoth Lakes has grown.

OPPOSITE ABOVE Relaxing in the dining room at the Tamarack Lodge & Resort.

OPPOSITE BELOW A cozy cabin in the snow. Lodging options include condos, cabins, and hotel rooms.

down free samples before filling up their growlers with IPA 395, a local favorite, or grabbing kegs and cases to go. A favorite spot among Mammoth's growing international crowd is **Shea Schat's Bakery** (3305 Main Street; 760-934-6055), which feels, and smells, like the inside of a gingerbread house. The shop serves up steaming hot chocolate and stocks rows of pastries — cinnamon nut bread, ginger cakes, and bread pudding.

9 *Mid-Mountain Dining* 6 p.m.

The swanky restaurant **Parallax** (800-626-6684; mammothmountain.com; $$$$) takes up almost half of the cafeteria at McCoy Station, a midmountain gondola station up from the Main Lodge. Its modern décor and Asian-themed trimmings, including white bark walls, would not look out of place in downtown Manhattan, save, perhaps, for the tacky TV Yule log fireplace. Yet at 9,600 feet, it is reachable by only

snowcat, which picks people up at the **Mammoth Mountain Inn** (10001 Minaret Road; 760-934-2581; mammothmountain.com). Hop aboard a heated snowcat that feels like a spaceship as you gaze up at the stars through its glass roof. Then feast on a satisfying entree — perhaps New Zealand lamb or grilled chicken with risotto. For optimal views, get there as night falls.

10 *Rockies Meets Hollywood* 9 p.m.

Never mind the gondola D.J. booth and vintage lanterns above the bar. **Hyde Lounge** (6201 Minaret Road; 760-934-0669; sbe.com/hydemammoth) lives up to its Sunset Boulevard forefather. There

are bottle-service-only booths, lasers everywhere, and Mammoth's version of a strict door policy (no snowboard gear). The crowd sipping pricey cocktails is a mix of slovenly clad snowboarders and dressed-to-impress partygoers, all crammed within its fire-engine

ABOVE With over 3,500 acres of trails, Mammoth has more variable terrain than most ski mountains.

OPPOSITE A summer view of the wild beauty at Twin Lakes near the village at Mammoth Lakes.

red walls. Warm up with a burning mango, a jalapeño and vodka concoction, and settle in for a night of people watching.

SUNDAY

11 *Olympic Workout* 9 a.m.

In recent years, Mammoth Lakes has become a year-round hub for Olympic and pro athletes attracted to the high altitudes and easygoing ethos. A nice byproduct is the state-of-the-art facilities at the Snowcreek Athletic Club, which resembles a giant barn just outside town. The club recently opened the **Double Eagle Spa** (51 Club Drive; 760-934-8511; snowcreekathleticclub.com), with earthy massage rooms, Vichy showers, and a yoga studio.

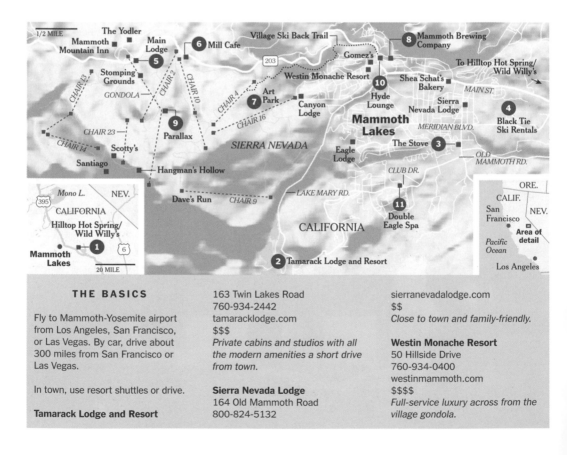

THE BASICS

Fly to Mammoth-Yosemite airport from Los Angeles, San Francisco, or Las Vegas. By car, drive about 300 miles from San Francisco or Las Vegas.

In town, use resort shuttles or drive.

Tamarack Lodge and Resort

163 Twin Lakes Road
760-934-2442
tamaracklodge.com
$$$
Private cabins and studios with all the modern amenities a short drive from town.

Sierra Nevada Lodge
164 Old Mammoth Road
800-824-5132

sierranevadalodge.com
$$
Close to town and family-friendly.

Westin Monache Resort
50 Hillside Drive
760-934-0400
westinmammoth.com
$$$$
Full-service luxury across from the village gondola.

Big Sur

Running southward from Carmel, 150 miles south of San Francisco, to San Simeon, Big Sur's mass of tight mountains pushes brazenly against the Pacific swell. Kelp forests sway at the feet of the rugged sea cliffs. Deep valleys shelter some of California's southernmost redwoods. Writers, artists, dreamers, and hippies have all been drawn here; Henry Miller described it as "a region where one is always conscious of weather, of space, of grandeur and of eloquent silence." Although the rich and famous are now building homes here, the geography prevents sprawl and most development is invisible, preserving the feeling of solitude. Big Sur still rewards serendipity, but this is no place to rely upon it: the few lodgings fill quickly. Make reservations well in advance, allow plenty of time for the drive, and then let the ocean and the mountains take over.

— BY GREGORY DICUM

FRIDAY

1 *View from the Road* 2 p.m.

The only way into and through the Big Sur coast is along winding, breathtaking **California Highway 1**. Its construction here in the 1930s was controversial (sheer cliffs and constant rockfalls attest to the project's audacity), but today it is a testament to the ambition of New Deal public works projects. Though Big Sur is as much an idea as a place, you will know you have arrived when, driving south from Monterey, you cross **Bixby Bridge**. A marvel of concrete spanning a deep coastal gorge, it has appeared in a thousand car commercials, and it's worth a stop if you're into infrastructure: turn out at either end of the span. Other viewpoints abound on the road, so keep your camera at the ready and expect to stop frequently.

2 *Waterside* 5 p.m.

Though the Pacific is everywhere in Big Sur, the enfolding coast guards access like a jealous lover. Beaches nestle in coves backed by fearsome cliffs, and in only a few places is it easy — or even possible — to set foot on them. **Pfeiffer Beach** is one. Take a sharp right turn a quarter-mile south of the Big Sur Ranger Station onto the unmarked Sycamore Canyon Road, and follow it down to a bay sheltered from the ocean's full force by chunky offshore rocks. The fine tan sand there is streaked with purple minerals. Wander in the warm sun and test a toe in the cold water. On one sunny late afternoon, handfuls of college students basked in sweatshirts and sunglasses like style-conscious sea lions. An arch in the rocks serves as a proscenium for the lowering sun and the backlit orange seawater splashes of gentle swells.

3 *Sunset Sustenance* 7 p.m.

Big Sur has remarkably few dining options for a place so visited. Fortunately, some of them are sublime. **Cielo**, the restaurant at **Ventana Inn** (48123 Highway One; 831-667-4242; ventanainn.com; $$$) takes archly appropriate ingredients — wild Dungeness crab, seasonal local organic vegetables, Sonoma duck, bison from a Wyoming ranch — and turns them into finely wrought California cuisine. Get a table by the big windows, or outside, and enjoy a view of the sun dropping into the rippling waves. Unless it's foggy, of course.

OPPOSITE McWay Falls pours 80 feet onto a perfect, though inaccessible, beach around a blue Pacific cove.

BELOW A yurt at Treebones Resort, a mid-priced lodging option. Land-use restrictions both keep Big Sur beautiful and limit places to stay.

SATURDAY

4 *Grandpa's Eggs Benedict* 9 a.m.

One of Big Sur's heartiest breakfasts is at **Deetjen's** (48865 Highway 1; 831-667-2378; deetjens.com; $$), this coast's original roadhouse. The inn dates to the 1930s, when Grandpa Deetjen built a redwood barn here that grew into a cluster of cabins. The restaurant, open to all, has an unpretentious but efficient and friendly feel that seems the epitome of Big Sur at its best. Eggs Benedict are a specialty, but there's a varied menu that also includes smoked salmon and huevos rancheros. If you're lucky, you can eat by the fire, but resist the urge to sit there all day: it's time to work off that breakfast.

5 *The Redwoods Are Waiting* 10 a.m.

State parks are strung up and down the coast. Many offer short hikes to astounding coastal vistas, while others permit access to the rugged mountain wilderness of the interior. At **Pfeiffer Big Sur State**

Park (26 miles south of Carmel on Highway 1), trails lead through dense, damp groves of redwoods and oaks to coastal overlooks, a waterfall, and up to open ridges and mountaintops. The three-mile Oak Grove Trail gives hikers a taste of the diversity of Big Sur landscapes and, with luck, the wildlife: Big Sur is one of the places where majestic California condors have been reintroduced following their near-extinction.

6 *Go for the View* 1 p.m.

Nepenthe (48510 Highway 1; 831-667-2345; nepenthebigsur.com; $$–$$$), has long been a favorite tourist aerie. It is worth a visit on sunny days for the magnificent views and cheery crowd,

ABOVE A cabin in a redwood grove at Deetjen's, an inn that dates to the 1930s.

RIGHT At Pfeiffer Big Sur State Park, trails lead through dense redwood groves to open ridges and mountaintops.

OPPOSITE Pfeiffer Beach, one of the few accessible Big Sur beaches. Most are below fearsome cliffs.

although the food is undistinguished. Think of it as the price of admission.

7 *Waterfall to the Sea* 2 p.m.

Julia Pfeiffer Burns State Park (on Highway 1, 831-667-2315; parks.ca.gov, not to be confused with Pfeiffer Big Sur State Park) is an all but requisite stop: from the parking area it's an easy stroll to view McWay Falls. The 80-foot-high cataract pours onto a perfect, though inaccessible, beach around a blue Pacific cove. It's the image most likely to come to mind later as you reminisce about Big Sur.

8 *Enlightenment* 3 p.m.

"There being nothing to improve on in the surroundings," Miller wrote of Big Sur in 1957, "the tendency is to set about improving oneself." He could have been describing the **Esalen Institute** (55000 Highway 1), a sort of New Age Harvard founded in 1962, whose campus tumbles down toward a precipitous cliff above the ocean. Seekers and celebrities come for "energy" and Atlantis, registering for workshops in yoga, meditation, and various kinds of self-realization. Participants stay overnight. To get a taste of the place in a shorter time — and work away any lingering stress that has managed to survive Big Sur so far — book a massage (831-667-3002; esalen.org/info/massage; time slots limited and reservations essential; $165). It's a rare chance to enter the Esalen grounds without booking for a longer stay. You're allowed to arrive an hour early and stay an hour afterward to experience the hot springs.

9 *The Soak* 5:30 p.m.

By now you've emerged refreshed from your bodywork and are soaking (nudity optional, but de rigueur), in the **Esalen Hot Springs Baths** (esalen.org/place/hot_springs.html). Esalen is known for these legendary tubs. Hugging a seaside cliff, the complex of baths momentarily captures natural hot springs before they pour into the Pacific. Board-formed concrete walls, warm and grippy sandstone floors, and floor-to-ceiling windows look out to sea. Outdoor soaking pools and a living roof lend the baths a sense of belonging in the landscape. From the hot water bathers can look down on sea otters lounging in the kelp. If your brief soak isn't enough, sign up to return between 1 a.m. and 3 a.m., when the baths are open to the public for $20. The hours are inconvenient (the nighttime drive over corkscrew Highway 1 will instantly undo the baths' restorative effects), but breakers below shake the cliff and thousands of stars shine out of a black sky, giving the place the feel of a celestial point of embarkation.

10 *Above It All* 8 p.m.

On the ridgeline hundreds of feet above Pfeiffer Beach, the **Post Ranch Inn** perches in unobtrusive luxe, its cottages spread tactfully over rolling acres of grass and woods. But like the rest of Big Sur, the inn has a charm that has as much to do with its attitude as with the landscape — not every thousand-dollar-a-night resort has an in-house shaman. Even if your wallet places you in a different category from the establishment's target clientele, you will find a welcoming spirit at the inn's restaurant, the **Sierra Mar** (831-667-2800; postranchinn.com; $$$$). Seek a table on the outdoor deck and order the four-course prix fixe dinner.

OPPOSITE A hot spring pool at the Esalen Institute, where you can seek enlightenment or just a relaxing massage.

11 *Literary Nexus* 11 a.m.

The **Henry Miller Memorial Library** (Highway 1; 831-667-2574; henrymiller.org) maintains a reference collection of Miller's work, a bookshop, and a big wooden deck where visitors can enjoy coffee and Wi-Fi. Special events include readings, concerts, art shows, performances, and seminars. It's hardly monumental — little more than a house in the woods before a grassy yard strewn with sculptures and bric-a-brac that might be sculptural. Like much of the rest of Big Sur, the library is a casual place where lounging and artistic pursuit go hand in hand.

THE BASICS

Drive at least three hours from San Francisco, or fly into San Jose or Monterey. Plan on slow-paced driving over Highway 1's curves and switchbacks.

Deetjen's
48865 Highway 1
831-667-2377
deetjens.com
$$-$$$
A cluster of rough-hewn cabins under the boughs of a redwood grove; unpretentious and friendly.

Esalen Institute
55000 Highway 1
831-667-3005
esalen.org
$$$$
Pricey and spartan, but comfort isn't the point. To rent a room, sign up for a one-night Personal Retreat.

Post Ranch Inn
Highway 1
831-667-2200
postranchinn.com
$$$$
Room rates in four figures buy privacy and peace on a beautiful coast.

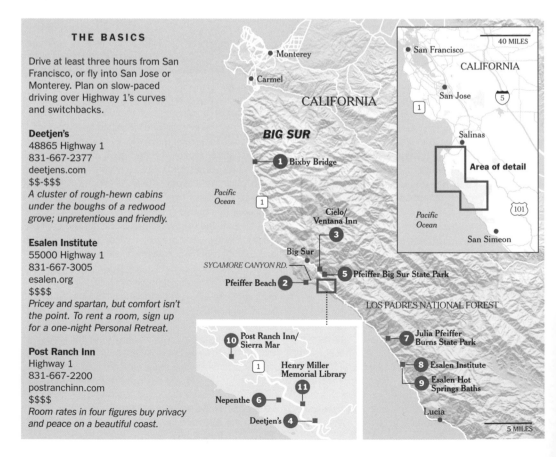

Carmel

With its architectural mishmash of storybook English cottages and Swiss Alpine chalets, the small California town of Carmel-by-the-Sea resembles a Disneyland version of Europe. You half expect a bereted Parisian to saunter out of one of the ridiculously cute Euro-themed bistros. But walk a few blocks to Carmel's steep, sandy beach and the view is pure California: a rugged Pacific coastline spangled with rocky outcroppings, ghostly cypress trees, and the electric green slopes of the famed Pebble Beach golf course. The one-square-mile village has no street lights, parking meters, or numbered addresses, but you wouldn't call it low-key. Once a bohemian outpost for people like Jack London, Carmel today is prime real estate, and the surrounding valley is abuzz with top-notch restaurants, boutique wineries, and precious shops. — BY JAIME GROSS

FRIDAY

1 *Cocktails with Clint* 6 p.m.

Carmel has had its share of boldfaced residents, but few more enduring or beloved than Clint Eastwood, who was the town's mayor from 1986 to 1988 and still lives in the area. You might catch a glimpse of him at his restaurant at **Mission Ranch** (26270 Dolores Street; 831-624-6436; missionranchcarmel.com), his 22-acre property just outside of town, where he's been known to eat with his family and greet old-timers at the piano bar. Order a glass of wine and snag a seat on the heated restaurant patio overlooking a striking tableau: sheep meadows, rolling hills, and the shimmering ocean in the distance.

2 *California French* 8 p.m.

For an intimate dinner with plenty of foodie appeal, try Aubergine, the restaurant at the Relais & Châteaux hotel **L'Auberge Carmel** (Seventh Avenue and Monte Verde Street; 831-624-8578; laubergecarmel.com; $$$$). The French-influenced menu reflects the availability of fresh local produce, celebrating the seasons with dishes like roasted lamb with cranberry bean cassoulet.

OPPOSITE The Point Lobos State Reserve.

RIGHT A landscape painter at Bernardus Winery in vineyard country near Carmel-by-the-Sea.

SATURDAY

3 *Biking for a View* 8 a.m.

Beat the gawking motorists and entry fee for cars by waking early and biking the **17-Mile Drive**, the jaw-dropping corniche that hugs the rocky coastline between Carmel and Pacific Grove. **Adventures by the Sea** (299 Cannery Row, Monterey; 831-372-1807; adventuresbythesea.com) rents bikes for $7 an hour and is an easy five miles from the drive's most scenic stretches, which are lined with sandy beaches, golf courses, and a 250-year-old cypress tree sprouting from a seaside boulder.

4 *Mission Museum* 11 a.m.

The **San Carlos Borroméo del Rio Carmelo Mission** (3080 Rio Road; 831-624-1271; carmelmission.org) was founded at its present site in 1771 by Father Junipero Serra and was once the headquarters for the entire California mission system. Known more simply as the Carmel Mission, the site includes a poppy-filled garden, an abalone-strewn cemetery, and a stone Basilica with original 18th-century artworks. At the Mission's **Convento Museum**, you can peer into Father Serra's spartan living quarters—with a table, a chair, and a highly uncomfortable-looking wooden bed— and check out his book collection, identified as "California's first library."

5 *In-Town Tastings* 12:30 p.m.

Pick up lunch on a walking tour of some of Carmel's best food shops. Here's a cheat sheet: **Bountiful Basket** (San Carlos Street off Ocean Avenue; 831-625-4457; bountifulbasketcarmel.com)

imports more than 100 olive oils and vinegars from around the world; **Bruno's Market and Deli** (Sixth Avenue and Junipero Avenue; 831-624-3821; brunosmarket.com) has gourmet tri-tip and barbecued chicken sandwiches; and the **Cheese Shop** (Carmel Plaza, Ocean Avenue and Junipero Avenue, lower level; 800-828-9463; thecheeseshopinc.com) stocks picnic fixings, wine, and about 300 cheeses. They'll let you taste as many as you like, or they can assemble a customized cheese plate that you can nibble at the cafe tables out front.

6 *Sip the Valley* 2 p.m.

Thanks to its coastal climate and sandy, loamy soil, Carmel Valley is gaining renown for its wines. Most of the tasting rooms are clustered in Carmel Valley Village, a small town with a handful of restaurants and wineries 12 miles east of Carmel-by-the-Sea. **Bernardus** (5 West Carmel Valley Road; 800-223-2533; bernardus.com), the granddaddy of area wineries, is known for the breadth and quality of its wines. A relative newcomer, **Boekenoogen Wines** (24 West Carmel Valley Road; 831-659-4215; boekenoogenwines.com), is a small family-owned winery with a few varietals. Teetotalers can opt for topical wine treatments at **Bernardus Lodge** (415 Carmel Valley Road; 831-658-3560; bernardus.com), where a spa offers chardonnay facials and grape seed body scrubs.

7 *Stuff for Home* 4 p.m.

Walk off the buzz back in town, where 42 hidden courtyards and alleys shelter a plethora of stylish new galleries and boutiques. **Trouvé** (San Carlos Street and Sixth Avenue; 831-625-9777; trouvehome.com) is a well-curated collection of modern housewares and global antiques. The whimsical **Piccolo** (Dolores Street between Ocean and Seventh Avenues; 831-624-4411; piccolocarmel.com) is packed to the gills with handmade glassware, pottery, stationery, and jewelry. And the working studio and gallery of **Steven Whyte**, a local sculptor (Dolores Street

between Fifth and Sixth Avenues; 831-620-1917; stevenwhytesculptor.com), sells his hyper-realistic cast bronze portraits. Looking for something humbler? The **Carmel Drug Store** (Ocean Avenue and San Carlos Street; 831-624-3819; carmeldrugstore.com) has been selling handmade Swiss combs, grandma colognes, and Coca-Cola in glass bottles since 1910.

8 *Casual Flavors* 8 p.m.

For dinner, make a beeline for one of Carmel's über-charming French or Italian restaurants. **La Bicyclette** (Dolores Street at Seventh Avenue; 831-622-9899; labicycletterestaurant.com; $$$) resembles a rustic village bistro. The compact menu spans Europe with dishes like beef with Gorgonzola-red wine sauce or German sausage with homemade sauerkraut. Also worth a try is **Cantinetta Luca** (Dolores Street between Ocean and Seventh Avenues; 831-625-6500; cantinettaluca.com; $$$), an Italian restaurant popular for its wood-fired

ABOVE The Cheese Shop stocks picnic fixings, wine, and about 300 different cheeses.

BELOW Trouvé, a housewares and antiques shop downtown.

OPPOSITE Cycling on the winding 17-Mile Drive, which hugs the rocky coastline between Carmel and Pacific Grove.

pizzas, homemade pastas, all-Italian wine list, and a dozen types of salume aged on site in a glass-walled curing room.

SUNDAY

9 *Sea Life* 11 a.m.

Legend has it that Robert Louis Stevenson hit on the inspiration for the 1883 novel *Treasure Island* while strolling the beach near Point Lobos. Retrace his steps at **Point Lobos State Reserve** (Route 1, three miles south of Carmel; 831-624-4909; pt-lobos.parks.state.ca.us), a majestic landscape with 14 meandering trails. Don't forget binoculars: you can spot sea otters, seals, and sea lions year-round, and migrating gray whales December through May. Scuba divers take note: 60 percent of the reserve's 554 acres lies underwater, in one of the richest marine habitats in California. Scuba diving, snorkeling, and kayaking

reservations can be booked through the park's Web site.

10 *Poodles and Scones* 2 p.m.

In a town known for being dog-friendly, the **Cypress Inn** (Seventh Avenue and Lincoln Street; 831-624-3871; cypress-inn.com) takes the cake with poop bags at the door, bone-shaped biscuits at the front desk, and a *Best-in-Show*-worthy tea service. In addition to serving scones and crustless cucumber sandwiches, the tea service draws a head-spinning parade of Shih Tzus, toy poodles, and other impeccably groomed pups taking tea with their equally well-coiffed owners.

THE BASICS

Carmel-by-the-Sea is a scenic two-hour drive south of San Francisco.

L'Auberge Carmel
Seventh Avenue and Monte Verde Street
831-624-8578
laubergecarmel.com
$$$$
Winding staircases lead to 20 rooms, many with Japanese soaking tubs.

Cypress Inn
Seventh Avenue and Lincoln Street
831-624-3871
cypress-inn.com
$$$
Co-owned by Doris Day, whose songs are piped through the hotel.

Carmel Valley Ranch
1 Old Ranch Road
831-625-9500
carmelvalleyranch.com
$$$$
Fireplaces, terraces, golf course.

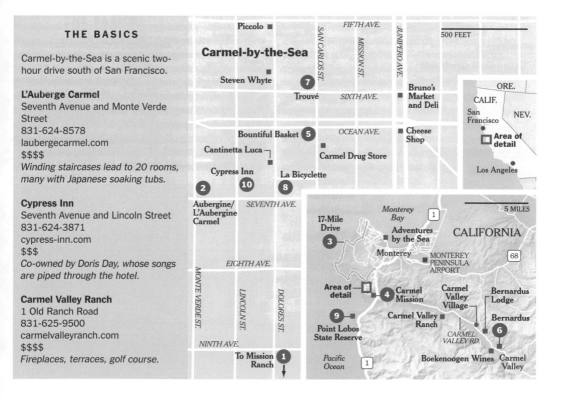

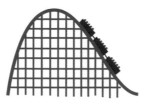

Santa Cruz

Santa Cruz has Mediterranean weather and an artfully skewed sense of reality. Yes, there are world-class surf breaks, sidewalk cafes, and a seaside amusement park, but on the city's streets you will also see jugglers, a saw player, and a street accordionist named the Great Morgani who dresses like an alien robot. This town has a high tolerance for eccentricity. And don't mistake it for a Southern California beach town. There isn't much in the way of glitz, celebrities, or pushy talent agents. Instead, the temperate weather, the Pacific Ocean, and the University of California, Santa Cruz, have attracted a mixture of surfers, street musicians, intellectuals, bookworms, authors, professors, and young professionals, all happy to share the sun and the salt air.
— BY DAN WHITE

FRIDAY

1 *Pacific Cruise* 4 p.m.

Once the domain of seedy bars and bong displays, the southern section of Pacific Avenue is now a more fashionable strip where the city's lust for vintage is on display. **Idle Hands Dry Goods** (803 Pacific Avenue; 831-466-9305; idlehandsdrygoods.com) feels like an updated Rolling Stones track, melding vintage American outlaw looks (cowboy boots, belt buckles) with rock-'n'-roller attitude (graphic T-shirts, Pendleton shirts). **True Love Antiques & Vintage** (805 Pacific Avenue; 714-847-3961) is a wonder cabinet of curios, art, and odd-ends. And on nearby Cedar Street, **MetaVinyl** (320 Cedar Street; 831-466-9027; metavinyl.com) carries new and old LPs, turntable gear, and rare finds like a mint-condition copy of 2 Live Crew's "As Nasty as They Wanna Be."

2 *Haut Kebabs* 7 p.m.

The dining scene in downtown Santa Cruz got a jolt with the arrival of **Laili** (101B Cooper Street; 831-423-4545; lailirestaurant.com; $$), a stylish Afghan restaurant. With its nattily dressed waiters, soaring ceilings and wall-size photo display of precious Afghan jewelry, this is no hole-in-the-wall kebab joint. A cross-section of Santa Cruz can be found on a given night, sampling Persian chive-stuffed Aushak dumplings and the braised lamb shank with kabuli rice and yogurt. Ask for a seat at the communal table, where you can rub elbows with surfers and techies, and watch a cook in an open kitchen preparing naan dough with a giant rolling pin.

3 *Latin Rhythms* 9 p.m.

The spiciest spot downtown is arguably the weekly salsa dance party at the historic **Palomar Ballroom** (1344 Pacific Avenue; 831-426-1221; palomarballroom.com), where dancers swirl in tight dresses, miniskirts, and high heels. If you know your salsa moves, pay $5 at the door. If you need to brush up, a $10 fee covers a salsa class and the dance party.

4 *Deep Red* Midnight

A crimson glow beckons late-night patrons upstairs to the **Red Restaurant & Bar** (200 Locust Street; 831-425-1913; redsantacruz.com), a curiously dark lounge with hidden nooks that stays open until 2 a.m. Unless you sit by the fire, reading the menu can be a challenge, so try the Winnie, a house-infused rose tea vodka with fresh lemon and simple syrup. Don't confuse this spot with the Red Room, which occupies the floor below and is a rite of passage for college students.

OPPOSITE Sand, surf, and a sunset, all commodities in generous supply in Santa Cruz.

BELOW Even if you're a novice at salsa, consider joining the weekly salsa dance party at the Palomar Ballroom. If you don't know the moves, you can pay $5 extra for a class.

SATURDAY

5 *Warm Brioche* 10 a.m.

Stock up for an outdoor picnic along the scenic coastline. True to its name, the **Buttery** (702 Soquel Avenue; 831-458-3020; butterybakery.com) specializes in butter-rich comfort foods like lemon cheese pockets and blueberry muffins. It also sells French baguettes. Round out your supplies across the street at **Shopper's Corner** (622 Soquel Avenue; 831-423-1398; shopperscorner.com), a local institution with a neon clock, local wines, hard cheeses, and tapenades.

6 *Take a Hike* 11 a.m.

A slow ride on West Cliff Drive offers views of cypress trees, eroded cliffs, and epic surf breaks. Park at the **Wilder Ranch State Park** (1401 Old Coast Road; 831-423-9703; parks.ca.gov), a 7,000-acre park with numerous hiking trails that tunnel through misted forests of alders, Douglas firs, and coastal redwoods. The park is also home to bobcats, feral piglets, and the occasional cougar.

7 *Green Hedonists* 3 p.m.

Once home to a frozen-vegetable processing plant, the **Swift Street Courtyard** (402 Ingalls Street) has been transformed into a kind of epicurean food court. The bittersweet Black IPA is a specialty at **Santa Cruz Mountain Brewing** (Suite 27; 831-425-4900; santacruzmountainbrewing.com), an organic microbrewery with a tiny tap room. If you're hungry, order a platter of fish tacos delivered to the bar from the shop next door, **Kelly's French Bakery** (831-423-9059; kellysfrenchbakery.com). Or, if you want to sample biodynamic wines, head to the tasting room at **Bonny Doon Vineyard** (328 Ingalls Street; 831-425-4518; bonnydoonvineyard.com), where a metal spaceship hovers overhead. A flight may include wines like

a white Spanish varietal called albariño or a dry muscat, both made from Monterey County grapes.

8 *Seabright Salumi* 6:30 p.m.

At **La Posta** (538 Seabright Avenue; 831-457-2782; lapostarestaurant.com; $$), the flavors might hail from Italy, but the ingredients are local. This handsome restaurant, which opened a few years ago in a former general store, draws locavores to the hushed neighborhood of Seabright. Examples of its farm-to-table ethos include the ortiche brick-oven pizza with wild nettles foraged at Route 1 Farm in Santa Cruz, and an escarole salad topped with a boiled egg that comes from the chickens out back.

9 *Music Boxes* 8 p.m.

With its large college population, Santa Cruz has long been a hub for indie music. One of the best spots to hear live music is the **Rio Theatre** (831-423-8209; 1205 Soquel Avenue; riotheatre.com), a former movie house from the 1940s that reopened 10 years ago as a concert hall and features acts like Neko Case and Cat Power. Another reliable option is the **Crepe Place** (1134 Soquel Avenue; 831-429-6994; thecrepeplace.com), a small venue housed in a century-old Victorian building, where acts like Erin McKeown and the cult favorite Dan Bern perform under the original stamped-tin ceiling.

SUNDAY

10 *Beach Walk* 10 a.m.

After ordering a butter-slathered hot cinnamon roll at **Linda's Seabreeze Cafe** (542 Seabright

ABOVE The Walton Lighthouse near Seabright State Beach.

Avenue; 831-427-9713; seabreezecafe.com), walk to nearby **Seabright State Beach** (East Cliff Drive at Seabright Avenue), a long stretch of tan-white sand with a midget lighthouse, a foghorn, and a cave. The **Municipal Wharf** (21 Municipal Wharf; 831-420-6025; santacruzwharf.com), a large pier built in 1914 that draws fishermen and pods of barking sea lions, is nearby. Don't trust your eyes: that set of "islands" is a fog-bound stretch of coastline.

11 *Deep Freeze* 2 p.m.

Two scoops of celery raisin ice cream? You won't find that in the freezer case of the local supermarket, but it is among the eccentric flavors that have been dreamed up at the **Penny Ice Creamery** (913 Cedar

Street; 831-204-2523; thepennyicecreamery.com). The shop changes its menu daily, so you never know whether it will have familiar options like rum raisin and dark chocolate or something wacky like black sesame or mandarin creamsicle.

OPPOSITE BELOW Sea lions under the municipal wharf, which dates back to 1914.

ABOVE Idle Hands Dry Goods on Pacific Avenue.

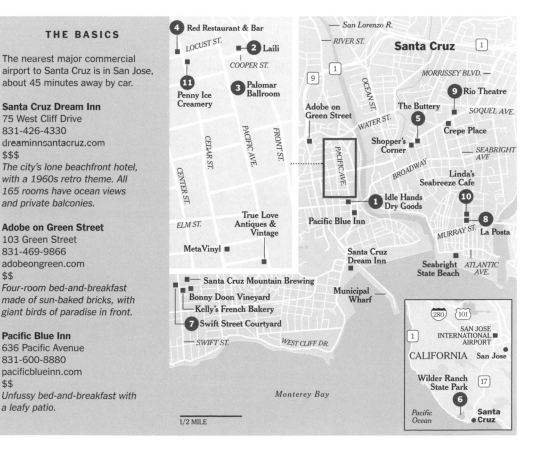

THE BASICS

The nearest major commercial airport to Santa Cruz is in San Jose, about 45 minutes away by car.

Santa Cruz Dream Inn
75 West Cliff Drive
831-426-4330
dreaminnsantacruz.com
$$$
The city's lone beachfront hotel, with a 1960s retro theme. All 165 rooms have ocean views and private balconies.

Adobe on Green Street
103 Green Street
831-469-9866
adobeongreen.com
$$
Four-room bed-and-breakfast made of sun-baked bricks, with giant birds of paradise in front.

Pacific Blue Inn
636 Pacific Avenue
831-600-8880
pacificblueinn.com
$$
Unfussy bed-and-breakfast with a leafy patio.

4 Red Restaurant & Bar
LOCUST ST.
2 Laili
COOPER ST.
11 Penny Ice Creamery
3 Palomar Ballroom
CEDAR ST.
PACIFIC AVE.
CENTER ST.
FRONT ST.
ELM ST.
True Love Antiques & Vintage
MetaVinyl
Santa Cruz Mountain Brewing
Bonny Doon Vineyard
Kelly's French Bakery
7 Swift Street Courtyard
SWIFT ST.
WEST CLIFF DR.

1/2 MILE

San Lorenzo R.
RIVER ST.
Santa Cruz 1
1
9
MORRISSEY BLVD. —
OCEAN ST.
WATER ST.
Adobe on Green Street
9 Rio Theatre
SOQUEL AVE.
The Buttery
5
Crepe Place
Shopper's Corner
SEABRIGHT AVE.
PACIFIC AVE.
BROADWAY
Linda's Seabreeze Cafe
1 Idle Hands Dry Goods
10
Pacific Blue Inn
MURRAY ST. La Posta
8
Santa Cruz Dream Inn
Seabright State Beach
ATLANTIC AVE.
Municipal Wharf

Monterey Bay

280 101
1
SAN JOSE INTERNATIONAL AIRPORT
CALIFORNIA San Jose
Wilder Ranch State Park
17
6
Pacific Ocean
Santa Cruz

Silicon Valley

Like the high-tech companies that give this hyper-prosperous region its name, Silicon Valley thrives on reinvention. Situated just south of San Francisco Bay, the valley was once home to orchards and vineyards. These days, of course, it bears fruit of a different sort, as the home of tech giants like Apple, Google, and Intel. Buoyed by the resilience of tech companies, the valley's dozen or so cities, which include Mountain View and Palo Alto, continue to evolve from corporate strip malls to urban hubs. The valley now buzzes with cultural spaces, lively restaurants, and the energy of a hyper-educated workforce that has no problem keeping up.
— BY ASHLEE VANCE

FRIDAY

1 *Small Town Downtown* 4 p.m.

San Jose may still call itself the capital of Silicon Valley, but picturesque **Los Gatos** is emerging as its trendier downtown, with historic cottages and upscale boutiques. The chains have begun an invasion, but dozens of independent shops remain, selling fashion, children's clothing, baby duds, shoes, accessories, home decor, and collectors' items. Start your prospecting on North Santa Cruz Avenue at West Main Street and follow your whims as you head north. The people cruising the streets in Los Gatos give off a vibe that matches the bright, charming town, which is full of surprises off the main drag.

2 *Pitch Your Venture* 6 p.m.

Sand Hill Road is one the valley's main arteries, cutting through Palo Alto, Menlo Park, and Stanford University. As the weekend gets under way, follow the stream of Prius hybrids, Mercedes coupes, and the occasional Tesla electric car to **Madera** (2825 Sand Hill Road, Menlo Park; 650-561-1540; maderasandhill.com), at the Rosewood Sand Hill hotel. The indoor-outdoor bar is a hot spot for venture capitalists to unwind and gossip as they survey their domain on a terrace that looks out on the surrounding mountains. Down

a cocktail or three, and find your pluck to pitch that brilliant Web idea you had.

3 *American Fare* 8 p.m.

St. Michael's Alley (140 Homer Avenue, Palo Alto; 650-326-2530; stmikes.com; $$) seized a page straight out of the valley playbook when it reinvented itself and moved to an ambitious new home, a few blocks off crowded University Avenue in Palo Alto, in 2009. Two and a half years in the making, the new incarnation has three elegant dining areas, including a bar anchored by an artful hunk of walnut. The business casual attire matches the informal cuisine, which leans toward Californian and American fare.

4 *Choose Your Libation* 10 p.m.

Shame on Stanford students for allowing such tame bars along their home turf, University Avenue. For a more energized crowd, head to nearby California Avenue. A favorite among Silicon Valley's young titans is **Antonio's Nut House** (321 California Avenue, Palo Alto; 650-321-2550; antoniosnuthouse.com), a low-key neighborhood place where patrons can chuck their peanut shells on the floor, scribble on the walls, and take a photo with a peanut-dispensing gorilla. Down the road is **La Bodeguita del Medio** (463 California Avenue, Palo Alto; 650-326-7762; labodeguita.com), a Cuban-style bar and restaurant that serves tall glasses of rum, along with hand-rolled cigars.

SATURDAY

5 *Ogle Google* 9 a.m.

Unless you're the next Mark Zuckerberg, the high-tech campuses that dot the valley are off-limits.

OPPOSITE A view over the high-tech hotbed of Silicon Valley toward San Francisco Bay, from Thomas Fogarty Winery.

RIGHT Checking out a 1970s-era Microchess game at the Computer History Museum in Mountain View.

But there are ways to sneak a look. For a glimpse of the **Googleplex** (1600 Amphitheatre Parkway, Mountain View), the headquarters-cum-playground of Google, drive north on Shoreline Boulevard until you see a pair of colorful towers rising on your left. There's a small public park next to the entrance that peeks inside the laid-back campus. Grander views can be found through **Airship Ventures** (Building 20, South Akron Road; Moffett Field; 650-969-8100;

ABOVE The garage where Hewlett-Packard began.

BELOW The circuit board of an Apple I, the first Apple computer, at the Computer History Museum.

OPPOSITE ABOVE The Airship Ventures zeppelin.

OPPOSITE BELOW Google's headquarters.

airshipventures.com), a tour company that offers rides aboard a 246-foot-long airship. Plan on shelling out at least $200 for a 30-minute ride, but you'll glide over geek hot spots like Apple's shimmering headquarters and Larry Ellison's 23-acre Japanese-style compound. The airship travels along the West Coast, so check its Web site to be sure it's in town.

6 *Cafeteria Lunch* Noon

Some chefs parlay a reality show into a restaurant. Charlie Ayers used his stint as the top chef of the Googleplex cafeteria — and a few of his Google shares — to open **Calafia Café** (855 El Camino Real, Palo Alto; 650-322-9200; calafiapaloalto.com). It is split down the middle between a sit-down restaurant and to-go counter. The fare is a lunch-style version of Californian comfort food: tacos, salmon, lamb hash, turkey meatloaf, and, of course, a vegetarian menu.

7 *Computers 101* 3 p.m.

The name Silicon Valley may have been coined in the early 1970s, but the tech timeline goes even further back here. For a self-guided tour of computer lore, start at 367 Addison Avenue in Palo Alto, site of the humble wood garage where Bill Hewlett and Dave Packard started their company in 1939. Next, drive by 391 San Antonio Road in Mountain View, a squat, dilapidated produce shop that housed the first true silicon start-up — Shockley Semiconductor

Laboratory — in 1955. Finally, swing by 844 Charleston Road in Palo Alto, an office building where Fairchild Semiconductor invented a commercial version of the integrated circuit in 1959. Much of that history is now lovingly captured at the **Computer History Museum** (1401 North Shoreline Boulevard, Mountain View; 650-810-1010; computerhistory.org), where you'll get a sense of how we got from room-filling mainframes to nanochips.

8 *Vietnamese Plates* 8 p.m.

Thanks to Google and its army of millionaires, Castro Street, the main drag in Mountain View, has undergone a culinary and nightlife revival. Among the bubblier spots is **Xanh** (110 Castro Street, Mountain View; 650-964-1888; xanhrestaurant.com; $$), a sprawling Vietnamese fusion restaurant with a handsome patio and dining rooms bathed in green and blue lights. The playful names on the menu — Duck Duck Good, Truth Serum cocktails — fail to capture the elegance of the dishes, plated in delicate fashion with exotic sauces. On weekends, the bar/lounge turns into a quasi-nightclub, with D.J.'s and more cocktails.

9 *Geek Talk* 10 p.m.

Back in 2010, an Apple software engineer lost an iPhone 4 prototype at **Gourmet Haus Staudt** (2615 Broadway; 650-364-9232; gourmethausstaudt.com), a German beer garden in Redwood City. Images of the prototype were splattered on Gizmodo, foiling the company's well-known obsession with secrecy. The beer garden has since shaken off its notoriety and remains a low-key place for engineers to gab about the newest products of their wizardry.

SUNDAY

10 *Local Harvest* 9 a.m.

Farmers' markets dot the valley on Sundays. One of the most bountiful is the **Mountain View Farmers' Market**, in the parking lot of the town's Caltrain Station (600 West Evelyn; 800-806-3276;

cafarmersmkts.com), where flowers, fruits, and vegetables are sold along with locally raised meats and artisanal cheeses. You can pick up prepared foods to munch on as well, including homemade pork dumplings and fresh samosas.

11 *Up to the Hills* 11 a.m.

It's called a valley for a reason. The Santa Cruz Mountains rise along the valley's western edge and provide a treasure hunt for people willing to explore. Wineries, including the **Thomas Fogarty Winery** (19501 Skyline Boulevard; Woodside; 650-851-6777;

fogartywinery.com) sit atop the mountains, offering unrivaled views of the valley. Hikes abound. The **Windy Hill Open Space Preserve** (openspace.org), a 15-minute drive from Stanford in Portola Valley, has a range of trails that cut through 1,312 acres of grassland ridges and redwood forests. By the end of the hike, you'll be able to spot Stanford, the NASA Ames Research Center, and the mega-mansions like a valley pro.

ABOVE Gourmet Haus Staudt found a place in valley lore when an iPhone prototype was carelessly left behind there.

OPPOSITE The Googleplex, headquarters of Google, spreads out over a campus in Mountain View. Visitors can access the small public park at the entrance

THE BASICS

Fly into San Jose or San Francisco. Rent a car.

Rosewood Sand Hill
2825 Sand Hill Road, Menlo Park
650-561-1500
rosewoodsandhill.com
$$$$
On a 16-acre estate with stunning rose gardens overlooking the hills.

Avatar Hotel
4200 Great America Parkway,
Santa Clara
408-235-8900
avatarhotel.com
$$
Newly remodeled, with Wi-Fi and iPod docks.

Larkspur Landing Sunnyvale
748 North Mathilda Avenue,
Sunnyvale
408-733-1212
larkspurhotels.com
$$
All-suite hotel catering to business travelers.

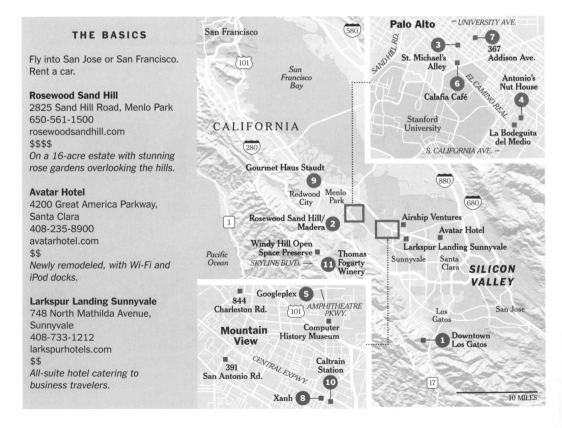

San Francisco

San Francisco typically wows visitors with its heights. The hills sear themselves into memory after a few up-and-down-and-up-again cable car rides or punishing walks. Then there are the hilltop sights: the sweeping vistas and the picturesque Victorians. But surrounding all of that is coastline, miles of peninsula shore along the Pacific Ocean and the expansive natural harbor of San Francisco Bay. Once a working industrial area with pockets of outright blight, much of the city's waterfront has been polished into another of its pleasures. To sample what it offers, start exploring in the east, south of the Bay Bridge, and loop your way west to the Golden Gate and then south to Ocean Beach. In one weekend romp, you'll join San Franciscans in many of the places they love best—and see what remains of their city's maritime heart. —BY JESSE MCKINLEY

FRIDAY

1 *A Ride along the Water* 4 p.m.

China Basin, south of the Bay Bridge, is home to an entirely new neighborhood since big changes began around 2000. The University of California, San Francisco has developed its **Mission Bay Campus**, adding handsome new buildings and public art including two soaring steel towers by Richard Serra, a San Francisco native. And the opening of **AT&T Park**, the baseball field that's home to the San Francisco Giants, brought new energy and new monuments including tributes to greats like Willie Mays and Willie McCovey (the basin is often called McCovey Cove). Rent a bike at the **Bike Hut**, a non-profit outlet at Pier 40 (415-543-4335; thebikehut.org), and pedal the wide promenade along the water.

2 *Embarcadero Imbibing* 5:30 p.m.

Once the home to a raised freeway—demolished after the 1989 Loma Prieta earthquake—and before that a busy wharf area receiving cargo from around the world, the **Embarcadero** is now one of San Francisco's most inviting Friday night spots, filled

OPPOSITE On the Embarcadero near the San Francisco Oakland Bay Bridge. Outdoor workouts, often including jogging near the water, are a theme of San Francisco life.

RIGHT The Bay Bridge view from Waterbar.

with workweek-wearied downtown workers ready to relax. Two inviting spots for a drink and appetizers are **Waterbar** (399 Embarcadero; 415-284-9922; waterbarsf.com) and **Epic Roasthouse** (369 Embarcadero; 415-369-9955; epicroasthouse.com). Views of the Bay Bridge are unbeatable at either, but oysters at Waterbar can really set the mood.

3 *Boat to a Bistro* 8 p.m.

Forbes Island (off Pier 39; 415-951-4900; forbesisland.com; $$$) is not an island, but it is an experience. Created from a 700-ton houseboat, it's a floating restaurant complete with an underwater dining room (with portholes), a 40-foot lighthouse, and an outdoor bar within barking distance from local sea lions. Its nautically minded creator and owner, Forbes Thor Kiddoo, pilots the pontoon boat that brings patrons from a nearby pier. The fish chowder is briny and yummy, as is an assortment of turf (including flat steak in a cognac cream sauce) and surf (organic salmon). Kiddoo, a houseboat designer who combines Gilligan's mirth with the Skipper's physique, is a charming host. Don't miss the 360-degree view from the top of the lighthouse; it may be the best—and the most unusual—vantage point in the city.

SATURDAY

4 *Flip, Flop, Fly* 9 a.m.

Yearning for a Saturday-morning workout? Go for a run at **Crissy Field**, once a waterfront airfield and now San Francisco's weekend outdoor gym, with

masses of joggers, walkers, and cyclists cruising its paths. It's part of the **Presidio**, formerly a military complex guarding San Francisco Bay and the strategic strait at its entrance—the Golden Gate. Now it's all part of the Golden Gate National Recreation Area. Activities run from the quirky (crabbing classes at the Civil War-era Fort Point, under the Golden Gate Bridge) to the caffeinated (outdoor coffee at the **Beach Hut**, 1199 East Beach; 415-561-7761). But the bounciest option is the **House of Air** (926 Mason Street; 415-345-9675; houseofairsf.com), a trampoline center in one of the repurposed buildings on the main Presidio post. Flanked by a kids' swimming school and an indoor climbing center, the House of Air also features a dodgeball court, a training center, and an old-fashioned bouncy castle for tots.

5 *Chow Time* Noon

Dining at the Presidio has come a long way since the days of reveille at dawn. Several restaurants now dot the northeastern corner, where much of the Presidio's development has occurred since it was transferred to the National Park Service in the mid-

1990s. One spot that retains the old military feel is the **Presidio Social Club** (563 Ruger Street; 415-885-1888; presidiosocialclub.com; $$$). As unpretentious as an Army grunt, the club offers old-time drinks (the rye-heavy Sazerac, which dates to 1840) and a pleasantly affordable brunch. A dessert of beignets with hot cocoa can fuel you up for your next offensive.

6 *Union Street Stroll* 2 p.m.

Detour off base to Union Street, long a shoppers' favorite for its locally owned boutiques and home furnishings stores. The owner of **Chloe Rose** (No. 1824; 415-932-6089; chloeroseboutique.com), who lives upstairs, has a keen eye for silk dresses, chiffon blouses, and gold jewelry. Nearby are **Sprout San Francisco** (No. 1828; 415-359-9205; sproutsanfrancisco.com), which carries clothing, toys, and other items for children, and more women's wear at **Ambiance** (No. 1864; 415-923-9797; ambiancesf.com) and the nearby **Marmalade** (No. 2059; 415-673-9544; marmaladesf.com). The **San Francisco Surf Company** (No. 2181; 415-440-7873; sfsurfcompany.com), run by a local wave rider, stocks surf wax candles and all manner of aquatic accoutrements.

7 *Nature and Art* 4 p.m.

Take a walk through the hills and woods on the Pacific coast side of the Presidio, where miles of hiking trails lead to scenic overlooks (presidio.gov). You may also find an artwork or two. The Presidio

ABOVE The downtown skyline under a ceiling of clouds. The gold dome crowns the Palace of Fine Arts, built for a 1915 exposition.

LEFT The wind can be biting, but the mood is usually warm as groups gather for impromptu fires on Ocean Beach.

OPPOSITE ABOVE The House of Air, a trampoline center in one of the repurposed buildings of the Presidio.

OPPOSITE BELOW *Spire*, a sculpture by Andy Goldsworthy, at the Presidio. Miles of trails lead to ocean views.

doesn't need much help being beautiful, but that hasn't stopped artists who have placed installations and sculpture on the grounds. One is Andy Goldsworthy, an environmental British sculptor whose ephemeral pieces in the park include *Spire*—a soaring wooden spike—and *Wood Line*, a serpentine forest-floor sculpture made of eucalyptus.

8 *Dinner at the Edge* 8 p.m.

The **Cliff House** (1090 Point Lobos; 415-386-3330; cliffhouse.com) has been serving visitors at the end of the continent since the Civil War. Still perched on the same rocks, facing shark-fin-shaped Seal Rock and the crashing waves below, the Cliff House underwent a major renovation in 2004. The result was a vastly improved dining experience on two levels, each with commanding views of the Pacific. The **Bistro** ($$), upstairs, serves entrees and cocktails under the watchful eyes of celebrity headshots (Judy Garland, for one, on an autographed glamour shot,

sending her "best wishes"). Downstairs is the higher-end **Sutro's** ($$$), where the specialty is seafood dishes like a two-crab sandwich or grilled scallops. Try a Ramos Fizz, a gin cocktail—and purported hangover cure—made with egg whites, half-and-half, and orange juice.

9 *Burning, Man* 10:30 p.m.

Few things say California more than beach bonfires, a proud tradition up and down the coast. In San Francisco, free spirits keep it going at **Ocean Beach**, the wide sand expanse south of Baker Beach (the spot where Burning Man, the now Nevada-based arts fest, was born). While the wind can be biting, the mood at the impromptu fires is usually warm

as groups congregate with guitars, pipes, and good vibes. Take a blanket and a pullover and watch the stars, surf, and sparks collide.

SUNDAY

10 *Other Side of the Park* 11 a.m.

The western edge of **Golden Gate Park**, facing Ocean Beach, has a Rodney Dangerfield feel, less known and appreciated than the park's cityside flanks. But its offerings are impressive, including a cheap

and public nine-hole, par-3 golf course, a lovely bison enclave, and serene fly-fishing ponds. A good place to convene for any park adventure is the **Park Chalet** (1000 Great Highway; 415-386-8439; parkchalet.com; $$$). In this somewhat hidden spot just off Ocean Beach, kids run free in the wilds of the park and parents enjoy a brunch buffet that advertises "bottomless champagne."

ABOVE On the trail that leads from Fort Point, under the Golden Gate Bridge, along the bay to Crissy Field.

OPPOSITE A 21st-century addition, *Cupid's Span*, by Claes Oldenburg and Coosje van Bruggen, frames a view of the Ferry Building clock tower, a more traditional San Francisco landmark.

THE BASICS

Take the BART train from San Francisco International Airport to downtown.

Use taxis and public transportation.

Hotel Vitale
8 Mission Street
415-278-3700
hotelvitale.com
$$$$
Style and luxury on the Embarcadero, across from the landmark Ferry Building.

Harbor Court Hotel
165 Steuart Street
415-882-1300
harborcourthotel.com
$$
Boutique hotel with bay views.

Union Street Inn
2229 Union Street
415-346-0424
unionstreetinn.com
$$$
Quiet and charming bed-and-breakfast.

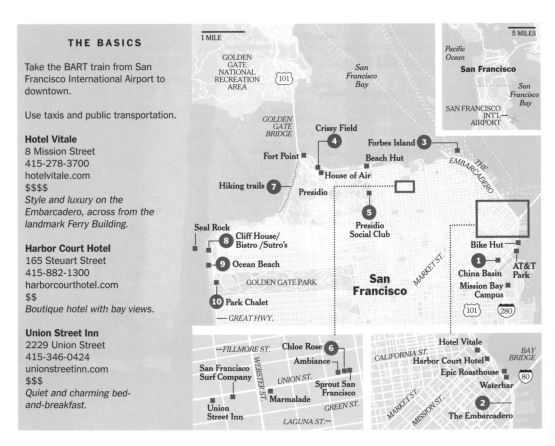

The Mission
San Francisco

For much of the 1990s, San Francisco's Mission District maintained a precarious balance between its colorful Latino roots and a gritty bohemian subculture. Then came the overfed dot-com years. Rising real estate prices threatened the Mission's status not only as a working-class enclave, but also as the city's center of all things edgy and artsy. Sleek bars moved next door to divey taquerias. Boutiquey knick-knack shops came in alongside fusty dollar stores. But prosperity did not sap the district of its cultural eclecticism. With a population that is about half Latino, a third white, and an estimated 11 percent Asian, the Mission still remains a wonderful mishmash. Where else can you find epicurean vegan cafes, feisty nonprofits, and a Central American butcher shop that, for a memorable time, anyway, had women's undergarments in the window?
— BY CHRIS COLIN

FRIDAY

1 *Illicit Doughnuts* 4 p.m.

It's one thing to operate a pirate radio station, with foul-mouthed D.J.'s hopping from rooftop to rooftop to hide the transmitter. But the ever-defiant Pirate Cat Radio, now called the **PCR Collective**, went and opened a cafe (2781 21st Street; 415-341-1199). Now you can stick it to the man over a spot of tea or vegan doughnuts. The grungy décor and sparse offerings are true to pirate form — the fun lies in watching the broadcasts (now confined to the Internet, to appease the FCC) through the smudged window.

2 *Eat with the Fishes* 6:30 p.m.

Don't let the trendiness fool you: the food at **Weird Fish** (2193 Mission Street; 415-863-4744; weirdfishsf.com; $$) is actually terrific. Situated on chaotic Mission Street, this guppy-sized spot serves inspired dishes like sweet-and-spicy rainbow trout, local cod with cauliflower puree and young chestnuts, and something called the Suspicious Fish Dish (varies). There's often a line, but you can wait outside on the street, enjoying that singular pleasure

of sipping wine beside the bus stop that serves as the restaurant's de facto lounge.

3 *Acting Out* 8 p.m.

On a good Friday night, the neighborhood is theatrical in its own right. For more distilled drama, catch a performance at the **Marsh** (1062 Valencia Street; 415-826-5750; themarsh.org), a small theater devoted to small stagings. Award-winning productions have included *Squeezebox* and *Tings Dey Happen*, a one-man show about Nigerian oil politics. Seating is first come, first served, so buy tickets in advance and arrive early.

4 *Hot Diggity* 10 p.m.

It can seem that one hears indie rock or Mexican polka in the Mission, and little else. But **Savanna Jazz** (2937 Mission Street; 415-285-3369; savannajazz.com) has live sets every night but Monday in its cozy, New Orleans-style room. When the last chord is struck and you're still longing for something late-night and local, discover the bacon dog craze on your walk home. Vendors sell them — a food best consumed in the dark — on the sidewalk along Mission.

SATURDAY

5 *Art and Noble Pie* 10 a.m.

You'll never sample all the creative galleries, shops, and restaurants in the Mission. Carve out a few hours for strolling, concentrating on Valencia, Mission, 16th, and 24th Streets. **Aquarius Records** (1055 Valencia Street; 415-647-2272; aquariusrecords.org) is the city's oldest independent record store and a sanctuary for

OPPOSITE San Francisco has a storied mural tradition, and the Mission has a vast, ever-changing collection.

RIGHT Burritos and a skyline view at Dolores Park.

music lovers. For a flavorful snack, take your taste buds to **Mission Cheese** (736 Valencia Street; 415-553-8667; missioncheese.net). The hot pressed sandwiches are good, but for now, just buy a gorgeous loaf of levain—a bread that's a cousin to sourdough—and pair with a selection of artisanal cheeses.

ABOVE At first glance, the Mission District might seem perennially 23, but it has a long history.

BELOW Aquarius Records, a haven for music lovers.

OPPOSITE ABOVE St. Francis Fountain.

OPPOSITE BELOW Mission Dolores.

Galería de la Raza (2857 24th Street; 415-826-8009; galeriadelaraza.org) showcases projects by Chicano and Latino artists and activists. And check out **Creativity Explored** (3245 16th Street; 415-863-2108; creativityexplored.org), a nonprofit studio where developmentally disabled men and women make and sell beautiful art.

6 *Gorging in the Grass* 2 p.m.
What you've heard about Mission burritos is true: they're big and everyone eats them. Arguing over the best is a popular sport, but you won't go wrong with **Taquería Cancún** (2288 Mission Street; 415-252-9560), a no-frills joint that packs a crowd. Take a Super Veggie up 19th Street to **Dolores Park**, and enjoy the downtown views among the Frisbeeing, smuggled-beer-drinking multitudes. If it's the last Saturday of the month, scout out the **Really Really Free Market** (reallyreallyfree.org), a haphazard and funky exchange that's worth investigating. The prices are really really unbeatable.

7 *Where It All Began* 3 p.m.
At first glance, the Mission District might seem perennially 23, with a Pabst Blue Ribbon fixed forever in its collective fist. But there's real history in this youthful quarter. Two blocks from Dolores Park is the city's oldest landmark and the district's namesake, **Mission Dolores** (3321 16th Street; 415-621-8203;

missiondolores.org). Founded before San Francisco itself, it remains a hub of cultural and religious life. It's a quick tour, but the bright frescoes and hushed basilica balance the surrounding hoopla with a welcome calm. Hitchcock buffs will recall its cameo in *Vertigo*.

8 *Cocktail Hour* 6 p.m.

San Francisco is a cocktail-before-dinner kind of town—just ask Sam Spade. Among Mission's grooviest bars are the **Latin American Club** (3286 22nd Street; 415-647-2732), **Doc's Clock** (2575 Mission Street; 415-824-3627; docsclock.com), and **Papa Toby's Revolution Cafe** (3248 22nd Street; 415-642-0474). The combination of ambience, music, and robust gawking make these perfect run-ups to dinner.

9 *Dinner and a Movie* 8 p.m.

It may sound gimmicky, but the dinner-and-a-movie at **Foreign Cinema** (2534 Mission Street; 415-648-7600; foreigncinema.com; $$$) is an elegant, white tablecloth affair. If the weather's nice, snag an outdoor table in the austere, vaguely Soviet cement courtyard. Start with oysters before carving into the likes of bavette steak or delicate tombo tartare with ginger-lime vinaigrette. When the sun sets, a foreign film is projected silently on the far wall with subtitles. Heat lamps keep you toasty and, if you want to follow the dialogue, the waiter will even bring vintage drive-in speakers.

10 *Sweating to the Music* 10:30 p.m.

Hot, sweaty bodies shaking it on a plywood floor in a thimble of a room with holes in the ceiling. If that's your cup of tea—and, in a way, that sums up the Mission perfectly—head over to **Little Baobab** (3388 19th Street; 415-643-3558; littlebaobabsf.com).

The bass thumps and an international crowd sloshes around admirably.

SUNDAY

11 *On the Wall* 11 a.m.

San Francisco has a storied mural tradition, and the **Precita Eyes Mural Arts Center** (2981 24th Street; 415-285-2287; precitaeyes.org) runs casual yet informative tours of the Mission's vast, ever-changing collection. They include scenes of a bloody Honduran massacre and of weeping families pushed out by

developers. But perhaps most poignant are the simple portraits of neighborhood figures — the flower seller, the bakery owner, the guy who break-dances. After your tour, stop by **St. Francis Fountain** (2801 24th Street; 415-826-4200; stfrancisfountainsf.com; $) for brunch. Look past the trendy crowd's tattoos and leggings and you'll see a fastidiously preserved ice cream parlor from 90 years ago. They still make a terrific egg cream, and the eggs Florentine aren't bad, either. According to legend, the San Francisco 49ers were founded on the back of a napkin in one of the booths.

ABOVE The food is good at Weird Fish — and that includes the daily Suspicious Fish Dish.

OPPOSITE Dinner and a show at Foreign Cinema.

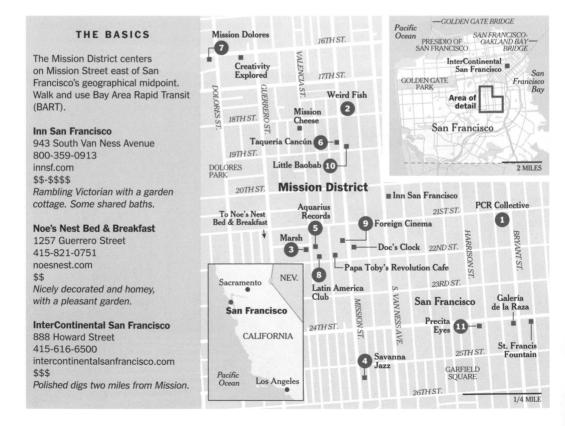

THE BASICS

The Mission District centers on Mission Street east of San Francisco's geographical midpoint. Walk and use Bay Area Rapid Transit (BART).

Inn San Francisco
943 South Van Ness Avenue
800-359-0913
innsf.com
$$-$$$$
Rambling Victorian with a garden cottage. Some shared baths.

Noe's Nest Bed & Breakfast
1257 Guerrero Street
415-821-0751
noesnest.com
$$
Nicely decorated and homey, with a pleasant garden.

InterContinental San Francisco
888 Howard Street
415-616-6500
intercontinentalsanfrancisco.com
$$$
Polished digs two miles from Mission.

Berkeley

Berkeley, California, sticks in the collective memory as a hotbed of '60s radicalism and '70s experimentation. But anyone who thinks that's the whole picture is in for a surprise. From the main gate of the flagship campus of the University of California to revamped sophisticated boutiques, this city overlooking San Francisco Bay offers variety few towns can match. On College Avenue, the main drag, costumed hipsters mix with high-tech geeks in training, and freelance philosophers rub elbows with label-conscious materialists. Not that the spirit of 1969 has completely gone away. Walk down Telegraph Avenue, and along one block you may encounter activists for Free Tibet, patchouli-scented advocates of homeopathic medicine, and crusty purple-haired free-love followers still eager to convert you to their cause.

— BY JOSHUA KURLANTZICK

FRIDAY

1 *Bookmark This* 5 p.m.
   Old and new Berkeley, activists and achievers, all head to **Moe's Books** (2476 Telegraph Avenue; 510-849-2087; moesbooks.com). Founded in 1959 and piled high with used books, Moe's is a place to wander for hours, flipping through choices from out-of-print tomes on 1950s African history to kabbalah manuals. The store also hosts frequent readings.

2 *Comfort Soba* 8 p.m.
   Berkeley's food scene has blossomed well beyond student hangouts. Consider the local favorite **O Chamé** (1830 Fourth Street; 510-841-8783; $$). Its classy Japanese fusion fare is decidedly un-college-town, but the slightly beaten-up tables and unpretentious crowd make you feel like you're eating in someone's home. And dishes like onion pancakes, soba platters, and grilled eel are as satisfying as Japanese comfort food gets.

3 *Cinema Paradise* 10 p.m.
   The **Pacific Film Archive** (2621 Durant Avenue; 510-642-0808; bampfa.berkeley.edu) at the Berkeley Art Museum offers one of the most refreshingly unpredictable moviegoing experiences in the Bay Area. At the archive's theater across the street from the museum, you might find a French New Wave

festival followed by a collection of shorts from West Africa. The archive is particularly strong on Japanese cinema — and grungy-looking grad students.

SATURDAY

4 *Hill Country* 8 a.m.
   This is California, so you'll have to get up early to have prime walking paths to yourself. Wander through the main U.C. Berkeley campus, quiet at this time, and into the lush Berkeley hills overlooking the university. You'll pass sprawling mansions that resemble Mexican estates, families walking tiny manicured poodles, and students running off hangovers along the steep hills. It's easy to get lost, so take a map; Berkeley Path Wanderers Association (berkeleypaths.org) offers one of the best. If you want a longer walk, try nearby **Tilden Park**, a 2,000-acre preserve that includes several peaks and numerous trails open for mountain biking. Or head to the **University of California Botanical Garden** (200 Centennial Drive; 510-643-2755; botanicalgarden.berkeley.edu), a home for more than 12,000 species of plants.

5 *Veggie Bounty* Noon
   It's tough choosing from the many farmers' markets in the San Francisco Bay Area, but for the real deal, head to the **Berkeley Farmers' Market** (Center Street at Martin Luther King Way). The

OPPOSITE At Moe's Books, the stock spills off the tables and all of Berkeley streams in the door.

BELOW Berkeley Bowl, a fruit-and-vegetable heaven.

Berkeley market is run by actual farmers and has a workingman's vibe. Afterward, stop by the **Berkeley Bowl Marketplace** (2020 Oregon Street; 510-843-6929; berkeleybowl.com) for a comparison. A veritable fruit-and-vegetable heaven, the Bowl offers a staggering array of peaches, apples, and rows of heirloom tomatoes — pudgy, lumpy, flavorful. Grab a roasted chicken and fresh beet salad at the deli counter, and snack on it while arguing with the various activists who congregate outside the Bowl's doors.

6 *Snake Pit* 3:30 p.m.

For a shopping experience not easily duplicated, drop in at the **East Bay Vivarium** (1827-C Fifth Street; 510-841-1400; eastbayvivarium.com), perhaps the city's strangest attraction. But don't come with a fear of snakes: the massive gallery and store, which specializes in reptiles, amphibians, and arachnids, is like a living nightmare. Strolling through, you'll pass gargantuan boas and more scorpion species than you'd ever imagined.

7 *Rock Out* 5 p.m.

The best views of campus aren't from the 10-story Evans Hall, but from **Indian Rock Park**. Wedged in a residential neighborhood along the city's northeast, the park has large rock outcroppings that offer 360-degree views across Berkeley and Oakland, and over the Bay into San Francisco. For more spectacular

sunset views, bring some rope and carabiners: the main outcropping, Indian Rock, is a practice site for rock climbers.

8 *Homage to Alice Waters* 6:30 p.m.

Scoring a reservation at **Chez Panisse** (1517 Shattuck Avenue; 510-548-5525; chezpanisse.com; $$$$), the renowned restaurant created by the groundbreaking chef Alice Waters in 1971, can be a labor-intensive project. A creative, casual alternative is **Gather** (2200 Oxford Street; 510-809-0400; gatherrestaurant.com; $$), very much built on the Waters tradition but heading down its own contemporary organic/local ingredients/eco-chic path. The stated aim is to please both vegetarians and omnivores, and even the pizzas, nicely blistered and chewy, shed

light on the concept. How about morel pizza topped with fontinella, stinging nettles, and braised leeks?

9 *Berkeley Roots* 8 p.m.

Berkeley may be the perfect town for roots music. The genre of the '60s is not forgotten, although there's no objection to some updating. Shows at **Freight and Salvage Coffeehouse** (2020 Addison Street; 510-644-2020; freightandsalvage.org) feature nationally known musicians performing folk, blue-grass, and modern takes on traditional music like jazz folk and Celtic jazz. Be warned. There's no alcohol. It really is a coffeehouse.

SUNDAY

10 *Fourth and Long* 11 a.m.

Fourth Street is not far from Telegraph, but it's miles away in style. This trendy shopping district has become a chic, open-air mall with funky home décor, local art, and designer fashions. One of the most interesting of the shops and galleries is the **Stained Glass Garden** (1800 Fourth Street; 510-841-2200; stainedglassgarden.com), which carries elegantly curved glassware, dangly jewelry that resembles Calder mobiles, and kaleidoscope-like lampshades.

OPPOSITE ABOVE Sather Gate, leading into the central campus of the University of California.

OPPOSITE BELOW The Pacific Film Archive.

ABOVE California hills from Tilden Park.

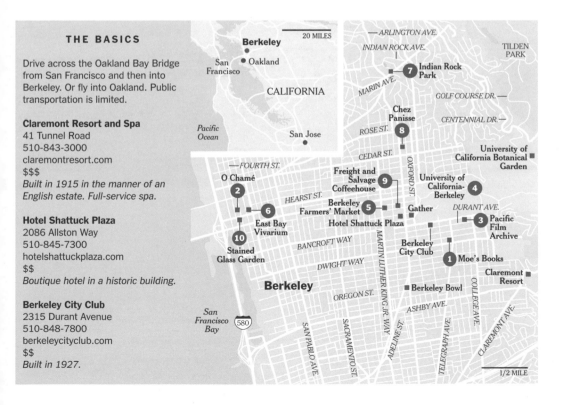

THE BASICS

Drive across the Oakland Bay Bridge from San Francisco and then into Berkeley. Or fly into Oakland. Public transportation is limited.

Claremont Resort and Spa
41 Tunnel Road
510-843-3000
claremontresort.com
$$$
Built in 1915 in the manner of an English estate. Full-service spa.

Hotel Shattuck Plaza
2086 Allston Way
510-845-7300
hotelshattuckplaza.com
$$
Boutique hotel in a historic building.

Berkeley City Club
2315 Durant Avenue
510-848-7800
berkeleycityclub.com
$$
Built in 1927.

Napa Valley

If you don't know where to look, the Napa Valley of California can seem uninspiring: big, Disney-ish wineries, lines four deep at the tasting rooms, and one too many tour buses. But nudge just a little off the tourist track, and you're instantly back in the rolling, bucolic paradise that first beckoned wine growers decades ago—quirky little vineyards, tiny towns, and a genuinely slower pace, despite the massive industry all around. In the bright days of summer and the misty moodiness of winter, this 30-mile-long region hums with life—and invites an air of reflection perfectly suited to those big California reds. — BY CHRIS COLIN

FRIDAY

1 *Vintage Cycling* 3 p.m.

Rent a bicycle at the **Calistoga Bike Shop** (1318 Lincoln Avenue, Calistoga; 707-942-9687; calistogabikeshop.com) and do some exploring. Some of the prettiest roads are found around Calistoga, a funky and unstuffy town on the northwest tip of the valley—a bit of whiskey before the pinot. For your first taste of Napa Valley wine, pedal two miles to the Michael Graves-designed **Clos Pegase Winery** (1060 Dunaweal Lane, Calistoga; 707-942-4981; clospegase.com) and feel the terroir under your tires.

2 *The Food Is Local, Too* 7 p.m.

Stay in Calistoga for dinner at **JoLe Farm to Table** (1457 Lincoln Avenue; 707-942-5938; jolerestaurant. com; $$), which aims to live up to its name with seasonal cuisine made from organic locally farmed ingredients. Selections change frequently, but you might find scallops with leeks, mushrooms, and pancetta or chicken fried quail with Cobb salad. The wine list, naturally, also leans local.

3 *Bring Your Earplugs* 10 p.m.

Beer in Napa? It might sound like blasphemy, but the **Calistoga Inn Restaurant & Brewery** (1250 Lincoln Avenue, Calistoga; 707-942-4101; calistogainn.com) makes a mean Pilsener, along with various ales and stouts. There's live music every night at this wood-paneled watering hole—and who wants to drink merlot while dancing to rock? Besides, there will be plenty of other wines this weekend.

SATURDAY

4 *Sling Some Mud* 9 a.m.

Calistoga's name has been mud, or at least synonymous with it, ever since the Gold Rush pioneer Sam Brannan dipped into the Wappo tribe's ancient mud baths. Some claim the volcanic ash and geothermally heated water rejuvenate the pores; others find relief from aches and pains. At a minimum, it's fun and weird to float in hot goop with cucumbers on your eyes. With a manicured lawn and white cottages, the **Indian Springs Resort and Spa** (1712 Lincoln Avenue; 707-942-4913; indianspringscalistoga.com) resembles a colonial hill town under the British Raj and claims the title of the oldest continually operating spa in California.

5 *Sizing Up the Grapes* 11 a.m.

Time to hit the vineyards. With hundreds to choose from in this valley, there's no perfect lineup. But some stand out for personality, memorable wines, or both. Stop first at **Casa Nuestra** (3451 Silverado Trail North, St. Helena; 707-963-5783; casanuestra.com; appointments required). This is a small family winery, and with your sips of chenin blanc or tinto you can expect a taste of old California informality—just ask the goats out front that clamor for snacks, emboldened by having a blend named after them (Two Goats Red). From there it's a short drive to the **Culinary Institute**

OPPOSITE Ballooning over the Napa Valley, an exhilarating adventure for a Sunday morning.

RIGHT Grapes on the vine at a Napa vineyard.

of America at **Greystone** (2555 Main Street, St. Helena; 707-967-1010; ciachef.edu/california), the California campus of the chef-training school in Hyde Park, New York. It's not a winery, but it occupies a picturesque century-old stone building that was originally the Christian Brothers' Greystone Cellars, and its shop and the campus are worth a look around.

6 *Main Street Retail* Noon

You could have lunch at the Culinary Institute's restaurant, but you'll want to stop anyway in the precious town of St. Helena, a shopaholic's delight. Have an avocado and papaya salad or a burger with house-made pickles at **Cindy's Backstreet Kitchen** (1327 Railroad Avenue; 707-963-1200;

cindysbackstreetkitchen.com; $$). Then shop Main Street. **Footcandy** (No. 1239; 877-517-4606; footcandyshoes.com) carries Jimmy Choos and Manolo Blahniks with heels as high as stemware. **Woodhouse Chocolate** (No. 1367; 707-963-8413; woodhousechocolate.com) sells handmade artisanal chocolates in an elegant space that looks more like a jewelry shop. And the local interior designer Erin Martin has bronze sculptures, porcelain lamps, and other housewares at her shop, **Martin Showroom** (No. 1350; 707-967-8787; martinshowroom.com).

7 *Back to the Grapes* 2 p.m.

Large wineries often suffer in the character department, but not **Quintessa** (1601 Silverado Trail; Rutherford; 707-967-1601; quintessa.com). From the graceful crescent facade to the fascinating tours of its production facilities, this 280-acre estate makes a great stop—and it produces wonderful Bordeaux-style wines. For drop-dead gorgeous scenery, swing

ABOVE The misty moodiness of the Napa Valley in December.

LEFT Cycling the quiet roads near Calistoga, the unstuffy town on the valley's northwest tip.

OPPOSITE Mustard, a winter crop growing amid the rows of leafless vines.

by **Frog's Leap** (8815 Conn Creek Road, Rutherford; 707-963-4704; frogsleap.com) and its five acres of lush gardens, orchards, beehives, chickens, photovoltaic cells, and everything else that puts this among Napa's more forward-thinking operations. And for unforgettable architecture, visit **Quixote Winery** (6126 Silverado Trail, Napa; 707-944-2659; quixotewinery.com). Its turreted, multicolored, cartoonlike building was designed by Friedensreich Hundertwasser, Vienna's late 20th-century answer to Antoni Gaudí. Appointments are required at each of these vineyards, and all have tasting fees.

8 *Riverfront Dining* 8 p.m.

For memorable fare and setting, go to **Angèle** in the city of Napa (540 Main Street; 707-252-8115; angelerestaurant.com; $$$), a converted boathouse on the Napa River where locals and tourists come to get away from the tourists. French brasserie classics like braised rabbit and cassoulet are served under a

beamed ceiling and warm lighting. Regulars can be spotted ordering the off-menu burger with blue cheese. Needless to say, the wine list is varied and extensive.

9 *Make It Swing* 9:30 p.m.

The city of Napa rolls up its sidewalks after dark, but **Uva** (1040 Clinton Street; 707-255-6646; uvatrattoria.com) makes an exception for free live jazz every Saturday until midnight. Photos of old jazz greats crowd the walls, and you can tap along from the swanky dining room or the crowded bar.

SUNDAY

10 *The Overview* 6 a.m.

By this time, you've noticed that the Napa Valley is beautiful country, with corduroy-pattern vineyards carpeting its rolling golden hills and the Napa River easing its way from north to south. There's no better way to see it than from a slow-floating hot-air balloon.

Several companies will take you up and away for $200 to $300 per person; one standby is **Napa Valley Balloons** (1 California Drive, Yountville; 707-944-0228; napavalleyballoons.com). After a ride lasting about an hour, you will be served a Champagne brunch. The balloons leave early in the morning to catch favorable air currents.

11 *Art of Winemaking* 11 a.m.

For a nontipsy perspective on wine, drive up the winding, woodsy road to the ivy-covered **Hess**

Collection (4411 Redwood Road, Napa; 707-255-1144; hesscollection.com), the winery and contemporary art museum built by the Swiss multimillionaire Donald Hess. Tours of the bright gallery, which are self-guided and free, take you past works by Frank Stella, Robert Motherwell, and Francis Bacon. At one point, a window provides a view of the fermentation tanks — the suggestion that wine equals art is not lost. Judge for yourself: the tasting room, just off the lobby, specializes in mountain cabernets.

ABOVE Dining at the Calistoga Inn Restaurant & Brewery, an outpost of beer in the wine country.

OPPOSITE Oak barrels in a cave at Quintessa. Stop in to see how its Bordeaux-style wines are made.

THE BASICS

The Napa Valley is about 50 miles north of San Francisco, just over an hour's drive. Make someone in your group the designated driver.

Indian Springs Resort and Spa
1712 Lincoln Avenue, Calistoga
707-942-4913
indianspringscalistoga.com
$$$
Retro glamour in an authentic, century-old spa. Olympic-size mineral springs pool.

River Terrace Inn
1600 Soscol Avenue
707-320-9000
riverterraceinn.com
$$$
Well-appointed rooms; close to riverside walks.

Auberge du Soleil
180 Rutherford Hill Road, Rutherford
707-963-1211
aubergedusoleil.com
$$$$
Spa, pool, tennis court, and terraces with valley views.

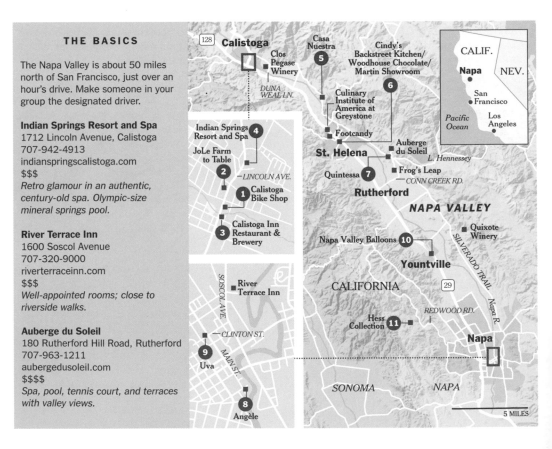

Sonoma County

If you're looking for a chocolate pinot noir sauce, keep driving. The rustic region of Sonoma County, California, may be a wine lovers' playground, but it lacks many of the touristy trappings of its more upscale and better-known neighbor, Napa. Not that Sonomans are complaining. Bumper stickers carry messages like "Kill Your TV" and "Subvert the Dominant Paradigm," and people here mean it. The freethinking tradition is being nurtured by a new generation of oenophiles who appreciate Sonoma's low-key charms, filling its beautiful historic towns with upscale boutiques, art galleries, and Old World-style restaurants. — BY KABIR CHIBBER

FRIDAY

1 *Young Blood* 4 p.m.

Wineries in Sonoma still tend to be small, young, and family-owned. One of the youngest is **Scribe Winery** (2300 Napa Road, Sonoma; 707-939-1858; scribewinery.com), started by Andrew Mariani and his family in 2007 on an estate of almost 200 acres that used to be a turkey farm. The winery, with its dusty driveway and artfully rundown hacienda, is so new the first wines from these vineyards, a pinot noir and chardonnay, could not be released until 2011. Early visitors to the winery tasted blends made from grapes grown nearby.

2 *Tragedy Loves Company* 7 p.m.

The hills of Sonoma come alive with music in the summer and fall. The town of **Cloverdale** has free evening concerts in its main square, next to the farmers' market (cloverdaleartsalliance.org). For a dose of high culture, the **Sonoma City Opera** (484 East Napa Street, Sonoma; 707-939-8288; sonomaopera.org) holds concerts, and the **Sonoma County Repertory Theater** (104 North Main Street, Sebastopol; 707-823-0177; the-rep.com) produces plays from Shakespeare to contemporary fare.

3 *La Bella Sonoma* 9 p.m.

Sondra Bernstein's first restaurant, the Girl and the Fig, is an institution. In 2008 she opened another, **Estate** (400 West Spain Street, Sonoma; 707-933-3663; thegirlandthefig.com; $$-$$$), in a historic home, serving regional Italian cuisine using Northern Californian ingredients. Sit outside and start with the prosecco spritzer and the burrata with homemade olive oil. Some favorite past entrees have been porchetta with polenta served in pork jus and Pacific rock cod with wood-fire roasted Yukon golds.

SATURDAY

4 *Farmer's Choice* 10 a.m.

A bit too early to be an oenophile? Luckily, there's much more to Sonoma than wine. The local food movement is long-established here, and Sonomans are as passionate about what they eat as what they drink. Sample the locally produced cheeses and kefirs using goat's milk at **Redwood Hill Farm** (2064 Highway 116 North, Sebastopol; 707-823-8250; redwoodhill.com) and organic wildflower honey from **Quivira Vineyards & Winery** (4900 West Dry Creek Road, Healdsburg; 707-431-8333; quivirawine.com). And **La Michoacana** (18495 Highway 12, Sonoma; 707-938-1773) makes soft, creamy ice creams with flavors like caramel and mango, just like those found in Tocumba, Mexico, where the owner, Teresita Carr, grew up.

OPPOSITE Sonoma, a wine region of low-key charms.

BELOW Estate, a restaurant in the former home of a daughter of Mariano Vallejo, a governor in Mexican California.

5 *Canvases and Fans* 12:30 p.m.

Healdsburg, one of Sonoma's main towns, is full of boutiques and second homes of the San Francisco Bay Area's beautiful and wealthy, but it retains a youthful vibe. It also has a sizable collection of modern art. The **Healdsburg Center for the Arts** (130 Plaza Street; 707-431-1970; healdsburgcenterforthearts.com) features a rotating cast of local and regional artists, while **Hawley Tasting Room and Gallery** (36 North Street; 707-473-9500; hawleywine.com) displays the landscape paintings of Dana Hawley, who is the wife of the respected local winemaker John Hawley. The Capture gallery (105 Plaza Street; 707-431-7030; capturefineart.com) has high-end photography of the Sonoma terrain. And don't leave without checking out the **Hand Fan Museum** (219 Healdsburg Avenue; 707-431-2500; handfanmuseum.com), the first in the country dedicated to the once popular accessory.

6 *The Padrino (of Wine)* 2:30 p.m.

Around here, Francis Ford Coppola is known more as a winemaker than as an Oscar-winning director, having been a vintner for decades at the Rubicon Estate in Napa. In 2010 Coppola opened the **Francis Ford Coppola Winery** in Sonoma (300 Via Archimedes, Geyserville; 707-857-1471; franciscoppolawinery.com). The 88-acre estate has a restaurant called Rustic featuring some of Coppola's favorite dishes, two outdoor swimming pools to keep things child-friendly, and Hollywood memorabilia like Vito Corleone's desk from *The Godfather*. Best of all, some tastings of standard wines are free—a rarity in California.

7 *Bubble Bath* 5:30 p.m.

Sonoma has its fair share of high-end resorts for feeling sequestered from the world. But it's better to take advantage of the excellent day spas in the area that let you pop in and out at your leisure. **A Simple Touch Spa** (239C Center Street, Healdsburg; 707-433-6856; asimpletouchspa.com) lets you lie in a bath of sparkling wine, mustard, or fango mud and then enjoy a half-hour massage. The stylish spa at **Hotel Healdsburg** (25 Matheson Street, Healdsburg; 800-889-7188; hotelhealdsburg.com) has a reviving body wrap using wine and local honey.

8 *Polished Classics* 7 p.m.

In 2004, when the French chef Bruno Tison took over the restaurant **Santé** at the historic **Fairmont Sonoma Mission Inn and Spa** (100 Boyes Boulevard, Sonoma; 707-938-9000; fairmont.com/sonoma; $$$), he set his sights high, with a creative menu that paired French flavors with American favorites. The gamble seems to have paid off: the restaurant received a Michelin star in 2009—one of only four in Sonoma County to be awarded the distinction. Expect dishes like macaroni and cheese with Maine lobster and black truffles, or roasted duck breast in a "dirty rice" of mushrooms and foie gras, accompanied by a duck confit. There's an extensive selection of regional wines.

9 *Cocktail Tasting* 10 p.m.

Wine country is not renowned for its night life, but that doesn't mean you can't have fun. The cocktail bar at the sleek and minimalist **El Dorado Hotel** (405 First Street West, Sonoma; 707-996-3220;

ABOVE At the Francis Ford Coppola Winery, taste the vintages made by the renowned film director. Then pop into the Movie Gallery for a look at props like the Godfather's desk and this Tucker car.

eldoradosonoma.com) exudes an effortless glamour and gets particularly lively during the Sonoma Jazz Festival. Try the peach jalapeño, a mix of peppers and peach vodka. The town of Santa Rosa is also filled with bars, though many can feel fratty. An exception is **Christy's on the Square** (96 Old Courthouse Square, Santa Rosa; 707-528-8565; christysonthesquare.com), which draws an older, sophisticated clientele.

SUNDAY

10 *Salt Air* 9 a.m.

Leave the vineyards behind and head to the coast, about an hour away at Bodega Bay. **Campbell Cove**, by the Bodega Head, is a secluded beach that feels as though it was made just for you and the seagulls. Spend some time on the sand and chill.

Then take a little time to drive up a few miles along the rugged Sonoma coast.

11 *Yeast Notes* Noon

Tired of pondering the finer points of merlot versus pinot noir? Well, get ready to debate the terroir of malted barley and hops — Sonoma has a fine collection of microbreweries. **Dempsey's** (50 East Washington Street, Petaluma; 707-765-9694; dempseys.com) has a stout called Ugly Dog — because the annual World's Ugliest Dog Contest is held in town. **Bear Republic Brewing Co.** (345 Healdsburg Avenue, Healdsburg; 707-433-2337; bearrepublic.com) serves special brews available only on draft, including the ultra-creamy Black Raven Porter and a pale ale called Crazy Ivan that's been mixed with a yeast used by Trappist monks.

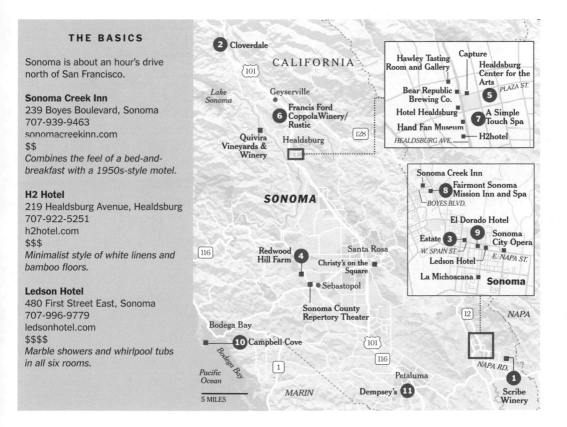

THE BASICS

Sonoma is about an hour's drive north of San Francisco.

Sonoma Creek Inn
239 Boyes Boulevard, Sonoma
707-939-9463
sonomacreekinn.com
$$
Combines the feel of a bed-and-breakfast with a 1950s-style motel.

H2 Hotel
219 Healdsburg Avenue, Healdsburg
707-922-5251
h2hotel.com
$$$
Minimalist style of white linens and bamboo floors.

Ledson Hotel
480 First Street East, Sonoma
707-996-9779
ledsonhotel.com
$$$$
Marble showers and whirlpool tubs in all six rooms.

Sacramento

California's governors and legislators may argue aggressively at its center, but the rest of Sacramento, California's capital city, has a gentle, small-town charm. Situated at the confluence of the Sacramento and American Rivers, it grew into a city as the gateway to the California Gold Rush and prospered as the home of railroad barons. What visitors will notice today is a strong theater tradition, delightful restaurants, a vibrant art scene, and a wealth of greenery — residents proudly claim that Sacramento has more trees per capita than any city in the world besides Paris. — BY BETH GREENFIELD

FRIDAY

1 *What Could Go Wrong?* 4 p.m.

Who says California's capital is prone to disarray? A stroll through the **California State Capitol** (10th and L Streets; 916-324-0333; capitolmuseum.ca.gov) — a neo-Classical confection of Corinthian and other classic columns, parget plasterwork, and mosaic floors — conveys the feeling that everything is in grand order. Painstakingly restored in the 1970s, the interior is graced with numerous artworks, including presidential portraits, WPA murals, and a stunning marble statue of Columbus and Queen Isabella by Larkin Goldsmith Mead. Outside, there's a lush park. A 250-pound bronze statue of a grizzly bear was brought by Arnold Schwarzenegger to guard the door to the governor's office. Wander at a leisurely pace while government employees rush by.

2 *Farm to Table* 6:30 p.m.

To dine in modern elegance, head a few blocks to the **Ella Dining Room and Bar** (1131 K Street; 916-443-3772; elladiningroomandbar.com; $$), which is draped with dramatic scrims of white linen. The restaurant emphasizes local produce, a sensible choice given that Sacramento sits amid some of the world's richest farmland. The menu includes dishes like pappardelle with poached egg and prosciutto in preserved lemon butter sauce or Sonoma duck breast with lentils and roasted pears. You could also have a soothing elderflower gimlet and a chocolate-rich dessert.

3 *Act Three* 8 p.m.

Sacramento has a healthy theater scene, judging by the well-chosen plays at the intimate **B Street Theatre** (2711 B Street; 916-443-5300; bstreettheatre.org). Past productions have included *The Maintenance Man*, a comedy about divorce by Richard Harris, a prolific British playwright, and *Entertaining Mr. Sloane*, a tale of seduction and sibling rivalry by Joe Orton. Draw out the drama with a nightcap at **Harlow's** (2708 J Street; 916-441-4693; harlows.com), where you'll find live rock or jazz downstairs and purple backlighting and plush and inviting seats in the Momo Lounge upstairs.

SATURDAY

4 *Mimosa Brunch* 10 a.m.

The **Tower Cafe** (1518 Broadway; 916-441-0222; towercafe.com; $$) sits across the street from the original (and, sadly, defunct) Tower Records. Get there early, and you'll have a better chance of snagging an outdoor table under the shady mimosa tree. But you could also do a lot worse than sitting indoors — where you'll be surrounded by an eclectic collection of objets d'art including African beaded belts, Mexican Day of the Dead sculptures, and 1930s travel posters. Dive into toothsome specialties like the Mexican scramble, blueberry cornmeal pancakes, or chorizo burrito.

OPPOSITE The California State Railroad Museum.

RIGHT Bond with the American River by riding along the 32-mile Jedediah Smith Memorial Bike Trail.

5 *Buffet of Art* 11:30 a.m.

The **Crocker Art Museum** (216 O Street; 916-808-7000; crockerartmuseum.org) is the perfect museum for a weekend getaway: compact yet diverse, including works from prehistoric to modern times. Oswald Achenbach's painting *Festival and Fireworks by Moonlight*, circa 1855, has a fiery luminescence so true that you expect to feel heat rising off the canvas.

ABOVE The rotunda in the California State Capitol, both working center of government and restored landmark.

BELOW Dry hills and green oaks on the bike trail.

In the contemporary gallery, the Mexican artist Rufino Tamayo's *Laughing Woman*, from 1950, is dark and whimsical. The original building, an 1872 Victorian Italianate mansion, is absolutely grand, and a 2010 addition that tripled the museum's size works in tasteful counterpoint.

6 *Boats and Trains* 1:30 p.m.

Old Sacramento (oldsacramento.com), a historic district with costumed cowboys and Old West facades, is a hokey, tourist-mobbed scene. But two spots stand out: the **Pilothouse Restaurant** (1000 Front Street; 916-441-4440; deltaking.com; $$) and the **California State Railroad Museum** (Second and I Streets; 916-445-6645; californiastaterailroadmuseum.org). The restaurant is on the *Delta King*, a 1920s riverboat-turned-floating-hotel, and offers dishes like a Shrimp Louie salad or fish and chips. The museum contains restored locomotives and railroad cars that you can climb aboard, including a 1937 stainless-steel dining car with white linen, fancy china, and a vintage menu offering a "lamb chop, extra thick" for 80 cents.

7 *Shop Midtown* 4 p.m.

Midtown, the area bordered roughly by 17th and 29th Streets and H and P Streets, is Sacramento's hippest district. Stop into boutiques like **Dragatomi** (2317 J Street; 916-706-0535; dragatomi.com) for designer collectibles like Kidrobot. Midtown is also

home to art galleries, so if you're not in town for a Second Saturdays Art Walk, pop into a few, including **b. sakata garo** (923 20th Street; 916-447-4276; bsakatagaro.com) or the **Center for Contemporary Art Sacramento** (1519 19th Street; 916-498-9811; ccasac.org).

8 *Capital Cuisine* 6:30 p.m.

For a taste of Sacramento's new culinary scene, make reservations at **Grange** (926 J Street; 916-492-4450; grangesacramento.com; $$$), an airy restaurant in the Citizen Hotel. Michael Tuohy uses local ingredients to make seasonal dishes like risotto with morels and fava beans, grilled sturgeon with polenta and shiitake mushrooms, or slow-smoked pork shoulder with turnips.

9 *Closer to Wine* 8:30 p.m.

If the art gods are on your side, you'll be in town for a **Second Saturdays Art Walk**, when galleries stay open until 10 p.m. with live music, food vendors,

and, of course, vino. Though most of the action is in Midtown, around K Street, galleries in other neighborhoods get involved, too; it's best to check in with the art walk's map, on its Web site (2nd-sat.com). Any other Saturday, remind yourself how close you are to California wine country with a trip to **Revolution Wines** (2831 S Street; 916-444-7711; revolution-wines.com), a tiny industrial-chic winery with free tastings, or **L Wine Lounge and Urban Kitchen** (1801 L Street; 916-443-6970; lwinelounge.com), which has at least 20 wines by the glass.

ABOVE A gallery at the Crocker Art Museum.

BELOW Old Sacramento, a historic district with touristy shops behind Old West facades.

10 *Paint the Town Green* 10 p.m.

Sacramento isn't known for night life, but there are a few surprises. One is the glossy and upscale **Lounge on 20** (1050 20th Street; 916-443-6620; loungeon20.com), where a seat on the patio, glass of emerald absinthe in hand, conjures up South Beach — without the limos, celebrities, and models. Across the street is **Faces** (2000 K Street; 916-448-0706; faces.net), one of five gay clubs clustered near K and 20th Streets.

SUNDAY

11 *Bike the River* 10 a.m.

Bond with the American River by riding along the **Jedediah Smith Memorial Bike Trail**, a 32-mile route that snakes along the water and through a series of parks featuring sand dunes, oak groves, picnic areas, and fishing nooks. **Practical Cycle** (114 J Street; 916-706-0077; practicalcycle.com), in Old Sacramento, has rentals.

ABOVE An indoor-outdoor view of passersby and reflected diners at the Grange restaurant in the Citizen Hotel.

OPPOSITE The skyline and the Sacramento River.

THE BASICS

Fly into Sacramento International Airport or drive about 80 miles from San Francisco. Drive or ride a bicycle on the smooth, flat streets.

The Citizen Hotel
926 J Street
916-447-2700
citizenhotel.com
$$
Designer boutique hotel in California's Joie de Vivre collection, site of popular Grange restaurant and Scandal bar.

Inn & Spa at Parkside
2116 6th Street
916-658-1818
innatparkside.com
$$$
Eleven elegant rooms and a spa in a 1936 mansion.

Delta King
1000 Front Street
800-825-5464
deltaking.com
$$
Hotel aboard a riverboat in Old Sacramento.

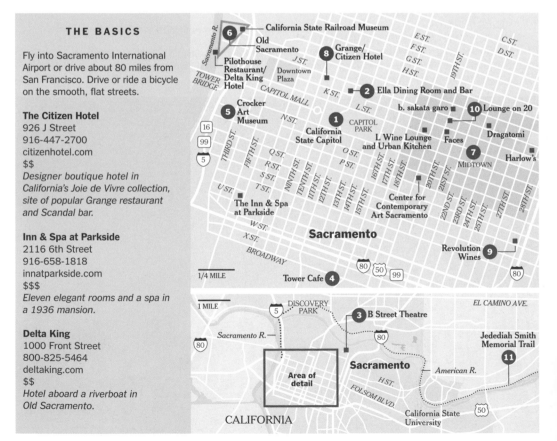

Sutter Creek

In California, the name "Sutter" means gold. And although John Sutter's sawmill, where something was seen glinting in 1848, was about 40 miles away, Sutter Creek is in the heart of California Gold Country. Sutter made camp here for a while, trying to avoid the gold rush crowds, but miners soon spilled in and made the town. Mining boomed and then faded (although there's some talk of a comeback as the gold price skyrockets), making way for today's contagion: wine fever. Vineyards now blanket hills that once swarmed with 49ers, and weekenders journey to the still-rustic towns of the Mother Lode to tour and taste. In and around Sutter Creek (population 2,600), you can mosey along sidewalks shaded by filigreed balconies or bicycle through blissfully empty Amador County countryside. Belly up to the bar in an 1880s saloon or sip Sierra Foothills vintages at the source.
— BY CONSTANCE JONES

FRIDAY

1 *Gold Rush Downtown* 4 p.m.

Amble through downtown Sutter Creek — it won't take long. The abbreviated **Main Street** may remind you of a tourist trap, but the buildings are mostly authentic, and 125 years ago, shoppers may have been looking at tools and provisions where you're now seeing antiques and designer jeans. For a map and background, consult the history section under "About" at suttercreek.org, or find the small visitors' center just off Main Street. Call in advance (209-267-1344) for the center's hours or to schedule a visit at the adjoining museum.

2 *Wines of the Foothills* 6 p.m.

Off an arbor-shaded courtyard, the wine bar at **Susan's Place** (15 Eureka Street; 209-267-0945; susansplace.com) pours a rotating list of Sierra Foothills picks. You'll want to try a side-by-side comparison of the region's powerful zinfandels, but there's more than just zin here. The gold rush

legacy of Italian immigrants lives on in barbera and sangiovese, and Rhone varietals are emerging as well. Take home a bottle of whatever strikes your fancy.

3 *Pesto and Amador Red* 7 p.m.

The decor is simple and the cuisine straightforward at the **Twisted Fork** (53 Main Street; 209-267-5211; $$). Meals start promisingly, with fresh bread served and a good dipping pesto, and proceed to unsurprising but satisfying entrees: grilled salmon, basil chicken, or flatiron steak with mashed potatoes, a variety of pastas. Local Amador and Eldorado County wines are well represented on the wine list.

4 *Sweet Music* 9 p.m.

Walk your sugar cravings next door to the **Sutter Creek Ice Cream Emporium** (51 Main Street; 209-267-0543) and have a scoop of nostalgia. At the original mirror-backed soda fountain and the long shelves crammed with candies, cookies, and fudge, families make sticky choices. Ask the owner, Stevens Price, for a ragtime tune on the upright piano; he organizes the Sutter Creek Ragtime Festival each August.

SATURDAY

5 *In a Cavern* 10 a.m.

It's up into the hills and underground this morning, not for gold but to see nature's work. In **Black Chasm National Natural Landmark** (15701 Pioneer-Volcano Road, Volcano; 209-736-2708;

OPPOSITE Black Chasm, a cave in Gold Country.

RIGHT Tools at the Western Hardrock Mining Museum in Amador. Miners swarmed here after gold was found at Sutter's Mill, but today's fortune seekers are vintners.

caverntours.com), rare and delicate helictites snake out from subterranean walls like mineralized tentacles, kinking and squirming into bizarre formations. The guided tour along stairways and catwalks shows off your ordinary stalactites and stalagmites, too, plus an unearthly aquamarine cave lake.

6 *Volcano, Still Active* 11:30 a.m.

Prospectors misnamed the settlement of **Volcano**, misinterpreting the craterlike shape of the valley that surrounds it, but the hottest thing ever to come out of here was $90 million in gold. Almost 5,000 in 1858, the population now hovers around 100, give or take, but the old limestone and false-front buildings still house real businesses. The plain, no-nonsense **Country Store** (16146 Main Street; 209-296-4459) cooks hamburgers for customers and displays vintage dry goods alongside batteries and beer nuts. Behind a ruined rock facade lies the open-air **Volcano Amphitheater** (Main Street; 209-296-2525; volcanotheatre.org), where community theater plays in summer; in the fall, the same theater company performs at the Cobblestone Theater, a small stone building put up as a cigar emporium in the 1850s. The colonnaded **St. George Hotel** (16104 Main Street; 209-296-4458; stgeorgehotel.com) operates a restaurant and the Whiskey Flat Saloon. But for a quick Saturday lunch, duck into the **Volcano Union Inn** (21375 Consolation Street; 209-296-7711; volcanounion.com; $$) for a burger or a pear and arugula salad.

7 *Wine Valley* 1:30 p.m.

After half an hour of twisting mountain roads and a turn at barely-there Fiddletown, you might feel as if you've made it all the way to Virginia. This is the other Shenandoah Valley (yes, that's the name), one of California's lesser-known wine regions, increasingly attractive to Napa-weary Bay Area and Sacramento weekenders. Taste old-vine zinfandels at **Sobon Estate** (14430 Shenandoah Road; 209-245-6554; sobonwine.com), founded in 1856, and

then poke around the homegrown museum's frontier and wine-making artifacts. With big reds poured in its barrel room, **Dobra Zemlja** (12505 Steiner Road; 209-245-3183; dobraz.com) is the antithesis of wine country slickness; **Vino Noceto** (11011 Dickson Road; 209-245-6556; noceto.com) focuses on sangiovese. In all, the eight-mile-long Shenandoah Valley has about two dozen producers.

8 *Culinary Outpost* 6 p.m.

In one-horse Plymouth, a humble time-warp at the foot of the Shenandoah Valley, **Taste** (9402 Main Street; 209-245-3463; restauranttaste.com; $$$) is an utter surprise. To step off the gritty sidewalk into the simple frame buildings is to go through a looking glass and into the hoped-for future of Sierra Foothills dining. In the sleek space, "small tastes" like foie gras with Kilt Lifter beer gastrique and "large tastes" like double cut pork chop with pear walnut bleu cheese, sauteed pears, and calypso beans may not push any culinary envelopes, but the execution is first-rate. After a day of touring the wine trail or tending the vineyards, patrons appreciate the extensive beer selection and the substantial wine list of Old World as well as local options.

BELOW The Sutter Creek Ice Cream Emporium.

9 *Footlights in the Foothills* 8 p.m.

Drive the nine miles back to town in time for the show at **Sutter Creek Theater** (44 Main Street; 916-425-0077; suttercreektheater.com), which presents live folk, jazz, country, or world music many Saturday nights year-round. With only 216 seats, the theater seldom books big names, but it brings in high-quality acts from around California and beyond. The Italianate 1919 building, once a silent-movie house, has been renovated from top to bottom.

SUNDAY

10 *Wide Spot in the Road* Noon

On your way back north to Highway 50, stop in tiny Amador City, a couple of blocks of shops along Old Highway 49. Spend a little time in the **Amador Whitney Museum** (No. 14170 Highway 49; amador-city.com/amador_museum/index.html), where displays emphasize the role of women in the gold rush days,

and then look through the vintage clothing and textiles, some dating back to those times, next door at **Victorian Closet** (No. 14176; 209-267-5250; antique-adventures.com). **Miner's Pick Antiques** (No. 14207; 209-267-0848; minerspick.com) specializes in mining artifacts and has its own tiny museum, the **Western Hardrock Mining Museum**. On the hillside behind the revamped 1879 **Imperial Hotel** (No. 14202; 209-267-9172; imperialamador.com), stroll through a 19th-century graveyard and read the headstones. Before you leave town, you can put together a take-away lunch at **Andrae's Bakery and Cheese Shop** (No. 14141; 209-267-1352; andraesbakery.com): fresh bread, artisanal cheese, charcuterie, and cacao-flecked nibby cookies.

OPPOSITE ABOVE On the hillside behind the revamped 1879 Imperial Hotel in Amador, stroll through a 19th-century graveyard and read the headstones.

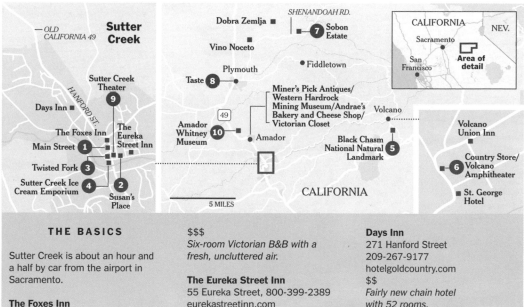

THE BASICS

Sutter Creek is about an hour and a half by car from the airport in Sacramento.

The Foxes Inn
77 Main Street
800-987-3344
foxesinn.com

$$$
Six-room Victorian B&B with a fresh, uncluttered air.

The Eureka Street Inn
55 Eureka Street, 800-399-2389
eurekastreetinn.com
$$
Four rooms in a richly detailed 1914 Craftsman bungalow.

Days Inn
271 Hanford Street
209-267-9177
hotelgoldcountry.com
$$
Fairly new chain hotel with 52 rooms.

Lake Tahoe

Politics and religion aside, 200,000 people can't be wrong. According to the California Tahoe Conservancy, that's the estimated crowd at Lake Tahoe on a busy summer weekend. That's enough people to make you rethink your vacation plans, but Tahoe never feels too frantic. Maybe it's the enormous mountain lake standing center, proudly straddling California and Nevada, that lets you know right away who's in charge, but the weekenders who flood the 72 miles of shoreline instinctively bow to nature's pace. And there's that other little fact, too—far less provable, but widely asserted: There's nothing quite like a weekend spent circling Tahoe. The endless activities of summer are standard enough, but they're set to a Sierra backdrop of soaring evergreens and crystalline water worthy of a thousand poets. Throw in the late-night siren call of the Nevada casinos, and it's a tough act to follow.
— BY CINDY PRICE

FRIDAY

1 *Deeper Shades of Blue* 3 p.m.

Wordsmiths have beat themselves silly trying to capture the true color of Lake Tahoe, so take your pick—cobalt, azure, electric, sapphire. Suffice it to say that it's pretty darn blue. And cold. Even in late summer, the water averages 65 to 70 degrees, given the many mountain streams that slither into it. Judge for yourself on a guided kayak trip out of Sand Harbor, Nevada, with the **Tahoe Adventure Company** (530-913-9212; tahoeadventurecompany.com), which offers individual tours that are part geology lesson and part history lesson. Paddle out past the children cannonballing off the rocks, and learn about the lake's underlying fault lines—and the tsunami that may have burst forth there sometime in the last 10,000 years.

2 *Drama on the Sand* 7 p.m.

Shake yourself dry, slip on your flip-flops, and head up the beach to the **Lake Tahoe Shakespeare Festival**

OPPOSITE Set high in the Sierra Nevada, Lake Tahoe is the largest alpine lake in North America.

RIGHT The lake straddles California and Nevada. At the Cal Neva Resort, the border divides a fireplace chimney.

(Sand Harbor State Park, Nevada; 800-747-4697; laketahoeshakespeare.com). Patrons pile up on the inclined sand banks, carrying towels, wine, and fat dinner spreads. You can bring your own, or check out the food court and beer garden. The plays are staged at dusk, the lake deftly employed as a silent witness to the unfolding action. If you miss the play, you don't have to miss the beautiful park.

SATURDAY

3 *Frank's Joint* 10 a.m.

Frank Sinatra owned what is now the **Cal Neva Resort, Spa, and Casino** (2 Stateline Road, Crystal Bay, Nevada; 800-233-5551; calnevaresort.com) for three short years (from 1960 to 1963), but he left a wealth of scandal in his wake. The resort, called the Cal-Neva Lodge when Sinatra owned it, rests on the state line, and the property is marked down the center. Poke your head into the old Celebrity Showroom, where Frank and his buddies performed. Marilyn Monroe often sat up front, and members of the hotel staff say she overdosed on sleeping pills here two weeks before her death, amid a swirl of rumors of sex and foul play. Find the Indian Room yet? Secret passages run below it that lead to the closets of Cabin 3 (Marilyn's) and Cabin 5 (Frank's). The Chicago mobster Sam Giancana is said to have used the tunnels to conduct business.

4 *High Noon* 12 p.m.

It's noon on the lake, and you're 6,225 feet above sea level. A cheeseburger washed down with an

ice-cold Anchor Steam is not only agreeable; it's mandatory. You're now in California, coming down the west side of the lake. Find your way through Tahoe City and take a right just past Fanny Bridge (called "rump row" for the line of backsides that forms as people lean over the railing to stare at the Truckee River and its fish). **Bridgetender Tavern and Grill** (65 West Lake Boulevard, Tahoe City; 530-583-3342; $) is home to one of the juiciest cheeseburgers on the lake as well as a generous outdoor patio that winds along the Truckee.

5 *Just Drift Away* 2 p.m.

Follow the hoots of laughter across Fanny Bridge and arrive at the **Truckee River Raft Company** (185 River Road, Tahoe City; 530-584-0123; truckeeriverraft.com) for a lazy afternoon on the river. You can paddle, but the ride is best enjoyed as one long floating party. Families drift alongside groups of friends with tubes lashed together as they bask and pass each other beer. A little more than halfway, you might find a shallow, standing-room-only party complete with makeshift stickball games (the paddles double as bats).

6 *Cocktail of the Brave* 7 p.m.

South Lake Tahoe isn't known as a gastronomic hotbed, but a seat at the sushi bar at the **Naked Fish** (3940 Lake Tahoe Boulevard, South Lake Tahoe; 530-541-3474; thenakedfish.com; $$) offers up ace rolls and a frisky pre-casino crowd. Kick your night off with an appetizer of barbecued albacore and the surprisingly tasty house drink, the Money Shot, which involves a bolt of hot sake, a drizzle of ponzu sauce, fish eggs, a Japanese mountain potato, and a few other nerve-racking ingredients.

7 *Poker Faces, Old and New* 10 p.m.

Itching for the dull tumble of dice on felt, or the shudder and snap of a fresh deck of cards being shuffled? You'll have no trouble finding it. South Tahoe's casinos are snugged up against each other

along the border of Stateline, Nevada. Refurbishing has made them sexier. Witness the vampy **MontBleu Resort Casino & Spa** (55 Highway 50; 775-588-3515; montbleuresort.com), a k a the old Caesar's sporting a slap of paint and a fresh attitude, or the swank bar at **Harveys Resort Casino** (18 Lake Tahoe Boulevard; 775-588-2411; harveystahoe.com). Still, old-timers and hipsters might enjoy the old-school ambience and low-limit tables at the **Lakeside Inn and Casino** (168 Highway 50, 800-624-7980; lakesideinn.com).

SUNDAY

8 *Now That's Venti* 10 a.m.

Ride the touristy but must-do **Heavenly Gondola** (Heavenly Mountain Resort; 4080 Lake Tahoe Boulevard, South Lake Tahoe; 775-586-7000; skiheavenly.com), a ski lift that doubles as a sight-seeing excursion in summer. Hop on board when it opens and cruise 2.4 miles up the mountain to the observation deck. Grab a very decent mocha at the cafe and soak in the stunning views of the Carson Valley and the Desolation Wilderness—not to mention that big blue thing in the center.

BELOW Warming up at the Bridgetender Tavern and Grill. In the winter, Tahoe turns into ski country.

9 *Pesto Bread, Just Like Mom's* Noon

There's an art to gathering beach provisions, and Tahoe regulars know there's good one-stop shopping at the **PDQ Market** (6890 West Lake Boulevard, Tahoma, California; 530-525-7411; $), where customers can secure not only the usual Coke and sun block, but also one of the tastiest sandwiches in town. Press through the store, and you'll find a little homegrown operation pushing out delicious sandwiches on fresh-baked breads like jalapeño or pesto. The half-size sandwich, loaded high with shaved meats like pastrami or turkey, is a steal.

10 *Decisions, Decisions* 2 p.m.

Trying to pick the right Tahoe beach is a bit like plucking a date off the Internet. Zephyr Cove is young and likes to party. Meeks Bay is into poetry and likes long walks on the beach. The good news is that each is better looking than the next. For those given to fits of polarity, try **D. L. Bliss State Park** (Highway 89, South Lake Tahoe; 530-525-7277; parks.ca.gov), a camping ground with sheltered coves for swimming and lazing, as well as a few bracing hikes for the restless. The pristine beaches make it hard to resist the former, though. Imagine you've found the turquoise waters of Vieques in the middle of the Black Forest of Germany. Until you dip your hand in, of course.

OPPOSITE ABOVE Learning about the lake on a kayaking tour with Tahoe Adventure Company.

ABOVE A ski lift does summer duty ferrying sightseers.

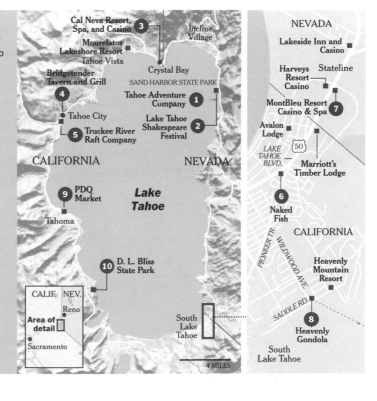

THE BASICS

Fly to Reno and drive 60 miles or to Sacramento and drive 100 miles.

Mourelatos Lakeshore Resort
6834 North Lake Boulevard,
Tahoe Vista, California
530-546-9500
mlrtahoe.com
$$$
Cute hotel on the lake, with a private beach.

Avalon Lodge
4075 Manzanita Avenue,
South Lake Tahoe, California
530-544-2285
avalonlodge.com
$$$
Walking distance to casinos.

Marriott's Timber Lodge
4100 Lake Tahoe Boulevard,
South Lake Tahoe, California
530-542-6600
$$$
Pool, private beach, fitness center.

The Oregon Coast

You could drive down the southern third of the Oregon coast in a couple of hours, and you'd think, How beautiful! Highway 101, the Oregon Coast Highway, hugs the shoreline enough to give you views of the sand and windblown trees, rocks and crashing waves that give this stretch its fame. But to instill memories that will make these gorgeous seascapes your own, plan a leisurely weekend of detours and side trips with plenty of time to stop at the beaches and lighthouses, gulp the salt air, and kick back in the harbor towns.
— BY DAVID LASKIN

FRIDAY

1 *Park Land* 1 p.m.

In North Bend, leave Highway 101 to pick up Route 540 and head south as it leaves city streets behind to become the **Cape Arago Highway**. You'll descend quickly into Charleston, a tiny place with a working harbor, a fish-and-chips shack, and tidal shallows raked by whitecaps on windy days. The road—despite its "highway" designation, it's only a few miles long—leads from there to a series of three adjoining oceanside state parks (oregonstateparks.org). Stop at the first, **Sunset Bay**, for beachcombing and your first photo ops, but don't be tempted to stay too long. You'll need time at the next one, **Shore Acres**, to sniff the luxe ivory Elina roses in the well-kept garden of a former private estate perched atop a forbidding cliff.

2 *Cape Arago* 3 p.m.

The last stop on the road, before it loops around to point you back toward Charleston, is **Cape Arago State Park**, where you'll find the rocky headland, topped by a lighthouse, that all of this has been leading to. Hike on one of the cove trails down to the beach and look for seals and tide pools. When you've seen enough, drive back to Charleston and pick up Seven Devils Road, which will lead you to West Beaver Hill Road to complete the loop back to Highway 101.

OPPOSITE Highway 101 winds close to the water's edge along rocky coast south of Cape Sebastian State Park.

RIGHT Surf fishing in Port Orford, a town where every street seems to end in a view of the sea.

3 *Old Town Wine List* 4 p.m.

Find a little West Coast slice of Nantucket in **Bandon**, a town of 3,100 people with terrific beaches to the west and the silvery estuary of the Coquille River to the north and east. Check out the shops and galleries in the compact Old Town before heading to dinner at the **Alloro Wine Bar** (375 Second Street Southeast; 541-347-1850; allorowinebar.com; $$-$$$). It serves superb dishes like feather-light lasagna, sautéed local snapper, and fresh fava beans. Relax over a Walla Walla cabernet or another of the Northwest vintages on its wine list.

SATURDAY

4 *Sea Stacks* 10 a.m.

Take the lightly trafficked **Beach Loop Road** south of town. It parallels the coast for four and a half miles, and although there are a few too many cottages and motels, you forget all about them when you stop to wander on the beach amid fantastically carved sea stacks and watch colorful kites slashing against the sky. After the loop rejoins Highway 101, follow it as it leaves the coast for an inland stretch past ranches and cranberry bogs. When you come to Route 250, the Cape Blanco Road, turn right and drive through rolling sheep pastures reminiscent of Cornwall. It's not far to the sea.

5 *Blown Away* 11 a.m.

State parks are strung along this coast, and you can't hit them all. But **Cape Blanco** is a must-stop — the farthest west point on the Oregon coast, the state's oldest lighthouse, one of the windiest spots in the United States. Be prepared for that wind as you walk toward the stark circa-1870 lighthouse. The view at the headland is worth it, so stand and stare as long as you can withstand the blast.

6 *On the Edge* 1 p.m.

Imagine the shabby picturesque waterfront of an outer Maine island fused onto the topographic drama of Big Sur: that's **Port Orford**. Mountains covered with Douglas firs plunge down toward the ocean, and you feel how truly you are at the continent's

edge. The town itself has a salty, dreamy, small-town vibe; every street ends in blue sea framed by huge dark green humps of land. Look around and then find lunch. **Griff's on the Dock** (490 Dock Road; 541-332-8985; $$) and the **Crazy Norwegian's** (259 Sixth Street; 541-332-8601; $$) are good bets for fish and chips.

7 *End of the Rogue* 3 p.m.

The Rogue River, known for the whitewater along its 200-mile journey from the Cascades, looks wide, tame, and placid as it meets the sea in **Gold Beach**. The bridge that carries Highway 101 over it is a beauty, multiple-arched, elegant, and vaguely Deco. The city isn't particularly inviting — utilitarian motels hunkering along the strand, a drab dune obstructing views of the ocean. But don't miss the well-stocked **Gold Beach Books** (29707 Ellensburg Avenue; 541-247-2495; oregoncoastbooks.com), which in addition to covering every literary genre has an art gallery and coffee house. **Jerry's Rogue River Museum** (29880 Harbor Way; 541-247-4571; roguejets.com/museum.php) is worth a look around and has an unusual feature — you

ABOVE The harbor in Crescent City, a town just south of the Oregon state line in California.

LEFT Driftwood piled up by the surf at a beach along Beach Loop Drive in Bandon, Oregon.

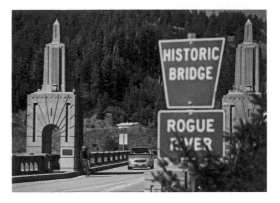

can book a jetboat trip on the Rogue there. There's also good hiking just outside town at **Cape Sebastian State Park**, with miles of trails and views down the coast to California.

8 *Gold Beach Dining* 7 p.m.

If you can get a reservation, head out of town for dinner at the **Tu Tu' Tun Lodge** (96550 North Bank Rogue River Road; 541-247-6664; tututun.com; $$$), a fishing resort a few miles upstream on the Rogue. If you're staying in town, **Spinner's Seafood Steak and Chophouse** (29430 Ellensburg Avenue; 541-247-5160; $$$) features hefty portions of entrees like grilled duck breast, Alaska halibut, and ribeye steak.

SUNDAY

9 *More and More Scenic* 9 a.m.

Have a filling breakfast at the **Indian Creek Café** (94682 Jerry's Flat Road; 541-247-0680) and get back on the road. From here on it just keeps getting better.

About 14 miles south of Gold Beach you will enter **Samuel H. Boardman Scenic Corridor**, a nine-mile roadside corridor along Highway 101 with turnouts overlooking natural stone arches rising from the waves, trailheads accessing the Oregon Coast Trail, and paths winding down to hidden beaches and tide pools. The scenic summa may be **Whaleshead Beach**, a cove with the mystical beauty of a Japanese scroll—spray blowing off the crest of a wave, massive sea rocks dazzled in the westering sun, and maybe a kid or two making tracks in the sand.

ABOVE The Patterson Bridge in Gold Beach, completed in 1931, crosses the Rogue River just before it meets the sea.

BELOW Kite flying on a windy beach in Bandon.

10 *Tsunami Zone* 11 a.m.

Glance around in **Brookings**, by far the toastiest town on the Oregon coast. Its curious microclimate — winter temperatures in the 80s are not unheard of — is a point of pride, as is its park devoted to preserving native wild azaleas. Then push on south into California to **Crescent City**, a place distinguished by its unfortunate history. In 1964 it was struck by a tsunami that destroyed 300 buildings and killed 11 residents. The vulnerability

remains in this region of the Pacific coast. In 2011, the harbors in both Brookings and Crescent City were severely damaged by the tsunami that swept away cities in coastal Japan. You're tantalizingly close to California's towering redwoods here, so turn a few miles inland and make a final stop at **Jedediah Smith Redwoods State Park**, where you can wander among 200-foot-tall trees. Their majesty matches that of the rocky windswept coast you've just left behind.

ABOVE Along Beach Loop Drive south of Bandon.

OPPOSITE Veer a few miles off the coast near Crescent City, south of the California state line, for a look at the giants of Jedediah Smith Redwoods State Park.

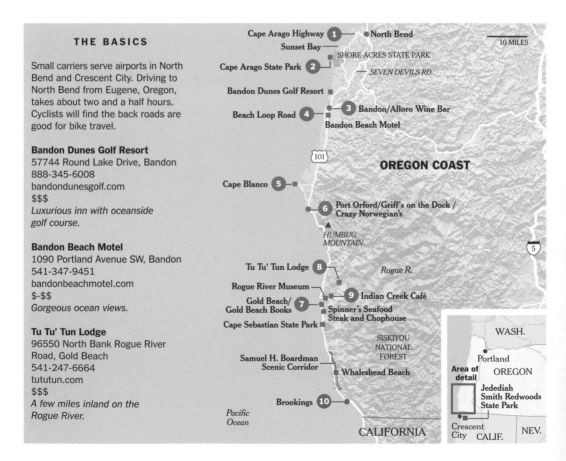

THE BASICS

Small carriers serve airports in North Bend and Crescent City. Driving to North Bend from Eugene, Oregon, takes about two and a half hours. Cyclists will find the back roads are good for bike travel.

Bandon Dunes Golf Resort
57744 Round Lake Drive, Bandon
888-345-6008
bandondunesgolf.com
$$$
Luxurious inn with oceanside golf course.

Bandon Beach Motel
1090 Portland Avenue SW, Bandon
541-347-9451
bandonbeachmotel.com
$-$$
Gorgeous ocean views.

Tu Tu' Tun Lodge
96550 North Bank Rogue River Road, Gold Beach
541-247-6664
tututun.com
$$$
A few miles inland on the Rogue River.

Portland
Oregon

"Nice" is an adjective that Portland, Oregon, can't seem to shake. But below the fleece-clad and Teva-wearing exterior lurks a cool and refreshingly unneurotic city that marches to its own cosmopolitan beat. Truth is, Portland doesn't want to be Seattle, its highly caffeinated neighbor to the north. With less traffic, better public transportation, and Mount Hood in its backyard, this self-styled City of Roses doesn't stand in anybody's shadow. Its vibrant downtown overflows with urban pleasures like chic restaurants, funky nightclubs, and sprightly neighborhoods crackling with youthful energy, but nobody's boasting. That's another nice thing about Portland.

— BY DAVID LASKIN

FRIDAY

1 *Fresh Orientation* 6 p.m.

The pastel roses peak in the late spring at the **International Rose Test Garden** (850 SW Rose Garden Way; 503-227-7033; rosegardenstore.org), but the blooms last for months and the view from this hillside terraced garden is fantastic year-round. Even if clouds keep you from seeing Mount Hood, you still get a bird's-eye view of colorful wood-frame houses surrounding a tidy grove of skyscrapers. Breathe in the pine-scented air and stretch your legs on the hillside paths of this precipitous chunk of green, five minutes from downtown by car, or 15 minutes on the efficient MAX Light Rail.

2 *Bright Brasserie* 7:30 p.m.

The trendy Pearl neighborhood has evolved rapidly from a raw industrial zone to a neighborhood of galleries, parks, and condos. Take in the district's new maturity at the French restaurant **Fenouil** (900 NW 11th Avenue; 503-525-2225; fenouilinthepearl.com; $$$). A sleek, soaring space, Fenouil makes the most of its location overlooking Jamison Park with big windows that roll up like garage doors in nice weather. Local and regional ingredients come with a French touch in dishes like

OPPOSITE There's a vista at the International Rose Test Garden even when the roses aren't in bloom.

RIGHT Portland's skyline from the outskirts.

Sonoma foie gras or duck breast with rillette, beets, and onions.

3 *Downtown Jazz* 9:30 p.m.

Portland's nightlife scene offers plenty of choices, from torchy lounges to high-decibel indie hang-outs. A much-loved institution is **Jimmy Mak's** (221 NW 10th Avenue; 503-295-6542; jimmymaks.com), an intimate jazz club with a national profile. You'll see high-quality local musicians or jazz stars like Joey DeFrancesco or Louis Hayes. Reserve if you want a table.

SATURDAY

4 *Market to Teahouse* 10 a.m.

Even if you can't stand handcrafted soaps, dangly earrings, gauzy scarves, chunky ceramics, fancy pet bowls, messy street food, and the people who make them, the **Portland Saturday Market** is worth visiting (portlandsaturdaymarket.com). Tucked under the Burnside Bridge, the market is a perfect starting point for a leisurely walk amid the cast-iron buildings of Old Town and into Chinatown. Drop in at stores like **Seven Planet** (412 NW Couch Street; 503-575-9455; sevenplanet.com), a good match for green Portland with its bamboo pashminas and cutlery made of recycled plastic, or **Floating World Comics** (20 NW 5th Avenue; 503-241-0227; floatingworldcomics.com), a shop that approaches comic books as an art form. Wend your way to the serene **Lan Su Chinese Garden** (239 NW Everett Street; 503-228-8131; portlandchinesegarden.org), where you can refuel with a cup of tea in the ornate teahouse beside Zither Lake.

5 *Walk to Lunch* Noon

Downtown Portland has about five neighborhoods, each with its own mood and flavor, but it isn't very big. In 20 minutes, you can walk from Chinatown in the northwest to the cultural district in the southwest. Which brings you to lunch. At **Southpark Seafood Grill & Wine Bar** (901 SW Salmon Street; 503-326-1300; southparkseafood.com; $$), you can plunk down at the bar for a quick meal and ask for sightseeing suggestions from the young downtown crowd. Seafood holds center stage; check the menu for bouillabaisse or fried calamari with spicy aioli.

6 *How Nice* 1 p.m.

South Park takes you to the **Portland Art Museum** (1219 SW Park Avenue; 503-226-2811; portlandartmuseum.org), which has an impressive collection of photographs. They run the gamut from 19th-century daguerreotypes to contemporary landscapes. Another strong point in the permanent collection is Japanese scrolls from the Edo period. If you'd like to buy art objects to take home as well as look at them, proceed to the nearby **Russian Art Gallery** (518 SW Yamhill Street; 503-224-5070; russiangalleryportland.com), which carries religious

icons for several hundred to several thousand dollars, along with nesting dolls and Gzhel pottery, all imported from Russia.

7 *Roll Out of Town* 3 p.m.

Stash your stuff, don your Spandex and rent a bicycle at **Waterfront Bicycles** (10 SW Ash Street No. 100; 503-227-1719; waterfrontbikes.com) for a ride along the Willamette River. If you're feeling mellow, ride the three-mile loop that goes north on the Waterfront Bike Trail in **Tom McCall Waterfront Park**, across the river via the Steel Bridge to the **Vera Katz East Bank Esplanade**, and back across on the Hawthorne Bridge. For a tougher workout, stay on the East Bank Esplanade and continue south on the **Springwater Corridor** for an 18-mile ride through the city's semirural outskirts. The trail terminates at the town of Boring (its slogan: "An Exciting Place to Live").

8 *Hot Reservation* 8 p.m.

Serious foodies head to **Park Kitchen** (422 NW Eighth Avenue; 503-223-7275; parkkitchen.com; $$$). In a former garage, the restaurant has a warren of dark and cozy rooms that faces an open kitchen. The chef and owner, Scott Dolich, combines elements of French, Italian, and Northwestern cooking in an imaginative fusion all his own. The menu changes with the season, but the tastes are always superb.

ABOVE The Portland Saturday Market in full swing. Portland's vibrant downtown overflows with youthful energy.

9 *Hang Out, Rock On* 10:30 p.m.

Check out the latest indie bands at **Doug Fir Lounge** (830 East Burnside Street; 503-231-9663; dougfirlounge.com), connected to the trendy Jupiter Hotel. It is Portland's primo spot to hang out, drink good local beer, rub shoulders with the young and pierced, and catch emerging groups from all over the country. The room is surprisingly modern and woodsy for a dance club, with gold-toned lighting, a fire pit, and walls clad in Douglas fir logs.

SUNDAY

10 *Petit Dejeuner* 10 a.m.

For a taste of Paris, pop over to **St. Honoré Boulangerie** (2335 NW Thurman Street; 503-445-4342; sainthonorebakery.com; $-$$), a French-style bakery where Dominique Geulin bakes almond croissants, apricot tarts, and Normandy apple toast, a mix of

French toast, brioche and custard. The cafe is airy, with huge windows and lots of wicker. Equally important, the coffee is among the city's finest.

11 *City of Books* 11 a.m.

It says a lot about Portland that **Powell's City of Books** (1005 West Burnside; 503-228-4651; powells.com) is one of the city's prime attractions — a store so big that it provides maps. The dusty, well-lighted store is larger than many libraries, with 68,000 square feet of new and used books. Plan to stay a while.

ABOVE Comb the shelves at Powell's City of Books.

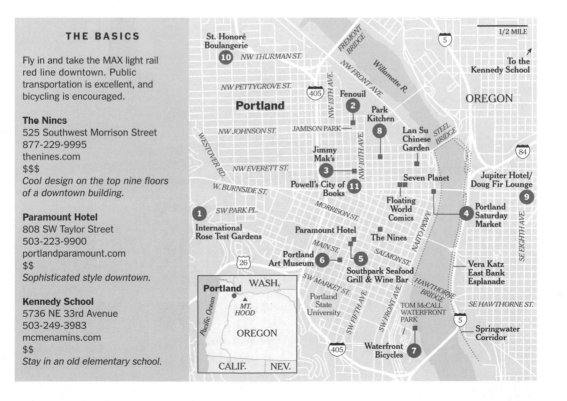

THE BASICS

Fly in and take the MAX light rail red line downtown. Public transportation is excellent, and bicycling is encouraged.

The Nincs
525 Southwest Morrison Street
877-229-9995
thenines.com
$$$
Cool design on the top nine floors of a downtown building.

Paramount Hotel
808 SW Taylor Street
503-223-9900
portlandparamount.com
$$
Sophisticated style downtown.

Kennedy School
5736 NE 33rd Avenue
503-249-3983
mcmenamins.com
$$
Stay in an old elementary school.

St. Honoré Boulangerie

10 NW THURMAN ST.

NW PETTYGROVE ST.

Portland

NW JOHNSON ST.   JAMISON PARK

NW EVERETT ST.

W. BURNSIDE ST.

1 SW PARK PL.

International Rose Test Gardens

Paramount Hotel

Portland Art Museum

6

SW MARKET ST.

Portland WASH.

MT. HOOD

OREGON

CALIF.   NEV.

FREMONT BRIDGE

NW FRONT AVE.

Willamette R.

405 Fenouil **2** Park Kitchen

8 Lan Su Chinese Garden

STEEL BRIDGE

Jimmy Mak's

3

Powell's City of **11** Books

Floating World Comics

MORRISON ST.

Seven Planet

The Nines

SALMON ST.

Southpark Seafood Grill & Wine Bar

5

Portland State University

TOM McCALL WATERFRONT PARK

405 Waterfront Bicycles **7**

1/2 MILE

5

To the Kennedy School

OREGON

84

Jupiter Hotel/ Doug Fir Lounge **9**

4 Portland Saturday Market

Vera Katz East Bank Esplanade

HAWTHORNE BRIDGE

SE HAWTHORNE ST.

5

Springwater Corridor

SE EIGHTH AVE.

NAITO PKWY

Seattle

Seemingly overnight, whole swatches of downtown Seattle, Washington, and close-in neighborhoods — notably South Lake Union and the Pike-Pine Corridor — have transformed themselves into vibrant enclaves of restaurants, bars, and galleries. With so many converted and repurposed buildings, Seattle's cityscape is starting to look as layered as the wardrobes of its inhabitants. The tarry pitch of this old timber port city has never disappeared; it was just plastered over with grunge flannel, tech money, yuppie coffee, Pacific Rim flavors, and more recently the backyard chickens and chard of urban pioneers. Don't let one of Seattle's famous rainshowers keep you from entering the mix. This is one of the rare American cities where you can be outdoors year-round without either shivering or sweating. — BY DAVID LASKIN

FRIDAY

1 *Park Tower View* 4 p.m.

Volunteer Park (1247 15th Avenue East; 206-684-4075; seattle.gov/parks), a 10-minute cab or bus ride from downtown at the north end of Capitol Hill, has gardens designed a century ago by the Olmsted Brothers, a conservatory bursting with plants from regions around the world, and a squat brick water tower that you can ascend for terrific views of the city below and the mountains and sea beyond. Rain or shine, it's the ideal place for orientation. If hunger strikes, stroll a couple of blocks east through one of Seattle's oldest and prettiest neighborhoods for a slice of lemon Bundt cake and a Stumptown coffee at the cozy, humming **Volunteer Park Cafe** (1501 17th Avenue East; 206-328-3155; alwaysfreshgoodness.com; $$).

2 *Coolest Corridor* 6 p.m.

The Pike-Pine Corridor is Seattle's happiest urban makeover: from a warren of shabby flats and greasy spoons to an arty but not oppressively gentrified hamlet just across the freeway from downtown. When the locally revered **Elliott Bay Book Company** (1521 10th Avenue; 206-624-6600; elliottbaybook.com)

abandoned Pioneer Square downtown to relocate here, the literati gasped — but now it looks like a perfect neighborhood fit, what with the inviting communal tables at **Oddfellows** (1525 10th Avenue; 206-325-0807; oddfellowscafe.com; $$) two doors down, and a full spectrum of restaurants, vintage clothing shops, and home décor stores in the surrounding blocks. When it's time for a predinner drink, amble over to **Licorous** (928 12th Avenue; 206-325-6947; licorous.com). Behind the shack-like facade is a soaring, spare, just dark and loud enough watering hole that serves creative cocktails (Bound for Glory, with Bacardi, allspice, lime juice, and Jamaican bitters) and bar snacks like a salumi plate.

3 *Fresh and Local* 7:30 p.m.

One of the most talked-about restaurants in town, **Sitka & Spruce** (1531 Melrose Avenue East; 206-324-0662; sitkaandspruce.com; $$), looks like a classy college dining room with a long refectory table surrounded by a few smaller tables, concrete floors, exposed brick, and duct work. But there's nothing sophomoric about the food. The chef and owner, Matt Dillon, who moved the restaurant to the Pike-Pine Corridor in 2010, follows his flawless intuition in transforming humble local ingredients (smelt, nettles, celery root, black trumpet mushrooms, turnips, pumpkin) into complexly layered, many-textured but never fussy creations like beer-fried smelt with aioli, spiced pumpkin crepe with herbed labneh, and salmon with stinging nettles. Heed your server's advice that entrees are meant to be shared — you will have just enough room for dessert (try warm dates, pistachios, and rose-water ice cream), and you will be pleasantly surprised by the bill.

SATURDAY

4 *Art and Water* 9 a.m.

There used to be two complaints about downtown Seattle: it offered no inspiring parks and no waterfront access worthy of the scenery. The **Olympic Sculpture Park** (2901 Western Avenue; 206-654-3100; seattleartmuseum.org), opened four years ago by the Seattle Art Museum, took care of both problems in one stroke. Masterpieces in steel, granite, fiberglass, and bronze by nationally renowned artists have

OPPOSITE Alexander Calder's red steel *Eagle*, at the Olympic Sculpture Park, upstages Seattle's iconic Space Needle.

wedded beautifully with maturing native trees, shrubs, ferns, and wildflowers. Wander the zigzagging paths and ramps past the massive weathered steel hulls of Richard Serra's *Wake* and Alexander Calder's soaring painted steel *Eagle* until you reach the harborside promenade. From there continue north to a pocket beach and into the adjoining grassy fields of waterfront **Myrtle Edwards Park**. It's all free.

5 *Urban Village* 10:30 a.m.

The development of South Lake Union into a thriving urban village, brainchild of the Microsoft tycoon Paul Allen, is finally alive and kicking. This former industrial no man's land now houses the city's best galleries, an ever increasing collection

of dining spots, some nifty shops, and the spanking new Amazon campus. Use the South Lake Union Streetcar to hop from **Gordon Woodside/John Braseth Gallery** (2101 Ninth Avenue; 206-622-7243; woodsidebrasethgallery.com), which specializes in Northwest landscapes, to **Honeychurch Antiques** (411 Westlake Avenue North; 206-622-1225; honeychurch.com), with museum-quality Asian art and artifacts, and on to the **Center for Wooden Boats** (1010 Valley Street; 206-382-2628; cwb.org), where you can admire the old varnished beauties or rent a rowboat or sailboat for a spin around Seattle's in-city lake. Need a (really rich) snack? The newly renamed **Marie & Frères Chocolate** (2122 Westlake Avenue; 206-859-3534; claudiocorallochocolate.com) has some of the most exquisite chocolate macaroons ever confected.

6 *Lunch beside the Chief* 1 p.m.

Tilikum Place, with its imposing fountain statue of the city's namesake, Chief Sealth, is Seattle's closest thing to a piazza, and the **Tilikum Place Café** (407 Cedar Street; 206-282-4830; $$) supplied the one

ABOVE AND LEFT A dock and a tool shop at the Center for Wooden Boats, where you can admire classic boats or rent a rowboat or sailboat for a spin around Lake Union, Seattle's in-city lake. The center also offers boatbuilding workshops and other woodworking classes.

missing element — a classy informal restaurant — when it opened. Understated elegance is the byword here, whether in the delicate purée of butternut squash soup with bits of tart apple, the beet salad with arugula and blue cheese, or the light and piquant mushroom and leek tart.

7 *Walk on Water* 4 p.m.

You don't have to leave the city limits to immerse yourself in the region's stunning natural beauty. Drive or take a bus 15 minutes from downtown to the parking lot of the **Museum of History and Industry** (2700 24th Avenue East; 206-324-1126; seattlehistory.org) and pick up the milelong **Arboretum Waterfront Trail**. A network of well-maintained paths and boardwalks takes you through thickets of alder, willow, and elderberry into marshy islands alive with the trills of red-winged blackbirds and marsh wrens, and over shallows where kayakers prowl amid the rushes and the concrete pillars of the freeway overhead. If the sun is out, you'll want to prolong the outing with a stroll through the flowering fruit trees in the adjoining **Washington Park Arboretum** (depts.washington.edu/uwbg).

8 *La Dolce Vita* 8 p.m.

Maybe it's the stylish Italian vibe or the pretty people basking in the soft glow of dripping candles, or maybe it's the sumptuous, creatively classic food — whatever the secret ingredient, **Barolo**

Ristorante (1940 Westlake Avenue; 206-770-9000; baroloseattle.com; $$$) always feels like a party. The pastas would do a Roman mother proud — gnocchi sauced with braised pheasant, leg of lamb ragù spooned over rigatoni. The rack of lamb with Amarone-infused cherries is sinfully rich, and the seared branzino (sea bass) exhales the essence of the Mediterranean. Don't leave without at least a nibble of cannoli or tiramisù.

TOP The beach at Myrtle Edwards Park next to the Olympic Sculpture Park in downtown Seattle.

ABOVE Sitka & Spruce looks like a classy college dining room, but there's nothing sophomoric about the food.

ABOVE See Sound Lounge, where Saturday night house music goes into Sunday morning.

OPPOSITE A streetcar rolls along Westlake Avenue in the South Lake Union area, a thriving urban village.

rowdy in the wee hours, but inside the beat and liquor flow smoothly.

9 *The Beat Goes On* Midnight

At **See Sound Lounge** (115 Blanchard Street; 206-374-3733; seesoundlounge.com) young and not so young Seattle join forces to party to house music spun by a revolving cast of D.J.'s. There's a small dance floor — but the compensation is lots of booths and sofas to crash on. The scene outside can get

SUNDAY

10 *Bayou Brunch* 10:30 a.m.

Lake Pontchartrain meets Puget Sound at **Toulouse Petit** (601 Queen Anne Avenue North; 206-432-9069; toulousepetit.com; $$), a funky bistro-style spot near the Seattle Center in Lower Queen Anne. Grab a booth and settle in with a basket of hot, crispy beignets; then indulge in something truly decadent, like pork cheeks confit hash topped with a couple of fried eggs or eggs Benedict with crab and fines herbes. You can cleanse your system afterward with a brisk walk up the hill to **Kerry Park** (211 West Highland Drive) for a magnificent farewell view.

THE BASICS

The best, cheapest way to get from the airport to downtown is the new Link Light Rail. Around town, drive or walk and take the bus.

Hyatt at Olive 8
1635 Eighth Avenue
206-695-1234
hyatt.com
$$
New in 2009, with pool, fitness center, and city views.

Pan Pacific Hotel Seattle
2125 Terry Avenue
206-264-8111
panpacific.com
$$$
Light and airy; a 15-minute walk to downtown.

Fairmont Olympic
411 University Street
206-621-1700
fairmont.com/seattle
$$$
The grande dame of Seattle hotels.

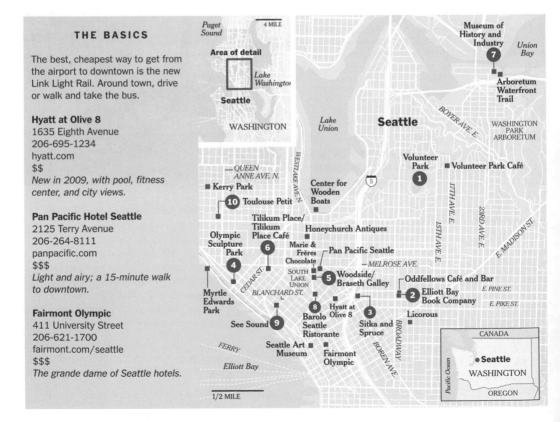

Map labels: Puget Sound; 4 MILE; Area of detail; Lake Washington; Seattle; WASHINGTON; Lake Union; Seattle; Museum of History and Industry; Union Bay; Arboretum Waterfront Trail; BOYER AVE. E.; WASHINGTON PARK ARBORETUM; QUEEN ANNE AVE. N.; Kerry Park; WESTLAKE AVE. N.; Center for Wooden Boats; Volunteer Park; Volunteer Park Café; 17TH AVE. E.; 23RD AVE. E.; E. MADISON ST.; 10 Toulouse Petit; Tilikum Place/Tilikum Place Café; Honeychurch Antiques; 15TH AVE. E.; Olympic Sculpture Park; 6 Marie & Frères Chocolate; Pan Pacific Seattle; MELROSE AVE.; CEDAR ST.; SOUTH LAKE UNION; 5 Woodside/Braseth Galley; Oddfellows Café and Bar; E. PINE ST.; Myrtle Edwards Park; BLANCHARD ST.; 2 Elliott Bay Book Company; E. PIKE ST.; FERRY; 8 Barolo Seattle Ristorante; Hyatt at Olive 8; 3 Sitka and Spruce; Licorous; BROADWAY; CANADA; See Sound 9; Seattle Art Museum; Fairmont Olympic; BOREN AVE.; Elliott Bay; Seattle; WASHINGTON; Pacific Ocean; OREGON; 1/2 MILE

SEATTLE

658

Northwest
Seattle

Long ago the expanding city of Seattle swallowed up two of its neighbors, and neither of them has ever forgotten. Fremont and Ballard, once cities in their own right, are now Seattle neighborhoods of a particularly independent-minded kind. They're close together, though not contiguous, and still have unique character that resists complete assimilation — arty and free-spirited in Fremont; Nordic and proudly maritime in Ballard. Each is undergoing a kind of 21st-century renaissance, with shops and restaurants moving in, and a new, often young crowd arriving to live or just to play. But in either one, you can still lose yourself so thoroughly that you will barely even remember you're in the same town as the Space Needle.
— BY DAN WHITE

FRIDAY

1 *Welcome to Fremont* 3 p.m.

As they cross the orange-and-blue Fremont Bridge on their way from downtown Seattle, drivers are met by a neon Rapunzel, a sign proclaiming Fremont the Center of the Universe, and instructions to set their watches back five minutes. From there on, it's a cross between a family-friendly bohemian enclave and a larger-than-life-size hipster sculpture garden. Don't be surprised if the cast-aluminum commuters standing near the bridge, waiting for a train that has not run for years, are wearing flamboyant clothes and headgear. Ever since **Waiting for the Interurban** was installed in 1979, whimsical Fremonters have clad them in continually changing costumes. (During the Abu Ghraib scandal someone put hoods over their heads, but it's not usually that political.) A block to the southeast, beneath the busy Aurora Bridge, the two-ton **Fremont Troll** crouches beneath a support wall, staring with his one eye and squashing a Volkswagen Bug in his left hand. Children sometimes crawl up his forearms and wedge their hands into his nostrils while parents take pictures.

2 *Scrap Art* 3:30 p.m.

You'll see a variety of outdoor art around Fremont — clown statues, dinosaur topiaries, a street sign pointing to Atlantis — but don't miss two more high spots. The seven-ton bronze **statue of Lenin** (Evanston

Avenue North and North 36th Street), rescued from an Eastern European scrapyard after the Soviet collapse, loses some of its symbolic power when adorned with lights at Christmas or dressed in drag during Gay Pride Week. Another must-see is the **Fremont Rocket** (601 North 35th Street), a reborn piece of cold war junk pointing 53 feet into the sky. Some Fremontians, still pining for their lost independence, claim that it is aimed at Seattle's City Hall.

3 *Retail Trail* 4 p.m.

Do some exploring on foot. Beneath the rocket, check out **Burnt Sugar and Frankie** (206-545-0699; burntsugarfrankie.com), selling handbags, books, and more. Walk west on 35th Street to **Theo Chocolate** (3400 Phinney Avenue North; 206-632-5100; theochocolate.com), a chocolate factory that offers tours and has a retail shop. A bit farther south, find the entrance to the **Burke-Gilman Trail** near where Phinney Avenue intersects with North Canal Street and walk southeast along the Lake Washington Ship Canal amid the joggers and cyclists. Just before you reach the Fremont Bridge, head back north on Fremont Avenue to find shops like **Jive Time Records** (3506 Fremont Avenue North; 206-632-5483; jivetimerecords.com), **Ophelia's Books** (3504 Fremont Avenue North; 206-632-3759; opheliasbooks.com)

OPPOSITE Autumn shopping at the Farmers Market in Ballard, a Seattle neighborhood with an independent streak.

BELOW Cocoa beans at Theo Chocolate in Fremont, another part of town with its own quirky identity.

and **Show Pony** (702 North 35th Street; 206-706-4188; showponyseattle.com), a clothing boutique.

4 *Fremont Fodder* 7:30 p.m.
Assess your mood and choose a place for dinner. **The Red Door** (3401 Evanston Avenue North; 206-547-7521; reddoorseattle.com; $) has outdoor patio dining year-round (think burgers and salads) and a wide selection of craft brews. Or go upscale at the **35th Street Bistro** (709 North 35th Street; 206-547-9850; 35bistro.com; $$-$$$), where you can sip a martini made with seasonal ingredients and order wine pairings with entrees like chicken confit or herb-crusted trout.

SATURDAY

5 *Eggs of the Universe* 9 a.m.
Start the day at **Silence-Heart-Nest** (3508 Fremont Place North; 206-633-5169; silenceheartnest.com; $), a vegetarian cafe. It's a total-immersion experience in itself, with sari-clad wait staff asking diners to ponder business cards printed with inspirational verses while serving up sesame waffles and Center of the Universe scrambled eggs. After breakfast, it's time to leave Fremont. Drive northwest on Leary

ABOVE The bar at King's Hardware on Ballard Avenue.

Way, which becomes Northwest 36th Street, and into Ballard, where neighborhood assertion goes in a different direction.

6 *Nordic Pride* 10:30 a.m.
Follow the mazelike layout of the surprisingly beguiling **Nordic Heritage Museum** (3014 Northwest 67th Street; 206-789-5707; nordicmuseum.org) as it snakes through three floors of a former schoolhouse, guiding you past a centuries-old fishing boat and a life-sized replica of an Icelandic sod house. Seafaring Scandinavians were the heart of old Ballard, and although ethnicities are mixed up now, the neighborhood still celebrates Norwegian Constitution Day every May 17 with a parade and much flag-waving. It was water that persuaded reluctant Ballardites to accept annexation in 1907 by a narrow margin—they needed access to Seattle's freshwater supply. Not everyone is reconciled to it even now. On the 100th anniversary, some people wore black armbands.

7 *Cohos on the Move* Noon
The nearly century-old **Hiram M. Chittenden Locks** (3015 Northwest 54th Street; 206-783-7059) help keep the salt water of Puget Sound from despoiling freshwater Lake Washington. They also lift boats from sea level to the lake's 26-foot elevation. Watch yachts and fishing boats steadily rise as the locks fill like a giant bathtub—a sight that can seem surreal.

But the irresistible flourish is the glass-lined tunnel that, if you're here in salmon spawning season, lets you spy on cohos and chinooks as they make their way up the fish ladder, a series of ascending weirs. You can press your face a few millimeters away from the fat fish, which clunk into each other, form traffic jams, and sometimes turn their vacant expressions on the humans.

8 *The Sound of Lunch* 1:30 p.m.

Ballard's southern boundary is the Washington Lake Ship Canal, its western boundary is Puget Sound, and **Ray's Cafe**, at Ray's Boathouse Restaurant (6049 Seaview Avenue Northwest; 206-789-3770; rays.com) sits right about where they meet. Grab a table on the outdoor deck and order fish for lunch.

9 *Dunes in the City* 3 p.m.

The maritime spirit feels alive at **Golden Gardens Park** (8498 Seaview Place Northwest; 206-684-4075),

arguably the loveliest picnic spot in all of Seattle, with sand dunes, a lagoon, secluded benches, occasional sightings of bald eagles, and heart-stopping views of the distant Olympic Mountains at sunset. Walk the paths, find a spot for relaxing, and chill.

10 *Hometown Ravioli* 8 p.m.

Combine Northwestern with Italian in a dinner at **Volterra** (5411 Ballard Avenue Northwest;

ABOVE Underwater windows let curious humans spy on salmon at the Hiram M. Chittenden Locks.

BELOW The Fremont Troll peers out from under the Aurora Bridge. His left hand is squashing a Volkswagen Bug.

bar. "Everyone comes here," Brian Plonsky, the bartender, said. "This has been a bar for 100 years."

SUNDAY

206-789-5100; volterrarestaurant.com; $$), where the Dungeness Crab ravioli is made using house-made pasta. Then finish out the evening with drinks in the area around Ballard Avenue Northwest. One choice is **King's Hardware** (No. 5225). Another is **Hattie's Hat** (No. 5231). Students, fishermen, professionals, and laborers gather at its hand-carved

11 *Sunday Shoppers* 11 a.m.

Ballard's eastern edge feels more contemporary, with dining, shopping, and a lively social scene. Year-round, the **Ballard Sunday Farmers Market** (Ballard Avenue between Vernon Place and 22nd Avenue; ballardfarmersmarket.wordpress.com) brings out vendors and shoppers in a scene that some Ballardites insist surpasses Seattle's well-known Pike Place Market. Spend some time people watching and checking out the quintessentially Pacific Northwestern products on offer: giant radishes, tiny potatoes called spud nuts, jugs of homemade cider, milk from purebred Boer goats, and spiced blackberry wine.

ABOVE Music at Ballard Sunday Farmers Market, which is open year-round.

OPPOSITE Golden Gardens Park, one of the loveliest places for an afternoon escape in all of Seattle.

THE BASICS

Fremont and Ballard are easily reachable from downtown. Drive a car and park to walk.

Watertown Hotel
4242 Roosevelt Way Northeast
206-826-4242
watertownseattle.com
$$
Lodging is scarce in both Fremont and Ballard; this stylish alternative is nearby in the University district.

University Inn
4140 Roosevelt Way Northeast
206-632-5055
universityinnseattle.com
$$
Another University District option.

Courtyard Seattle Downtown/Lake Union
925 Westlake Avenue North
206-213-0100
marriott.com
$$
Reliable chain hotel nearby.

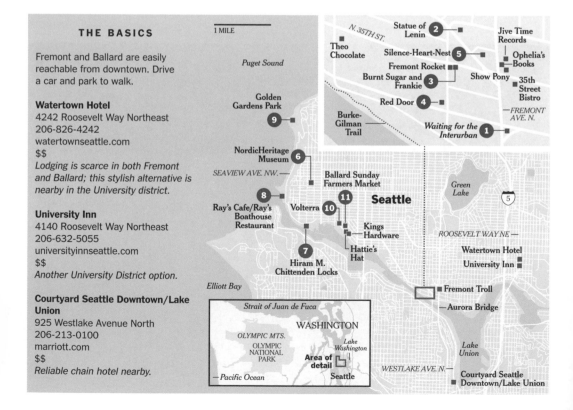

The San Juan Islands

You could spend years getting to know the more than 170 San Juan Islands of Washington, but it's easy to become acquainted with three of the biggest. Lopez, Orcas, and San Juan are jewels of the Pacific Northwest, great for sailing, kayaking, hiking, biking, diving, or just relaxing. Visit, and you'll find out how a quarrel over the killing of a farm animal in the 19th century nearly led to war, spot wildlife in a way you've probably never done before, and find yourself drifting onto island time. — BY BOB MACKIN

FRIDAY

1 *To Lopez for Dinner* 6 p.m.

After the pleasant 40-minute passage by car ferry (206-464-6400, wsdot.wa.gov/ferries) from Anacortes, Washington, to quiet Lopez Island, take a quick drive to Lopez Village for dinner. The view is fantastic from a window seat at the **Bay Café** (9 Old Post Road; 360-468-3700; bay-cafe.com; $$), and so is the food. Look out on the bay and the islands beyond as you dig into fresh local fish or locally raised beef or lamb. Make a reservation in advance. Residents of other islands make the trip to Lopez just to dine.

2 *To Orcas for Dessert* 7:30 p.m.

After dinner, head back to the ferry landing. The timetable is often more theoretical than actual, so your boat to Orcas Island is likely to be late. But after 30 minutes across the water and a 25-minute drive, you'll be at the **Rosario Resort & Spa** (1400 Rosario Road, Eastsound; 360-376-2222; rosarioresort.com). The waterside resort is built around the Moran mansion, which was completed in 1909 by a ship-building magnate and former mayor of Seattle. Order dessert in the lounge — selections change often, but one day's standout was a marionberry cobbler. A special treat is the music room, where the musician and mansion curator, Christopher Peacock, offers tours and demonstrates the 1,972-pipe organ.

SATURDAY

3 *Sea to Summit* 10 a.m.

At 2,409 feet, Mount Constitution on Orcas Island is the highest point in the San Juans. The 15-minute drive to the top is full of hairpin turns on a narrow road. But if the weather cooperates, you'll be rewarded with breathtaking views as far as Vancouver, British Columbia; the Cascade and Olympic ranges; and the islands and ships in Puget Sound. Mount Constitution is part of **Moran State Park** (3572 Olga Road, Olga; parks.wa.gov), granted to Washington in 1921 by Robert Moran, whose mansion you visited last night. He built that house when doctors told him to retire early, but he wound up living to 86, thanks, it is said, to the serene beauty of Orcas.

4 *Pig War* Noon

Take the boat to San Juan Island to hear the strange tale of the Pig War. In 1859, an American settler killed a Hudson's Bay Company pig. Within two months, more than 400 American troops, dispatched to protect the settler from arrest, faced off against some 2,000 British soldiers, sailors, and marines. But no shots were fired, and small detachments from each nation remained until 1872, when Kaiser Wilhelm I, acting as arbitrator, awarded the islands to the United States, not British Canada. Today, the British and American camps make up the **San Juan Island**

OPPOSITE The view from the highest vantage point in the San Juans, Mount Constitution on Orcas Island.

BELOW Boats docked near Eastsound on Orcas Island.

National Historical Park (360-378-2902; nps.gov/sajh). During summer, it comes alive as local history buffs don period costumes for historical recreations.

5 *Whale Watch, Minus Boat* 1 p.m.

Pack a picnic, keep binoculars handy, be patient. That's the three-pronged strategy for enjoying your time at **Lime Kiln Point State Park** (1567 Westside Road, Friday Harbor; 360-378-2044; parks.wa.gov). The 36-acre park has Douglas fir, arbutus and even cactuses along its forest trails. But from late spring to early fall, it may be the world's best place to see orca whales from land. Park your car in the lot and hike the lighthouse trail to the rocky outcrop in the shadow of the Lime Kiln Point lighthouse. Set up your picnic on the rocks and watch for the shiny black and white orcas. If you're lucky, they'll come close enough that they can also see you. If you miss a pod on parade, you're still likely to see seals and eagles. The lighthouse, built in 1919, is now a whale behavior research center. In summer, park staff members are often available to provide information on the whales and also offer evening tours of the lighthouse; day tours can be arranged.

6 *Purple Pleasure* 4 p.m.

Lavender farming has made its way to the San Juans, so ask if there's lavender oil available when you choose hot stone massage, Swedish massage, reiki, or all three at **Lavendera Day Spa** (440 Spring Street, Friday Harbor; 360-378-3637; lavenderadayspa.com), ideal after a spell of hiking and sitting on rocks. When you've achieved blissful relaxation, make a visit to the **Pelindaba Lavender Farm** (33 Hawthorne Lane, off Wold Road; 360-378-4248; pelindabalavender.com), where you're welcome to tour the rippling purple in flowering season.

7 *San Juan Locavore* 6 p.m.

This is Washington, and salmon should be on the menu. Expect it at **Coho Restaurant** (120 Nichols Street, Friday Harbor; 360-378-6330; cohorestaurant.com; $$$), along with shellfish from the Straits of Juan de Fuca, meat from a Lopez Island farm, and local produce from several island growers. The desserts are house-made, and the wine list is filled with vintages from Washington, Oregon, and California.

8 *Sculptured Trail* 8 p.m.

A visit to the **IMA Sculpture Park** (Roche Harbor Road, Roche Harbor, overlooking Westcott Bay), a location of the **San Juan Islands Museum of Art & Sculpture** (360-370-5050; sjima.org), is a great way to spend the late, late afternoon. Scattered along the trails are more than 100 sculptures (by artists from the Pacific Northwest and beyond) looking magical in their open-air setting as the light fades.

SUNDAY

9 *Whale Talk* 10 a.m.

A modest two-story building, the former Odd Fellows Hall in Friday Harbor, is the home of the **Whale Museum** (62 First Street North; 360-378-4710; whale-museum.org), a remarkable collection of whale photographs, skeletons, and even some brains. Take a few minutes to listen to the library of whale vocalizations in a phone booth.

10 *A Drink of Lavender* 11 a.m.

The proprietors of the lavender farm you visited yesterday have cleverly opened the **Pelindaba Lavender shop** in downtown Friday Harbor near the ferry terminal (First Street; 360-378-4248; pelindabalavender.com). The lavender-infused lemonade is the perfect drink to quaff on a summer day's cruise among the San Juans as you return to the mainland.

OPPOSITE Sunset and serenity in the San Juans.

ABOVE A busy ferry system, carrying passengers and cars, keeps the islands connected and tied to the mainland.

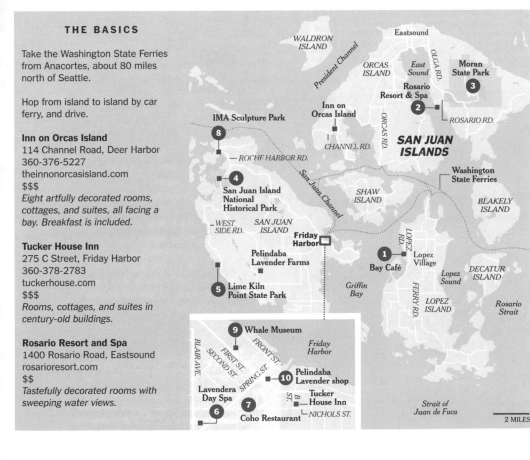

THE BASICS

Take the Washington State Ferries from Anacortes, about 80 miles north of Seattle.

Hop from island to island by car ferry, and drive.

Inn on Orcas Island
114 Channel Road, Deer Harbor
360-376-5227
theinnonorcasisland.com
$$$
Eight artfully decorated rooms, cottages, and suites, all facing a bay. Breakfast is included.

Tucker House Inn
275 C Street, Friday Harbor
360-378-2783
tuckerhouse.com
$$$
Rooms, cottages, and suites in century-old buildings.

Rosario Resort and Spa
1400 Rosario Road, Eastsound
rosarioresort.com
$$
Tastefully decorated rooms with sweeping water views.

WALDRON ISLAND

Eastsound

President Channel

ORCAS ISLAND

East Sound

OLGA RD.

Moran State Park

3

Rosario Resort & Spa

2

ROSARIO RD.

Inn on Orcas Island

ORCAS RD.

CHANNEL RD.

SAN JUAN ISLANDS

IMA Sculpture Park

8

ROCHE HARBOR RD.

San Juan Channel

Washington State Ferries

4

San Juan Island National Historical Park

SHAW ISLAND

BLAKELY ISLAND

WEST SIDE RD.

SAN JUAN ISLAND

Friday Harbor

Pelindaba Lavender Farms

Bay Café

LOPEZ RD.

1 Lopez Village

DECATUR ISLAND

5 Lime Kiln Point State Park

Griffin Bay

Lopez Sound

LOPEZ ISLAND

FERRY RD.

Rosario Strait

9 Whale Museum

Friday Harbor

BLAIR AVE.

FIRST ST.

SECOND ST.

FRONT ST.

SPRING ST.

Pelindaba Lavender shop

10

Lavendera Day Spa

6

7

B ST.

Tucker House Inn

NICHOLS ST.

Coho Restaurant

Strait of Juan de Fuca

2 MILES

Vancouver

Vancouver, British Columbia, is often heralded as one of the world's most livable cities. It is blessed with a snowcapped mountain backdrop and crystal blue harbors. It is a gateway to the Inside Passage — the marvelous maze of glacier-carved fjords and forested islands that are a cruise lover's delight. In the city itself and close by, outdoor lovers will find miles of scenic hiking and biking trails. But what really sets Vancouver apart is its urban density. With sprawl kept in check by geography, the city thinks vertically. Neighborhoods overlap, apartments rise. That seems to heighten the city's international mix. — BY DENNY LEE

FRIDAY

1 *Assembly Point* 4 p.m.

Blame the great outdoors, but Vancouver lacks a central square where citizens turn inward and visitors feel they have arrived. A quirky stand-in is the **Mount Pleasant** district, which is becoming cooler by the minute. Scattered among dingy bingo parlors are trendy boutiques like **Lark** (2315 Main Street; 604-879-5275; lark.me), which carries Chimala jeans from Japan, and **Jewellerbau** (2408 Main Street; 604-872-7759; jewellerbau.blogspot.com), with modern industrial jewelry. The local designer Hajnalka Mandula spins lacy and brooding finery for *Twilight* goths at **Mandula** (206 Carall Street; 604-568-9211; mandula.com). An anchor is the artist-run **Western Front** (303 East Eighth Avenue; 604-876-9343; front.bc.ca), which has galleries, stages, and arch architecture. Look up while you're there: those are the North Shore Mountains looming over the faux cornice.

2 *Pigging Out* 7:30 p.m.

With salmon-rich waters out front and heritage pig farms out back, locavore eating is a way of life in Vancouver. The barn-to-bistro ethos is buoyed by

Refuel (1944 West Fourth Avenue; 604-288-7905; refuelrestaurant.com; $$), a casual restaurant in the affluent Kitsilano district. Start with an irresistible bowl of spiced pork ribs and offal, rubbed with cayenne, citric acid, paprika, and other spices and then deep-fried to crunchy bliss. Your cardiologist won't understand. For the main course, a recent favorite included salmon (wild and local, of course), grilled and served in a pool of fragrant leeks and clams.

3 *Club Corner* 10 p.m.

Vancouver isn't known for nighttime debauchery, thanks partly to tough liquor laws. If you insist on getting dolled up, a party train of 20-somethings forms along Granville Street, a still-seedy strip with a cluster of velvet-roped bars like **Granville Room** (957 Granville Street; 604-633-0056; granvilleroom.ca), which has a handsome interior of brick walls and chandeliers. A skip away is Davie Street, the city's gay strip, with plenty of night spots to choose from.

SATURDAY

4 *Granola Island* 10 a.m.

Take a water taxi across False Creek to the tiny peninsula known as **Granville Island** (granvilleisland.com), which has a popular food market brimming with farmers, butchers, and fishmongers.

OPPOSITE Outdoor lunch on Granville Island, with a metropolitan view across False Creek.

RIGHT Fresh merchandise at Lobster Man, a vendor at the popular food market on Granville Island. The market brims with farmers, butchers, fish sellers, and artisans.

It also has a hippie side—from yoga and crafts studios to a pottery gallery and theater. Grab a multigrain loaf at **Terra Breads** (terrabreads.com) and stroll through the island's jam-packed aisles and alleys. Look for the **Lobster Man** (1807 Mast Tower Road; 604-687-4531; lobsterman.com), with its tanks of kayak-size lobsters, and the **Artisan Sake Maker** (1339 Railspur Alley; 604-685-7253; artisansakemaker.com), which makes small batches of junmai sake on the premises and, for a couple of dollars, will let you taste.

5 *Creative Curries* 12:30 p.m.

Mark Bittman, the *New York Times* columnist and longtime food writer, once called **Vij's** (1480 West 11th Avenue; 604-736-6664; vijsrestaurant.ca; $$$), which serves regional interpretations of familiar Indian foods, "among the finest Indian restaurants in the world." But for lunch, pop in next door to its colorful sister, **Vij's Rangoli** (1488 West 11th Avenue; 604-736-5711; vijsrangoli.ca; $$), which looks like a takeout diner. Memorable combinations included a goat meat and jackfruit curry with a coconut cabbage salad.

6 *Photoconceptualism* 2 p.m.

Before Vancouver's film industry was nicknamed Hollywood North, the city's cultural high point may have been the Vancouver School of post-conceptual photography, led by artists like Jeff Wall and Roy Arden, who blurred the line between documentation and artifice. The school lives on at a pair of galleries in the South Granville district. **Monte Clark Gallery** (2339 Granville Street; 604-730-5000; monteclarkgallery.com) represents Arden, Stephen Waddell, and others. Down the block is the **Equinox Gallery** (2321 Granville Street; 604-736-2405; equinoxgallery.com), where you're likely to see Fred Herzog's vintage mid-20th-century photographs, reprinted using color-saturated inkjets.

7 *Where Olympians Trod* 4 p.m.

Before hosting the Winter Olympics in 2010, Vancouver built a billion-dollar waterfront Olympic Village to house the athletes. Afterward, it reinvented the jumble of elegant towers as **Millennium Water**, a new residential district clustered around a central square. The recession and housing bust hurt sales, but the neighborhood is beating with a bohemian pulse. Have an uber-healthy snack at **OrganicLives** (1829 Quebec Street; 778-588-7777; organiclives.org; $), where you may hear customers raving about the macaroons. Then drop in at the **Beaumont** (316 West Fifth Avenue; 604-733-3783; thebeaumontstudios.com), a 7,000-square-foot, two-story collective of studios

ABOVE The seawall path at Stanley Park, a favorite spot for strolling, running, and biking.

in a former denture manufacturing plant, to watch the artists work and see what's for sale.

8 *Neo-Fusion* 8 p.m.

From Tokyo-style izakayas to banh mi cafes, the flavors of Asia are well represented in Vancouver. The large Asian population has also raised the bar on fusion. For haute interpretations of humble Thai dishes, **Maenam** (1938 West Fourth Avenue; 604-730-5579; maenam.ca; $$) has drawn comparisons to the Michelin-starred Nahm in London, where its chef and owner apprenticed. The pink-and-bamboo spot draws a foodie set with playful dishes like spicy braised duck with sweet longans, confit potatoes, and cucumber relish. Another option is **Bao Bei** (163 Keefer Street; 604-688-0876; bao-bei.ca; $$), an upscale Chinese brasserie in Chinatown.

9 *Drink Sets* 10:30 p.m.

A smattering of high-concept watering holes — the kind serving wine and beer flights — have opened in Gastown. Popular with the Hollywood North set is the **Alibi Room** (157 Alexander Street; 604-623-3383; alibi.ca), a loft-like space with wooden

ABOVE Make your way to Maenam for haute interpretations of humble Thai dishes.

BELOW Its setting on the calm waters of the Burrard Inlet, a long coastal fjord, made Vancouver a prosperous port.

tables and a long list of bottled and draft beers. Wine imbibers head to the **Salt Tasting Room** (45 Blood Alley; 604-633-1912; salttastingroom.com), a cellar-like bar with a large chalkboard menu that lists eclectic wines, cheeses, and exotic cured meats.

SUNDAY

10 *The Rainforest* 10 a.m.

To experience one of the largest and most diverse urban parks in North America—and be reminded that this area is naturally a temperate rain forest—spend a few hours at **Stanley Park**

(vancouver.ca/parks/parks/stanley), a gloriously green peninsula. A six-mile walking and cycling bicycle path on a sea wall rings the park's 1,000 acres of gardens and majestic cedar, hemlock, and fir trees, tracing much of the seafront. Bicycle rentals are close by at several shops, including **Denman Bike Shop** (710 Denman Street; 604-685-9755; denmanbikeshop.com) and **Bayshore Bike Rental** (745 Denman Street; 604-688-2453; bayshorebikerentals.com). Don't miss the totem pole display at Brockton Point, which according to the park's Web site is the most visited tourist attraction in British Columbia.

ABOVE Vij's Rangoli, the more colorful, affordable sister restaurant of the acclaimed Vij's next door.

OPPOSITE Western Front, a gallery and performance space in the gentrifying bohemian Mount Pleasant district.

THE BASICS

Vancouver is 140 miles north of Seattle, Washington. Flights arrive from cities around the world. Use public transportation in the city; drive a car for exploring.

Fairmont Pacific Rim
1038 Canada Place
604-695-5300
fairmont.com/pacificrim
$$$
High-style and new in 2010. You will want to stay for the view alone.

Shangri-La Hotel Vancouver
1128 West Georgia Street
604-689-1120
shangri-la.com/vancouver
$$$$
Zen-like rooms and polished service.

Loden Vancouver
1177 Melville Street
604-669-5060
theloden.com
$$$
Bright and stylish.

Whistler

Whistler, British Columbia, North America's biggest ski resort, invites a listing of statistics. A mile of vertical drop, 37 lifts, 8,100 skiable acres, 200 runs spread across its two mountains, Whistler and Blackcomb. In 2010, the Winter Olympics, lured by all that snow, brought skiers to town from around the planet. But this steep mountain valley is home to a diversity that has nothing to do with international competitions. Walk down the main promenade and see everyone from rich urban castaways and old-school hippies to stylish French-speaking Québécois and weathered dropouts shouldering skis the size of ironing boards. It makes Whistler feel worldly and cosmopolitan, even when gold medals aren't being handed out. — BY CHRISTOPHER SOLOMON

FRIDAY

1 *Cultural Powder* 4 p.m.

Before you hit the snow, pay homage to the ground underneath: for thousands of years, Whistler Valley was the hunting and berry-picking grounds of the Squamish and Lil'wat First Nations. Explore the rich history of the land you'll be skiing at the **Squamish Lil'wat Cultural Center** (4584 Blackcomb Way; 866-441-7522; slcc.ca). While the hand-carved canoes, baskets, and smoked-salmon bannocks (kind of a local panini) are diverting, what really makes this 30,000-square-foot museum shine are the friendly aboriginal "youth ambassadors," who welcome visitors with native songs and totem-carving exhibitions.

2 *Carbo Load* 8 p.m.

It's easy to spend money in Whistler. Those watching their loonies should follow the local ski bums to **Pasta Lupino** (4368 Main Street, Whistler Village North; 604-905-0400; pastalupino.com; $$). Tucked near a 7-Eleven at the edge of the resort, the small, cheery restaurant serves fantastic fresh pastas with homemade Bolognese and Alfredo sauces. And the budget-friendly prices for pastas, soup or salad, and freshly baked focaccia make it easy to indulge.

3 *Pre-Ski Cocktails* 10 p.m.

Maybe it's all the snow, but Whistler doesn't skimp when it comes to watering holes. They run the spectrum from hockey sports bars to "ice" bars where you can chill your drink between sips. For the latter, head to the august **Bearfoot Bistro** (4121 Village Green; 604-932-3433; bearfootbistro.com; $$$$). There you can have your flute of B.C. bubbly with a side of tinkling piano music and appetizers by Melissa Craig, an award-winning chef. For a more boisterous setting, stomp your Sorel boots over to **Crystal Lounge** (4154 Village Green; 604-938-1081), a basement bar in the village center festooned with TVs and hockey sweaters. It's packed with local skiers and boarders eating chicken wings and drinking pitchers of Granville Island English Bay Pale Ale.

SATURDAY

4 *Where to Schuss* 8 a.m.

Which mountain, Whistler or Blackcomb? Skiers used to have to pick one, but thanks to the **Peak 2 Peak Gondola**, this whole behemoth resort is now within easy reach. If the snow is good, Whistler will be packed, so here's a plan. In the morning, avoid the crowded Village Gondola at Whistler and go to

OPPOSITE The Peak 2 Peak Gondola links Whistler and Blackcomb Mountains, the two peaks whose 8,100 skiable acres make Whistler North America's largest ski area.

BELOW Quattro at Whistler, a spot for Italian cuisine.

Blackcomb's base area to ride the Wizard Express and Solar Coaster Express lifts. The lines are shorter, and they get you right up Blackcomb Mountain. Warm up on the gentle Jersey Cream run and check the lighted boards to see which mountaintop lifts are open. When you reach the top, take your pick of ego powder runs like Showcase or the mettle-testing Couloir Extreme. When you're ready, swoop across to Whistler on the Peak 2 Peak, which is an event in itself: the cabins, which fit 28 passengers, dangle up to 1,427 feet high over a span of almost three miles.

5 *Belgian Waffles and BBQ* Noon

Come lunchtime, the huge lodges can feel like rush hour. So seek out the lesser-known on-

mountain restaurants. On Blackcomb, the **Crystal Hut** (whistlerblackcomb.com/todo/MountainDining) is a small log cabin near the top of the Crystal Chair that serves Belgian waffles all day and lunch specialties from a wood-burning oven. On Whistler, the **Chic Pea** near the top of the Garbanzo Express lift serves toasted sandwiches, pizza, and barbecue on its outdoor deck.

6 *Heaven on Skis* 2 p.m.

If the sun is smiling, head over to Blackcomb's **7th Heaven** area, which has great views and is warmed by the afternoon's rays. It also has something for everyone: long, bumpy runs like Sunburn and Angel Dust, harder-to-reach powder stashes like Lakeside Bowl, and lingering intermediate groomers like Hugh's Heaven and Cloud Nine, which seem to meander to the valley floor.

7 *Boards at the Source* 4 p.m.

Independent ski and snowboard makers like Igneous Skis and Never Summer Snowboards have sprung up all over in recent years. One of the oldest is **Prior Snowboards and Skis** (104-1410 Alpha Lake

ABOVE The new timber-and-stone Nita Lake Lodge.

LEFT The shooting range for biathletes at Whistler Olympic Park, a sprawling Nordic playground.

Road; 604-935-1923; priorskis.com), founded 20 years ago in Whistler. Every Wednesday at 5 p.m. and Saturday at 4 p.m., the company offers free one-hour tours of the factory floor. See how fiberglass layers are glued with epoxy and pressed together under enormous heat and pressure to create a springy, responsive snow toy.

8 *Playtime for All* 6:30 p.m.

A ski resort can be tricky for parents. At day's end the kids are still wound up, but the adults are ready for a cocktail. Before you push off for a good pour, drop the kids off for more vertical fun at the **Core** (4010 Whistler Conference Centre; 604-905-7625; whistlercore.com), a climbing gym and fitness center in the middle of the village with an indoor wall. Try the nightly Climb & Dine program for kids — three hours of supervised rock climbing and a pizza dinner. Reservations required.

9 *Dinner for Grownups* 7 p.m.

Yes, you had Italian last night, but this is different. The snug and romantic **Quattro at Whistler** (Pinnacle International Hotel, 4319 Main Street; 604-905-4844; quattrorestaurants.com; $$$) serves entrees like glazed wild salmon with orange, honey, pickled fennel, and baby arugula. And yes, there

ABOVE Nordic skiing maneuvers on the biathlon course at Whistler Olympic Park.

BELOW At Prior Snowboards and Skis, see how fiberglass layers are bonded together under enormous heat and pressure to create a springy, responsive snow toy.

is pasta. One example: ravioli made with smoked pork cheek and ricotta, served with parsnip chips.

10 *What Wipeout?* 9:30 p.m.

Everyone from weary locals to visiting ski-film royalty (sometimes just returned from nearby backcountry heli-skiing) ends up at the **Garibaldi Lift Company**, fondly known as GLC (4165 Springs Lane; 604-905-2220). The crowd is big and rowdy, favoring beer by the pitcher. Count on a band or D.J. playing, a fire roaring, and hockey on the flat screen. With its floor-to-ceiling windows overlooking the slopes, the GLC is the kind of place to embellish the day's stories and make outsize promises for tomorrow.

SUNDAY

11 *Nordic Dreams* 11 a.m.

Yesterday you barreled down Whistler Mountain pretending to be Lindsey Vonn. Now go for the Walter Mitty experience. About 12 miles southwest of the resort, in the Callaghan Valley, is the **Whistler Olympic Park** (5 Callaghan Valley Road; 877-764-2455; whistlerolympicpark.com), a sprawling Nordic playground. Strap on a pair of cross-country skis, toss a firearm over your shoulder, and become a biathlete for an hour. On the open trails and snow fields among towering, moss-draped hemlocks, there's plenty of room to fulfill your Nordic gold-medal fantasies.

ABOVE A bright day on Blackcomb Mountain.

OPPOSITE Drop the kids off at the Core, a new climbing gym and fitness center that has a rock-climbing wall.

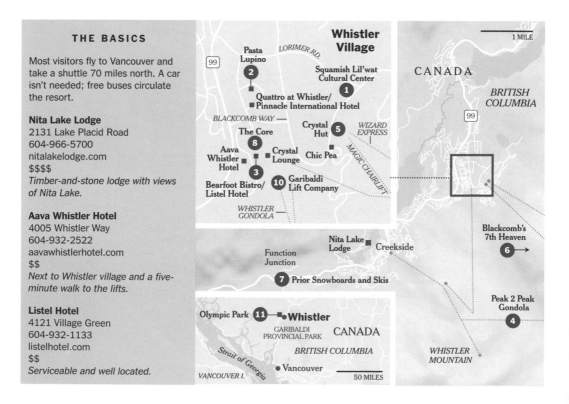

THE BASICS

Most visitors fly to Vancouver and take a shuttle 70 miles north. A car isn't needed; free buses circulate the resort.

Nita Lake Lodge
2131 Lake Placid Road
604-966-5700
nitalakelodge.com
$$$$
Timber-and-stone lodge with views of Nita Lake.

Aava Whistler Hotel
4005 Whistler Way
604-932-2522
aavawhistlerhotel.com
$$
Next to Whistler village and a five-minute walk to the lifts.

Listel Hotel
4121 Village Green
604-932-1133
listelhotel.com
$$
Serviceable and well located.

The Okanagan Valley

Glacier-formed and fertile, the Okanagan Valley is the British Columbia of popular imagination, all steep-walled mountain valleys and spectacular snow-fed lakes. But there's a bonus — it's also a wine region, with more than 100 wineries and counting, striving to hold its own with the famous California valleys to the south. Part old-fashioned summer lake resort, part cycling center, and traditionally fruit-growing country, the valley is changing fast as cherry orchards and nut farms lose ground to the vineyards and as tourism grows along with the grapes. — BY BONNIE TSUI

FRIDAY

1 *A Sheet of Blue* 2 p.m.

Kelowna, the Okanagan Valley's gateway city, combines a pedestrian-friendly waterfront and mountain views with tracts of gas stations and big-box stores. Head straight for Lake Okanagan, a sheet of blue that is the defining signature of this region, and rent a kayak from the marina at the **Hotel Eldorado** (500 Cook Road, Kelowna; 250-763-3625; hoteleldoradokelowna.com). Sailboats and canoes skim the water as you paddle, while back at the marina, margarita drinkers from the hotel bar watch the buzzing watercraft leaving the slips. As you near the middle of the lake, the steep walls of the valley rise up dramatically on either side, one shade of green fusing subtly into the next. Look for the telltale corduroy of the vineyards.

2 *Go to the Grapes* 4 p.m.

A wine tour of the 120-mile-long Okanagan Valley satisfies many tastes. The southern end delivers big reds like merlots and cabernet sauvignons that are robust and jammy, with soft, pleasing finishes. In the north, near Kelowna, crisp, fresh whites have fruity characteristics reminiscent of the orchards they are displacing. Drive a few miles out of town to the **Cedar Creek Estate Winery** (5445 Lakeshore Road; 250-764 8866; cedarcreek.bc.ca), where you'll find vines producing pinot noir, pinot gris, chardonnay,

gewürztraminer, ehrenfelser, riesling, and merlot grapes. The tasting room and a terrace restaurant occupy a Mediterranean-style building, and as a tourist experience, the winery has a polished, yet intimate air, with service that puts it on a par with most wineries of northern California.

3 *Where It Came From* 7 p.m.

Long before the current bloom of wineries, the Okanagan Valley was known for its produce, and in recent years small vegetable farmers have begun supplying discriminating buyers from lovingly tended plots. **RauDZ Regional Table** (1560 Water Street, Kelowna; 250-868-8805; raudz.com; $$$) takes advantage of this local bounty, as well as meats and fish raised or caught nearby, in cuisine featuring regional and seasonal ingredients. Its ever-changing menu lists the origin of the main ingredient in each dish — salmon from the Fraser River, ling cod from Queen Charlotte's Sound north of Vancouver Island, lamb tenderloins from Okanagan, wild boar from nearby Enderby.

SATURDAY

4 *Shoreline Drive* 9 a.m.

Start early to cross the bridge across Lake Okanagan in Kelowna and drive 40 miles south on its western shore to **Penticton**. You'll have lake and winery views and a good perspective on Okanagan Mountain, a giant rock rising dramatically out of the water. At Penticton, scones, pastries, eggs, and coffee await at the **Bench Artisan Food Market** (368 Vancouver Avenue, Penticton; 250-492-2222;

OPPOSITE Mission Hill, the valley's largest winery.

RIGHT Fruit for sale along Highway 97. Before wine took center stage in the Okanagan Valley, orchards were supreme.

thebenchmarket.com; $$). You have come to the end of Lake Okanagan, but not the end of the valley, which stretches south along two smaller lakes. You have also reached the fertile Naramata Bench, just north of town on the lake's east side.

5 *Fruit Basket* 11 a.m.

As you drive north toward **Naramata**, the center of the Okanagan wine region, every visible square mile of land you see seems to be growing, blooming, bearing fruit. Tucked away among the wineries, at the ends of dirt roads, are small specialty producers: a blueberry farm here, a fruit orchard there. Taste the two themes combined at **Elephant Island Orchard Wines** (2730 Aikins Loop, Naramata; 250-496-5522; elephantislandwine.com), which specializes in fruit wines: cherry, crabapple, pear, raspberry. Some are for dessert, but others are dry dinner wines. Next make your way to **Lake Breeze Winery** (Sammet Road, Naramata; 250-496-5659; lakebreeze.ca) for a taste of icy whites. And in the town of Naramata, stop at the **Naramata General Store** (225 Robinson Avenue,

ABOVE The lights of Kelowna glow on Lake Okanagan.

BELOW The Naramata Heritage Inn.

OPPOSITE The Lake Okanagan view at Quails' Gate Estate Winery, which specializes in pinot noir and chardonnay.

Naramata; 250-496-5450) for a deli sandwich or an ice cream cone and a choice of many local wines for sale.

6 *The Pioneer* 1 p.m.

There is no road around the lake. That mountain —in Okanagan Mountain Provincial Park, and happy home for mountain goats—is in the way. So drive back to Penticton and then repeat your morning drive in the reverse direction. There are plenty of wineries along the way. You may want to visit one of the oldest in the valley, **Sumac Ridge Estate Winery** (17403 Highway 97 North, Summerland; 250-494-0451; sumacridge.com), which released its first vintage in 1980 and was the first to introduce blends with traditional Bordeaux varietals.

7 *The Biggest* 3 p.m

A few miles shy of the lake bridge, you'll come to the valley's largest winery, **Mission Hill Family Estates** (1730 Mission Hill Road, Kelowna; 800-957-9911; missionhillwinery.com), which has big buildings, a big and thriving business, and a breathtaking setting. This is a temple to wine, with manicured grounds, a concert amphitheater, a reception room with a Chagall tapestry, a terrace restaurant set high above the valley, and a state-of-the-art tasting room. Tours are offered at several different prices and levels of access.

8 *Vinotherapy* 5 p.m

Feeling a bit weary from all the driving and tasting? Revitalize at **Beyond Wrapture** (in the Coast Capri Hotel, 1171 Harvey Avenue Richter Street, Kelowna; 250-860-6060; kelownaspa.ca), a day spa next to a shopping center. Its vinotherapy massages take advantage of antioxidants found in local grapes, using seeds, skins, wine, and honey.

9 *Dine by the Lake* 7 p.m.

Cross the bridge again for the short drive to **Quails' Gate Estate Winery** (3303 Boucherie Road, Kelowna; 250-769-4451; quailsgate.com). It was a valley pioneer and specializes in chardonnays and

pinot noir. More to the point tonight, it is the home of the lakefront **Old Vines Restaurant** ($$$), where the menu offers multiple excellent choices. And of course, wines will be recommended to complement your roasted sirloin with saffron pearl couscous, black olive sauce, and pomegranate reduction, or Yukon Arctic char with vegetables and citrus-mustard cream.

SUNDAY

10 *Cycle B.C.* 9 a.m.

Breakfast on a spinach and cheddar omelet or a BC Benedict, with sockeye salmon, at the **Bohemian Cafe & Catering Company** (524 Bernard Avenue, Kelowna; 250-862-3517; bohemiancater.com/cafe;

$$). Then meet up with **Monashee Adventure Tours** (1591 Highland Drive North, Kelowna; 888-762-9253; monasheeadventuretours.com; reserve in advance) for a bicycle tour. Biking is big in the Okanagan; extensive trail networks crisscross the hills and mountains above the valley. A challenging 108-mile trail follows an abandoned section of the Kettle Valley Railway through terraced slopes (you can also hike the trail). Laid-back cruiser routes wind through provincial parks around the lakeshore. Choose your preference and pedal away.

THE BASICS

Fly into Kelowna International Airport or drive four hours from Vancouver.

A car is essential for your wine tour.

Hotel Eldorado
500 Cook Road, Kelowna
250-763-7500
hoteleldoradokelowna.com
$$
On the lake, with private boardwalk and marina.

Naramata Heritage Inn
3625 First Street, Naramata
866-617-1188
naramatainn.com
$$$
Polished wood floors, antique furnishings, and a spa.

Cove Lakeside Resort
4205 Gellatly Road, West Kelowna
877-762-2683
covelakeside.com
$$$$
On the lake's edge, with a pool and boat or kayak rentals.

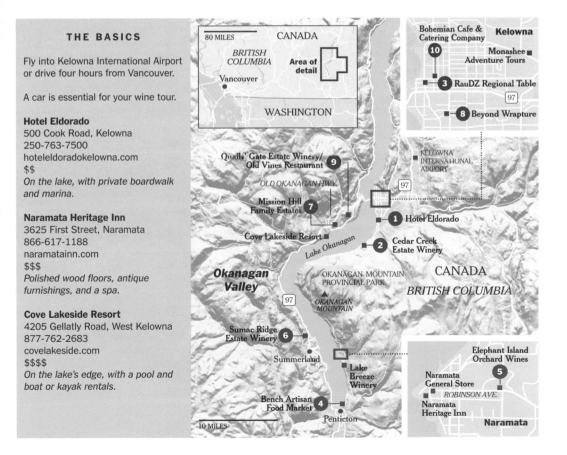

Boise

Boise, Idaho, once ruled by the bait-and-bullet crowd, has embraced the Lycra lifestyle. Sitting at the junction of the arid plateau of the high desert and the western foothills of the Rocky Mountains, Boise, Idaho's capital, offers all the outdoor advantages of more ballyhooed Western towns but with less, well, ballyhoo. Boise may have a population of more than 200,000, but it is still a mining and farming town at heart, and it attracts active professionals and young families who will tell you that theirs is a great hometown—just don't let too many people know. They wouldn't want those trailheads or hot springs to get too crowded. A rejuvenated downtown and a budding arts community mean that after a day of rafting on the Payette River, mountain biking in the foothills, or carving at Bogus Basin Ski Resort you don't have to turn in once the sun fades behind the Snake River.
— BY MATTHEW PREUSCH

FRIDAY

1 *The Idaho Story* 4 p.m.

It's best to educate before you recreate, so check out the pioneer days reconstructions and Lewis and Clark artifacts at the **Idaho Historical Museum** (610 North Julia Davis Drive; 208-334-2120; history.idaho.gov/museum.html) in **Julia Davis Park**. From there, walk down the **Boise River Greenbelt** (cityofboise.org), a much-loved and gloriously scenic public corridor of parks and trails snug against the Boise River. It stretches for 23 miles, but you won't be going that far tonight.

2 *Big Game* 7 p.m.

Emerge at the **Cottonwood Grille** (913 West River Street; 208-333-9800; cottonwoodgrille.com; $$) to reward yourself with drinks and dinner. Have a cocktail or a glass of wine on the patio overlooking the river and, of course, cottonwoods. Check out the game menu. This is your chance to try elk sirloin, bison with cabernet sauce, or grilled pheasant. If

OPPOSITE Rafting on the South Fork of the Payette River north of Boise.

RIGHT Join the Boiseans browsing amid carrots and lettuces near the Capitol dome at the Capital City Public Market.

you're feeling more conventional, there's always the pasta or Idaho trout.

SATURDAY

3 *Breakfast Builders* 8 a.m.

Put your name on the list at **Goldy's Breakfast Bistro** (108 South Capitol Boulevard; 208-345-4100; goldysbreakfastbistro.com; $$) and stroll two blocks north to the domed Capitol to contemplate the statue of Governor Frank Steunenberg. He was killed in 1905 by a bomb planted near his garden gate; the perpetrators were enraged by his rough handling of labor uprisings in upstate mines. But don't let that assassination ruin your appetite. Return to Goldy's and examine the menu to see which elements of the build-your-own breakfast you'd like to have with your scrambled eggs. Red flannel hash? Black beans? Salmon cake? Blueberry pancake? Be creative.

4 *Bumper Crop* 10 a.m.

Join stroller-pushing Boiseans gathered near the Capitol dome at the **Capital City Public Market** (280 North 8th Street; capitalcitypublicmarket.com). Browse amid the lettuces—not to mention the fruit, flowers, desserts, and art glass—and reflect that Idaho grows more than potatoes.

5 *Basque Brawn* 11 a.m.

A century ago, Basque shepherds tended flocks in the grassy foothills around Boise. Today the mayor and many other prominent Idahoans claim Basque heritage. Learn about aspects of the Basques' culture,

ABOVE Downtown and the Boise Mountains.

OPPOSITE Hikers, runners, and cyclists share the 130 miles of paths in the Ridge to Rivers trail system.

including their love of a stirring strongman competition, at the **Basque Museum and Cultural Center** (611 Grove Street; 208-343-2671; basquemuseum.com). Don't drop the theme when you leave the museum in search of lunch. Grab a table at **Bar Gernika Basque Pub & Eatery** (202 South Capitol Boulevard; 208-344-2175; bargernika.com; $). The lamb grinder is a safe bet, but for something more spirited, brave the beef tongue in tomato and pepper sauce. Wash it down with Basque cider.

6 *Rapid Transit* 1:30 p.m.

Join the weekend exodus of pickups hauling A.T.V.'s and Subarus bearing bikes as they head over the brown foothills of the Boise Front to outdoor adventure. Drive 45 minutes north to Horseshoe Bend and hook up with **Cascade Raft and Kayaking** (7050 Highway 55; 208-793-2221; cascaderaft.com) for a half-day raft trip through Class III and IV rapids on the Lower South Fork of the Payette River. There's also a milder trip with Class II and III rapids. If even that seems like whiter water than you're up for, stay in town, buy an inner tube, and join lazy locals floating down the relatively placid Boise River for six miles

between **Barber Park** (4049 Eckert Road) and **Ann Morrison Park** (1000 Americana Boulevard). Avoid the river if the water is high.

7 *How about a Potato-tini?* 7 p.m.

Swap your swimsuit for town wear and find an outdoor table on the pedestrian plaza outside the overtly cosmopolitan **Red Feather Lounge** (246 North 8th Street; 208-429-6340; justeatlocal.com/ redfeather; $$), where the focus is on post-classic cocktails, like the Tangerine Rangoon: Plymouth gin, fresh tangerine juice and homemade pomegranate grenadine. Pair that with sockeye salmon or truffled duck egg pizza, and you might forget that you're in laid-back Boise. That is, until you spot the guy in running shorts and a fanny pack sitting at the bar.

8 *Bard by the Boise* 8 p.m.

Borrow a blanket from your hotel and find a spot on the lawn at the **Idaho Shakespeare Festival**, overlooking the Boise River east of town (5657 Warm Springs Avenue; 208-336-9221; idahoshakespeare.org), which runs June to September. It features productions of Shakespeare as well as more contemporary works at an outdoor amphitheater. As the sun sets and the stars come out, you might start to think that Boise's status as one of the most isolated metro areas in the lower 48 states is not a bad thing.

SUNDAY

9 *Pedal for Your Coffee* 9 a.m.

Head to **Idaho Mountain Touring** (1310 West Main Street; 208-336-3854; idahomountaintouring.com), rent a full-suspension mountain bike, and head north on 13th Street to Hyde Park, a neighborhood of bungalows and tree-lined streets. Park your bike with the others in front of **Java Hyde Park** (1612 North 13th Street; 208-345-4777) and make your way past the dogs tied up outside to order your favorite caffeinated creation.

10 *Up, Down, Repeat* 10 a.m.

Fortified, and perhaps jittery, remount your rented ride and pedal a few blocks farther up 13th

Street to **Camel's Back Park** (1200 West Heron Street). Look for the trailhead east of the tennis courts, one of many entrances to the Ridge to Rivers trail system (ridgetorivers.cityofboise.org), a single- and double-track network that covers 80,000 acres between the Boise Ridge and Boise River. Climb the Red Cliffs Trail to open vistas of the Treasure Valley below, then loop back down on the rollicking Lower Hulls Gulch Trail. Repeat as necessary.

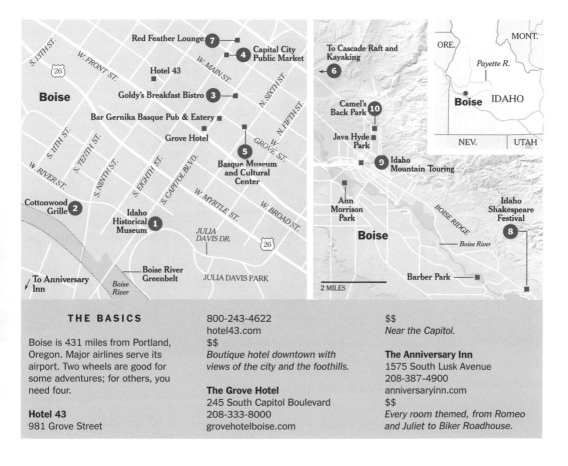

THE BASICS

Boise is 431 miles from Portland, Oregon. Major airlines serve its airport. Two wheels are good for some adventures; for others, you need four.

Hotel 43
981 Grove Street

800-243-4622
hotel43.com
$$
Boutique hotel downtown with views of the city and the foothills.

The Grove Hotel
245 South Capitol Boulevard
208-333-8000
grovehotelboise.com

$$
Near the Capitol.

The Anniversary Inn
1575 South Lusk Avenue
208-387-4900
anniversaryinn.com
$$
Every room themed, from Romeo and Juliet to Biker Roadhouse.

Sun Valley

Nostalgia can feel like the dominant mode at the Sun Valley Resort near Ketchum, Idaho, which was founded by W. Averell Harriman in 1936 to bring passengers to the West on the Union Pacific Railroad. Just check out the photographs in the hallways at the Sun Valley Lodge — isn't that Gary Cooper, Janet Leigh, Lucille Ball? All were high-glam-quotient visitors to this resort during its Hollywood glory days. Ernest Hemingway was also a Ketchum regular, and bought his own local ranch. These days you're likely to mingle with less-photogenic tech moguls and their pals, but the guest rooms are updated along with the clientele, and so are the slopes. At Bald Mountain, the bigger of Sun Valley's two ski areas, the Roundhouse gondola has enhanced the experience. At Dollar Mountain, the terrain parks have new rails and jibs. Some things haven't changed. It's a short hop from the resort hotels to the slopes, and "Sun Valley Serenade" still plays, free, on guest room TVs. — BY AMY VIRSHUP

FRIDAY

1 *Skate under the Lights* 6 p.m.

Make like Michelle Kwan and hit the ice at the **Sun Valley Lodge**'s outdoor rink (208-622-2194). This oval has seen performances by all manner of Olympic gold medalists, from Peggy Fleming to Evan Lysacek. So lace up a pair of rental skates and practice your triple lutz. (If your tastes run more to Alex Ovechkin, there are hockey skates available, too.) And if you hear Scott Hamilton doing the commentary in your head, well, you won't be the first — or last. The evening session ends at 8.

2 *Slow Cooker* 8 p.m.

The wood-frame cottage that's home to the **Ketchum Grill** (520 East Avenue North; 208-726-4660; ketchumgrill.com; $$) dates back to Ketchum's first boom industry — silver mining, which briefly fueled development here in the 1880s. There are lots of old-fashioned touches at this cozy, cheerful place:

OPPOSITE A snowboarder waits to start a run at the Sun Valley Ski Resort in Ketchum, Idaho.

RIGHT Looking down at the town of Ketchum, where skiers from Sun Valley descend to find all sorts of sustenance.

the oversize rodeo poster as you walk in, the kayak suspended overhead in the back dining room, the rustic apple tart with homemade ice cream on the dessert menu. But the owners Scott Mason, chef, and his wife, Anne, pastry chef, are up on the latest trends. There's always a "slow cooked food of the day" entree: stuffed pork loin, short ribs or maybe house-cured corned beef with cabbage and boiled potatoes. And the steak of the day might come with pomegranate sauce, gorgonzola butter, or mushrooms.

SATURDAY

3 *Breakfast with a View* 8:30 a.m.

The slopes don't officially open until 9, but you can get an early start by riding the gondola to the **Roundhouse** for breakfast (about $15 for those with lift tickets; $30 for those without). Perched 7,700 feet up Baldy, the Roundhouse was the first day lodge on the mountain, and its exposed rafters, four-sided fireplace and antler chandeliers feel as if they've barely changed since it opened in 1939. The breakfast is continental — fruit, Danish, artisan breads, juices, and coffee — and the views are striking. A good number of your fellow diners may have really worked up an appetite, as it's a popular stop for skiers who have walked up the mountain with climbing skins on their boards. If you time things right, you can be first in line at the **Christmas chair** lift when it opens.

4 *Hit the Slopes* 9 a.m.

Some mountains require elaborate strategizing to avoid the lift lines, but at Sun Valley that's rarely

a problem. What does take some thought is working around Bald Mountain's relatively low elevation, which means that the lower half of the mountain can get slushy in the afternoon sun and then freeze overnight. So start your morning up high at the **Seattle Ridge** area. The slopes up here, named for Sun Valley's Olympic stars and their medals — Gretchen's Gold, Christin's Silver — are mostly greens, but their consistent pitch down the fall line makes them eminently swooshable on morning legs. Once you've warmed up, Christmas Bowl, from the top of the Christmas chair, is the longest run on the mountain, starting out as a blue and then turning into an expert run down below. Feel ready? The **Mayday chair** takes you up to the Easter, Lookout, and Mayday bowls. If you feel overwhelmed, keep going left to the easier Broadway Face or Sigi's Bowl.

5 *Refresh Your Look* 4 p.m.

If your skiwear needs a little sprucing up, knock off early and head to the **Gold Mine Thrift Store** (331 Walnut Avenue, Ketchum; 208-726-3465), where

ABOVE Skis as fencing: themed architecture along the road between the Sun Valley resort and Ketchum.

BELOW Downhill is not the only kind of skiing around Sun Valley. Extensive networks of cross-country trails wind through the countryside.

the used stock runs heavily to the brand-name and all but brand-new. Among the finds: a men's Giorgio Armani jumpsuit for $75; numerous Bogner parkas and ski pants for women for about $80 each; and enough children's Obermeyer bibs to outfit a ski school, plus Burton snowboards, skis from K2, Rossignol, and Salomon, and vintage ski sweaters. Proceeds benefit the Community Library. Around the corner, **Iconoclast Books** (671 Sun Valley Road, Ketchum; 208-726-1564; iconoclastbooks.com) has current adult and children's books, but its real strength is its Hemingway-related collection, including selected first editions of many of his novels plus biographies and memoirs by far-flung members of the clan. Or discover other Idaho writers, like Vardis Fisher, whose 1965 novel *Mountain Man* was the basis for the film *Jeremiah Johnson*, with Robert Redford.

6 *Cross-Cultural Eating* 8 p.m.

Derek Gallegos, the chef and owner of **310 Main** in Ketchum's scruffier neighbor, Hailey, grew up in the restaurant business. His family owned an Idaho chain of Mexican places called Mama Inez; later he worked in Deer Valley, Utah, and at the Sun Valley Brewing Company. In this tidy 35-seat spot on Hailey's main drag (310 North Main, Hailey; 208-788-4161; threetenmain.com; $$), Gallegos mashes up his influences to create starters like Shanghai Tacos or Homa Homa oysters with habanero and lime sorbet. And there's always the rib-eye steak with mashed potatoes. You're in Idaho, after all.

7 *Drink with the Wildlife* 10 p.m.

Back in Ketchum, the **Pioneer Saloon** (320 North Main Street; 208-726-3139) is probably as famous for its décor as it is for its food. There's taxidermy galore — heads of deer (the one over the dining room entrance is named Fred and was shot in 1927), elk, and bison; stuffed grouse and pheasant; and even trophy trout (the enormous one is actually a fiberglass replica of a record steelhead). That's not to mention the birch-bark canoe hanging in the bar, or the numerous bullet and rifle displays. Admire them all while having one of the Pioneer's signature bartender margaritas or a draft Sun Valley ale at the bar.

SUNDAY

8 *Brunch by the Fire* 9 a.m.

Tucked away on a side street but worth finding, **Cristina's** (520 Second Street East; 208-726-4499; cristinasofsunvalley.com; $$) is a Sun Valley institution. It serves homey food in a trim salmon-pink cottage where a fire burns all winter long in the fireplace. The Sunday brunch menu mixes classic breakfast fare like French toast and omelets with items like 10-inch thin-crust pizzas. The breads are homemade—prune walnut is a house specialty.

9 *Time for Skinny Skis* 10 a.m.

Downhill is not the only kind of skiing in Sun Valley. There are extensive networks of cross-country trails that wind through the countryside. Get outfitted at the **Elephant's Perch** (280 East Avenue; 208-726-3497; elephantsperch.com), where a touring package rents for about $15 for a half day. (You'll also need a day pass for the trails, which costs about the same.) Head north and pick up the Harriman Trail near the Sawtooth National Recreation Area headquarters (seven miles north of Ketchum on Route 75). It's gentle and flat and runs along the banks of the Big Wood River. Farther north you can try the Prairie Creek Loop, with views of the Boulder and Smoky Mountains. For trail information, check with the Blaine County Recreation District (208-578-9754; bcrd.org).

THE BASICS

Fly into Boise and rent a car or use the Sun Valley Express Shuttle for the two-and-a-half-hour drive to Sun Valley. In town, the Mountain Fairy (208-720-0776; mtnfairy.blogspot.com) offers rides to outdoor-sports locations

The Sun Valley Resort
800-786-8259
sunvalley.com
$$$
The biggest game in town, with a lodge and inn, cottages, apartments, and condos.

Knob Hill Inn
960 North Main Street, Ketchum
208-726-8010
knobhillinn.com
$$$-$$$$
High-end rooms and good views.

Best Western Tyrolean Lodge
260 Cottonwood Street, Ketchum
208-726-5336
bestwesternidaho.com
$$
A less expensive alternative.

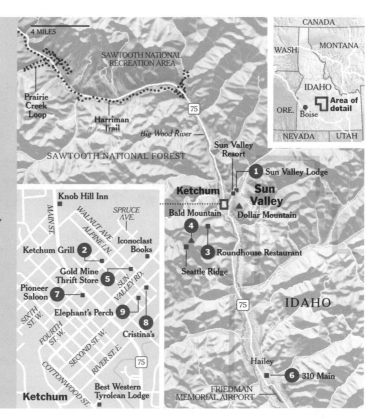

Jackson

At the edge of Grand Teton National Park, among other natural wonders, Jackson, Wyoming (often confused with the wider valley in which it rests, Jackson Hole) has avoided becoming a sprawling tourist trap thanks to its quirk of geography: hemmed in by public land, the town has no room to expand. And the new money drawn here has added cosmopolitan flair without loss of respect for the town's Old West tradition. Sometimes it seems as if you're as likely to see a Buddhist prayer flag as a pickup truck. Add an ever-expanding list of adventure sports, and you've got a destination that packs in enough adrenaline, scenery, and culture per square mile to keep anyone coming back. — BY TOM PRICE

FRIDAY

1 *Western Style* 6 p.m.

Get oriented with a ramble around the town square, which is framed by four arches made from elk horns gathered in nearby forests. Duck into the **Million Dollar Cowboy Bar** (25 North Cache Street; 307-733-2207; milliondollarcowboybar.com) to look over the spur collection and 70 years' worth of other accumulated Westernalia. Then check out some of the nearby shops. **Terra Jackson Hole** (105 East Broadway; 307-734-0067; terrajh.com) stocks designer clothes for women, including strapless dresses, glittery tops, and plenty of denim. For something completely different, walk down the street to **Stone's Mercantile** (50 West Broadway; 307-733-3392; stonesboots.com) for Western boots and hats, motorcycle chaps, and gun belts.

2 *Night Sights* 8 p.m.

Climb the steps to the **Snake River Grill** (84 East Broadway; 307-733-0557; snakerivergrill.com; $$$) and settle down at one of the tables in the log-walled dining room. It's one of Jackson's best-known restaurants — reservations are recommended — and the menu is kept dynamic while maintaining worthy

OPPOSITE Fishing the Snake River. Jackson attracts a well-to-do crowd that loves getting outdoors.

RIGHT Open land just outside of town. Nearby is publicly owned wilderness including Grand Teton National Park.

traditions. Expect dishes like crispy pork shank with orzo, salsa verde, and tomato jam. After dinner, stroll north, toward the **National Elk Refuge**, which abuts town. If the season is right, you may find southbound geese asleep on the grass roof of the visitors center (532 North Cache Street; 307-733-9212; fws.gov/nationalelkrefuge). But look up higher. Away from the lights and neon, you'll have a striking view of the night sky.

SATURDAY

3 *And Wear a Helmet* 9 a.m.

Get fitted for a mountain bike rental at **Hoback Sports** (520 West Broadway; 307-733-5335; hobacksports.com), buy a trail map, and start pedaling. Ride east toward the 20-mile Cache Creek-Game Creek loop through the **Bridger Teton National Forest**. Take either the smooth dirt road or the parallel single-track Putt-Putt Trail, winding along a shaded stream. At the Game Creek turnoff, crank up a short steep climb, and you'll be rewarded with a five-mile descent down sage- and aspen-covered hills before connecting with a paved path back to town.

4 *Picnic with the Tetons* Noon

For all its worldliness, Jackson is a tiny town of about 9,000 full-time residents. Grab picnic fixings at **Backcountry Provisions** (50 West Deloney Street;

307-734-9420; backcountryprovisions.com) and then get a side order of scenery at **Snow King Resort** (corner of Snow King Avenue and King Street; 307-733-5200; snowking.com), the in-town ski area. Hike the piney switchbacks 1.8 miles and 1,571 vertical feet to the summit (45 minutes if you're huffing, but remember you're starting at 6,200 feet). The view stretches 50 miles to Yellowstone, and it's the best place in the valley to see both the town and the Tetons.

5 *Drive-By Shooting* 2:30 p.m.

Relax with a behind-the-wheel wander through **Grand Teton National Park** (307-739-3300; nps.gov/grte). Best bet for scenic photos: loop north on Route 191 past the Snake River Overlook, where you can frame the river that carved the valley and the mountains behind it in one shot. Then head south along Teton Park Road past Jenny Lake. On your way back, stop at **Dornan's** in the town of Moose (200 Moose Street; 307-733-2415; dornans.com) for cocktails on the deck, about as close as you can get to the Tetons and still have someone bring you a drink.

6 *Japanese Plus* 7 p.m.

At **the Kitchen** (155 North Glenwood Street; 307-734-1633; kitchenjacksonhole.com; $$$), a Japanese bistro in a casual, contemporary space, you can start with truffle fries or sashimi and move on to veal in a chile-miso broth or an organic burger. The drinks menu has similar mixed influences. There's a wide selection of sakes and 19 different types of tequila.

7 *Moose Music* 10 p.m.

Drive the 12 miles to Teton Village to join the locals crowding into the **Mangy Moose Restaurant and Saloon** (Teton Village, Village Road; 307-733-4913;

mangymoose.net), where the live music includes national and local acts. Order a draft beer and elbow into a seat at the bar — no matter who's playing.

SUNDAY

8 *Never Toasted* 7:30 a.m.

Join the lineup for coffee at **Pearl Street Bagels** (145 West Pearl Avenue; 307-739-1218). Purists, rejoice; even after pranksters nailed a dozen toasters to Pearl Street's pink facade several years ago, it still serves its bagels warm from the oven but always untoasted. And with bagels this fresh and good, it seems a little unfair to quibble.

9 *Big Red Box* 9 a.m.

If the caffeine didn't get you going, this ride will. From the Teton Village base, the **Jackson Hole Mountain Resort tram** (tram-formation.com) will whisk you up 4,139 feet to the summit of Rendezvous Mountain. (Pack a jacket — it can be gorgeous in

the valley but snowing up top.) Coming down, press against the front window for a stomach-dropping pass over the skier's jump known as Corbet's Couloir. There's been a "big red box" on this mountain since 1966, but the beloved original was retired and replaced by this newer, larger, more streamlined version in 2008. The new version holds 100 people, twice the old one's capacity. But the view is still spectacular.

10 *The Compleat Angler* 10 a.m.

Not every full-service hotel is likely to have a director of fishing, but this is Jackson Hole, and you'll find one at the **Four Seasons Resort** (7680 Granite Loop Road, Teton Village; 307-732-5000; fourseasons.com/jacksonhole). In the resort's

handmade wooden dory, he'll take you down one of the secluded braids of the Snake River and offer expert advice on how to reel in some of the Snake's 2,500 fish per mile. You don't have to be a guest, even first-timers are welcome, and it's safe to feel very surprised if you don't land a fish. A day trip will set you back several hundred dollars, and if it's a couple of hundred too many, you can look for a less expensive guide back in town.

OPPOSITE ABOVE The Westernalia on display at the Million Dollar Cowboy Bar includes a collection of spurs.

OPPOSITE BELOW Arches downtown are made from antlers, a material the local elk obligingly shed each spring.

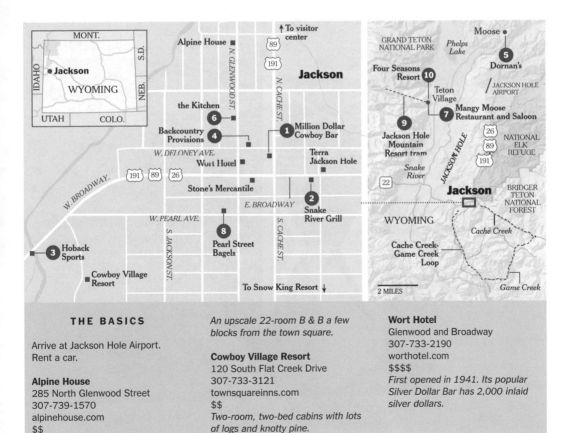

THE BASICS

Arrive at Jackson Hole Airport. Rent a car.

Alpine House
285 North Glenwood Street
307-739-1570
alpinehouse.com
$$

An upscale 22-room B & B a few blocks from the town square.

Cowboy Village Resort
120 South Flat Creek Drive
307-733-3121
townsquareinns.com
$$
Two-room, two-bed cabins with lots of logs and knotty pine.

Wort Hotel
Glenwood and Broadway
307-733-2190
worthotel.com
$$$$
First opened in 1941. Its popular Silver Dollar Bar has 2,000 inlaid silver dollars.

Juneau

Residents of Juneau, Alaska, brag that their town is the most beautiful state capital city in America, and they have a strong argument. Juneau is inside the Tongass National Forest, part of the world's largest temperate rain forest. Old-growth groves and glaciers lie within the municipal limits, snow-capped mountains loom overhead, and whales and other marine wildlife are a short boat ride away. The town itself is a working state capital with a utilitarian feel, but gold rush-era buildings, art galleries, quality regional theater, and fresh seafood make for pleasant companions to Juneau's stunning surroundings. — BY CORNELIA DEAN

FRIDAY

1 *Back to the Ice Age* 3 p.m.

Nature beckons. But some preparations are required. On your way into town, stop at **Western Auto-Marine** (5165 Glacier Highway; 907-780-4909; westernautojuneau.com) for a pair of brown rubber, calf-high Xtra Tuf Boots, a must-have item in any Alaskan's wardrobe. A good place to start your trek is the entrance to the **Switzer Creek and Richard Marriott Trails** (midway on Sunset Street). On the hillside, evergreens in even ranks give way to a hodge-podge of trees of different species, sizes, and shapes. This change marks the boundary between second-growth timber, on land logged decades ago, and an old-growth forest, untouched since the end of the last ice age. Hike up the trail — it's not too strenuous — and discover for yourself why environmentalists are so keen to save these ancient woods, home to an amazingly rich variety of plant and animal life. (Keep to the wooden planks at the base of the trail, and be glad you have your boots. The bog, or muskeg, is plenty wet.)

2 *Fish Don't Get Fresher* 6:30 p.m.

Locals say Juneau is not much of a restaurant town because so many people dine on fish they catch themselves. But when they want fish prepared for them, they head to the **Hangar on the Wharf Pub & Grill** (2

Marine Way; 907-586-5018; hangaronthewharf.com; \$\$-\$\$\$). The building's exterior of plain blue clapboard isn't designed to impress, but the harborside location offers dazzling views of the Gastineau Channel and the mountains of Douglas Island west of downtown. There's halibut on the menu, of course, and salmon (guaranteed wild-caught) and king crab.

3 *Indoor Drama* 8 p.m.

Take in a play at the **Perseverance Theatre**, a nonprofit repertory company across the Gastineau Channel on Douglas Island (914 Third Street, Douglas; 907-364-2421; perseverancetheatre.org). A pillar of Juneau's cultural life for more than 30 years, it stages high-quality classic and contemporary plays, and the prices are low.

SATURDAY

4 *Seeing Sea Life* 9 a.m.

What better way to start your Saturday than with some close-up views of Juneau's wildlife? A number of companies offer whale-watching trips from Auke Bay, a short car (or bus) ride north of downtown. Find one offering a trip up the Lynn Canal to **Berners Bay**, and you are sure to see Steller sea lions basking on a rocky haul-out, harbor seals bobbing in the water, and harrier hawks, geese, and ducks. Also watch for eagles nesting along the shores. Most companies guarantee you will see whales; chances of spotting humpbacks are best in late spring when the herring-like fish called eulakon ("hooligan" in a local native language) are running.

OPPOSITE A navigational buoy near Juneau makes a convenient perch for Steller sea lions and a bald eagle.

RIGHT Cruise ships turn their sterns toward town at the end of daylong stops in Juneau's harbor.

5 *Up North, Down South* Noon

Back in town, enjoy a taste of old Juneau at the **Triangle Club** (251 Front Street; 907-586-3140; triangleclubbar.com; $). Order a hot dog and some Alaskan Amber — one of the local beers brewed and bottled right in town. If the Triangle looks a bit louche for your tastes, try **El Sombrero** around the corner (157 South Franklin Street; 907-586-6770; $$), a Juneau institution. The modest place has been dishing out generous helpings of Mexican standards since the oil boom began in the 1970s.

6 *They Came First* 1:30 p.m.

For some historical perspective, visit the **Alaska State Museum** (395 Whittier Street; 907-465-2901; museums.state.ak.us), which houses a collection covering the Athabascans, Aleuts, and other Alaska natives, the state's history as a Russian colony, and the 1880s gold rush that helped create Juneau. The museum's store stocks native crafts including baskets, prints, and dolls. Keep walking farther from the port and you'll come upon what is probably Juneau's least-known gem: the lichen-covered tombstones in **Evergreen Cemetery** (601 Seater Street; 907-364-2828). Joseph Juneau and Richard Harris, the prospectors who founded the city, are buried there, and the cemetery was also the site of the funeral pyre of Chief Cowee, the Auk who led them to Juneau's gold.

7 *Arts and Crafts* 3 p.m.

When cruise ships are in town, the locals say they stay out of "waddling distance" of the piers. And with good reason: most of the shops that line the streets of downtown are filled with mass-produced "native" items for the tourist trade. But not all. The **Juneau Artists Gallery** (175 South Franklin Street; 907-586-9891; juneauartistsgallery.net), a co-operative shop, sells jewelry, prints, pottery, drawings, and other work. Be sure to chat with the gallery staff — each is an artist and a member of the co-op. For apparel a little more exotic than the ubiquitous Alaska-themed sweatshirt, try **Shoefly & Hudsons** (109 Seward

Street; 907-586-1055; shoeflyalaska.com), which offers unusual designs in footwear, handbags, and accessories. (People in Juneau say it was one of Sarah Palin's favorite shops when she was the governor.) But the city's most unusual retail outlet is **William Spear Design** (174 South Franklin Street; 907-586-2209; wmspear.com), a purveyor of tiny enamel pins, zipper pulls, and other items — many with edgy political messages.

8 *On the Page* 4:30 p.m.

If your shopping interests are geared more toward the written word, you are in luck: Juneau is friendly to independent bookstores. One in downtown is the **Observatory** (299 North Franklin Street; 907-586-9676; observatorybooks.com), perched up the hill from the harbor. From a tiny blue house not much younger than the town itself, the shop's proprietor, Dee Longenbaugh, offers an extensive stock of books on Alaska, particularly the southeast region. She prides herself on her collection of maps and charts as well as works on regional plants, animals, and geology.

9 *Alaskan Mediterranean* 7 p.m.

With its high ceiling and wood floors, **Zephyr** (200 Seward Street; 907-780-2221; $$$) is Juneau's most elegant restaurant. It serves fish, of course,

ABOVE AND BELOW Spectacular scenery courtesy of Juneau's in-town glacier, the Mendenhall Glacier. Downstream, Nugget Falls cascades from the glacial melt, while upstream the glacier itself holds onto its frozen grandeur.

but Mediterranean style, for example the halibut provençale, with tomatoes and olives. Nonseafood options include the mushroom risotto. The crème brûlée and other desserts are rich, so save some appetite. After dinner, you can get back into the gold rush mood with a game of pool and an Alaskan pale ale in the bar of the **Alaskan Hotel** (167 South Franklin Street; 907-586-1000; thealaskanhotel.com).

SUNDAY

10 *Coffee and a View* 9 a.m.

Grab a coffee and a pastry at the downtown location of the **Heritage Coffee Company** chain (174 South Franklin Street; 907-586-1087; heritagecoffee.com) before donning your boots and heading out to Juneau's in-town glacier, the **Mendenhall Glacier**, off Glacier

Spur Road. Dress warmly—cool air flows constantly off the 12-mile stream of ice, and it is typically 5 or 10 degrees cooler there than in town. In part because of global warming, the glacier is retreating perhaps as much as 100 feet a year. Even from the visitor center (8510 Mendenhall Loop Road; 907-789-0097), you can see the kinds of rock and soil it deposited as it moved inland. But if you are feeling energetic, try the Moraine Trail for a first-hand look at what glaciers leave behind.

ABOVE Tourists cruise South Franklin Street.

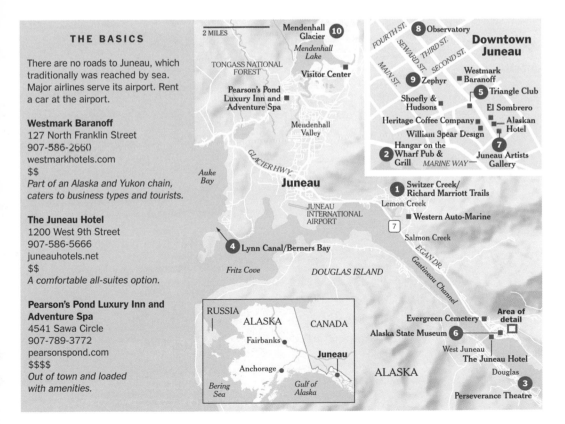

THE BASICS

There are no roads to Juneau, which traditionally was reached by sea. Major airlines serve its airport. Rent a car at the airport.

Westmark Baranoff
127 North Franklin Street
907-586-2660
westmarkhotels.com
$$
Part of an Alaska and Yukon chain, caters to business types and tourists.

The Juneau Hotel
1200 West 9th Street
907-586-5666
juneauhotels.net
$$
A comfortable all-suites option.

Pearson's Pond Luxury Inn and Adventure Spa
4541 Sawa Circle
907-789-3772
pearsonspond.com
$$$$
Out of town and loaded with amenities.

Homer

As you round the final bend on the Sterling Highway in Alaska and reach the town of Homer, the view of Kachemak Bay stops you dead. Across the water, jagged mountains cut by fjords lead right to the rocky coastline, and forests lead to alpine tundra, then glaciers that glint in the sunlight. On the Homer side of the bay, fields full of purple lupine, white yarrow, and goldenrod lead to beaches; snow-capped volcanoes across a nearby inlet come into view. Homer is called the End of the Road, the Halibut Fishing Capital of the World, or the Cosmic Hamlet by the Sea, depending on whom you happen to ask. Located on the Kenai Peninsula, a 220-mile drive south of Anchorage, Homer is a small town of homesteaders and artists, fishermen and ex-hippies, with a sprinkling of outlaws and seers. These categories frequently overlap, creating a funky, dynamic community that is a bit eccentric even by Alaskan standards. — BY MARIA FINN

FRIDAY

1 *Across the Water* 4:30 p.m.

The road on the Homer Spit, a four-mile-long sliver of land jutting into the bay, leads to the boat harbor and **Kachemak Bay Ferry** (907-399-2683; halibut-cove-alaska.com/ferry.htm). Catch the ferry, the *Danny J*, for a ride across Kachemak Bay to **Halibut Cove**, a small community that has no roads, only wooden boardwalks. The *Danny J* has a wildlife tour to Halibut Cove at noon and a 5 p.m. service that takes people there for the evening. Before dinner, stroll the boardwalks and drop in at the **Halibut Cove Experience Fine Art Gallery** (907-296-2215; halibutcoveexperience.com), which showcases the works of Halibut Cove artists. Many of them also fish commercially, a way of life reflected in the salmon mosaics and drawings and the occasional halibut or herring painting.

2 *Taste of the Bay* 6:30 p.m.

The **Saltry** restaurant in Halibut Cove (907-399-2683; halibut-cove-alaska.com; $$$) serves

OPPOSITE Homer, Alaska, a city of about 5,000 people on the Kenai Peninsula, has been called the the End of the Road, the Halibut Fishing Capital of the World, and the Cosmic Hamlet by the Sea.

locally caught seafood and vegetables grown in a patch out back. There is seating indoors or outside on a covered deck that overlooks the moored boats. The Saltry has a brief list of wines to go with its main event, the seafood. Try a huge appetizer platter of tart pickled salmon or mildly spiced halibut ceviche, and an entree of grilled pesto halibut or Korean barbecued salmon.

3 *Beer on the Spit* 9 p.m.

To while away a few hours in an atmosphere of conviviality (if not urbanity), drop in at the **Salty Dawg Saloon** (4380 Homer Spit Road; 907-235-6718; saltydawgsaloon.com), a dive bar and Alaska institution. It's the place where tourists and locals drink, sing, and get silly together.

SATURDAY

4 *Tempting Aromas* 8 a.m.

Anyone cutting back on carbs should avoid **Two Sisters Bakery** (233 East Bunnell Avenue; 907-235-2280; twosistersbakery.net) in Homer's Old Town near Bishop's Beach. But the salty ocean air carrying wafts of pecan sticky buns, savory Danishes, and fresh-brewed coffee makes this place hard to resist.

5 *Natural Alaska* 10 a.m.

Get into the forest on a guided hike at the **Wynn Nature Center** (East Skyline Road; 907-235-6667; akcoastalstudies.org/wynn-nature-center.html; $7), part of the nonprofit Center for Alaskan Coastal Studies, established in 1982. The bears and moose may be elusive, but the wildflowers and trees stay in place, ready for your guide's interpretation. (The coastal studies center also offers full-day, $120 nature tours from its Peterson Bay Field Station, leaving from Homer Harbor and including a forest hike, talks about indigenous people and fantastical rock formations, and a glimpse of the sea life exposed at low tide.)

6 *Lunch and a Book* Noon

You'll be back in town in time for lunch at the cozy **Mermaid Cafe** (3487 Main Street; 907-235-7649; mermaidcafe.net; $$), where specialties include quiche

and Thai chowder. After your meal, browse next door at the **Old Inlet Bookshop** (oldinletbookshop.com), located at the same address.

7 *Paddling Tour* 2 p.m.

From the Homer harbor, take a water taxi ride across the bay to **Yukon Island**, where you can launch a kayak into the smooth waters of Kachemak Bay. There, translucent jellyfish pulse below the sea's surface and bald eagles perch on rocky balustrades. On clear days the volcanoes Iliamna and Augustine can be seen. Alison O'Hara, owner of **True North Kayak Adventures** (5 Cannery Row Boardwalk, Homer Spit Road; 907-235-0708) and a longtime guide in Kachemak Bay, teaches how to approach the sea otters resting in kelp beds and identifies the seabirds. You may see porpoises, whales, and seals. The half-day tour is about $100. (There are also full-day and three-quarter-day options.)

8 *The Homestead* 8 p.m.

Locals describe the **Homestead Restaurant** (at the 8.2-mile marker on East End Road; 907-235-8723; homesteadrestaurant.net; $$$) as the best in the state. Menus change weekly, but expect a variety of local seafood: perfect oysters, clams, Alaska scallops, Alaskan king crab. Another specialty is halibut, Homer's favorite fish. Dishes are nicely presented, and the wine list is extensive.

SUNDAY

9 *Cosmic Cuisine* 7:30 a.m.

Brother Asaiah Bates, a follower of South Asian mysticism, arrived in Homer in 1955 from California. He and others with him vowed not to wear shoes or cut their hair until world peace had been achieved and world hunger eradicated. They were called Barefooters. Although the group broke up, Brother Asaiah stayed on, becoming a local sage. He dubbed Homer "the Cosmic Hamlet by the Sea," and although he died in 2000, a small cafe, the **Cosmic Kitchen** (510 Pioneer Avenue; 907-235-6355; cosmickitchenalaska.com; $), shows that his legacy lives on in many forms, even in the breakfast burrito. A homemade salsa bar offers condiments

ABOVE The beach at Kachemak Bay. In the bay, translucent jellyfish pulse below the sea's surface. On rocky overlooks, bald eagles find perches.

LEFT A fresh catch of halibut is prepared for market on a dock along the Homer Spit.

OPPOSITE Catch the ferry to Halibut Cove, a community that has boardwalks instead of roads but offers visitors a good restaurant and a gallery of works by local artists.

for the breakfasts of burritos with chorizo or huge plates of huevos rancheros accompanied by fresh hash browns.

10 *Head of the Bay* 8:30 a.m.

Just about the only way to get to the head of Kachemak Bay is on horseback, and it's worth it for the trip. **Trails End Horse Adventures** (53435 East End Road; 907-235-6393) takes visitors down a steep switchback that leads to the beach, and then past the Russian Orthodox village of Kachemak Selo. The tour continues on to the Fox River Flats. Turning toward the Homer Hills, the horses follow a narrow path flanked by elderberry bushes that open into a breathtaking site that was a Barefooters homestead in the 1950s and is now abandoned. Bald eagle chicks peer down from cottonwood trees and clusters of wildflowers dot the open fields. It feels like timeless Alaska.

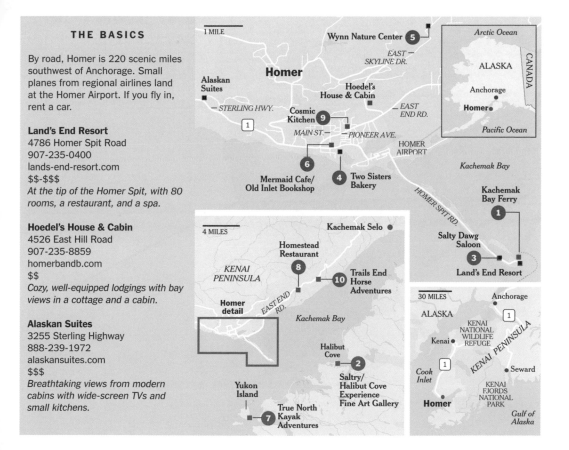

THE BASICS

By road, Homer is 220 scenic miles southwest of Anchorage. Small planes from regional airlines land at the Homer Airport. If you fly in, rent a car.

Land's End Resort
4786 Homer Spit Road
907-235-0400
lands-end-resort.com
$$-$$$
At the tip of the Homer Spit, with 80 rooms, a restaurant, and a spa.

Hoedel's House & Cabin
4526 East Hill Road
907-235-8859
homerbandb.com
$$
Cozy, well-equipped lodgings with bay views in a cottage and a cabin.

Alaskan Suites
3255 Sterling Highway
888-239-1972
alaskansuites.com
$$$
Breathtaking views from modern cabins with wide-screen TVs and small kitchens.

Whitehorse

In his poem "The Spell of the Yukon," Klondike bard Robert W. Service wrote of the beauty and serenity of the "great, big, broad land 'way up yonder." Spend a winter weekend in Whitehorse (population: 26,000), and you'll find that the spell is truly contagious. Whitehorse, the capital of Canada's Yukon Territory, got its name when gold rush stampeders found that rapids in the Yukon River reminded them of the flowing manes of stallions. Whitehorse is sub-Arctic, so winter is obviously cold, with temperatures often down around zero degrees Fahrenheit (pack very warm clothes). But dark it is not. You could enjoy more rays on an abbreviated February day than in an entire week down south in the Pacific Northwest. The clear nights are often highlighted by the symphony of color produced by the Northern Lights (don't visit during a full moon if you want the best chance of seeing them). The people? Friendly—and hardy indeed.

— BY BOB MACKIN

FRIDAY

1 *Fire on the Lake* 1 p.m.

Arrive in the Great White North and be whisked from your hotel (call ahead to arrange for an early check-in) to ice fishing at Fish Lake, just outside town, by **Up North Adventures** (103 Strickland Street; 867-667-7035; upnorthadventures.com; expect to pay about $150 to $200 in either U.S. or Canadian currency). Hop on a snowmobile and skim across the frozen waters of a lake you've surely seen on many a TV commercial, then onto shore and up a trail to a log cabin built for *The Last Trapper*, a 2004 French film, for a quick hot drink. From there, return to the lake and drill a hole with an auger. Drop your line and hope to hook arctic grayling or lake trout. Your guide will build a fire on the ice to keep everyone warm and serve as a makeshift cookout for your catch. Worry not: with the chilly temps and thick ice, the flames will do little damage.

2 *Mediterranean Thaw* 7 p.m.

Should the big one get away at Fish Lake, take your hunger to **Giorgio's Cuccina** (206 Jarvis Street;

OPPOSITE Drop a line through the ice at Fish Lake.

867-668-4050; giorgioscuccina.com; $$), a corner of the Mediterranean in the North. The Italian- and Greek-inflected menu includes seafood fettuccine, lamb souvlaki, and penne with asparagus. Most of the bottles on the wine list have made the long trip here from the Southern Hemisphere.

3 *The Lights Fantastic* 9:30 p.m.

Fill a flask with something hot and get out of town. A scant five minutes up the Alaska Highway, and you're beyond Whitehorse's lights. Bundle up, gaze heavenward, and if the conditions are right, you'll see the undulating ribbons of the Northern Lights, caused when clouds of ions from the sun strike the atmosphere. For about $125 to $150, you can pursue the lights more comfortably on a Northern Lights tour with **Aurora Borealis & Northern Lights Tours Yukon** (867-667-6054; auroraborealisyukon.com). Out in the blackness, you'll sit by a campfire and drink something warm as you watch the shimmering aurora.

SATURDAY

4 *Ride the Takhini Express* 9:30 a.m.

It would cost you plenty to shoot hoops with Michael Jordan or flip a puck to Wayne Gretzky at one of those celebrity sports camps, but it's relatively cheap to mush with a living legend of sled-dog racing, Frank Turner. From his **Muktuk Adventures** (15 miles north of Whitehorse off the Alaska Highway; 866-968-3647; muktuk.com), Mr. Turner runs a pooch-powered excursion along the frozen Takhini River. That six-mile route happens to make up part of the trail for the 1,000-mile-long premier dog-sled competition—the annual Yukon Quest International Sled Dog Race between Fairbanks, Alaska, and Whitehorse. Mr. Turner won it in record time in 1995 (10 days 16 hours 20 minutes). He'll outfit you in mushing gear and set you up with a sled and a quartet of eager dogs, then lead the way in another sled or on a snowmobile for the 90-minute-or-so jaunt.

5 *The Exotic North* Noon

The motto of the **Kebabery** (302 Wood Street; 867-393-2522; thekebabery.ca; $-$$) is "The Middle East Up North," and if the shish-kebabs, shawarma,

and falafel seem a little incongruous this close to the Arctic Circle, don't let that stop you from ordering a hearty lunch. The place feels more granola than exotic, although it has sometimes spiced things up at the dinner hour with belly dancers.

6 *Inspired by the Yukon* 1 p.m.

View the current exhibitions at **Yukon Arts Centre Public Gallery** (300 College Drive; 867-667-8575; yukonartscentre.com), which emphasizes the work of Yukon artists. Then check the schedule to see what's coming up in the arts centre's theater; performances there have ranged from Montreal ballet companies to Mongolian dancers and German experimental theater. Proceed next to **Mac's Fireweed Books** (203 Main Street; 867-668-2434; macsbooks.ca), a Yukon-centric bookstore with an extensive stock of classic and contemporary works by the North's men and women of letters. Look for Service's poetry; Jack London's novels and stories based on his time in the Yukon; and *Klondike*, an eye-opening and readable account of the Yukon Gold Rush by Whitehorse-born journalist and historian Pierre Berton.

7 *Yukon Gold* 3 p.m.

After gold was found in 1896 near Dawson City and the gold rush prospectors flooded in, order was maintained under the watchful eye of the North-West Mounted Police, that era's Mounties and the precursor of today's Royal Canadian Mounted Police. The **MacBride Museum of Yukon History** (1124 First Avenue; 867-667-2709; macbridemuseum.com) recounts that pivotal time in territory history. On the rounds are an N.W.M.P. station, Engine 51 from the White Pass & Yukon Route Railroad, and Sam

McGee's original 1899 log cabin. Service invoked poetic license to use McGee's name in "The Cremation of Sam McGee."

8 *All Under One Roof* 4:30 p.m.

The **Canada Games Centre** (867-667-4386; canadagamescentre.whitehorse.ca) is the territory's largest building. It could comfortably accommodate all 30,000 Yukoners, but was built for 2007's Canada Winter Games. The center includes Olympic- and N.H.L.-size hockey rinks, indoor soccer fields, a swimming pool, a waterpark, and an elevated running track. It's all open for use by the public. The drop-in schedule varies, so call ahead.

9 *Turn by the Mountie* 6 p.m.

A cold local brew and a hot Northern meal await you in the **Deck**, the heated, enclosed bar and restaurant that adjoins the popular summertime outdoor deck at the **High Country Inn** (4051 Fourth Avenue; 867-667-4471; highcountryinn.yk.ca; $$). You'll know you're at the right place when you see the 40-foot wooden Mountie statue. Have a draft Chilkoot Lager and enjoy the Alaska halibut or arctic char.

10 *Chilled Coiffure* 7:30 p.m.

Drive out to **Takhini Hot Springs** (867-633-2706; takhinihotsprings.yk.ca), 18 miles north of Whitehorse at the end of Hot Springs Road. The experience of soaking in a naturally hot outdoor mineral pool in the midst of a snowy landscape is both exhilarating

ABOVE Downtown Whitehorse. Check out the restaurants, the Public Gallery, and Mac's Fireweed Books.

RIGHT The Gold Rush exhibit at the MacBride Museum of Yukon History. After gold was found in 1896 near Dawson City, hopeful prospectors flooded into the Yukon.

and surreal. (The management has been known to sponsor wet hair contests. To compete, you dip your head into hot water and then emerge to let your hair freeze; the winner has the most eye-catching results.) If you missed the Northern Lights last night, you might catch them tonight while floating in the soothing pool.

SUNDAY

11 *Stop by the Woods* 9 a.m.

Have coffee and a scone or a breakfast panini at **Baked Cafe and Bakery** (108-100 Main Street; 867-633-6291; bakedcafe.ca; $) and assess your remaining time and energy level. If you're game for

one more wintry activity, drive or take the bus five minutes from downtown to **Whitehorse Cross Country Ski Club** (200-1 Sumanik Drive; 867-668-4477; xcskiwhitehorse.ca), which has more than 45 miles of wide groomed trails. Rent some skis and glide out into the quiet of the snow-covered woods.

ABOVE Dogsledding with a team from Muktuk Adventures. The frozen Takhini River makes a good roadway.

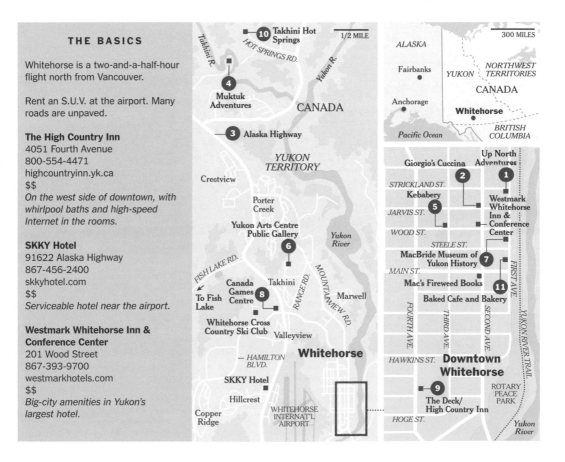

THE BASICS

Whitehorse is a two-and-a-half-hour flight north from Vancouver.

Rent an S.U.V. at the airport. Many roads are unpaved.

The High Country Inn
4051 Fourth Avenue
800-554-4471
highcountryinn.yk.ca
$$
On the west side of downtown, with whirlpool baths and high-speed Internet in the rooms.

SKKY Hotel
91622 Alaska Highway
867-456-2400
skkyhotel.com
$$
Serviceable hotel near the airport.

Westmark Whitehorse Inn & Conference Center
201 Wood Street
867-393-9700
westmarkhotels.com
$$
Big-city amenities in Yukon's largest hotel.

Honolulu

It's a cosmic irony that the longest, most grueling nonstop in the United States ends in the sweetest arrival of all. Jet-lagged, rumpled mainland travelers land in Honolulu having flown 2,500 miles from California — 5,000 miles if from the East Coast. But they will have flown past Diamond Head and over the surfers and paddlers of Waikiki Beach, and their first inhalations of Hawaiian air are likely to be scented with tuberose and plumeria. Add to these timeless enchantments the ethnic restaurants and fine art galleries and hula dancers at sunset, and you have a city in full bloom. So what if you miss the mangos of summer? There are whales and surf meets in the winter, gardenias in the spring, and cultural festivals and farmers' markets year-round.
— BY JOCELYN FUJII

FRIDAY

1 *Hula and a Mai Tai* 6 p.m.
There is no better cure for jet lag than **Halekulani's House Without a Key** (2199 Kalia Road; 808-923-2311; halekulani.com), where a dancer of traditional hula (perhaps the elegant Kanoe Miller) performs at sunset, on the oceanfront and with a view of Diamond Head. Under a 125-year-old kiawe tree, as superb mai tais stream from the bar, she undulates as if dancing for the first time, and just for you.

2 *An Iron Chef Dinner* 8 p.m.
Yes, there is an act to follow. It's **Morimoto Waikiki** (1775 Ala Moana Boulevard; 808-943-5900; morimotowaikiki.com; $$$$), an indoor-outdoor aesthetic fantasy of soft greens accented with large sculptures of farmed coral and aquarium-tables of suspended moss. It's as imaginative as it is pricey, living up to the Iron Chef's reputation as a culinary wizard. Nearly drafted in Japan as a baseball catcher, Masaharu Morimoto is now in the culinary big leagues, expanding his empire with dishes like the lightly spiced organic Angry Chicken, a lunch and dinner staple, and the Wagyu beef in several

iterations (including golf-ball sized mini-burgers at lunch). Other winners: the signature sushi and raw dishes, including lamb carpaccio and several types of seafood tartare, and the always appealing chirashi, sashimi served over sushi rice. Tofu cheesecake is lighter and more delectable than it sounds.

SATURDAY

3 *From the Good Earth* 8 a.m.
Arrive early at the **Saturday Farmers' Market** at **Kapiolani Community College** (4303 Diamond Head Road; 808-848-2074; kapiolani.hawaii.edu/object/farmersmarket.html), and take your pick of lush orchids from the Big Island, fresh corn from Waimanalo, persimmons from Kula (in season), or beans and brews from coffee farms throughout Hawaii. You can have an open-air breakfast (beignets, oat cakes, omelets) and sample local agricultural products — all on the slopes of Diamond Head.

4 *The Heiress's Treasures* 11 a.m.
To glimpse the private passions of the late reclusive billionaire Doris Duke, take a peek at **Shangri La** (shangrilahawaii.org), her oceanfront estate on the other side of Diamond Head. Two-hour tours of the Islamic museum there begin and end at the **Honolulu Academy of Arts** (900 South Beretania Street; 808-532-8701; reservations required). A 15-minute shuttle ride takes you to the site, where a Mughal garden quiets the mind and 13th-century Persian tiles line the walls of the central courtyard. The 8th- to 20th-century artifacts are integrated into

OPPOSITE A paddleboarder near Diamond Head.

RIGHT Waikiki Beach, flanked by hotels and curving toward Diamond Head.

the architecture, so you can stand at a 13th-century prayer niche, called a mihrab, and then sit in the gleaming Turkish Room, where Duke, a tobacco heiress, entertained guests after dinner.

5 *Fresh Fish Daily* 1:30 p.m.

Nico's (Pier 38, 1133 North Nimitz Highway; 808-540-1377; nicospier38.com; $), at the Honolulu waterfront, is just the place for a post-museum lunch: fresh fish plucked from an auction a few feet away and served on foam plastic plates under a cheerful awning a few feet away from the boats, with live blues or Hawaiian music. There are fresh fish specials at plate-lunch prices, and a pleasing open-air atmosphere. Order a grilled ahi sandwich, fish and chips, or even beef stew while yachts and fishing boats bob nearby. At the fish auction, chefs from Honolulu's upscale restaurants stock up on the day's catch, then often head to Nico's for breakfast or lunch.

6 *Art of the Garden* 3 p.m.

The Contemporary Museum, Honolulu (2411 Makiki Heights Drive; 808-526-1322; tcmhi.org) swaddled in green and with a panoramic view, features a setting and architecture that are as much a draw as its art collection — some of which is displayed outdoors. The gardens, built by a Japanese garden master, the Rev. K. H. Inagaki, in the 1920s, encourage contemplative strolls around a gracious estate built in 1925 by Alice Cooke Spalding, founder of the Honolulu Academy of Arts. The green serenity complements George Rickey's kinetic sculptures and Deborah Butterfield's larger-than-life signature horse.

7 *Stroll and Sniff* 5 p.m.

Follow the scent of jasmine, plumeria, and tuberose to the lei stands that line **Maunakea Street**, where vendors sell fragrant garlands among the ethnic restaurants, Chinese herb shops, Asian grocery stores, and Vietnamese pho houses. A burgeoning arts scene has peppered the area with galleries like **ARTS at Marks Garage** (1159 Nuuanu Avenue; 808-521-2903; hawaiiartsalliance.org/index.php/marks), the **Louis Pohl Gallery** (1111 Nuuanu Avenue; 808-521-1812; louispohlgallery.com), and the **Pegge Hopper Gallery** (1164 Nuuanu Avenue; 808-524-1160; peggehopper.com). All over the neighborhood, ethnic shops and small plazas brim with local products and contemporary local artists display their stone and native-wood sculptures, mixed-media collages, and abstract paintings.

8 *Seafood Hong Kong Style* 7 p.m.

At the busy **Little Village Noodle House** (1113 Smith Street; 808-545-3008; littlevillagehawaii.com; $), the sizzling scallops have a kick and the tofu pot stickers have a following. Vegetarian choices abound, and even traditional Chinese offerings like broccoli beef and noodles, kung pao chicken, and walnut shrimp are tastier — and healthier — than the norm.

9 *Jazz with a Dragon* 9 p.m.

The Dragon Upstairs (1038 Nuuanu Avenue; 808-526-1411; thedragonupstairs.com), an intimate jazz club, is a Chinatown hotspot in a former tattoo parlor lined with red walls, dragon masks, and glass-shard sculptures by Roy Venters, the Andy Warhol of Honolulu. Affixed to the wall is a large glittery dragon, a former stage prop for opera. While the mood is friendly and upbeat, it's the music that soars:

ABOVE Hike up Diamond Head for 360-degree views.

BELOW The lights of downtown Honolulu, a metropolitan enclave in an island paradise.

some of the best jazz in town can be heard here, and because many in the audience are musicians, you can count on hearty improv and guest artists.

SUNDAY

10 *Under the Sea* 10 a.m.

Snorkeling cures all ills, particularly early in the morning before the crowds arrive, when the water is glassy at tiny **Sans Souci Beach** in front of the **New Otani Kaimana Beach Hotel** (2863 Kalakaua Avenue). To the right and left of the sandy area, butterfly fish, Picasso fish (humuhumunukunukuapuaa), and yellow tangs flit and flash among the reefs, making for surprisingly good snorkeling at the Diamond

Head end of Waikiki. Across the street, Kapiolani Park is a recreational hub, with many of its joggers, tennis players, and yoga practitioners adding a swim and snorkeling session to their regimen.

11 *Windward Walk* Noon

No trip to Honolulu is complete without a drive to the easternmost point, **Makapuu**, about 30 minutes from Waikiki. Once past the suburban towns, the Ka Iwi coastline is a marvel of steep cliffs, tidal-pool-dotted shoreline, and the treacherous bodysurfing magnet **Sandy Beach**. A new scenic lookout at Makapuu has parking and improved access to a trail that leads to the Makapuu Lighthouse and its sprawling — and breathtaking — views of the windward coast.

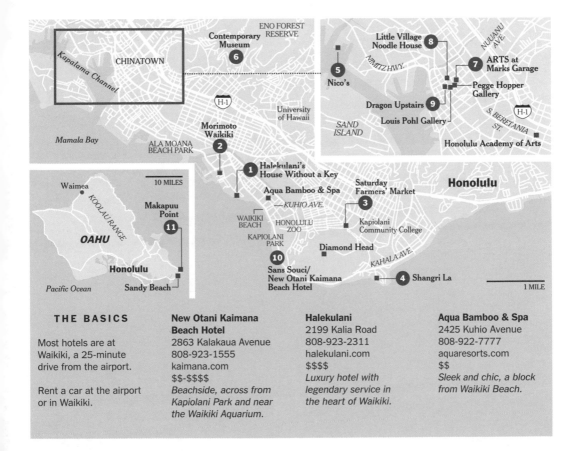

THE BASICS

Most hotels are at Waikiki, a 25-minute drive from the airport.

Rent a car at the airport or in Waikiki.

New Otani Kaimana Beach Hotel
2863 Kalakaua Avenue
808-923-1555
kaimana.com
$$-$$$$
Beachside, across from Kapiolani Park and near the Waikiki Aquarium.

Halekulani
2199 Kalia Road
808-923-2311
halekulani.com
$$$$
Luxury hotel with legendary service in the heart of Waikiki.

Aqua Bamboo & Spa
2425 Kuhio Avenue
808-922-7777
aquaresorts.com
$$
Sleek and chic, a block from Waikiki Beach.

Molokai

You've got to really want to go to Molokai, a steppingstone Hawaiian island between Oahu and Maui. Its stunning beaches and rugged jungle interior invite exploration, and the tragic tale of its leper colony, where native Hawaiians used to be summarily exiled, inspire an unavoidable curiosity. But hotel rooms are few, tourist amenities scarce, and developers actively discouraged. Yet for those who remember an older Hawaii — magical, sensuous, isolated — or for those who want to find some sense of how things were on Maui, the Big Island, and Kauai before they were drawn into the hustle and flow of Oahu, Molokai is more than worth the trouble. Its lifestyle is more traditionally Polynesian, its people reserved, but when their veneer is cracked, warm and full of an ancient joie de vivre. — BY CHARLES E. ROESSLER

FRIDAY

1 *The Moccasin* 1 p.m.

Pick up your rental car in the lava-rock terminal of tiny **Hoolehua Airport**, in the center of Molokai, and drive west on Highway 460 to **Maunaloa**, an old cattle ranching settlement. You won't encounter much traffic on these 10 miles of road, or anywhere on Molokai, which has 7,400 residents. The island is shaped roughly like a moccasin, 10 miles wide and 38 miles long from east to west. While eastern Molokai has a wet climate and junglelike foliage, the west end is arid with scrub vegetation. But it is rich in Hawaii's mythical history. Puu Nana, east of Maunaloa, is revered as the birthplace of the hula, which its practitioners consider to be a sacred dance, and every May dancers arrive to celebrate it. Molokai is also famous for its kahuna, powerful priests who could either provide life-giving herbal remedies or pray a healthy person to death.

2 *Clear Waters* 3 p.m.

Go for a swim at tiny **Dixie Maru Beach** at the lower end of a string of idyllic beaches that line the west coast. Ignore the temptation to swim at

OPPOSITE AND RIGHT Kaluapapa National Historic Park, the former leper colony that forms the core of Molokai's story of beauty and tragedy. A limited number of visitors are allowed; they arrive by mule ride or on foot.

Papohaku, two gorgeous miles of 100-yard-wide sandy beach; it harbors danger from sharp hidden coral reefs and swift, treacherous rip currents. Dixie Maru, not much more than a protected cove, is enticing in its own way: clear, deep-blue water with a calming undulation. If you take a careful walk over the lava rocks framing the left side of the bay, you may get lucky and spot a honu (a sea turtle) bobbing and weaving along the shoreline. This area was once dominated by a resort called Molokai Ranch, but it closed in 2008 after Molokai residents rejected a plan for its expansion.

3 *Try the Opakapaka* 6 p.m.

A bare-bones place reminiscent of a '50s diner, with old Coca-Cola decals on the wall, the **Kualapuu Cookhouse** (102 Farrington Avenue, Highway 470; 808-567-9655; $$-$$$) is a Molokai institution, serving fresh fish, beef, pork, and chicken dishes. Mahi-mahi and opakapaka (pink snapper) are local catches, subject to availability. The restaurant does not sell alcohol, but you can bring your own wine. Eat outdoors — you might share a picnic table with other customers who can tell you about life on the island. There may be live music — perhaps a ukelele and a one-string, gut-bucket bass — but be warned: the restaurant closes early.

SATURDAY

4 *Island Market* 10 a.m.

Saturday morning offers an opportunity to mix with the locals at the **Molokai Farmers Market**

(Alamalama Street) in what passes for a downtown in tiny Kaunakakai, the island's largest town. On a short street lined with stands, browse for papaya and poi, T-shirts, animal carvings, and shell jewelry in a convivial, relaxed atmosphere. Molokai never surrendered to tourist-first faux aloha spirit: the people here are genuine. They call Molokai the Friendly Island, but it can turn into the surly island to the outsider who ignores local protocol. The outdoor market is an opportunity to take in the local color and meet the locals on neutral ground.

5 *Fishponds and Spears* Noon

Have lunch at **Molokai Pizza** (15 Kaunakakai Place, just off Highway 460, Kaunakakai; 808-553-3288), which boasts the best pan pizza on the island, along with deli sandwiches on its own bread. Then set out to explore the south shore, driving east from Kaunakakai on Route 450, the East Kamehameha V Highway. In the first 20 miles you'll see 19th-century churches and some of the 60 ancient fishponds that dominate the southern coast. The Hawaiians who built

ABOVE The verdant, isolated Halawa Valley.

OPPOSITE ABOVE An ancient Molokai fishpond.

OPPOSITE BELOW A fisherman casts his net on a school of fish in Honouli Wai Bay.

them seven or eight centuries ago used lava rocks to surround and trap fish attracted to underground streams. At Mile Marker 20, stop at **Murphey's Beach**, a popular snorkeling spot. Watch locals spearfishing for dinner while children frolic on the sand, shouting and laughing.

6 *Old Ways* 2 p.m.

The last seven miles of the trip to the east end rival Maui's famous Road to Hana in adventure and beauty. The pulse quickens as you drive inches away from the ocean on the one-lane road. Inland views are a window onto a traditional Hawaii. Foliage is dense, and families have their horses and goats tied close to the road. On many of their one-acre plots, gardens and fruit trees vie for space with chickens, dogs, rusted car skeletons, and modest homes. Fishing nets and hunting accouterments, including dog kennels, attest to the survival of old ways of finding food; wild pigs, goats, and deer are the hunters' prey.

7 *The Far East* 3 p.m.

The road ends at **Halawa Park** in the spectacular Halawa Valley, surrounded by mountains and ocean. The isolated beaches in the bay are good for a dip in summer and great for big-wave surfing in winter. In the verdant valley, an ancient complex of terraces and taro patches, built by the Polynesians who first settled this island, helped sustain life on Molokai

from about 650 A.D. to the mid-20th century, when other job opportunities lured residents away. What remained of the taro was destroyed by a tsunami in 1946 and floods in the 1960s. You can learn about attempts to restore it — and can hike to lovely Moalua Falls — if you have some extra time and arrange a private tour (book at Hotel Molokai in Kaunakakai; about $80). On your drive back, go a half-mile or so past Kaunakakai to **Kaiowea Park** to see the **Kapuaiwa Coconut Grove**, a cluster of tall coconut palms that remain from 1,000 of their kind planted here in the 1860s by King Kamehameha V.

8 *Night Life* 7 p.m.

Find Molokai's weekend social scene at the casual **Hula Shores** restaurant in the Hotel Molokai (1300 Kamehameha V Highway, Kaunakakai; 800-535-0085; hotelmolokai.com; $$). Try a local dish like kalua pork and cabbage or hibachi chicken

and listen to live music, likely to feature ukeleles. The adjoining tiki bar, only yards away from the tranquil Pacific, conveys a feeling of timelessness as you sway in a hammock, one of three catching the slight breeze. If you're still out and about at 10, join the line at **Kanemitsu Bakery** (79 Ala Malama Avenue; 808-553-5855) waiting for hot French bread. It's what's happening Saturday night in Kaunakakai.

SUNDAY

9 *The Colony* 10 a.m.

Drive up Highway 470 to the north shore. Much of it is impenetrable, with soaring cliffs pitched

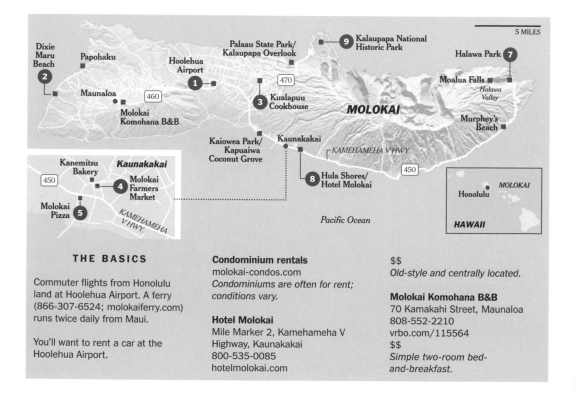

straight down 2,000 feet. In the center is **Kalaupapa National Historic Park** (nps.gov/kala), a small peninsula where native Hawaiian victims of leprosy were dropped off by ship and isolated. It was also the home of Father Damien, now St. Damien of Molokai, the 19th-century priest and Hawaiian folk hero who worked with the lepers until he contracted their disease and died. The unique community that developed there has a small-town New England feel, with tidy churches and modest homes belying past horrors. It is open to small numbers of visitors by permit; they can hike a cliff trail down or go with **Molokai Mule Ride** (800-567-7550; muleride.com; about $200) Monday through Saturday. Get a good

view from the **Kalaupapa Overlook**, 1,700 feet above the peninsula in **Palaau State Park**. If you know the story, the sight of the village below sets the mind racing with searing images of lepers being tossed overboard offshore and ordered to sink or swim to the peninsula—never to leave again.

ABOVE Ignore the temptation to swim at Papohaku, two gorgeous miles of 100-yard-wide sandy beach. It harbors danger from sharp hidden coral reefs and rip currents.

OPPOSITE Make a stop at Kaiowea Park to see the Kapuaiwa Coconut Grove, a cluster of tall coconut palms planted in the 1860s by King Kamehameha V.

THE BASICS

Commuter flights from Honolulu land at Hoolehua Airport. A ferry (866-307-6524; molokaiferry.com) runs twice daily from Maui.

You'll want to rent a car at the Hoolehua Airport.

Condominium rentals
molokai-condos.com
Condominiums are often for rent; conditions vary.

Hotel Molokai
Mile Marker 2, Kamehameha V Highway, Kaunakakai
800-535-0085
hotelmolokai.com

$$
Old-style and centrally located.

Molokai Komohana B&B
70 Kamakahi Street, Maunaloa
808-552-2210
vrbo.com/115564
$$
Simple two-room bed-and-breakfast.

Maui

"I went to Maui to stay a week and remained five,"
wrote Mark Twain in 1866. Whether lazing on a warm
sugary beach, gazing awestruck at a Haleakala sunrise,
or snorkeling to the song of humpback whales, visitors
to Maui today would likely feel the same. And while it
is known for its sparkling coastline and fertile green
interior, Hawaii's second-largest island appeals equally
to the urbane. Resorts hugging the south and west
shores claim some of the state's finest restaurants,
shops, and spas. A thriving arts community keeps
culture and creativity in high gear. In upcountry
Maui, on the slopes of the 10,000-foot Haleakala, you
can sample just-picked fruit or walk among fields of
lavender. Mark Twain had it right: it's not an easy
island to leave. — BY JOCELYN FUJII

FRIDAY

1 *Beauty and the Beach* 2:30 p.m.
   Tucked between the condo-studded town of Kihei
and the upscale resort of Wailea, the white-sand beach
of **Keawakapu** is south Maui's hidden jewel. Lined with
lavish Balinese- and plantation-style homes, this half-
mile playground has gentle waves, talcum-soft sands,
and free public parking along South Kihei Road. If it's
winter when you take a dip there, listen for the groans
and squeaks of the humpback whale, a haunting,
mystifying song.

2 *Drive-by Birding* 4 p.m.
   For a glimpse of Maui's remarkable biodiversity,
take a stroll on the boardwalk at the **Kealia Pond**
National Wildlife Refuge (Milepost 6, Mokulele
Highway 311; 808-875-1582; fws.gov/kealiapond),
a 700-acre natural wetland and seabird sanctuary.
Among the birds that shelter here are endangered
Hawaiian stilts, black-crowned night herons, and
Hawaiian coots, as well as migrating birds like
ruddy turnstones.

3 *Fairway Pizza* 6 p.m.
   There is no shortage of expensive restaurants
in Wailea packed with well-heeled tourists, which
makes **Matteo's Pizzeria** (100 Ike Drive, Wailea;
808-874-1234; matteospizzeria.com; $) all the more
inviting. An affordable joint that is wildly popular
with the locals, this casual restaurant is run by an

Italian couple who serve fresh thin-crust margherita
pizza, zesty penne in vodka sauce, and meaty lasagna.
After ordering at the counter, grab one of the tables
that overlook a golf course.

4 *Fine Arts* 7 p.m.
   The stellar collection of contemporary art
(including Jun Kaneko, Toshiko Takaezu, and a bevy
of island superstars) at **Four Seasons Resort Maui**
at Wailea (3900 Wailea Alanui Drive; 808-874-8000;
fourseasons.com/maui) is reason enough to go there.
Add designer cocktails, live Hawaiian music, hula, and
jazz in the open-air Lobby Lounge, and it becomes a
seduction. Take the self-guided audio tour through half
of the 68-piece art collection, then settle in for martinis
and musical magic at the bar by the grand piano.
Live nightly entertainment covers a gamut of musical
tastes. (If you want a romantic view, time your visit to
catch the setting sun.)

SATURDAY

5 *Upcountry Adventures* 9 a.m.
   Jump start your morning at **Grandma's Coffee**
House in the village of Keokea (9232 Highway 37, or
Kula Highway; 808-878-2140; grandmascoffee.com),
on the slopes of Haleakala volcano. On a wooden deck

OPPOSITE A windy beach on Maui, an island known for its
sparkling coastline and fertile green interior.

BELOW Kula Farm Stand sells just-picked fruit, like pineapple
and guavas, along with homemade mango bread.

with million-dollar views, you can sip Grandma's Original Organic, an espresso roasted blend from the family's fifth-generation coffee farm. Then move on to the **Kula Country Farm Stand** (Highway 37, or Kula Highway, across from Rice Park; 808-878-8381), a green-and-white produce stand selling just-picked fruit. Here's a chance to pick up fresh mangos (in season), rare pineapple guavas, and homemade mango bread before heading to lavender fields a few twists and turns away. With its view, acres of lavender, and fragrant jellies, scones, potions, and creams, **Ali'i Kula Lavender Farm** (1100 Waipoli Road; 808-878-3004; aklmaui.com), is a multisensory delight.

6 *Hot Art* Noon

Art is hot in **Makawao**, the cowboy town turned art colony that is about 1,600 feet above sea level on the slopes of Haleakala. Here you will find old wooden storefronts, mom-and-pop restaurants, chic boutiques, and hippie herb shops. At **Hot Island Glass** (3620 Baldwin Avenue; 808-572-4527; hotislandglass.com), the furnace burns hot and glass-blowing is performance art as molten glass evolves into jellyfish, bowls, and oceanic shapes. Next door, Maui artists display their work in the airy plantation-style space of **Viewpoints Gallery** (3620 Baldwin Avenue; 808-572-5979; viewpointsgallerymaui.com).

7 *Put the Top Down* 3 p.m.

The hourlong drive from Maui's hilly upcountry to Lahaina, a popular resort town on the island's west coast, provides nonstop entertainment. With the shimmering Pacific on your left and the chiseled valleys of the West Maui Mountains to the right, you will be hard-pressed to keep your eyes on the road. Once you reach **Black Rock**, a lava outcropping north of Lahaina in the resort named Kaanapali, you'll find equally compelling underwater sights.

RIGHT Jumping off the cliffs of Black Rock, a lava outcropping just north of Lahaina.

Grab a snorkel and explore this Atlantis-like world of iridescent fish, spotted eagle rays, and giant green sea turtles.

8 *Farm to Fork* 7:30 p.m.

Peter Merriman of **Merriman's Kapalua** (One Bay Club Place; 808-669-6400; merrimanshawaii.com; $$$) is a pioneer in Hawaii regional cuisine, a culinary movement blending international flavors with local ingredients. The oceanfront restaurant features jaw-dropping views of Molokai island, and the menu highlights local ingredients, whether chèvre from upcountry goats, Maui lehua taro cakes, or line-caught fish from nearby waters. Look for kalua pig ravioli or wok-charred ahi so fresh that it tastes as if it were cooked on the beach. With the opening of his newer Monkeypod Kitchen in Wailea, featuring handcrafted beers and food (housemade hamburger buns, made-from-scratch pies and juices), Merriman has both coastlines covered.

9 *Tiki Torches* 9:30 p.m.

The old Hawaii—tikis and plumeria trees around buildings without marble and bronze—is elusive in today's Hawaii, but you'll find it at **Kaanapali Beach Hotel**'s oceanfront **Tiki Courtyard**, where the **Tiki Bar** (2525 Kaanapali Parkway; 808-667-0111; kbhmaui.com) offers authentic Hawaiian entertainment nightly. Hula by Maui children, lilting Hawaiian music by local entertainers, and the outdoor setting under the stars are a winning combination, especially when warmed by genuine aloha.

SUNDAY

10 *Make It to Mala* 9 a.m.

Brunch at **Mala Ocean Tavern** (1307 Front Street, Lahaina; 808-667-9394; malaoceantavern.com; $$) is like being on the ocean without leaving land. At this casual restaurant, you're practically sitting on the water, enjoying huevos rancheros with black beans or lamb sausage Benedict while dolphins frolic in the ocean and turtles nibble at the shore. Ask for a table outdoors.

11 *Fly Like an Eagle* Noon

For an adrenaline finish, head to the heights of West Maui, where **Kapalua Adventures** (2000 Village Road; 808-665-3753; kapaluaadventures.com) offers an unusually long zip-line course. Beginners need

not fear, as the two-and-a-half-hour zip (about $150) requires virtually no athleticism. The four-hour trip (about $250) is not for the weak-kneed. The zip line takes you over bamboo forests, gulches, and ridges, with the luscious coastline in the distance.

OPPOSITE ABOVE Find a touch of the old Hawaii — tikis and plumeria trees under the stars — at Kaanapali Beach Hotel's tiki bar. The lilting Hawaiian music is genuine.

ABOVE At Black Rock, grab a snorkel. Below the surface are iridescent fish, spotted eagle rays, and giant turtles.

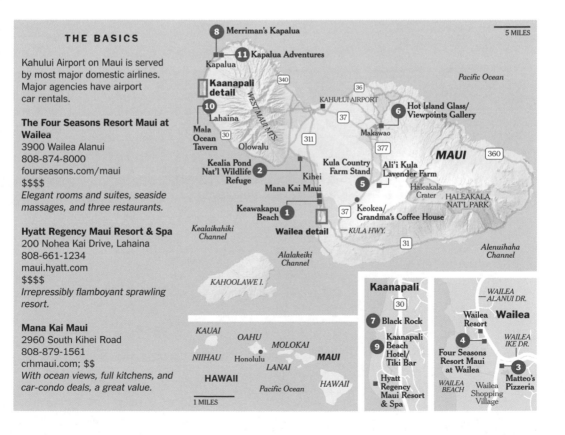

THE BASICS

Kahului Airport on Maui is served by most major domestic airlines. Major agencies have airport car rentals.

The Four Seasons Resort Maui at Wailea
3900 Wailea Alanui
808-874-8000
fourseasons.com/maui
$$$$
Elegant rooms and suites, seaside massages, and three restaurants.

Hyatt Regency Maui Resort & Spa
200 Nohea Kai Drive, Lahaina
808-661-1234
maui.hyatt.com
$$$$
Irrepressibly flamboyant sprawling resort.

Mana Kai Maui
2960 South Kihei Road
808-879-1561
crhmaui.com; $$
With ocean views, full kitchens, and car-condo deals, a great value.

Hilo

Of all the tropical postcard places in the Hawaiian Islands, Hilo, on the Big Island of Hawaii, may have the least to offer the traditional tourist. And that's exactly the reason to go. The center of power of Kamehameha the Great, the king who unified the islands in the early 19th century, Hilo combines history and raw natural power to offer a rich alternative to the resort scene. Orchids and anthuriums, fostered by the wet climate, grow amid some of the most magnificent geographic features on Earth, and the city exudes a genuine, small-town warmth and prototypical aloha spirit. No one works the tourist hustle, and the visitors don't come to vegetate. There's too much to see and do in a natural wonderland where some of the tallest mountains on Earth, as measured from sea bottom, dominate magnificent landscapes of beach and garden, rain forest and desert, with flowing lava adding more territory every day. — BY CHARLES E. ROESSLER

FRIDAY

1 *Down by the Banyans* 5 p.m.

Cruise down **Banyan Drive**, through a cathedral of monstrous banyan trees labeled with the names of celebrities who planted them, including Babe Ruth and Amelia Earhart. Park near Queen Liliuokalani Gardens, a 30-acre formal Japanese garden with a teahouse and pond, and cross the footbridge to Coconut Island for a good late-afternoon photo op looking back at the city and bay, with Mauna Kea volcano in the background. Back on the bayfront, keep walking, passing young boys fishing with bamboo poles while elders work two or three large rods. It's O.K. to watch, but don't talk. These locals don't work for a tourist bureau; they come down here for peace and solitude — and maybe dinner. Out on the bay, you may see teams of paddlers in 45-foot outriggers. The King Kamehameha statue in **Wailoa River State Park** is similar to the famous one in Honolulu, minus the mob.

2 *Fish Worth Flying For* 8 p.m.

Islanders sometimes fly in from Honolulu for the aholehole, or Hawaiian flagtail, a reef fish raised in ponds for the tables at the **Seaside Restaurant and Aqua Farm** (1790 Kalanianaole Avenue; 808-935-8825; seasiderestaurant.com; $$-$$$). Ask to be seated on the patio and watch the egrets roosting in a

small tree for the night. You can't go wrong with the catch of the day, which might be ahi, mahi-mahi, or opakapaka (blue snapper).

SATURDAY

3 *The Blissful Mist* 8 a.m.

Get up early and take a five-minute ride up Waianuenue Avenue to **Rainbow Falls**, where early morning affords the best chance to catch an ethereal rainbow rising from the mist. Refreshed with negative ions, head back to town and park near the **Hilo Farmers Market** at the corner of Mamo Street and Kamehameha Avenue (hilofarmersmarket.com). You won't be early; vendors begin to arrive at 3 a.m. to set up stalls selling exotic produce like atemoya and jackfruit. Sample a suman, a Filipino sticky-rice sweet wrapped in a banana leaf and cooked in coconut milk.

4 *Another Side of Paradise* 9:30 a.m.

Stroll Kamehameha Avenue, checking out **Sig Zane Designs** (122 Kamehameha Avenue; 808-935-7077;

OPPOSITE Hawaii Volcanoes National Park near Hilo on the island of Hawaii — the Big Island.

BELOW The statue of King Kamehameha I, the unifier of the Hawaiian islands, in Hilo. The city was the king's power base.

sigzane.com), with floral-themed contemporary Hawaiian fashions, and **Burgado's Fine Woods** (808-969-9663), with exquisite koa furniture, and the **Dreams of Paradise Gallery** (808-935-5670; dreamsofparadisegallery.com), both in the S. Hata Building (308 Kamehameha Avenue). Take a few steps to the **Pacific Tsunami Museum** (130 Kamehameha Avenue; 808-935-0926; tsunami.org), particularly poignant after the disastrous tsunami in Japan in 2011 and the Indian Ocean tragedy in 2004. The museum explains the physics of these "harbor waves" and documents tsunami devastation in Hilo in 1946 and 1960. A 25-minute video recounts the terror of the survivors, some of whom are docents at the museum.

5 *Munching the Mochi* Noon

Pick up an inexpensive two-course lunch to go, starting with a deliciously authentic bento at the **Puka Puka Kitchen** (270 Kamehameha Avenue; 808-933-2121). For dessert, walk to the **Two Ladies Kitchen** (274 Kilauea Avenue; 808-961-4766) and get the best mochi in the islands. You can see this glutinous rice sweet being made in the tiny shop as five workers scurry around with the hot mixture sticking to big ladles. All the flavors are ono (Hawaiian for delicious), but savor the strawberry, if it's available. Pack the food in the car and make the 45-minute drive southwest to **Hawaii Volcanoes National Park** (Highway 11; 808-985-6000; nps.gov/havo), where you can dine alfresco in the picnic area.

6 *Look Out for the Lava* 1 p.m.

Get information on current conditions from the visitor center at the park entrance. Though lava is likely to be flowing somewhere in the park, the 45-minute drive on Chain of Craters Road can end in frustration if Madame Pele, the temperamental Fire Goddess, isn't sending it that way. Another choice is

ABOVE Clouds of steam and gases surge into the night sky as lava from the Kilauea volcano pours into the ocean.

LEFT Shopping at Sig Zane Designs on Kamehameha Avenue for Zane's floral-themed Hawaiian clothing and textiles.

11-mile **Crater Rim Drive**, which circles the Kilauea Caldera. Stop at the park's **Thomas A. Jaggar Museum** for a refresher course in volcanology. You'll pass through desert flora, moonscapes, and rain forest and find incredible crater views. Take in the **Thurston Lava Tube**, formed as a lava flow left behind a hardened outer crust.

7 *Free-Range and Local* 7 p.m.

Find your way to the **Hilo Bay Cafe** (315 East Makaala Street; 808-935-4939; hilobaycafe.com; $$), a local favorite and locavore haven located incongruously in a strip mall — it grew out of a health food store there, the owners explain. Start with cocktails and dine on the likes of pan-seared

ABOVE A steaming volcanic cone near Hilo.

BELOW Hiking in the lava fields at the end of Chain of Craters Road in Volcanoes National Park.

scallops with crème fraîche, black truffle tomato relish, capellini in brown butter, and tobiko. Or perhaps the coconut-crusted tofu with sauteed vegetables, rice, and sweet chili sauce. The menu suggests wine pairings — or, in the case of the local free-range beef burger, a beer pairing: Guinness.

SUNDAY

8 *Back to the Garden* 9 a.m.

Drive north on Route 19 and turn onto the Scenic Route at Onomea Bay. Drive slowly past distortions of normal plants — huge Alexandra palms, king-size gingers, and hearty African tulip trees — to the **Hawaii Tropical Botanical Garden** (27-717 Old

Mamalahoa Highway; 808-964-5233; htbg.com). You're ahead of the crowd, so relish the peace in a tropical wonderland resplendent with bromeliads, heliconias, brilliant gingers, and delicate, buttery orchids. The garden holds more than 2,000 exotic species from all over the tropics.

9 *Water Rush* 11 a.m.

Akaka Falls State Park (end of Akaka Falls Road; 808-974-6200; hawaiistateparks.org) provides a final

opportunity to inhale nature's gifts on the Big Island. It's a short drive off Route 19 through the tiny former plantation town of Honomu. Take the 20-minute circular hike through bamboo groves, fern banks, and jungle flowers to view two beautiful waterfalls. The more impressive is Akaka, which tumbles 420 feet into a turbulent gorge eaten away by centuries of aquatic pounding. It's a no-frills tourist spot breathtaking in its raw simplicity—a perfect last taste of Hilo.

ABOVE Inside the Thurston Lava Tube, formed as a lava flow left behind a hardened outer crust.

OPPOSITE Hike through bamboo groves, fern banks, and jungle flowers to Akaka Falls, which tumbles 420 feet.

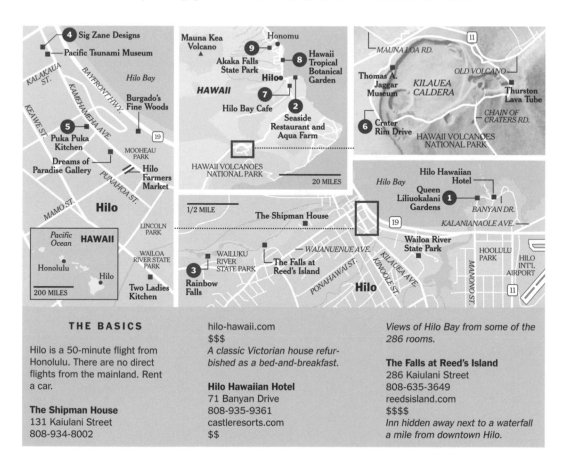

THE BASICS

Hilo is a 50-minute flight from Honolulu. There are no direct flights from the mainland. Rent a car.

The Shipman House
131 Kaiulani Street
808-934-8002

hilo-hawaii.com
$$$
A classic Victorian house refurbished as a bed-and-breakfast.

Hilo Hawaiian Hotel
71 Banyan Drive
808-935-9361
castleresorts.com
$$

Views of Hilo Bay from some of the 286 rooms.

The Falls at Reed's Island
286 Kaiulani Street
808-635-3649
reedsisland.com
$$$$
Inn hidden away next to a waterfall a mile from downtown Hilo.

Kauai

Kauai is a hot spot, and its beautiful North Shore, where majestic mountains meet the surging sea, is hottest. Two or three decades ago, when Maui was the place, Kauaians grinned and thought, "Good, we've got ours and we're going to keep it that way." Now, residents make their livings catering to tourists and pampering the movie stars and magnates who are collecting North Shore trophy homes. But with 60,000 people, this is still the least populated of the four major Hawaiian islands, and its spacious white beaches ring a lush, untrammeled interior. Kauai roads may not be marked, and numbers are rarely posted, so it helps to memorize the two most important directional words—mauka, meaning toward the mountains, and makai, for toward the ocean. When you ask directions, be ready for an answer like this: "Go a mile to the big mango tree, take a left, and head makai."
— BY CHARLES E. ROESSLER

FRIDAY

1 *Big Stretch* 5 p.m.

Your drive from the airport, north and then west on the Kuhio Highway following the curves of the coast, will take you through small towns and lush tropical countryside, with the bonus of a few coastal views, all the way to Hanalei, the last town on the North Shore. (Don't be surprised if you also see a rooster or two—wild chickens, descendants of escapees from domesticated flocks, are abundant on Kauai.) But for the best reward, stay with the highway past Hanalei, all the way until it ends at Kauai's northwest tip. On the last stretch, the road narrows, shrinking to one-lane bridges over inlets and streams, against a misty backdrop of volcanic hills and cliffs. It ends at **Haena State Park** (hawaiistateparks.org), where reef-protected Ke`e Beach offers a serene spot to take in the remains of the day. If there's time and conditions are mellow, it's a short swim out to the reef for some quality snorkeling.

2 *Feast at Sunset* 6:30 p.m.

When you enter the **St. Regis Princeville** (5520 Ka Haku Road; 808-826-9644; princeville.com) make your way straight to the **Makana Terrace** (stregisprinceville.com/dining/makana-terrace; $$$) to take in the sweeping Hanalei Bay view. Settle in, order the signature cocktail, blending passion fruit and Champagne, and look out across the water. The mountains on the other side stood in for Bali Hai in the movie *South Pacific.* (Be sure to arrive before sunset.) You may also see some surfers if the waves are right—the North Shore is popular for surfing and all of its relatives—windsurfing, body-boarding, stand-up paddling. Stay for a buffet dinner ($$$), or move indoors in the hotel to the **Kauai Grill** ($$$), where the frequently changing menu includes entrees like soy-glazed short ribs with papaya-jalapeno puree. After dinner, walk down to the beach, spectacular under a full moon.

SATURDAY

3 *Morning by the Sea* 7:30 a.m.

Take a stroll on the Princeville walking path, paralleling the road leading into the planned community of **Princeville**, and look out over the Robert Trent Jones Jr. golf course. At this time of day there is a good chance of seeing double rainbows in the direction of the misty mountains.

OPPOSITE AND BELOW Hanalei Bay and the pier at Hanalei on a cloudy day in December. Magnates and movie stars have arrived, but Kauai is still the least populated of the four main Hawaiian islands.

4 *A Flyover* 9 a.m.

Get on board with **Sunshine Helicopters** (808-245-8881; sunshinehelicopters.com/kauai) at the tiny Princeville Airport on Highway 56 and soar

ABOVE Houses along the golf course in the North Shore planned community of Princeville.

BELOW Kauai is popular for surfing and all of its relatives — windsurfing, body-boarding, stand-up paddling.

OPPOSITE The cliffs of the Na Pali Coast, inaccessible by road. One way to see them is on a scenic helicopter ride.

into the heart of Kauai. The trip takes just 50 minutes, but you'll revisit it in dreams. You fly along the dark walls of Waialeale Crater, home to the Hawaiian gods and shoulder to the wettest spot on Earth (more than 450 inches of rain a year), Mount Waialeale (pronounced way-AH-lay-AH-lay). Among the waterfalls plunging around and below you as you sweep along the mountain faces is one that appeared in *Jurassic Park*. You soar over Waimea Canyon; knife into valleys once inhabited by the ancient Hawaiians, now home to wild pigs and goats; and glide along the dramatic Na Pali Coast. Expect to pay in the neighborhood of $300 per person.

5 *Nene Spotting* 11 a.m.

Jutting out from the North Shore, the **Kilauea Lighthouse** (end of Kilauea Lighthouse Road;

808-828-0168; fws.gov/kilaueapoint) provided a life-saving beacon for the first trans-Pacific flight from the West Coast in 1927. Now it is part of the **Kilauea Point National Wildlife Refuge** and offers both an unobstructed view of striking shoreline and a chance to spot dolphins, sea turtles, and whales. Birders who visit here check off species like the red-footed booby, the great frigatebird, and the nene, or Hawaiian goose.

6 *Saddle Up* Noon

Grab an ono (delicious) ahi wrap or other takeout lunch at **Kilauea Fish Market** (4270 Kilauea Lighthouse Road, Kilauea; 808-828-6244; $) to eat a few miles mauka as you listen to instructions for your two-hour horseback ride at the **Silver Falls Ranch** (2888 Kamookoa Road; 808-828-6718; silverfallsranch.com). Imagine what life must have been like for the cowboys who raised cattle for islanders in years past. As you meander through fern and eucalyptus toward Mount Namahana, the stately peak of an extinct volcano, listen for the small streams that trickle along, hidden by the ferns. This is the Kauai that most visitors miss and most locals love (about $100 to $125; call ahead for directions and reservations).

7 *Kauaians' Favorite Beach* 4 p.m.

Another local favorite is **Kalihiwai Beach**, at the end of Kalihiwai Road, where a wide river empties

into the ocean, and joggers, boogie boarders, and dog owners share a piece of the shore. There are no amenities but you can take a dip or body surf in the shore break. And this late in the afternoon, you shouldn't need sun block if you want to stretch out and catch a few Z's or watch the seabirds work the ocean.

8 *Laid-Back Fine Dining* 7 p.m.

Postcards (5-5075 Kuhio Highway; 808-826-1191; postcardscafe.com; $$-$$$) offers mostly organic food in the picturesque town of Hanalei. Start with the taro fritters with pineapple ginger chutney, and try grilled fish with peppered pineapple sage or shrimp enchiladas. The modest portions leave room for a piece of banana and macadamia nut pie.

SUNDAY

9 *Botanicals* 9:30 a.m.

Limahuli Gardens in Haena (5-8291 Kuhio Highway; 808-826-1053; ntbg.org/gardens/limahuli.php), one of five National Tropical Botanical Gardens in the country, is in a valley where, 1,800 years ago, the first Hawaiians, with taro as their staple, developed a complex, hierarchical social system. On your self-guided tour, amid native plants like the ohia lehua tree and imports from Polynesia like breadfruit and banana trees, you can see the lava-rock terraces where taro was grown, fed by a series of

fresh-water canals. You will also find exquisite vistas; the Polynesians chose a lovely spot. Guided tours are at 10 a.m.; reservations are required.

10 *Ship the Orchids Home* 11 a.m.

As you head back to the Lihue Airport, stop in the town of Kapaa for high-end aloha shirts and skirts at **Hula Girl the Vintage Collection** (4-1340 Kuhio Highway, 808-822-1950); glass art at **Kela's** (4-1354 Kuhio Highway; 808-822-4527; glass-art.com);

or works by Hawaii-based artists at **Aloha Images** (4-1383 Kuhio Highway; 808-821-1382). At **Mermaids Cafe** (4-1384 Kuhio Highway; 808-821-2026; mermaidskauai.com; $$), order a focaccia sandwich or a tofu coconut curry plate. Make one last stop at **Orchid Alley** (4-1383 Kuhio Highway; 808-822-0486; orchidalleykauai.com) and have some tropical flowers shipped home to meet you on the mainland.

ABOVE Sunset at Ke'e Beach in Haena State Park, the last stop on the road west on the North Shore.

OPPOSITE The road to Ke'e narrows in the last stretch, shrinking to one-lane bridges over inlets and streams, against a misty backdrop of volcanic hills and cliffs.

THE BASICS

Lihue, the Kauai airport, is a 25-minute flight from Honolulu. The North Shore is a 40-minute drive north from the airport along Route 56.

Rent a car.

Princeville at Hanalei
5-3900 Kuhio Highway
808-826-9644
stregisprinceville.com
$$$$
Overlooks Hanalei Bay and has hosted many a celebrity.

Sealodge Condominiums
3700 Kamehameha Road
808-826-6751
hestara.com
$$
In Princeville, condo units with sea views.

Hanalei Bay Resort
5380 Honoiki Road
808-826-6522
tradingplaces.com/rentals
$$
156 rooms and condo units.

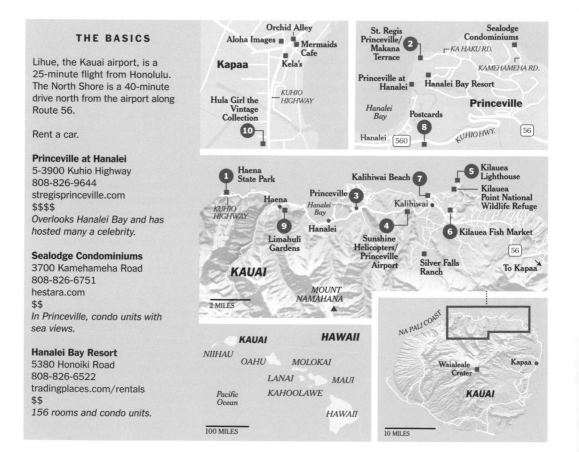

Indexes

Contributors

All images and text in this volume are © *The New York Times* unless otherwise noted. Any omissions for copy or credit are unintentional and appropriate credit will be given in future editions if such copyright holders contact the publisher.

Additional photo credits: Ethan Miller/2011 Getty Images, 8; Stan Grossfeld/*The Boston Globe*, 134; City of St. John's, 194; The Colonial Williamsburg Foundation, 210; Virginia Beach Convention and Visitors Bureau, 214; photo courtesy Town of Cary (photo by Roger May), 218; Visit Savannah (VisitSavannah.com), 226, 227; Dan Dry, 302; Nashville Convention and Visitors Bureau, 308; State of Tennessee, 312, 315; Traverse City Convention & Visitors Bureau (www.traversecity.com), 352; Jumper/Getty Images, 356; Photo Courtesy of Arkansas Parks & Tourism, 384; Jennifer Patrick 522-524, 534, 535, 537 (above), 538; Tom Brewster Photography, 562; Gregg Felsen, 563; courtesy of Palm Springs Bureau of Tourism, 564 (below); Ethan Miller/2011 Getty Images 566; Lake Tahoe Visitors Authority, 640.

Acknowledgments

We would like to thank everyone at *The New York Times* and at TASCHEN who contributed to the creation of this book.

For the yearlong book project itself, special recognition must go to Nina Wiener and Eric Schwartau at TASCHEN, the dedicated editor and assistant behind the scenes; to Natasha Perkel, the *Times* artist whose clear and elegantly crafted maps make the itineraries comprehensible; to Phyllis Collazo of the *Times* staff, whose photo editing gave the book its arresting images; and to Olimpia Zagnoli, whose illustrations and illustrated maps enliven every article and each regional introduction.

Guiding the deft and artful transformation of newspaper material to book form at TASCHEN were Marco Zivny, the book's designer; Josh Baker, the art director; and Horst Neuzner, production manager. Also at TASCHEN, David Martinez, Jessica Sappenfeld, and Anna-Tina Kessler provided production assistance, and at the *Times*, Heidi Giovine helped at critical moments. Craig B. Gaines copy-edited the manuscript.

But the indebtedness goes much further back. This book grew out of the work of all of the editors, writers, photographers, and *Times* staff people whose contributions and support for the weekly "36 Hours" column built a rich archive over many years.

For this legacy, credit must go first to Stuart Emmrich, who created the column in 2002 and then refined the concept and guided its development over eight years, first as the *Times* Escapes editor and then as Travel editor. Without his vision, there would be no "36 Hours."

Great thanks must go to all of the writers and photographers whose work appears in the book, both *Times* staffers and freelancers.

And a legion of *Times* editors behind the scenes made it all happen, and still do.

Danielle Mattoon, who took over as Travel editor in 2010, has brought her steady hand to "36 Hours," and found time to be supportive of this book as well.

Suzanne MacNeille, now the column's direct editor, and her predecessors Jeff Z. Klein and Denny Lee have all superbly filled the role of finding and working with writers, choosing and assigning destinations, and assuring that the weekly product would entertain and inform readers while upholding *Times* journalistic standards. The former Escapes editors Amy Virshup and Mervyn Rothstein saw the column through many of its early years, assuring its consistent quality.

The talented *Times* photo editors who have overseen images and directed the work of the column's photographers include Lonnie Schlein, Jessica DeWitt, Gina Privitere, Darcy Eveleigh, Laura O'Neill, Chris Jones, and the late John Forbes. The newspaper column's design is the work of the *Times* art director Rodrigo Honeywell.

Among the many editors on the *Times* Travel and Escapes copy desks who have kept "36 Hours" at its best over the years, three who stand out are Florence Stickney, Steve Bailey, and Carl Sommers. Editors of the column on the *New York Times* web site have been Alice Dubois, David Allan, Miki Meek, Allison Busacca, and Danielle Belopotosky. Much of the fact-checking, that most invaluable and unsung of skills, was in the hands of Rusha Haljuci, Nick Kaye, Anna Bahney, and George Gustines.

Finally, we must offer a special acknowledgment to Benedikt Taschen, whose longtime readership and interest in the "36 Hours" column led to the partnership of our two companies to produce this book.

— BARBARA IRELAND AND ALEX WARD

Editor Barbara Ireland
Project management Alex Ward
Photo editor Phyllis Collazo
Maps Natasha Perkel
Spot illustrations and region maps Olimpia Zagnoli
Editorial coordination Nina Wiener and Eric Schwartau
Art direction Marco Zivny and Josh Baker
Layout and design Marco Zivny
Production Horst Neuzner

To stay informed about upcoming TASCHEN titles, please request our magazine at www.taschen.com/magazine or write to TASCHEN, Hohenzollernring 53, D–50672 Cologne, Germany, contact@taschen.com, Fax: +49–221–254919. We will be happy to send you a free copy of our magazine which is filled with information about all of our books.

© 2012 TASCHEN GmbH
Hohenzollernring 53, D–50672 Köln, www.taschen.com

ISBN 978-3-8365-2639-5 Printed in China

TRUST *THE NEW YORK TIMES* WITH YOUR NEXT 36 HOURS

"The ultimate weekend planner for the literate by the literate — where even Oklahoma City can be as alluring as Paris." —AMAZON READER REVIEW

AVAILABLE IN *THE NEW YORK TIMES* 36 HOURS SERIES

150 WEEKENDS IN THE USA & CANADA*

Weekends on the road. The ultimate travel guide to the USA and Canada

125 WEEKENDS IN EUROPE*

(Re)discovering Europe: dream weekends with practical itineraries from Paris to Perm

* also available for iPad and iPhone

USA & CANADA REGION BY REGION

NORTHEAST   SOUTHEAST   MIDWEST & GREAT LAKES   SOUTHWEST & ROCKY MOUNTAINS   WEST COAST